DRAMA
for Students

Advisors

Jayne M. Burton is a teacher of English, a member of the Delta Kappa Gamma International Society for Key Women Educators, and currently a master's degree candidate in the Interdisciplinary Study of Curriculum and Instruction and English at Angelo State University.

Mary Beth Maggio teaches seventh grade language arts in Schaumburg, Illinois.

Tom Shilts is the youth librarian at the Okemos branch of Capital Area District Library in Okemos, Michigan. He holds an MSLS degree from Clarion University of Pennsylvania and an MA in U.S. History from the University of North Dakota.

Amy Spade Silverman has taught at independent schools in California, Texas, Michigan, and New York. She holds a bachelor of arts degree from the University of Michigan and a master of fine arts degree from the University of Houston. She is a member of the National Council of Teachers of English and Teachers and Writers. She is an exam reader for Advanced Placement Literature and Composition. She is also a poet, published in *North American Review*, *Nimrod*, and *Michigan Quarterly Review*, among others.

Mary Turner holds a BS in Secondary Education from East Texas State University and a Master of Education from Western Kentucky University. She teaches English 7 and AP English 12 literature and composition at SBEC in Southaven, Mississippi.

Brian Woerner teaches English at Troy High School in Troy, Ohio. He is also a Program Associate of the Ohio Writing Project at Miami University.

DRAMA
for Students

**Presenting Analysis, Context, and Criticism
on Commonly Studied Poetry**

VOLUME 29

Sara Constantakis, Project Editor

Foreword by Carole L. Hamilton

GALE
CENGAGE Learning·

Detroit • New York • San Francisco • New Haven, Conn • Waterville, Maine • London

Drama for Students, Volume 29

Project Editor: Sara Constantakis

Rights Acquisition and Management:
 Leitha Etheridge-Sims, Tracie Richardson

Composition: Evi Abou-El-Seoud

Manufacturing: Rhonda Dover

Imaging: John Watkins

Product Design: Pamela A. E. Galbreath,
 Jennifer Wahi

Content Conversion: Katrina Coach

Product Manager: Meggin Condino

For product information and technology assistance, contact us at
Gale Customer Support, 1-800-877-4253.
For permission to use material from this text or product,
submit all requests online at **www.cengage.com/permissions.**
Further permissions questions can be emailed to
permissionrequest@cengage.com

While every effort has been made to ensure the reliability of the information presented in this publication, Gale, a part of Cengage Learning, does not guarantee the accuracy of the data contained herein. Gale accepts no payment for listing; and inclusion in the publication of any organization, agency, institution, publication, service, or individual does not imply endorsement of the editors or publisher. Errors brought to the attention of the publisher and verified to the satisfaction of the publisher will be corrected in future editions.

Gale
27500 Drake Rd.
Farmington Hills, MI, 48331-3535

ISBN-13: 978-0-7876-8125-8
ISBN-10: 0-7876-8125-3

ISSN 1094-9232

This title is also available as an e-book.
ISBN-13: 978-1-4144-4941-8
ISBN-10: 1-4144-4941-0
Contact your Gale, a part of Cengage Learning sales representative for ordering information.

Printed in Mexico
1 2 3 4 5 6 7 16 15 14 13 12

Table of Contents

The Study of Drama

We study drama in order to learn what meaning others have made of life, to comprehend what it takes to produce a work of art, and to glean some understanding of ourselves. Drama produces in a separate, aesthetic world, a moment of being for the audience to experience, while maintaining the detachment of a reflective observer.

Drama is a representational art, a visible and audible narrative presenting virtual, fictional characters within a virtual, fictional universe. Dramatic realizations may pretend to approximate reality or else stubbornly defy, distort, and deform reality into an artistic statement. From this separate universe that is obviously not "real life" we expect a valid reflection upon reality, yet drama never is mistaken for reality—the methods of theater are integral to its form and meaning. Theater is art, and art's appeal lies in its ability both to approximate life and to depart from it. For in intruding its distorted version of life into our consciousness, art gives us a new perspective and appreciation of life and reality. Although all aesthetic experiences perform this service, theater does it most effectively by creating a separate, cohesive universe that freely acknowledges its status as an art form.

And what is the purpose of the aesthetic universe of drama? The potential answers to such a question are nearly as many and varied as there are plays written, performed, and enjoyed. Dramatic texts can be problems posed, answers asserted, or moments portrayed. Dramas (tragedies as well as comedies) may serve strictly "to ease the anguish of a torturing hour" (as stated in William Shakespeare's *A Midsummer Night's Dream*)—to divert and entertain—or aspire to move the viewer to action with social issues. Whether to entertain or to instruct, affirm or influence, pacify or shock, dramatic art wraps us in the spell of its imaginary world for the length of the work and then dispenses us back to the real world, entertained, purged, as Aristotle said, of pity and fear, and edified—or at least weary enough to sleep peacefully.

It is commonly thought that theater, being an art of performance, must be experienced—seen—in order to be appreciated fully. However, to view a production of a dramatic text is to be limited to a single interpretation of that text—all other interpretations are for the moment closed off, inaccessible. In the process of producing a play, the director, stage designer, and performers interpret and transform the script into a work of art that always departs in some measure from the author's original conception. Novelist and critic Umberto Eco, in his *The Role of the Reader: Explorations in the Semiotics of Texts* (Indiana University Press, 1979), explained, "In short, we can say that every performance offers us a complete and satisfying version of the work, but at the same time makes it incomplete for us, because it cannot simultaneously give all the other artistic solutions which the work may admit."

Thus Laurence Olivier's coldly formal and neurotic film presentation of Shakespeare's *Hamlet* (in which he played the title character as well as directed) shows marked differences from subsequent adaptations. While Olivier's Hamlet is clearly entangled in a Freudian relationship with his mother Gertrude, he would be incapable of shushing her with the impassioned kiss that Mel Gibson's mercurial Hamlet (in director Franco Zeffirelli's 1990 film) does. Although each of performances rings true to Shakespeare's text, each is also a mutually exclusive work of art. Also important to consider are the time periods in which each of these films was produced: Olivier made his film in 1948, a time in which overt references to sexuality (especially incest) were frowned upon. Gibson and Zeffirelli made their film in a culture more relaxed and comfortable with these issues. Just as actors and directors can influence the presentation of drama, so too can the time period of the production affect what the audience will see.

A play script is an open text from which an infinity of specific realizations may be derived. Dramatic scripts that are more open to interpretive creativity (such as those of Ntozake Shange and Tomson Highway) actually require the creative improvisation of the production troupe in order to complete the text. Even the most prescriptive scripts (those of Neil Simon, Lillian Hellman, and Robert Bolt, for example), can never fully control the actualization of live performance, and circumstantial events, including the attitude and receptivity of the audience, make every performance a unique event. Thus, while it is important to view a production of a dramatic piece, if one wants to understand a drama fully it is equally important to read the original dramatic text.

The reader of a dramatic text or script is not limited by either the specific interpretation of a given production or by the unstoppable action of a moving spectacle. The reader of a dramatic text may discover the nuances of the play's language, structure, and events at their own pace. Yet studied alone, the author's blueprint for artistic production does not tell the whole story of a play's life and significance. One also needs to assess the play's critical reviews to discover how it resonated to cultural themes at the time of its debut and how the shifting tides of cultural interest have revised its interpretation and impact on audiences. And to do this, one needs to know a little about the culture of the times which produced the play as well as the author who penned it.

Drama for Students supplies this material in a useful compendium for the student of dramatic theater. Covering a range of dramatic works that span from 442 BCE to the 1990s, this book focuses on significant theatrical works whose themes and form transcend the uncertainty of dramatic fads. These are plays that have proven to be both memorable and teachable. *Drama for Students* seeks to enhance appreciation of these dramatic texts by providing scholarly materials written with the secondary and college/university student in mind. It provides for each play a concise summary of the plot and characters as well as a detailed explanation of its themes. In addition, background material on the historical context of the play, its critical reception, and the author's life help the student to understand the work's position in the chronicle of dramatic history. For each play entry a new work of scholarly criticism is also included, as well as segments of other significant critical works for handy reference. A thorough bibliography provides a starting point for further research.

This series offers comprehensive educational resources for students of drama. *Drama for Students* is a vital book for dramatic interpretation and a valuable addition to any reference library.

Sources

Eco, Umberto, *The Role of the Reader: Explorations in the Semiotics of Texts*, Indiana University Press, 1979.

Carole L. Hamilton
Author and Instructor of English at Cary Academy, Cary, North Carolina

Introduction

Purpose of the Book

The purpose of *Drama for Students* (*DfS*) is to provide readers with a guide to understanding, enjoying, and studying dramas by giving them easy access to information about the work. Part of Gale's "For Students" literature line, *DfS* is specifically designed to meet the curricular needs of high school and undergraduate college students and their teachers, as well as the interests of general readers and researchers considering specific plays. While each volume contains entries on "classic" dramas frequently studied in classrooms, there are also entries containing hard-to-find information on contemporary plays, including works by multicultural, international, and women playwrights. Entries profiling film versions of plays not only diversify the study of drama but support alternate learning styles, media literacy, and film studies curricula as well.

The information covered in each entry includes an introduction to the play and the work's author; a plot summary, to help readers unravel and understand the events in a drama; descriptions of important characters, including explanation of a given character's role in the drama as well as discussion about that character's relationship to other characters in the play; analysis of important themes in the drama; and an explanation of important literary techniques and movements as they are demonstrated in the play.

In addition to this material, which helps the readers analyze the play itself, students are also provided with important information on the literary and historical background informing each work. This includes a historical context essay, a box comparing the time or place the drama was written to modern Western culture, a critical essay, and excerpts from critical essays on the play. A unique feature of *DfS* is a specially commissioned critical essay on each drama, targeted toward the student reader.

The "literature to film" entries on plays vary slightly in form, providing background on film technique and comparison to the original, literary version of the work. These entries open with an introduction to the film, which leads directly into the plot summary. The summary highlights plot changes from the play, key cinematic moments, and/or examples of key film techniques. As in standard entries, there are character profiles (noting omissions or additions, and identifying the actors), analysis of themes and how they are illustrated in the film, and an explanation of the cinematic style and structure of the film. A cultural context section notes any time period or setting differences from that of the original work, as well as cultural differences between the time in which the original work was written and the time in which the film adaptation was made. A film entry concludes with a critical overview and critical essays on the film.

To further help today's student in studying and enjoying each play or film, information on audiobooks and other media adaptations is provided (if available), as well as suggestions for works of fiction, nonfiction, or film on similar themes and topics. Classroom aids include ideas for research papers and lists of critical and reference sources that provide additional material on each drama. Film entries also highlight signature film techniques demonstrated, as well as suggesting media literacy activities and prompts to use during or after viewing a film.

Selection Criteria

The titles for each volume of *DfS* are selected by surveying numerous sources on notable literary works and analyzing course curricula for various schools, school districts, and states. Some of the sources surveyed include: high school and undergraduate literature anthologies and textbooks; lists of award-winners, and recommended titles, including the Young Adult Library Services Association (YALSA) list of best books for young adults. Films are selected both for the literary importance of the original work and the merits of the adaptation (including official awards and widespread public recognition).

Input solicited from our expert advisory board—consisting of educators and librarians—guides us to maintain a mix of "classic" and contemporary literary works, a mix of challenging and engaging works (including genre titles that are commonly studied) appropriate for different age levels, and a mix of international, multicultural and women authors. These advisors also consult on each volume's entry list, advising on which titles are most studied, most appropriate, and meet the broadest interests across secondary (grades 7–12) curricula and undergraduate literature studies.

How Each Entry Is Organized

Each entry, or chapter, in *DfS* focuses on one play. Each entry heading lists the full name of the play, the author's name, and the date of the play's publication. The following elements are contained in each entry:

Introduction: a brief overview of the drama which provides information about its first appearance, its literary standing, any controversies surrounding the work, and major conflicts or themes within the work. Film entries identify the original play and provide understanding of the film's reception and reputation, along with that of the director.

Author Biography: in play entries, this section includes basic facts about the author's life, and focuses on events and times in the author's life that inspired the drama in question.

Plot Summary: a description of the major events in the play. Subheads demarcate the play's various acts or scenes. Plot summaries of films are used to uncover plot differences from the original play, and to note the use of certain film angles or techniques.

Characters: an alphabetical listing of major characters in the play. Each character name is followed by a brief to an extensive description of the character's role in the play, as well as discussion of the character's actions, relationships, and possible motivation. In film entries, omissions or changes to the cast of characters of the film adaptation are mentioned here, and the actors' names—and any awards they may have received—are also included.

Characters are listed alphabetically by last name. If a character is unnamed—for instance, the Stage Manager in *Our Town*—the character is listed as "The Stage Manager" and alphabetized as "Stage Manager." If a character's first name is the only one given, the name will appear alphabetically by the first name. Variant names are also included for each character. Thus, the nickname "Babe" would head the listing for a character in *Crimes of the Heart,* but below that listing would be her less-mentioned married name "Rebecca Botrelle."

Themes: a thorough overview of how the major topics, themes, and issues are addressed within the play. Each theme discussed appears in a separate subhead. While the key themes often remain the same or similar when a play is adapted into a film, film entries demonstrate how the themes are conveyed cinematically, along with any changes in the portrayal of the themes.

Style: this section addresses important style elements of the drama, such as setting, point of view, and narration; important literary devices used, such as imagery, foreshadowing, symbolism; and, if applicable, genres to which the work might have belonged, such as Gothicism or Romanticism. Literary terms are explained within the entry, but can also be found in the Glossary. Film entries cover how the director conveyed the meaning, message, and mood of the work using film in comparison to the author's use of language, literary device, etc., in the original work.

Historical Context: in play entries, this section outlines the social, political, and cultural climate in which the author lived and the play was created. This section may include descriptions of related historical events, pertinent aspects of daily life in the culture, and the artistic and literary sensibilities of the time in which the work was written. If the play is a historical work, information regarding the time in which the play is set is also included. Each section is broken down with helpful subheads. Film entries contain a similar Cultural Context section, because the film adaptation might explore an entirely different time period or culture than the original work, and may also be influenced by the traditions and views of a time period much different than that of the original author.

Critical Overview: this section provides background on the critical reputation of the play or film, including bannings or any other public controversies surrounding the work. For older plays, this section includes a history of how the drama or film was first received and how perceptions of it may have changed over the years; for more recent plays, direct quotes from early reviews may also be included.

Criticism: an essay commissioned by *DfS* which specifically deals with the play or film and is written specifically for the student audience, as well as excerpts from previously published criticism on the work (if available).

Sources: an alphabetical list of critical material used in compiling the entry, with full bibliographical information.

Further Reading: an alphabetical list of other critical sources which may prove useful for the student. It includes full bibliographical information and a brief annotation.

Suggested Search Terms: a list of search terms and phrases to jumpstart students' further information seeking. Terms include not just titles and author names but also terms and topics related to the historical and literary context of the works.

In addition, each entry contains the following highlighted sections, set apart from the main text as sidebars:

Media Adaptations: if available, a list of audiobooks and important film and television adaptations of the play, including source information. The list may also include such variations on the work as musical adaptations and other stage interpretations.

Topics for Further Study: a list of potential study questions or research topics dealing with the play. This section includes questions related to other disciplines the student may be studying, such as American history, world history, science, math, government, business, geography, economics, psychology, etc.

Compare and Contrast: an "at-a-glance" comparison of the cultural and historical differences between the author's time and culture and late twentieth century or early twenty-first century Western culture. This box includes pertinent parallels between the major scientific, political, and cultural movements of the time or place the drama was written, the time or place the play was set (if a historical work), and modern Western culture. Works written after 1990 may not have this box.

What Do I Read Next?: a list of works that might give a reader points of entry into a classic work (e.g., YA or multicultural titles) and/or complement the featured play or serve as a contrast to it. This includes works by the same author and others, works from various genres, YA works, and works from various cultures and eras.

The film entries provide sidebars more targeted to the study of film, including:

Film Technique: a listing and explanation of four to six key techniques used in the film, including shot styles, use of transitions, lighting, sound or music, etc.

Read, Watch, Write: media literacy prompts and/or suggestions for viewing log prompts.

What Do I See Next?: a list of films based on the same or similar works or of films similar in directing style, technique, etc.

Other Features

DfS includes "The Study of Drama," a foreword by Carole Hamilton, an educator and author who specializes in dramatic works. This essay examines the basis for drama in societies and what drives people to study such work. The essay also discusses how *DfS* can help teachers show students how to enrich their own reading/viewing experiences.

A Cumulative Author/Title Index lists the authors and titles covered in each volume of the *DfS* series.

A Cumulative Nationality/Ethnicity Index breaks down the authors and titles covered in each volume of the *DfS* series by nationality and ethnicity.

A Subject/Theme Index, specific to each volume, provides easy reference for users who may be studying a particular subject or theme rather than a single work. Significant subjects from events to broad themes are included.

Each entry may include illustrations, including photo of the author, stills from stage productions, and stills from film adaptations, if available.

Citing Drama for Students

When writing papers, students who quote directly from any volume of *DfS* may use the following general forms. These examples are based on MLA style; teachers may request that students adhere to a different style, so the following examples may be adapted as needed.

When citing text from *DfS* that is not attributed to a particular author (i.e., the Themes, Style, Historical Context sections, etc.), the following format should be used in the bibliography section:

> "*Our Town.*" *Drama for Students*. Vol. 1. Ed. David Galens and Lynn Spampinato. Detroit: Gale, 1998. 227–30.

When quoting the specially commissioned essay from *DfS* (usually the first piece under the "Criticism" subhead), the following format should be used:

Fiero, John. Critical Essay on *Twilight: Los Angeles, 1992*. *Drama for Students*. Vol. 2. Ed. David Galens and Lynn Spampinato. Detroit: Gale, 1998. 247–49.

When quoting a journal or newspaper essay that is reprinted in a volume of *DfS*, the following form may be used:

> Rich, Frank. "Theatre: A Mamet Play, *Glengarry Glen Ross*." *New York Theatre Critics' Review* 45.4 (March 5, 1984): 5–7. Excerpted and reprinted in *Drama for Students*. Vol. 2. Ed. David Galens and Lynn Spampinato. Detroit: Gale, 1998. 51–53.

When quoting material reprinted from a book that appears in a volume of *DfS*, the following form may be used:

> Kerr, Walter. "*The Miracle Worker*." *The Theatre in Spite of Itself*. Simon & Schuster, 1963. 255–57. Excerpted and reprinted in *Drama for Students*. Vol. 2. Ed. David Galens and Lynn Spampinato. Detroit: Gale, 1998. 123–24.

We Welcome Your Suggestions

The editorial staff of *Drama for Students* welcomes your comments and ideas. Readers who wish to suggest dramas to appear in future volumes, or who have other suggestions, are cordially invited to contact the editor. You may contact the editor via e-mail at: **ForStudentsEditors@cengage.com.** Or write to the editor at:

Editor, *Drama for Students*
Gale
27500 Drake Road
Farmington Hills, MI 48331-3535

Literary Chronology

1849: August Strindberg is born on January 22 in Stockholm.

1889: August Strindberg's *The Stronger* is first performed at Strindberg's Scandinavian Experimental Theater in Copenhagen Denmark.

1891: Sidney Howard is born on June 16 in Oakland, California.

1897: Jo Swerling is born on April 8 in Baridchov, Russia.

1909: Ketti Frings is born on February 28 in Columbus, Ohio.

1910: Abe Burrows is born on December 18 in New York, New York.

1910: Frank Loesser is born on June 29 in New York, New York.

1912: August Strindberg dies of cancer on April 12 in Stockholm.

1920: Reginald Rose is born on December 10 in New York, New York.

1924: Sidney Howard's *They Knew What They Wanted* is produced.

1925: Sidney Howard is awarded the Pulitzer Prize for Drama for *They Knew What They Wanted.*

1930: Lorraine Hansberry was born May 19 in Chicago, Illinois.

1939: Sidney Howard dies in a farming accident on August 23 in Tyringham, Massachusetts.

1940: Luis Valdez is born on June 26 in Delano, California.

1950: David Ives is born on January 1 in Chicago, Illinois.

1950: Jo Swerling, Abe Burrows, and Frank Loesser's *Guys and Dolls* premieres on Broadway.

1950: Wendy Wasserstein is born on October 18 in Brooklyn, New York.

1951: Jo Swerling, Abe Burrows, and Frank Loesser' *Guys and Dolls* wins Tony Awards for Best Musical, Best Actor in a Musical, Best Featured Actress in a Musical, Best Director, and Best Choreography.

1953: Milcha Sanchez-Scott is born in Bali, Indonesia.

1954: Reginald Rose's *12 Angry Men* is performed on September 20 for the first time for a live nationwide audience on *Studio One*, a show on the CBS television network.

1957: David Henry Hwang is born in Los Angeles, California.

1957: Ketti Frings's *Look Homeward, Angel* is first performed at the Ethel Barrymore Theatre on Broadway.

1957: The film *12 Angry Men* is released.

1958: Ketti Frings is awarded the Pulitzer Prize for Drama for *Look Homeward, Angel.*

1959: Lorraine Hansberry's *A Raisin in the Sun* is first performed on Broadway.

1961: The film *A Raisin in the Sun* is released.

1964: Jo Swerling dies.

1964: Lynn Nottage is born in Brooklyn, New York.

1965: Lorraine Hansberry dies of cancer on January 12 in New York, New York.

1967: Luis Valdez's *Los Vendidos* is first performed by El Teatro Campesino in San Juan Bautista, California.

1969: Frank Loesser dies of lung cancer on July 26.

1981: Ketti Frings dies of cancer on Feburary 11 in Los Angeles.

1982: Milcha Sanchez-Scott's *The Cuban Swimmer* is performed by L.A. Theatre Works.

1985: Abe Burrows dies of pneumonia on May 17.

1988: David Henry Hwang is awarded a Tony Award for *M. Butterfly*.

1989: Wendy Wasserstein is awarded a Tony Award for *The Heidi Chronicles*.

1989: Wendy Wasserstein is awarded the Pulitzer Prize for Drama for *The Heidi Chronicles*.

1993: Lynn Nottage's *Poof!* is first performed at the Actors Theatre of Louisville, Kentucky.

1995: Wendy Wasserstein's *Workout* is produced.

1996: David Henry Hwang's *Trying to Find Chinatown* is produced at the Humana Festival, Actors Theatre in Louisville, Kentucky.

1997: David Ives's *Time Flies* is first produced onstage at Primary Stages, an off-Broadway theater in New York City.

2002: Reginald Rose dies of heart failure on April 19 in Norwalk, Connecticut.

2006: Wendy Wasserstein dies of lymphoma on January 29 in New York, New York.

2009: Lynn Nottage is awarded the Pulitzer Prize for Drama for *Ruined*.

Acknowledgements

The editors wish to thank the copyright holders of the excerpted criticism included in this volume and the permissions managers of many book and magazine publishing companies for assisting us in securing reproduction rights. We are also grateful to the staffs of the Detroit Public Library, the Library of Congress, the University of Detroit Mercy Library, Wayne State University Purdy/ Kresge Library Complex, and the University of Michigan Libraries for making their resources available to us. Following is a list of the copyright holders who have granted us permission to reproduce material in this volume of DfS. Every effort has been made to trace copyright, but if omissions have been made, please let us know.

COPYRIGHTED EXCERPTS IN *DfS*, VOLUME 29, WERE REPRODUCED FROM THE FOLLOWING PERIODICALS:

American Theatre, v. 9.7, November, 1992; v. 12.1, January, 1995; v. 16.4, April, 1999; v. 22.8, October, 2005; v. 27.8, October, 2010. © 1992, 1995, 1999, 2005, 2010 by Theatre Communications Group. All reproduced by permission of the publisher.—*Commentary*, v. 128.3, October, 2009. Copyright © 2009 by Commentary, Inc. Reproduced by permission of the publisher.—*Literary Review: An International Journal of Contemporary Writing*, v. 42.2, 1999 for "Making His Muscles Work for Himself: An Interview with David Henry Hwang" by Bonnie Lyons. Copyright © Fairleigh Dickinson University, 1999. Reproduced by permission of the author.—*Literature Film Quarterly*, v. 14.2, 1986. Copyright © 1986 by Salisbury State College. Reproduced by permission of the publisher.—*Literature Film Quarterly*, v. 37.3, July, 2009. Copyright © 2009 by Salisbury University. Reproduced by permission of the publisher.—*Modern Drama*, v. 6.3, December, 1963. Copyright © 1963 by University of Toronto Press, Inc. Reproduced by permission of the publisher.—*Quarterly Journal of Speech*, v. 90.1, February 1, 2004 for "'Fearful of the Written Word': White Fear, Black Writing, and Lorraine Hansberry's 'A Raisin in the Sun'" by Lisbeth Lipari. Copyright © 2004 Taylor & Francis Group. Reproduced by permission of the author and publisher (Taylor & Francis Group, http://www.informaworld.com).—*Scandinavian Studies*, v. 68.3, Summer, 1996, for "The Strindbergian One-Act Play" by Egil T—rnqvist. Copyright © 1996 Society for the Advancement of Scandinavian Studies. Reproduced by permission of the publisher and the author.—*Variety*, v. 392.1, August 18, 2003. Copyright © 2003 by Reed Business Information. Reproduced by permission of the publisher.

COPYRIGHTED EXCERPTS IN *DfS*, VOLUME 29, WERE REPRODUCED FROM THE FOLLOWING BOOKS:

Blahnik, Jeremy. From *Necessary Theater: Six Plays about the Chicano Experience*. Edited by Jorge Huerta. Arte Público Press, 1989.

Copyright © 1989 Arte Público Press-University of Houston. Reproduced by permission of the publisher.—Carlson, Harry G. From *Out of Inferno: Strindberg's Reawakening as an Artist*. University of Washington Press, 1996. Copyright © 1996 by the University of Washington Press. Reproduced by permission of the publisher.— Clark, Barrett H. From *Intimate Portraits, Being Recollections of Maxim Gorky, John Galsworthy, Edward Sheldon, George Moore, Sidney Howard and Others*. Edited by Barrett H. Clark. Dramatists Play Service, 1951. Copyright © 1951, Dramatists Play Service. Reproduced by permission of the Literary Estate of the author.—Craig, Carolyn Casey. From *Women Pulitzer Playwrights: Biographical Profiles and Analyses of the Plays*. McFarland & Company, 2004. Copyright © 2004, Carolyn Casey Craig. Reproduced by permission of McFarland & Company, Inc., Box 611, Jefferson, NC 28640. www.mcfarlandpub.com.—Hwang, David Henry. From *The State of Asian America: Activism and Resistance in the 1990s*. Edited by Karin Aguilar-San Juan. South End Press, 1994.

Copyright © 1994, Karin Aguilar-San Juan. Reproduced by permission of the publisher.— Savran, David. From *In Their Own Words: Contemporary American Playwrights*. Edited by David Savran. Theatre Communications Group, 1988. Copyright © 1988, David Savran. Reproduced by permission of the publisher.—Strindberg, August. From *Plays, Second Series*. Charles Scribner's Sons, 1913.—Valdez, Luis. From *Luis Valdez—Early Works: Actos, Bernabe and Pensamiento Serpentino*. Arte Público Press, 1990. Copyright © 1990, Arte Público Press. Reproduced by permission of the publisher.— White, Sidney Howard. From *Sidney Howard*. Twayne Publishers, 1977. Copyright © 1977, Gale, a part of Cengage Learning, Inc. Reproduced by permission of the publisher. www.cengage.com/ permissions.—Whitfield, Stephen J. From *Daughters of Valor: Contemporary Jewish American Women Writers*. Edited by Jay L. Halio and Ben Siegel. University of Delaware Press, 1997. Copyright © 1997, University of Delaware Press. Reproduced by permission of the publisher.

Contributors

Bryan Aubrey: Aubrey holds a PhD. in English. Entry on *They Knew What They Wanted*. Original essay on *They Knew What They Wanted*.

Kristy Blackmon: Blackmon is a writer and critic from Dallas, Texas. Entries on *The Cuban Swimmer* and *Los Vendidos*. Original essays on *The Cuban Swimmer* and *Los Vendidos*.

Rita M. Brown: Brown is an English professor. Entry on *Look Homeward, Angel*. Original essay on *Look Homeward, Angel*.

Catherine Dominic: Dominic is a novelist and a freelance writer and editor. Entries on *Guys and Dolls* and *Poof!*. Original essays on *Guys and Dolls* and *Poof!*.

Sheri Metzger Karmiol: Karmiol is a university lecturer in interdisciplinary studies. Entry on *A Raisin in the Sun*. Original essay on *A Raisin in the Sun*.

David Kelly: David Kelly is an instructor of creative writing and literature. Entry on *12 Angry Men*. Original essay on *12 Angry Men*.

Michael J. O'Neal: O'Neal holds a Ph.D. in English. Entry on *Time Flies*. Original essay on *Time Flies*.

April Dawn Paris: Paris is a freelance writer who has an extensive background working with literature and educational materials. Entry on *Trying to Find Chinatown*. Original essay on *Trying to Find Chinatown*.

Laura B. Pryor: Pryor is a professional writer with more than twenty-five years of experience and a special interest in literature. Entry on *Workout*. Original essay on *Workout*.

Bradley A. Skeen: Skeen is a classicist. Entry on *The Stronger*. Original essay on *The Stronger*.

12 Angry Men

1957

Sidney Lumet's 1957 film *12 Angry Men* has stood as the standard bearer for Hollywood courtroom drama for over fifty years. The story concerns twelve jurors from various walks of life deliberating about the fate of a young man accused of murdering his father. They enter the jury room convinced that the defendant is guilty, but one lone holdout persuades them to reconsider the facts that have been presented, and minute by minute, through argument and discussion, the meaning of the phrase "beyond a reasonable doubt" makes each man give careful consideration to what he knows. While other films rely on action and special effects to keep audiences interested, *12 Angry Men* does the same with strong basic dramatic tools: one room, a dozen skillful actors, a masterful script, and precise directing.

The film was written by Reginald Rose, who wrote the first version specifically for television. After a critically acclaimed live broadcast in 1954, Henry Fonda, the film's star, bought the rights, and he and Rose recruited Lumet, who had directed several of Rose's scripts on television, making it the first feature film in the director's long and distinguished career, which ultimately spanned half a century. In the 1960s, Rose wrote several stage versions of the story. Over the years, it was adapted to fit alternate circumstances, for a female cast (*Twelve Angry Women*) and for a mixed-gender cast (*Twelve Angry Jurors*), and it has been performed in

LIFE IS IN
THEIR HANDS—DEATH IS ON
THEIR MINDS!

IT
EXPLODES
LIKE
12
STICKS
OF
DYNAMITE!

HENRY FONDA

12
ANGRY MEN

hundreds of theater productions. The last version Rose wrote was for the play's Broadway debut in 2004, fifty years after its initial live broadcast.

PLOT SUMMARY

The film begins with an outside scene. It is a common technique to add outdoor footage to a filmed version of a stage play, opening the film up beyond the limits of live theater.

To the sound of street traffic, the camera pans up the pillars in front of the New York Supreme Court building in Manhattan to show a portion of the motto inscribed above the door: "The true administration of justice is the firmest pillar of good government."

A brief scene in the hall of the court building then shows several people: a man with a briefcase, then a nervous man, and then a jaunty man

leaving a phone booth and uniting with a happy family. None of these people are relevant to the story to come.

In courtroom 228, the judge gives the jury its final instructions before its members go into deliberation after a six-day trial. He explains the parameters of the case: one man is dead and another man's life is in the balance, since a death penalty is mandatory in the case of a guilty verdict. The judge also explains the principle of "reasonable doubt," which will play an important role in the discussions to come. Two alternate jurors are excused, and the jurors retire to the jury room. The credits roll as they enter it.

They open the windows, since it is expected to be the hottest day of the year. When the guard leaves, he locks them in, which Juror #5 comments on.

They elect to sit around the deliberation table in the order of their juror numbers. The general consensus is that the defendant will be found guilty. Juror #12, for instance, comments that he was impressed with the case the prosecuting attorney put forth, which Juror #11 supports with the comment that he "did an expert job."

They are so certain that they all agree to start with a vote. That first vote, however, produces one vote for "not guilty" from Juror #8. Jurors #3, 7, and 10 are very vocal in their amazement at #8's vote. Juror #8 admits that he is not convinced of the defendant's guilt or innocence, that he just wants to talk about it.

At Juror #8's suggestion, they all agree to deliberate for an hour before rushing to judgment. When Juror #8 lists the hardships of the defendant's life, Juror #10 counters with the claim that "they" have it too easy, a comment that seems to refer to poor people in general. Juror #12 suggests that they each speak for a moment, telling everyone, "It's up to us to convince this gentleman that he's wrong and we're right."

Juror #3 takes out his notebook and lists the facts of the case. An old man who lived downstairs from the crime scene heard a fight between a father and his eighteen-year-old son. He heard the defendant shout, "I'll kill you," then he heard a body hit the floor. He ran to his front door in time to see the defendant running down the stairs.

Juror #4 follows up with inconsistencies with the defendant's story: he claimed to have

FILM TECHNIQUE

- One technique that Lumet employs often in this film is the use of a wide-angle lens, which allows cinematographer Boris Kaufman to capture all of the actors at once. This technique appears early, in the courtroom. One shot shows all twelve jurors, two alternates, the judge, the bailiff, the guard, and the court stenographer. Throughout the film, the film shows jurors clustered together in groups of two or three, but it frequently reverts to the wide shot, showing all twelve jurors, either from the head of the table (shot from behind Juror #1) or from the foot (shot from behind Juror #7).

- A panning shot occurs when the camera moves horizontally, scanning slowly across a subject that is not moving. This film is about the jurors' reactions, so the panning shot is important for capturing a sequence of their faces. Lumet uses a similar technique for the first vote after Juror #3 nearly attacks Juror #8: the camera goes around the table showing each man's face, but it does not film them with one continuous shot, instead showing a new shot for each juror.

- During the jury's first vote, before the jurors have had a chance to individualize themselves to the audience, Lumet uses a foreshortened focal length: all twelve men are in the scene, but the camera squeezes them together. On film, the table, which must be at least ten feet long, looks no more than about three feet long. Another example of this technique occurs when the diagram of the murder scene is held up at the end of the table: the diagram is in focus, and the camera uses a wide lens to capture the jurors gathered around it.

- Lumet alternates medium shots, which show a few jurors at a time or show one juror from the waist up, with close-ups, which bring the camera in for a tight shot that fills the screen with an actor's face. Sometimes the camera jumps to a close-up, as when it shows the enraged face of Juror #3 when he lunges at Juror #8. Oftentimes the camera moves smoothly into the close-up, such as with the shot when the jurors leave and the camera swings around to show the defendant's face. This also occurs when Juror #11 changes his vote from "guilty" to "not guilty": the camera shows the table in general and then zooms forward to capture the emotions on Juror #11's face as he makes his decision. The close-up is also used to dramatic effect when Juror #8 thrusts his switchblade into the table next to the murder weapon.

- For the first half of the jury's deliberation, until the votes are tied, the jury room is supposedly lit by the lighting that is coming through the window. Ambient lighting generally refers to light sources that are naturally occurring before the cinematographer lights the set. If the effect that Lumet were going for was true ambient lighting, everyone would be lit from the side, with shadows of the window frame visible. The lighting in the first half of the film appears ambient, however, when it is contrasted with that in the second half. In the middle of the film, the set darkens as a storm approaches, and the overhead lights are snapped on and become the supposed light source. The film looks little different under the supposed glare of light bulbs than it did under supposed sunlight, though Rose's script for the play specifies that the final scenes be played with a flicker of fluorescent lighting.

---

gone to a movie that night but could not state what show he saw. Others pitch in to recall the testimony of the woman across the street, who testified that she actually saw the defendant kill his father while an empty elevated train passed between their two apartments.

Other facts, which come out later in the discussion, are that the father was stabbed with a switchblade knife and that a store owner remembers selling that exact kind of knife to the defendant earlier that night, after witnesses recalled seeing the father hit the defendant. The defendant claimed that the murder weapon was not his. He explained that he had lost his knife after it fell through a hole in his pocket. Most of the jurors presume that he returned to the scene of the crime hours after the murder to retrieve this piece of incriminating evidence.

Juror #6 explains that he was convinced of the defendant's guilt when he found a reasonable motive in the testimony of neighbors who saw the two arguing earlier that evening. Juror #7 runs down the defendant's record, from rock throwing to assault to mugging to knife fighting.

A general discussion about youth violence moves Juror #3 to discuss his personal life. When he was young, he was afraid of his father and called him "Sir." His own son is now twenty-two years old. After his son ran away from a fight at age nine, Juror #3 was ashamed. "I said I'll make a man out of you if I have to break you in two trying," he tells them. The result was that his son left and has not been in touch for two years. As the discussion continues, he stares at a photograph of himself with his son.

Juror #8 explains the crux of his uncertainty: there were only two witnesses for the prosecution, and they might be wrong. Juror #3 brings up the knife and the person who said he sold it to the defendant the night of the killing. The discussion turns to whether the knife is unique, and they ask the guard to bring it in. Juror #3 says that it is impossible that the murder weapon could be a knife that is only similar to the knife the boy bought, but Juror #8 then pulls an identical knife from his pocket. He says he bought it in the defendant's neighborhood the night before, showing that the defendant may also have owned the same model without it necessarily being the murder weapon.

Rather than declare the jury deadlocked, Juror #8 proposes that they take a secret ballot. If all eleven jurors who voted "guilty" the first time still vote that way, he will agree to a guilty verdict, but if any votes have changed they will have to stay and continue the discussion. Indeed, one new "not guilty" comes from Juror #9: he still thinks the defendant is guilty, but he respects Juror #8 and is willing to continue the discussion.

Juror #7 approaches Juror #8 in the restroom to try to persuade him to give up and vote guilty. Juror #6 then has a discussion with #8, leaving him with the uncomfortable suggestion that he might be working to free a person who killed his own father.

While he is trying to make a point about the evidence, Juror #8 sees two other jurors playing tic-tac-toe. He tears their paper away, which angers Juror #3.

Juror #8 questions the others about the testimony from the woman who says she saw the murder occur through the windows of a passing elevated train. They agree that such a train is deafeningly loud. How, then, Juror #8 asks, could the old man downstairs have heard the boy threaten to kill his father, and also have heard the body hit the floor?

The question is raised about why the old man would lie in his testimony. Juror #9, who is an old man himself, proposes that the apartment dweller might be ignored by society and starved for attention: he was dressed in a ragged jacket but trying to hide his lame leg, in shame. He does not suggest that the man lied, but that he fooled himself into believing that he was a witness to make himself important.

Juror #5 changes his vote to "not guilty." This makes Juror #7 angry, accusing Juror #8 of arguing the defendant's case for him.

Juror #11 stands up and raises a question about why the boy came back to the apartment, if he killed his father a few hours earlier: if the boy ran out in a panic after the killing, then why would he have wiped his fingerprints from the knife? It does not seem plausible that he was both panicking and calculating.

Another vote is taken, and Juror #11 joins as the fourth "not guilty" vote.

A discussion about the old man's testimony raises the question of how he could have gotten to his front door quickly enough to see the killer fleeing. A diagram of the apartment is brought in, showing how far the lame old man would have had to walk to reach his front door in a matter of seconds. Juror #8 measures off a similar distance in the jury room and walks that distance, taking three times the time the old man had to walk it, unlock his door, and open it.

His logical argument upsets Juror #3, who admits that he wants to see the defendant die. When Juror #8 accuses him of being a sadist,

Juror #3 lunges for him and shouts that he wants to kill him—demonstrating that the boy may have likewise shouted those words at his father without actually meaning to commit homicide.

Juror #11 stands up to quell the anger. He talks about his faith in the jury system, an observation based in his immigrant background. With the next vote, the total is six to six.

The intense heat of the day is dispelled when a thunderstorm breaks out, driving the jurors to close the windows and turn on the lights. Juror #7 tries the fan again and is delighted to see that it does work, despite the fact that he tried it unsuccessfully upon first entering the jury room; the fan's power is connected to the light switch. The congenial discussion about the rain that takes place between Juror #1 and Juror #8 is contrasted with a conversation between two of the jurors most interested in a guilty verdict, #3 and #4. Juror #3 tries to make Juror #8 look bad, but #4 will not join him in ostracizing #8, and he snubs #3.

Juror #8 raises the point made in the trial that, at the time of his arrest, the defendant could not remember the movies he had just come home from. He quizzes Juror #4 about what he has done in the previous few nights. When he mentions a movie he went to a few nights earlier and gets the title wrong, the point is made that he was having difficulty remembering even without the emotional stress faced by the defendant.

Juror #2 raises a question about the stab wound being at a downward angle, even though the father was almost seven inches taller than the defendant. Juror #3 stands in front of Juror #8, who by this time is his nemesis, and shows how an overhand swing of the arm would make the knife arc downward. For a moment, when he swings the knife toward Juror #3, it looks like he might actually stab him, and all of the men in the room gasp. But Juror #5, who has some experience with switchblade knives, makes the case that a person using such a knife would not swing it overhand, as that would require changing one's grip after snapping it open, defeating the quickness of the switchblade's spring action.

Juror #7 changes his vote to "not guilty" because he wants to leave, but Juror #11 calls him to task, insisting that he cannot vote that way unless that is what he believes. With the next vote, the tally is nine "not guilty" and just three "guilty"—Juror #3, Juror #4, and Juror #10.

Juror #10 explodes with a tirade about "these people." As he rants, shouting out one bigoted cliché after another, the other men walk from the table, one at a time, standing with their backs to him. The only one left at the table in the end is Juror #4, who, though he is voting with him, tells Juror #10 with disgust to sit down and not open his mouth again. This dramatic scene is toned down in the stage play, with the other jurors standing up to Juror #10 but not symbolically (and unrealistically) shutting him out by turning their backs.

Juror #4 makes the logical case for a guilty verdict, based on the testimony of the woman across the street. Juror #12 changes his vote back to "guilty."

Juror #9 notices Juror #4 rubbing the bridge of his nose when he takes off his glasses. This reminds him that the witness, who said she was in bed when she saw the boy kill his father, did the same thing, which makes several jurors remember that she had marks on her nose that came from glasses. Assuming that the woman wears glasses but did not wear them in court because of vanity, three holdouts change to "not guilty," leaving only Juror #3.

Pressed to explain why he is so sure the defendant is guilty, Jury #3 paces in rage, insisting that everything that was presented against him was correct. He takes out his notebook and slams it on the table: when he does, the photograph of his son falls out. The more he shouts, the more the others look at him with pity, and the less they respond, the angrier he becomes, until he takes the photograph and tears it to pieces.

That makes Juror #3 realize that he has been responding to this case with his personal feelings, projecting his anger toward his son onto the defendant. He breaks into tears and agrees to vote "not guilty." The guard is summoned, and the men take their jackets from the closet and leave. Juror #8 brings Juror #3 his jacket, as a conciliatory gesture.

Outside, the rain has stopped as the jurors leave the court building. Juror #9 calls out to Juror #8 to stop him. He asks his name. Juror #8 tells him it is Davis, and Juror #9 says his is McCardle, and they shake hands. After that brief moment of camaraderie, McCardle awkwardly says good-bye, and they head off in separate directions.

CHARACTERS

The Accused

The accused is only on-screen for a few seconds in the first scene. He does not appear in the play at all. When the jury retires for deliberating, several jurors sneak glances at him. He is a dark-eyed, thin young man.

Later in the discussion the jurors discuss the accused's difficult history. He is eighteen years old, though in the script published in 2003 his age has been lowered to sixteen, possibly to reflect changing social trends about who can be considered a "boy." His mother died when he was nine, and he grew up in a slum with an abusive father. He lived in an orphanage for more than a year while his father was in jail for forgery. Still, there is no question that he has become a petty criminal, with a record of arrests and a reputation for being good with a knife.

Davis

See Juror #8

Guard

The guard, played by James Kelly, brings the jurors into the jury room and locks them in. Throughout the film, he brings them exhibits from the trial that they want to reexamine, such as the murder weapon and the diagram of the apartment.

Judge

The judge, played by Rudy Bond, gives the jury its instructions in the first scene and, in the film, is not seen again.

Juror #1

Martin Balsam plays Juror #1, the foreman of the jury. He is in charge of organizing the discussion, and he takes his job seriously. When Juror #10 questions his ability and calls him a "kid," Juror #1's feelings are hurt. He offers to let Juror #10 be foreman. Juror #12 tries to calm him and tell him that he is doing fine, and Juror #1 offers to let #12 be the foreman, indicating that he is very uncomfortable with his position and is looking for a way out of his responsibility.

He is an "assistant head football coach" for a high school football team, a position that he discusses with pride, even though it does not have much status. Relating this little bit of his background to Juror #8 is his way of reaching out to the holdout juror, to make him feel less isolated. Juror #1 is diligent in his attempts to get the other men all working together.

Juror #2

John Fiedler, a well-known character actor, plays Juror #2. He is a meek, mild-mannered bank clerk who often will adopt the position voiced by the person who spoke before him. He is always trying to calm heated emotions in the jury room, but he tells one surprising story about a verbal fight he had once, when he had threatened to kill a coworker for calling him an idiot. Often, though, Juror #2 is forced to absorb insults from the more boisterous men: several times he starts to raise objections, only to find his objections ignored.

As a short man, Juror #2 is the one to raise the question of the angle of the wound.

Juror #3

Lee J. Cobb gives a powerful performance as the loud, angry Juror #3, who has built his own business up from scratch, a messenger service named the Beck and Call Company (he is quick to point out that the name was his wife's idea).

Early in the film Juror #3 notes how disrespectful children are in the modern world, turning his anger on the defendant for being a delinquent. He tells the story of how his son showed weakness by losing a fight and how, humiliated by the boy, he took him and made a man out of him, teaching him to be violent. His son turned this toughness against him, though: when he was eighteen he had a fistfight with Juror #3. Now that the son is grown, Juror #3 has not seen him in years. After he tells his story, the conversation moves on, but he sometimes stares wistfully at the photograph of himself with his son.

In the end Juror #3 is the lone, angry holdout against a "not guilty" verdict. His insistence on finding the defendant guilty turns out to be based upon his unrealized feelings about his son, much to his own surprise. He finds this out as he is shouting that the defendant killed his own father: in his rage, he rips up the photo of his son on the table before him, showing that he is mixing his feelings about his son with his feelings about the defendant. After that enlightening moment, he breaks down in tears, agreeing to vote "not guilty" with the others.

Juror #4

Juror #4 is a cool, passionless stockbroker, played by E. G. Marshall. He is one of the few to keep his jacket on throughout the deliberations. At one point Juror #5 asks him if he ever sweats, and he says calmly that no, he does not. That statement is belied later in the film when, pressed to remember his past few nights and finding that his memory is not as good as he expects the defendant's to be, his face is shiny with perspiration, which he dabs off with a handkerchief.

Throughout the prolonged discussion, Juror #4 shows that he has no vested interest in convicting the defendant. He is not a bigot, like Juror #10, and he is not angry, like Juror #3. He is calm and logical, driven by facts and reason. When Juror #10 tries to draw him into his hate-filled rant, Juror #4 listens and then insults him, telling him to sit down and keep his mouth shut.

Juror #4 is finally convinced that there is reasonable doubt about the defendant's possible guilt when the others point out that the female witness was rubbing her nose, the same way that he does when he takes off his glasses. His barrier of logic and belief in the witnesses is punctured by an appeal to his personal experience.

Juror #5

Jack Klugman plays Juror #5 as a timid, guarded man. When he is called on to explain his view of the trial, he quietly asks to pass.

As the story develops, Juror #5's history comes out. He was raised in poverty, like the defendant. He is a nurse at Harlem Hospital, working to save the same poor people that others on the jury try to dismiss as being criminal by nature.

He is shy about his background but becomes more and more vocal as he realizes that it makes the others listen to him as an expert. For instance, his background in poverty qualifies him to show the others with certainty how a switchblade knife would be handled, because he is the only one in the room who has used one.

Because he is intelligent and can empathize with the defendant's position, Juror #5 is one of the earliest jurors to change over to a "not guilty" verdict.

Juror #6

Juror #6 is a house painter by profession. He is played by Edward Binns. He is a hesitant, slightly confused man who is struggling to do the right thing. When he talks to Juror #8 alone, he admits that, as a working man, he is used to letting his boss do all of the thinking for him.

Because of his conciliatory nature, Juror #6 is often lost in the shuffle as stronger personalities shout across the jury room.

Juror #7

Juror #7, played by Jack Warden, is a jaunty, wise-cracking salesman, as indicated early on by his striped sport coat, his straw hat, and the gum he chews. From the start, the others give him patronizing glances, and it is obvious that they are unimpressed with his lack of seriousness. As the deliberation process goes on, he annoys them all.

He is impatient to reach an early verdict because he has tickets to a baseball game that evening, though in the original stage version, this is changed to tickets to a Broadway play.

After the first vote, Juror #7 says that he honestly believes the defendant is guilty and that nothing could change his mind. Later, though, he does change his vote to "not guilty." When Juror #11 accuses him of changing without any strong convictions about the defendant's innocence, he defends his right to vote for superficial reasons. He does, at the end of the conversation, admit that he truly believes that the defendant is innocent.

Juror #8

Juror #8 is an architect, played by the film's star and producer, Henry Fonda. He is distinguished from the others visually from the very start by his light-colored suit coat, and he quickly shows himself to be different from the others by standing up to the other eleven men when he votes "not guilty" on the initial ballot. He does not claim that the defendant is innocent, only that he has questions about the prosecution's case.

As the film progresses, the other jurors become more and more friendly toward Juror #8. Even those who do not change over to his side right away, like Juror #7, can appreciate his calm, rational demeanor. The exception in this is Juror #3, who focuses his anger and frustration on Juror #8. The animosity between the two men is so strong that the other men actually fear for a second that Juror #3, demonstrating how the death blow was struck, might stab Juror #8 before their eyes. At the end, when Juror #3 has agreed to a "not guilty" verdict, Juror #8 brings him his jacket, to show that there are no hard feelings, and helps him put it on.

Juror #8 is one of only two jurors identified by name—Davis—when Juror #9 asks for his name on the courthouse steps as they leave. After one second of mutual admiration, they walk away from each other.

Juror #9

Played by Joseph Sweeney, who also played the part in the original telecast, Juror #9 is an older man in his seventies. For the film, Sweeney gives this character a level of dignity that he did not have in the original version, where he was described as being defeated by life and waiting to die. In the television version, he is played as more befuddled than wise.

Juror #9 is the first one to change his vote, during the initial secret ballot. While discussing the old man who lived in the apartment below the victim, Juror #9 explains what he believes would motivate him to stretch the truth. The way that he describes the man's pride and loneliness, his need for attention from a society that has forgotten him, makes clear that Juror #9 has felt the same emotions.

At the end of the film, when the others have gone their separate ways, Juror #9 approaches the lone, brave holdout, Juror #8, on the courthouse steps. He shakes his hand and asks Juror #8 his name, a sign that he understands that the depersonalizing process of acting as a jury is over and that he wants to honor the other man. He also offers his own name, McCardle, but when the moment of friendship is over, he feels awkward, and he quickly says goodbye and leaves.

Juror #10

Played by Ed Begley, Juror #10 is a garage operator. Begley gives his character a distinguishing mannerism by playing him with a cold, often coughing and drying his nose with a handkerchief.

Throughout the deliberations, Juror #10 holds fast to the idea that the defendant is guilty and is irritated with the others as they change to the "not guilty" position. His position seems based at first in logic, but then later in the commonly held position that the boy's background

in poverty is what made him able to kill his own father. In a climactic moment for this character, he goes into an impassioned rant about "them," and it becomes clear to all that his judgment is based on racial prejudice, though he does not use any specific racial slurs in the film. As the other jurors come to understand his true feelings, they walk away, separating themselves from Juror #10 physically as well as emotionally.

Juror #11

Juror #11 is an immigrant, by trade a watchmaker. His country of origin is never named, but the play specifies that he speaks with a German accent. He is played with an accent by George Voskovec, who also played the role in the original 1954 television broadcast.

As an immigrant, Juror #11 is more impressed than the others with the complex efficiency of the American jury system. He gives a speech about how the jury system is supposed to work. He is also, though, at the mercy of the prejudices of the other men, who do not feel that he has a right to tell them about how justice in America should be administered. For example, Juror #7 laughs and dismisses #11's suggestion that he might not fully understand the concept of "reasonable doubt," finding it funny that an immigrant could know more about the English language than he could.

Aside from Juror #8, Juror #11 is the most analytical juror when it comes to questioning the prosecution's case, as he shows when he raises the question of why the boy would come back to the murder scene.

Juror #12

Juror #12, played by Robert Webber, works in advertising. He smiles often and does not always take the deliberations seriously; for instance, during the beginning of the debate, when the vote is still eleven to one, he has a side discussion with Juror #11 about a package that he designed for a product, Rice Pops. Early in the film he amuses the other jurors with his observations in the kind of jargon that advertising executives use when they speak, couching ideas in clichéd expressions like "Let's run it up the flagpole and see who salutes it." His words come back to him later when, during a tense moment, he says of an idea he is throwing out, "Let's throw it out on the stoop and see if the cat licks it up," a nonsensical expression that makes the other men break out in laughter.

Juror #12 is the only juror to change his vote often: he starts as a "guilty" vote, changes to "not guilty," and then goes back to "guilty" before settling on "not guilty."

McCardle

See Juror #9

THEMES

Justice

Justice is a word that stirs up the drive for nobility in human beings. Although this film does focus on the personal, petty motivations that people bring into the jury room, as with the juror who wants to leave to catch a baseball game or the juror who is acting out of his own repressed feelings for his son, its overall point is to make audiences believe in justice.

These jurors are from all walks of life, with diverse histories. They have nothing to do with the young defendant, and they certainly have not met him before. Still, despite the various factors that tell them to behave in their own self-interest, a few of them believe in their mission: to dispense justice. That faith in a higher mission spreads from Juror #8 to the others, who gradually put aside their own concerns and focus on what it will take to serve a higher calling. Audiences who might have come to the film doubting the wisdom of putting a person's life in the hands of twelve randomly chosen strangers are encouraged to believe that the jury system is the best way to ensure that justice will be served.

Prejudice

Early in the film, Juror #10 gives a speech about some unspecified category to which the defendant belongs, stating that "they" do not have the same standards about murder that other people have.

Juror #8 uses his words against him a few moments later, questioning why he would find the testimony of the woman across the tracks so credible, considering that she is "one of them" too. The script does not specify what group either of them is referring to, whether it is the defendant's ethnicity or the people living in the slum that Juror #10 has insulted by his statements, but it does not really matter. In a literal example of

prejudice, he is pre-judging the defendant, finding him to likely be guilty because of his ethnic or social class. Later, Juror #4 adds to the prejudice by commenting that people raised in slums are inclined toward violence, a theory that Juror #5, who was raised in a slum himself, refutes.

The simmering issue of prejudice cracks open late in the film when Juror #10 makes a long speech denouncing "them." Although this was filmed in the 1950s, when civil rights was considered a controversial issue, there is no controversy here: every one of the jurors rejects Juror #10's prejudiced language. Not only do they refuse to acknowledge his speech, but they all move away from him and turn their backs to him, providing audiences with visual proof of their rejection. Juror #10 believes that the one man who stayed at the table with him, Juror #4, might agree with him, but he is quickly, cuttingly insulted. For the rest of the film he sits at a side table, ostracized because of his hatred.

For the stage play performed in the twenty-first century, the bigoted tirade is still against an unspecified group of "them." These views are even more socially unacceptable in the modern world, and so the play does not need to show the other jurors turning against Juror #10: their disgust with his views is assumed.

Identity

The fact that the men in this jury room do not introduce themselves to one another by name makes a point about the legal system: they are not there to think as individuals but to operate as anonymous cogs in the machinery of justice. They do tell each other their professions, but they give information about their backgrounds hesitantly, such as when Juror #5 admits that he has lived in slums all his life. Rose's script keeps their identities from each other with casual uses of language, such as the way they will sometimes refer to "this man" while pointing, or when Juror #3 refers to Juror #8 as "that tall man." Viewers of the film or the play will not necessarily pick up on the fact that names are not used.

The film draws attention to this pattern of hidden identities at the end, when Juror #9 asks Juror #8 his name. Exchanging names is a sign of respect and friendship, and they shake hands as they do it. Juror #9, McCardle, then leaves, showing that speaking their names, establishing the identities they have outside of the jury room, has

READ, WATCH, WRITE

- Watch *12 Angry Men* again, paying close attention to the character of any one of the twelve jurors. Then look for pictures of strangers, choosing ten strangers who you think could be chosen to play that part. Create a chart or digital presentation that contains a written explanation of what aspects of the character you see in each person's appearance.

- How do you think the argument in the jury room in *12 Angry Men* would have been different if one or two characters had been of an ethnic or racial minority? How would it have changed if *most* of the jurors were from ethnic minorities? Use sources about race relations in social settings in the 1950s to support your ideas in an essay.

- Watch Sidney Lumet's final film, *Before the Devil Knows You're Dead*, released in 2007, fifty years after *12 Angry Men*. Take notes on the various directorial techniques displayed in this motion picture. Use footage from both films to explain to your class some techniques that you think Lumet learned in his fifty years of filmmaking, as well as techniques that he knew from the start were successful.

- Young adults often find themselves forming emotional relationships with characters in Jodi Picoult's fiction. Read *My Sister's Keeper*, Picoult's 2005 novel about a thirteen-year-old girl who sues her parents to stop them from using her organs to help her older sister battle leukemia. Write a script in which some of the jurors from the film argue the merits of the girl's case, using lines of dialogue from the novel when appropriate.

- Watch the highly acclaimed documentary about the Mexican legal system *Presumed Guilty* (*Presunto Culpable*), which follows the struggles of a wrongly convicted man as he is processed through the courts and prison. Write an essay about whether you think the principle of "guilty beyond a reasonable doubt" is the main difference between the legal systems of the United States and Mexico, or if there are other aspects that make more important differences.

- Lumet added a few outdoor scenes to *12 Angry Men* to differentiate it from a stage play. Imagine that you had to add ten more minutes of footage taking place outside the jury room. Write a script for these scenes, and include with each scene a synopsis that explains how the scene will help viewers understand or enjoy the overall story.

- Gary Fleder's 2003 film *Runaway Jury*, based on a John Grisham novel, shows corruption in jury selection in a high-profile case, with a wealthy corporation studying the backgrounds of prospective jurors to ensure a favorable outcome. After watching both movies, write an opinion essay about how you think technology has affected and will affect the jury system.

---

completed their friendship. The play, by contrast, ends with Juror #3 agreeing to vote "not guilty" and Juror #8, his assumed nemesis, showing him mercy. No names are ever mentioned.

Responsibility
Juror #8 is the main character in this film because he most fully understands the responsibility that he, as a juror, has to the legal system. He knows that if he has any doubts about the defendant's guilt, then he is obliged to examine those doubts. As he explains to the other jurors after the initial vote, he does not necessarily believe that the defendant is innocent, but he believes that the matter should be discussed.

© *Photos 12 | Alamy*

This puts him in the position of keeping the conversation on track, a responsibility that should be fulfilled by the jury foreman but is not because Juror #1 is too insecure about his authority to offend the others. Juror #8 flies into a rage when he finds two other jurors playing tic-tac-toe while they are supposed to be involved in discussions that could save the defendant's life.

Juror #8's sense of responsibility slowly rubs off on the others, who begin to police themselves so that, as a group, they can focus. Even meek, soft-spoken Juror #2 snaps at boisterous Juror #7 when he feels that the matter at hand is not being carefully tended in a responsible manner.

Compassion

Compassion for the defendant is handled awkwardly by the men of the jury, though not by the filmmakers. Early on, Juror #8 focuses on the difficult life the defendant has led. He has never known stable living conditions, having lost his mother young and having been raised by a father who beat him, within terrible surrounding social conditions. Juror #8 mentions these facts to remind the other jurors that there might be

reasons for the boy to carry a knife, to fight with his father, and to have the criminal record that he has.

However, compassion is not all there is to the jurors' task. Juror #6, who is meek and does not have any particular interest in persecuting the boy, reminds Juror #8 of the horrible consequences of standing up for the boy and being wrong: he might be involved in freeing a boy who is so violent that he would murder his own father.

STYLE

Single Set

Plays adapted as films often take advantage of the mobility available to cameras by adding new scenes that take place beyond the confines of the stage set. This film adds a few such scenes, but they only amount to a few minutes of its running time. They are clustered at the beginning of the film and at the end, and they never stray beyond the courthouse's front steps.

By confining the cameras to the jury room, Lumet is able to give his audience an experience that resembles what the confined jury must feel. The story takes place on the hottest day of the year, and the characters become more and more soaked with sweat as deliberations go on, giving the oppressive heat in the room a visual form.

Confining the action could make the film visually static, but Lumet and his director of photography, Boris Kaufman, used a wide array of camera angles and motions to keep viewers visually engaged. Keeping the cameras moving entails precision work in moving the actors around the set, changing camera lenses, and zooming in and out on faces. Walls were made to move away quickly to accommodate the motion of bulky cameras, and in some cases cameras were hidden behind opaque set walls, so that they would not show up on film shot by other cameras at the same time. The methods are complex, but they were necessary to achieve the film's uniquely claustrophobic style.

Black-and-White Film

By 1957, color photography was common in film. It was more expensive, however, than black and white. Films that were released in black and white either were made on a limited budget or, like black-and-white releases today, used gray scale as part of their artistic style.

Releasing *12 Angry Men* in black and white served as a reminder to viewers that there may be realistic elements to the story but that it is, after all, a parable. A deliberation like the one the film presents could possibly happen, but the movie is not trying to make viewers believe in the actuality of the situation. Several elements indicate a symbolic, nonrealistic type of story: the jurors are known only by their numbers and not by names, the proceedings occur during a heat wave (broken by a thunderstorm once the vote is tied), and two knives are plunged into the jury-room table. Similarly, black-and-white photography is not realistic. It takes viewers out of the realm of reality and puts them into the special, very specific world of the story.

CULTURAL CONTEXT

Television Anthology Drama Series

As television became popular after the end of World War II in 1945, there came a need for new programming. One source of material was adapting stage dramas to television shows, as radio had been doing for decades. These shows were broadcast on an individual basis at first, but broadcasters soon saw the benefits of creating a regular schedule of televised plays, or "teleplays." In 1947, *Kraft Theater* became the first weekly television series to be broadcast regularly on a television network and the first regularly scheduled anthology series. The following year saw the premieres of several programs following the format, such as the *Ford Television Theater*, *Philco Television Playhouse*, *Actors' Studio*, and *Studio One*. These shows, broadcast live out of New York City, brought the prestige of Broadway drama to the small screen, and they were a hit with critics. Networks tried to reproduce the format with live broadcasts from Hollywood, taking advantage of the talent gathered on that side of the country for the filmmaking industry, but they were less successful. Eventually, the Hollywood productions became standardized as half-hour broadcasts, often filmed in advance. Many of these anthology programs were named after particular stars who hosted and introduced each broadcast, such as with *The Loretta Young Show*, *Douglas Fairbanks Presents*, *The Barbara Stanwyck Show*, and *Crown Theatre with Gloria Swanson*.

The growth of the television industry created the necessity of filling the expanding broadcast schedules with regular scripted dramas and situation comedies (sitcoms) that had recurring characters who returned each week. These series gained in popularity as producers found the market for reruns and syndication. Live anthology dramas, meanwhile, continued throughout the 1950s.

One of the most successful and respected of the live anthology drama programs was *Studio One*, the show for which Reginald Rose wrote the first version of *12 Angry Men*. This program had a ten-year run, from 1947 to 1957, having begun as a radio series in the mid-1940s. It distinguished itself from the other programs in the same vein with its technological innovations in camera angle and placement, accomplishing the illusion of a closed room (instead of a three-walled set) and switching live from one set to another to weave such elements as flashbacks into the story. In the 1950s, writers for the series, such as Rose, moved away from adapting existing properties and toward producing original

stories, of which *12 Angry Men*, broadcast in 1954, was one of the first.

Standardization of the industry made filmed shows with continuing characters more financially lucrative than live broadcasts of individual stories, and the anthology drama series died out by the end of the decade, with *Kraft Television Theater*, the last of the kind, going off the air after its 1957–1958 season. By then, all television production moved to the Hollywood soundstages, where film had been for decades. The anthology format stayed on in a half-hour form with series such as *Twilight Zone* and *Thriller*, and it returns from time to time to this day.

Youth and Justice

In the years after World War II, when the country was enjoying a level of prosperity that it had never known before, there arose a fear of the dangers posed by juvenile delinquents—young people who committed crimes.

Fear of juvenile delinquency was a long time coming. Its roots came in the social reforms of the nineteenth century. Education and psychology experts recognized that it was counterproductive to treat children the same way adults were treated—that is, to expect them to work—pushing for public education. In the early twentieth century, reformers pushed for laws regulating child labor, though it was a difficult battle: a minimum age for being sent to work was not established until 1937, when the labor market was awash with potential workers during the Great Depression.

While reformers were pushing for new standards for children in education and labor, there was also a drive to establish separate courts for juvenile offenders. The first such court, established in Illinois in 1899 through the efforts of the Chicago Women's Club, provided for a separate courtroom, judge, and records process for young lawbreakers. These measures were seen as being necessary to nurture, not punish, children, with the hope of rehabilitation. The new system proved popular and quickly spread to other jurisdictions.

The early juvenile courts took on the legal and moral role of parents: the judge was seen not as a punisher but rather as someone who was there to protect the youthful offender. This view was countered by some who felt that young criminals were only emboldened by easy treatment. These different viewpoints are both on display in *12 Angry Men*, with some jurors focusing on the home life that might have driven the defendant to crime and others feeling that, regardless of the causes, a young criminal should be treated the same way an adult criminal would be. It was not until the 1980s that the U.S. Supreme Court ruled against executing anyone age fifteen or younger. In 1992, the United States ratified the International Covenant on Civil and Political Rights, which has a provision against using the death penalty on offenders under the age of eighteen, but the United States specified in its ratification that it reserved the right to continue executing juvenile offenders, a practice the Supreme Court eventually outlawed in 2005. The eighteen-year-old defendant of the film would be eligible for the death penalty today, but not the sixteen-year-old defendant of Rose's stage play.

CRITICAL OVERVIEW

The film *12 Angry Men* was a hit with reviewers from the moment it was released in April 1957. It did not win any of the three Academy Awards for which it was nominated—Best Film, Best Director, and Best Adapted Screenplay—but the competition was particularly strong that year, with *Bridge on the River Kwai* taking those three awards plus four more. Nonetheless, *12 Angry Men* was recognized internationally, winning the Golden Bear, the highest award available for a film, at the Berlin International Film Festival in 1958. It did not sell many tickets that year, likely because of its serious subject matter and the fact that it was filmed in black and white at a time when color film had been available for two decades; still, the relatively low

budget ($350,000, or about $3 million in current dollars) was made back over the years.

More important than ticket sales was the recognition of film critics, such as that of A. H. Weiler in the *New York Times* of April 15, 1957:

> Reginald Rose's excellent film elaboration of his fine television play ... is a penetrating, sensitive and sometimes shocking dissection of the hearts and minds of men who obviously are something less than gods. It makes for taut, absorbing and compelling drama that reaches far beyond the close confines of the jury room setting.

A contributor to *Variety*, a publication geared toward show business, makes a point of drawing attention to Lumet's work in directing his first feature film, stating that he "cleverly maneuvered his players in the small area. Perhaps the motivations of each juror are introduced too quickly and are repeated too often before each changes his vote. However, the film leaves a tremendous impact."

As the *Variety* reviewer reveals, there were some critics who found flaws in the film. Jonathan Baumbach wrote one of the rare negative reviews of the film in *Film Culture* in 1957. In the article "*Twelve Angry Men* Is a Shallow Call to Civic-Mindedness," Baumbach admires the film's technique but finds that its message is less than it appears to be at first glance. He calls it "undoubtedly a melodrama of the first rank if one is willing to accept it solely on its presentational level" but holds that once one searches "beneath its shiny surface," the film is on "less solid ground." Even with his dissatisfaction, however, Baumbach admits that "within its simplicity there is a freshness and ingenuousness about *Twelve Angry Men* uncommon in a slickly sophisticated film industry." It is that central honesty, in spite of the film's more awkward emotional devices, that has kept *12 Angry Men* on lists of important Hollywood productions for decades.

CRITICISM

David Kelly

Kelly is an instructor of creative writing and literature. In the following essay, he examines the placement of the jurors at the jury table in 12 Angry Men *and how their locations with respect to one another enforce the story's message.*

WHAT DO I SEE NEXT?

- Lumet's cinematic version of *12 Angry Men* is based on the television play that was broadcast live on September 20, 1954, as part of the *Studio One* anthology series on CBS. This version, also written by Reginald Rose, starred Robert Cummings as Juror #8, Franchot Tone as Juror #3, and Edward Arnold as Juror #10. For nearly half a century it was thought to be lost, but a copy was found in 2003, and it is now available on DVD.

- Generations of young adults have grown up remembering the lesson in social compassion learned from Gregory Peck as Atticus Finch, the father of two young children, in *To Kill a Mockingbird* (1962), directed by Robert Mulligan and based on the classic novel by Harper Lee. Peck's trial defense of a black man accused of murder in a hostile environment rivals the legal nuances explored in Lumet's film.

- William Friedkin directed an updated version of *12 Angry Men* for the Showtime network in 1997, with a star-studded cast including Jack Lemmon, Ossie Davis, James Gandolfini, and William Peterson. Reginald Rose wrote a new version of his script for this broadcast. Orion Home Video released a VHS version of this film in 1998, but it has not yet been released on DVD in the United States.

- A courtroom drama that is often compared to Lumet's film for its psychological complexity is Otto Preminger's 1959 production of *Anatomy of a Murder*, concerning an army officer charged with killing a man who allegedly molested his wife. The film was lauded for performances by Ben Gazzara, Lee Remick, George C. Scott, and James Stewart, as well as for the innovative jazz soundtrack by Duke Ellington.

- In 1960, Stanley Kramer directed *Inherit the Wind*, based on a play by Jerome Lawrence and Robert Edwin Lee. It is loosely based on the famed "Scopes Monkey Trial" of the 1920s, in which internationally famed lawyers Clarence Darrow and William Jennings Bryan squared off over the issue of a schoolteacher in Dayton, Tennessee, being fired for discussing Darwinian evolution in class. Spencer Tracy and Fredric March star in the film.

- In 1982, Lumet directed Paul Newman in *The Verdict*, a film about a drunk, self-loathing lawyer who rises up to fight for the cause of justice against a hospital that permanently damaged his low-income client. The film also stars Charlotte Rampling, James Mason, and, from *12 Angry Men*, Jack Warden and Edward Binns.

- Nikita Mikhalkov's film *12*, nominated for an Academy Award for Best International Film in 2008, follows the same basic shape as Lumet's film. It concerns a Chechen youth accused of killing his father and a jury of twelve arguing the facts of the case. The Russian production has little else in common with its inspiration, though, with more intensity and more focus on current events in eastern Europe. The DVD, with subtitles, is available from Sony International.

At the start of Sidney Lumet's film version of *12 Angry Men*, the camera looks up at the entrance to the state supreme court building in New York City's Foley Square, showing the inscription carved in stone above the door: "The true administration of justice is the firmest pillar of good government." The rest of the film is a case study of how unsteady that pillar can be. The camera moves into the courthouse, and for a few minutes it wanders around the building, scanning from one face to another, as if shooting from the point of view of a lost child or someone

> THE PERSONALITY TRAITS OF THE
> CHARACTERS SEATED TOGETHER ARE ESTABLISHED
> IN THE SCRIPT AND INTENSIFIED BY THE FILMING.
> CHARACTERS WALK AROUND THE JURY ROOM AND
> STRIKE UP CONVERSATIONS, BUT WHEN THEY ARE AT
> THEIR PLACES AT THE TABLE, LUMET
> STRATEGICALLY FRAMES THEM TOGETHER."

who is there for an appointment with someone, perhaps the serious man with the expensive hat; the sweaty, nervous man; or the smiling man who leaves a phone booth to join a joyous family.

This opening is odd and seemingly superfluous, as it does nothing to introduce any of the film's twelve main characters. It does, though, introduce the setting as well as Lumet's fluid filming style. It prepares viewers to keep their eyes moving around the screen in case they might miss something important, to not focus too long on any particular character's story. It lays the groundwork for the idea that this film will be a composite of different stories, all blended together.

In a few minutes, this pattern carries over into the jury room, where more than 90 percent of the film will play out. Some of the jurors draw more attention than others, particularly Juror #8, the lone holdout for a verdict of not guilty (played by the film's star, Henry Fonda), and Juror #3 as the final holdout for the guilty verdict (played by Lee J. Cobb). Overall, though, the film obscures the jurors' individual identities by calling these characters by their appointed numbers and going no deeper than their professions—the architect, the salesman, the house painter, and so forth. As far as the script is concerned, these are not distinguished individuals, they are just typical Americans.

The problem for the overall project is that the filmmakers want to make these characters seem ordinary, typical, and anonymous, but at the same time they want to show that the jury system hinges on human interaction. The secret,

it seems, is the collusion between Lumet's direction and Rose's script. Rose created twelve distinct characters and stipulated the order in which they sit around the big table that dominates the jury room, and Lumet's framing makes viewers aware, even if only subconsciously, of geometric patterns of alliances and opposition when these men are seated at their places.

It is easy to identify the like-minded characters who are seated together. Fonda's Juror #8, the one whose "not guilty" vote ensures that this will not be a ten-minute-long film, is seated beside Juror #9, the old man, played by Joseph Sweeney. Both men are studious and soft-spoken. They even look somewhat alike, dressed in light colors and light fabrics, thin and tall. Their faces are brightly lit. If there were any question about the bond they share, the film settles the issue in its final moments, when these two exchange names and shake hands.

Just as clearly a pair are Jurors #3 and #4, played by Cobb and E. G. Marshall, respectively. They are often shown in a dual shot, beside one another, though their temperaments could not be more different. Cobb's character is scowling, angry, and wet with sweat, while Marshall's character is so calmly dispassionate that Juror #5 feels compelled to ask him, incredulously, "Pardon me, but, don't you ever sweat?" Despite their differences, or maybe because of them, these two characters jointly represent the drive for a "guilty" verdict, showing how emotions without reason and reason without emotions can lead to the same conclusion.

Jurors #5 and #6 are an obvious pair, two working-class guys who sit down at the table with the inclination to vote "guilty" but who are willing to let the questions raised in deliberations swing them. Jack Klugman and Edward Binns, the actors who play these men, look nearly interchangeable, with their dark features, slumped shoulders, and similar builds. They both have darting eyes that hungrily take in the conversation when they are not participants. The film solidifies their function as two earnest men with boyish curiosity in one scene, when the possibility that the man downstairs could have heard what happened in the murder apartment is questioned. For a moment, Klugman and Binns separate themselves from the main conversation to confer with each other. The script has Klugman state—not to the room in general but to Binns, his partner—"Y'know, I don't think he could have heard it." Lumet's direction has him turn to Binns and poke him with his index finger as he says it, the kind of gesture that one would make toward an old friend. Jurors #5 and #6 clearly represent the best of the jury system: congenial yet curious, willing to let the facts come first. They serve as the audience's representatives in the room.

There are other groupings to be found at the table as well, but only through some stretches of the imagination. Martin Balsam's Juror #1, the foreman, for instance, is a nervous man with weak convictions, eager to put others at ease: Does that make him more akin to John Fiedler as Juror #2, who has the wits to press back when he questions the seriousness of the phrase "I'm going to kill you"? Or does it align him with Robert Webber's Juror #12, an advertising man who changes his vote three times? Or should Webber's character be paired with the immigrant sitting to his other side, played by George Voskovec, whom he tries several times to entertain with stories from the ad business, possibly sensing that the foreign man can be enchanted by his insight into American culture—even though Juror #11 is a sharp inquisitor and a duty-bound citizen, more like Jurors #8 and #9.

The grouping of these jurors is problematic, but it can be considered useful from a critical perspective. Two jurors, however, cannot be grouped with those around them. Ed Begley's Juror #10 is ostracized by the others after losing control and unleashing a bigoted rant that proves him unwilling to listen to any line of reason. After Juror #9, seated to his right, he is the oldest man in the room, but age gives them no common bond. Once the others have seen his ugly side and turned their backs on him, Begley sits off at another table and hardly ever speaks again.

Juror #7 occupies the foot of the table. Jack Warden's wise-cracking persona shows that Juror #7 wants to be liked, but his temper gives him a hard edge that makes him unapproachable. His crooked smile, as much as his jaunty hat, makes him stand out. He socializes with the men to either side of him as much as he does with the other men in the room, but he makes no particular connection with them.

The personality traits of the characters seated together are established in the script and intensified by the filming. Characters walk around the jury room and strike up conversations, but when they are at their places at the table, Lumet strategically frames them together. They lean toward one another to show cohesion or away from each other to show tension, as Jurors #3 and #4 do. The layout of the set and the way the action is filmed also serve to show complexities in their relationships. The jury foreman, for instance, is as unsure of himself as Juror #7, sitting opposite him, is assertive.

The center of compassion, Fonda and Sweeney, is to the bottom left side of the table when the camera shoots toward the foreman's seat. From the same point of view, the stalwarts for a guilty verdict are to the upper right. Placing them nearly as far apart as possible makes viewers take in the whole table when they argue, showing all of the varied reactions at once.

Similarly, the groupings of uncertainty are at the far corners from each other, at the top left and bottom right from the same camera angle. This means that Jurors #11 and #12, as they are trying to make up their minds, are looking across the table at the hard-core "guilty" voters Jurors #3 and 4, while Jurors #5 and #6 are looking at the "not guilty" bloc of Jurors #8 and #9. This visual alignment is reflected in the way their votes change: Juror #5 shifts to a "not guilty" vote quickly, while Juror #11 struggles hard before giving up his "guilty" vote.

These geometric arrangements undoubtedly ramp up the tension of the story in unmeasurable ways. Just as unmeasurable is the extent to which these alliances were part of Rose's plan when he wrote the script and how much was Lumet's realization as he brought the script to life. Film is a visual medium, and it is the director's job to make the concepts come alive before the audience's eyes, just as it is the scriptwriter's job to have ideas that are worth presenting. The film *12 Angry Men* is an outstanding example of one in which the parts all work together in harmony, from the characterizations to the staging to the shooting. Whether or not the groupings of the characters around the jury table were planned, they amount to another sign of the skill that went into telling this story.

Source: David Kelly, Critical Essay on *12 Angry Men*, in *Drama for Students*, Gale, Cengage Learning, 2012.

Frank Cunningham

In the following excerpt, Cunningham maintains that Sidney Lumet reflects the liberal principles of democracy in the way he filmed 12 Angry Men.

© *AF Archive | Alamy*

Twelve Angry Men (1957), Lumet's first feature film after seven years of outstanding television production, stands to this date as one of his most thematically rich and cinematically evocative films. Treating such typical Lumet concerns as the necessity for personal responsibility if democratic processes are to survive, and the tendency for man's illusions, guilts, and prejudices to endanger his legal systems, *Twelve Angry Men* goes beyond the well-intentioned "message picture" to make a remarkable cinematic statement on the nature of the limitations both of the American jury system and of the American democratic process itself.

Reginald Rose's screenplay (expanded considerably from his 1954 teleplay) treats the jury deliberation in a murder trial of an 18-year-old minority youth accused of the premeditated killing of his father. We do not hear or see of the trial itself beyond the judge's direction to the jury. Nor do we witness the boy on trial except for one wordless shot of him near the beginning of the film. Lumet is uninterested in the legal attack and defense system, in the sometimes pyrotechnical emotional displays by both

counsel and witness in American courtrooms. To the contrary, as is so frequent in his film, Lumet is far more interested in human character, in the nuances of the ways that people make up their minds about things (or think they do), than he is in the more obvious spectacle level of such legal melodramas as *Kramer vs. Kramer* or *And Justice For All*. *Twelve Angry Men* takes place in one small room for almost all its length, a jury room in which sit twelve ordinary men, chosen at random by a human institution that entrusts them with a decision that determines the future of a human life. To all but one of the jurors (all but two of whose names are never known to us), the boy seems clearly guilty as charged on the abundance of circumstantial evidence, and their responsibility seems obvious—to put a guilty man into the electric chair, despite his youth and the impoverished environment from which he has come and which may well have contributed to his alleged crime. But Juror #8 (Henry Fonda), a softspoken architect in his outside life, is not certain that the evidence is sufficiently clear or ample to establish, beyond reasonable doubt, the boy's guilt. To the surprise of almost all the other eleven jurors—and the anger of a few who feel that the case is so clear that they should be permitted to be about their business—Fonda insists that the case be discussed for awhile, that a little of their time is called for before a terminal decision is made regarding a human life.

For the approximately one and a half hours of the film (congruent with the elapsed time of the jury's deliberations), Lumet reveals the processes of thought and feeling of the twelve men as they grapple with the facts of the case, facts that seem to become less clear, more elusive the more carefully they are reflected upon. Ultimately, the young defendant's guilt or innocence is never conclusively known to them, nor to us. To Lumet the boy's eventual fate, important as it is, is less significant than the ways in which it affects the minds and sensibilities of the twelve chosen to decide that destiny. Lumet's storied skill with actors is evident even in this early film, as all the jurors—even those with smaller speaking parts—emerge as recognizable human beings with whose conflicts and weaknesses we can identify. Though a cross-section of middle-class and lower middle-class New Yorkers, they are individualized by Lumet's unobtrusive yet sharply probing camera eye, sometimes seen from behind Fonda's shoulder as the man of reason and deliberation attempts to argue some jurors out of their prejudices and to persuade others out of their unconsidered conformity or fear. Several of the jurors (John Fiedler, Edward Binns, Martin Balsam, Jack Klugman) are "average" men, some more intelligent and reflective than others, who wish justice to be done, yet whose natural tendency to follow others leads them often to defer to the ill-considered judgments of the impatient and careless (Jack Warden, Robert Webber), the intemperate (Ed Begley), or the deeply conflicted (Lee J. Cobb). As pivotal to the decisions and conflicts of these less self-realized jurors is E. G. Marshall, whose greater insight and intelligence sometimes is as endangered by his own preconceptions and illusions as by the dogmatism and prejudice of those more fearful and dependent than he. A superior actor's picture, *Twelve Angry Men* provides a fine contrast "between alliances formed for intellectual reasons and for emotional needs."

At a sociological level, Lumet's film clearly reflects strong concern with the constituent parts of a living democracy, as the wiser and more emotionally stable jurors must responsibly lead those men with less self-awareness and self-knowledge than they, if democracy is to have any chance to work fairly and justly. Though there is little doctrinaire preaching on the subject of democracy, the audience is led to respond favorably to those jurors—Fonda, Sweeney, Voskovec—for whom reason, the liberal vision of the world and of man, are paramount. Nowhere is Rose's screenplay more subtly eloquent than in the scene in which Voskovec, an East European immigrant watchmaker now proud of his American citizenship, berates Warden, the successful marmalade salesman, for casting a crucial vote out of no more considered motive than simple indifference and haste, so that he can get to his baseball game on time. Whenever Voskovec speaks of democracy he does so simply, out of the harsh experience of a

man who has seen another political system up close and has found it wanting. He insists that if men are to govern themselves and their social relationships fairly and reasonably, they must be guided by principle. As he forces Warden for the first time to state his convictions for casting his vote, to ask questions of himself, Lumet frames Voskovec coming toward Warden's seat into an extremely tight close-up, but with the camera tilted only slightly up at the watchmaker, as if to minimize the European's "heroism" and to make him less important than the convictions for which he stands. The subtlety of this low-angle shot in an emotionally heightened scene underscores visually that though Voskovec may regard Warden with contempt, he does not consider himself—nor does Lumet consider him—intrinsically superior to the all-American baseball fan.

Earlier in the film, as a few of the jurors take a break from the sometimes angry debate, Lumet's meditative camera follows Fonda and Binns to the washroom, where Binns, an earnest working man who honestly disagrees with Fonda, states his conviction of the boy's guilt. After a critical comment about the irrationality and unfairness of some of the jurors who support his own position, Binns says, "I'm not used to supposin', I'm just a workin' man, my boss does all the supposin'." Yet he calls Fonda back as he is about to return to his seat in the jury room with, "But supposin' you do talk us all out of this and the kid really did knife his father?" The well-intentioned juror misses the point, of course, in that the entire thrust of the jury system is at least as much to protect the innocent as to convict the guilty. Holding Binns in steady mid-shot during this brief scene, Lumet suggests more, however, than the intellectual vacuity of this decent man, the fact that men who do not exercise their imaginative faculty, who do not "suppose," make weak cogs in a social system based supposedly upon the imaginative use of reason. That this sequence takes place in the most mundane location of the film underscores the basic importance of the theme of democracy in *Twelve Angry Men*. Lumet further emphasizes his concern by the last shot of this sequence, as Warden chatters aimlessly to Fonda about baseball and his success selling marmalade: as Warden talks on, Lumet holds Fonda in frame left, standing at the wash basin, cleaning his nails so long that it seems almost obsessive. Lumet plays no favorites in *Twelve Angry Men*; here its "hero" shows a penchant for fastidious cleanliness. It is not the character of Juror #8 that Lumet celebrates in the film, but rather the man's reasoned use of principle.

Lumet visually enhances his concern with the workings of the liberal democratic system early in the film when, having walked into the barren, sultry jury room Warden and Binns manage, with a difficulty emblematic of the film's action, to raise the window together. Moments later, it is Robert Webber, a slogan-spouting advertising executive in private life and one of the least sympathetic of the jurors, who hits on the democratic idea that each of the eleven convinced of the defendant's guilt present their reasons in turn and in order in an attempt to convince Fonda of the rightness of a guilty verdict. But it is the four-minute opening sequence of the film that most impressively and succinctly (and wordlessly) represents the principles of reason and liberalism that *Twelve Angry Men* upholds. After an establishing shot of the city courthouse, Lumet's camera tilts very slowly upward at its four framing pillars, with a huge lamp hanging down from the exact center of the frame, at the top of which is seen a motto carved in stone: "Administration of Justice is the Firmest Pillar of Good Government." Against the background sound of city traffic noise, Lumet cuts to an equally slow downward tilt from inside the courthouse, from a large chandelier at ceiling level down to the center cupola, again perfectly framed between four inner pillars. Pausing at the second landing level, the camera observes five people passing slowly near one another from several directions and converging at a point directly beneath the hanging chandelier. Their carefully orchestrated passage, reminiscent of the ballet-like passing sequence in Welles's *Magnificent Ambersons*, offers a symmetrical arrangement that parallels the carefully framed backdrop against which they move; by his formal composition and intra-shot montage, Lumet suggests a tone of almost classical stateliness and rationality to the forthcoming action. The extraordinarily leisurely camera movements featuring but one cut in almost four minutes, ending in a slow tracking shot to the outside of the courtroom where the boy's trial is being conducted, imply that the course of human justice is glacially slow, and that only the classical values of ordered, reasoned, meditative inquiry will possibly defeat the irrational prejudice that we are soon to see dominating the jury room.

Typically, Lumet's cinematic technique does not call attention of itself here, but its union with the film's thematic and moral meaning serves to remind the film viewer that the point of technique in any art form is less for spectacle than for serving the thematic values of the work of art itself. Rarely a pretentious, self-conscious artist, Lumet here reveals, quite early in his directorial career, that his central aesthetic interests lie in joining artistic content and form as closely as possible into a mutually integrative web of meaning. . . .

Source: Frank Cunningham, "Sidney Lumet's Humanism: The Return to the Father in *Twelve Angry Men*," in *Literature Film Quarterly*, Vol. 14, No. 2, 1986, pp. 112–21.

SOURCES

12 Angry Men, DVD, MGM, 2001.

Batt, Marissa N., "Just Verdicts? A Prosecutor Extols Jury Service for Women," in *Ms.*, Summer 2004, http://www.msmagazine.com/summer2004/justverdicts.asp (accessed August 17, 2011).

Baumbach, Jonathan, "*Twelve Angry Men* Is a Shallow Call to Civic-Mindedness," in *Readings on "Twelve Angry Men,"* edited by Russ Munyan, Greenhaven Press, 2000, pp. 109–12; originally published in *Film Culture*, 1957.

"Child Labor in U.S. History," in *Child Labor Education Project*, University of Iowa Labor Center, http://www.continuetolearn.uiowa.edu/laborctr/child_labor/about/us_history.html (accessed August 23, 2011).

Empey, LaMar T., and Mark C. Stafford, *American Delinquency: Its Meaning and Construction*, 3rd ed., Wadsworth Publishing, 1991, p. 59.

Jacobs, Jason, "Studio One," in *The Museum of Broadcast Communications*, 2011, http://www.museum.tv/eotvsection.php?entrycode=studioone (accessed August 17, 2011).

"Limiting the Death Penalty," in *Death Penalty Information Center*, 2011, http://www.deathpenaltyinfo.org/part-ii-history-death-penalty (accessed August 23, 2011).

Review of *12 Angry Men*, in *Variety*, December 31, 1956, http://www.variety.com/review/VE1117795934?refcatid=31 (accessed August 18, 2011).

Ritrosky-Winslow, Madelyn, "Anthology Drama," in *The Museum of Broadcast Communications*, 2011, http://www.museum.tv/eotvsection.php?entrycode=anthologydra (accessed August 17, 2011).

Rose, Reginald, *Twelve Angry Men*, introduction by David Mamet, Penguin Books, 2006.

Trojanowicz, Robert C., and Merry Morash, *Juvenile Delinquency: Concepts and Control*, 4th ed., Prentice-Hall, 1987, p. 12.

Weiler, A. H., "*12 Angry Men*: Jury Room Drama Has Debut at Capitol," in *New York Times*, April 15, 1957, http://movies.nytimes.com/movie/review?res = 9f02e3de 1730e23bbc4d52dfb266838c649ede (accessed August 18, 2011).

FURTHER READING

Bogdanovich, Peter, "An Interview with Sidney Lumet," in *Sidney Lumet: Interviews*, edited by Joanna E. Rapf, University Press of Mississippi, 2006, pp. 3–11.

> In this interview early in his career, Lumet talks about *12 Angry Men* and, in particular, the switch from directing television shows to directing films.

Bowles, Stephen E., *Sidney Lumet: A Guide to References and Resources*, G. K. Hall, 1979.

> Though parts of this book, such as the cast and credits for each film, have been made irrelevant by Internet sources, the long biography that opens the book is thorough and relevant to Lumet's career, and the sources to which Bowles refers are useful for researchers who are studying the director in depth.

Cunningham, Frank, "Sidney Lumet's Humanism: The Return to the Father in *Twelve Angry Men*," in *Literature Film Quarterly*, Vol. 14, No. 2, 1986, pp. 112–21.

> Despite the seemingly narrow focus indicated by the title, this article gives a sound overview of many of the film's themes and how they fit into Lumet's body of work as a whole.

———, "Lumet at Zenith: In the American Film Pantheon," in *Sidney Lumet: Film and Literary Vision*, 2nd ed., University Press of Kentucky, 2001, pp. 108–85.

> This section of a book by one of the most respected Lumet scholars offers readers in-depth analysis that shows why Lumet is considered one of the great American artists of the twentieth century. The section concerning *12 Angry Men*, subtitled "Toward an Imaginative Use of Reason," gives a careful reading of some specific scenes and the choices the director made in filming them.

Garfinkle, Ely, "Psychic Barriers to Truth in *Twelve Angry Men*," in *Canadian Journal of Psychoanalysis*, Vol. 11, No. 1, 2011, pp. 169–83.

> The author uses events in the film to explain a wide range of complex psychoanalytical ideas that might not be apparent to the casual viewer.

Lumet, Sidney, *Making Movies*, Alfred A. Knopf, 1995.

> With chapters about script, style, the actor, the camera, and other areas of his craft, this work is Lumet's thorough explanation of the process of putting together a film.

Rose, Reginald, "The Challenges of Screenwriting the 1957 Film Version," in *Readings on "Twelve Angry Men,"* edited by Russ Munyan, Greenhaven Press, 2000, pp. 40–43.

> This short piece, excerpted from a piece originally published in 1957, talks about how the author came to know the characters he had created for the teleplay and how he fit them to the film's actors.

SUGGESTED SEARCH TERMS

12 Angry Men OR Twelve Angry Men

12 Angry Men AND theatrical film

teleplay AND film AND 12 Angry Men

Sidney Lumet AND 12 Angry Men

12 Angry Men AND theatrical production

12 Angry Men AND trial system

Lumet AND jury room

Lumet AND urban drama

murder AND Lumet AND jury

Reginald Rose AND Fonda AND Lumet

Reginald Rose

Fonda AND producer

The Cuban Swimmer

MILCHA SANCHEZ-SCOTT

1982

The Cuban Swimmer, by Milcha Sanchez-Scott, is a one-act play that uses elements of the magical realist style in order to portray struggles for identity among the members of one Cuban immigrant family in America. The action of the play centers on Margarita Suárez and a race in which she is competing: a swim from San Pedro to Santa Catalina Island, off the California shore. Her father, mother, brother, and grandmother follow behind her in a boat, and together the family crosses this span of the Pacific Ocean in an attempt to win not only prize money but also respect for themselves.

Several times in the play, the characters come up against socially constructed identities. They struggle with questions of ethnicity, religion, gender, and assimilation, among others. Each character represents a unique identity quest. Central to the success of the play is its use of magical realism and elements of mysticism evident throughout. Also important is the tradition of mysticism that is passed down through the female members of this family.

Sanchez-Scott was one of the first Latina playwrights to win national attention for her work. In the early 1980s, she wrote prolifically and collaborated with other famous Latino and also Chicano writers in the United States to produce a style of theater uniquely suited to the experiences of immigrants of Hispanic descent. *The Cuban Swimmer* is a work exemplary of the

identity quests of these immigrants and the tradition developed in the Chicano and Latino theater communities to tell these stories.

The Cuban Swimmer was first performed in 1982 by L.A. Theatre Works. It was published in 1984 when performed at the INTAR (International Arts Relations) Hispanic American Arts Center in New York City.

AUTHOR BIOGRAPHY

Sanchez-Scott was born in Bali in 1953. Her mother was of Indonesian, Chinese, and Dutch descent, and her father was Colombian. The family traveled internationally a great deal during Sanchez-Scott's childhood, and her time was split primarily among Colombia, Mexico, and England, where she attended a school outside London. The family immigrated to the United States and settled in La Jolla, California, when Sanchez-Scott was thirteen. Here, she first encountered discrimination because of her ethnicity. Ironically, this discrimination against her as a "Mexican" and her later classification as a Chicana (Mexican) playwright occurred despite the fact that she has no Mexican ancestry. La Jolla, however, is close to the Mexican border and home to a large Mexican community, and she was quite often assumed to be Chicana.

Sanchez-Scott graduated from the University of San Diego and moved to Los Angeles. She took work with different theater companies and eventually found a place for herself in television, in a number of small roles playing poor women of Hispanic descent. She began to think about her own experiences and those of the women she portrayed. In 1980, she took those accounts and wrote her first play, *Latina*, to high critical acclaim.

This success encouraged her to write other productions about the roles of women in Latino and Chicano communities, often shining a spotlight on the contrasts between the traditional roles these women were typically expected to fill within the family and the opportunities that came with being an American. In 1982, she wrote two one-act plays, *Dog Lady* and *The Cuban Swimmer*, and the latter was performed by L.A. Theatre Works that year. Both plays use the female protagonists' struggle for athletic success as a symbol for success as an American

woman of Hispanic descent. Again, Sanchez-Scott's work received excellent reviews.

In 1984, Sanchez-Scott joined María Irene Fornés's prestigious Hispanic Playwrights in Residence Laboratory in New York. While studying with Fornés, Sanchez-Scott began to write her most famous play, *Roosters*, about a Chicano family living in the southwestern United States. Like her other work, *Roosters* utilizes magical realism to make pointed commentaries about her subject matter. It also continues her experimentation with language as a way of exploring the intersection of Hispanic and American culture. In 1987, *Roosters* was co-produced by INTAR Theatre and the New York Shakespeare Festival, cementing her reputation as a legitimate voice in feminist Latina theater. *American Theatre* magazine featured *Roosters* in its September 1987 edition, and that year Sanchez-Scott won the First Level Award for American playwrights from the Rockefeller Foundation.

Sanchez-Scott continued to write and be well-received into the 1990s, but she has produced little in the twenty-first century. Winner of seven Dramalogue awards for *Latina*, the Vesta Award for a West Coast female artist, and a Le Compte du Nouy Foundation Award, Sanchez-Scott is considered a pioneer in Latina and Chicana theater in America.

PLOT SUMMARY

Scene 1
A boat appears on the horizon and crosses the stage twice, growing larger each time. There is no dialogue and no sight of any characters in this scene. It serves only to illustrate that the action of the play takes place in the middle of the ocean, with no land in sight on the stage.

Scene 2
Nineteen-year-old Margarita Suárez is swimming at midday in the Pacific Ocean. A boat follows her. Onboard, her father, Eduardo, counts in time to the rhythm of Margarita's swimming, shouting both encouragement and direction through a megaphone to her. Her brother, Simón, sits shirtless on the cabin wearing punk sunglasses. A pair of binoculars hangs from his neck. As Eduardo counts in rhythm to Margarita's swimming strokes, Simón takes off

his sunglasses and looks through the binoculars directly at the sun, challenging it to "zap" his eyes and show him something. Abruptly, he yells for his father to stop. Aída and Abuela (which means "grandmother" in Spanish), Margarita's mother and grandmother, come running from the back of the boat. At first they are panicked, thinking there is a shark, but Simón quickly corrects them. He says they have reached the halfway mark in the race. When Aída asks him to explain how he knows this, he points to San Pedro behind them and then to Santa Catalina Island, the destination, in front of them, and says it "looks halfway."

Suddenly, they hear a helicopter approaching. There is confusion onboard, and Margarita calls to her father to explain what is happening. Simón looks at the helicopter through his binoculars and realizes they are being filmed. Aída scolds him to put on his shirt, fluffs her hair, and waves to the helicopter. The audience hears the voices of two reporters, Mel Munson and Mary Beth White. They serve to fill the audience in on the back story and characters. Mel remarks that "the little Cuban swimmer . . . is our Cinderella entry" in a race to Catalina that, should she win, would result in a prize of two thousand dollars and a gold cup. Mel and Mary Beth interrupt each other constantly, and through them the audience learns that Eduardo is not himself a swimmer; he owns a sea salvage yard. Aída is a former Miss Cuba.

The reporters decide to try to get a closer look at the family, and the helicopter moves closer. This frightens Margarita, and Aída urges Eduardo to deal with the press. He calls to Margarita to ignore them. Abuela calls to the helicopter in Spanish, cheering on her granddaughter and "all the Cubans" in the United States. She therefore draws a symbolic parallel between Margarita and all Cuban Americans, which makes clear that Margarita's race to Santa Catalina is a metaphor for the struggles of her people. She gets so excited that she asks Simón to translate for her, and with his help she gives "a big hug" to her friends all over the country, from Long Beach to Miami. She tells of her son, Carlos, living "in Brooklyn with a Puerto Rican woman in sin." She is ashamed that he has brought indecency to the family name by not marrying his live-in girlfriend. Her traditional beliefs and limited English define her as a symbol of the old country and the old ways. Mel makes disparaging comments

about Margarita's efforts, saying he hopes her family "won't be too disappointed" when she loses. When Mary Beth points out that Margarita is in fact doing well, he dismisses it by saying that "it takes all kinds to make a race," a play on words since, of course, in the ethnic sense, a race by definition consists of only one specific type of people. Mel calls Margarita and her family amateurs, which upsets them.

Simón and Abuela curse the reporters as they fly off, and Aída is offended that he called them all "simple." "If my daughter was simple," she says, "she would not be in that water swimming." Aída, the Suárezes, and the audience understand that this is not only a test of physical prowess and endurance but as well a chance to prove something more complex than Mel and Mary Beth can understand. Aída wants Eduardo to call the television station for an apology when they get to Santa Catalina, but he grumbles at his family for breaking Margarita's concentration. He scolds them, saying that a race is won in the head, and tells them to go do "something practical." The scene ends as Abuela and Aída pray and the sun appears brighter.

Scene 3

The family is shown in tableau (a still and quiet scene): Eduardo is counting strokes per minute with a timer in hand, Simón is steering, and Abuela and Aída are muttering Spanish prayers with their heads bowed. Eduardo calls out that Margarita is doing seventy-two strokes per minute and remarks that it is a beautiful day to win. Abuela and Aída thank God for the beautiful weather; Simón sings in the background. Abuela thinks she sees a rainbow in the water, but Eduardo quickly realizes it is an oil slick. Margarita is covered in oil, and Aída begs Eduardo to pull her out of the water, but he says that if they touch her, she is disqualified. Margarita is surrounded by dead birds floating with their wings glued to their sides, and the entire family urges her to keep swimming so that she is not trapped in the sludge. Those on the boat begin to chant direction together in rhythm as a family, pointing Margarita in the direction of clear, clean water. The lights go down on the boat, highlighting Margarita in the water and Abuela standing over her. Abuela tells a mystical legend about Margarita's great-grandmother Luz Suárez. Back in Bolondron, Cuba, one day it began to rain blood. All of the villagers ran inside their houses crying, but Luz looked up into the sky and challenged the devil to come and take her if he wanted before opening her mouth and drinking the blood. Abuela addresses this story to Margarita, saying that she "will be another to save us" like Luz.

Scene 4

Aída and Eduardo watch Margarita swim, and the sound of her increasingly louder breathing, the lapping sound of her movements, and her heartbeat are heard over the dialogue of the scene. Aída and Eduardo reminisce about how Margarita has always come alive in the water, so much so that she resembles a seal. While Eduardo claims her talent is due to the intense training he put her through as a child, Aída says that the spirit of the ocean must have invaded Margarita. In the background, Margarita's breathing and heartbeat speed up, while onboard, Aída and Eduardo poetically remember the boat trip from Cuba to America. Aída claims that Eduardo kidnapped her from her home without her consent, but he protests that it was so they could be married. However, Aída calls him a liar and talks about how he seduced her on the boat. The lights go down on everyone but Aída as she tells of a dream she had that night "of a big country with fields of fertile land and big, giant things growing." She crosses herself as she watches her daughter in the water, and Margarita asks Aída to pray for her.

Scene 5

The weather has changed to foggy, misty air and howling wind. Margarita has started drifting because of the wind, and the unstable weather reflects the mood between the family members. They draw together only in their encouragement of her. Margarita stops, and so does the boat. The others assume Margarita is tired, and Eduardo and Simón start clowning around. Simón goes too far, and Eduardo slaps him so that he falls to the deck of the boat. Abuela runs to hold back Eduardo as Aída rushes to her son's side. Margarita cries out that it is her fault; the fish are taunting her, and she is exhausted and cold. The cold has numbed her, and she asks Eduardo if she has died. Simón is the first to realize that Margarita wants to quit and needs to get out of the water, but she cannot make herself ask. She needs Eduardo to tell her that it is all right if she does not finish the race, but instead, he says that the key is only "mind over matter" and that she needs to concentrate. He

curses, asking God why Cubans must go everywhere with their families. Abuela and Simón lower a water bottle to Margarita in the sea, and it seems to refresh her a bit. She begins to swim backstroke, but as the lights focus on her, she stops in pain. Disoriented, she sinks to the bottom of the sea. She calls out for her father, asking for both his forgiveness and his instruction. She begins to swim in rhythm with the Hail Mary she is praying. The scene ends in blackout with her saying, "I don't want to die, I don't want to die."

Scene 6

The scene opens with radio static and an outline of Abuela in the heavy mists. The voices of Margarita's parents are overheard telling the radio operator that they have lost Margarita. Simón calls out to the sea, urging Margarita to return. In his ensuing monologue, he remembers how Margarita was always told to watch out for him, and he blames his father for her disappearance. He says he will send sonar signals, like the ones dolphins use, to get her to come home. Real dolphin noises drown him out and fade into the sound of Abuela praying as the lights rise slowly.

Scene 7

Eduardo and Aída sob and blame themselves while Abuela stares calmly ahead. Simón says he is going in after Margarita, but Eduardo holds him back, begging God to take him instead. He calls his children his "illusions" and says that Simón holds all of the parts of him that cannot be seen. Mel, the reporter, is heard over the radio, announcing the tragedy of Margarita being lost at sea. Suddenly, Mary Beth interrupts to announce that there is a winner. In shock, she says that the winner is Margarita. The Suárez family cheers, euphoric over her "resurrection." The scene ends with cheering crowds and Mel proclaiming, "This is a miracle!"

CHARACTERS

Abuela

Abuela is Eduardo's mother and Margarita's grandmother. She speaks primarily in Spanish, espouses the traditional beliefs of Cuban culture, and is devoutly religious. She seems innocent in comparison with the rest of the characters and is unwavering in her belief and pride in her granddaughter. *Abuela* means "grandmother" in Spanish, which places her as a symbol of nurturing and tradition. (Although Aída calls her by her first name, Cecilia, a couple of times, her character is consistently referred to as Abuela.) When first confronted with Mel and Mary Beth in the helicopter, she exhibits childlike delight in her surprise appearance on television, jumping and waving at them and shouting her pride in Margarita. Of all the characters, she is the least assimilated. She is quick to pray and invoke the blessings of God, the Virgin Mary, and various saints. She is also the most mystical of the group, and her dialogue often evokes a poetic lyricism. To Abuela, Margarita "will be another to save us."

Even though Abuela seems naive and as if she needs protecting herself from the alien culture in which she lives, she demonstrates more strength and faith than any other character, and she recognizes the importance of the responsibility they have all placed upon Margarita. When everyone else believes Margarita has been drowned at sea, Abuela says that her "little fish is not lost." Her faith in Margarita is unfailing.

Cecilia
See Abuela

Mel Munson
Mel is one of the two television reporters covering the race whom readers hear. His is the voice of the superior, prejudiced, mainstream American society. He patronizes Margarita and her family, calling them amateurs despite the fact that she is doing well in the race. Mel places Margarita and the role of the Cubana within the constructs of America as portrayed by the mainstream media. "It takes all kinds to make a race," he notes condescendingly. While he acknowledges Margarita's participation in the race, it is clear he does not consider her a valid contender. He gives lip service to encouraging her "long-shot chance to victory" while simultaneously dismissing it. In his Anglo (white), stereotypical final metaphor of Margarita, though, he expresses the theme of the play: "It's a resurrection!" Margarita has been resurrected in his eyes, just as a successful Cuban American is reborn in the eyes of society as a whole.

Aída Suárez
Aída is Margarita's mother. She is caught between the traditional role of the wife and mother in the Cuban familial structure and her desire to fit into American culture. As a former Miss Cuba, Aída is extremely feminine and somewhat shallow at times. Appearances are very important to her, as evidenced by her primping for the camera, her desire for her son and Abuela to make a good showing for Mel and Mary Beth, and the way she takes offense at their dismissive and disparaging attitudes toward her family. More than any other character, Aída seems to embody both feminine strength and submissiveness to Eduardo's authority. Though she nags him, she tends to back down when Eduardo turns his anger and frustration on her. There is no thought of going against Eduardo to pull Margarita from the race even when her life is in danger. This would be a transgression of Eduardo's authority.

Aída has moments of mysticism that are reminiscent of Abuela's. She makes the best of her situation, but there is a longing for the home she left behind that underlies her character. Speaking to Eduardo, she says, "I see the lights of Havana in your eyes. That's when you seduced me." Where Eduardo is excited and seduced by the promise of America, it is the memory of Cuba that moves Aída. All she knows to do is to bring her knowledge of how to be a Cuban woman to her new country and apply it as best she can while still clinging to her pride—her pride in her country, in her children, and in herself. Although she cannot directly connect to the mystic tradition of faith that Abuela so strongly symbolizes, she manages to do so through dreaming of her children. Thus, she is a step removed from Abuela's firm and unbreakable ties to Cuba but also is unable to fully accept America as her new country; she is caught in the middle.

Eduardo Suárez
Margarita's father, Eduardo, is her self-named coach, and throughout the play he struggles with reconciling his paternal role of protector and guide with his desire to use Margarita to secure a place for the Suárez family in American society. Though he time and time again insists that he is in charge and has everything under control, it is clear that he controls nothing. Margarita is the one doing the swimming, and all Eduardo can do is encourage her and push her to continue. Only Margarita can uphold the family name by winning the race, so he pushes her even harder. "You must win," he tells her, "*por la familia*"—for the family. He constantly chides

his family for breaking Margarita's concentration, but it is his own focus he is afraid to shift. It is almost as though if for one moment he stops concentrating on Margarita's winning the race, she will be destined to lose. In contrast to Abuela's effortless faith, Eduardo must assert to himself and the others over and over that Margarita must win.

There is a desperation to Eduardo that hints at a much larger and stronger desire to once again find a position from which he can truly lead and protect his family in the traditional way, a way that is denied to him by virtue of the socially impotent role he occupies in America. During a conversation with Aída, he seeks reassurance from his wife, asking for confirmation that he was a good lover and husband. His confusion can be seen elsewhere: in his dogged insistence that Margarita stay in the water and finish the race even when he is scared for her life, in his strange relationship with his son, in the clear juxtaposition of his verbal claims as head of the family with his powerlessness to protect them. His relationship with his children is complicated. Despite being female, Margarita carries the responsibility of upholding the family honor with a good showing. Simón, on the other hand, is left almost to his own devices. Eduardo treats his son as though the sole reason for his existence is to help his sister succeed. He says that his children hold all of his dreams and illusions. These are his last lines of dialogue in the play, and they encompass his character. As Simón says to Margarita, her winning the race is Eduardo's dream. Stripped of the traditional patriarchal authority that is his legacy from his Cuban culture, he is desperate for Margarita to do what he cannot: to make a place for them in this new world that seems to have no room for his success.

Margarita Suárez

Margarita is the title character of *The Cuban Swimmer*. She is competing in a race to swim from San Pedro, California, to the island of Santa Catalina. The prize is two thousand dollars and a gold cup, but it is really her family's honor that is at stake. The daughter of Cuban immigrants, Margarita is tasked with proving to American society that the Suárez family deserves recognition as a valid part of the culture. She is followed in her swim by a boat containing her mother, father, grandmother, and brother, and it is through her interactions with these characters that Sanchez-Scott attempts to define Margarita's identity. Margarita's dialogue is in large part mystical and dreamlike, and it is mostly directed toward her father, Eduardo, who also acts as her coach. When Mel Munson and Mary Beth White appear in the helicopter, Margarita turns to her father for reassurance. Although he tells her that he has everything under control, it is clear that nothing in this play is under his control except for his family, especially Margarita. Margarita is in motion for the entire play, pulling herself through the water toward Santa Catalina Island and her first-place prize. She defers constantly to Eduardo's authority as her father and the male head of the family. This gender power dynamic is typical of many Hispanic traditions; however, the United States in the 1980s was embracing women's rights. Margarita, therefore, is caught between two gender identities: that of the strong, American woman of power and responsibility and that of the traditional, submissive woman of her family's ethnic heritage. She understands that the burden of proof is on her to show that the Suárez family and indeed all Cuban immigrants are strong enough to survive this test of endurance.

Margarita does not race for herself. She does it for her father, her family, and her people. However, though she races for others, she survives and wins for herself. The last words in the play that she speaks are "I don't want to die." This is the first indication that Margarita wants anything for herself, and what she wants is not to make her father proud or make a name for her family; she wants to survive. It is this survival instinct that propels her to push beyond the limits of her physical ability and not only make it to shore but even win. The Cuban swimmer, in the end, has become Margarita Suárez: separated from the other characters, she is no longer seen as a daughter, sister, or amateur. She is triumphant in her own right, seizing her win alone and winning not just a trophy and some prize money but respect and independence.

Simón Suárez

Margarita's younger brother, Simón, represents the male side of the identity struggle that Margarita faces. Bound by traditional expectations from his Cuban cultural roots but forced to live in a society that throws all those beliefs into question, Simón is left without a clear-cut gender role within the power structure of his family. His father, Eduardo, made essentially powerless by his Cuban immigrant status, places all of his hopes for a resurrection of the family honor on his daughter Margarita. Simón is demoted to the status of Eduardo's assistant; his only importance lies in how effective he is in helping Margarita win the race. Where *The Cuban Swimmer* confines the action to the Suárez family's boat and limits the character interaction to solely among family members, Simón represents the young, American popular culture in which he partly exists, in contrast to the traditional, confined familial culture that is found on the boat. Simón, with his punk sunglasses, American slang, and fondness for curse words, wants desperately to be a part of something instead of just an observer and a helper.

Simón often plays the scapegoat for Eduardo, such as when Margarita swims into the oil slick. Despite the fact that Eduardo, who is acting as Margarita's coach, does not see the oil, he blames Simón for not paying attention. When the wind picks up and Margarita begins to drift away from the boat, again Eduardo blames Simón. The dynamic between father and son is complicated and confusing. Eduardo depends heavily upon Simón yet does not give him any respect as his own person. Simón recognizes that Eduardo is living vicariously through Margarita and that her success or failure will be a personal success or failure for Eduardo. Of all of the members of the family, Margarita is the one Simón is closest to. His vulnerable side comes out when he fears that she has drowned, and he begs her not to leave him behind, reminding her that when they were little, adults always told her to watch out for him.

Mary Beth White

Mary Beth is a reporter in the helicopter who, along with Mel Munson, is covering the Wrigley Invitational Women's Race to Catalina. Though certainly not sensitive or a person who can in any way relate to Margarita Suárez, Mary Beth is not as dramatic in her portrayal of the Suárez family as Mel is. It is Mary Beth who keeps her focus on the "family effort" that is behind Margarita's success thus far. Hers is a more sympathetic point of view than Mel's, and she is willing to recognize Margarita's individuality.

THEMES

Feminism

Feminism first began to emerge as a theme in literature and drama in the late nineteenth century. However, it was not until the activist movements of the 1960s that feminism as a critical theory truly came into its own. Along with minority rights and the antiwar movement, feminist ideas took deep root in the youth culture of America in the 1960s and 1970s. By the 1980s, feminism had moved beyond college campuses and into every aspect of American society, from federal government to the workplace. As with all literary criticism, feminist theories question the way people understand and portray the world through the lenses of literature and drama. Feminism radically changed the face of artistic expression.

The Cuban Swimmer uses ideas of feminist theory but focuses on a specific ethnicity, thus exploring issues of gender on a deeper and more complex level. The play questions the dominance of the father, emphasizes the roles of the women in the family as both caretakers and holders of traditional spirituality (such as with Abuela's mysticism and Margarita's prayers), and contrasts the actions and attitudes of Margarita with those of her brother, Simón. According to Tiffany Ana Lopez in *The Oxford Companion to Women's Writing*,

> Theatre has become an important artistic arena for Latinas working through issues of women's identity and cultural development, particularly in regard to their representation of two marginalized groups in American society: women and people of color.

Far from attempting to distract the cultural critic from the struggles of ethnic minorities in America, Sanchez-Scott is adding another layer of social criticism by positioning her protagonist as oppressed both racially and because of her gender. *The Cuban Swimmer* explores the issue of gender both within the familial structure governed by Latino power dynamics and within the broader aspect of the American worldview.

Identity

The Cuban Swimmer explores the fundamental questions of cultural identity: what it is, how it is defined, and how one person is able to find a voice and identity unique to him- or herself amongst the chaos and confusion of identity imposed by outside forces. All people are defined

TOPICS FOR FURTHER STUDY

- Read *Maniac Magee*, a young-adult novel by Jerry Spinelli, the story of a young boy struggling with racism and other cultural issues. The book is written in the magical realist style, weaving metaphor, fantastical situations, and realistic portrayals together to tell Maniac's struggle to find his way in the world. Find three instances of magical realism at work in the book. How does the use of this style work to enhance the story or more clearly show the themes in the book? How would the story change if told in a purely realistic style as opposed to magical realism? Write an essay discussing your findings.

- With your class, explore and identify the role of language as a construct of societal roles. Be creative. Although you and your parents may alike speak English, in all probability it would be accurate to say that you at times do not "speak the same language." Slang, formal language used in the workplace, foreign languages, and language hybrids such as "Spanglish" are some examples of variance in language. Discuss how language can be used as an identifying factor in American society. Create a blog that pulls examples from popular media, such as television, film, advertising, and real footage from sites such as YouTube to explore your discoveries. Have your classmates comment on the blog about the findings of the class.

- Although magical realism is not officially recognized as a genre in film, there are many examples of this style in the movies. Movies such as *Big*, *Whale Rider*, *Groundhog Day*, *Chocolat*, and *Moulin Rouge!* can all be classified as magical realism: they mix elements of fantasy into a mostly realistic

setting. Choose a film to watch that could fall under the heading of magical realism, and identify and isolate elements of this technique in the film. How do each of the elements help the filmmaker present the main theme of the film? How would the film be different if the "magic" was removed? Write a paper explaining your findings.

- In *The Cuban Swimmer*, Margarita struggles with the different roles that have been assigned to her by her family, her ethnicity, and the American culture in which she lives. She is so weighed down trying to fulfill all of these identities that she finally gives in to exhaustion and sinks to the bottom of the ocean. It is only there, isolated from other influences, that she is able to shed these assigned roles and discover who she truly is. In what ways have you undergone a similar process? How have you discarded an identity that was assigned to you in order to create your own? Create a multimedia presentation using music, video, and images found online to show this transformation.

- In a group, identify the key identity issues with which you and your classmates struggle daily. Be specific. In what ways does your gender define your socially constructed role in American culture? How does your race or ethnicity factor into your struggle both to fit in and to stay unique in our society? Are you particularly religious or spiritual? With the other members of your group, write a one-act play in which each of you plays a character representing a particular identity struggle. Using elements of magical realism as discussed in this chapter, tell the story of these identity quests and how they are resolved.

by their environments. The people and social structures that form the environment provide a starting point, but ultimately it is up to individuals to decide how they will both identify themselves and allow others to identify them. Sanchez-Scott explores Margarita's identity through her interactions with the other characters in the play. Through them, Margarita is presented with multiple identities: daughter, sister, granddaughter, savior, Cuban, immigrant, American, female, and athlete are some of the more obvious ones. Margarita must sift through these identities and roles as well as explore her own feelings about where she feels she belongs in the world.

Sanchez-Scott explores identity on multiple levels in *The Cuban Swimmer*. Margarita must define herself in terms of her family, her Cuban heritage, the American social structure in which she lives, and, perhaps most difficult, in terms of how she views herself. What labels will she accept from among those that are proffered, which will she reject, and what labels will she create on her own? Drama is a medium uniquely suited to the theme of the identity quest. Since individual identity is created by interactions with others and the culture in which the individual resides, the stage is an ideal vehicle through which to explore these relationships via dialogue and visual representation. Rita E. Urquijo-Ruiz, in her essay "Drama" in *Inside the Latin@ Experience: A Latin@ Studies Reader*, says that Sanchez-Scott addresses "issues of assimilation into the mainstream, Anglo society." The audience comes to understand the different identities that Margarita has to reconcile through the other characters in the play. The three broad areas of cultural identity she must explore are represented by the three worlds in which the play takes place. There is Margarita's search for self-identity, which occurs in the water. The Suárez family on the boat represents the traditional world of her Cuban heritage and her familial ties and obligations. Finally, mainstream America is represented by the reporters in the helicopter, who give a running commentary on what they feel is her role within the social structure of American culture.

As Urquijo-Ruiz points out, "The protagonists struggle to find pride within their cultural and ethnic identities while managing their lives in the mainstream, [and] they each reach a compromise in the end." By portraying that struggle between identities as a metaphorical race, the play tells the story of this search for compromise. As she struggles to win the competition, Margarita tries to fulfill the expectations of her family, as well as those of the American news reporters and their audience. By the play's end, when she drifts beneath the surface and her family and the reporters believe that she has drowned,

Margarita has separated herself from all outside influences. She discovers who she is, and the act of defining her own identity literally saves her life.

Mysticism

Mysticism is an elevated sense of spirituality, the feeling that one is, or can be, in direct contact with God or the core meaning of the universe. It is similar to transcendence, the experience of passing beyond ordinary human experience to something higher or more meaningful. There have always been mystics in every major religion, including Buddhism, Hinduism, Islam, and Christianity. A mystic is a person who, through intense focus and personal expression of faith, is able to reach a higher spiritual plane than others. Buddhists call these people "enlightened," and the term is an apt description for mystics of all faiths. Springing from the spiritual rather than the rational realm, mysticism is difficult to define, yet characteristics of it can be easily recognized.

In *The Cuban Swimmer*, for instance, Abuela has several mystic moments when the basis of her reasoning seems to come from her faith and not from logic. For example, Abuela's tale of Luz Suárez carries mystic tones. The story is meant to reach the audience on a spiritual and emotional level and to illustrate the meaning of Margarita's struggle in a way that transcends mere facts. Abuela likens Margarita to her ancestor by comparing their respective confrontations with forces that seek to defeat them. Through courage and strength, both Margarita and Luz are able to triumph over challenges of spirit. By couching Margarita's efforts in terms of religion, faith, and spirituality, Abuela both represents and reinforces the mystic, almost unknowable strength of the women in the Suárez family that is drawn from a connection to God. Aída, too, has moments of mysticism, such as when she recounts the dream she had the night she conceived Margarita. The symbolic nature of the dream springs from emotion and an instinctual spirituality rather than from logic or reason, and it draws a connection between Aída, Margarita, and forces such as God that are larger and more infinite than any one human. In the Christian tradition, mystics are people who have, through intense dedication, purity, or divine intervention, been able to experience spiritual transcendence in one way or another. Margarita's resurrection at the end of the play is representative of her ability to overcome the

Margarita Suarez, the main character, is in a swimming competition throughout the entire play. *(emin kuliyev | Shutterstock.com)*

pressures that almost cause her to drown through supplication to God, the saints, and the Virgin Mary.

In *The Cuban Swimmer*, the women of the Suárez family are the ones who exhibit mystic overtones. Where Eduardo is stern and at times unfeeling, Abuela, Aída, and Margarita all turn eventually to their religious faith when things appear desperate. They are the holders of traditional spirituality in their family, and they therefore claim a vital piece of Hispanic culture as belonging to the realm of women. They rest their faith ultimately in God, and it is this steadfast faith that allows them to believe in each other and in divine providence.

STYLE

Magical Realism

According to Enrique Grönlund and Moylan C. Mills in "Magic Realism and García Márquez's *Eréndira*," German art critic Franz Roh first introduced the term *magic realism* in 1925 as a definition for postexpressionist art. Since then, the term has expanded to include a number of definitions, and it has come to describe a style of writing that incorporates miraculous or magical elements with a degree of realism, accepting the magical elements as a normal part of the world. The term also incorporates a conflict of perspectives, where the supernatural elements of the work are approached through the perspective of the average and mundane. This process adds a nuanced layer to the final product, which gives it a sense of mystery. Mills and Grönlund make a point of emphasizing the success of this genre, especially in Latin American literature: "Latin American reality [is] so infused with an inherent . . . wonderment that writers need not conjure artificial adornments in order to express this element."

Magical realism contrasts situations found in everyday life with fantastical imagery and lyrical, almost poetic language. Allegory—the use of events or characters to represent other ideas, often with the aim of teaching a lesson—is an important feature of the genre. For example, in *The Cuban Swimmer*, Sanchez-Scott uses the swim race as an extended metaphor for the girl's real-life struggle for success. Symbols abound in the play, all coming together to form the allegory wherein the race and the fantastical situations in the play represent Margarita's very real struggle for identity. The magical or mysterious aspects of a work are often the result of closely and carefully examining the reality of any situation and discovering what is already inherently mysterious about it. Since the magical element is already present in the depiction of reality, it neither needs nor receives elaborate description. Though the language of the style and of this play is sometimes lyrical, the tone is often matter-of-fact or even distant. Supernatural or dreamlike elements are presented as if they were reality, and reality is presented as if it were dreamlike, so that the two become the special reality of the play.

In *Chicano Drama: Performance, Society and Myth*, Jorge Huerta quotes director Peter Brosius as saying that magical realism is a genre in which Sanchez-Scott seems particularly comfortable: "For Milcha, magic realism is not a genre so much as it is a way of life.... It's just a part of the perceptual apparatus she brings to the world every day." Her work in this regard is similar to the fiction of Jorge Luis Borges and Gabriel García Márquez in that it combines history with dreams for the future and contrasts them with the sometimes harsh realities of the present. The play itself is written to be staged in a way that forces the audience into a separated series of worlds, each directly advancing the narrative but also representing a different aspect of the play's perspective. The fractured narrative style gives the audience a richer perspective on the influences of the Latino and American worlds on the protagonist.

Miracle Play

Mystery plays originated in Europe in or around the twelfth century as a way for the church to teach the gospel and stories of the Bible to a largely illiterate citizenry. Miracle plays are a sub-genre of mystery plays that specifically reenact the miraculous intervention of saints in ordinary people's lives. In modern terms, a "miracle play" is loosely defined as one in which dire circumstances are turned around in a mysterious way, and the protagonist is saved from doom without much explanation, if any.

Margarita's miraculous emergence from the sea at the end of *The Cuban Swimmer* qualifies the play, in this sense, as a miracle play. Huerta, in *Chicano Drama: Performance, Society and Myth*, describes this work as Sanchez-Scott's interpretation of the miracle play. In large part because of the mysticism the Roman Catholic Church teaches throughout much of the Spanish-speaking world, the concept of miracles, especially those with biblical connotations such as a resurrection, is a common theme in South American and Latin American life. *The Cuban Swimmer* incorporates traditional and faith-driven aspects of Hispanic culture into a modern context, including elements of miracle plays.

Language

The importance of language in *The Cuban Swimmer* cannot be overstated. Sanchez-Scott is able to use the language of the characters as yet another symbol. Above Margarita in the helicopter, the impersonal, sensationalistic, and clichéd dialogue of the American newscasters symbolizes the country in which she lives yet quite obviously does not belong. The Suárez family's means of communication is a fascinating study of gender, generational, and cultural identifications. Simón speaks in slang, using the unique blend of Spanish and English common to so many Latino youths with Spanish-speaking family members living in an English-speaking world. The grandmother, simply called Abuela (which means "grandmother"), speaks the most Spanish in the play. Spanish, then, becomes the language of family, mysticism, and tradition, while English becomes an almost foreign tongue, symbolizing an alien world that does not accept the Suárez family. The language of the play serves as a vehicle for the exploration of what it means to Margarita to be a bilingual and bicultural woman, caught between her heritage and her home.

HISTORICAL CONTEXT

Mariel Boatlift

Amid a plummeting economy and persisting social inequities in Cuba, a small group of Cubans rammed a bus through the gates of the Peruvian embassy in Havana in April 1980, seeking asylum from Castro and his administration. Castro withdrew all Cuban guards from the embassy after the Peruvian government decided

COMPARE & CONTRAST

- **1980s:** In 1980, the Mariel boatlift (so called because of the departure point in Mariel Harbor) brings a large number of Cuban immigrants to the United States. However, tensions rise because of suspicions that the majority of these immigrants are criminals, mentally ill, or otherwise "undesirable" and have been sent to American shores by Cuban president Fidel Castro as a form of sabotage.

  Today: Cuban Americans have established respected communities throughout the United States, primarily in Florida but also across the rest of the country, and are a vibrant and integral part of the American social system.

- **1980s:** Women of all ethnic traditions struggle to be recognized as valuable and autonomous individuals in their own right, capable of holding their own in what is still largely considered a culture dominated by men.

  Today: Having won hard-fought battles for equal rights and recognition both legally and socially since the women's liberation movement began in the 1960s, women hold positions of power in all facets of American society, and American culture remains highly sensitive to instances of discrimination based on gender.

- **1980s:** Postmodernist literature and drama seeks to expose the realities of social truths and patterns within a culture, valuing innovative approaches to the construction of artistic works as a way of symbolically exposing these truths.

  Today: While the artistic movements of the twenty-first century have yet to be defined under a single umbrella term (though some critics have proposed the awkward term "post-postmodernism"), a return to more intimate and lyrical storytelling as a means of exposing the truths of the human condition seems to be an ever-growing trend in literature and the performing arts.

---

to grant the refugees asylum, and within days thousands of Cubans had crammed themselves into every available space on the embassy grounds. Castro granted permission for any Cuban who wanted to leave the country to leave from the nearby port of Mariel. When news of this announcement reached Cuban Americans in the United States, hundreds of people set off in watercraft of all sorts and sizes to go rescue their relatives from Cuba in what later came to be known as the Mariel boatlift. Between April and October 1980, an estimated 125,000 Cubans found asylum in the United States. The wave of immigrants was so overwhelming that the Coast Guard was sent to assist in search-and-rescue missions to help Cubans who were stranded in the journey. President Jimmy Carter and his administration came under harsh criticism from Americans who believed that Castro was sending convicted criminals and mentally unstable people to the United States to undermine the foundation of American society, but later estimations showed that only a small percentage of these immigrants were in fact such "undesirables."

Feminism

Feminism as an activist movement began in earnest in the 1960s. Dissatisfied with their marginalized roles in American culture and yet conditioned to feel that questioning those roles was subversive and unnatural, a generation of young women was living in a world that was becoming more modernized every day, and they wanted to be a part of it. Like other social protest movements at the time, feminism focused

The competition involves swimming from Long Beach, California, to Catalina Island. (Sim Creative Art / Shutterstock.com)

on equal rights. These women (mostly white, middle-class women, at first), many of them housewives or workers confined to low-status "women's work," were using their voices for the first time to speak up against societal discrimination against females. By the late 1970s and early 1980s, the feminist movement had spread to encompass Americans who were disenfranchised in other ways, as well. Minority women and homosexual women had a platform from which to speak out against the particular brand of oppression they suffered within their social and cultural identities. After the massive achievements of women in the 1960s and early 1970s, cultural attention was focused on what any and all women had to say for the first time.

Latinas and Chicanas, even more so than other women, were fighting this battle not only with American society but within their own familial units. The traditional power structure in families of Hispanic origin firmly placed women in a position of vulnerability. Men were almost universally held as the head of the household and the ultimate voice of power. This was reinforced by the strong influence that Roman Catholicism held over these cultures. Therefore, these women

were attempting to find a place for themselves not only in contemporary American society but also within their own ethnic cultures, often going against long-held beliefs in the subordination of women to men. *The Cuban Swimmer* provides examples of this dynamic. The dialogue of the women is mystical and emotional, while Margarita's father is relentless in his domination. Margarita symbolizes the "new woman" caught between the expectations of her family and her own desperation to find a separate identity as an independent, successful Cuban woman.

Postmodernism

Postmodernism is a post–World War II movement in philosophy, art, and literature that was a reaction against the modernist era in the earlier twentieth century. While modernism focused on finding meaning in a rapidly changing era of industrialization, class restructuring, and the aftermath of World War I, postmodernism's concentration is more about the construction of the art—whether visual art, performing art, or literature—and the reflections of the artist's world in the final work. In *The Cuban Swimmer*, a style known as magical realism is prevalent. This is a postmodern phenomenon that explores the predicaments of modern society not by simply looking for meaning but by twisting the reality of any situation to show the absurd or encourage the audience to question the "truths" they have been shown. Irony, deceptive playfulness, and satire are other tools of postmodernism, and they can all be seen in *The Cuban Swimmer*. Often, postmodern works play on traditional structures and give them a new twist. Sanchez-Scott, for example, takes the centuries-old form of the miracle or mystery play and modernizes it in forms such as Margarita's magical resurrection at the end of the play. Postmodernism almost always carries a hidden (or not so hidden) story within a story, sometimes called metafiction. The embedded story may be obvious (for example, a novel about the process of writing a novel), or it may be cleverly disguised. Sanchez-Scott, in *The Cuban Swimmer*, has used several subtle versions of this technique. The reporters in the helicopter narrate the action in the water for their American viewers, while simultaneously the family in the boat is giving much of Margarita's backstory and insights into her character and her struggle. Postmodernism seeks to show a truth or reality through unconventional means. *The Cuban Swimmer* is not a realistic play; rather, it seeks to show a truth through an unrealistic event. Postmodernism seeks to use everything from language to themes to setting in slightly new ways. Some critics point to the rise of television and film, and the fantastic and unrealistic characteristics with which they are imbued, as an inspiration behind postmodernist work.

It is unclear whether the postmodern movement is at or near its end. References have been made to "post-postmodernism" in the early 2010s, but postmodern fiction and drama are still unmistakably prevalent in contemporary literature.

CRITICAL OVERVIEW

When Sanchez-Scott burst onto the literary scene in 1980 with *Latina*, she grabbed the attention of critics, who widely hailed her as a great voice for the Latina woman along the lines of María Irene Fornés. *Latina*, her first play, received seven Dramalogue awards and provided her with opportunities to study and work with some of the preeminent Hispanic playwrights of the 1980s. The quick succession in which *Latina*, *Dog Lady*, *The Cuban Swimmer*,

and *Rooster* were written and produced speaks to her ability to hit upon socially relevant and often highly sensitive subjects in a style that manages to enchant rather than offend. In 1987, Mel Gussow, in a *New York Times* review, wrote that "Ms. Sanchez-Scott has a natural theatrical talent and an ability to ensnare an audience in a tale—both comic and poignant."

Her fascination with magical realism as a medium for addressing the cultural issues faced by Latinas and Chicanas allowed her, in Gussow's words, to "maintain balance and humor" while somehow making "the bizarre seem everyday." This style is vital to the success of her work, and her drama, while obviously meant to illustrate identity struggle on many levels, seems almost as dedicated to magical realism as to her ultimate message. Jorge Huerta, in *Necessary Theatre: Six Plays about the Chicano Experience*, notes that "this Latin American magical realism seems to come naturally to Ms. Sanchez-Scott."

In the same *New York Times* review, Gussow praises Sanchez-Scott for her "fanciful imagery," and indeed her work brims over with symbolism and allegory. In *The Cuban Swimmer*, the beauty of the magical realism genre is exemplified perfectly in the symbols she uses and the images she creates: the all-seeing, ever-scrutinizing American media hovering over the scene; Margarita's family in a boat beside her, isolated from the mainland, from the destination, and from Margarita herself; and ultimately the exhausting swim that Margarita must undertake, a physical struggle to gain success for herself, on her own terms, in the culture of America. "The illusory becomes tangible," Gussow states. Sanchez-Scott took abstract ideas and gave them concrete form in what was to become a trademark style both for her and for Latin American writers in general. As Catherine Casiano and Elizabeth C. Ramírez point out in *La Voz Latina: Contemporary Plays and Performance Pieces by Latinas*, Sanchez-Scott imbues "her work with imaginative language and interesting themes and ideas to draw new and multifaceted characters that [represent] her Latina and Latino world."

CRITICISM

Kristy Blackmon

Blackmon is a writer and critic from Dallas, Texas. In the following essay, she examines Sanchez-Scott's use of magical realism in The Cuban

WHAT DO I READ NEXT?

- *Cool Salsa: Bilingual Poems on Growing Up Latino in the United States*, edited by Lori Colson, is a popular 1994 collection of thirty-six poems by famous Latino poets, including Sandra Cisneros, Gary Soto, and Martín Espada. The theme of the collection is the experience of being young and Hispanic in American society.

- Sociologist Judy Miller explores the realities of young African American women in her 2008 book *Getting Played: African American Girls, Urban Inequality, and Gendered Violence*. This award-winning volume closely examines the problems faced by young black women in urban America, frankly and sometimes shockingly exposing the mental, emotional, and physical danger present in their everyday lives.

- Sanchez-Scott's 1998 award-winning play *Roosters* examines the power dynamic in a Chicano family in the southwest United States. The play examines gender roles and the problems that arise from the conflicts of tradition and expectation in one family's experience of being Hispanic in America.

- *The House on Mango Street*, by Sandra Cisneros, is a young-adult coming-of-age novel published in 1984. Cisneros tells the story of Esperanza Cordero, a young Latina girl who is determined to leave the drama and psychological trauma of her Chicago home behind her.

- Julia Alvarez's 1992 collection of stories *How the García Girls Lost Their Accents* chronicles the experiences of four sisters, exiled from the Dominican Republic and trying to come to grips with life in the Bronx. The book begins when the sisters are adults and describes, in reverse chronological order, their journey from a wealthy Dominican home to the United States, where they must find their own identities in a new country.

- Cuban writer Yoani Sánchez documents life under the Castro regime in Cuba in her 2011 book *Havana Real: One Woman Fights to Tell the Truth about Cuba Today*. Sánchez risked persecution by her own government to tell of the harsh reality of living under a Communist dictatorship, being the victim of state censorship, and lacking a private world for individual thoughts, dreams, and opinions.

- María Irene Fornés's 2008 collection of plays *What of the Night?* includes her 1987 play *Abingdon Square*. Fornés served as Sanchez-Scott's mentor and teacher in her time with INTAR, and this collection represents the talent and insight that has made Fornés one of the preeminent Latina playwrights of the twentieth century.

Swimmer as an ideal stylistic vehicle for expressing the uniqueness of the Latina identity struggle in America.

Much literature and drama that centers on the Chicano or Latino immigrant experience has, at its core, a clear identity quest. Torn between the traditional, even mystical culture of their homelands and the modern, mostly alien society they find in America, many immigrants struggle to keep their grasp on their ethnic heritage while still trying to find a place in the American social structure they can call their own. The pull of mysticism in *The Cuban Swimmer* is especially evident in the females of the Suárez family. To varying degrees, Abuela, Aída, and Margarita all turn to their tradition of faith in times of crisis as a basis for their core identity. This conflict between tradition and modernism, between mysticism and pragmatism, is a topic that lends itself well to the style of magical realism. The yearning for

The Cuban Swimmer

> SANCHEZ-SCOTT USES MAGICAL REALISM TO EXPLORE THE MYSTICAL TRADITION OF LATINA IMMIGRANTS STRUGGLING WITH A SEARCH FOR IDENTITY BOTH WITHIN THEIR TRADITIONAL FAMILIAL UNITS AND AS INDIVIDUALS UNSURE OF THEIR ROLES IN A NEW SOCIAL STRUCTURE."

something which is so difficult to articulate can be beautifully illustrated through showing the unreal in a situation; something that is strongly felt but remains unseen cannot be accurately portrayed through realism alone. Readers and audience members must be willing to accept that the impossible is possible during the course of the story. In *The Cuban Swimmer*, Sanchez-Scott "treats the supernatural as if it were a perfectly acceptable and understandable aspect of everyday life," as Christopher Warnes describes the genre in his essay "Naturalizing the Supernatural: Faith, Irreverence and Magical Realism." Sanchez-Scott uses magical realism to explore the mystical tradition of Latina immigrants struggling with a search for identity both within their traditional familial units and as individuals unsure of their roles in a new social structure.

Warnes writes that magical realism is a genre that manages to reconcile the "modern, rational, 'disenchanted' subject of the West with forgotten but recoverable spiritual realities." Unlike some other styles, magical realism is defined very loosely, and no one critic or scholar seems to have been able to pin down the precise qualities that define a work as part of the genre. At its core, magical realism is "literature in which real and non-real exist in a state of carefully contrived equivalence," according to Warnes. This elusive quality, which manages to produce such a specific result as the melding of the real and the supernatural, may make it the perfect vehicle for identity quests and searches for meaning in an alien world. As Warnes points out, magical realism expresses both a sort of "primitivism" and a modern search for "cultural emancipation." The conflict in the identity quest of many Latina immigrants is between the desire

to be accepted and recognized as part of American culture and the desire to retain the cultural aspects of a heritage that makes them unique.

Jorge Huerta believes that Sanchez-Scott's own South American heritage and the environment in which she was raised have been big contributors to her use of magical realism to successfully depict the strange reality of the Latino or Hispanic American situation. "Sanchez-Scott has always been fascinated by occurrences that defy logic and she delights in bringing these moments into her theatre," he writes in his book *Chicano Drama: Performance, Society and Myth*. The style of magical realism is what allows Sanchez-Scott to connect the dots between the pragmatic reasons behind the race and the mystical implications it holds for the family. While needing to explain the logistics and portray the realities of life as a Cuban living in America— and in the case of this particular story, especially a Cuban woman—Sanchez-Scott knows that the true meaning in the story lies in finding a way to hold on to the tradition of Latina culture in a society that places little to no value on it. That is, the Suárez family's world is so much broader than just this race or even their lives in California. Their world is made up of an ingrained tradition of faith in the inexplicable and pride in a shared heritage. This unique combination of elements results in a culture perfectly suited to magical realism as a means by which to illustrate its particular struggles and successes. Kenneth Reeds, in "Magical Realism: A Problem of Definition," says it is "natural to Latin America's history, geography, people, and politics that unlikely combinations of events occurred producing marvelous results."

The most mystical character in the play is Abuela, Margarita's grandmother. Abuela represents the old country, the intrinsic faith in God, the church, and a long line of tradition. In a play that revolves around confused gender roles, Abuela is notably both the strongest and the most vulnerable of characters. She cannot speak much English, and the fact that the majority of her dialogue is in Spanish places her as an outsider in America and adds to her strangeness or otherness. However, Abuela believes in the sanctity of her heritage completely, and she grounds herself as the holder of a familial tradition that places the woman as the center of spiritual strength in the Suárez family. When Margarita is caught in the oil slick, Abuela's

Drama for Students, Volume 29

3 7

faith in her does not falter. She is worried about her granddaughter, but she calmly recites the tale of Luz Suárez, Margarita's great-grandmother, who was similarly challenged by evil back in Cuba. The story tells of blood raining from the sky and Luz's defiance toward the *Diablo* (Devil). Luz confronted the evil, telling the Devil that if he wanted her, all he had to do was look. She was not afraid. Several times, Abuela calls Margarita "*sangre de mi sangre*" (blood of my blood). She claims Margarita, in a way she never claims her grandson Simón, as part of her lineage. Abuela thus traces her heritage through Margarita's strength, recognizing in her another great spirit like Luz, like Abuela herself. The story illustrates the faith and dependence the family has placed in Margarita to be their savior more than any realistic dialogue could. Eugene L. Arva notes in his essay "Writing the Vanishing Real: Hyperreality and Magical Realism" that "fantastic re-presentation (imaginative reconstitution) works where realistic representation (descriptive mimesis) has apparently failed." It is through the mystical tale that the audience understands the depth and importance of Margarita. She will be her family's savior in the tradition of women in the Suárez family. By recounting the legend, Abuela is able to give the audience a taste of that generational and inbred belief in otherworldliness, in success despite evil, in defiance in the face of terror, and in the ability of the Suárez women to protect the family on a spiritual level.

To a lesser extent, Aída exhibits some of the same mysticism. Aída plays a role partway between those of Abuela and Margarita. She defers constantly to Eduardo's authority, yet there are moments in the play that clearly show that she possesses at least some of the mystical faith of Abuela. Where Eduardo is excited and seduced by the promise of America, it is the memory of Cuba that moves Aída. She fears for her children but is unable to defy traditional gender roles and stand up to Eduardo to effectively protect them. For example, when she notices the oil slick, and the family realizes the danger Margarita is in, she demands of Eduardo, "Get my daughter out of the water." Despite her frantic concern for her daughter, however, there is no thought of defying her husband and pulling Margarita from the race when he says that she must continue. Instead of standing up to Eduardo at times like these, she joins Abuela in prayer, and she invokes religious blessings almost as much as her mother-in-law. It is not just her reliance on religion that shows her connection with the mystical, female tradition of the Suárez family. The conversation between her and Eduardo in the fourth scene illustrates her unique position as the rightful heir to the family's tradition of faith while at the same time illuminating her utter helplessness in the face of Eduardo's authority. She describes how Eduardo "stole" her from her family and her country to take her to Miami: "I left everything behind. . . . You took me, you stole me from my home." These lines make explicit to the audience her loss of identity in America. Watching Margarita in the water, Aída tells of the night her daughter was conceived. Where Abuela retold a mystical familial legend, Aída recounts a dream she had that night "of a big country with . . . big, giant things growing." She describes finding a pea pod that, when she opened it, was full of baby frogs, which she feels symbolized Margarita's immediate connection with the water. The story shows Aída's connection to her traditional faith in the unknowable. As Arva puts it, "magical realist fiction must look beyond the realistic detail and accept [that] the natural and the supernatural, the explainable and the miraculous, coexist side by side in a kaleidoscopic reality."

Abuela's story and Aída's dream both use fantastic imagery to show the juxtaposition of timelessness and mysticism against Eduardo's intense concentration on the here and now. The family members are part of the same world, but they all experience it differently—they are all holders of different aspects of their culture, and only together as a family can they represent the whole. By exposing that which is unreal or fantastical, Sanchez-Scott also shows the audience the spaces where reality by itself fails to represent the entirety of human existence. The experiences of this family, both the members as individuals and the familial unit as a whole, is an amalgam of Abuela's mysticism, Aída's longing, Simón's loneliness, Eduardo's obsession, and Margarita's desperation to please. Each character sees his or her own reality, and through them, the audience is able to draw conclusions about a larger picture that encompasses all of their experiences. "Magical realism constitutes an attitude toward and a way of approaching reality—a reality that is rarely what it seems and is seldom perceived in the same way" by any two people, states Arva.

Margarita encounters many obstacles, including an oil slick, during the competition. *(Oleksandr Kalinichenko /*
Shutterstock.com)

Margarita's race is metaphorical on multiple levels. It symbolizes the struggle that Cuban immigrants faced in crossing the ocean to seek asylum on American shores. It stands for the struggle of Cuban Americans to make a place for themselves in the American social structure. It represents her family's hopes and dreams, especially those of her father, Eduardo. At the most personal level, it signifies Margarita's own search for validation from both her family and a country that marginalizes her on the basis of her gender and her ethnicity, as well as her ultimate reliance on the faith-based traditions of her homeland as a source of perseverance. Margarita carries the responsibility of upholding the family honor by winning this race. She is to be the savior of the Suárez family. Through her near martyrdom, Margarita succeeds where no one else in the family can: she resurrects them from their marginal status as immigrants and gives them something in which to feel pride.

It is important to remember that in this play, Margarita holds the power, though she may not realize it. Eduardo may be the driving force behind the action, but in the end only Margarita can win the race, and she must do it essentially alone. "You must win," Eduardo tells her—"give it everything... *por la familia*." Unlike Simón, who understands that the race is Eduardo's dream and thinks that Margarita should not have to make her father's ambitions her own, Margarita assumes responsibility. "*Es mi culpa*," she laments as her body gives out at the end of scene 5. She begs her father not to leave her and accuses her mother of letting her go to be lost amongst the waves. She knows that by leaving her in the water after the point when it would have made sense to take her out, her parents have in essence abandoned her to succeed or fail on her own. As she sinks beneath the water to the bottom of the sea, she asks her father's forgiveness.

Margarita is resurrected when she arrives at Santa Catalina Island. *La Havana*, her family's boat, is no longer at her side. Instead, there is a "flotilla of boats to meet her" on her arrival as she, like Christ, is "walking on the waters, through the breakers." Margarita, though she set out in the race on a mission given to her by her family, has succeeded in her own right, on her own behalf. Her family's absence is representative of her breaking away from the overwhelming responsibility that Eduardo has placed on her shoulders. Swimming only for her father and her family exhausts her to the point where she sinks to the bottom of the ocean. She is stripped of the identities thrust upon her by the other characters in the play by the will to survive, and it is only when she begins to swim solely for herself that she prevails.

The play is set in the middle of the ocean in what is obviously an unrealistic situation. However, it is unimportant whether or not the Suárez family could actually follow Margarita in the water so closely, whether or not the stories told by Abuela and Aída are true, and whether or not it is possible for Margarita to seemingly drown and then suddenly end up winning the race. These elements, among others, are the things that allow Sanchez-Scott to impart a dreamlike quality to the action. This dreamlike feel is the only accurate way of depicting the sense of mysticism that is so vital to understanding the family dynamic and the influences of tradition on the female Suárezes. The implausibility of the logistics of the story allows the meaning behind the story to be seen. "By virtue of its subversive character," says Arva, "magical realism foregrounds... the falsehood of its fantastic imagery exactly in order to expose the falsehood—and the traumatic absence—of the reality" that it is attempting to portray. Magical realism is a style that Sanchez-Scott has been able to claim, along with other Latin American writers, as part of her own heritage. It is a means of expression that can accurately capture both the realities that immigrants face and the pull of their heritage that cannot accurately be explained through realistic dialogue alone. *The Cuban Swimmer* is an extremely successful example of not only the mechanics of magical realism but also the reasons behind its use.

Source: Kristy Blackmon, Critical Essay on *The Cuban Swimmer*, in *Drama for Students*, Gale, Cengage Learning, 2012.

Howard Allen

In the following review of The Old Matador, *Allen examines the cultural conflict at the heart of Sanchez-Scott's work.*

A short, pudgy boy of 15 pulls his broken bike up in front of a small wood-frame house dominated by one of those famous Southwestern sunset-filled skies. He switches off the radio rap music, while inside the voices of his aging parents rise to an angry pitch. "I don't believe it," blurts out the mother. "I'm not going! No, señor, I'm not."

The father shouts back, "Ah you, you know nothing! You believe in nothing!" (We will learn he wants to return to the Spain of his youth to fulfill his passionate dream of facing a proud bull in the ring.)

The voice of the mother grows louder and more fierce. "And where's the money coming from... Dios mio!! You took our money out of the bank. Ahh! Come back, I'm talking to you." (We will learn she is the practical Mexican woman who "tamed" the now-old matador.)

In the front yard, meanwhile, the teenager turns on the radio news from "the vampire poet and midnight cabajellero," El Bonito: "After scouring the rocky slopes of the San Jacinto Mountains for three days, searchers are still hopeful of finding a 12-year-old Boy Scout lost in the wilderness. Come on, homes, don't get all sad. They'll find him, they got the Los Gatos Search and Rescue, the Chino Fire Department, volunteers from the 7th Day Adventists Church in La Hambra."

The tension-fraught atmosphere evoked by this collision of old world and new will strike a familiar chord for those who have followed the career of playwright Milcha Sanchez-Scott. Her newest play, *The Old Matador*, returns to the same mythic neighborhood she created in such earlier plays as *Dog Lady*, *The Cuban Swimmer* and *Roosters*. The Arizona Theatre Company debuts the play Jan. 7–28 at its Tucson theatre, and at its Phoenix theatre Feb. 3–18.

Like Horton Foote's South Texas and Faulkner's Yoknapatawpha County, Sanchez-Scott's southwestern territory has proven a rich dramatic landscape. The author rejects such cliché-laden labels as "latina" or "feminist" or even "magic realism" for her work, which is—despite her disavowal of the latter term—rich in spells and miraculous cures. All these identities, however, play their part in shaping the bicultural milieu of her plays.

Sanchez-Scott could, in fact, be a standard-bearer for multiculturalism. Born on the island of Bali to an Indonesian, Chinese and Dutch mother and Colombian father, she spent her school-age years at a Catholic girls' school near London, and her holidays back at the family ranch in Colombia. Her family later moved to southern California, where she went to high school in La Jolla and to the University of San Diego. Her first play, *Latina*, was inspired by the immigrant maids she met while working for a Beverly Hills employment agency after college.

"I try to keep her connected to her heart and her deep personal sources," says director Peter Brosius, her collaborator on three recent shows and the current project. "The collision of cultures is an important part of her work."

The Old Matador teems with ideas and cultural signifiers on a collision course. Enrique, the dissatisfied father of the play's title, wants to celebrate the life of the heart and the passions of a distant cultural perspective; the mother, Margarita, embodies a more reasoned and rational life force. The rap music in the opening moments will soon contrast with Enrique's flamenco dreams when his quest for the world of his youth takes him to the play's other setting, a Spanish bar called El Cid.

The local priest, Father Stephan, must contend with a language barrier between himself and his Hispanic parishioners while the battle between secular and spiritual forces rages around him. Enrique and Margarita's teenaged daughter Jesse (a character who originally appeared, aged some five years younger, in Sanchez-Scott's 1984 *Dog Lady*) cannot make her mother comprehend her fear that her own dreams of escape will be crushed after her engagement to a Cuban boy in the neighborhood falls through.

It is Jesse's brother Cookie, who often finds himself caught in the middle between his practical mother and dreamer father, who witnesses the play's most extreme manifestation of magic realism: the arrival of an angel. For Brosius, the angel is a key example of how Sanchez-Scott conflates the material and metaphysical worlds in magical ways that make some people uncomfortable. "For Milcha, magic realism is not a genre so much as it is a way of life," he argues. "One isn't grafted onto the other. It's just part of the perceptual apparatus she brings to the world every day."

The arrival of an angel in *The Old Matador* is not, however, an occasion for comparisons to Tony Kushner's *Angels in America*, Brosius insists. "Angels existed before Mr. Kushner's

wonderful plays, and they will exist in theatre afterwards. The only connection we might make is one of synchronicity between writers. There is something about the approaching millennium that is, perhaps, creating a greater hunger for the divine in everyday life."

For Sanchez-Scott, who wrote the first draft of the play "in a rush" after her mother's death from leukemia, *The Old Matador* is meant to address that hunger directly. "Everyone wants resolution," she says. "At the end of the play, that opportunity is given. The play is a collision of this world and the next."

Source: Howard Allen, Review of *The Old Matador*, in *American Theatre*, Vol. 12, No. 1, January 1995, p. 12.

Jorge Huerta

In the following excerpt, a short discussion of Sánchez-Scott and her early works is provided.

Milcha Sánchez-Scott was born in 1955 on the island of Bali, the daughter of a Colombian father and an Indonesian, Chinese and Dutch mother. Her father was raised in Colombia and in Mexico, and Ms. Sánchez-Scott grew up in a variety of international settings, because her father's work as an agronomist required him to travel a great deal. During her early school years Ms. Sánchez-Scott attended a Catholic girls school near London, where she learned to speak English.

Although Ms. Sánchez-Scott is admittedly not a Chicana by virtue of her ancestry, she was introduced to the harsh realities of being brown-skinned in the United States when her family moved to La Jolla, California. She was about fifteen and was waiting for the school bus on the first day of classes when, "A smart-alecky boy threw a pebble at me and said, 'This isn't the Mexican bus stop. You have to go to the Mexican bus stop,'" and to her chagrin, the other students joined in with the same insulting chant. Her parents immediately enrolled her in an Episcopalian girls school. "I had never experienced racial tension, but in La Jolla we saw incredible—to us—prejudice."

Having experienced her adolescence and young adulthood in Southern California, close to the Mexican border and in an area rich with Mexican customs, Ms. Sánchez-Scott could not escape the influences of her environment. One year after graduating from the University of San Diego with a degree in Literature, Philosophy and Theatre, Ms. Sánchez-Scott moved to Los

Angeles where she worked in an employment agency for maids in Beverly Hills.

After the job with the maid's agency, Ms. Sánchez-Scott began to work as an actress with a variety of professional theaters in Los Angeles, including the Mark Taper Forum (*Savages*) and the Loft Studio (*A Doll's House*). Like the protagonist in the play she would soon write, Ms. Sánchez-Scott also appeared in various television programs playing "a variety of barrio women." It was while performing in a women's prison, recreating the inmates' experiences as dramatized by Doris Baizley, that Ms. Sánchez-Scott realized that some of the stories she had heard from the Latina women at the employment agency could also be dramatized. Ms. Sánchez-Scott recalls, "The idea to write *Latina* was born in a traffic jam on the Pomona Freeway. I mentioned then to Jeremy [Blahnik] that I had kept some journals and notes on Latin women. I asked her if she would put them into play form. She turned the tables on me, however, and soon I was writing *Latina* with Jeremy as my guide and mentor."

Commissioned by Susan Lowenberg, Producing Director of the New Works Division of Artists in Prison and Other Places (AIPOP), the actress/playwright then created *Latina*, her first play. *Latina* was first produced in 1980 to great critical acclaim.

The success of *Latina* encouraged Ms. Sánchez-Scott to continue writing and she was then commissioned by Ms. Lowenberg to write another play. This commission led to two one-acts, *The Cuban Swimmer* and *Dog Lady*. Most importantly, perhaps, Ms. Sánchez-Scott was invited to join Maria Irene Fornés' Hispanic Playwrights-in-Residence Laboratory during the year of 1983. "That year was the best thing that ever happened to me," Ms. Sánchez-Scott recalls. "I met some extraordinary Hispanic writers. And I felt more accepted." It was during that residency that Ms. Sánchez-Scott began to write *Roosters*.

Roosters is a Southwestern play about the struggles within a Chicano family in crisis: a father and son vying for dominance and a daughter looking for significance in a too brutal reality. It is a play about survival, told in a poetic style that evokes images of pure beauty and grace, contrasted with the severity of poverty and the desert. In a mixture of naturalism and the surreal, *Roosters* evokes images of magical realism both visually and linguistically. In the playwright's words, "*Roosters* is a word play."

In the introduction to *Roosters*, Ms. Sánchez-Scott tells how her youth was spent in a world of fantasy, creating images in her mind, as all children do, but with a distinctly Latin American flavor. This Latin American magical realism seems to come naturally to Ms. Sánchez-Scott, who recalls such imagery on a visit to the town in Colombia where she had spent Christmas holidays and summers in her youth: "Do you remember the summer all the birds flew into the bedroom?" someone asked, reminding her of "the way we say things in Colombia."

Roosters is Ms. Sánchez-Scott's best-known play to date, with professional and community productions across the country. After initial development in Ms. Fornés' workshop and at the Sundance Institute in Utah, *Roosters* was co-produced by INTAR and the New York Shakespeare Festival in 1987. This extraordinary play will reach millions of people on PBS's American Playhouse in 1989.

Adding to an exceptionally busy year for Ms. Sánchez-Scott, her play, *Evening Star*, was produced by New York's Theatre for a New Audience in the spring of 1988 under the direction of Paul Zimet. That same year she was Playwright-in-Residence for the Los Angeles Theater Center's Latino Lab, working closely with director José Luis Valenzuela and a core of professional Hispanic actors. This group worked collectively with Ms. Sánchez-Scott on *Stone Wedding*, a parable in the magical realism style about a Southwestern Chicano wedding in the 1950's. The play was included in the LATC's 1988 season, following the success of *Roosters*. Most recently, Ms. Sánchez-Scott has begun work on the book and lyrics for a musical in collaboration with Gold McDermit, the composer of *Hair*. This play, as yet unnamed, will be produced by INTAR.

Ms. Sánchez-Scott has received a number of distinctive awards, including a first-level Rockefeller Foundation Playwriting Grant, a Vesta Award, given each year to a West Coast dramatist, and the Le Compte du Nouy prize. She is also a member of New York's prestigious New Dramatists. Through her plays, Ms. Sánchez-Scott is becoming an exceptional spokeswoman for Chicano and Hispanic-American issues.

Source: Jorge Huerta, "Milcha Sanchez-Scott," in *Necessary Theater: Six Plays about the Chicano Experience*, edited by Jorge Huerta, Arte Público Press, 1989, pp. 82–84.

SOURCES

Arva, Eugene L., "Writing the Vanishing Real: Hyperreality and Magical Realism," in *Journal of Narrative Theory*, Vol. 38, No. 1, Winter 2008, pp. 60–61, 68.

Bruneau, Marie-Florine, *Women Mystics Confront the Modern World*, State University of New York Press, 1998.

Casiano, Catherine, and Elizabeth C. Ramírez, *La Voz Latina: Contemporary Plays and Performance Pieces by Latinas*, University of Illinois Press, 2011, p. 34.

De La Roche, Elise, *Teatro Hispano! Three New York Companies*, Garland Press, 1995, p. 159.

García, María Cristina, *Havana USA: Cuban Exiles and Cuban Americans in South Florida, 1959–1994*, University of California Press, 1996, pp. 46–54.

Grönlund, Enrique, and Moylan C. Mills, "Magic Realism and García Márquez's *Eréndira*," in *Literature/Film Quarterly*, Vol. 17, No. 2, 1989, p. 114–15.

Gussow, Mel, "Stage: *Roosters* at INTAR," in *New York Times*, March 24, 1987, p. C15.

Huerta, Jorge, *Chicano Drama: Performance, Society and Myth*, Cambridge University Press, 2000, pp. 108, 110–11.

——, "*Latina*," in *Necessary Theater: Six Plays about the Chicano Experience*, edited by Jorge Huerta, Arte Público Press, 1989, p. 83.

López, Tiffany Ana, "Drama," in *The Oxford Companion to Women's Writing*, edited by Cathy N. Davidson and Linda Wagner-Martin, Oxford University Press, 2011, p. 481.

Reeds, Kenneth, "Magical Realism: A Problem of Definition," in *Neophilologus*, Vol. 90, 1996, p. 182.

Sanchez-Scott, Milcha, *The Cuban Swimmer*, in *Plays in One Act*, edited by Daniel Halpern, Harper Perennial, 1991, pp. 407–20.

Siegel, Robert, "Postmodernism," in *Modern Fiction Studies*, Vol. 41, No. 1, Spring 1995, pp. 165–94.

Urquijo-Ruiz, Rita E., "Drama," in *Inside the Latin@ Experience: A Latin@ Studies Reader*, edited by Norma E. Cantú and María E. Fránquiz, Palgrave Macmillan, 2010, p. 160.

Warnes, Christopher, "Naturalizing the Supernatural: Faith, Irreverence and Magical Realism," in *Literature Compass*, Vol. 2, No. 1, January 2005, pp. 1–2, 7, 12.

FURTHER READING

Campbell, Richard C., *Two Eagles in the Sun: A Guide to U.S. Hispanic Culture*, Two Eagles Press, 2003.
   Campbell presents an in-depth look at the value systems, language, traditions, and history of Hispanics living in America. The volume serves as an encyclopedia of sorts for those struggling to understand the nuances of Chicano and Latino culture.

Cantú, Norma E., and Nájera-Ramírez, Olga, *Chicana Traditions: Continuity and Change*, University of Illinois Press, 2002.
   This anthology of personal and scholarly essays focuses on Chicana culture and the ways women continue to reinvent themselves professionally within that culture.

Cocchiarale, Michael, *Upon Further Review: Sports in American Literature*, Praeger Publishers, 2004.
   Cocchiarale's book explores the use of sports figures and athletic events by American writers as a means of commenting on social issues such as race, class, and gender.

Faris, Wendy B., and Lois Parkinson Zamora, *Magical Realism: Theory, History, Community*, Duke University Press, 1995.
   This volume treats magical realism as an international phenomenon, and literary contexts as diverse as Europe, Asia, North and South America, the Caribbean, Africa, and Australia are brought together under the rubric of the term.

Taylor, Diana, *Negotiating Performance: Gender, Sexuality and Theatricality in Latin/o America*, Duke University Press, 1994.
   Taylor widens the typical scope of theatrical criticism to include performance art, indigenous theater, living installations, and public protests by a multiplicity of further marginalized groups within Latin and Latino America, such as Mayans, women, and homosexuals.

SUGGESTED SEARCH TERMS

Milcha Sanchez-Scott

The Cuban Swimmer

Milcha Sanchez-Scott AND The Cuban Swimmer

Milcha Sanchez-Scott AND feminism

Latina AND feminism

Milcha Sanchez-Scott AND magical realism

The Cuban Swimmer AND identity

Latina AND America AND cultural identity

INTAR AND Sanchez-Scott

Latino theater

Chicano theater

Guys and Dolls

JO SWERLING
ABE BURROWS
FRANK LOESSER

1950

Guys and Dolls is a work of musical theater that premiered in 1950. Inspired by short stories by Damon Runyon that were published in 1932 under the same title, *Guys and Dolls* was adapted for the stage by Jo Swerling and Abe Burrows. Frank Loesser wrote the music and lyrics.

Set in New York City, the play does not specify its time frame, but references in the story suggest that the play's writers updated the setting to make the play contemporary with its 1950 production. The story explores the world of illegal gambling and betting, and its action is generated by a bet between Nathan Detroit, who is seeking a location for an illegal dice game but needs money to pay a bribe, and Sky Masterson, a worldly and wealthy gambler known for taking on bizarre bets. Nathan bets Sky that Sky cannot get Sarah, the prim and devout Christian of the Save-a-Soul Mission, to go to Havana, Cuba, with him. Sky takes the bet, setting off a chain of events that leads through improbable maneuvering to a happy ending. Throughout the play, the notion of romantic love is at once the source of derision and the butt of jokes but also an ideal for which the main characters all strive.

The Guys and Dolls Book, which contains the full text of the play as well as the lyrics to all of the songs, was published in 1982. The play won five Tony Awards in 1951, including Best Musical.

AUTHOR BIOGRAPHY

Abe Burrows

Burrows adapted Swerling's draft of the script for the theatrical version of *Guys and Dolls* around Loesser's songs, and he is credited with writing the bulk of the playbook. Burrows was born on December 18, 1910, in New York. After writing for radio and television, he began writing for the stage in his debut effort, *Guys and Dolls*, revising and completing the script begun by Jo Swerling. Following the successful run of *Guys and Dolls*, Burrows continued to work as both a playwright and director, writing and directing his first post–*Guys and Dolls* effort, *Can-Can*, in 1954. By the mid-1960s, Burrows focused on directing. Burrows died of pneumonia on May 17, 1985.

Frank Loesser

Loesser wrote the music and lyrics to *Guys and Dolls*. According to Caryl Brahms and Ned Sherrin, who wrote a biographical essay on Loesser for *The Guys and Dolls Book*, "It was Loesser who threw out Swerling's original book, but perversely he still wrote his score around it."

Loesser was born on June 29, 1910, in New York. In the early portion of his career, Loesser wrote lyrics and sketches for both radio and live vaudeville productions. He collaborated with a number of other songwriters for screen and stage. Loesser wrote the music and lyrics for *Guys and Dolls*, working with Burrows, who wrote the final version of the playbook begun by Swerling. Loesser also worked on the 1955 film adaptation of *Guys and Dolls*, composing several new numbers for this production. Loesser continued to compose for both film and theater, writing the music and lyrics for the 1961 Broadway production *How to Succeed in Business Without Really Trying*, another award-winning play. It won the 1962 Tony Award for Best Musical, along with the Pulitzer Prize for Drama. Loesser died of lung cancer on July 26, 1969.

Jo Swerling

Swerling was originally hired to write the playbook for *Guys and Dolls*, but he was replaced by Burrows, who revised and built upon what Swerling had begun.

Swerling was born on April 8, 1897, in Baridchov, Russia. As a child, he and his family escaped the czarist regime and landed in New York. Swerling moved to Chicago and secured a position with the *Chicago Herald and Examiner* newspaper. He began writing for the theater after writing a review for the Marx Brothers' vaudeville act. His early plays include *One of Us* (1918) and *Kibitzer* (1929). The success of his plays encouraged him to pursue a career in screenwriting, and he wrote a number of films in the 1930s and 1940s. In 1950, Swerling began a playbook inspired by characters and stories in Damon Runyon's 1932 collection *Guys and Dolls*. Burrows completed the playbook Swerling began, but Swerling is still credited for his early work on the play. Swerling died in 1964.

PLOT SUMMARY

Act 1, Scene 1

Guys and Dolls is divided into two acts. The first act opens with a musical number, "Runyonland," playing as various individuals make their way across the stage, which is set as Broadway, the famous street in the theater district of New York City. The stage directions refer to "bobby soxers" crossing the stage. The use of this term suggests that the time frame in which the play is set is contemporary with its production in 1950. The term refers to teenage girls of the 1940s and 1950s who dressed in skirts paired with a short cuffed style of sock known as bobby socks. Other figures moving across the stage include police officers, chorus girls from a Broadway show, prostitutes, an elderly female street vendor, a boxer and his manager, an actress, and sightseers. Benny Southstreet enters reading a racing form and is shortly joined by Nicely-Nicely Johnson and Rusty Charlie, all gamblers. The three sing a number about horse racing and betting, "Fugue for Tinhorns." This number is shortly followed by the entrance of Sarah and the Mission Band, who sing "Follow the Fold." Sarah then preaches to the people still gathered on the street, including the gamblers, to repent. Everyone ignores her or walks away, and Sarah and the other missionaries leave, dejected. Her good looks are noticed by Nicely and Benny. Another gambler, Harry the Horse, enters, and the men discuss the difficulties that Nathan Detroit is having in finding a place to hold a crap game. (Craps is a dice game in which bets are placed on the outcome of a player's roll.)

MEDIA ADAPTATIONS

- In 1955, Swerling, Burrows, and Loesser's stage musical *Guys and Dolls* was adapted for the big screen. The film adaptation was written and directed by Joseph L. Mankiewicz and starred Frank Sinatra as Nathan, Vivian Blaine as Adelaide, Marlon Brando as Sky, and Jean Simmons as Sarah. The film was released on DVD in 2006 by MGM Studios.

- The original cast recording of the songs from the 1950 musical version is available as an MP3 download. The album was released in 1992 by RCA Victor.

- The cast recording from the 1992 Broadway revival of *Guys and Dolls* starring Nathan Lane is available as a CD and MP3 download; it was released in 2009 by Masterworks Broadway.

Lieutenant Brannigan is trying to find and arrest gamblers, and he has reminded business owners that it is illegal to allow their premises to be used for gambling. Nathan enters, looking depressed, and after Brannigan's departure reveals to his friends that he has found a place to host the high-stakes crap game, but the owner of Biltmore Garage, Joey Biltmore, wants one thousand dollars in payment, which Nathan does not have. A number of other crap shooters enter gradually, and together they sing about Nathan's unfailing ability to find a place for "the oldest established permanent floating crap game in New York," in the musical number "The Oldest Established." One of the dice players informs Nathan that Sky Masterson is in town; his reputation as a high-stakes player is discussed.

Adelaide arrives on the scene, and she and Nathan discuss their fourteen-year anniversary of being engaged. Nathan rushes her off as she begins to talk about marriage, and Sky arrives. Sky observes, when Adelaide's name comes up, that Nathan is "trapped." He advocates a freer

lifestyle and assures Nathan that he could take any woman he wanted with him to Havana. As the Save-a-Soul Mission Band, led by Sarah, reappears, Nathan seizes an opportunity for a bet he believes he cannot lose: he bets Sky that he cannot get Sarah to go with him to Havana.

Act 1, Scene 2

At the Save-a-Soul Mission, Sarah Brown and Arvide Abernathy, who is Sarah's grandfather and who also works for the Save-a-Soul Mission, discuss the apparent futility of trying to get sinners to repent in this part of town. Sky enters the mission and begins to try and convince them that he would like to give up gambling. Arvide leaves the two of them to talk. Sky flirts with Sarah, assuring her that he is such a sinner he will need private instructions to overcome his ways. Aware that the mission has not been successful in bringing in sinners, he promises Sarah that he will fill the place with sinners if she only has dinner with him—in Havana. In the number "I'll Know," Sarah sings about what her true love will be like. Sky joins in, after chastising Sarah on her unwillingness to take chances, and describes the chemistry he will feel with his true love when he meets her. He then kisses Sarah. The stage directions indicate that Sarah looks entranced and moved by what has happened but nevertheless "belts him one across the chops."

Act 1, Scene 3

In this brief scene, Nathan is talking on the phone to Joey Biltmore, the owner of the Biltmore Garage, where Nathan would like to host the next crap game. Joey insists on receiving one thousand dollars up front.

Act 1, Scene 4

This scene opens at the Hot Box, the nightclub where Adelaide sings and dances with the Hot Box girls. After Adelaide performs the number "Bushel and a Peck," she sits with Nathan, who has come to see her, and tells him of her impending raise, such that now they can get married. She also informs him of the elaborate fiction she has conveyed to her mother: she married Nathan long ago and they now have five children. Another dancer, Mimi, enters, looking for an earring. Seeing Nathan, she angrily reproaches him because her boyfriend, Society Max, has broken a date with her to attend Nathan's dice game. After Mimi leaves, Nathan hurriedly reassures Adelaide that they will get married; he then rushes off. Adelaide, who has been fighting a cold since the play began, reads from a book the doctor has given her, alternating between speaking and singing in the number "Adelaide's Lament." She discovers that her symptoms may have developed as a result of the emotional struggle she endures owing to Nathan's failure to marry her.

Act 1, Scene 5
On a street off Broadway, Nicely and Benny discuss the way women unnecessarily distract men. Nicely has just observed Sky following Sarah and the Mission Band when Benny comments that Nathan is probably trying to see Adelaide, as she is angry with him again. The two sing the number "Guys and Dolls" and observe the way men behave irrationally or outlandishly in their pursuit of women.

Act 1, Scene 6
Back at the mission, Sarah and Arvide are approached by General Cartwright, a mission administrator. She informs them that the mission will have to close. Sky, who has wandered by, overhears the conversation and persuades General Cartwright to wait until after the next meeting to make her decision. Sarah personally guarantees the presence of a dozen sinners at the next meeting.

Act 1, Scene 7
On a street off Broadway, Benny and Harry the Horse are ready for the crap game, but Nathan has still not received the money he thought Sky would have delivered by now. Consequently, he has not been able to pay Joey Biltmore for the use of the Biltmore Garage. Another high-stakes gambler, Big Jule, has also arrived, and he threatens Nathan, who tries to placate him with promises that he will still find a place for the dice game. Lieutenant Brannigan approaches, suspicious of the men. As he begins to question them, Adelaide appears, and Benny attempts to deter Brannigan by telling him that everyone is gathered for Nathan's bachelor dinner, as he is about to marry Adelaide. Nathan tries to dampen Adelaide's eagerness by informing her that they still need to get a license and blood test, but he is dismayed to hear Brannigan suggest they drive upstate to Buffalo, New York, where they would not need a blood test, and elope.

Act 1, Scene 8
The scene opens in a café in Havana, Cuba, where Sarah is ordering a ham sandwich. The stage directions indicate a quick change in the scenery to indicate that Sky and Sarah are now sightseeing. They sit down at a street café where Sky orders Sarah a drink that she thinks is a type of milk shake but is really a rum-based cocktail. She innocently gulps down two. After another quick scene change, Sky and Sarah are seen entering another bar, where Sarah orders two more "dulce de leche" drinks. A female Cuban dancer begins to flirt with Sky, and a male Cuban dancer flirts with Sarah, until a fight breaks out with some of the other Cubans at the bar. Sarah smashes a bottle on someone's head before Sky forcibly drags her out.

Act 1, Scene 9
In the street outside the bar, Sky asks Sarah how she is feeling. She replies by singing the number, "If I Were a Bell," demonstrating her inebriation and elation. Sky begins to feel guilty and confesses that he brought her to Havana on a bet. Sarah does not seem to care. Although Sarah expresses a wish to stay in Havana, Sky picks her up and exits, heading for their plane.

Act 1, Scene 10
Sarah and Sky are standing outside the mission at four in the morning. Sarah thanks Sky for returning her safely. Adelaide enters, and after Sky introduces Sarah and Adelaide, Adelaide explains that her friends have just given her a wedding shower and that she and Nathan are eloping the next night. Sky sings the number "My Time of Day," confiding to Sarah that this predawn hour is his favorite, and she is the only one with whom he would want to share it. He also tells her that his real name is Obediah; she is the first person he has ever told this. He then sings "I've Never Been in Love Before," and she joins in. They then kiss, but they are soon interrupted by the arrival of Arvide and the Mission Band, who have been out all night. Suddenly, as Sky opens the door, Benny, Nicely, and Nathan hurry out of the mission. Other gamblers emerge as well, and everyone rushes away, but Sky grabs Nathan, who explains that they were gambling. Big Jule yells angrily after Nathan that he is losing ten thousand dollars. Brannigan arrives with two other officers and informs Sarah that the mission was being used for Nathan's floating crap game. Sarah is shocked, and Sky explains to

her that he knew nothing of Nathan's plans for the mission. When Sky asks when he will see her again, Sarah tells him they are through.

Act 2, Scene 1

The second act opens at the Hot Box, where Adelaide and the Hot Box Girls sing the number "Take Back Your Mink." Sky and Nicely are in the audience, and Nicely asks Sky to tell Adelaide that Nathan had to go to Pittsburgh to help a sick aunt, an obvious lie. Nicely tells Sky the game is still going on, and Sky wants the location. Nicely shouts a botched version of Nathan's message to Adelaide before he leaves. Adelaide rushes over to Sky, expressing her dismay, telling Sky that Nathan promised to change. Sky admonishes her for wanting to change Nathan, and Adelaide scolds him and men like him who refuse to settle down like other people. Sky asks her why she does not just find another man, and Adelaide explains that she loves Nathan; when Sky falls in love someday, she says, he will understand. Sky exits, and Adelaide sings "Adelaide's Second Lament," a reprised (repeated, sometimes with variations) version of her earlier song.

Act 2, Scene 2

On 48th Street, Sarah and Arvide discuss what happened with the gamblers using the mission. Arvide attempts to assure Sarah that they can still help such people and points out that even a man like Sky Masterson came to the mission seeking refuge. Sarah counters that Sky came to the mission seeking her. Arvide says that he knew Sky had his eye on Sarah, but he did not anticipate her falling for Sky. Sarah assures him she will get over Sky, but Arvide asks her why she would want to. Arvide sings the number "More I Cannot Wish You," insisting that all he wants for her is to find love. Sky arrives and confesses that the gamblers—the sinners to be saved, showing the necessity of keeping the mission open—will not be at the mission after all. Seeing that Sarah is angry with him, Sky insists he will still try and convince twelve sinners to be at the mission for the meeting that night. Sarah dismisses him, but Arvide threatens to expose Sky as a man who does not honor his bets if he does not deliver the men he promised.

Act 2, Scene 3

The scene opens in the sewer, where the crap game continues. Many of the men are getting ready to depart, but Big Jule wants to keep playing. In Nathan's conversation with Big Jule, Nathan implies that Big Jule, who will use only his own dice, is not playing fairly. After directly accusing Big Jule of cheating, Nathan is warned by Harry about what Big Jule could do to him. Nathan assures him that even death would be welcome at this point, since he has lost all his money, after risking so much to put the game together and even promising to get married in order to arrange the game.

Sky and Nicely arrive. When Big Jule threatens to prevent Sky from talking to the other men, Sky punches him and takes his gun away. Sky asks the men to come to the mission, but they scoff. As he turns to leave, Nathan apologizes for not yet having the money to pay him for losing the bet on Sarah. Instead, Sky pays Nathan, telling him that Nathan won the bet after all. Again, Sky turns to leave, and Nathan tells Big Jule that he now has enough money to play him—but they will use Sky's dice this time. Harry tells Nathan that without using his own (loaded) dice, Big Jule cannot make a winning roll "to save his soul." This gives Sky an idea: he tells the men he will roll them for their souls, that is, if he wins, they come with him to the mission; if he loses, he pays them each one thousand dollars. Sky sings "Luck Be a Lady Tonight," and the other men join in, each hoping for luck to be with him in the dice game to follow.

Act 2, Scene 4

The crap shooters are all making their way through the streets when Nathan runs into Adelaide. Despite her initial indignation with him, Adelaide warms up and shortly persuades him to still elope. However, when Nathan sees Benny and Nicely, he realizes he must go to the mission. Adelaide does not believe him when he tells her he is going to a prayer meeting. The two sing a duet, "Sue Me," in which Nathan pleads for her understanding and Adelaide accuses him of making false promises.

Act 2, Scene 5

Inside the mission, Sarah, Arvide, and the Mission Band members are gathered, and General Cartwright begins to wonder whether the promised sinners will appear. Moments later, Sky arrives with the gamblers. When the men are called upon to confess their sins, Harry the Horse reveals that they are only at the mission because Sky beat them in a dice game. Sarah is dismayed as she makes the matter clear to

Guys and Dolls

General Cartwright, but the general is pleased, feeling as though having gotten the sinners to the mission in this fashion is a great accomplishment. The men continue to testify to their sinful natures. Brannigan appears, but he is hushed by Nathan and made to sit and join the group. When it is Nicely's turn, he sings the number "Sit Down, You're Rockin' the Boat." The other men join in. At the end of the number, Brannigan reveals that he is there to arrest the men for gambling in the mission the previous night. He asks Sarah whether she can identify the men, but she replies that she has never seen them before. Frustrated, Brannigan leaves. Nathan confesses to the missionaries that he and the other men did gamble at the mission and that they are all sorry. He then apologizes to Sarah for making the bet with Sky about being able to take her to Havana.

Act 2, Scene 6

Adelaide and Sarah run into each other near Times Square. They talk about the ways they wish Sky and Nathan were different and how they wish they could change them. Sarah reveals that Nathan was at the prayer meeting at the mission, so Adelaide finds out that this time Nathan has not actually lied to her. Adelaide and Sarah realize that they have been approaching the matter the wrong way. In the number "Marry the Man Today," they discuss a new philosophy: marry the man today, and change him afterward.

Act 2, Scene 7

On Broadway, many of the same people who bustled across the stage when the play opened are present once again. Adelaide, dressed in a wedding gown, arrives at a newsstand looking for Nathan. Brannigan is buying a paper. Nathan appears from behind the newsstand, and when he pulls down the shade on the stand, it reads "Nathan Detroit's News Stand." He emerges dressed for his wedding, but he soon frets that he has not found a place for it to take place. The Mission Band enters, and Sky is now dressed in one of the mission's uniforms as well. Nathan asks Sky if he and Adelaide can get married at the mission, but Arvide replies instead. Arvide recently performed the marriage ceremony for Sky and Sarah at the mission; he would be happy to perform the ceremony for Nathan and Adelaide as well. The play closes with a reprise of the "Guys and Dolls" number.

CHARACTERS

Arvide Abernathy

Arvide is Sarah's grandfather. Like Sarah, he works at the Save-a-Soul Mission. He encourages Sarah when she despairs that the mission is not having a positive effect on the sinners in the area. Realizing Sarah is in love with Sky, he suggests that she overlook the fact that Sky is a gambler and encourages her to follow her heart.

Adelaide

Adelaide is Nathan Detroit's fiancée. A performer at the Hot Box, Adelaide has been engaged to Nathan for fourteen years, and she has created an elaborate fiction of their life together for her mother, to whom she has written about a wedding that never happened and children that do not exist. She repeatedly pleads with Nathan to marry her and give up gambling, and she takes him back every time he apologizes for lying to her. Throughout the play, she has a cold that, after consulting a medical book, she attributes to the fact that she loves a man who will not marry her. She and Sarah resolve to forget about changing their men until after they marry them.

Agatha

Agatha is a member of the Mission Band.

Angie the Ox

Angie the Ox is one of the crap shooters.

Brandy Bottle Bates

Brandy Bottle Bates is one of the crap shooters.

Joey Biltmore

Joey Biltmore does not appear on stage; only his voice is heard. Joey talks to Nathan on the phone, insisting that Nathan may only use the Biltmore Garage for the crap game if Nathan pays him one thousand dollars first.

Lieutenant Brannigan

Brannigan is a police officer who attempts to shut down the illegal gambling ring run by Nathan. Although he succeeds in making it difficult for Nathan to set up a game, he is unable to prosecute any gamblers during the course of the play.

Sergeant Sarah Brown

Sarah is a missionary who is focused on compelling the sinners of New York City to repent their sins and renew their faith at the Save-a-Soul Mission where she works. Despite her prim demeanor, she longs for love. Sky Masterson believes that her notion of love is one that few men could live up to. Sky propositions Sarah, promising her sinners to fill up the mission if she will accompany him to Havana. She initially refuses. After Sky kisses Sarah, she slaps him, but she eventually agrees to accompany him on the condition that he can actually bring in a dozen sinners to the mission; she needs to prove to her superiors that the mission is necessary and should not be closed. In Havana, Sarah unwittingly drinks alcohol, becomes tipsy, and begins to open up to the possibility of a romance with Sky. When the two return to New York, they profess their love for one another. Sarah, however, comes to the realization that she and Sky are too different to be a suitable match. He nonetheless delivers on his promise to bring the sinners to the mission, thereby saving it from being closed. Sarah resolves to pursue her relationship with Sky, and they marry at the end of the play.

Calvin
Calvin is a member of the Mission Band.

General Cartwright
General Cartwright is an administrator for the mission. She tells Arvide and Sarah and the others that the mission will be closing. Sky persuades her to wait until after the next meeting (to which he has promised Sarah he will bring a dozen sinners) to make her decision.

Rusty Charley
Rusty Charley is a gambler who appears in the first scene, singing with Benny and Nicely.

Nathan Detroit
Nathan is a gambler. He runs a floating crap game, that is, a game that moves from location to location to protect the gamblers from being discovered by the police. Nathan repeatedly professes his love for Adelaide, but he is obviously reluctant to commit to marriage, given that the couple's engagement has lasted fourteen years. Much of the play's action is generated by a bet Nathan makes with Sky. Seeking a location for the dice game, Nathan needs money to pay Joey Biltmore for the use of his garage. Consequently, Nathan bets Sky that Sky cannot get Sarah to go to Havana with him. Sky's pursuit of Sarah parallels Nathan's pursuit of a location for his

crap game. After the prayer meeting at the mission—a meeting that Nathan, along with the other gamblers, is forced to attend after losing a bet to Sky—Nathan appears to seek a respectable way of living. He buys a newsstand and is finally prepared to marry Adelaide.

Harry the Horse
Harry the Horse, another gambler, arrives in New York with Big Jule and serves as one of his underlings.

Hot Horse Herbie
Hot Horse Herbie is one of the crap shooters.

Hot Box Girls
The Hot Box Girls are Adelaide's fellow performers at the nightclub, the Hot Box. They throw her a bridal shower when it appears as though Nathan and Adelaide are going to elope.

Nicely-Nicely Johnson
Nicely is one of Nathan's friends and fellow gamblers. With Benny Southstreet, Nicely attempts to help Nathan as much as possible, by running errands and delivering messages for him or helping to keep Adelaide at bay. Nicely and Benny both feel that Adelaide is a distraction for Nathan.

Big Jule
Big Jule is a high-stakes gambler from Chicago. He threatens Nathan with physical violence if Nathan cannot find a place for a game of craps. During the game, Big Jule cheats, leaves everyone broke, and threatens Nathan when Nathan stands up to him. Like the other gamblers, he loses his game with Sky and must report to the prayer meeting at the mission.

Liverlips Louis
Liverlips Louis is one of the crap shooters.

Martha
Martha is a member of the Mission Band.

Sky Masterson
Sky Masterson is a high-stakes gambler. Depicted as cool-headed and suave, Sky is known for taking on strange bets. He is wise to Nathan's attempt to trick him into taking a rigged bet regarding the number of desserts sold at a local café. He accepts Nathan's bet that he cannot take any woman he chooses with him to Havana;

Nathan selects Sarah. Sky initially pursues Sarah only to win the bet, but he has fallen in love with her by the time they return from Havana. He persuades her to go by promising her a mission full of sinners, and Sarah agrees to the Havana trip only to keep the mission open. Although Sky is disheartened by Sarah's decision to stop seeing him after the gamblers are discovered at the mission, Sky follows through on his promise: after winning a series of dice rolls, he delivers the gamblers to the mission. Because his efforts are successful, General Cartwright decides that the mission may remain operational. When Nathan and Adelaide are looking for a place to have their wedding, Arvide informs them that he has recently performed the wedding of Sky and Sarah at the mission. Sky is seen at the play's end working as a missionary, dressed in uniform and preaching to people on the street about changing their ways.

Society Max

Society Max is one of the crap shooters. He breaks a date with Mimi to play in Nathan's dice game.

Mimi

Mimi is a performer at the Hot Box. She dates the gambler Society Max and is angry with Nathan that Max has broken off a date to play craps.

Joey Perhaps

Joey Perhaps is one of the crap shooters.

Regret

Regret is one of the crap shooters.

Sky Rocket

Sky Rocket is one of the crap shooters.

Scranton Slim

Scranton Slim is one of the crap shooters.

Benny Southstreet

Benny Southstreet is a gambler and friend of Nathan's. Along with Nicely-Nicely Johnson, Benny attempts to help Nathan find a place for the crap game. He and Nicely lament the fact that Nathan gets distracted by Adelaide.

THEMES

Love

Throughout *Guys and Dolls*, the notion of romantic love is often derided. Nathan repeatedly professes his love for Adelaide, but he has resisted marrying her for well over a decade. His friends regard him as caught, trapped by his relationship with her. Adelaide likewise views herself as caught, unable to break away from Nathan and find someone who might settle down and marry her because she is trapped by her love for him.

The musical number "Guys and Dolls," sung by Nicely and Benny in the first act, depicts love as something that compels men to behave in a way counter to their instincts. They cite a movie about a man who "sacrifices everything" for a woman. Discussing a story in the newspaper, they sing about a man who bought his wife a ruby with his union dues and about men who used to see a number of women and are now stuck watching television. Nicely and Benny describe the unique way men become "insane" when in love. A man who buys wine he cannot afford is likely doing it because he "is under the thumb of some little broad," they sing. In the lyrics to this song, the sentiment, expressed throughout the play as well, is conveyed that love makes men blind to the way women manipulate them. Love makes men helpless and women miserable.

Adelaide and Sarah both express angst, sadness, and frustration at loving men who disappoint them either through their behavior or character. Adelaide, in fact, is physically ill throughout the play seemingly because of her love for Nathan and his inability to follow through on promises to marry her. In song, Sky and Sarah describe the "helpless haze" they are in. Nathan similarly describes a feeling of helplessness. When Adelaide rages at him in the number "Sue Me," Nathan replies with a shrug, "Sue me, sue me, / What can you do me? / I love you / Give a holler and hate me, hate me, / Go ahead hate me / I love you." He seems genuinely baffled by his own feelings, knowing he loves Adelaide but not knowing how to change for her. At the play's end, he succumbs and agrees to marry her, but his sneeze suggests that he feels some reluctance. Love, as the play demonstrates, seems to require that Nathan change, and while he may be certain of his feelings, he doubts his ability to change.

TOPICS FOR FURTHER STUDY

- *Guys and Dolls* is based on the short fiction of Damon Runyon. "The Idyll of Miss Sarah Brown" is the inspiration for the play's story line, but the play's writers were said to have also been inspired by other characters developed by Runyon, as well as by his style of dialogue. Read "The Idyll of Miss Sarah Brown" and compare it with *Guys and Dolls*. What elements appearing in the original were retained in the musical? What was changed, and what was left out? How successful were the musical writers in capturing the sounds of the characters' speech patterns as depicted by Runyon? Write a comparative essay in which you analyze these issues.

- As musical theater, *Guys and Dolls* integrates musical numbers within the play's narrative, often using a song to replace dialogue or to convey a character's private thoughts to the audience. Compose a scene into which you incorporate a short song sung between two characters or used to express one character's thoughts. Consider the ways in which the writers of *Guys and Dolls* created dialogue to introduce each song, thereby making them seem integrated with the play rather than simply added to the existing dialogue. Perform your scene for your classmates or record it and post to your Web page or YouTube. Invite classmates to review your production.

- In 1957, C. Y. Lee wrote the best-selling novel *Flower Drum Song*, which inspired the Rodgers and Hammerstein musical adaptation that premiered in 1958. In 1961, this story of a Chinese immigrant family was once again adapted, as the Rogers and Hammerstein musical was adapted for film. In 2002, Asian American playwright David Henry Hwang wrote a revival of the original musical for Broadway, attempting to make it more accessible for modern audiences. Read Lee's original novel and compare it with the 1961 film, which Hwang has stated inspired his own interpretation of Lee's novel. How are the Chinese characters presented in the novel and on film? In what ways does the film perpetrate stereotypes of Asian Americans? How accurately do you think the film represents Lee's original characterizations? How do you think the movie would be perceived today in terms of its depiction of Chinese immigrants? Write an essay in which you discuss your opinions of the book and movie, giving specific evidence from both, or create a visual presentation, either with PowerPoint or as a Web page accessible by your classmates, in which you present your comparison.

- Set in the 1950s, Cynthia Kadohata's young-adult, Newbery Award–winning novel *Kira-Kira*, published in 2006, portrays the experiences of a Japanese American family living in Georgia. In examining their struggles with poverty and racial injustice, Kadohata depicts an entirely different world than that portrayed in *Guys and Dolls*, which is set in the same time period. With a small group, read *Kira-Kira*. Consider the way Kadohata portrays the setting of Georgia in the 1950s. Is it vividly described, and docs it play an essential role in the story? From which character's point of view is the story narrated? Does the author switch narrators during the course of the story? Are there characters in the story to whom you relate on some level? Give some thought to the way the author portrays the racism that the characters experience, and think about your responses as you read these sections of the story. Discuss these issues with the members of your group, or create an online blog in which you share your ideas and analyses with one another.

Marquee from the 1953 West End premiere of
Guys and Dolls *(© Trinity Mirror | Mirrorpix | Alamy)*

able to transform himself for Sarah. At the play's conclusion, after his marriage to Sarah, he is dressed as a missionary and now preaches to anyone who will listen about the dangers of sin.

Sarah and Adelaide come to the conclusion that the personal transformations they had hoped for in Sky and Nathan are not possible. Having believed that Sky and Nathan should and would change because they love Sarah and Adelaide, the women transform their attitudes and determine that they can induce changes in their men after they have married them. They still believe that they can compel others to change rather than accept the notion that personal transformation arises out of a desire to behave differently. Nathan's sneeze at the play's conclusion suggests that he still doubts his ability to be the man Adelaide wants him to be.

Sky, on the other hand, not only promises to change his ways but apparently follows up on his promises, as indicated by his membership in the Mission Band at the play's end.

Transformation

The personal transformation that love apparently inspires or requires is referred to repeatedly in the play. It is indicated, for example, in the "Guys and Dolls" number that Nicely and Benny sing, as they describe the way love changes men. Despite the fact that Benny and Nicely regard Adelaide as problematic in that she distracts Nathan, Nathan nevertheless changes little about his behavior in order to please her. Nathan makes promises to Adelaide, and she expects him to change, but then he continues to gamble and to apologize to her. Benny's and Nicely's fears about the way love changes men are unfounded in Nathan's case, as he seems unable to change. The futility of personal transformation also appears to be underscored by the perpetually empty Save-a-Soul Mission. Despite Sarah's and Arvide's proselytizing, none of the sinners to whom they preach seem interested in repenting or changing their ways. When the gamblers do arrive, it is because of a dice game rather than a desire to transform. Yet Sky appears to be ready and

STYLE

Musical Theater

As a work of musical theater, *Guys and Dolls* incorporates song and dance into the fabric of the play's narrative. The musical numbers serve as a way for the characters to express feelings, and the lyrics often stand in for spoken dialogue. There are three types of musical numbers in *Guys and Dolls*. Some numbers are songs that the characters are actually performing for one another, as when the Mission Band sings "Follow the Fold" or when Adelaide and the Hot Box Girls perform "Bushel and a Peck" and "Take Back Your Mink." Other songs represent dialogue among a number of characters. "Fugue for Tin Horns," for example, sung by Benny, Nicely, and Rusty Charley, includes comments about the horse upon which the characters are betting; the song also serves as a means of introducing the play's focus on gambling. Similarly, "The Oldest Established" is performed by the gamblers in the play as they discuss Nathan Detroit's reputation for hosting crap games. Other numbers are more intimate and are sung between two characters expressing feelings for one another, as when Sky and Sarah sing "I've Never Been in Love Before." Adelaide additionally sings two solos, "Adelaide's Lament" and a reprise of this number in the second act. In these songs, Adelaide sings as a way of expressing private feelings of sadness and frustration with Nathan.

Romantic Comedy

Guys and Dolls is written in the style of a romantic comedy. It lightly and humorously treats the romances of Nathan and Adelaide, who are perpetually engaged, and of Sarah and Sky, who as a missionary and a gambler form an unlikely couple. The two romances are approached quite differently. Nathan and Adelaide entertain the audience through Adelaide's silly, naive nature and Nathan's fumbling excuses. After Nathan sends a message to Adelaide about not being able to elope because his aunt in Pittsburgh has come down with a tropical disease, Adelaide gives Sky a nonsensical message for Nathan: "Tell him I never want to talk to him again and have him phone me here."

The playwrights structured the play's romance between Sky and Sarah in such a way as to generate both comedy and conflict. Nathan bets Sky that he cannot get Sarah to go to Havana with him. She eventually does so, and the two begin to fall in love, so much so that Sarah is not even angry with Sky when he reveals that Nathan's bet was the only reason he approached her. Later, however, Sarah determines that as a "Mission doll," she cannot be involved with a gambler. She then tells Arvide rather angrily that Sky came to the mission not seeking salvation, but seeking her, seeming now to feel uneasy at having been sought out in this manner. After the quick resolution of their differences, Sarah and Sky marry. His complete reversal from gambler to missionary serves as another comic element in their unlikely romance.

Similarly, Nathan stops stalling and agrees to marry Adelaide, but his sneeze at the play's conclusion reminds the audience of Adelaide's cold, which she believed was caused by being strung along by Nathan for so long. Nathan seems to be developing a similar ailment, now that he is about to wed. The play's use of lighthearted, upbeat musical numbers, along with jokes about the way love makes men behave as though they are insane, contribute to the comedic elements of the story line.

HISTORICAL CONTEXT

1950s Broadway Musicals

During the 1950s, the Broadway musical as a genre enjoyed enormous popularity. As a genre, the musical play was born in the 1940s, beginning with the 1943 production of *Oklahoma!* written by composers Richard Rodgers and Oscar Hammerstein. The duo went on to write a number of other musicals in the 1940s and 1950s. As Stacy Ellen Wolf observes in *Changed for Good: A Feminist History of the Broadway Musical*, "While in fact fewer musicals opened in the 1950s [than in other decades], more made a profit and more have continued to be performed in revivals and school and community productions." A dominant theme of the musicals of this time period is romance. Popular productions of the 1950s featuring romantic relationships included Swerling, Burrows, and Loesser's *Guys and Dolls* and Rodgers and Hammerstein's *The King and I*, *My Fair Lady*, and *The Sound of Music*. Such productions were enormously popular among critics and audiences and frequently were adapted for film productions. Not only did theatrical musical productions spawn film adaptations, but the soundtrack albums topped the music charts as well and became an integral part of the American popular music scene.

As Ethan Mordden comments in *Coming Up Roses: The Broadway Musical in the 1950s*, "The musical then was central to American culture." A popular form of entertainment, the Broadway musical accounted for fifteen of the fifty-one shows during the 1949–1950 season. In his book, Mordden traces the ways the musicals of this time period transformed the conventions of the genre as well as where they honored them. *Guys and Dolls*, Mordden observes, like the traditional musical, features two romantic couples, but in *Guys and Dolls* it is difficult to ascertain which couple—Sky and Sarah or Nathan and Adelaide—takes the primary role in the narrative. Some 1950s musicals, such as 1950's *Call Me Madam*, typically incorporated wry references to topical, contemporary themes. Mordden notes that *Guys and Dolls* resisted this trend and instead "holds to the boundaries of its timeless Runyonland."

Literature in the 1950s

Trends in fiction in the 1950s represented a move away from the experimental modes that thrived during the years between World War I (1914–1918) and World War II (1939–1945) and that continued to prevail in new forms in the postwar years. Writers such as Ernest Hemingway, who published *Across the River and Into the Trees* in 1950 and *The Old Man and the Sea* in 1952, and John Steinbeck, who published *East of Eden* in

COMPARE & CONTRAST

- **1950s:** *Guys and Dolls* debuts on Broadway in 1950. The musical runs for 1,194 performances and wins five Tony Awards: Best Musical, Best Actor in a Musical, Best Featured Actress in a Musical, Best Director, and Best Choreography.

  Today: *Guys and Dolls* has been revived numerous times on Broadway, most recently in 2009. This production is much less well received than the original 1950 production. *New York Times* reviewer Ben Brantley describes the work as "paralyzed by self-consciousness." Although the play is nominated for a 2009 Tony Award for Best Revival, the play runs for only 113 performances.

- **1950s:** American cultural tastes are broad. Musicals featuring romantic, comedic story lines are popular on Broadway, as evidenced by the success of such plays as *Guys and Dolls* and *My Fair Lady*. In fiction, genre works are popular, as mass-market paperback production increases in the postwar years. Mickey Spillane's crime novels, such as *My Gun Is Quick* (1950), are a part of this trend, as are feminine middlebrow novels designed to appeal to middle-class women, such as Margaret Kennedy's *The Feast* (1950). The combination of literary themes and accessible writing also broadens the appeal of such authors as Ernest Hemingway and John Steinbeck, while those of the literary movement known as the Beat movement experiment with form and language and explore themes of freedom and experience.

  Today: Like the literature and culture of the 1950s, twenty-first-century drama, film, and

literature offer a range of stylistic varieties. Popular films entertain audiences with romantic and alternatively comedic or dramatic story lines, while in fiction the lines between popular fiction and literary fiction blur. Acclaimed works of literary fiction, such as Muriel Barbery's *The Elegance of the Hedgehog* (2006), as well as novels that become mainstays of the book-club set, including Kathryn Stockett's *The Help* (2009), are adapted for the screen. The popularity of the musical is seen not only on Broadway, which routinely features a number of musicals (many of which are revivals of earlier productions), but on television as well, such as in the widely popular television series *Glee*, which centers on a high-school glee club.

- **1950s:** The world of illegal gambling comes under the scrutiny of the U.S. Senate via the Kefauver Committee, which is established in 1950 to investigate organized crime and which subsequently reveals the extent to which local officials are involved in illegal gambling and racketeering, among other crimes.

  Today: The world of gambling has expanded to include online gambling, some of which is legal and some of which is not. This realm has proved difficult to regulate. Additionally, since the 1950s, the U.S. government has expanded the category of legalized gaming, allowing regulated casino-type games and lotteries. There has also been an increase in the number of casinos operated by Native American tribes, to which different rules apply.

1952, were popular; their approaches to literature were regarded as innovative and literary yet accessible. Martin Halliwell observes in *American Culture in the 1950s* that the mass paperback

market grew rapidly after World War II, and genre fiction, such as crime writing and murder mysteries, became popular. In the world of poetry, new experiments with form were taking place.

American actress Vivian Blaine played Miss Adelaide in both the original stage productions and the 1955 film production. (© *Trinity Mirror /*
Mirrorpix / Alamy)

and examines which types of gambling were most popular; these included betting on sporting events, in particular on horse racing. In exploring legal and illegal gambling, Havemann compares the fees and licenses paid by legal clubs to the bribes paid to officials by racketeers. Summarizing the activities and recommendations of the Kefauver Committee, named after the senator who headed the committee, Estes Kefauver of Tennessee, Havemann is critical of their efforts. He notes that senators investigating gambling and crime in the nation praised the city of New York for reducing the prevalence of bookmaking (betting) in the city. But Havemann insists that this reduction was due to the fact that the bribes demanded by the police were so high that the bookmakers took their business elsewhere, fleeing the city. The investigations of the Kefauver Committee were later applauded and have since been credited with revealing the extent to which organized crime families had infiltrated state and local governments at this time period in American history.

Poets such as Allen Ginsberg, Gary Snyder, Lawrence Ferlinghetti, Michael McClure, and Gregory Corso, among others, became known as the Beat poets, seeking new modes of poetic expression through experiments with sound, language, and form. Halliwell asserts, "This emphasis on poetic form was not a retreat into modernist experimentation, but the attempt to discover a new vocal range to speak to the rapidly transforming postwar nation." Such innovations and rejection of conventions stand in stark contrast to the Broadway musicals of the time period, which, though exploring new modes of marrying dramatic storytelling with musical numbers, presented society, culture, gender roles, and relationships in traditional, familiar ways.

New York Gambling in the 1950s

Ernest Havemann reported in *Life* magazine in June 1950 on the U.S. Senate's "full-scale probe of gambling and crime" that was then under way. According to Havemann, in the previous year, "about 50 million adult Americans as well as quite a number of minors" participated in "some form of gambling." Surveying the heavy losses suffered in the realm of legalized casino gambling, Havemann in his article also discusses gamblers from whom gambling racketeers profit

CRITICAL OVERVIEW

Upon the 1950 Broadway debut of *Guys and Dolls*, *New York Times* critic Brooks Atkinson commented, "With a well-written book by Jo Swerling and Abe Burrows, and a dynamic score by Frank Loesser, it is a more coherent show than some that have higher artistic pretensions." Atkinson praises the play's "form, style and spirit," describing it as "gusty and uproarious" and stating that "it is not too grand to take a friendly, personal interest in the desperate affairs of Broadway's backroom society." In the *Dictionary of Literary Biography* volume *American Song Lyricists, 1920–1960*, Michael Lasser discusses the collaborative nature of the relationship between Burrows and Loesser. Lasser assesses Loesser's score, observing the ways in which it "combines comedy and skepticism, advances plot, and creates both atmosphere and character."

The nature of the creation of the playbook is sometimes a source of debate among theater critics. Caryl Brahms and Ned Sherrin, in an essay on Loesser for *The Guys and Dolls Book*, assert (as does Lasser) that Swerling's contribution to the play was minimal compared with that of Burrows. In their words, Loesser was "teamed with Abe Burrows (after an abortive book by Jo Swerling)." Yet Swerling's name is typically listed along with Burrows as writer, without any caveats or reservations. Swerling's son, Jo Swerling, Jr., defended his father in a 1992 letter to the editor in the *New York Times*. The junior Swerling insisted that "the book was written, the money was raised, and the show was cast and in rehearsal with the director before Burrows started on the project. He was brought in... to snap up the dialogue." Yet Geoffrey Block, in *Enchanted Evenings: The Broadway Musical from "Show Boat" to Sondheim*, concurs that Swerling's work was minimal compared to that of Burrows. Block first describes the way the play's producers "commissioned Hollywood script writer Jo Swerling to write the book, and Loesser wrote as many as fourteen songs to match." Block then indicates that the producers and director George S. Kaufman were unhappy with Swerling's draft, as it "failed to match their vision of Runyonesque comedy. Burrows was then asked to come up with a new book to support Loesser's songs." Richard Hornby, in *Mad about Theatre*, emphasizes not the perceived rift between Swerling and the rest of the production but also the role of Kaufman in the development of the story in *Guys and Dolls*. Hornby asserts that in the play, "Swerling, Burrows and Kaufman flesh out the story in impressive ways."

CRITICISM

Catherine Dominic

Dominic is a novelist and a freelance writer and editor. In the following essay, she examines what she maintains is the deterioration of two characters in Guys and Dolls, *Sarah and Adelaide, who establish themselves as unique individuals with distinct values and beliefs but who, in the end, are transfigured by the required happy ending of the genre into the flat, stereotypical "dolls" the male characters had earlier, and unfairly, perceived them to be.*

In postwar America, when *Guys and Dolls* was first staged, the feminist movement had not yet blossomed. Gender roles were distinct, and women were largely expected to become wives and mothers. *Guys and Dolls* was designed as entertainment, as musical theater, not as experimental or controversial drama, and it cannot be expected to have challenged the status quo.

> WHEN THE PLAY DRAWS TOWARD THE HAPPY ENDING REQUIRED OF THE MUSICAL GENRE, HOWEVER, THE WOMEN SUDDENLY EMBRACE A VIEW OF THEMSELVES, MARRIAGE, AND THE MEN THEY LOVE THAT IS INCONSISTENT WITH THEIR CHARACTERS BUT WHICH MOLDS THEM PERFECTLY INTO THE GENERIC, UNDIFFERENTIATED DOLLS THE MEN BELIEVE THEM TO BE."

Indeed, the lead female characters in *Guys and Dolls*, Adelaide and Sarah, do little to challenge conventional notions of gender roles. Both regard marriage as an ideal to which they strive, although the pictures they paint for themselves about what marriage will be like are quite different. Yet the women both possess qualities that define them as individuals with distinct personal opinions about love. The women stand out not as the generic "dolls" the male characters in the play perceive them to be, but as unique women. When the play draws toward the happy ending required of the musical genre, however, the women suddenly embrace a view of themselves, marriage, and the men they love that is inconsistent with their characters but which molds them perfectly into the generic, undifferentiated dolls the men believe them to be. Discarding their previously held beliefs, Adelaide and Sarah now seek to manipulate men, to dupe them by marrying them with the intention of changing them later. Some critics have suggested that this union of purpose and seizing of power stands in opposition to the male dominance of the play; yet Adelaide and Sarah transform themselves from women with a clear view of themselves and their ideals into women who succumb to the prescriptions of society, becoming diminished versions of themselves by the end of the play.

Sarah is introduced early in the first act. With the Mission Band accompanying her, Sarah is preaching to the citizens of New York, pleading with them to give up gambling and to repent. She encourages them to come to the

WHAT DO I READ NEXT?

- *Jelly's Last Jam* is an example of musical theater written and performed by African Americans. Based on the life of jazz musician Jelly Roll Morton, the play premiered in 1991 and was published in 1993. The playbook was written by George C. Wolfe and the lyrics by Susan Birkenhead, while the production utilized Morton's music for the score.

- The Rodgers and Hammerstein musical *The King and I*, which premiered and was published in 1951, features an Asian setting, as an English governess travels to Siam (now Thailand), where she is employed to instruct the king's offspring. Produced during the same period as *Guys and Dolls*, the musical adheres to the same theatrical and plot conventions and presents Siamese society from the point of view of English speakers.

- Like *Guys and Dolls*, *Bat 6*, a young-adult novel by Virginia Euwer Wolff, published in 2000, takes place shortly after World War II. Wolff's novel is set in Oregon and concerns the relationships of young teens preparing for a series of baseball games among rival towns. Two of the girls have been affected by the war more than the others; one lost her father in the Japanese attack on Pearl Harbor, and the other spent much of the war in a Japanese internment camp.

- *Broadway: The American Musical*, by Michael Kantor and Laurence Maslon, published in 2004, explores the history of the musical genre and serves as a companion resource to a Public Broadcasting System television series on the same subject.

- Mary Rose Wood's young-adult novel *My Life: The Musical*, published in 2008, uses musical theater as a basis for portraying not only friendships among teens but also the rich interior world they inhabit.

- Abe Burrows's memoir, *Honest, Abe: Is There No Business Like Show Business?* (1980), recounts the details of his career as a writer and includes his recollections about the creation of the playbook for *Guys and Dolls*.

- *Where's Charley?* is a musical by George Abbott and Frank Loesser, produced in 1948. The work represented Loesser's Broadway debut and established his reputation as a songwriter.

- Vaikom Mohammad Basheer's novella *Me Grandad 'ad an Elephant*, originally published in 1980, was produced as a musical play in 2011. The story focuses on a young Muslim-Malayali girl and her coming-of-age in a village in North Malabar.

---

mission and "seek refuge from this jungle of sin." Watching her, Benny describes Sarah as "a beautiful doll," and Nicely agrees, lamenting that she "wastes all her time being good." Having taken Nathan's bet that he cannot get Sarah to go to Havana with him, Sky approaches Sarah at the mission and flirts with her, offering twelve sinners to populate the mission if she comes with him to Havana. Sarah is outraged. When Sky presses her, asking her what type of man would appeal to her, Sarah sings the number "I'll

Know." In it, she describes the "strong moral fibre" and "wisdom" of her ideal mate. She insists that she will take no chances. She will not have to because she will know such a man when she sees him. He will be precisely what she needs, "not some fly-by-night Broadway romance." Sky scoffs at her ideals, insisting that she is trying to plan what cannot be planned. Yet Sarah has not imagined an impossible mate. Although she thinks of her future love as a pipe smoker, an aspect of her characterization at which Sky pokes fun, the rest of Sarah's portrait of her future love is not frivolous or unreasonable. Sarah resolves to wait for a man whose moral beliefs are compatible with her own. Sky, on the other hand, states that he is interested more in physical attraction. Once Sky compels Sarah to go with him to Havana (as she believes it is the only way she can save the mission), Sky plies her with alcohol. He succeeds in getting her tipsy enough to participate in a bar fight and throw herself at him. Sarah now indulges herself, giving in to her attraction for Sky and then calling it love, as he does. When she is reminded of who he really is, as Nathan and the other gamblers exit the mission, Sarah pushes Sky away, reasserting her sense of herself, but describing this notion in terms Sky will understand. After she insists that their relationship is "no good," Sky angrily asks her what kind of doll she is. Sarah responds, "I'm a Mission doll!"

Adelaide appears in the first act shortly after Sarah's departure. She presents Nathan with an anniversary gift. The two are clearly affectionate with one another, although when Adelaide brings up her disapproval of Nathan's floating crap game, he begins to pull away. Adelaide grows suspicious of Nathan when Benny, Nicely, and Harry the Horse approach, asking him, "Nathan, are you trying to get rid of me?" After Nathan's friends escort Adelaide offstage, Sky, who has just walked over, asks Nathan about Adelaide. When Nathan indicates that they will eventually marry, Sky admonishes, "Nathan, we can fight it. Guys like us, Nathan—we got to remember that pleasant as a doll's company may be, she must always take second place to aces back to back." Sky goes on to tell Nathan that Adelaide has him cornered, but Nathan insists, "Maybe I don't want to unload her." Stating that he loves Adelaide, Nathan then slips into speaking about Adelaide as if she is like any other woman. "When a guy walks into a restaurant it looks nice if there is a doll behind him. A doll is a necessity," he glibly tells Sky.

Later, Adelaide reveals to Nathan that, because they have been together so long without getting married, she has had to lie to her mother. She has created a tale in which she and Nathan have been married for twelve years and have five children. Nathan assures her that he wants to be married, wants them to be "the happiest married couple that there is in the world," which, he states, is why "I give up the crap game."

Significantly, Nathan states this in the present tense. He does give up the crap game, repeatedly, but goes back to running it again as well. He can no more make a permanent commitment to the crap game than he can to Adelaide, but she loves him nonetheless, and she has clearly accepted the situation, as it has remained unchanged for fourteen years. Adelaide comes to believe, after reading what purports to be a medical book, that being an "average unmarried female, basically insecure," she can develop a cold, "just from worrying whether the Wedding is on or off." Adelaide describes her state as being "single, just in the legal sense," and one must wonder if Adelaide would feel more satisfied with her relationship with Nathan if society's views on the necessity of marriage were different. After all, she has been with Sky for fourteen years in a presumably committed relationship. Although unmarried, she is not, in another sense, single. After Nathan again promises marriage and again lets Adelaide down, she, like Sarah, reasserts her sense of her own desires. Whereas Sarah, in stating, "I'm a Mission doll," emphasizes her status as a Christian seeking a man with similar moral values, Adelaide, as a woman only single "in the legal sense," emphasizes her desire to be with Nathan, married or not, with Nathan running the crap game or not. She tells Sky to tell Nathan, "I never want to talk to him again and have him phone me here." In this statement, she expresses her continued frustration but also her devotion. She will follow her heart, even if it means society will frown upon her for not being married, and even if it means she seems a fool to everyone else. Sky asks her, "Why don't you find yourself another guy?" "I can't," she replies; "I love Nathan." Despite the fact that she has one more fight with Nathan, where she lashes out about his gambling, and despite the time that has elapsed while she has waited for him to change, Adelaide has not thus far strayed from her loyalty to Nathan, not in fourteen years; it is not reasonable to believe that she would truly walk away from him at this point, even though she sings in "Sue Me" that they are through. This is certainly a song Nathan has heard before.

Throughout the play, the male characters have expressed their regard for women as "dolls," a term that indicates the way the men view the women as objects, rather than people. Nathan and Sky have discussed women as accessories, things to make a man look better when he

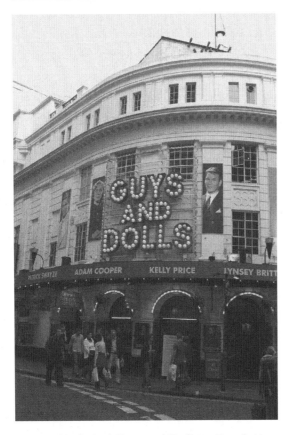

A 2005 revival of Guys and Dolls *in London's West End featured Patrick Swayze as Nathan Detroit for part of the run. (© Meeyoung Son / Alamy)*

walks into a bar. When Benny and Nicely bemoan Nathan's distraction with Adelaide, they sing, in "Guys and Dolls," about the way men become insane when they are in love and the way women trick men into spending all their money on them. In the view of Benny and Nicely, women trap men into marriages that transform the lives of lusty, roving, gambling men into dull existences spent in front of the television. Nicely and Benny characterize women as controlling and manipulative "broads."

When Adelaide and Sarah meet in act 2, scene 6, on a street near Times Square, they have both recently resigned themselves to a course of action that, while difficult, is aligned with the principles they have professed and upheld throughout the play. Adelaide, for fourteen years, has stuck by Nathan, realizing that marriage might never be in the cards for her and that Nathan might never give up craps. She loves him and has no desire to be without him, even if it

means sacrificing the portrait of their life together that she has painted for her mother. Sarah, though missing Sky and no doubt having enjoyed her trip to Havana with him, devotes herself again to her dream of finding someone with whom she can share a life based on common values and moral beliefs. Unlike Adelaide, who simply frowns upon Nathan's illegal gambling, Sarah believes gambling is a sin. Reconciling this way of life with her own would be impossible for a woman who, as a missionary for the Save-a-Soul Mission, is clearly a devout Christian with firm views on what constitutes right and wrong. Pondering their fates, the women wonder whether or not Sky and Nathan can change. Adelaide, experienced in this area, insists that they cannot. However, the stage direction indicates that suddenly, "Two girls look at each other for a moment." In that instant, the play is propelled forward toward the happy ending musical audiences expect; yet it progresses in a way that distorts the characters of Adelaide and Sarah. Although both women have demonstrated their willingness and desire to follow the paths they have created for themselves, despite setbacks or moments of unhappiness or discontent, in "Marry the Man Today" the women suddenly reject their previously held beliefs. During the play, although they expressed a desire for their men to change, the women seemed to have developed an understanding that a man cannot be compelled to change, and a woman can either choose to remain with him anyway, loving him for what he is rather than for what he could be, as Adelaide chose, or to move forward alone and be willing to wait for a more suitable mate, as Sarah chose. In "Marry the Man Today," the women take on the role of doll that many of the male figures in the play have ascribed to them all along. Suddenly, a man has become, to Sarah and Adelaide, comparable to an article of clothing or a vegetable; a buyer cannot alter it or squeeze it until after the purchase is completed. They now vow to "Marry the man today / And change his ways tomorrow." They describe the way they will use their "girlish laughter" to lure their men and will then gradually, after they are married, domesticate them, introducing them to "respectable" elements of daily life, like "golf" and "galoshes." If he shows signs of straying, the women advise presenting him with a pot roast, withholding sex ("have a headache"), or using sex and domesticity ("have a baby," or two, or six, or nine) to trap him into staying.

As the play concludes, the women's efforts have succeeded. Nathan appears to have purchased a newsstand, and he and Adelaide are on their way to get married. Sky and Sarah have already wed, and Sky has undergone an almost incomprehensible transformation. The former gambler not only supports his new wife's efforts as a missionary but has become one himself. He is dressed in the mission uniform and is preaching to the gamblers on the street about the temptations of the devil, temptations that must be resisted. Although this ending conforms to the conventions of the genre and of the time period, Sarah and Adelaide are transformed by it in ways that are difficult to come to terms with. Not only do they discard their previously held beliefs, they do so incredibly quickly, with nothing to prompt the change at all. They change from women to dolls with a glance and a song.

Source: Catherine Dominic, Critical Essay on *Guys and Dolls*, in *Drama for Students*, Gale, Cengage Learning, 2012.

Terry Teachout

In the following essay, Teachout reviews Frank Loesser's career with an eye to the importance of Guys and Dolls *to his success.*

Among connoisseurs of popular song, Frank Loesser is universally regarded as a master. Not only did he write the scores for two major Broadway musicals, *Guys and Dolls* (1950) and *How to Succeed in Business Without Really Trying* (1961), but he also wrote or co-wrote numerous songs that became standards after being introduced in Hollywood films, including "Baby, It's Cold Outside," "I Don't Want to Walk Without You," and "On a Slow Boat to China." In addition, *Guys and Dolls* and *How to Succeed in Business Without Really Trying* were both turned into hit movies, and *How to Succeed* won a Pulitzer Prize for drama.

Yet Loesser is less well known to the public at large than any of his peers, and even at the peak of his success, he was obscure by comparison with such popular-music celebrities as Irving Berlin, George Gershwin, and Cole Porter. Nor has he attracted the attention of scholars of American popular song. No full-scale biography of Loesser has been written, and it was only last year that the first monograph devoted to his life and work, Thomas L. Riis's *Frank Loesser*, was published.

> LOESSER'S SCORE IN PARTICULAR IS A MIRACLE OF CONSISTENCY, AN UNBROKEN SUCCESSION OF IMMACULATELY CRAFTED SONGS, NEARLY ALL OF THEM COMIC, IN WHICH WORDS AND MUSIC FUNCTION IN FLAWLESS TANDEM."

Why is Loesser's personal profile so low? One reason is that even the best Hollywood songwriters (except for Irving Berlin, who was already famous when he began writing for films) were treated as craftsmen, not stars, and were billed accordingly. Because Loesser came late to the stage and wrote only two musicals that continue to be revived with any regularity—and because he spent most of his Hollywood years working on second-rate pictures that are no longer remembered save for the songs he contributed to them—he failed to establish himself as a songwriter whose name alone could sell music. Moreover, he was and is best known for his comic songs, whereas the popular reputations of the other great songwriters of the pre-rock era were based mainly on their romantic ballads.

Even so, Loesser's standing as a giant of American popular song would be secure even if he had written nothing but *Guys and Dolls*, one of a handful of postwar musicals to have received three Broadway revivals, the second of which ran almost as long as the original production. It is the quintessential Broadway show, a vade mecum of theatrical craft—and the long road that led Loesser to its opening night is in some ways as interesting as the show itself.

Born in Manhattan in 1910, Frank Loesser was the child of cultivated and fully assimilated middle-class German Jews with serious musical interests, and he spent his adult life rebelling against their starchy influence. His father was a piano teacher and accompanist, and Arthur Loesser, his older half-brother, became a concert pianist, music critic, and cultural historian whose best-known book, *Men, Women and Pianos: A Social History* (1954), continues to be read. But Frank, whose musical gifts were no less obvious than his sibling's, refused to study piano or acquire any formal knowledge of music.

Instead of interesting himself in classical music, Frank became a Tin Pan Alley lyricist, explaining in a letter to Arthur that his new line of work was a "trade" rather than an art: "It is all contact, salesmanship, handshaking, etc.—not a bit different from cloaks and suits or any other industry." By 1937 he had moved to Hollywood to work for Paramount Pictures, and a year later he produced his first hit songs with Hoagy Car-michael, who wrote the music for "Heart and Soul" and "Two Sleepy People."

In addition to rejecting his parents' milieu, Loesser simultaneously immersed himself in a different kind of Jewish culture. As Thomas Riis explains:

> For Loesser, embracing the milieu of New York popular music also meant embracing the world of working-class, Yiddish-speaking Lower East Side Jews, who figured promi-nently in the entertainment business. . . . They were swing dancers, fans of Tin Pan Alley and burlesque who had little use for high art, culti-vated sensibilities, or the classical legacy valued by Loesser's family.

More than any of the other Jewish song-writers who shaped American popular song in the 20s and 30s, Loesser incorporated the sound of Yiddish-flavored English into his lyrics. On occasion he did so explicitly, as in "Sue Me," sung in *Guys and Dolls* by a Jewish gambler: "Alright already, I'm just a nogoodnik/ Alright already, it's true, so nu?" In addition, he filled his songs with virtuoso wordplay and rhymes of the utmost intricacy: "When you find a doll with her diamond in hock/ Rest assured that the rock has gone to restock/ Some gentleman jock." Yet he also had an uncanny sense of verbal economy, as well as an understanding of how the best song lyrics function as miniature dramas. In the 60s he served as a mentor to Dave Frishberg, a jazz pianist and aspiring songwriter who set down his elder's artistic credo: "Loesser's objective in writing a lyric was to make the words work throughout so that the end provides a payoff rather than a repetition of what comes before."

Starting in 1939, Loesser began writing music for some of his own lyrics, and it soon became evident that he was as gifted a tunesmith as he was a wordsmith. The uniqueness of this achievement is not sufficiently appreciated: except for Stephen Sondheim, he is the only songwriter to have established himself as a first-tier composer after having won fame as a lyricist. "Spring Will Be a Little Late This Year"

(1944), the best of his pre-Broadway songs, is an atypically melancholy ballad with an expansive melody whose long leaps suggest a deeper knowledge of classical music than he cared to admit.

Loesser spent World War II working on a series of musical revues designed to be per-formed by overseas servicemen, an experience that introduced him to the special problems of writing theatrical songs. After the war, he went back to Paramount, but in 1948 he returned to New York to write his first Broadway score, *Where's Charley?*

Though this musical version of Brandon Thomas's 1892 farce has not become part of the theatrical repertory, it was commercially suc-cessful as a starring vehicle for Ray Bolger. Not long after it opened, Loesser agreed to collabo-rate with Abe Burrows, a radio comedy writer, on a musical based on "The Idyll of Miss Sarah Brown," a short story by Damon Runyon, a news-paperman whose half-comic, half-sentimental tales of the gangsters and gamblers of Broadway were wildly popular in the 30s.

Guys and Dolls was put together in an unor-thodox fashion. In the modern "integrated" Broadway musical pioneered by Richard Rodg-ers and Oscar Hammerstein II with *Oklahoma!* (1943) and *Carousel* (1945), the songs are all derived from the book of the show and usually (though not always) serve to advance the action. To facilitate this integration of story and song, the book of such a musical is drafted before the musical numbers are written. But several of the best-known songs in *Guys and Dolls*, including "Luck Be a Lady Tonight" and "Sit Down, You're Rockin' the Boat," were written before Burrows went to work on the book, while the others were composed by Loesser after the show was sketched but before the dialogue was writ-ten. "Loesser's songs," Burrows explained, "were the guideposts for the libretto."

Under normal circumstances, this would have resulted in a dramatically static musical with untheatrical, action-stopping songs. But Burrows—undoubtedly guided by George S. Kaufman, the veteran playwright-director who staged the first production of *Guys and Dolls*—took special care to ensure that his book would carry the action of the show, thus freeing Loesser to write songs that illuminated the personalities of the various characters rather than moved the plot forward.

The result was a pop-culture masterwork, a raffishly nostalgic evocation of a never-never land of crapshooting sharpies in snap-brimmed hats who prowl Times Square in search of action. Brooks Atkinson put it best in his *New York Times* review of the original production when he called *Guys and Dolls* "a perfectly-composed and swiftly-paced work of art." It is, in fact, one of the greatest pieces of musical theater, irrespective of genre, to be created by an American. Even when staged ineptly, as were Samuel Goldwyn's 1955 film version and Des McAnuff's 2009 Broadway revival, *Guys and Dolls* remains irresistible.

Loesser's score in particular is a miracle of consistency, an unbroken succession of immaculately crafted songs, nearly all of them comic, in which words and music function in flawless tandem. From the thrusting syncopations of "The Oldest Established Permanent Floating Crap Game in New York" to the tipsy ecstasy of "If I Were a Bell" ("Pal, if I were a salad / I know I'd be splashing my dressing"), Loesser makes the personality of each character stand out in high relief. He even finds room for a bit of vernacular lyricism that rises to the level of poetry: "My time of day is the dark time:/ A couple of deals before dawn."

For all his genius at writing songs of character, Loesser had only a limited grasp of what makes a musical-comedy book work, and he proved it with his next show, *The Most Happy Fella* (1956), a musical version of *They Knew What They Wanted*, Sidney Howard's 1924 play about a middle-aged Italian immigrant who falls in love with a young waitress. Loesser wrote the book himself, following the advice of the screenwriter Samuel Taylor: Any time you have doubts about what you're doing, write a song." The result was an opera-length musical that contained many more songs and much less spoken dialogue than *Guys and Dolls*.

While *The Most Happy Fella* was not a mere succès d'estime—the original Broadway production ran for 676 performances—its revival life has been limited, partly because the show is too long to produce economically and partly because it feels more like an opera than a musical. To be sure, Loesser insisted that *The Most Happy Fella* was not an opera, preferring to call it "a musical with a lot of music." In fact, it is an awkward cross between a musical and an evening-long song cycle in which the dramatic action is carried by the songs rather than the fragmentary dialogue. Therein lies its flaw: popular-song form, with its dosed circles of repeating choruses, lacks the musical momentum necessary to propel a large-scale dramatic structure. As a result, *The Most Happy Fella*, despite the kaleidoscopic variety of its musical numbers, is slow-paced, unlike *Guys and Dolls*, in which Abe Burrows's dialogue keeps the action flowing briskly from song to song.

It is unlikely that Loesser could have written a full-fledged opera had he wished to. Like Duke Ellington, he had the natural talent but not the grasp of large-scale musical form that can be obtained only from close study of the classics. Yet the failure of his next show, *Greenwillow* (1960), a pastoral fantasy that closed on Broadway after 97 performances and has never been successfully revived, proved that he was no more able to write a conventional musical without a collaborator who knew how to make the best use of his talents.

Loesser found that collaborator when he rejoined with Abe Burrows to write *How to Succeed in Business Without Really Trying*, a satirical portrait of corporate America in the age of *Mad Men*. Unlike *Guys and Dolls*, *How to Succeed* is a fully "integrated" musical whose songs are so deeply rooted in Burrows's book (which was written first) that only one of them, "I Believe in You," can be sung effectively outside the context of the show. It is for this reason that *How to Succeed* has proved to be less popular than *Guys and Dolls* and that Loesser himself claimed not to like the show as much as its predecessor. But if *How to Succeed* lacks the immediate appeal of *Guys and Dolls*, it is no less sharp-witted and well-crafted, and the 1967 film version (which preserves the performances of Robert Morse and Rudy Vallée, the stars of the Broadway production) is one of the few movies based on a Broadway musical that does more than merely hint at the impact of the original show.

By 1967, Loesser found his career at a standstill. He never succeeded in opening another musical on Broadway, and by the time of his death in 1969, he had given up songwriting entirely. His disillusion stemmed from the fact that he, like the vast majority of his songwriting contemporaries, believed—not altogether without reason—that rock was an amateurish idiom unworthy of the old-style professional tradition that had dominated American popular song into the 50s and beyond. Unwilling to acknowledge the possibility that rock might offer a serious alternative to the professional songwriting tradition, he came to the understandable conclusion that his time had come and gone.

In one sense, of course, it had. Loesser was (with Jule Styne, another of his collaborators) the last of the great songwriters of the pre-rock era, and when his career came to an end, the era ended with it. Though individual songs of high quality continue to be written by tradition-oriented songwriters like Dave Frishberg, there is no reason to suppose that the professional tradition, at least as Loesser knew it, will ever be revived.

On the other hand, there is also no reason to suppose that *Guys and Dolls* will disappear from the musical-comedy pantheon any time soon. To the contrary, it now appears to be of permanent interest, and its enduring popularity is a tribute to a craftsman of genius who believed in and understood the expressive potential of American popular song. It may even be that the creator of *Guys and Dolls* will someday come to be seen as an exemplary figure of American art—a man who, like so many other Americans, took up a trade to earn a living and ended up becoming an artist in spite of himself.

Source: Terry Teachout, "The Greater of Two Loessers: How a Songwriting Craftsman Became an Artist," in *Commentary*, Vol. 128, No. 3, October 2009, pp. 69–72.

SOURCES

Atkinson, Brooks, Review of *Guys and Dolls*, in *New York Times*, November 25, 1950.

Banner, Lisa, "Feminism," in *The Concise Princeton Encyclopedia of American Political History*, edited by Michael Kazin, Rebecca Edwards, and Adam Rothman, Princeton University Press, 2011, pp. 233–36.

Block, Geoffrey, *Enchanted Evenings: The Broadway Musical from "Show Boat" to Sondheim*, Oxford University Press, 1997, pp. 197–224.

Brahms, Caryl, and Ned Sherrin, "Frank Loesser," in *The Guys and Dolls Book*, Methuen, 1982, pp. 21–33.

Brantley, Ben, "It's a Cinch That the Bum Is Under the Thumb of Some Little Broad," in *New York Times*, March 2, 2009.

"Burrows, Abe," in *The Oxford Companion to American Theatre*, edited by Gerald Martin Bordman and Thomas S. Hischak, Oxford University Press, 2004, p. 102.

Carlan, Philip, Lisa Nored, and Ragan A. Downey, *An Introduction to Criminal Law*, Jones and Bartlett, 2011, p. 112.

Friedman, John S., "Introduction to the Kefauver Committee Report," in *The Secret Histories: Hidden Truths That Challenged the Past and Changed the World*, edited by John S. Friedman, Picador, 2005, pp. 151–52.

"*Guys and Dolls* Revival to Close on Broadway June 14," in *Broadway.com*, June 10, 2009, http://www.broadway.com/buzz/99654/guys-and-dolls-revival-to-close-on-broadway-june-14/ (accessed August 28, 2011).

Halliwell, Martin, *American Culture in the 1950s*, Edinburgh University Press, 2007, pp. 51–84.

Havemann, Ernest, "Gambling in the U.S.," in *Life*, Vol. 28, No. 25, June 19, 1950, pp. 96, 108–109, 112–19, 121.

Hornby, Richard, *Mad about Theatre*, Applause, 1996, pp. 187–93.

Lasser, Michael, "Frank Loesser," in *Dictionary of Literary Biography*, Vol. 265, *American Song Lyricists, 1920–1960*, edited by Philip Furia, The Gale Group, 2002, pp. 336–53.

Loesser, Frank, Jo Swerling, and Abe Burrows, *Guys and Dolls*, in *The Guys and Dolls Book*, Methuen, 1982, pp. 44–124.

Mordden, Ethan, *Coming Up Roses: The Broadway Musical in the 1950s*, Oxford University Press, 1998, pp. 3–27, 28–36.

Naden, Corinne J., *The Golden Age of American Musical Theatre: 1943–1965*, Scarecrow Press, 2011, pp. 80–81.

Slater, Thomas, "Jo Swerling," in *Dictionary of Literary Biography*, Vol. 44, *American Screenwriters, Second Series*, edited by Randall Clark, Gale Research, 1986, pp. 363–69.

Swerling, Jo, Jr., "*Guys and Dolls*; Abe Burrows: Undue Credit?" Letter to the Editor, in *New York Times*, May 3, 1992.

Wolf, Stacy Ellen, *Changed for Good: A Feminist History of the Broadway Musical*, Oxford University Press, 2011, pp. 25–52.

FURTHER READING

Barlow, Judith E., ed., *Plays by American Women: 1930–1960*, Applause Books, 2001.
　　Barlow's collection gathers the work of prominent female American dramatists of the mid-twentieth century. In her introduction, Barlow discusses the influences of these women on contemporary American theater.

Breslin, Jimmy, *Damon Runyon: A Life*, Houghton Mifflin, 1991.
　　Breslin's biography of Damon Runyon explores his career as a journalist and short-story writer

and discusses the way Runyon came to be associated with New York's Broadway scene.

Durham, Steve, and Kathryn Hashimoto, *The History of Gambling in America*, Prentice Hall, 2009.

Durham and Hashimoto's volume offers an assessment of gambling in the United States, discussing gaming among European settlers and the role of organized crime in developing the gambling industry in modern America.

Kenrick, John, *Musical Theatre: A History*, Continuum, 2008.

Kenrick's history of musical theater explores the ancient predecessors of the genre in Greece and Rome and arrives at the modern American Broadway musical, also discussing the way musical theater evolved in other countries throughout the centuries.

Loesser, Susan, *A Most Remarkable Fella: Frank Loesser and the Guys and Dolls in His Life; A Portrait by His Daughter*, Donald I. Fine, 1993.

This book, by Loesser's daughter, functions as both biography of Loesser and as her personal memoir about her father and her childhood. The work includes Susan Loesser's account of the controversy surrounding Jo Swerling's role in the writing of the *Guys and Dolls* playbook.

Runyon, Damon, *Guys and Dolls: The Stories of Damon Runyon*, Penguin, 1992.

This collection of Runyon's short fiction includes the pieces that inspired the creators of the musical *Guys and Dolls*. William Kennedy offers an introduction to Runyon's stories.

SUGGESTED SEARCH TERMS

Swerling, Burrows, Loesser AND Guys and Dolls

Guys and Dolls AND Broadway AND 1950

Guys and Dolls AND Broadway AND 1992

Guys and Dolls AND Broadway AND 2009

Loesser AND Guys and Dolls AND musical theater

Loesser AND Guys and Dolls AND film

Guys and Dolls AND 1950 AND gender roles

Guys and Dolls AND 1950 AND gambling

Guys and Dolls AND 1950 AND romantic comedy

Guys and Dolls AND Burrows AND Swerling AND authorship

Look Homeward, Angel

KETTI FRINGS

1957

Ketti Frings's Pulitzer Prize–winning 1957 play *Look Homeward, Angel* is an adaptation of Thomas Wolfe's 1929 novel *Look Homeward, Angel: A Story of the Buried Life*. The novel is a remarkably autobiographical work that established Wolfe's reputation as one of the greatest writers of his generation, alongside William Faulkner, F. Scott Fitzgerald, and Ernest Hemingway. The work is an exposé of small-town American life that reveals a far different understanding of that culture than the sanitized Norman Rockwell stereotype. In particular, it is the story of a family destroyed by the greed and narcissism of the mother, playing on archetypal themes that go back to the Greek myth of King Midas.

The play was first performed at the Ethel Barrymore Theatre on Broadway in 1957. Despite the play's tremendous popular and critical success at the time of its premiere, *Look Homeward, Angel* is today something of a lost play, rarely performed anymore. It was published by the Samuel French Publishing Company in 1958. Once a regular in anthologies of best plays of the decade or the century, it has not been reprinted since the 1980s, and no full text of it exists on the Internet.

The title of the play refers to the role of a statue of an angel that Oliver sees in a cemetery. (Neale Cousland / Shutterstock.com)

AUTHOR BIOGRAPHY

Frings was born on February 28, 1909, in Columbus, Ohio. Born Katherine Hartley, her professional name, Ketti Frings, combines her nickname and her name after marriage to Hollywood agent Kurt Frings in 1938. While she was growing up, her family moved about once a year because of her father's work as a salesman. After attending Principia College, in southern Illinois, she moved to New York and worked as an advertising copywriter. After a failed attempt to become a Broadway actress, she moved to California and worked as a freelance journalist covering Hollywood celebrities. She later traveled in Europe and met and married her husband Kurt.

Returning to the United States in 1940, Frings published the autobiographical novel *Hold Back the Dawn* and immediately sold it as a screenplay. It was produced as a film the next year. After writing an unsuccessful allegorical Broadway play, *Mr. Sycamore*, in 1942, Frings became a full-time screen writer, turning out a dozen more projects that were filmed, including *Come Back Little Sheba* (1952) and *The Shrike* (1955), both based on Broadway plays.

In 1957, Frings's adaptation of *Look Homeward, Angel* premiered on Broadway at the Ethel Barrymore Theatre and ran for more than five hundred performances, followed by a successful national tour. *Look Homeward, Angel* won the Pulitzer Prize that year—marking only the fifth time a woman had received the award for drama—as well as receiving numerous Tony Award nominations and winning the New York Drama Critics' Circle Award for Best Play. Besides the quality of Frings's effort in shaping the play out of Wolfe's long novel, the play was a success because Wolfe's popularity was then at its height (as seen in his influence on 1950s authors such as Ray Bradbury and Jack Kerouac) and because of the innovative, television-like direction of George Roy Hill (who would go on to become a film director, making *Slaughterhouse-Five* in 1972, among other projects) and the performance of Anthony Perkins as the protagonist, Eugene.

Paradoxically, Frings's writing career virtually came to an end after she reached the pinnacle of success and recognition with her Pulitzer Prize. She wrote several more Broadway plays without notable success, including a musical adaptation of *Look Homeward, Angel* that closed after a week in 1978. Frings died of cancer on February 11, 1981, in Los Angeles, California.

PLOT SUMMARY

Act 1

SCENE 1: A FALL AFTERNOON

Look Homeward, Angel is set in the year 1916 in Altamont, North Carolina (a fictionalized stand-in for Thomas Wolfe's native Asheville). The first act begins at the Dixieland Boarding House, which is owned by the Gant family. The narrator describes what is happening on stage. Seventeen-year-old Eugene Gant is writing. His older brother, Ben, is chatting with his girlfriend "Fatty" Pert, a boarder, while their sister, Helen, is preparing dinner for the boarders.

MEDIA ADAPTATIONS

- In 1972, a filmed performance of Frings's *Look Homeward, Angel*, directed by Paul Bogart, was broadcast on CBS television, as the first installment of its *Playhouse 90* series. Frings wrote a new, shorter version of the script for the television production.

- In 1978, Frings revisited *Look Homeward, Angel* to adapt it as a musical, with lyrics by Peter Udell and a score by Gary Geld. It ran on Broadway for less than a week.

Eliza, matriarch of the Gant family, sends Eugene to the train station to hand out business cards for the boardinghouse to arriving passengers. Ben argues with his mother over this, insisting that Eugene needs to stop being made to waste his time on such trivial occupations and go to college. Ben becomes enraged when he sees that his brother is wearing hand-me-down clothes, including shoes that Ben himself had thrown away. Eliza had fished the shoes out of the trash for Eugene, on whom they are painfully small.

After dinner, Laura James, newly arrived in town, comes to rent a room in the boardinghouse. Eliza is impressed by her superior manners and behavior. As they are negotiating, Eugene comes onto the scene to announce that his father, W. O. Gant, has become drunk at a local bar and, loud and combative as he is, is being escorted home by Dr. Maguire. At first he refuses to enter the boardinghouse, insisting that he lives in the stone house he built himself for his family, but which Eliza actually forced him to sell some years ago. Once inside, he insults the boarders and overturns furniture in a drunken fury (a carefully chosen word, spoken by Gant himself, whose origins imply being in the grip of divine inspiration). Helen is able to calm him, and he begins to recite poetry. He becomes alarmed, though, when Maguire tries to sedate him, denouncing the practice of surgery as quackery.

Gant then has a vision of death coming for him before he passes out and is carried upstairs. Despite this scene, Laura takes a room in the house.

Ben comes home, having heard of his father's binge, and Eugene asks him why he thinks their father does not simply leave, since it seems clear he is reduced to these bouts of drinking by a deep unhappiness. Ben thinks his question is naive and suggests to him that none of them can leave, any more than they could walk out of a photograph after it had been taken. Nevertheless, when he sees Maguire, Ben pesters him, as he evidently has been doing for some time, to write a letter of recommendation attesting to his good health so that he can join the Canadian air force: he, too, is desperate to leave. Maguire briefly examines him and confirms what he has long known about Ben, that he has tuberculosis. Although Maguire tells Ben that he is unfit for military duty, he does not tell him that he has the fatal disease. It was a common practice at the time to conceal such news, since there was no effective treatment.

Ben gives Eugene money to buy new shoes and advises him to get away from their mother as quickly as he can, whatever he has to do. He confesses that it is too late for him, and even for their brother Luke, who is in the navy.

SCENE 2: THAT EVENING

As the boarders and the Gant family lounge around the house after dinner, Laura begins to talk to Eugene. He is so nervous that he replies to everything she says with a long list of relevant facts, as if he were doing a psychoanalytical word association exercise, but she seem impressed by his knowledge. Eugene gives Laura a lyrical description of trains as a symbol of the freedom to wander. They lie to each other about their ages, Eugene making himself older and Laura making herself younger.

Eliza suggests to her husband that he ought to sell his stonecutting yard; the bank is offering twenty thousand dollars (a huge sum of money in 1916). He refuses, trying to explain to her the spiritual significance that the Carrara angel (a beautiful Italian sculpture, made of prized Carrara marble, that he acquired long ago—the angel of the play's title) has for him and what the significance of his work is to him, but Eliza is incapable of understanding. Temporarily defeated, Eliza takes her frustrations out on Ben and Fatty. They argue most sharply about the way Eliza is neglecting Eugene and his education. Late in the evening, Eugene and Laura go for a walk.

Act 2

SCENE 1: ONE WEEK LATER

Eliza visits the marble yard and is surprised to find Eugene working there. His father has agreed to pay him wages as an assistant, but because she provides his clothes, food, and shelter, Eliza cannot imagine what else Eugene could possibly need money for. She leaves since her husband is not in.

Gant returns and is visited by Madame Elizabeth. She runs the local brothel; one of her prostitutes, Lilly (whom she regards almost as her daughter and as her successor in running the business), has died, and Madame Elizabeth wants to buy a headstone. In fact, she wants the angel, but W.O. refuses to sell it to her. She finally realizes its special significance to Gant and agrees to take a sculpted lamb marker instead.

Later, Eliza returns, to repeat her demand that her husband sell out to the bank. Surprisingly, he agrees and signs the check she has brought. However, he does not intend to sign the check over to his wife as she insists, but rather to use the money to take Eugene and leave, sending the boy to college. This drives Eliza into a blind rage, and she struggles with her husband to seize the check and then tears it to shreds. She cannot let the family be separated, but her husband and sons cannot understand why she wants to keep them, since they clearly do nothing but cause her pain.

SCENE 2: TWO DAYS LATER

Ben's condition has worsened, and he is lying in his bed at the boardinghouse, drowning in the blood filling up his lungs. He wants Fatty to be near him, but Eliza orders her out, though Dr. Maguire sends her back in. Luke, the elder Gant boy, has returned from the navy to be with his brother. Ben soon dies, after saying that it will be a relief, his only way out of the photograph. Dr. Maguire and Eugene both try, in their own ways, to come to terms with Ben's death.

Act 3

Eugene and Laura lie awake in her bed. They have made detailed plans for their future: Eugene will take the job working in his mother's real-estate office, and then they will be married. The first step is to go to Richmond and announce their plans to Laura's parents. Eugene has some money that Ben left to him.

First, though, Eugene makes the announcement to Eliza. The shock is like a physical blow to her, as she believes she is losing control over her son. Eliza insists that Eugene give up his plans for marriage, and instead she will find the money to send him to the university in Chapel Hill, North Carolina. But it is too late, and Eugene's mind is made up. Eliza seeks out Laura, intending to buy her off, but Laura confesses that she had come to Altamont to think over the prospect of marrying her fiancé back in Richmond. She fell in love with Eugene and realized that she is not in love with her betrothed; still, she is going to leave Eugene to go back to the other man, to try to learn to love him, because she realizes that she would only hold Eugene back from the great things that he seems destined for.

Eliza concedes that she will send Eugene to Chapel Hill anyway. But before he leaves, he makes clear to his mother every soul-crushing thing she has done to him over the years, announcing that he may never be healed of it.

Gant comes onto the scene, and he and Eliza begin to release decades of pent-up aggression and frustration by attacking the Dixieland, taking axes to the woodwork and threatening the boarders with murder. Their energy and rage are soon spent without doing any serious damage. When Eugene leaves, his father congratulates him on being the only one who has succeeded in getting away.

CHARACTERS

Helen Barton
Although Helen is married and a member of the Gant family, Eliza essentially uses her daughter as a domestic worker at the Dixieland.

Hugh Barton
Hugh is Helen's husband, who lives with her at the Dixieland. He is generally in the background, little different from the other boarders, but he acts as a marginal member of the family; for instance, he helps carry a drunken W. O. Gant up to his room, and he is hovering in the background when Ben dies.

Madame Elizabeth

Elizabeth's title is a reference to the fact that she runs the town brothel. When one of her prostitutes dies, Elizabeth wants to buy the Carrara angel as her gravestone, but she is persuaded otherwise when she realizes that Gant wants it for his own grave marker. Her character merits a pointed comparison with Eliza (short for Elizabeth) Gant's, since they both express the belief that life consists of nothing more than buying and selling. Madame Elizabeth, however, is wise enough to know that this philosophy has a limit and that some things cannot and should not be bought.

Ben Gant

Ben is the oldest Gant brother living at home. He works at a low-paying job as a reporter for the local newspaper. He dreams of getting away from his existence under his mother's thumb by joining the Royal Canadian Air Force, but his small size and ill health make this impossible. He has transferred his hopes of escape onto his younger brother Eugene, whom he wants to see go to college. Ben considers the Gant family trapped, like the figures in a photograph, unable to move, change, or escape. The subtitle of the original novel refers to a "buried life," and Ben's sense of being trapped expresses this idea: under their mother's domination, Ben and Eugene are like ghosts trapped in a tomb. As Ben dies of tuberculosis, he is by no means displeased but instead looks on his fate as the only way he has left to escape the photograph.

Eliza Gant

Eliza, whose maiden name was Pentland ("pent" means closed up or confined), is the second wife of W. O. Gant and the mother of Luke, Ben, Helen, and Eugene. She is a more prominent character in the play than in the original novel and might even be said to be the dominant character of the play, though as the antagonist rather than the protagonist.

Eliza is obsessed with the control of her family. In the first scene of the play, she already observes that her children and husband all want something different than she does—though what that might be she does not care and cannot imagine. Their desires are irrelevant, since she can only conceive of there being one dominant spirit in the family: her own. As the stress on the family increases, Eliza becomes more strident on this issue and is baffled by the rebellion of her

husband and children. She finally reveals her own understanding of what the true relationship within the family has been and the way it ought to continue when she tells them, "You should all get down on your knees and be grateful to me!" Eliza's narcissism blinds her to the possibility that her children and husband might have desires and ambitions—lives—of their own. The only relationship that she has with her family is one of control. She manipulates her husband into giving up the home he built with his own hands, and then she unsuccessfully tries to get him to give up his work as a stone carver, work that provides meaning to his life. She treats her children as menial laborers and employees, Helen as a cook and Eugene as an errand boy. She has spiritually crippled her older sons, Ben and Luke, so that the small measures of independence they have gained are irrelevant to her overall control. Frings caricatures this aspect of Eliza's personality, making it even more marked than in the original novel. Eliza becomes a vampire, sucking the life out of her family. Gant tells his wife, "As I get weaker and weaker, you get stronger and stronger!"

Eliza is utterly at a loss to understand her son Eugene's ambitions and sensibilities as a young artist. She imagines that she is engaging him when she accidentally speaks a rhyme and tells him, "You see, Eugene, I'm a poet, too—'A poet and I don't know it, but my feet show it—they're longfellows!'" Unable to perceive the suffering of anyone else, Eliza is caught entirely by surprise by her son Ben's death, denying it up until the last moment. Once the doctor has pronounced him dead, she is called to come away from the body, but she refuses, seemingly preferring him in this condition: "He doesn't turn away from me any more," she says. Eliza has no interest in giving Eugene a college education, except as another means of control. She prevents the possibility of the tuition coming from any other source, and she finally agrees to his going away to school only when it seems Eugene is leaving one way or another and she comes to see it as her last anchor line on him. She joins with her husband in the frenzied, though brief, destruction of the Dixieland as a release for the anxiety she feels about the loss of control over Eugene.

Eugene Gant

Eugene Gant is the autobiographical stand-in for Thomas Wolfe, the novelist. At the beginning of the play, Eugene is leading two unconnected lives: one as his mother's flunky, doing the most menial jobs she can find for him, and in the other reading and writing every spare moment. The death of Ben and Eugene's realization of the degree to which his father is trapped make clear to him that if nothing changes, he will remain under his mother's control forever. Even more horrible to him is the future profession envisioned for him by his mother, that of a real-estate broker like her. His affair with the new boarder Laura, who acts as his muse, magnifies the better part of himself so that Eugene can overcome his mother's control. Although it is clear by the end of the play that she intends to pay for his university degree, this will not extend her control over Eugene as she hoped. He is leaving no matter what happens. He finds the inner strength to tell her, "By God, I shall spend the rest of my life getting my heart back, healing and forgetting every scar you put upon me when I was a child."

Helen Gant
See Helen Barton

Luke Gant
Luke is the oldest of the surviving Gant children. He has become a sailor in the navy, but he returns home briefly to attend his brother Ben's deathbed.

W. O. Gant
The father of the family in Wolfe's novel is named W. O. Gant, while Wolfe's real father was named William Oliver Wolfe. In the text of the play, the father is usually called simply Gant or Mr. Gant, but in the dramatis personae (the listing of characters at the beginning of a printed play), Frings calls him W. O. Gant, and Madame Elizabeth, for one, addresses him as W.O.

Eliza's opinion, and the audience's initial impression, is that Gant is a raging alcoholic. But an intoxicated man does not become a different person. Rather, he releases the parts of himself that he usually represses, often violent and irrational impulses that are disturbing to others. Gant embarrasses himself with actions of this kind, but he also releases other feelings that are quite different. He is highly cultured, for example, and is a devoted reader of poetry, so at the height of his drunken rampage he invites his daughter, Helen, "Sit and talk. Would you like to hear some Keats...beautiful Keats?" But why must he repress such noble feelings? Eliza immediately puts a stop to it. She is cowed by

literature because she knows nothing about it and so considers the recitation of poetry an attempt to embarrass her.

In the traces of his own life that are left to him, Gant is a creative artist whose identity is tied up in work. He has a passion to learn and travel and enjoy life, which Eliza dismisses as mere idle dreaming. He tries to seize such a life back for himself and Eugene but is unable to overcome Eliza, either physically or spiritually.

Laura James
Laura is a boarder at the Dixieland who briefly becomes Eugene's amour. Her name is the Greek word for laurel, the plant sacred to the god Apollo, who was responsible for inspiring poets. It would be wrong to view her as an older woman who toys with and then jilts Eugene. Rather, she inspires him with the courage he needs to break free of Eliza and then quietly departs once her role is fulfilled.

Dr. Maguire
Dr. Maguire is the family physician to the Gants. He escorts W. O. Gant home during his bout of drunkenness and attends Ben on his deathbed. Given the relatively primitive state of medical science in 1916, his failure to provide a true cure to Ben is well justified.

Will Pentland
Will is Eliza's brother and partner in her real-estate dealings.

Marie "Fatty" Pert
Fatty is Ben's girlfriend and a boarder at the Dixieland. She is separated from her husband, but this background is never explained. She seems to be everything that Eliza is not: curvaceous, passive, and inoffensive. Ben tells Eugene that he goes with her because she does not carry a burden of pain that she must inflict on other people. She might fairly be described as motherly. Eliza hates her as a rival and humiliates her by ordering her away from Ben's deathbed.

THEMES

Work
The work ethic, the idea that honest labor brings meaning to life and is virtuous in itself, has always been an important part of the American

TOPICS FOR FURTHER STUDY

- Look over a young-adult manga (Japanese comic book) such as *20th Century Boys* (2010) by Naoki Urasawa, which in the background of its science-fiction plot examines the life of a group of young men living in poverty who are only sustained by their memories of their happier childhoods. Draw and write your own manga based on a scene from *Look Homeward, Angel*.

- Frings reproduced much of the vivid language of Wolfe's *Look Homeward, Angel* for the play, but not without extensive changes. A detailed stylistic study of the changes Frings implemented reveals much about her approach to the text. Find several parallel passages between the play and the novel, and, in an essay, comment on the changes Frings made. Compare and contrast the specific differences of language in the passages that Frings closely paraphrases.

- Read Wolfe's novel *Look Homeward, Angel* and adapt a few scenes into dramatic form. Specifically focus on material that Frings did not have room to deal with, for example, Mr. Gant's nurturing of his family in the early phase of his second marriage. This text may be performed for your class or posted online on your blog or Web page.

- Adapt a scene from the play as a Flash animation to share with your class. While almost any scene could be treated in this manner, the technique might be best suited to showing things that cannot be seen onstage, such as Ben's fantasy of becoming a fighter pilot in the Royal Canadian Air Force. You might also choose a scene of intense dialogue, calling for a more stripped-down animation style, or Eugene's almost ecstatic vision about getting away from home on the railroad.

---

identity. In *Look Homeward, Angel*, W. O. Gant has tried to define himself by this traditional standard. He describes himself in his passing from youth to adulthood in this way: "I was a man who set out to get order and position in life." And indeed, he became very successful in his work as a stone carver: his monuments are sought after throughout North Carolina. He used his own skills and labor to build a house for his family, an accomplishment that was a natural source of pride. Gant is respected by his family and community because of the quality and success of his work. There is one exception: her husband's work is meaningless to Eliza. While it is no doubt profitable, Gant's business is not under Eliza's control, so she views it as a waste of resources. She not only forces him to sell the house he built (using the money to buy the Dixieland Boarding House, where she is decidedly in control) but also schemes to force him to sell his shop and give up his work. This would leave him with no identity of his own, completely under her control. When Gant declares that no such thing will happen and that he will use the money from any sale of his business to get away from her, she physically attacks him to destroy the check and his last hope of freedom.

The pressures that Eliza puts upon her husband have made him into a binge drinker: he drinks only once every few weeks, but then becomes so intoxicated that he is prone to embarrassing, even violent scenes. His drinking allows him to release the pent-up aggression that he must repress in daily life, but, more to the point, it does not interfere with his work because it is limited in time. In this way, he is able to preserve his identity built around his work. Even so, Gant must concede that his life has been a failure and that his hard work has done nothing to protect himself or his family. Conversely, Eliza sees herself as a success, and so she is, at least as measured by the small fortune she has accumulated as "the vigorous real-estate operator, proud of her reputation for being the smartest trader in town." But in another sense, she does no work in the sense of creation at all, merely buying a commodity at one price and selling it later for another. As she hoards her real estate, it becomes more valuable in the rapidly expanding industrial economy of the early twentieth century, not through any effort of her own. She is unable to conceive that it is actually possible to make or produce anything; rather, she tells Eugene, "we are all ... all of us ... selling something." Her success is built on anything except productive, meaningful work.

The play is a bildungsroman about Eugene Gant, who wants to leave North Carolina during the Depression. (Jorgo (Ryan Jorgensen) / Shutterstock.com)

Religion

Small-town America of a century ago, represented in the popular imagination by the paintings of Norman Rockwell, is often seen as an uncomplicated place of traditional virtues. Among these might be included faith, particularly Christian faith and more particularly Protestant faith. *Look Homeward, Angel* is a reminder that the situation was never quite so simple. Today, the America of 1916 seems not so much unified by faith as divided by religious intolerance. Many people even at the time realized this. It is, for example, the theme of D. W. Griffith's 1916 film *Intolerance*. *Look Homeward, Angel* highlights the plurality of religious thought that actually existed in the America of that time.

No character in the play expresses the idea that Ben is going to his reward in heaven. Dr. Maguire is not certain of anything except that Ben's physical body is no more than a few dollars' worth of chemicals and that his existence in

which he was known by those who loved him is what matters. Eugene manages to bring himself to pray for his brother, but his prayer is deistic, expressing a belief in a god but not a specific religion, rather than Christian: "Whoever You are, be good to Ben tonight." He has little certainty that a god exists and evidently none that it is the Christian God. The recurrence of these ideas in Frings's play is especially important considering the time when it was published. The anti-Communist feeling of the 1950s solidified the myth that the United States was a necessarily Christian country, since Communists were seen as lacking or opposing religion. It was in this decade that the motto "In God We Trust" was added to the coinage and the phrase "Under God" was added to the Pledge of Allegiance.

STYLE

Metatheater

Although drama is by its nature an artificial imitation of reality, a common impulse is to make a production as realistic as possible; certainly, the most superficial response of the audience is to judge a play by its realism. This realism is embodied in the idea of the dramatic unities, by which an ancient Greek drama was supposed to show events in a specific location in real time, as if the audience were watching the tape from a surveillance camera. But dramatists have always used other techniques, calling attention to the artificiality of the theatrical production, in order to create realism in a different way, by reminding the audience that their real experience is of watching a play. This pattern is called metatheatricality; "meta-" indicates a distance or a second layer of study, such that the theater itself may be used to examine or understand theater, for example. These techniques have only recently received systematic attention from critics, beginning with Lionel Abel's *Tragedy and Metatheatre: Essays on Dramatic Form*. Greek dramas frequently began with a narration, in which a character (usually a god or a slave, both of which classes were commonly believed to know everything that went on in people's lives), spoke to the audience directly, explaining background information necessary to understanding the play about to unfold. In sixteenth-century England, William Shakespeare continued this convention but used new techniques, such as the play-within-a-play, in which the characters on the stage watch a play as a secondary audience, which is fully staged and also viewed by the primary audience. Not surprisingly, postmodernism, a twentieth- and twenty-first-century artistic movement that plays with the audience's expectations of form and genre, has witnessed a renewed interest in metatheater.

This postmodern spin on dramatic technique is best represented by Thornton Wilder's *Our Town* (1938), which was very likely an inspiration for Frings's version of *Look Homeward, Angel*. In Wilder's play, the audience watches a dress rehearsal for a play, with the stage director acting both as a narrator throughout the play and as a character, as well as, it seems, the creator or arranger of the drama as he gives instructions to the other actors. Frings wrote a first draft of *Look Homeward, Angel* using very similar techniques, introducing Thomas Wolfe himself as a character to narrate and oversee the action of relatively unconnected scenes from the novel. Although this approach was abandoned, more than half the text of the finished play remains narrative text, often with lines of dialogue spoken by the characters embedded in it, just as in the text of the novel. With no specific instructions in the text, the individual directors of productions would be free to have these lines spoken by a narrator or circulated in the text of the play given to the audience. The play is rarely performed any longer, though, and then generally by high-school drama clubs, which often simply omit the narration, making for a very disconnected drama.

The original director of the Broadway production, George Roy Hill, had spent his career in television (though he later became a prominent film director) and introduced other metatheatrical techniques, meant to recreate the experience of watching television. (In 1958, television shows were frequently live productions, not broadcasts of something recorded earlier.) The stage was dominated by a circular revolving floor that could quickly swing around to change scenes before the eyes of the audience. Another part of the stage decoration was a backdrop of the boardinghouse that could be moved around the stage to create different perspectives, akin to moving a camera to reframe a scene. Other backdrops were images projected onto a screen lowered from the rafters. Spotlights were used to approximate the effects of close-ups and rapid cutting between scenes. In effect, Hill was showing the audience a dramatic recreation of a television show, a novelty at the time.

Prose Poetry

Many sections of the dramatic version of *Look Homeward, Angel* stand out from the rest as rising far above the level of the realistic dialogue that dominates the text. They are poetic in tone, form, and style. Indeed, since meter need not play a great role in modern poetry, these passages resemble prose only in not being offset (indented on the page). Here is an example, with Eugene explaining to Laura how locomotives symbolize for him freedom and the whole world outside of the little trap in which he finds himself (ellipses are in the original):

> You feel the shining steel rails under it ... and the rails send a message tight into your hand ... a message of all the mountains that engine ever passed—all the flowing rivers, the forests, the towns, all the houses, the people, the washlines flapping in the fresh cool breeze—the beauty of the people in the way they live and the way they work—a farmer waving from his field, a kid from the school yard—the faraway places it roars through at night, places you don't even know, can hardly imagine.

One might expect that this text had been lifted directly from the novel, inasmuch as Wolfe is widely praised for the lyrical beauty of his prose, but in fact, no such text occurs in the novel. The explanation for this is that Frings complained that she found Wolfe's prose clichéd and often felt she had to improve it (just as when she worked as a script doctor in Hollywood, polishing others' rough work). What one does find is a passage on the same theme that Eugene thinks while he is traveling around the country with his parents in 1903 (many years before the play is set):

> And he had heard thus the far retreating wail of a [train] whistle in a distant valley, and faint thunder on the rails; and he felt the infinite depth and width of the golden world in the brief seductions of a thousand multiplex and mixed mysterious odors and sensations, weaving, with a blinding interplay and aural explosions, one into the other.

One of Frings's stated goals was to use the play to sample the best of the novel, even though her work is limited to only a small part of the chronological range of the novel, so it is expected that she would draw from every part of the book.

COMPARE
&
CONTRAST

- **1910s:** Antibiotics have not yet been discovered, modern surgical procedures are in their infancy, and any encounter with a physician is likely to be at least as dangerous as the medical condition the patient is experiencing. Tuberculosis is completely incurable and is the center of a large quack medicine industry.

    1950s: Antibiotics make medical practice generally effective for the first time in history. Tuberculosis is easily curable.

    Today: Despite the evolutionary development of antibiotic-resistant strains of tuberculosis, the wide availability of treatment and public health measures have largely wiped out tuberculosis in the United States.

- **1910s:** Women only rarely have lifelong careers in businesses such as real estate. Most women who are employed are teachers.

    1950s: The feminist movement begins to open doors for women in positions of power and authority in the workforces.

    Today: Women are fully integrated into the American workforces in all industries and make up more than half of all workers.

- **1910s:** Only relatively small numbers of the socially, economically, and intellectually elite attend college.

    1950s: Programs such as the G.I. Bill make a college education more widely available. Tuition, even at most private schools, is largely affordable on a working-class income.

    Today: Although a college education is recognized as a virtual necessity for almost everyone in the workforce, tuition is spiraling out of control, and many traditional liberal arts institutions are being refashioned into professional schools.

Since the two passages really contain the same information and have the same lyrical style, it seems probable that Frings rewrote it (and many others in the play) to give it a more concrete texture, showing specific examples of the abstracted categories Wolfe preferred.

HISTORICAL CONTEXT

Thomas Wolfe

Frings's play is based on Thomas Wolfe's novel *Look Homeward, Angel*. Wolfe, born on October 3, 1900, is one of the most prominent American novelists of his generation, along with figures such as William Faulkner and Ernest Hemingway.

Look Homeward, Angel was his first novel and a notable success. The material of the novel is decidedly autobiographical. The author's father, William Oliver Wolfe, was a sculptor of funerary monuments in Asheville, North Carolina. His mother, Julia Elizabeth, was a real-estate dealer who ran a series of boardinghouses. In 1904, she opened one in St. Louis, Missouri, to coincide with the World Fair being held there. The death of Wolfe's brother Grover from typhoid there (observed when the author was four years old) is the model for the death of Ben in the novel and play.

Wolfe earned an undergraduate degree from the University of North Carolina at Chapel Hill, starting at age fifteen (less unusual then than it would be now), and eventually earned a master of fine arts degree in drama from Harvard University in 1922. His original intention was to become a playwright, but after several plays failed in production, he turned to novels with *Look Homeward, Angel*. The mass of autobiographical prose that he wrote had to be carefully chiseled into shape by his editor at Scribner's, Maxwell Perkins (although the original version, *O Lost*, has since also been published).

Eugene Gant's father, Oliver, makes a decision to become a stonecutter. *(mrfotos / Shutterstock.com)*

The book was published a few days before the stock-market crash of 1929, but it became a critical and financial success anyway, especially in Europe. The book was vilified, however, by Wolfe's family and the citizens of Asheville because of its unflattering depiction of easily identifiable real persons. Wolfe did not return to Asheville for many years and lived for the most part in New York or in Europe.

Wolfe could not maintain personal or private relationships for long, an inability often attributed to his repeating the disappointment he felt with his parents. He published nine novels, all highly autobiographical. Wolfe's most important work is *You Can't Go Home Again* (1940), a novel that reflects on the writing and publishing of *Look Homeward, Angel.* He also produced more plays, collections of short stories, and travel writing. Wolfe's letters have been published in several collections, of which the most important was in 1956, perhaps spurring the production of Frings's play. Wolfe's works have remained popular, although critical opinion has varied and recently has not been very favorable.

Wolfe fell ill on a tour of the American West and was found to suffer from an unusual infection of the brain caused by tuberculosis. He underwent surgery at Johns Hopkins Hospital in Baltimore, Maryland, but his condition was too advanced to be treated (effective antibiotics did not exist at the time), and he died on September 15, 1938.

CRITICAL OVERVIEW

Frings's *Look Homeward, Angel* was tremendously well received by critics and by the public in 1958, enjoying more than five hundred performances on Broadway and a national tour and going on to win the Pulitzer Prize for Drama that year. The favorable newspaper reviews are reflected in Henry Popkin's survey of the year on Broadway written for the *Kenyon Review* in 1958, but with a little more critical distance than the newspaper reviewers, he is able to see some of the play's flaws as well. He notes that the play is episodic and disconnected, but then, he admits, so is the novel, and both must rely on the beauty of Wolfe's prose to cover over many flaws. In particular, 1958 had been a political year on Broadway. At the height of the cold war, Molly Kazan's *The Egghead* attacked Communism and defended the political witch hunts of the era. In such an atmosphere, even Leonard Bernstein's *West Side Story*, a musical based loosely on *Romeo and Juliet*, took on political overtones. But Popkin singles out Frings's play as refreshingly nonpolitical.

Much of the appeal of *Look Homeward, Angel* was visual, stemming from the production's imitation of television, then a novelty on the stage. This effect soon lost its charm, though, and the essential effect of the play could be had by reading the novel. As a consequence, Frings's play soon fell into relative obscurity and was at best infrequently performed or read. Accordingly, there has been very little critical attention given to the play.

The only substantial work to deal with it, in fact, is the chapter on Frings in Carolyn Casey Craig's *Women Pulitzer Playwrights*. Craig provides the most extensive published biography of Frings, a summary of the play, and a brief critical appreciation. Craig explains how Frings isolated herself from other sources of information or criticism about the novel and worked directly from the original text: "An appropriate analogy was that Frings had played the stonecutter to the monumental rock which was Wolfe's novel. She had carved from it a perfectly featured and balanced Carrara angel of a play." Craig views the play as revolving around the spiritual stifling of the dreamers W. O. Gant, Ben, and Eugene by Eliza, who has become a monster by abandoning her nurturing role as a woman and mother and adopting an entirely masculine set of goals and ideals. Craig sees Ben's death as a symbol of Eliza squeezing the life out of her family. Craig largely contextualizes Frings's play within the corpus of Pulitzer Prize–winning female dramatists that is her ultimate concern.

CRITICISM

Rita M. Brown

Brown is an English professor. In the following essay, she examines the character of Eliza Gant in Look Homeward, Angel *in terms of Freudian psychology.*

Psychoanalysis, the science of the mind developed by the Viennese psychologist Sigmund Freud and his followers beginning in the

> GOLD, AND HENCE MONEY, IS A SYMBOL FOR THE WASTE OF HUMAN LIFE."

1890s, was a highly influential conceptual framework in the 1920s among intellectuals and artists in Europe and the United States. It was certainly a framework that Thomas Wolfe studied at Harvard. Psychoanalysis again rose to prominence in the 1950s in America, as the influence of analysts who had fled Nazi persecution before and during World War II became felt and as a new generation of analysts advanced psychoanalytical theory outside of Freud's shadow. Psychoanalysis excited interest far outside the medical sphere because, for the first time, it offered a scientific explanation and description of the human capacity to create art and literature. At the same time, many artists, notably the surrealists, used psychoanalytical ideas as a basis for artistic creativity in every field. It remains doubtful that psychoanalytic insight affected Wolfe's experiences within his own family that are the basis of *Look Homeward, Angel*, but it must have shaped his interpretation and understanding of his experiences in retrospect (as indeed all memories are shaped by later thoughts and beliefs). Frings, for her part, consciously avoided making her own interpretation of the novel so that in writing the play of *Look Homeward, Angel*, she might more simply serve Wolfe's purposes and intentions. So it is certainly possible to find Wolfe's authentic voice in the play and to use psychoanalytic theory as a means of understanding the deeply troubled relationships that exist within the Gant family.

Although in many senses Eugene is the protagonist or main character of the play (which is, after all, about his transition from one stage of life to another), in other senses the dominant character of the play is his mother Eliza: the dominant relationship of each major character is with her, and each one is struggling, with greater or lesser success, against her control. While it is true that in well-written literature, as in psychoanalysis, character cannot be reduced to simple types, there are nevertheless groups of characteristics that tend to occur together in

WHAT DO I READ NEXT?

- In 2004, Lucy Conniff and Richard S. Kennedy edited a publication of Wolfe's original notebook in which he outlined his novel. It is titled *The Autobiographical Outline for "Look Homeward, Angel."*

- Nathaniel Hawthorne's *A Wonder-Book for Girls and Boys* (1852) retells Greek myths for young adults. It includes "The Golden Touch," a version of the myth of King Midas.

- Yukio Mishima's 1958 memoir *Confessions of a Mask* recalls the youth during the 1920s and 1930s of one of Japan's most distinguished novelists. The young Mishima finds himself at the mercy of his controlling and manipulative grandmother, must explore his ambivalent attitude to joining the military, and struggles with tuberculosis, ultimately finding his way to independence as a professional writer.

- Thomas Mann's 1924 novel *The Magic Mountain* examines the aggressive and destructive impulses that lie underneath polite bourgeoisie (middle-class) society in the setting of a tuberculosis sanitarium (a therapy center) in the Swiss Alps.

- Paul A. Firestone's 2008 study *The Pulitzer Prize Plays: The First Fifty Years, 1917–1967, a Dramatic Reflection of American Life*, sets the history of Broadway, reflected in its most notable productions, in the larger context of contemporary American history.

- William Inge's 1950 Broadway play *Come Back Little Sheba* was adapted for film with a screenplay by Frings. Reading the play and then viewing the film will demonstrate a type of adaptation different from the one Frings undertook in *Look Homeward, Angel*, adapting from stage to film rather than from a novel to the stage.

- *A Southern Appalachian Reader*, edited by Nellie McNeil and Joyce Squibb in 1988, is intended to introduced young-adult readers to the distinctive culture and language, especially the dialects, of the Carolina mountains. Wolfe's work makes the single largest contribution to the anthology.

---

many people and that do so for common and comprehensible reasons. Eliza shares many traits with a character type that Freud encountered in his analytical work and described in his essays. Eliza is obsessed by the need to control everything and, in particular, everyone around her. From a perspective outside the family, she is a real-estate dealer through and through. Although she carries out a pretense that the real-estate office belongs to her brother Will, it is clear that she is the one in charge. She is highly successful: when she wants to, she sells one of the many properties she owns to get the money to pay for four years of tuition and living expenses for Eugene at the University of North Carolina at Chapel Hill. In today's terms, she probably has a net worth of several million dollars. In her daily life, she wears cheap clothing as if she were poor, but she has a special wardrobe of expensive and fashionable clothes she wears when conducting her real-estate dealings.

Eliza makes her children Helen and Eugene work for her as servants. Helen is the cook in the boardinghouse Eliza owns, where the family lives, and Eugene is made to spend his time at the town railroad station attracting business for the boardinghouse. She does not pay them for this work because she cannot imagine what they would need money for. Her children wear cast-offs and hand-me-downs, whether they fit or not, and they eat the leftovers from the meals prepared for the boarders and drink a cheaper grade of coffee. Eugene, at least, does not even have a room or a bed but must sleep wherever he can find a space in the house. Eliza thinks that all of these measures are in the children's best interests, because they all limit the expenditure of money. The accumulation of wealth is the only good that she can think of, and the only use she has for the wealth is the control of other people. This she justifies to her son Eugene by telling him, "If I hadn't tried to accumulate a little something, none of you would have had a roof to call your own." The huge hoard of property she owns is much more than "a little something." Eugene replies to her that in fact they have nothing to call their own, only things that are hers, as they are constantly reminded. Eliza believes that once she has beaten her children down in this way, there is no way that they can try to rebel against her or disobey her. Ben must have been in the same situation once, but he now has a low-paying job at the local newspaper that provides him some independence. However, he still lacks either the resources or the spirit to leave completely, and he still lives at the boardinghouse. (Although the matter is not discussed in the play, one would expect he must pay for the privilege.)

Eliza's relationship with her husband is not very different. The symbolic expression of their marriage in the play is the fact that, as a master stonecutter, he built his own house for his family (the house where he yet claims to live when he is drunk), but Eliza forced him to sell it to buy the boardinghouse because she cannot tolerate anyone around her having their own independent accomplishments. Whatever the income W. O. Gant gets from his business, Eliza seems to control most of it. Nevertheless, she cannot tolerate her husband having anything of his own and makes arrangements within the scope of the play to sell the business to the bank for the value of its land and stock, planning to browbeat her husband into accepting this emasculation. (The way she hides the papers relating to the sale in her bosom hints that she initially used her sexuality to gain control of him.) That he is a successful and respected artisan and that the loss of his workshop would destroy his identity and the only meaning he has in his life are irrelevant to her, or perhaps this destruction is her chief aim. Gant's alcoholism can be seen as an attempt to anesthetize the pain he feels being trapped in this relationship.

For their part, Eliza's family can think of nothing but getting away from her control. Ben distanced himself as far as he could from his mother, though she made sure he would lack the power to truly get away. The oldest brother, Luke, succeeded in leaving by joining the military, and Ben dreams of doing the same, but his health will not allow it. Ben's dream of becoming a fighter pilot represents his wish to escape his mother and literally fly away. W. O. Gant is actually happy to have his workshop sold out from under him because he imagines he will be able to keep the twenty-thousand-dollar check (rather than sign it over to Eliza as she imagines); he intends to use part of it to send Eugene to college and the remainder to simply get away from his wife. Eugene, too, has no greater wish than to get away from his mother. He is ready to, like Ben, accept dependency on a longer tether, by taking a job in the real-estate office that would let him start his own household. Eugene tells his mother, "The first move I ever made after the cradle was to crawl for the door. And every move I ever made since has been an effort to escape." Whenever she is confronted in this way, Eliza has a stock answer: preserving the unity of the family is a good in itself that cannot be questioned. She repeatedly expresses the idea with the famous phrase "A house divided against itself cannot stand," famous both from the Bible and from an Abraham Lincoln speech. In the original context (Matthew 12:25), Jesus casts out a demon, and some Pharisees who witness it think to themselves that Jesus is able to exorcize because he is in league with the prince of the devils. But Jesus reads their mind and responds that if that is how he does it, then the whole structure of the demons' home must collapse in civil war. By quoting Jesus's line with reference to her own house and family, Eliza is implicitly comparing her house to the kingdom of the demons. She is admitting (without having to say it openly and perhaps without having to think it consciously) that she has turned the family house into hell on earth. Why?

Freud proposed an answer to the question of why Eliza, and many other people, would act in the way she does. In the essay "Beyond the Pleasure Principle," Freud observes that animals, including human beings, are driven by two contradictory instincts. One of them is the life instinct, which causes animals to expend their resources of energy on activities such as hunting or foraging, to get more energy, and on reproduction, which is a waste from the individual's point of view, even if the individual's genes are able to propagate themselves because of the expenditure. But there is another instinct, one Freud calls the death instinct, which leads an animal to rest to conserve its energy and to hide from predators to

A southern boarding house, "Dixieland, run by Eugene Gant's mother," is the setting for Look Homeward, Angel. *(Sam Strickler | Shutterstock.com)*

hoard up as much of its energy as it can for as long as it can, resulting in survival behaviors such as sleep and hibernation. These instincts have to exist in a balance in every individual, though in many cases one instinct is stronger than the other. In essays such as "Character and Anal Eroticism" and in the *Introductory Lectures on Psychoanalysis,* Freud suggests that these instincts are utilized as the infant's personality is formed. The life instinct first gives the newborn the desire to suckle in order to survive, but it is the death instinct that allows the infant to gain control of oneself, and the first step of this is control of the waste functions in toilet training. Freud therefore refers to adults whose inner lives are still organized around that primitive phase of development as anal-hoarding or anal-retentive (a phrase that has taken on a life of its own in popular culture). This is the personality type shown by Eliza. Money is too recent an invention for the instinctual drives of the unconscious mind that evolved over millions of years to have taken it in, so it is commonly understood as psychologically equivalent to human waste. This notion is expressed as early

as in the ancient myth of King Midas, whose fondest wish the god Dionysus granted: that everything he touched would turn to gold. To Midas's horror, he finds that he is doomed since he can no longer eat (the food turns to gold), and he kills his own daughter when she tries to comfort him by hugging him and is turned to gold. Gold, and hence money, is a symbol for the waste of human life. As the death instinct impels Eliza to hoard up her energy to survive, it takes the form of hoarding up money, symbol of the first thing she ever hoarded. Since the death instinct is the basis of self-control, it leaves her driven to control everything around her. To her, the people she ought to love are important only as objects to be controlled in an orderly fashion. She is not able to think about them in any other way.

For Freud, the purpose of explaining patterns like these to a patient to whom they applied was to provide insight that could become the basis of change. Frings is not so optimistic. Eliza finally does realize the enormity of the sins she has committed against Eugene, and her remorse fuels a manic episode in which she joins with her husband in destroying the boarding-house, the symbol of the web of control and manipulation she has woven around herself. This frenzy soon passes, though, and by the end of the play she has tried to reassert her control over Eugene. She is indeed paying for him to go to Chapel Hill, and she thinks that this will keep him in her power. W.O. knows better, though, and realizes that Eugene will finally be able to break free of Eliza.

Source: Rita M. Brown, Critical Essay on *Look Homeward, Angel,* in *Drama for Students*, Gale, Cengage Learning, 2012.

Carolyn Casey Craig

In the following excerpt, Craig examines Frings's adaptation of Thomas Wolfe's novel and analyzes the characters in the dramatic version of Look Homeward, Angel.

. . . When she sat down to adapt Thomas Wolfe's autobiographical novel *Look Homeward, Angel*, Ketti was already well known for her superb adaptations and her skillful handling of domestic drama. Her interest in the idea of adapting the novel began in 1950, although she had long been something of a "Wolfe idolater." Having read his novels and finding them "full of dramatic materials," she finally read his play *Mannerhouse*. "I hadn't known until then that Wolfe had wanted to be a playwright."

This was an understatement. Wolfe tried everything humanly possible to create a viable play. He studied playwriting at the University of North Carolina, acted with Carolina Playmakers, and became a member of George Pierce Baker's legendary playwriting workshop at Harvard. Wolfe did turn out a few plays, and submitted *Mannerhouse* to the Theatre Guild. They were mildly interested, but asked Wolfe to cut down the script. The compulsive over-writer crafted a "cut" version that was longer than the original.

Thomas Wolfe died in 1938, at age 37, without ever realizing his dream of writing a stage-worthy play. The task of forging a play from his massive novel was taken up by Ketti Frings 18 years after his death. The book's story spanned 20 years of Wolfe's life, and was 626 pages long. When Ketti undertook the project, friends asked her about it "with the same awe as if she were sweeping out the Augean Stables." John Toohey referred to it as "the Herculean task of jamming this steamer trunk of a book into the tight confines of the stage." But Frings claimed that she

did not find the task too difficult. She said that, for one thing, during the year that the project took, "I didn't read anything else about Wolfe or by Wolfe that might have confused me."

After getting the rights to *Look Homeward, Angel* from Wolfe's last editor, Edward Aswell, Ketti made a list of all the moments in the book that touched her the most. In distilling the time period down to a few pivotal weeks, Ketti searched for what she called the "point of not-blindedness. . . . In a play," she insisted, "the protagonist should have a blind spot about something. When that blind spot is removed for him, the play is over."

Ketti decided that for Wolfe's autobiographical protagonist, Eugene, the "blind spot is his feeling that he must accept the embraces of his family and be bound by the ties of family love." She felt that the moment of not-blindedness came in a talk that Gene had with his brother, Ben. Once she had hit on that moment, Ketti was able to reduce the play's action to the weeks surrounding Ben's death. She juggled sequences and speeches to increase the play's impact. Her innovations included having Ben say on his deathbed a speech he had made earlier in the book.

Originally, Frings wrote a prologue and epilogue that featured Thomas Wolfe as a shadowy narrator, describing the main characters before important speeches. She abandoned this device as slightly pretentious (and perhaps too similar to *The Glass Menagerie* in form). "Still," she maintained, "I'm glad I did it. . . . It helps define the characters in my mind, and all of those speeches now appear in actual scenes."

Ketti greatly enlarged the role of Eugene (Gene), as well as the romance between Gene and Laura, a vital ingredient in the build to the play's climax. She made no attempt to follow the novel's dialogue, and some of the favorite lines of her producer (Kermit Bloomgarden) were purely inventions of Frings.

"I hate to say this about Wolfe," Ketti confided, "but I had to work my way around an awful lot of clichés in the dialogue." On the other hand, she doubted there could be a more inspirational and "beautiful line for the theatre" than Thomas Wolfe's painful observation:

> I understand that men are forever strangers to one another, that no one really comes to know anyone, that imprisoned in the dark womb of our mother we come to life without having seen her face, that we are given to her arms a stranger, and that caught in the insoluble prison of being, we escape it never, no matter what arms may clasp us, what mouth may kiss us, what heart may warm us. Never, never, never, never, never.

This passage, part of which became Ben Gant's anguished enlightenment of his brother Gene, helped to convince Ketti that Wolfe's intent was best revealed in his novel's subtitle, *A Story of the Buried Life*. The stonecutter's angel was a symbol of the beauty that had been buried in the life of Gene's father, W. O. Gant. Beyond that, the angel stood for the pain of all misspent lives; but it was of special significance to artists, who agonize when their work falls short of their dreams. In this respect, the angel was evocative of Wolfe himself, whose work often depicted the torment of the artist in an insensitive world.

"I didn't worry about the number of different scenes," Ketti confessed. "I hoped that somehow the scene designer would work it out." Producer Kermit Bloomgarden took the script to Jo Mielziner who indeed worked it out, as he had worked out a similar challenge in designing *Death of a Salesman*. Mielziner's solution for letting scenes flow without stopping was to depart from literalness, and to use a revolving stage. A shift from the living room of the Gant Dixieland Boarding House to an upstairs bedroom was made by a turn of the revolve. The whole boarding house also moved back and forth, to allow for scenes to be played in front of it (against projections of locales). A fluid, cinematic feel was brought to the production's staging by George Roy Hill, "a television man." . . .

The family spotlighted in Frings' *Look Homeward, Angel* is the most brutal example, so far, of a family of strangers. This horribly divided house is nothing like a family home: In Eliza Gant's Dixieland, the material needs of the boarders come first. The spiritual and emotional

needs of the Gant family have been neglected or deeply buried. So much so, that the fight for survival of the three dreamers—W. O. Gant, Ben, and Eugene (Gene)—is well under way when the play begins.

Ben has already lost that fight before the opening curtain. Ben's story is the point to which Eugene's story is the counterpoint. The play's conflict and suspense derive from the question of whether or not Gene will manage to secure for himself what Ben could not, by pulling free of the forces of family. Gene does escape, with help from Ben and Laura. Both of these supportive people leave Gene; but not until they have helped to remove his blind spot—his belief that he must endure the embrace of family, the smothering grasp of Eliza.

As a matriarch, Eliza Gant is more aggressive and power-wielding than any patriarch found in these plays. She is the one, here, who has set up selfish and powerful myths to control her family. A match for Eliza is difficult to find in the whole body of prize-winning American drama. (Two other domineering wives are Harriet Craig of *Craig's Wife* by George Kelly, and Ann Downs in Joseph Kramm's *The Shrike*, which Frings adapted for the screen.)

What is so striking about Eliza is not that she shows the aggression and competitiveness usually associated with men; but that she is so devoid of the impulses toward nurturing and connection that are considered inherent in women. Eliza's children have lived and looked as if they were orphans, bereft of anything but the boarders' leftovers—in food, bedding, and above all, Eliza's attention. As Gene finally cries out near the end ". . . all these years—feeding us on *their* leftovers—do you know what it does to us? When it's . . . *you* we needed for us. Why? Why?"

The answer is that the boarders are the family that Eliza has created, to suit her own very material needs. The paying boarders feed her skewed sense of self-worth. Ketti Frings' stage version of Eliza comes off as more ruthless that the mother of Wolfe's original novel. In the book, Eliza's greed is given some mitigating explanation: While her husband was raised amid the plenty of a Northern farm, and knows nothing of the privation that plagued the South after the Civil War, Eliza knows it full well. This is behind the "insatiate love of property" among Eliza and her brothers. In Frings' play, only a brief line by Mme. Elizabeth hints at this:

"Mrs. Gant and I both understand that property is what makes a person hold one's head up!"

But Eliza has imposed the public sphere on her private family sphere with disastrous results. Her cold, consuming interest in the dollar value of Dixieland makes her the mortal foe of her idealistic sons and husband.

Ben has already relinquished his dream of writing, resigned to being a "hack on a hick newspaper." He divulges to Fatty Pert his fleeting, futile dream—to fly "up with the angels" and help "drive the Huns from the skies." Ben's dream is fueled by his desperate wish to escape from Dixieland and the family "photograph" in which he feels forever trapped.

Eliza is so oblivious to the needs of her son that Ben is dying before her eyes. He is being drowned by consumption, which Frings draws as an apt symbol for the consuming clutch of Eliza. As Ben tells Fatty, dying is "one way to step out of the photograph." Fatty Pert is Ben's created family: She sings to him, knits socks for him, and listens to his dreams. She fills for Ben the voids of mother, wife, friend, and confidant. A parallel relationship is formed between Gene and Laura.

Ironically, the women who become surrogate mothers and lovers to Eliza's sons both come from her hodgepodge of boarders. But they are not like the rest. These two are examples of the "outsider-strangers" who can be more kind than kin.

Laura has even been brought to Dixieland—and to Gene—by the business cards that his mother forces him to hand out at the depot. (Laura found a card that he'd rebelliously discarded.) The hawking of Dixieland is one of the degrading tasks that Eliza has foisted on Gene. "He hasn't anything else to do," she grumbles. "Spends his time up there dreaming, scribbling." In dismissing his dreams, Eliza negates the very essence of her son. She can't see in him what is so clear to a caring outsider. Laura genuinely loves Gene, but lets him go, knowing that he needs "the whole world to wander in," while she herself must go back and live by the "good rules for marriage."

Through Laura James, Ketti Frings questions the same biases about women and marriage that the previous playwrights have questioned. Laura does not relish the prospect of marrying her fiancé, Philip, back home. She says of herself "I never liked responsibilities. . . . I like music, I like to walk in the woods, I like—to dream." Yet, at age 23, she is getting married for practical reasons that are imposed, to a man she does not love but hopes she will grow to love. (Scores of young women in the era's audiences no doubt identified with this mind-set.)

Laura's part in saving Gene is not the usual role of a rescuer. Quite literally, by loving and then leaving him, she gives Gene the impetus to break away from family and Dixieland. Laura's warmth and caring let him know what love should be like. But his marriage to Laura would keep Gene trapped: To marry her, he is ready to take the menial office job with his Uncle. This choice would give a perverse victory to Eliza, and destroy Gene's dreams of college, and travel, and the writing that is his destiny.

Two sorrows, one on the heels of the other, bring about Gene's unblinding and escape. One is the death of Ben, the only family tie of affection for Gene. The other is Laura's departure. If it were not for these events, Gene might remain in Altamont, trapped in the family photograph by his anguished loyalty to family.

According to Ben, being stuck in this photograph is what has held their father here, long after his perfect marriage turned to perfect torture. All the passion and romance of Gant have dwindled down to "riot and confusion." His search for the intangible has been locked in demeaning combat with Eliza's avid pursuit of tangibles. All that remains of Gant's old dream is his precious angel statue, whose beauty he cannot replicate. (But Gant's work is still "clean and pure" to Gene.)

To Eliza, Gant's stonecutting is useless, either as art or business. She has already betrayed Gant by trading in their real family home—proudly built with Gant's hands—for what he calls the "bloody barn" of Dixieland. Now, she is determined to cash in Gant's marble yard for its cold dollar value, the only value Eliza sees.

Ultimately, Eliza is the most blind and wretched in the Gant family portrait: The more she counts her profits, the more she loses of all that matters. Even the death of Ben and the loss of Gene do not awaken her. For one chilling, uncharacteristic moment, she joins Gant in his violence upon the boarding house. Eliza seems to revel in their vengeance on the "miserable unholy house." "I'll kill you, kill you, house," she shrieks. And for that lightning moment, love and union exist between Gant and Eliza. But it is short-lived, a false hope. Snapping back to reality, Eliza surveys with horror what they have done, and sends Helen to placate the boarders.

Gant's final comfort comes with his son's departure. If Gene leaves, part of Gant will escape, too. Gene knows that his escape from Dixieland is the start of another fight. "I shall spend the rest of my life getting my heart back, healing and forgetting every scar." Still, a redeeming light has dawned for him: the realization that self-nurturing is far better than abuse at the hands of family. Gene can carry his dream within; this is Ben's final message to his brother. Look in, not out, counsels the spirit of Ben.

There is an appealing full-circle postscript attached to the story of the play's creation: Ketti Frings re-coined those closing thoughts of Thomas Wolfe in her favorite room at home, the room with a skylight and no windows—where she could "not look out, only in."

Source: Carolyn Casey Craig, "Ketti Frings and Her Stageworthy Angel," in *Women Pulitzer Playwrights: Biographical Profiles and Analyses of the Plays*, McFarland & Company, 2004, pp. 113–26.

SOURCES

Abel, Lionel, *Tragedy and Metatheatre: Essays on Dramatic Form*, Holmes & Meier, 2003, pp. 41–73.

Aristotle, *Poetics*, in *The Complete Works of Aristotle: The Revised Oxford Translation*, Vol. 2, edited by Jonathan Barnes, translated by I. Bywater, Princeton University Press, 1995, pp. 2315–20.

Craig, Carolyn Casey, "Ketti Frings and Her Stageworthy Angel," in *Women Pulitzer Playwrights: Biographical Profiles and Analyses of the Plays*, McFarland & Company, 2004, pp. 113–26.

Freud, Sigmund, "Beyond the Pleasure Principle," in *The Standard Edition of the Complete Psychological Works of Sigmund Freud*, Vol. 18, Hogarth, 1955, pp. 7–64.

———, "Character and Anal Eroticism," in *The Freud Reader*, edited by Peter Gay, W. W. Norton, 1995, pp. 293–97.

———, *Introductory Lectures on Psychoanalysis*, translated by James Strachey, W. W. Norton, 1977, pp. 405–406.

Frings, Ketti, *Look Homeward, Angel*, in *The Best Plays of 1957–1958*, edited by Louis Kronenberger, Dodd, Mead, 1958, pp. 249–302.

Gassner, John, "Introduction to *Look Homeward, Angel*," in *50 Best Plays of the American Theatre*, edited by Clive Barnes, Crown, 1969, p. 261.

Popkin, Henry, "Theatre II," in *Kenyon Review*, Vol. 20, No. 2, 1958, pp. 307–13.

Turnbull, Andrew, *Thomas Wolfe*, Charles Scribner's Sons, 1968.

Wolfe, Thomas, *Look Homeward, Angel: A Story of the Buried Life*, Charles Scribner's Sons, 1929, p. 84.

FURTHER READING

Bruccoli, Mathew J., and Park Bucker, eds., *To Loot My Life Clean: The Thomas Wolfe–Maxwell Perkins Correspondence*, University of South Carolina Press, 2009.
     This collection of letters covers the period during which Wolfe and Perkins edited Wolfe's manuscript into the publishable *Look Homeward, Angel* and the period following publication.

Donald, David Herbert, *Look Homeward: A Life of Thomas Wolfe*, Little, Brown, 1987.
     This Pulitzer Prize–winning biography of Wolfe focuses on his career and practice as a writer.

Lawlor, Clark, *Consumption and Literature: The Making of the Romantic Disease*, Palgrave Macmillan, 2006.
     Lawlor discusses the history of tuberculosis, also known as consumption, as a literary theme, particularly as a marker of an ethereal, spiritual character, too good for this world.

Wolfe, Thomas, *O Lost: A Story of the Buried Life*, text established by Arlyn and Matthew J. Bruccoli, University of North Carolina Press, 2000.
     This is an edition of Wolfe's original text that he submitted for publication before it was edited down, removing about a quarter of the pages, into *Look Homeward, Angel* by Wolfe and Perkins.

SUGGESTED SEARCH TERMS

Ketti Frings

Thomas Wolfe NOT The Bonfire of the Vanities

Look Homeward, Angel

Look Homeward, Angel AND Ketti Frings

Ketti Frings AND Thomas Wolfe

Southern renaissance

Thomas Wolfe Society

Carrara marble

tuberculosis

George Roy Hill

Maxwell Perkins AND Thomas Wolfe

Ketti Frings AND Broadway

Los Vendidos

LUIS VALDEZ
1967

Los Vendidos is a one-act play by Luis Valdez first performed in 1967 by El Teatro Campesino as part of the United Farm Workers (UFW) movement. The play helped pioneer the *acto*, which is the term coined by Valdez to describe a type of one-act play that uses stock characters and humor to emphasize social or political themes. Along with the leader of the UFW movement, Cesar Chavez, Valdez and El Teatro Campesino brought these *actos* to the migrant workers in the fields of California as a means to motivate the Mexican immigrant political base to fight for unionization and demand fair working conditions. *Los Vendidos* (*The Sellouts*) addresses the identity issues that Chicanos faced during the late 1960s as immigrants trying to find a place within American society while struggling to maintain their ethnic heritage.

The play highlights common stereotypes of Chicanos in the late 1960s, among them the *campesino*, the *pachuco*, the *revolucionario*, and an assimilated Mexican American man. Each of these characters embodies a different Anglo American view of Mexicans. In addition, there is a completely assimilated, anglicized Mexican American woman named Miss Jimenez (pronounced "JIM-enez") and a salesman who pointedly describes the traits of each of the stock characters. *Los Vendidos* is a satiric portrayal of the Chicano struggles with cultural stereotypes, and it and other *actos* like it helped form Chicano theater, of which Valdez is often said to be the father.

Luis Valdez (Getty Images)

First published in Valdez's collection *Actos* in 1971, *Los Vendidos* can also be found in numerous anthologies, collections, and textbooks on Chicano or drama studies such as *Luis Valdez—Early Works: Actos, Bernabé and Pensamiento Serpentino*, published in 1990, with accompanying notes and introduction.

AUTHOR BIOGRAPHY

Valdez was born on June 26, 1940, in Delano, California. A son of migrant farmworkers and the second of ten children, Valdez traveled as a child to wherever his family could find work. In elementary school, Valdez was assigned a leading role in a puppet show. Although his family moved on to the next camp before he could perform, it sparked in him an interest in theater. As a teenager, Valdez taught himself ventriloquism and was featured on KNTV, a local news channel, in 1956. After graduating from high

school, Valdez attended San Jose State University, where he earned a bachelor of arts degree in English and wrote award-winning plays that stressed ethnic pride, a growing issue among Chicanos. The Chicano migrant worker population was getting restless, incited in no small part by the efforts of the revolutionary labor leader Cesar Chavez, who organized the United Farm Workers movement of the late 1960s.

Valdez joined the San Francisco Mime Troupe after graduating from college, but the struggles of Chavez and his loved ones in the camps were always in the back of his mind. "I felt I needed some roots again and wanted to get to the Valley and people here," he told Beth Bagby in a 1967 interview with the *Tulane Drama Review*. Soon he became involved in Chavez's United Farm Workers movement. His contribution to the cause was El Teatro Campesino, or "The Farmworkers' Theater," a means of political expression as well as a tool to rally workers. El Teatro Campesino produced short, one-act plays, dubbed *actos* by Valdez, to urge unionization among workers and draw publicity to the exploitation of Chicano migrant workers.

By 1967, when *Los Vendidos* was produced, the efforts of Valdez and El Teatro Campesino had moved beyond the boundaries of the fields and into the outside world, as he toured with his plays and drew more attention to the plight of the Mexican immigrant. Valdez quickly rose in prominence, and today he is widely considered the father of Chicano theater, which centers on the struggle for ethnic identity combined with an American identity. In 1978, Valdez became the first Chicano director and playwright to have a play on Broadway with *Zoot Suit*, made into a film in 1981. In 1987, Valdez directed *La Bamba*, a film adaptation of the life of Richie Valens.

Throughout the 1990s, Valdez directed primarily in television while also teaching at California State University, Monterey Bay. He continues to give lectures on the importance of media to help combat stereotypes of Chicano culture. In 1968, Valdez received a prestigious Obie Award for off-Broadway theater. This was followed by Los Angeles Drama Critics Circle Awards in 1969, 1972, and 1978 and an Emmy Award in 1973 for his work in television. He received the 1987 Peabody Award for *Corridos: Tales of Passion and Revolution*. Valdez holds honorary doctorates from Colombia College, San Jose State University, and the California Institute of the Arts.

PLOT SUMMARY

Los Vendidos opens in Honest Sancho's Used Mexican Lot and Mexican Curio Shop. There are three "models" of Mexicans on display: the Farmworker, the Pachuco, and the Revolucio-nario. As the play opens, Honest Sancho, the Mexican proprietor, moves around dusting the models and using a mix of Spanish and English to describe his shop to the audience. A secretary, Miss Jimenez, enters looking for a "Mexican type" for administrative work in the governor's office. Though of Hispanic descent, the secretary insists that her name is pronounced "JIM-enez" and appears completely anglicized. She tells Honest Sancho that she desires a model that is suave yet a hard worker, and Honest Sancho leads her to the Farmworker.

In describing the Farmworker to Miss Jime-nez, Sancho highlights both the stereotypical traits of field hands and makes references to the very difficult working conditions they face. The Farmworker is friendly and deferential, made for efficient and economical manual labor— that is, he is cheap to maintain. Sancho says that this model will run on mere "pennies a day" and requires no decent lodging. The biggest selling point of the Farmworker is that he returns to Mexico in the fall and does not return until spring. Miss Jimenez is impressed, but when she asks if the Farmworker can speak English, she learns that not only does he only speak Spanish, he is programmed to go on strike at a moment's notice. She pronounces him unsuitable, and she and Sancho move on to the Pachuco.

Johnny Pachuco is a city model, sleek and fast. Although he is bilingual, he is violent and uses English mainly to curse at Miss Jimenez. His foul language offends her, and Sancho points out that he learned how to speak in that manner in American schools. The Pachuco is also economical, but instead of beans and tortillas like the Farmworker, the Pachuco runs on fast food, alcohol, and marijuana. However, Sancho is quick to point out that not only does the Pachuco have a programmed inferiority complex, but he is also made to take physical abuse, a trait he invites Miss Jimenez to test. She kicks him several times at Sancho's encouragement. However, the Pachuco steals, and Miss Jimenez does not want to add to the number of thieves already in the government. Plus, she is looking for a model that

MEDIA ADAPTATIONS

- Valdez's award-winning play *Zoot Suit* was adapted for film in 1981 by Universal Pictures. *Zoot Suit* was the first play either written or directed by a Mexican American to be performed on Broadway, and the film adaptation was nominated for the 1982 Golden Globe for Best Picture in the Musical or Comedy category. In 2001, L.A. Theatre Works released *Zoot Suit* as an audiobook.

- UCTV, the University of California television station, hosts an online video of a 2009 Valdez lecture on the problems of cultural identity (http://www.uctv.tv/search-details.aspx?show ID = 15561) in their archived videos.

- University of California at San Diego professor Jorge Huerta interviewed Valdez about his experiences with and views of Chicano theater in 2008. UCTV hosts an archived video of this interview (http://www.uctv.tv/search-details.aspx?showID = 3467), in which Valdez discusses El Teatro Campesino, the critically acclaimed play *Zoot Suit*, and the Chicano renaissance of the 1960s and 1970s.

- Valdez's El Teatro Campesino, still in existence today, maintains a Web site (http://www.eltea trocampesino.com/index.html) with information about their upcoming plays, their history, and the contemporary company itself.

will attract female voters. Sancho pronounces that he has just the product for her and leads her to the Revolucionario.

Versatile and durable, the Revolucionario can be anything from a rebel to a movie star. He is romantic and charming. Sancho tells Miss Jimenez that he is such a good lover because he is also cheap to maintain, needing only "raw horsemeat and tequila," which makes him manly. However, almost immediately the Rev-olucionario becomes unacceptable for Miss Jimenez because he was made in Mexico. She specifically asks for a Mexican American, and Sancho brings a model from the back room to show her.

This new Mexican American is educated, clean, and polite. He is capable of serving on any type of board of directors and is well suited to politics, a fact he demonstrates by giving a political speech about the "problems of the Mexican" in which he fervently praises America until partially collapsing. However, the Mexican American is not economical to maintain, and Miss Jimenez reacts with utter shock and horror at Sancho's asking price of $15,000. Sancho explains that it is expensive to produce a Mexican American and talks her into making the purchase.

Miss Jimenez hands Sancho the money and takes control of the Mexican American, eager to show him off at the governor's rally. However, when she snaps her fingers, instead of reacting as he did during the sales demonstration, the Mexican American begins speaking in Spanish about revolting against white authority. Sancho refuses to take the model back, saying that he is Miss Jimenez's problem now that she has purchased him. She snaps again to try to regain control, but this only makes him more zealous. He snaps his own fingers and one by one turns on the Farmworker, Pachuco, and Revolucionario. All four surround Miss Jimenez and shout rebel-rallying cries in Spanish. She flees the shop, and all of the characters freeze.

After she leaves, the four models begin to stretch while Sancho remains frozen. The models begin discussing the money that Miss Jimenez left behind, and soon it becomes clear that they are actual people, not robots. It is Sancho who is the robot. They split up the money and go their separate ways, with the Revolucionario taking Sancho with him to get serviced.

CHARACTERS

Farmworker

The Farmworker, or campesino, is the first model that Honest Sancho shows Miss Jimenez. The Farmworker's first big selling point is that he is a hard worker. Sancho points out all of the special tweaks made to the Farmworker to make him perfect for field labor. In describing the various attributes of the Farmworker, Sancho also illustrates the working conditions of Chicano migrant field workers, the same conditions

that Chavez and the UFW were trying to change. Never allowed to rest or even slow down, the Farmworker can pick anything from grapes to cotton to melons. The model secretes a special grease that enables him to move around in the typical "field when the vines or the branches get so entangled, it's almost impossible to move." He survives on one plate of tortillas, beans, and chiles per day and can be housed in a shack or simply left in the field overnight, so his owners never have to put much expense into his food or lodging. The best selling point is that "every year at the end of the season, this model goes back to Mexico and doesn't return, automatically, until next Spring." Therefore his owners don't have to worry about him once the farming season is over and he is not needed any longer. However, he cannot speak English at all, and this kills the deal for Miss Jimenez.

Miss Jimenez

Miss Jimenez is a secretary in the governor's office in California who comes to Honest Sancho to purchase a Mexican American for use in the administration. Although of Hispanic descent, she adamantly anglicizes her name and shows no trace of her ethnic heritage. She wants a model that is a "Mexican type" but was made in America. That is, she wants a model that can play the part of a Mexican but is really an American inside. Her superficial acceptance of only one side of the multifaceted Mexican American identity is representative of the way Valdez and his contemporaries believed mainstream America viewed Chicanos in the 1960s. Miss Jimenez is so believable, in fact, that at first glance she may seem to represent that "mainstream America."

However, it is vital to the play to note and understand that Miss Jimenez is a Mexican American herself, one who has completely adopted the attitudes of American culture, to the point of being repelled by people of her own ethnicity. As Maria Antónia Oliver-Rotger puts it in her 2002 book *Battlegrounds and Crossroads: Social and Imaginary Space in Writings by Chicanas*,

> Miss Jimenez, the only woman appearing in Valdez's popular *acto Los Vendidos* (1967)...is the stereotype of the completely assimilated Mexican American. She no longer understands Spanish and has forgotten about the struggles of the Mexican people in the U.S.

Even more, she has betrayed her fellow Chicanos and Chicanas by encouraging their exploitation and discrimination by the Anglo-American population. The villain in this play is not only America's preconceived notion of Chicano culture; it is moreover the refusal of those who are in advantageous positions both to understand the Chicano struggle and to speak up about it in hopes of affecting change. Miss Jimenez works for the same government whose lack of equal-rights legislation is oppressing the very people with whom she should be identifying. She is another stereotype—more subtle, perhaps, but nonetheless a key character in the rhetoric of the Chicano movement.

Mexican American

The last model Sancho brings from the back room is the Mexican American. Brand new, the Mexican American is built exactly like American models, just with darker skin tone. He speaks perfect English, is college educated, and is very hygienic. He is polite and programmed to fit in perfectly with the American political scene. He can make speeches and sit on boards and is extremely patriotic. He makes a small speech in which he blames Chicanos for their own predicament, calling them stupid and insinuating that they are lazy. He is much more expensive than the other three models, however, for he only runs on the same things that it takes to fuel an Anglo-American, including mom's apple pie.

Despite his exorbitant cost, Miss Jimenez buys him on the spot. As she tries to leave the store with him, however, he turns rebellious and incites a small revolution in the shop in which all of the models advance on Miss Jimenez and threaten to bring her down. At the end of the play, when it is revealed that the models are in fact live people, the Mexican American complains about having to play the same role all the time. Johnny Pachuco says, "That's what you get for finishing high school." Once a Chicano has been indoctrinated in the American school system, he is pigeon-holed into a role just as his fellow immigrants who are uneducated are.

Johnny Pachuco

When Miss Jimenez expresses a desire for a more "urban model," Sancho shows her Johnny Pachuco. The Pachuco is sleek and dandified. In her 2009 article "Reinventing the Pachuco: The Radical Transformation from the Criminalized to the Heroic in Luis Valdez's Play *Zoot*

Suit" published in the *Journal for the Study of Radicalism*, Ashley Lucas says that

> the *pachuco* as a cultural figure offers up dramatically captivating images...because the *pachuco* is alluring yet frightening, working class yet dressed in expensive clothes, representative of a real community yet one imagined from the outside.

The Pachuco is at first a study in contrasts. He dances yet knife fights. He sings yet swears violently. He commits crimes yet is a ready scapegoat for any crimes he did not commit. He, too, is economical; however, unlike the Farmworker, who survives on basic staples, the Pachuco survives on alcohol, fast food, and marijuana. Though he is bilingual, it seems the only English he is willing to speak entails insulting Miss Jimenez and all she stands for. The Pachuco is symbolic of the negative results of Americanization.

Conflicted between a Mexican identity that is unwelcome in America and an American identity that looks down on Mexicans, the Pachuco is assimilation gone wrong. Sancho says as much when Miss Jimenez objects to Johnny's cursing: "Well, he learned it in your school." In many ways, the assimilation of the Pachuco and the assimilation of Miss Jimenez serve as foils for each other. America has taught them both different ways of functioning within American culture. They have both carved a space for themselves in American society—unlike the Farmworker, who is permanently relegated to visitor status—but that space restricts their potential to grow out of the stereotype that they embody. Miss Jimenez is most enthralled by the fact that the Pachuco can be physically beaten in his role as a scapegoat and takes one or two very satisfying kicks at him, whereupon Johnny tries to steal her purse. She treats him as a criminal, and he reacts by acting like one.

Revolucionario

Miss Jimenez pronounces the Pachuco unsuitable, and she and Sancho move on to the Revolucionario. Charming, handsome, athletic, and versatile, the Revolucionario can fill any number of needs. One of the most popular uses for the Revolucionario is in film, where he plays stereotypes of Mexicans for the entertainment of American viewers. Therefore, he contributes to the prevailing view of Chicanos in the United States by turning the Mexican into a stock character. He also has a streak of savagery: he survives on tequila and raw horsemeat.

This model is assimilated in a unique way. He has found a place for himself by emphasizing the traits that make him different from Americans and encouraging their limited notions of what constitutes Chicano culture. His role in society and culture is dependent upon the very stereotypes that keep Chicanos oppressed and discriminated against. In this way, he is the least Americanized of them all, for rather than attempt to change or hide the characteristics that make him a Mexican, he exaggerates them. However, he is made in Mexico, and Miss Jimenez is adamant that the model she purchases be American made.

Honest Sancho

Honest Sancho is introduced as the owner and proprietor of Honest Sancho's Used Mexican Lot and Mexican Curio Shop, but at the end of the play he is revealed to be a machine. Sancho shows Miss Jimenez four different models of Mexicans she can buy, extolling the virtues of each. In his pitches for each model, Sancho touches explicitly on social issues and cultural barriers faced by Mexican immigrants in the late 1960s, such as worker exploitation, lack of education, and crime. Although he first lists all of the virtues of the different models, some of what he considers good characteristics turn out to be horrifying to Miss Jimenez. He coldly and almost cruelly speaks of how little care they require, calling each model except the Mexican American "economical." His descriptions reflect both the ethnic and cultural backgrounds of Mexicans and the ways in which they gain favor in American society. The Chicano struggle with this dual identity was a key focus of Valdez's work and the Chicano movement, and Sancho's character serves as a means to convey this conflict to audiences.

THEMES

Dialectical Materialism

Dialectical materialism is a philosophical approach to understanding reality developed by the nineteenth-century German social theorists Karl Marx and Friedrich Engels. In this sense, *materialism* is used as the opposite of *idealism*, meaning that any analysis of reality intrinsically depends upon the material—what we can see and touch—and does not originate in the mind independent of the material world.

Materialism does not negate the thought process or spiritual experience. Instead, it says that the thought process is a result of the material world in which the thinker lives. We are all products of the material world we inhabit.

Dialectics is rooted in the research of G. W. F. Hegel, who posited that everything is always changing and is always interdependent upon other influences. Nothing exists that can be taken solely on its own merits. Every idea, every discovery, every development is the result of the interaction of other ideas, discoveries, or developments and always leads to yet another idea, discovery, or development. Every concept carries within it tensions created by contradictory aspects of itself that are constantly conflicting. This conflict is the driving force behind any kind of change, and change—either transformation or dissolution—is absolutely inevitable. These changes always result in new conflicts, which in turn propagate more change. Hegel saw the dialectical process as the result of new ideas. Marx and Engels, in contrast, saw new ideas as the result of the dialectical process. In other words, Hegel believed that new ideas shaped the world; Marx and Engels believed that the world shaped new ideas.

Dialectical materialism, then, is a theory proposing that all change is a result of interaction with the material world. Any social development, ideology, or cultural process is inextricably linked to the immediate world in which it arose. For example, in *Los Vendidos*, Valdez expresses a theme of impending social change. This change—equal rights and protection for Mexican Americans—was instigated by the material conditions Valdez and his contemporaries experienced on a daily basis. American culture in the 1960s is a near-perfect example of dialectical materialism in action. There existed a material condition—discrimination against and exploitation of minority groups—that was in conflict with another condition—the desire of these minority groups to have equal rights. This conflict incited change in the material culture of America. Social development, therefore, is a constant process of tension, conflict, and the resolution of that particular conflict, which inevitably leads to new tension.

Social Satire

Satire is a way of using scathing humor to criticize individuals or institutions. Ridicule, irony, sarcasm,

TOPICS FOR FURTHER STUDY

- Working in groups, write and perform an *acto* that addresses a social issue you and your peers struggle with every day. Use your imagination for the topic. Is bullying a problem in the social structure of your school? Do you and many of your classmates struggle with divorced parents and extended families? Is there a clearly defined social class system in your school? In the tradition of Valdez's *actos*, break the issue down into its most basic parts. Write a brief paragraph outlining the problem, articulating the changes you wish to see and explaining what you feel needs to be done to effect those changes. Your play should feature elements of an *acto*, including stock characters, audience participation, and the use of humor to emphasize the social problem you are addressing. Perform your play for the class, and then discuss their reactions. Did they understand your message?

- As a class, develop a blog that addresses the issues of socially constructed identities and preconceived notions in American culture. Divide into groups, and assign each group an issue that revolves around identities. Gender, race, religion, ethnicity, and sexual orientation are some examples of factors influencing identity. Each week, post a blog entry that references an online news clip or article that is specific to your group. Include a link to the article followed by your group's interpretation of how the issue is framed within the relevant sociopolitical mindset. Invite your classmates to comment on your blog entries.

- Partner with a classmate with whom you do not typically have much interaction. Make a list of the differences between you, then a list of your similarities. Which list was easier to compile? Which was longer? What do the two lists tell you about your identities within mainstream American culture? Discuss your findings with the class.

- Pick a recent controversy in politics that has received widespread media attention. A good way to begin looking for ideas is to examine what positions politicians running for federal office take on different issues or on a recent news story that has drawn national attention. Use both print and Internet resources to find as much background information as you can on the subject. Find a person you can interview about their experience with the issue. For example, what does one of your teachers have to say about possible budget cuts in public education? Do you know someone who has personally been affected by the rise in unemployment in the beginning of this century? Record your interview and, using footage you find online, make a documentary about your topic and the personal effects it has on everyday people.

- Read the young-adult biography *Cesar Chavez: A Photographic Essay* (2009), by Ilan Stavans. Then research a prominent figure in a social, economic, or political movement from another period in American history. Create a photographic essay in the manner of Stavans's book, providing an overview of the movement, including any historical events that helped contribute to the call to action, and the role your chosen person played in it. Choose as your medium a paper or digital format.

---

and hyperbole are all elements of satire. Social satire directs the ridicule toward a particular cultural phenomenon, such as religion, politics, or class systems. The purpose of satire is not solely to make fun of something or someone, but to do so in order to emphasize inherent faults or abuses in the

Honest Sancho owns a curio shop that sells Mexican "mannequins." *(Vinicius Tupinamba | Shutterstock.com)*

hopes of affecting social change. Cleverness and wit are the tools the social satirist uses to reveal and attempt to correct injustice or oppression.

Los Vendidos is a perfect example of social satire. Valdez uses exaggerated characters as a mirror to show Anglo-Americans how destructive stereotyping an entire race can be. Interspersed in the humor are pointed remarks that make definitive political statements, such as when Honest Sancho tells Miss Jimenez that the Pachuco learned to curse and fight in American high schools. Other points are made more subtly. For example, Miss Jimenez's disgust of Mexican Americans "made in Mexico" and Sancho's assertion that the Farmworker can be fueled only by tortillas, beans, and chiles shine a metaphoric light on the low opinion mainstream America held of Chicanos and the exploitation and oppression that were the result.

Satire is almost always controversial, because it deals with controversial material. The mix of humor and outrage results in deliberately heightened tensions. It is also easy to miss the point of satire; if one does not understand the issues being

addressed or know the author's stance on them, satire is easily misunderstood. When executed well, however, for an informed audience, satire can be a powerful weapon in the arsenal of social change.

STYLE

Audience
The audience for which Valdez wrote *Los Vendidos* was a critical consideration. Writers express themselves through their work as a part of a dialogue, and thus audience is an important part of any work of literature or drama. But because these *actos* existed to convey a political message, the audience played almost as large a role as the actors. The original audience for *Los Vendidos* was the working-class Chicano community itself. In 1967, when the piece was first performed, the Chicano movement had yet to attract much widespread attention or garner public support. Thus, the audiences of Chicanos and Chicanas would have been really the only

ones to understand the symbolic nature of *Los Vendidos*. The allegorical aspects of the play would only have been recognizable to people who could relate to each of the characters, either personally or through someone they personally knew.

This was the purpose behind El Teatro Campesino—to speak directly to the migrant workers they were attempting to motivate. Only later, after the national spotlight was focused on Chavez and the UFW struggle, would the real meaning of the play have been evident to people outside of or unconnected with the Chicano community. As David Copelin emphasizes in "Chicano Theatre: El Festival de los Teatros Chicanos," "The idea of sharing a performance with an audience seems to be natural to the Chicano theatre; if an audience does not understand a stage action, it is the *teatro's* fault, not the spectators'."

Didactics

In 1967, when *Los Vendidos* was first performed, there was an incredibly intense sense of urgency to show people what it was like to be a Mexican American and to motivate the base of working-class Chicanos to action. Therefore, the *actos* written by Valdez during this time were meant to illustrate and to teach much more than to entertain. A work that is created with the intention of teaching is described as *didactic*. Valdez's goal was to incite social action and cultural change, and the vehicle through which he best knew how to do this was theater.

The sociopolitical implications of works like *Los Vendidos* are staggering in the way they challenged the workings of everyday American culture. Like many other protest movements of the 1960s, the Chicano movement wanted to throw back the curtain so that non-working-class and Anglo-Americans could see the exploitation, discrimination, and oppression Mexican Americans faced while simultaneously moving people to want to fight for change. In the 1990 collection *Luis Valdez—Early Works: Actos, Bernabé and Pensamiento Serpentino*, Valdez defined the mission of El Teatro Campesino: "Inspire the audience to social action. Illuminate specific points about social problems. Satirize the opposition. Show or hint at a solution. Express what people are feeling."

Setting

The setting of *Los Vendidos* is very specific. Valdez placed the action of the play in then-present-day Sacramento, the gubernatorial seat of California, and the significance of this should not be underemphasized. Valdez wanted the *acto* to be pointed and for the message to be clear. This is not a play set in an ambiguous time or place; it is *here* and *now*, and this serves to make evident the fact that the attitudes Chicanos face as portrayed in *Los Vendidos* were very real and present.

The setting of any play affects the mood of the drama, and there is a sense of urgency and immediacy conveyed in *Los Vendidos* that is due to the setting. Valdez allows no room for the audience members to distance themselves from the action. The sharpness of the action, the blunt dialogue, and the cold and dismissive attitude of Miss Jimenez are only relevant when placed in a context that does not allow the audience anywhere to hide from the truth Valdez is attempting to expose.

That the setting of the play remain socially and politically relevant is so important that most later productions of *Los Vendidos* have made at least minor alterations. Some have featured "Honest Sancha" rather than Sancho, with a female playing the part. Others have changed the ending altogether. In 1993, a televised version of the play ended with a call not to strike but to a permeation of Mexican Americans nationwide with the goal of changing the situation for Chicanos from within mainstream American culture.

Allegory

An allegory is a story in which the characters and plot stand for something else, usually an abstract idea or philosophy. The purpose of an allegory is usually to impart some moral lesson. The secondary meanings of the characters imbue the situation and plot with a deeper meaning that is revealed as the relationships in the story develop. Another way of thinking of an allegory is as an extended metaphor. In a metaphor, one thing or idea is substituted for another in order to draw parallels between the two. "He has a heart of stone" juxtaposes heart and stone and implies that the person is hard and cold. In an extended metaphor, the ideas may be more abstract and on a larger scale, but the basic concept is the same.

In *Los Vendidos*, Valdez uses Honest Sancho's Used Mexican Lot and Mexican Curio Shop as a metaphor for the contained identity that mainstream America imposed on the idea of Mexican Americans. Everything that occurs in the shop expands on that metaphor. The models, Miss Jimenez, the dialogue, and the action all serve to illustrate a situation that is never directly referenced in the play: the discrimination and exploitation of the Chicano people. Because the concept of an allegory is so broad and can be applied to such a wide variety of artistic expression, the term itself is not used to identify a genre as much as a style of expression and interpretation. It is the interaction between the symbols that is important to understand about the allegory. A single allegory could be interpreted numerous different ways depending on the reader and the connections that already exist in that reader's mind. *Los Vendidos* is allegorical only to those who have some sort of knowledge of the struggle for Chicano rights in America. Because the allegory must exist as much in the mind of the reader as in the intention of the author, it represents a communicative act between reader and writer. Though symbolism is an element of allegory, it is the combination of multiple cultural symbols and signifying systems of language and communication that makes an allegory work.

Stereotype

Valdez and El Teatro Campesino relied heavily on the use of stereotypes or stock characters to help connect the audience to the play. In *Los Vendidos*, every character is a stereotype of some sort: the Farmworker is the campesino; the Pachuco is the city thug; the Revolucionario is the social rebel; the Mexican American is the immigrant programmed to assimilate completely into American society; and Miss Jimenez is the traitor to her own race and people, so desperate to fit into American culture that she has become completely indoctrinated. These characters were instantly recognizable to Valdez's audiences and therefore required little or no background or character development. These are stereotypes that many Anglos believed about Chicanos and that some Chicanos (such as Miss Jimenez) believed about themselves. These stock characters do not represent different factual facets of Mexican American culture. They represent differing perceptions of Chicanos. It is important to note that Valdez wrote these characters in this manner very deliberately. His point was to illustrate the widely held biases against the Chicano community, to hold a mirror up to the people of American society and reflect back to them their own prejudices.

HISTORICAL CONTEXT

Mexican Americans and the Vietnam War

"*La batalla está aquí*" became a rallying cry in the Chicano community during the Vietnam War years among activists who believed that "the battle is here" in the United States, not in a foreign country. Much like the African American community in the 1960s and 1970s, the Chicano population was overrepresented in the military, and many resented America's involvement in an overseas war while the government was ignoring the war for equal rights at home. However, not all of the Chicano community was opposed to the war in the mid- to late 1960s. Many, in fact, saw military service as a way to show their patriotism as well as adhere to the traditional role of the Chicano male as warrior, as John Alba Cutler points out in "Chicana/o Authenticity and Viet Nam." Newly immigrated Mexican Americans had left behind a homeland that was itself in a near-constant state of war, and to many it was an honor and a responsibility to serve.

The allure of the military for the Chicano in the 1960s is not difficult to understand. As members of the military, Mexican Americans had a chance to prove their pride in their country, earn a steady income to send home to their families, and possibly raise their social status from "immigrant" to "veteran." Again, as with other protest movements of the 1960s, the Chicano movement and the antiwar movement combined at times, with many Mexican Americans loudly voicing their anger at an ongoing conflict that took focus and resources off of domestic issues and initiatives and that sent a disproportionate number of poor and minority citizens to Vietnam to fight and possibly die for a cause in which they did not believe. These two conflicting stances caused a "tension between assimilationist patriotism and radical antiwar protest" within the Chicano community, according to Cutler, providing another dividing line for Chicano identity.

Chicano Renaissance

The 1960s was a decade of change for many traditionally oppressed social groups, including Mexican Americans or Chicanos. The Chicano movement was particularly dedicated to the idea that artists were an integral part of the sociopolitical process. Through art, literature, and theater, Chicano artists developed a unique

COMPARE
&
CONTRAST

- **1960s:** The United States undergoes a massive social revolution, with multiple oppressed groups, such as African Americans, Mexican Americans, women, and antiwar activists, staging unprecedented acts of social protest outside of the legislative process to effect social change.

  Today: Groups wishing more representation in Washington or wishing to spread their message typically utilize an ever-growing network of lobbyists and special-interest groups to effect change from within the political and legislative process.

- **1960s:** Chicano theater is a brand new artistic form. For the first time, Mexican American voices can be heard through the medium of performance art.

Today: There are Chicano and Latino theater companies throughout the United States, in regional theater, many major urban centers, and a large number of universities. The experiences of Hispanics in America have been popularized through not only the theater but television and film as well.

- **1960s:** Social movements grow through word of mouth, media coverage, and letter writing. The amount of information the public receives about political unrest within a minority group is restricted to personal experience or traditional media outlets.

  Today: Social movements spread via social networking sites such as Facebook and Twitter. Vastly proliferating online media outlets and cable news channels allow access to breaking news on a constant basis.

---

iconography and a set of repeated themes that eventually came to represent the core problems that the movement sought to change.

Los Vendidos, for example, shines a bright light on one of the largest obstacles in the path of Mexican Americans: stereotypes and the roles that American culture expects Chicanos to fill. By placing the movement in terms of recognizable icons, slogans, and themes, the Chicano renaissance not only lent an intense focus on precise issues but also helped define Mexican American culture as its own entity, existing both within and outside of mainstream American culture.

The symbols that came to be associated with the Chicano movement inevitably came to be associated with Chicanos themselves, both among non-Mexicans and from within their own culture. Thus, the Chicano renaissance was more than an artistic movement. For the first time, Mexican Americans were not struggling to identify with either their ethnic heritage or the American culture of their adopted nature. Instead, they developed a unique voice

and identity of their own. Vendez's El Teatro Campesino is often cited as the first representative of the Chicano renaissance.

Cesar Chavez and the United Farm Workers Movement
The physical work done in the fields has traditionally been performed by the poorest and least educated of the workforce, who almost by default end up being immigrants and migrant workers. Initial attempts at unionizing farmworkers were short lived and seemed hopelessly doomed from the start. Because of the migratory nature of the work, it was extremely difficult to keep anyone in one place long enough to organize. In addition, there were no protections against employer retaliation for workers who joined unions, and many of them could not afford to face the very real threat that they would lose their jobs instantly were they to engage in collective bargaining.

In 1965, the Agricultural Workers Organizing Committee, a mostly Filipino workers' group,

Miss Jimenez come to Sancho's shop to buy a "Mexican type" mannequin to campaign for California gubernatorial candidate Ronald Reagan. (auremar | Shutterstock.com)

began a strike against California's grape growers in Delano, California. Within a week, the National Farm Workers Association, which served the migrant farmworker community in multiple ways outside of the labor movement, voted to join the strike. By 1966, the two groups merged to form the United Farm Workers (UFW).

Adopting the tactics of African Americans protesting for equal rights in the South, Chavez advocated nonviolence and sought to engage the public on an emotional level by involving students and church groups. The farm owners had an enormous amount of power and almost inexhaustible resources at their disposal, while the UFW depended on donations and volunteers. What they did have, however, was the attention of the public. A nationwide boycott of table grapes was in full swing by 1968. Not only would members of the UFW refuse to pick grapes, but a growing segment of the American people refused to buy or eat them.

In 1968 Chavez began a fast, in the tradition of India's renowned pacifist reformer Mahatma

Gandhi, at the UFW headquarters in Delano, attracting international attention. Finally, in 1969, the pressure became too much for the Delano grape growers to withstand, and they signed historic agreements with the unions that regulated the hiring process, gave protection from dangerous pesticides, raised wages, guaranteed improved working conditions, and provided medical care. It was a major victory in the fight for farmworkers' rights and served to draw attention to the plight of the largely Latino migrant worker population.

CRITICAL OVERVIEW

Few critics disagree regarding the importance of Luis Valdez and El Teatro Campesino in the creation of Chicano theater and, in turn, in inciting the Chicano renaissance. The impact of Valdez's *actos* on not only the UFW movement but also issues ranging from Chicano involvement in the Vietnam War to the condition of the barrios was enormous. In 1967, the same year that *Los Vendidos* was first performed and just as El Teatro was beginning to expand beyond the struggles of Chavez and the UFW, Bagby wrote in the *Tulane Drama Review* that "the Teatro has been limited to an audience of either farm workers or urban strike sympathizers, but its unwritten *actos* have established dramatic images which will last the lives of its audiences." El Teatro Campesino gave the Chicano population an audible, pointed sociopolitical voice that allowed the articulation of the issues with which Mexican Americans were struggling both in mainstream American society and within their own cultural ranks.

With the social and artistic explosion in the late 1960s and early 1970s, Chicanos broke free from their role as the so-called silent minority. "It is in this very spirit of asserting the importance of the values, traditions, and history of the community," states Oliver-Rotger in *Battlegrounds and Crossroads*, "that much of the literature by Chicanos and Chicanas was produced during and after the so-called 'Chicano Renaissance.'"

Some early critics were dubious about Valdez's claims regarding the inspiration behind the *actos*. In 1973, David Copelin wrote in his article "El Festival de los Teatros Chicanos" that there seemed to be very few influences Valdez did not claim:

> He cited improvisation, *Commedia dell'arte*, Naturalism, Symbolism, Old Comedy…and the theories and practice of Artaud, Brecht, the Bread and Puppet Theatre, the Open Theatre, the Living Theatre, Grotowski, and the agit-prop drama of the thirties.

Although Valdez had training in theater and exposure to artistic philosophies, his actors came primarily from the camps for which they performed. The two sensibilities—the uneducated enthusiasm of the actors and the intellectual political theories of Valdez—combined beautifully as a form of expression unique to the Chicano movement.

The limited role of women is an often-cited criticism of Chicano theater. Copelin reminds readers "that there is also a struggle within the Chicano liberation movement against the old sexist stereotypes of the traditional *macho* culture." Jorge Huerta echoes this sentiment in "When Sleeping Giants Awaken: Chicano Theatre in the 1960s": "The teatros were male-dominated, mirroring the

Chicano Movement, and few Chicanas, if any, were in leadership positions in the 1960s." If women were underrepresented in Chicano theater, then homosexuals were almost completely ignored. According to Huerta, "Within the community's patriarchal system of values, fueled by the Roman Catholic Church, gay and lesbian issues were not discussed openly in teatro, except through comic characters." Although later El Teatro would grapple with broader social issues such as the Vietnam War and educational opportunities, the Chicano movement did remain somewhat separate from other forms of activism of the time, including feminism and gay rights.

Los Vendidos signaled a turning point for Valdez and El Teatro Campesino. Having just moved away from *actos* specifically written for audiences of migrant workers, Valdez wanted to expand his reach into other social issues Chicanos faced. Rife with social satire, *Los Vendidos* directly addresses "the issues of the sellout and stereotyping in a humorous way, demonstrating the stereotypes and prejudices of people within and without" the Chicano community, writes Huerta; "it also demonstrates a subversive, economic act perpetrated against the System, however metaphorically."

The satirical nature of the *actos* is what allows for such penetrating insight into sensitive issues. In a review of *Los Vendidos* for *Theatre Journal*, Edit Villarreal calls the play a "classic acto" that masterfully utilizes "broad satire" to make its point about racial stereotyping. Huerta asserts that the stereotypes portrayed in *Los Vendidos* "are constructions of the dominant society (Hollywood imagery at its worst) even as they are also reflections of the colonized subject's internalized self-hatred." Thus, Valdez not only shows the audience how they are viewed by Anglo-Americans but also holds up a mirror to remind them that they, too, are responsible for the broad assumptions made about Chicanos.

CRITICISM

Kristy Blackmon

Blackmon is an independent writer who specializes in literature. In the following essay, she uses the theory of dialectical materialism to examine Luis Valdez's play Los Vendidos *and its role in social change for Chicanos in the late 1960s.*

WHAT
DO I READ
NEXT?

- *The American Dream in African American, Asian American, and Hispanic American Drama: August Wilson, Frank Chin, and Luis Valdez*, written by Tsui-fen Jiang in 2009, examines the concept of the American dream within the theatrical expressions of multiple minority groups. Three plays are examined for identity themes, cultural struggles, and the desire for minorities to find their own place within American culture.

- *Zoot Suit, and Other Plays*, published in 1992 by Luis Valdez, contains three of his later plays—*Zoot Suit, Bandido!* and *I Don't Have to Show You No Stinking Badges*—and includes an introduction by Jorge Huerta.

- *Decolonial Voices: Chicana and Chicano Cultural Studies in the 21st Century*, edited by Arturo J. Aldama and Naomi Quiñonez, is a 2002 collection of essays that focuses on interactions between Chicano artists and other groups both nationally and internationally and places specific emphasis on the role of the feminine voice in Chicano cultural productions.

- David Reyes and Tom Waldman expanded and updated their 1998 book *Land of a Thousand Dances: Chicano Rock 'n' Roll from Southern California* in 2009. The book chronicles the roots and accomplishments of Chicanos in rock music originating in California, from Richie Valens to Los Lobos. They examine how barrio culture influenced Mexican rock and roll's developments from a historical and cultural standpoint.

- *Mexican WhiteBoy* (2008), by Matt de la Peña, is the fictional story of a half-white, half-Mexican sixteen-year-old named Danny Lopez. In his American high school, he is ignored because he is considered Mexican. However, when he visits his family in Mexico over the summer, he finds that he cannot fit in there, either. This young-adult novel is a moving depiction of one teen's struggle to find a cultural identity that incorporates two very different worlds.

- *I Am the Darker Brother: An Anthology of Modern Poems by African Americans*, by Arnold Adoff, was originally published in 1968 and was one of the first poetry anthologies to specifically address the African American struggle for social acceptance. In 1997, Adoff expanded the collection to include newer works, essays, notes, and biographies.

The 1960s were a time of great social upheaval and change in America. Social revolution was everywhere, from minority struggles for equal rights to student protests of the Vietnam War and beyond. There existed a majority voice in mainstream American society—that of the Anglo middle class—against which any competing ideology or belief system was held as seditious and "other." The social philosophy of Karl Marx and Friedrich Engels called dialectical materialism provides an ideal framework upon which to construct a theory of why these minority social groups were able to enact change in American society.

Paying specific attention to the Chicano movement, we can see how Luis Valdez's El Teatro Campesino and the Chicano renaissance it inspired were the result of conflicting social identities that could no longer exist simultaneously without alterations in the cultural conditions. *Los Vendidos* is an example of dialectical materialism in action in that it reflects the material conditions in which Chicanos of the 1960s lived, illustrates the tension inherent in those conditions, and pushes toward societal change in American material culture.

"The issue of identity was and is central to most Chicano theatre precisely because of the marginalized position of its participants, both on- and offstage," Jorge Huerta wrote in his 2002 article "When Sleeping Giants Awaken:

> *LOS VENDIDOS* IS AN EXAMPLE OF DIALECTICAL MATERIALISM IN ACTION IN THAT IT REFLECTS THE MATERIAL CONDITIONS IN WHICH CHICANOS OF THE 1960S LIVED, ILLUSTRATES THE TENSION INHERENT IN THOSE CONDITIONS, AND PUSHES TOWARD SOCIETAL CHANGE IN AMERICAN MATERIAL CULTURE."

Chicano Theatre in the 1960s." Mexican Americans in the 1960s faced many of the same issues that African Americans and other minority groups faced in their searches for identity. What does it mean to be "Chicano"? Conversely, what does it mean to be "American," and to what extent must the Chicano change in order to be considered American? Finally, does becoming American mean that the Chicano must give up all identification with a Mexican ethnic heritage?

Ethnic identity is not easily defined. C. W. E. Bigsby articulates the problem in his book *A Critical Introduction to Twentieth-Century Drama: Beyond Broadway*: "Pushed to the periphery of the American political, economic and cultural system [the Chicano] has found himself asserting his rights to be included in the very society whose hostility has led to his exclusion." That is, Chicanos had to find a way to both stand up for their individuality, including their Mexican heritage, and also demand to be recognized as American citizens.

One of the problems Chicanos faced in this identity struggle was the issue of how to combat stereotypical depictions of Mexican Americans within mainstream culture, because in order to prove them wrong, the stereotypes first had to be recognized. Therefore, Chicanos had to acknowledge the different ways in which they were portrayed and admit to certain consistencies before being able to dismiss the stereotype as a shallow and insufficient picture of their identity. Further, as Valdez shows in *Los Vendidos*, the varying stereotypes of Mexican Americans were in many ways radically different from one another, having little in common beyond the color of their skin.

This phenomenon was not fully constructed by the Anglo-American majority. Huerta points out that "Chicano" is neither a Spanish nor an English term: "To call oneself 'Chicano' meant that you were neither Mexican nor 'American' but, rather, someone who recognized the various forms of oppression your communities were suffering." Chicanos looked down on those who identified themselves as Mexican Americans, such as Miss Jimenez in *Los Vendidos*, considering them traitors to their race. In turn, Mexican Americans scorned Chicanos for being troublemakers.

Even those who identified themselves as Chicano further divided themselves with sub-identities, as illustrated by Valdez. A pachuco held that he was in fact different from a campesino, for example. Valdez's aim was to unite all Chicanos under the umbrella of La Raza, or "The Race," regardless of where the individual stood within that Chicano social structure. Biliana C. S. Ambrecht and Harry P. Pachon describe in their 1974 study "Ethnic Political Mobilization in a Mexican American Community" that self-stereotyping is not uncommon in any minority culture. It allows the minority to show pride in their ethnicity and individuality. However, it also provides ample fodder for those who would discriminate against a "type."

With *Los Vendidos*, Valdez attacked this dilemma head on. In his essay "Actos," Valdez says that "the teatro archetypes symbolize the desire for unity and group identity" among Chicanos. By exposing and directly addressing stereotypes of Chicanos, Valdez and El Teatro wanted to show the absurdity of these stereotypes through the type of satire unique to the *acto* of the Chicano renaissance. He ridicules each Chicano stereotype without discrimination, though the most vitriolic of jokes are made at the expense of Miss Jimenez, the ultimate sellout. In his 1967 interview with Beth Bagby, Valdez says that the comedy works as a vehicle for making social observations because all of the stereotypes are easily recognizable as shallow reflections of real material conditions. "I think that is why farm workers laugh," he explains. "Not because it's funny, but because they recognize that reality. They've been caught."

By recognizing the existence of the stereotypes and admitting they have a basis in reality (as do all stereotypes) in a comedic way, Valdez took some of the sting out of them. *Los Vendidos* acknowledges the existence of campesinos, pachucos, revolucionarios, and assimilated Mexican Americans while simultaneously asserting the validity of their inclusion in American society. Thus, the play takes the conflicting material conditions for Chicanos in the America of the 1960s and shows that they simply cannot exist at the same time: Chicanos cannot be marginalized members of society while also receiving the privileges of fully fledged citizens. Mainstream American society wanted to deny them fundamental rights due to their lack of "Americanness," so to speak; Chicanos wanted the same rights as other Americans without having to completely ignore and lose their ethnic heritage. One of those competing scenarios had to lose, and Valdez was determined to use the theater as his weapon to ensure victory for equal rights for Chicanos.

The starkness, bluntness, humor, and honesty with which he expressed this passion led to the creation of the *acto* and served as the impetus for the entire Chicano renaissance. Lee Stacy articulates this in his 2003 book *Mexico and the United States*: "The central aim of Chicano theater was to form a collective identity among oppressed people of Mexican origin living in the United States. Chicano theater called for radical transformations in both the arts and in society."

The ultimate goal for Valdez was for Chicanos to rally under the one identity of La Raza. They could no longer attempt to identify themselves as either Mexican or American. Equally impossible was the notion of identifying as some hybrid of Mexican and American. The social conditions in which he produced his work clearly could not sustain both national identities; therefore, in accordance with dialectical materialism, a new identity had to be created and solidified: that of the Chicano, a member of La Raza living in the United States. Only when this identity was established could Valdez then move on to address the inequalities faced by the Chicano community.

As long as their minority group was considered unequal in the political spectrum, there was no way to make the legislative changes necessary to provide them with equal rights; Chicanos had to be recognized as part of the economic and political structure of America first. Speaking of the Chicano communities of the 1960s, Awam Amkpa states in his 2004 review of Harry J. Elam's book *Taking It to the Streets: Social Protest Theater of Luis Valdez and Amiri Baraka*

that "the causes their social protest theatres articulate center around race as markers of class subordination." It was through the medium of theater that Valdez and El Teatro aimed to motivate the Chicano political base into becoming a valid voice in the conversation about equal rights.

In dialectical materialism, situations are always in a state of constant tension leading to change. When two material social conditions conflict, a struggle ensues, and a victor is established. However, within this victory there is always and inevitably another inherent tension, another conflict, which leads to another struggle and another change, and so on. This is Marx and Engels's theory of social and cultural development. Though not specifically articulated as such, this theory further validates, for example, Valdez's move in 1967 away from solely performing in the fields for the benefit of the unionization movement of Cesar Chavez. His *actos* had assisted in resolving the conflict between oppressed workers and the growers that exploited them, and history has proven that El Teatro Campesino was successful in its efforts with the UFW.

With that success, however, came another challenge that prompted a shift of focus away from only the campesinos and onto the Chicano population as a whole. *Actos* such as *Los Vendidos* then engaged in another struggle, the struggle for Chicano identity as outlined above. In the late 1960s and early 1970s, widespread legislative change drastically altered the material conditions for minority groups such as Chicanos, and El Teatro could claim at least some credit for that victory. Inherent in that victory, however, was still more tension, more conflicts to be resolved, leading to further social change in a never-ending process of cultural evolution.

Thus, Valdez has had ongoing inspiration to continue his work of expression through theater and film on behalf of Chicano social issues. The role of Chicanos in Vietnam and the demand for cultural studies at the university level and equal education in the public-school sector were focuses of the 1970s. By the 1980s, the role of women had become a major focus of Chicano theater. Always there is the ceaseless battle over immigration legislation, an issue this nation is still hotly debating today. However, the fact that there will always be struggles on behalf of the Chicano people does not negate their victories.

Eric Garcia begins to lead a revolution, shouting "Viva la raza!" (*Richard Thornton | Shutterstock.com*)

Chicanos, Latinos, Mexican Americans, and Hispanics now have a strong and loud political voice that could not be heard in 1965 when Valdez first approached Chavez and Delores Huerta with the idea for a farmworkers' theater. The political goals of the Mexican American community continue to grow in ambition to provide voters with more Chicano candidates, generate support among non-Chicanos, support new legislation, and commit to community activism. The struggle only gets stronger, the voices of Chicanos only get louder, and the victories only get greater the longer the Chicano dialectic continues. As Valdez told Bagby, "You end with a bang, and certainly with hope. You show some kind of victory, even though victory is not immediately forthcoming."

Source: Kristy Blackmon, Critical Essay on *Los Vendidos*, in *Drama for Students*, Gale, Cengage Learning, 2012.

Ed Morales

In the following excerpt, Morales challenges Valdez's continuing influence in Chicano theater.

An outspoken new generation of Hispanic artists is widening the trail Luis Valdez blazed through Southern California.

Driving into San Juan Bautista, an old Spanish mission town about two hours south of San Francisco, is a little like going backwards in time. Having rushed past the Stanford Linear Accelerator Center (or SLAC, as it's known to particle physicists) and the bustling Silicon Valley megalopolis San Jose, the road begins to narrow and you slip into a valley, past an historic mission church and into the gravel driveway of a former produce packing shed that since 1981 has housed Luis Valdez's El Teatro Campesino. "One of the reasons we chose this site," grins Valdez, sporting his familiar mustache and chomping on his trademark cigar, "is that we could see whoever was approaching for miles."

Valdez is implying that his earlier days as a countercultural force made it imperative that he watch his back, but the impressive list of corporate sponsors in the program for 1990's Feathered Serpent Awards, given in celebration of the company's 25th anniversary, leaves no doubt that Valdez is an established survivor. From his brilliant self-described "synthesis of Brecht and Cantinflas" which produced the early analogs of commedia dell'arte that served as agitprop for

BUT AS MUCH AS VALDEZ HAS MEANT TO
CHICANO THEATRE'S ORIGIN, HOW MUCH DOES HE
HAVE A HOLD ON ITS FUTURE?"

the United Farm Workers' Union, through his landmark accomplishments with *Zoot Suit* and the feature film *La Bamba*, Valdez has no peer in the history of Chicano arts. But as much as Valdez has meant to Chicano theatre's origin, how much does he have a hold on its future?

Within two weeks of my arrival in California, two separate articles appear in the alternative *SF Weekly* containing disparaging comments about Valdez from Chicano artists. Richard Montoya, Valdez's godson and the iconoclastic leader of the San Francisco-bred, L.A.-based comedy troupe Culture Clash, complains that Valdez's recent PBS-TV special, *La Pastorela*, was a "piece of shit," proof that "Luis has lost his edge." And lesbian feminist playwright Cherrie Moraga, whose new play *Heroes and Saints* is being produced by Brava! for Women in the Arts in San Francisco, says flatly, "I have a great deal of respect for the origins of Luis Valdez's work, but I have never respected his sexism."

Moraga says this despite knowing that the two plays that Teatro Campesino had just sent out on tour were written by women—Evelina Fernandez and Josefina Lopez. While Moraga dismisses this fact as an exception, Valdez prefers to think of such internecine struggles as family quarrels. Rene Yanez, who works at San Francisco's Mexican Museum developing stage projects and who helped to start Culture Clash, explains it this way: "I think when Valdez came out with *Pastorela*, a lot of the criticism was a generational thing. People wanted something more nitty-gritty. Luis is in the forefront—and young people are impatient, they want him to do it for them sometimes. They want a lot of productions, a lot of theatre pieces, a lot of movies—and they want to get hired."

In fact, Valdez is forward-looking in the way he always has been. As one of the participants in the '60s gestation of "El Plan de Aztlan," a Chicano nationalist document which called for

renewed racial pride through recognition of the indigenous nation of Aztlan—whose borders stretched north into California, New Mexico and Arizona—Valdez likes to project the future by reaching back into the ancient past. "It's possible to be Mayan and live in a jet-age society, in a modern, sleek, sophisticated 20th-century world," he contends, as if to explain the poster that hangs in his office picturing a Meso-American figure typing away at a computer keyboard.

Valdez's passion for ancient teachings may have taken hold during his celebrated 1973 encounter in San Juan Bautista with members of Peter Brook's Paris-based Centre for International Theatre Research, a meeting which attempted to merge ninth-century Persian Sufism with the UFW class struggle. "They were birds, we were serpents," Valdez said at the time. "We needed desperately to fly, to put wings on our serpent." The constant identity struggle among Latino thinkers involves recognizing their indigenous past, so Valdez plunged into Mayan philosophy.

"Mayan understanding has sort of fed me philosophically. Once upon a time I was a math major—that's how I got to college, I had a scholarship in math. The mathematical basis of Mayan cosmology is something that's universal," says Valdez. Impatient with the propensity of theatre critics to view his work as agitprop—a tendency which he said diminished in importance in 1967, when he left the UFW—Valdez has developed the concept of Theatre of the Sphere as his central technique.

"The Mayan concept of zero was not two-dimensional, not just a ring—it was three-dimensional, so it's more like a sphere," explains Valdez. "And the sphere is both empty and full. That's the most basic state of life that there is. It's a sphere of potentiality. The very space that we articulate with our bodies is a sphere. Actors need to know this so that they know how to function within it. Everything is a sphere. The joints all circulate. And your head is one and your eyes are one. And when you walk, you're really rolling."

Despite his methodological breakthroughs, Valdez is involved in projects that have taken him away from theatre. He is contemplating the long-term development plan for Rancho las Americas, a 50-acre site on the rolling hills behind the existing Teatro Campesino building. "We want to build several buildings that will have state-of-the-art facilities for theatre, our offices and video-production space. The group has ventured into video in a big way. Last year when we did the *Pastorela* we turned into a small production company for the duration, and it was a good test of the capacity of the group."

When I interviewed him, Valdez was in the casting phase with New Line Cinema for a screenplay he and his wife Lupe had completed about the life of Frida Kahlo. Several months later, in late August, the revelation that Valdez had cast Italian-American Laura San Giacomo as Kahlo sparked angry protests by the Chicano theatre community. These protests created "an ugly mood of creative suppression," according to an El Teatro Campesino press release, which prompted Valdez both to shelve the movie project and postpone the world premiere of his new play, *Bandido! The American Melodrama of Tiburcio Vasquez, Notorious California Bandit.*

Although he is arguably the Latino director with the most credibility in Hollywood, it has been a difficult road for Valdez since his 1987 success with *La Bamba*, and the demands of his film career have interfered with his playwriting. "The playwright in me is a little frustrated," admits Valdez, "because the screenwriter is too busy to pay much attention to writing new plays, although I've had one cooking now for about seven years. It's a 'Major Work'—I don't know what it will be, but I can feel it. I persist in film because it's such a powerful medium, and in some ways it's a more democratic medium than the theatre. We've always done popular theatre and have taken it where the people are, but the professional theatre is another question altogether. I think that the professional theatre is still very white, urban and middle-class."

This spring Teatro Campesino went on the road for the first time since 1980. I managed to catch up with the tour in San Diego. The two works, *How Else Am I Supposed to Know I'm Alive?* by Evelina Fernandez (who was Edward James Olmos's co-star in his recent film *American Me*) and Josefina Lopez's *Simply Maria*, were staged before a full house in a San Diego theatre. Fernandez's play is a humorous exercise in which middle-aged Chicana women discuss their long-repressed sexuality; while *Simply Maria* is a wildly funny portrait of a young Chicana who aspires to leave the archaic mindset of her immigrant parents while still retaining a strong sense of her ethnicity. At 23, Lopez shows remarkable wit and understanding of absurdist humor, as well as the technique of using a media-

saturated postmodern narrative. "Josefina has gotten very good notices," says Valdez, "But she's young, and I don't know if it's that good to receive a lot of attention at that age. I'd have hated to have that much pressure on me when I was that age." . . .

Source: Ed Morales, "Shadowing Valdez," in *American Theatre*, Vol. 9, No. 7, November 1992, pp. 14–19.

Luis Valdez

In the following essay written in 1970, Valdez attempts to define uniquely Chicano theater.

What is Chicano theatre? It is theatre as beautiful, rasquachi, human, cosmic, broad, deep, tragic, comic, as the life of La Raza itself. At its high point Chicano theatre is religion—the huelguistas de Delano praying at the shrine of the Virgen de Guadalupe, located in the rear of an old station wagon parked across the road from DiGiorgio's camp #4; at its low point, it is a cuento or a chiste told somewhere in the recesses of the barrio, puro pedo.

Chicano theatre, then, is first a reaffirmation of LIFE. That is what all theatre is supposed to be, of course; but the limp, superficial, gringo seco productions in the "professional" American theatre (and the college and university drama departments that serve it) are so antiseptic, they are antibiotic (anti-life). The characters and life situations emerging from our little teatros are too real, too full of sudor, sangre and body smells to be boxed in. Audience participation is no cute production trick with us; it is a pre-established, pre-assumed privilege. "¡Que le suenen la campanita!"

Defining Chicano theatre is a little like defining a Chicano car. We can start with a low-riders' cool Merc or a campesino's banged-up Chevi, and describe the various paint jobs, hub caps, dents, taped windows, Virgin on the dashboard, etc. that define the car as particularly Raza. Underneath all the trimmings, however, is an unmistakable product of Detroit, an extension of General Motors. Consider now a theatre that uses the basic form, the vehicle, created by Broadway or Hollywood: that is, the "realistic" play. Actually, this type of play was created in Europe, but where French, German, and Scandinavian playwrights went beyond realism and naturalism long ago, commercial gabacho theatre refuses to let go. It reflects a characteristic "American" hang-up on the material aspect of human existence. European theatre, by contrast,

PACHUCOS, CAMPESINOS, LOW-RIDERS, PINTOS, CHAVALONAS, FAMILIAS, CUÑADOS, TÍOS, PRIMOS, MEXICAN-AMERICANS, ALL THE HUMAN ESSENCE OF THE BARRIO, IS STARTING TO APPEAR IN THE MIRROR OF OUR THEATRE."

has been influenced since around 1900 by the unrealistic, formal rituals of Oriental theatre.

What does Oriental and European theatre have to do with teatro Chicano? Nothing, except that we are talking about a theatre that is particularly our own, not another imitation of the gabacho. If we consider our origins, say the theatre of the Mayans or the Aztecs, we are talking about something totally unlike the realistic play and more Chinese or Japanese in spirit. *Kabuki*, as a matter of fact, started long ago as something like our actos and evolved over two centuries into the highly exacting artform it is today; but it still contains pleberías. It evolved from and still belongs to el pueblo japonés.

In Mexico, before the coming of the white man, the greatest examples of total theatre were, of course, the human sacrifices. *El Rabinal Achi*, one of the few surviving pieces of indigenous theatre, describes the sacrifice of a courageous guerrillero, who rather than dying passively on the block is granted the opportunity to fight until he is killed. It is a tragedy, naturally, but it is all the more transcendent because of the guerrillero's identification, through sacrifice, with God. The only "set" such a drama-ritual needed was a stone block; nature took care of the rest.

But since the Conquest, Mexico's theatre, like its society, has had to imitate Europe and, in recent times, the United States. In the same vein, Chicanos in Spanish classes are frequently involved in productions of plays by Lope de Vega, Calderón de la Barca, Tirso de Molina and other classic playwrights. Nothing is wrong with this, but it does obscure the indio fountains of Chicano culture. Is Chicano theatre, in turn, to be nothing but an imitation of gabacho playwrights, with barrio productions of racist works by Eugene O'Neill and Tennessee Williams? Will

Broadway produce a Chicano version of *Hello, Dolly* now that it has produced a Black one?

The nature of Chicanismo calls for a revolutionary turn in the arts as well as in society. Chicano theatre must be revolutionary in technique as well as content. It must be popular, subject to no other critics except the pueblo itself; but it must also educate the pueblo toward an appreciation of *social change*, on and off the stage.

It is particularly important for teatro Chicano to draw a distinction between what is theatre and what is reality. A demonstration with a thousand Chicanos, all carrying flags and picket signs, shouting CHICANO POWER! is not the revolution. It is theatre about the revolution. The people must act in *reality*, not on stage (which could be anywhere, even a sidewalk) in order to achieve real change. The Raza gets excited, simón, but unless the demonstration evolves into a street battle (which has not yet happened but it is possible), it is basically a lot of emotion with very little political power, as Chicanos have discovered by demonstrating, picketing and shouting before school boards, police departments and stores to no avail.

Such guerrilla theatre passing as a demonstration has its uses, of course. It is agit-prop theatre, as white radicals used to call it in the '30's: agitation and propaganda. It helps to stimulate and sustain the mass strength of a crowd. Hitler was very effective with this kind of theatre, from the swastika to the Wagneresque stadium at Nuremburg. At the other end of the political spectrum, the Huelga march to Sacramento in 1966 was pure guerrilla theatre. The red and black thunderbird flags of the UFWOC (then NFWA) and the standard of the Virgen de Guadalupe challenged the bleak sterility of Highway 99. Its emotional impact was irrefutable. Its political power was somewhat less. Governor Brown was not at the state capitol, and only one grower, Schenley Industries, signed a contract. Later contracts have been won through a brilliant balance between highly publicized events, which gained public support (marches, César's fast, visits by Reuther, Robert and Ted Kennedy, etc.), and actual hard-ass, door to door, worker to worker organizing. Like Delano, other aspects of the Chicano movement must remember what is teatro and what is reality.

But beyond the mass struggle of La Raza in the fields and barrios of America, there is an internal struggle in the very corazón of our people. That struggle, too, calls for revolutionary change. Our belief in God, the church, the social role of women, these must be subject to examination and redefinition on some kind of public forum. And that again means teatro. Not a teatro composed of actos or agit-pop, but a teatro of ritual, of music, of beauty and spiritual sensitivity. This type of theatre will require real dedication; it may, indeed, require a couple of generations of Chicanos devoted to the use of the theatre as an instrument in the evolution of our people.

The teatros in existence today reflect the most intimate understanding of everyday events in the barrios from which they have emerged. But if Aztlán is to become a reality, then we as Chicanos must not be reluctant to act nationally. To think in national terms: politically, economically and spiritually. We must destroy the deadly regionalism that keeps us apart. The concept of a national theatre for La Raza is intimately related to our evolving nationalism in Aztlán.

Consider a *Teatro Nacional de Aztlán* that performs with the same skill and prestige as the Ballet Folklórico de Méico (not for gabachos, however, but for the Raza). Such a teatro could carry the message of La Raza into Latin America, Europe, Japan, Africa—in short, all over the world. It would draw its strength from all the small teatros in the barrios, in terms of people and their plays, songs, designs; and it would give back funds, training and augmented strength of national unity. One season the teatro members would be on tour with the Teatro Nacional; the next season they would be back in the barrio sharing their skills and experience. It would accommodate about 150 altogether, with 20–25 in the National and the rest spread out in various parts of Aztlán, working with the Campesino, the Urbano, the Mestizo, the Piojo, etc.

Above all, the national organization of teatros Chicanos would be self-supporting and independent, meaning no government grants. The corazón de La Raza cannot be revolutionalized on a grant from Uncle Sam. Though many of the teatros, including El Campesino, have been born out of pre-established political groups, thus making them harbingers of that particular group's viewpoint, news and political prejudices, there is yet a need for independence

for the following reasons: objectivity, artistic competence, survival. El Teatro Campesino was born in the huelga, but the very huelga would have killed it, if we had not moved sixty miles to the north of Delano. A struggle like the huelga needs every person it can get to serve its immediate goals in order to survive; the teatro, as well as the clinic, service center and newspaper, being less important at the moment of need than the survival of the union, were always losing people to the grape boycott. When it became clear to us that the UFWOC would succeed and continue to grow, we felt it was time for us to move and to begin speaking about things beyond the huelga: Vietnam, the barrio, racial discrimination, etc.

The teatros must never get away from La Raza. Without the palomilla sitting there, laughing, crying and sharing whatever is onstage, the teatros will dry up and die. If the raza will not come to the theatre, then the theatre must go to the raza.

This, in the long run, will determine the shape, style, content, spirit and form of el teatro Chicano. Pachucos, campesinos, low-riders, pintos, chavalonas, familias, cuñados, tíos, primos, Mexican-Americans, all the human essence of the barrio, is starting to appear in the mirror of our theatre. With them come the joys, sufferings, disappointments and aspirations of our gente. We challenge Chicanos to become involved in the art, the life style, the political and religious act of doing teatro.

Source: Luis Valdez, "Notes on Chicano Theatre," in *Luis Valdez—Early Works: Actos, Bernabé and Pensamiento Serpentino*, Arte Público Press, 1990, pp. 6–10.

David Savran

In the following excerpt, Savran discusses with Valdez the development of his drama and the forces that have had an impact on his work and career.

One month into the 1965 Delano grape strike, which solidified the power of the United Farm Workers, Luis Valdez met with a group of union volunteers and devised a short comic skit to help persuade reluctant workers to join the strike. He hung signs reading *Huelgista* (striker) on two men and *Esquirol* (scab) on a third. The two *Huelgistas* starting yelling at the *Esquirol* and the audience laughed. Thus began Valdez's career as founder and director of El Teatro Campesino and author of a diverse and yet deeply interconnected collection of plays.

> IN THE 1970s VALDEZ DEVELOPED A THIRD DRAMATIC FORM, THE *CORRIDO* (BALLAD), WHICH, LIKE THE *MITO*, IS INTENDED TO CLAIM A CULTURAL HERITAGE RATHER THAN INSPIRE POLITICAL REVOLUTION."

For two years the Teatro remained actively involved in the union's struggle, performing in meeting halls, fields and strike camps. Drawing on *commedia dell'arte* and elements of Mexican folk culture, Valdez created *actos* (acts), short comic sketches designed to raise political awareness and inspire action. *Los Vendidos* (*The Sellouts*, 1967), for example, attacks the stereotyping of Chicanos and government-sanctioned tokenism. A Chicano secretary from Governor Reagan's office goes to Honest Sancho's Used Mexican Lot to buy "a Mexican type" for the front office. She examines several models—a farm worker, a young *pachuco* (swaggering street kid), a *revolucionario* and finally a Mexican-American in a business suit who sings "God Bless America" and drinks dry martinis. As soon as she buys the last, he malfunctions and begins shouting "*Viva la huelga*," while the others chase her away and divide the money.

At the same time that he was writing and performing agitprop for the Farm Workers, Valdez turned to examine his pre-Columbian heritage, the sophisticated religion and culture of the ancient Mayans. The Teatro settled in two houses in San Juan Bautista in 1971, where they farmed according to Mayan practices and Valdez developed the second of his dramatic forms, the *mito* (myth), which characteristically takes the form of a parable based on Indian ritual. For Valdez the *mito* is an attempt to integrate political activism and religious ritual—to tie "the cause of social justice" to "the cause of everything else in our universe." *Bernabe* (1970) is a parable about the prostitution of the land. It opposes the pure, mystical love for La Tierra (the Earth) by the mentally retarded *campesino* of the title against its simple possession by landowners and banks. At the play's end Bernabe is visited by La Luna (the Moon), dressed as a 1942

pachuco; La Tierra; and El Sol (the Sun), in the guise of Tonatiuh, the Aztec sun god. In a final apotheosis, the "cosmic idiot" is made whole and united with La Tierra, at last revealed to be Coatlicue, the Aztec goddess of life, death and rebirth.

In the 1970s Valdez developed a third dramatic form, the *corrido* (ballad), which, like the *mito*, is intended to claim a cultural heritage rather than inspire political revolution. The *corrido* is Valdez's reinvention of the musical, based on Mexican-American folk ballads telling tales of love, death and heroism. *Zoot Suit* (1978) is perhaps his best known *corrido* and was the first Hispanic play to reach Broadway, after a long and successful run in Los Angeles. Mixing narrative, action, song and dance, it is the story of members of a zoot suit-clad *pachuco* gang of the forties, their wrongful conviction for murder and the "Zoot Suit Riots" that followed. His 1983 piece, *Corridos*, featuring songs in Spanish and dialogue in English, has been videotaped for Public Television.

Valdez's most recent play is the comedy *I Don't Have to Show You No Stinking Badges*, which has been acclaimed in Los Angeles and San Diego. A play about the political and existential implications of acting, both in theatre and society, it takes place in a television studio in which is set the suburban southern California home of Buddy and Connie Villa, two assimilated, middle-class Chicanos, "the silent bit king and queen of Hollywood." Their son, Sonny, who has just dropped out of Harvard Law School and has returned home with his Asian-American girlfriend, tries to find work in Hollywood, but despairs at having to become one of the many "actors faking our roles to fit into the great American success story." With Pirandellian sleight of hand, Valdez uses a director to interrupt the scene (which it turns out is an episode of a new sitcom, *Badges!*) in order to debate the social function of art. "This isn't reality," Sonny protests. But the director assures him, "Frankly, reality's a big boring pain in the ass. We're in the entertainment business. Laughs, Sonny, that's more important than reality."

Although closer to mainstream comedy than mystery play, Valdez's exploration of role-playing represents more a development of than a break with the technique of his early *mitos*. Both *Bernabe* and *Badges* eschew naturalism in favor of a more theatrically bold style, the earlier play drawing upon a naive formal model and the later a sophisticated one. *Bernabe*, in keeping with the conventions of religious drama, opts for a simple, mystical ending, while *Badges* refuses the pat resolution of television sitcom by offering several alternative endings. Both examine the spiritual implications of material choices; both are celebratory despite their socially critical vision. This continuity over a fifteen-year period attests to the clarity of Valdez's intention: to put the Chicano experience on stage in all of its political, cultural and religious complexity; and to examine the interrelationship between the political and the metaphysical, between historically determined oppressive structures and man's transhistorical desire for faith and freedom.

[David Savran]: How did you get interested in theatre?

[Luis Valdez]: There's a story that's almost apocryphal, I've repeated it so many times now. It's nevertheless true. I got hooked on the theatre when I was six. I was born into a family of migrant farm workers and shortly after World War II we were in a cotton camp in the San Joaquin valley. The season was over, it was starting to rain, but we were still there because my dad's little Ford pickup truck had broken down and was up on blocks and there was no way for us to get out. Life was pretty meager then and we survived by fishing in a river and sharing staples like beans, rice and flour. And the bus from the local school used to come in from a place called Stratford—irony of ironies, except it was on the San Joaquin River [laughs].

I took my lunch to school in a little brown paper bag—which was a valuable commodity because there were still paper shortages in 1946. One day as school let out and the kids were rushing toward the bus, I found my bag missing and went around in a panic looking for it. The teacher saw me and said, "Are you looking for your bag?" and I said, "Yes." She said, "Come here," and she took me in the little back room and there, on a table, were some things laid out that completely changed my perception of the universe. She'd torn the bag up and placed it in water. I was horrified. But then she showed me the next bowl. It was a paste. She was making papier-mâché. A little farther down the line, she'd taken the paper and put it on a clay mold of a face of a monkey, and finally there was a finished product, unpainted but nevertheless definitely a monkey. And she said, "I'm making masks."

I was amazed, shocked in an exhilarating way, that she could do this with paper and paste. As it turned out, she was making masks for the school play. I didn't know what a play was, but she explained and said, "We're having tryouts." I came back the next week all enthused and auditioned for a part and got a leading role as a monkey. The play was about Christmas in the jungle. I was measured for a costume that was better than the clothes I was wearing at the time, certainly more colorful. The next few weeks were some of the most exciting in my short life. After seeing the stage transformed into a jungle and after all the excitement of the preparations—I doubt that it was as elaborate as my mind remembers it now—my dad got the truck fixed and a week before the show was to go on, we moved away. So I never got to be in the Christmas play.

That left an unfillable gap, a vacuum that I've been pouring myself into for the last forty-one years. From then on, it was just a question of evolution. Later I got into puppets. I was a ventriloquist, believe it or not. In 1956 when I was in high school, I became a regular on a local television program. I was still living in a *barrio* with my family, a place in San Jose called Sal Si Puedes—Get Out if You Can. It was one of those places with dirt streets and chuckholes, a terrible place. But I was on television, right? [laughs], and I wrote my own stuff and it established me in high school.

By the time I graduated, I had pretty well decided that writing was my consuming passion. Coming from my background, I didn't feel right about going to my parents and saying, "I want to be a playwright." So I started college majoring in math and physics. Then one day late in my freshman year I walked to the drama department and decided, "The hell with it, I'm going to go with this." I changed majors to English, with an emphasis on playwriting, and that's what I did for the rest of my college days.

In 1964 I wrote and directed my first full-length play, *The Shrunken Head of Pancho Villa*. People saw it and gave me a lot of encouragement. I joined the San Francisco Mime Troupe the following year, and then in '65 joined the Farm Workers Union and essentially started El Teatro Campesino. The evolution has been continuous since then, both of the company and of my styles of playwriting.

During that period, what was your most important theatre training—college, the Mime Troupe?

It's all important. It's a question of layering. I love to layer things, I think they achieve a certain richness—I'm speaking now about "the work." But life essentially evolves that way, too. Those years of studying theatre history were extremely important. I connected with a number of ancient playwrights in a very direct way. Plautus was a revelation, he spoke directly to me. I took four years of Latin so I was able to read him in Latin. There are clever turns of phrases that I grew to appreciate and, in my own way, was able almost to reproduce in Spanish. The central figure of the wily servant in classical Roman drama—Greek also—became a standard feature of my work with El Teatro Campesino. The striker was basically a wily servant. I'd also been exposed to *commedia dell'arte* through the San Francisco Mime Troupe, with its stock characters, the Brighellas, Arlecchinos and Pantalones. I saw a direct link between these *commedia* types and the types I had to work with in order to put together a Farm Workers' theatre. I chose to do an outdoor, robust theatre of types. I figured it hit the reality.

My second phase was the raw, elemental education I got, performing under the most primitive conditions in the farm labor camps and on flatbed trucks. In doing so, I dealt with the basic elements of drama: structure, language, music, movement. The first education was literary, the second practical. We used to put on stuff every week, under all kinds of circumstances: outdoors, indoors, under the threat of violence. There was a period during the grape strike in '67 when we had become an effective weapon within the Farm Workers and were considered enough of a threat that a rumor flashed across the strike camp that somebody was after me with a high-powered rifle. We went out to the labor camp anyway, but I was really sweating it. I don't think I've sweated any performance since then. It changed my perspective on what I was doing. Was this really worth it? Was it a life-and-death issue? Of course it was for me at the time, and still is. But I learned that in a very direct and practical way. I was beaten and kicked and jailed, also in the sixties, essentially for doing theatre. I knew the kind of theatre we were doing was a political act, it was art and politics. At least I hope I wasn't being kicked for the art [laughs].

What other playwrights had a major impact on you in those days?

Brecht looms huge in my orientation. I discovered Brecht in college, from an intellectual perspective. That was really the only way—no one was doing Brecht back in 1961. When Esslin's book *Brecht: The Man and His Work*, came out in 1960, I was working in the library, so I had first dibs on all the new books. Brecht to me had been only a name. But this book opened up Brecht and I started reading all his plays and his theories, which I subscribed to immediately. I continue to use his alienation effect to this day. I don't think audiences like it too much, but I like it because it seems to me an essential feature of the experience of theatre.

Theatre should reflect an audience back on itself. You should think as well as feel. Still, there's no underestimating the power of emotional impact—I understand better now how ideas are conveyed and exchanged on a beam of emotion. I think Brecht began to discover that in his later works and integrated it. I've integrated a lot of feeling into my works, but I still love ideas. I still love communicating a concept, an abstraction. That's the mathematician in me.

How has your way of writing changed over the years?

What has changed over the years is an approach and a technique. The first few years with the Teatro Campesino were largely improvisational. I wrote outlines. I sketched out a dramatic structure, sometimes on a single page, and used that as my guide to direct the actors. Later on, I began to write very simple scripts that were sometimes born out of improvisations. During the first ten years, from '65 to '75, the collective process became more complicated and more sophisticated within the company—we were creating longer pieces, full-length pieces, but they'd take forever to complete using the collective process.

By 1975, I'd taken the collective process as far as I could. I enjoyed working with people. I didn't have to deal with the loneliness of writing. My problem was that I was so much part of the collective that I couldn't leave for even a month without the group having serious problems. By 1975 we were stable enough as a company for me to begin to take a month, two months, six months, eventually a year. I turned a corner and was ready to start writing plays again.

In 1975 I took a month off and wrote a play. We did a piece called *El Fin del Mundo* (*The End of the World*) from 1974 through 1980, a different version every year. The '75 version was a play I sat down and wrote. I started with a lot of abstract notions—the mathematician sometimes gets in the way—but eventually I plugged into characters born of my experience. Those characters are still alive for me. Someday I'll finish all of that as a play or else it will be poured into a screenplay for a "major motion picture" [laughs].

Shortly after that, in 1977, I was invited by the Mark Taper Forum to write a play for their New Theatre for Now series. We agreed on the Zoot Suit Riots as a subject. *Zoot Suit* firmly reestablished my self-identity as a playwright. Essentially I've been writing nonstop since '75. That's not to say I didn't write anything between '65 and '75. *Soldado Razo*, which is probably my most performed play around the world, was written in 1970, as was *Bernabe*. *The Dark Root of a Scream* was written in 1967. These are all one-acts. I used to work on them with a sense of longing, wanting more time to be able to sit down and write.

Now I'm firmly back in touch with myself as a playwright. When I begin, I allow myself at least a month of free association with notes. I can start anywhere. I can start with an abstract notion, a character . . . it's rarely dialogue or anything specific like that. More often than not, it's just an amorphous bunch of ideas, impressions and feelings. I allow myself to tumble in this ball of thoughts and impressions, knowing that I'm heading toward a play and that eventually I've got to begin dealing with character and then structure.

Because of the dearth of Hispanic playwrights—or even American playwrights, for that matter—I felt it necessary to explore the territory, to cover the range of theatre as widely as I could. Political theatre with the Farm Workers was sometimes minimal scale, a small group of workers gathered in some dusty little corner in a labor camp, and sometimes immense—huge crowds, ten thousand, fifteen thousand, with banners flying. But the political theatre extends beyond the farm worker into the whole Chicano experience. We've dealt with a lot of issues: racism, education, immigration—and that took us, again, through many circles.

We evolved three separate forms: the *acto* was the political act, the short form, fifteen minutes; the *mito* was the mythic, religious play; and the *corrido* was the ballad. I just finished a full-length video program called *Corridos*. So the form has evolved into another medium. I do political plays, musicals, historical dramas, religious dramas. We still do our religious plays at the Mission here every year. They're nurturing, they feed the spirit. Peter Brook's response when he saw our Virgin play, years ago, was that it was like something out of the Middle Ages. It's religion for many of the people who come see it, not just entertainment. And of course we've gone on to do serious plays and comedies like *I Don't Have to Show You No Stinking Badges.* . . .

Source: David Savran, "An Interview with Luis Valdez," in *In Their Own Words: Contemporary American Playwrights*, Theatre Communications Group, 1988, pp. 257–71.

SOURCES

Ambrecht, Biliana C. S., and Harry P. Pachon, "Ethnic Political Mobilization in a Mexican American Community: An Exploratory Study of East Los Angeles, 1965–1972," in *Western Political Quarterly*, Vol. 27, No. 3, September 1974, p. 508.

Amkpa, Awam, Review of *Taking It to the Streets: Social Protest Theater of Luis Valdez and Amiri Baraka*, in *Drama Review*, Vol. 48, No. 4, Winter 2004, p. 198.

Bagby, Beth, "El Teatro Campesino: Interviews with Luis Valdez," in *Tulane Drama Review*, Vol. 11, No. 4, Summer 1967, pp. 72–73, 77–78, 80.

Bigsby, C. W. E., "Theatre of Commitment," in *A Critical Introduction to Twentieth-Century American Drama*, Cambridge University Press, 1985, p. 358.

Copelin, David, "Chicano Theatre: El Festival de los Teatros Chicanos," in *Drama Review: TDR*, Vol. 17, No. 4, December 1973, pp. 74–76.

Cutler, John Alba, "Disappeared Men: Chicana/o Authenticity and the American War in Viet Nam," in *American Literature*, Vol. 81, 2009, p. 587.

Fokkema, Douwe, and Elrud Ibsch, *Theories of Literature in the Twentieth Century*, C. Hurst, 1978.

Huerta, Jorge, "When Sleeping Giants Awaken: Chicano Theatre in the 1960s," in *Theatre Survey*, Vol. 43, No. 1, May 2002, pp. 23, 28, 32.

Lucas, Ashley, "Reinventing the Pachuco: The Radical Transformation from the Criminalized to the Heroic in Luis Valdez's Play *Zoot Suit*," in *Journal for the Study of Radicalism*, Vol. 3, No. 1, 2009, p. 63.

Oliver-Rotger, Maria Antónia, *Battlegrounds and Crossroads: Social and Imaginary Space in Writings by Chicanas*, Rodolpi BV, 2002, p. 245.

Stacy, Lee, ed., "Chicano Theater," in *Mexico and the United States*, edited by Chris King, Andrew Campbell, Emily Hill, and Mark Fletcher, Marshall Cavendish, 2003, p. 171.

Turco, Lewis, *The Book of Literary Terms: The Genres of Fiction, Drama, Nonfiction, Literary Criticism, and Scholarship*, University Press of New England, 1999.

Valdez, Luis, *The Actos*, in *Luis Valdez—Early Works: Actos, Bernabé and Pensamiento Serpentino,*, Arte Público Press, 1990, pp. 12–13.

———, *Los Vendidos*, in *Luis Valdez—Early Works: Actos, Pensamiento, Serpentino, and Bernabe*, Arte Público Press, 1990, pp. 40–52.

Villarreal, Edit, "Theatre Review," in *Theatre Journal*, Vol. 41, No. 2, May 1989, p. 231.

FURTHER READING

Ada, Alma Flor, and F. Isabel Campoy, *Voices (Gateways to the Sun)*, Alfaguara, 2002.

> This biographical book explains the importance of Valdez, muralist Judith Francisca Blanca, and Dr. Carlos Juan Finlay to the world and Hispanic culture in particular.

Beltran, Cristina, *The Trouble with Unity: Latin Politics and the Creation of Identity*, Oxford University Press, 2010.

> Beltran's book examines the growing presence of Latinos in the American political scene to try to determine what exactly the "Latin vote" is. Along the way, she looks at what constitutes a Latin identity within the domain of the political arena in regard to feminism and multiculturalism.

Chavez, Cesar, *An Organizer's Tale: Speeches*, Penguin Classics, 2008.

> This collection of essays and speeches by Chavez illustrates his belief in nonviolent protest and the changes it effected on society over the course of his decades as an activist for the Chicano movement.

Gutierrez, Manuel de Jesus Hernandez, and David Foster, *Literatura Chicana, 1965–1995: An Anthology in Spanish, English, and Calo*, Routledge, 1997.

> This anthology chronicles the evolution of modern Mexican American literature through a collection of essays, short stories, poems, plays, and two complete novels. Gutierrez and Foster

study themes such as identity, feminism, conservationism, and homoeroticism.

Maciel, David R., Isidro D. Ortiz, and Maria Herrara-Sobek, *Chicano Renaissance: Contemporary Cultural Trends*, University of Arizona Press, 2000.

> The authors examine visual art, literature, music, film, theater, and beyond to track changes in the Chicano movement as represented by these art forms. This collection of original essays shines a much needed light on the last two decades, a time period largely ignored in volumes of criticism on the Chicano movement.

Pawel, Miriam, *The Union of Their Dreams: Power, Hope, and Struggle in Cesar Chavez's Farm Worker Movement*, Bloomsbury Press, 2010.

> Through the presentation of primary source material alongside current interviews, Pawel takes a look back on the era of the farmworker movement. She analyzes the decline of involvement in the movement and puts special emphasis on the contradictory aspects of the Chicano movement as a whole.

Reyes, Luis, and Peter Rubie, *Hispanics in Hollywood*, Lone Eagle, 2000.

> Reyes and Rubie have compiled an extensive research reference guide on Hispanics in film and television. In addition, bibliographical information, essays, beautiful photographs, and plot summaries make this volume a valuable resource for any study on the subject.

SUGGESTED SEARCH TERMS

Luis Valdez

Los Vendidos

Chicano renaissance

El Teatro Campesino

Luis Valdez AND actos

Luis Valdez AND Los Vendidos

Luis Valdez AND Cesar Chavez

Luis Valdez AND Chicano movement

Luis Valdez AND satire

Luis Valdez AND Delano grape strike

El Teatro Campesino AND stock characters

Poof!

LYNN NOTTAGE
1993

Lynn Nottage's short play *Poof!* treats the serious theme of domestic violence while incorporating humor into the play through the dialogue between the characters Loureen and Florence. Their shocked and uncertain response to the fact that Loureen appears to have cursed her husband into nonexistence—he spontaneously combusts—is largely responsible for generating the play's often-comedic tone. Spontaneous human combustion, referred to in a note by Nottage just following the character list, is an unexplained, fantastical phenomenon in which a person appears to burn from the inside out. This strange event occurs in the opening moments of the play, after Loureen, once again threatened by her violent husband, yells, "Damn you to hell, Samuel!" This is followed by a flash of light and Loureen's discovery of the mound of "smoking ashes" in her kitchen, atop which rest her husband's eyeglasses.

The remainder of the play's action centers on Loureen's range of emotions. In a state of disbelief, she calls her friend Florence, who lives in the same building. Loureen has an immediate understanding of the fact that she caused Samuel's fate but cannot fathom how it happened. Florence is confused and wonders if Loureen has perhaps gone insane. A portion of their discussion reveals the hint that disposing of her abusive husband was something Loureen had considered in the past. At one point, Loureen concludes that she must be a witch to have made this happen. After reflecting on their mutual history as abused

Lynn Nottage (Getty Images)

women, Loureen and Florence contemplate what Loureen should do with Samuel's remains. Eventually, after Florence's departure, Loureen sweeps the ashes under the rug and eats her dinner. The bizarre event that sparks the action in this story creates an avenue for Nottage to approach the themes of domestic abuse and retribution in a nontraditional manner. At its heart, the play is also about the friendship and complicity of the two friends.

Under the direction of Jon Jory, *Poof!* premiered in Louisville, Kentucky, at the Actors Theatre of Louisville in 1993. In 2004, it was included in Nottage's collection *Crumbs from the Table of Joy, and Other Plays*.

AUTHOR BIOGRAPHY

Born in Brooklyn, New York, in 1964, Nottage graduated from New York's High School of Music and Art in Harlem in 1982. Nottage attended Brown University, in Providence, Rhode Island, where she received a bachelor of arts degree in 1986. In 1989, she earned a master of fine arts degree from the Yale University School of Drama.

After working for four years as the national press officer at Amnesty International, Nottage took up writing full time. Her short play *Poof!* premiered in 1993 at the Actors Theatre in Louisville, Kentucky. There, it won the Heideman Award. Three years later, Chicago's acclaimed Steppenwolf Theatre Company produced one of Nottage's best-known plays, *Crumbs from the Table of Joy*. For a period of several years Nottage took a break from writing, but she returned to the stage in 2003 with an award-winning play, *Intimate Apparel*.

Her subsequent awards and fellowships include the 2004 PEN/Laura Pels Award for Drama, a 2005 Guggenheim Fellowship, and a 2007 Lucille Lortel Foundation Fellowship. She also won a 2007 MacArthur Fellows grant, known as the "Genius Award," and a 2009 Pulitzer Prize for Drama for *Ruined*, about the suffering endured by women during the civil war in the Democratic Republic of Congo. Nottage was awarded the 2010 Steinberg Award for playwriting. The award, as the *New York Times* reported in an article on Nottage, is "the most lucrative prize in theater." As of 2011, Nottage was a visiting lecturer at the Yale University School of Drama.

PLOT SUMMARY

A short, one-act play, *Poof!* opens with stage directions indicating an unlit stage. In the darkness, Samuel roars at his wife that he does not want to see her by the time he counts to ten. When Samuel gets to four, Loureen fires back, also in darkness, shouting a curse, damning her husband to hell. The stage directions indicate that a "bright flash" is seen, and the stage lights come on. Loureen spies a mound of ashes on the kitchen floor, smoke rising from them. Perched on the ash mound are her husband's spectacles.

As she backs away from the ashes, Loureen glances around her, waiting for Samuel to reappear. She apologizes to him and promises to "be good" if he will only return. Loureen's abruptly halted chuckle suggests her shock and confusion. Begging Samuel not to be angry with her,

MEDIA ADAPTATIONS

- *Poof!* was adapted for television for the Public Broadcasting System *American Shorts* series in 2002. Rosie Perez and Viola Davis starred in this adaptation, which was directed by Fred Barzyk.

Loureen considers the reasons why he might be, assuring him that though she forgot to pick up his shirt, she can wash him another. Loureen then calls her friend Florence and asks her to come down to her apartment, explaining, "There's been a ... little ... accident."

While waiting for Florence, Loureen retrieves a broom and dustpan, then studies the ashes more closely and begins to grin. When Florence enters, Loureen finds herself speechless. She points to the ashes and can only grunt for a moment. She then tries to explain that the burnt smell Florence detects is in fact Samuel. Florence becomes convinced that Loureen has finally been driven completely insane by Samuel but grows frightened when Loureen tells her repeatedly to dial 911. Florence does so, but she hangs up when Loureen states, "I think I killed him."

Florence attempts to gather a comprehensible explanation from Loureen, who simply does not have one. The exchange reveals the confusion experienced by both women. Florence asks Loureen where Samuel's body is; she points to the ashes. "You burned him?" Florence prods. Loureen expresses her uncertainty and then her belief that she thinks she did. Florence's reply reveals the way this bizarre incident injects humor into a story rooted in domestic violence. She states, "Either you did or you didn't, what you mean you don't know? We're talking murder, Loureen, not oven settings."

As the conversation continues, Florence contemplates the number of times she listened to Loureen discuss the ways she would like to kill Samuel but concludes that Loureen has never acted on what Florence had believed, to this point, to be fantasies. Loureen assures her friend that she is not lying. She explains that Samuel had always told her that if she yelled then something awful would occur. She becomes certain that she must be a witch for something like this to happen.

Loureen begins to imagine what would happen if Samuel did come back from the dead and how it would seem as if she had then performed two miracles. She would be venerated as "Saint Loureen, the patron of battered wives." Still amazed at the power of her words, Loureen muses, "How often does a man like Samuel get damned to hell, and go?" The stage directions then indicate that Loureen "breaks down." As Florence comforts her, she discovers her friend is "actually laughing hysterically" and begins to wonder if Loureen is high on crack.

Loureen turns her mind to the immediate future. What should she do next, she wonders. She contemplates sweeping Samuel up, calling the police. She asks Florence if she thinks she will be sent to jail. Florence now begins to express despair and asks Loureen why she could not have just allowed herself to be hit one more time, endured this one last rage of Samuel's and then come to her. Florence assures her that she would have helped her pack, "like we talked about," suggesting that leaving was something the women had discussed before. However, Loureen does not feel regret. She marvels at the way she could just blow on the ashes and Samuel would disappear.

Her readily apparent relief upsets Florence, however. She rages at her, swearing at her for breaking their pact, stating "We agreed that when things got real bad for both of us we'd ... you know ... together ... Do I have to go back upstairs to that?" Florence underscores the fact of the women's complicity, that together, they endured the abuse they perhaps only talked about with one another, they shared plans for escape, and now Loureen has essentially escaped without her. Her sense of betrayal and despair is expressed in this speech and in the way she begins to pace the room, "nervously touching objects."

Defending herself, Loureen describes the way she never spoke out, never realizing why Samuel feared her words. "I've never been by myself," she admits, save for the time when Samuel vacationed in Reno without her. She goes on, contemplating the power she had always possessed but had never been aware of, had never been able to access because of her tremendous fear of Samuel's violence. "And out of my mouth those words made him disappear. All these years and just words, Florence. That's all they were."

Florence is certain she will never be able to express the words that Loureen said with the intent Loureen had possessed. Florence still feels victimized, powerless. Loureen encourages her and suggests that the "hundred things" she considers reasons to not leave will always be there. Florence then asks for Loureen's help, thinking that Loureen can somehow end her misery for her, end Edgar with words, but Loureen does not think it is possible. Accepting her fate, Florence guesses that things will not be any different for her, and Loureen agrees, telling her friend, "If you can say for certain, then I guess they won't be."

Florence's sense of hopelessness is what defeats her, Loureen suggests. Her certainty that things will not change ensures that they will not. Florence's mood shifts to one of resignation: Loureen has a body to dispose of, and she has a husband to return to. Together, they come up with a plan of sorts, deciding that soon, Loureen will tell the police that Samuel is missing. The women make plans to play cards together the next evening. After Loureen and Florence hug, Florence departs. Loureen sweeps Samuel's ashes under the carpet and sits down to have her dinner.

CHARACTERS

Edgar

Although he does not appear in the play, Edgar, Florence's husband, remains a force who guides Florence's actions through fear and intimidation. She loathes the thought of returning to him, although Florence describes Edgar as less of a threat to her than Samuel had been to Loureen, noting, "Edgar has never done me the way Samuel did you, but he sure did take the better part of my life."

Florence

Florence is Loureen's friend. She lives in the same building as Loureen and Samuel and comes to Loureen's aid quickly after Loureen calls her. The stage directions indicate that Florence, like Loureen, is "a housewife in her early

thirties." She is dressed in "a floral housecoat and a pair of oversized slippers." Florence attempts to sort through Loureen's unbelievable story, the physical evidence of the ashes, and the violent history she knows Loureen and Samuel shared. As she tries to discern whether or not Loureen is capable of having murdered her husband, she vacillates between wondering whether Loureen has gone insane, imagining that she has really done something, and facing the fact that Samuel is really gone.

Florence seems disappointed that Loureen did not act differently, that she did not simply take one more blow and then leave—"like we talked about," she says to Loureen. Growing increasingly angry at Loureen, Florence accuses her friend of breaking their pact, suggesting that the women had planned on leaving their husbands together. She is horrified to think that she has to return to face her own abusive husband, and Loureen attempts to encourage her to stand up to Edgar, to leave. Florence, however, remains uncertain about her own ability to confront her husband, stating, "I'm afraid won't anything change for me."

Loureen

Loureen is an abused wife who discovers that her husband has burned to ash after she curses him. She is described in the stage directions as "a demure housewife in her early thirties." Throughout the text of the play, Loureen expresses a sense of satisfaction at the turn of events but also dwells on the still-suffocating nature of the fear that has ruled her life for so long. She relishes a previously unknown feeling of power, as when she grins upon viewing the ashes and "proceeds to saunter back across the room" after letting Florence in.

However, Loureen is at times horrified and paralyzed with guilt, shame, and fear. Uncertain as to how to proceed now that Samuel is gone, Loureen comments that "Samuel always said if I raised my voice something horrible would happen. And it did. I'm a witch . . . the devil spawn!" After repeating this certainty that she is a witch, Loureen "looks at her hands with disgust," the stage directions indicate, demonstrating her contempt and shame for what she has done.

When Florence nervously fumbles with Samuel's jacket, Loureen responds with horror, "NO! No! Don't wrinkle that, that's his favorite jacket. He'll kill me." Samuel, even after his death, still has the power to instill fear in Loureen;

yet she begins to take steps toward a positive assessment of her actions, realizing that through all the years of abuse, it was words, her ability to respond and to strike back verbally, that made the difference in her life, that finally protected her from Samuel.

Samuel

Samuel is Loureen's abusive husband. He has only one line in the play, and within it is contained an implicit threat of violence. After he has been reduced to a pile of ashes, apparently having spontaneously combusted, Samuel is still feared by Loureen, a fact suggestive of the way he intimidated and controlled her through abuse. Throughout the play the women refer to Samuel with a mixture of apprehension and disgust. His repeated victimization of Loureen is referred to throughout the duration of the play, as when Loureen recounts the moments that led up to his odd disappearance. Florence asks Loureen if Samuel had struck Loureen again, and she replies, "He was shouting like he does, being all colored, then he raised up that big crusty hand to hit me, and poof, he was gone."

THEMES

Domestic Violence

In *Poof!* the theme of domestic violence is explored without any instances of violence ever being enacted on stage. The play opens during an argument between Loureen and her husband Samuel. Samuel's brief speech carries with it a subtle threat. "When I count to ten, I don't want to see ya! I don't want to hear ya!" he bellows, forcing the reader to wonder what will happen if Loureen is seen or heard when the counting has stopped, but Loureen's response and the subsequent spontaneous combustion of Samuel prevent Samuel from ever carrying out his threat.

As the play continues, however, Samuel's history of violence is revealed in Loureen's verbalization of her fears and in the hesitancy and defensiveness of her actions. Upon discovering Samuel's ashes, Loureen carefully backs away and pleads with Samuel to not be angry with her. She apologizes for not picking up his shirt and promises to wash another immediately. When she admits that perhaps she never intended to launder him a fresh shirt, Loureen, aware of the undercurrent of defiance in her

statement, imagines how Samuel would likely react. She responds instinctively, the stage direction indicating that Loureen "Pulls back as though about to receive a blow." This action is telling: it reveals that Loureen has learned that speaking out against her husband results in violence.

When Loureen is attempting to explain what happened to her friend Florence, Florence asks if Samuel, whom she describes in a flurry of expletives, has hit her again. As the conversation between the two women progresses, Loureen's statements underscore the way the violence she has endured has shaped the way she views herself. She states, "Samuel always said if I raised my voice something horrible would happen. And it did. I'm a witch . . . the devil's spawn!" Under constant physical threat and verbal abuse, Loureen has begun to accept a view of herself as something evil. Reflecting on how her history with Samuel has changed her, she observes, "He's made me a killer, Florence, and you remember what a gentle child I was."

Even after she has accepted the fact that Samuel is truly gone, Loureen retreats instinctively into fearfulness when Florence nervously fidgets with Samuel's jacket. "He'll kill me," she tells Florence. Eventually Loureen begins to encourage Florence to find a way to stand up to her own abusive husband, Edgar. Florence asks Loureen to help her, to come with her and curse Edgar and make him disappear, the way Loureen did with Samuel. Loureen is certain that Florence must accomplish the task on her own, beginning to understand that it was her verbalizing her defiance directly to Samuel at the play's beginning that led to her freedom from victimization.

Friendship

Throughout *Poof!* the friendship between Loureen and Florence is characterized in terms of the circumstances the women share. Both are abused by their husbands, although Florence points out, "Edgar has never done me the way Samuel did you." Florence, described in the stage directions as Loureen's best friend, is the first and only person Loureen contacts after the combustion of her husband. Loureen, confused and stunned herself, attempts to explain the course of events to Florence, who remains skeptical about the possibility that Samuel simply burst into flames and burned to ash. Despite

TOPICS FOR FURTHER STUDY

- *Poof!* begins with the spontaneous combustion of the abusive husband character. An unexplained and widely disputed phenomenon, spontaneous human combustion has played a role in the novels of Charles Dickens (*Bleak House*) and Nikolai Gogol (*Dead Souls*). Using sources such as the *Paranormal Encyclopedia* (http://www.paranormal-ency clopedia.com/s/spontaneous-human-combus tion/) and the chapter "Spontaneous Human Combustion" in *The Mammoth Encyclopedia of the Unsolved*, by Colin Wilson and Damon Wilson, research this phenomenon. Write a research paper in which you discuss both historical belief in and skepticism surrounding spontaneous human combustion. Include a review of the leading theories regarding the possible scientific causes for spontaneous human combustion, and summarize the arguments of scientists who discount the validity of the phenomenon. Be sure to cite all of your sources.

- Indian American novelist Swati Avasthi's young-adult novel *Split* (2010) focuses on a teenage boy who, after spending years watching his father abuse his mother, now abuses a young woman. With a small group, read *Split* and begin an online blog to use for a book discussion. Talk with members of your group about the way Avasthi depicts the domestic violence in the novel. Consider the ways that witnessing incidents in which their father abused their mother affected Jace and his brother Christian. How are the brothers similar? In what ways do they differ from one another? Analyze the way Avasthi structures the novel. From which character's viewpoint does Avasthi narrate the novel? Does she alternate between point-of-view characters? Share with other members in the group the way the novel made you feel. Did the book elicit sympathy for the characters? Think about the way the novel affected your views regarding domestic violence and its victims.

- In *Poof!* Nottage incorporates an element of the fantastic into a short, one-act play. In *Moon Marked and Touched by Sun: Plays by African American Women*, longer works by a number of playwrights are presented. Many of these playwrights, including Adrienne Kennedy, Suzan-Lori Parks, and Ntozake Shange, incorporate surrealist elements in their plays. These women explore a variety of issues, including African American identity and stereotypes. Select one of the plays from this collection and compare it with Nottage's *Poof!* In what ways and to what ends do the authors employ absurdist elements? Does the play you chose share similar themes to those that *Poof!* depicts? Consider the ways in which both playwrights crafted their characters. Does Nottage's play suffer from less concretely defined characterizations owing to her play's shorter length in comparison to the characters in your other play? How do the playwrights' styles compare? Is their language poetic or formal, or does it resemble everyday speech? Write a comparative essay in which you discuss the similarities and differences between the two plays.

- Write a second act for *Poof!* in which you portray what might have happened to Loureen. Did she call the police? Did they believe her story? Perhaps in your play Loureen does not tell anyone what happened, or perhaps she confesses to Florence or the police that she deliberately killed Samuel, through more conventional means than spontaneous combustion. Consider the variety of ways in which you could approach Loureen's fate, and do not rule out incorporating elements of the absurd. Perhaps Loureen actually possess powers she did not realize she had. After writing your second act to the play, work with other members of your class to either perform your act or give a dramatic reading of it. You may also record your performance and then stage a screening of it for your classmates.

Loureen causes her husband Samuel to spontaneously combust during a fight.
(runzelkorn | Shutterstock.com)

Florence's disbelief, however, she remains supportive of her friend. Initially she asks Loureen, "Did he finally drive you out your mind?" As Florence begins to grasp that Samuel is really dead, Florence attempts to assess Loureen's involvement, asking her to carefully recount everything that happened. She does not seem to believe the spontaneous combustion story, asking Loureen at one point if she is smoking crack. When Loureen describes herself as a killer, she asks Florence if she thinks she will go to jail or receive the death penalty, and Florence states, "Folks have done time for less." Loureen is upset that her friend responds so frankly, but Florence presses on, asking her, "What did you expect, that I was going to throw up my arms and congratulate you?" At the core of their friendship is total honesty, and Florence does not sugarcoat the likely outcomes of the situation.

Florence also perceives the consequence of Loureen's accomplishment on the friendship

between the two women. As she explains, she feels betrayed that Loureen acted without consulting her. Florence reminds Loureen, "We made a pact." Loureen has broken the promise the two women made to one another, although the details of this agreement remain obscure. Florence reminds Loureen of the promise in vague terms, stating that if both of them had to face an increasingly worse situation, "we'd ... you know ... together." While the scope of their plan remains hidden to the audience, the strength of the bond between Loureen and Florence, born out of the danger they both face, is clear. As the play concludes, Loureen encourages Florence to stand up to her husband, while Florence advises Loureen not to call the police. They continue to support each other despite their apparent uncertainty about the choices the other has made.

STYLE

Comedy

The subject matter of *Poof!* is, though grave, treated in a manner that is often comedic in tone. As Sandra G. Shannon notes in an essay for *Contemporary African American Women Playwrights: A Casebook*, the play's "whimsical tone is prone to draw laughter." The extremely bizarre nature of Samuel's death itself gives rise to much of the humor in the play, as Loureen attempts to explain to Florence something she herself does not understand. As this confusion unfolds, the tone of the play periodically grows lighthearted. When Loureen shows Florence Samuel's pile of ashes, Florence asks, "You burned him?" When Loureen responds that she does not know, but she thinks so, Florence is incredulous, saying, "Either you did or you didn't, what you mean you don't know? We're talking murder, Loureen, not oven settings."

As the conversation continues, Loureen contemplates the possibility of Samuel returning. Acknowledging that this would be a miracle, Loureen imagines herself as a saint, "the patron of battered wives." She envisions women making pilgrimages to see her, "laying pies and pot roast at my feet and asking the good saint to make their husbands turn to dust." Such comical images as Saint Loureen surrounded by offerings of pie and pot roast belie the seriousness of the situation, but prevent the play from being regarded as wholly tragic.

In one of the play's final humorous passages, Loureen comes to grips with the fact that Samuel is truly gone and can torment her no more. She begins to bid farewell to everything she despised about Samuel, from "the bourbon" to the "bologna sandwiches." She goes on, saying, "Good-bye to the smell of his feet, his breath and his bowel movements." Loureen then sweeps the ashes under the rug and sits down to dinner.

Magical Realism

Nottage opens *Poof!* with an element of the fantastic—the spontaneous combustion of Samuel following Loureen's curse—to introduce a realistic exploration of the psychological effects of domestic violence on its victims. Although Nottage's play does not fit precisely into certain definitions associated with the literary mode known as magical realism, in its positing of the absurd element of Samuel's spontaneous combustion within an otherwise realistic world, *Poof!* cannot be regarded as a strictly realistic drama. As Neil Ayres explains in an essay for the Man Booker Prize organization, a work of magical realism is characterized as possessing, among other things, "a reality similar to our own, in which the impossible can occur without comment." Samuel's combustion is commented upon, but it is accepted within the fabric of the story as an actual event. It is not associated with a dream, nor does it figure as a figment of Loureen's imagination, nor is it explained away in scientific terms.

Although the mysterious death of Samuel and Loureen and Florence's attempt to find a solution drive the plot, as the play progresses, the focus shifts from the way in which Samuel died to the event that seems to have either triggered or simply coincided with Samuel's spontaneous combustion, that is, Loureen's act of verbalizing her anger toward Samuel. Whether or not Samuel's reduction to ash was caused by his wife's statement "Damn you to hell, Samuel!" Loureen seems certain of her own agency. She states repeatedly her belief that she killed Samuel, that she damned him to hell, and obligingly, he went. However, this occurrence, the curse and the combustion, becomes associated with the power of words. Loureen states this emphatically, noting, "Out of my mouth those words made him disappear. All these years and just words, Florence. That's all they were."

HISTORICAL CONTEXT

African American Drama in the 1990s

In the 1990s, African American theater was rooted in traditions that developed during the 1960s and 1970s, when the Black Arts Movement took hold, in correspondence with the civil rights movement. As Yolanda W. Page observes in the *Greenwood Encyclopedia of Multiethnic Literature: A–C*, "The founders of the movement called for more positive images in plays by African American playwrights and advocated the use of drama as a weapon in the Black Power struggle." Page states that the plays written during this volatile time period were "controversial, as well as shocking and militant."

Playwright August Wilson was one of the most prominent African American dramatists of the 1980s and 1990s, and like other African American dramatists of these decades, Wilson built on the success of earlier African American dramatists. Although typically centering on African American characters, Wilson's plays explore universal themes. His play *The Piano Lesson* won the Pulitzer Prize for Drama in 1990. Upon Wilson's death in 2005, Charles Isherwood wrote in the *New York Times* that Wilson "chronicled the African American experience in the 20th century in a series of plays that will stand as a landmark in the history of black culture, of American literature and of Broadway theater."

African American theater in the 1990s was also stamped with the distinctive experimental style of a number of female African American playwrights, including Nottage, whose 1993 *Poof!* opens with the fantastic device of spontaneous human combustion. Playwright Robbie McCauley's work has been compared with that of Black Arts Movement dramatist Adrienne Kennedy, best known for her early plays and their surrealist, dreamlike structure and imagery. Surrealism is an artistic mode that focuses on the unconscious mind as a source of inspiration and meaning. Like Kennedy, whose work spans the Black Arts Movement in the 1960s through the present day, McCauley employs experimental methods to explore her personal past, racism, and other social problems.

Suzan-Lori Parks similarly draws "on Kennedy's avant-gardist precedent," as Eugene Nesmith observes in *A Sourcebook of African-American Performance: Plays, People, Movements.* In literature, experimentalism and avant-gardism, like

COMPARE
&
CONTRAST

- **1990s:** Domestic-abuse rates among women are higher among African American women than among white women during this time period, yet more white women than African American women are murdered by their partner. The Violence against Women Act passes in 1994, to institute changes in legislation regarding domestic assault crimes and provide funding for domestic-violence assistance organizations.

  Today: By the middle of the first decade of the twenty-first century, domestic-violence rates and related homicide rates for African American women and white women have fallen considerably. In 2000, a new Violence against Women Act reauthorizes programs created by the original 1994 legislation.

- **1990s:** Women African American dramatists, including Nottage, Adrienne Kennedy, Robbie McCauley, and Suzan-Lori Parks, explore the lives and concerns of African American women. Their works often employ experimental techniques, such as absurd devices, dreamlike symbolism and imagery, nonlinear storytelling, direct address or involvement of the audience, minimalist sets, and the incorporation of music and song in nontraditional ways.

  Today: Many female African American dramatists whose reputations were established in the 1950s and 1960s, such as Kennedy, and

whose works were just beginning to gain critical attention in the 1990s, such as Nottage, continue to write for the stage. Parks won the Pulitzer Prize for Drama in 2001 for *Topdog/Underdog*, while Nottage claimed the same award in 2009 for *Ruined*.

- **1990s:** The purported phenomenon of spontaneous human combustion has been a source of fascination, speculation, and skepticism at least since the nineteenth century. Various theories about the cause of the phenomenon are tested. In 1982, the British Broadcasting Corporation program *QED* attempts to test the validity of a theory known as the "wick effect," a theory posited by some as an explanation for spontaneous human combustion. The theory is shown to explain the state of remains of alleged victims of spontaneous human combustion, but it does not offer an explanation of the process by which a person's clothes ignite and one's body fat becomes the fuel in a slow burning process.

  Today: Spontaneous human combustion continues to inspire the scientific community to seek explanations. In a 2002 paper for the *Journal of Theoretics*, M. Sue Benford, discussing plant genome research, explores the possibility that gamma radiation could create a nuclear reaction inside the body, thereby causing combustion.

---

surrealism, are modes in which traditional approaches to narrative technique and dramatic structure are eschewed. The use of nonlinear storytelling, a heavy reliance on symbol and meaning, the incorporation of elements of the fantastic or absurd, and the use of minimalist set designs are some features common to this type of theatrical experience. Nesmith describes Parks's "use of poetic language, non-traditional characters, and extraordinary images" as a means of crafting drama with "a

dense structure that is often impenetrable for an audience." Her 1990 play *The Death of the Last Black Man in the Whole Entire World* exemplifies some of these features. In it, Parks seeks to dissect and explode the stereotypes often associated with African Americans.

Domestic Violence in the 1990s

In 1993, at the time Nottage's play was written and produced, about ten women in every thousand

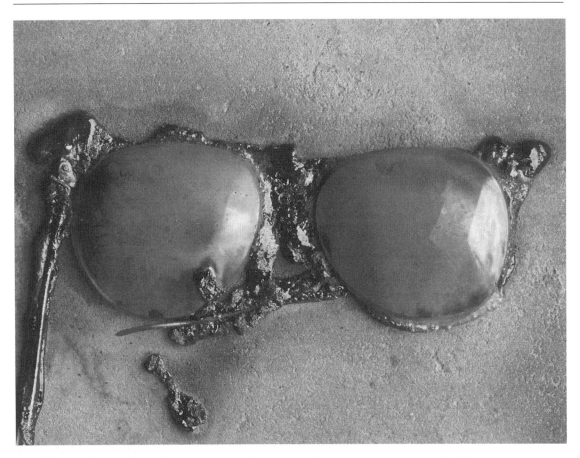

All that is left of Samuel are his eyeglasses. *(Kemeo | Shutterstock.com)*

were violently, but not fatally, victimized by what the U.S. Department of Justice labels an "intimate partner," that is, a boyfriend, girlfriend, or spouse. The figure was drastically smaller for male victims, with only about one male in every thousand being violently abused by such a partner. That same year, about fifteen hundred women were killed by their intimate partners, while approximately six hundred men were killed by their partners.

African American women suffered disproportionately from nonfatal domestic abuse compared to their white counterparts in 1993. About twelve African American women in every thousand were victimized, whereas about ten white women in every thousand were victimized. That same year, however, more white women than African American women were killed by their partner. There were nearly a thousand homicides of white women by their partner, compared with just over five hundred homicides of African American women by their partner. Despite some fluctuation, however, there was an overall

declining trend in victimization and homicide of women by their partners throughout the 1990s.

In the late 1980s, a new term, "battered women's syndrome," was used (unsuccessfully) to legally defend a woman who killed her partner. The term began to find its way into other cases in the 1990s. Battered women's syndrome was used both to obtain convictions of perpetrators of domestic violence and in the defense of women who killed their abusers. Despite the fact that, according to the Minnesota Center against Violence and Abuse, forty-eight states in 1990 "enacted or revamped injunctions that enable courts to refrain men from abusing, harassing and assaulting the women with whom they live," many women continued to suffer from domestic violence.

In 1992, spousal abuse was listed by the U.S. surgeon general as the "leading cause of injuries to women aged 15 to 44." In 1994, the Violence against Women Act was passed as part of the federal Crime Victims Act. The act funded a variety of services for victims of rape and domestic abuse. It broadened the scope of prosecutable domestic-violence crimes and closed loopholes in immigration laws that had previously allowed some immigrant abusers to go unpunished. The Office on Violence against Women was created in 1995 to administer Violence against Women Act programs.

CRITICAL OVERVIEW

Although Nottage is better known for her later works, including the Pulitzer Prize–winning *Ruined*, than she is for her early plays, the short one-act drama *Poof!* is attributed with drawing critical attention to the playwright's career, as Shante T. Smalls observes in an article on Nottage for the *Columbia Encyclopedia of Modern Drama*. Randy Gener, in *American Theatre*, describes *Poof!* simply as "a memorable one-act."

Sandra G. Shannon offers a lengthier analysis of the play in *Contemporary African American Women Playwrights: A Casebook*, observing that the play "is uncanny in its universality." Shannon maintains that Nottage "was careful that abused women not be given the message that homicide was an option for confronting violence leveled against them." Rather, Shannon insists, Nottage suggests that "through imaginative willpower," abused women may acquire a sense of "agency in initiating other more civil and more reality-based ways to negotiate intolerable relationships." Nevertheless, the play remains rooted in fantasy, as Shannon demonstrates.

The play has also been examined from a feminist standpoint. Mary Ellen Snodgrass, in the *Encyclopedia of Feminist Literature*, characterizes *Poof!* as a "surreal comedy" and reflects on Nottage's juxtaposition of Loureen's realization that words have given her her freedom with the notion of the "silencing of women through menacing words and gestures." The ambiguity inherent in *Poof!* is apparent in the comments made by Judy Flavell in her introduction to a discussion guide for the play, "*Poof!* From Drama to Discussion: A Tool for Talking about Domestic Violence." Flavell observes that the play's viewers are driven to discuss the play's "reflection or distortion of how the dynamics of domestic violence play out in real life."

CRITICISM

Catherine Dominic
Dominic is a novelist and a freelance writer and editor. In the following essay, she focuses on the ambiguous nature of the death of the abusive husband in Poof! *and criticizes Nottage's employment of a magical device in the work, as it transforms a potentially powerful play about finding one's voice and agency into a work rooted in fantasy and wish fulfillment.*

In *Poof!* Lynn Nottage explores the power of words, of one woman's voice, as an act of protest against the abuse she suffers. Through the device of the husband's spontaneous combustion, Nottage seemingly demonstrates the power of Loureen's ability to stand up for herself by speaking out. The play often employs comedy in its examination of these themes of abuse and resistance. The fact that the play opens with the death of the abuser and subsequently does not depict acts of violence allows Nottage the freedom to take a sometimes humorous approach to the subject of domestic violence, yet Loureen's fear remains a prevalent part of her character throughout the play. At the same time, Loureen experiences moments of jubilation at the thought of being free. Although Loureen's attitude toward her husband and his death vacillates throughout the play, her understanding of her complicity in his death remains constant.

A thorough examination of Loureen's conversations with Florence yields an understanding that Loureen has contemplated taking violent actions against her husband in retaliation for his abuse and as a measure of self-defense, but in the course of the play, Loureen never takes action. She speaks out, and magically, her abuser disappears. The playwright is quoted in "*Poof!* From Drama to Discussion: A Guide to Talking about Domestic Violence" as stating that the play is "about a woman discovering the power of her own voice." She goes on to assert that "a woman's voice can have a very powerful and magical effect."

Nottage seems to present two possible courses of action for victims of domestic abuse: speak out or act out. However, the playwright does not dramatize a realistic version of the first possible approach, as Loureen speaks out not to authorities or people in her community who can possibly help her, but to the man who, as the play hints, has never shown her an act of mercy

WHAT DO I READ NEXT?

- Nottage's latest play, *By the Way, Meet Vera Stark*, is slated for a 2012 release. The work, which focuses on a young African American maid and aspiring actress employed by a Hollywood star, explores the racial stereotyping of the entertainment industry and features time shifts between the 1930s and the present day.

- Charles Dickens's *Bleak House* was originally published in installments between 1852 and 1853. The work, available in a 2008 edition, contains an instance of spontaneous human combustion significant to plot developments.

- *Multicultural Theatre 2: Contemporary Hispanic, Asian and African-American Plays*, edited by Roger Ellis and published in 1998, collects theatrical work from new and diverse writers, some in their late teens. Many of the works are designed to be played by young actors and are targeted at young-adult audiences, including Jose Rivera's *Maricela de la Luz Lights the World* and *The Basement at the Bottom at the End of the World*, by Nadine Graham.

- Acclaimed Irish poet Eavan Boland examines the theme of domestic violence from a variety of perspectives in the 2008 poetry collection *Domestic Violence: Poems*.

- Pulitzer Prize–winning African American playwright Suzan-Lori Parks published the collection *The America Play, and Other Works* in 1994, just a year after the debut of Nottage's *Poof!* Parks is noted for her examinations of the struggles of African American women and men and for her use of experimental theatrical techniques.

- Geared toward a more mature young-adult audience, the nonfiction book *Domestic Violence*, part of the "Opposing Viewpoints" series, was published in 1999. Editor Tamara L. Roleff gathers articles and essays from a range of sources and explores factors that may contribute to domestic violence, the variety of forms domestic abuse may take, and legal issues pertinent to domestic-violence cases.

> NOTTAGE SEEMS TO HAVE UNDERCUT HER OWN SELF-STATED OBJECTIVE TO WRITE A PLAY ABOUT THE POWER OF ONE'S OWN VOICE THROUGH HER VERY USE OF THE FANTASTICAL SPONTANEOUS COMBUSTION OF SAMUEL."

or kindness. The effect of her speaking out and confronting Samuel is treated as magical, whereas in reality, the effect of a victim verbally challenging her abuser would most likely be continued abuse. Instead, in *Poof!* Loureen essentially makes a wish (for the damnation of her husband), and it comes true, without any action required on her part. As the play concludes, the mystery of Samuel's death remains, and ultimately, Nottage's own message is clouded. Nottage seems to have undercut her own self-stated objective to write a play about the power of one's own voice through her very use of the fantastical spontaneous combustion of Samuel.

In the course of the play, Nottage plants enough evidence of Loureen's plotting against Samuel and leaves enough unanswered questions for the audience to, like Florence, at least ponder the possibility that Loureen actually killed her husband. It is just as unlikely that in the space of the stage directions indicating the "bright flash" Loureen somehow intentionally murdered Samuel, reducing him to ashes, as it is that he spontaneously combusted. The play opens, then, with either a bizarre death or simply an unexplained one, for what the flash represents in terms of elapsed time is not specified. The flash could either represent Samuel's spontaneous combustion or hide a series of events occurring over a time period to which the viewer or reader is not privy. The audience is left to ponder two scenarios: either the bizarre incident of spontaneous combustion has actually occurred, or Loureen has killed her husband and has produced the ashes as a means of convincing Florence that Samuel simply exploded.

Through the ensuing dialogue, Nottage sows seeds of doubt regarding the fantastic spontaneous-combustion scenario. The audience, like

Florence, grows increasingly suspicious that Loureen has intentionally, rather than accidentally, killed her husband. Loureen's words and actions remain ambiguous throughout the play, however, and the audience is left only with the knowledge that Loureen wished her husband to be dead, spoke out against him in a way she has not before, and found her husband dead. That the spontaneous combustion of Samuel exists as reality within the world of the play is insisted upon throughout the course of the short drama, despite Florence's and the audience's suspicions.

Before the action of the play commences, a brief note introduces the play, in which Nottage states, "Nearly half the women on death row in the United States were convicted of killing abusive husbands. Spontaneous combustion is not recognized as a capital crime." Nottage here opens with a possible framework for understanding the events to follow. Women who kill abusive husbands may find themselves on death row. Spontaneous combustion, however, is not a crime punishable with the death penalty, the note informs.

The action of the play begins with the angry verbal exchange between Samuel and Loureen. Samuel's words are threatening, and Loureen's response is damning. Following a flash of light, Loureen stares at a mound of ashes. In the monologue that follows this discovery, Loureen appears confused, angry, and afraid, until, as the stage directions indicate, she "chuckles, then stops abruptly." She continues to address Samuel as if he can hear her, promising to wash a shirt because she forgot to pick his up, admitting she may not have intended to wash a fresh shirt after all, and then drawing back in fear as if Samuel is about to strike her. She appears to be genuinely stunned, a response that would be consistent with both possible causes of Samuel's death (spontaneous combustion or Loureen's act of murder). "I didn't mean it really," she insists, referring either to the angry words the audience has witnessed or, perhaps, a violent action she has taken in the open-ended interval of the "bright flash."

After Florence's arrival, Loureen attempts to explain that the pile of ashes is in fact Samuel. Florence alternately thinks that Loureen has gone insane or that she is joking. Then she pauses. The stage directions indicate that "she takes a hard look into Loureen's eyes" before asking, "Did you really do it this time?" This is the first indication the reader is given that Florence believes not only

that Loureen has contemplated killing Samuel, but also that she is strong enough to accomplish the task. The conversation continues, with Florence referring to Samuel's death as a possible "murder." Florence, responding to Loureen's seriousness, says, "How many times have I heard you talk about being rid of him. How many times have we sat at this very table and laughed about the many ways we could do it." However, her doubts are revealed as well. She goes on, "How many times have you done it? None."

As the women share a drink, Loureen explains how Samuel raised his hand to hit her and "poof, he was gone. . . . I barely got the words out and I'm looking down at a pile of ash." It is worth noting that the viewer or reader is unable to verify this account, because this portion of the play happens in darkness. Florence exhibits clear disbelief and says that she hopes Loureen is lying; not long after, she wonders if Loureen has been smoking crack. Loureen states repeatedly that she is a killer, and Florence, whether or not she believes Loureen's story about the way in which Samuel died, begins to accept that he is in fact dead and grows afraid of what might happen to Loureen next.

When Florence assumes that Samuel must have done something truly horrific to Loureen this time for her to respond by killing Samuel (either accidentally or intentionally), Loureen states that she simply could not tolerate "being hit one more time." Florence responds, "You've taken a thousand blows from that man, couldn't you've turned the cheek and waited. I'd have helped you pack. Like we talked about." In this statement, Florence presents an alternative scenario that the women clearly had discussed before: escape. She is dismayed that her friend resorted to other, more aggressive means to free herself.

Florence, feeling betrayed in a way, accuses Loureen of breaking their pact: "We agreed that when things got real bad for both of us we'd . . . you know . . . together." Florence, locked in the horror of her own situation, cannot even say the words and suggest that they leave together. Loureen insists that all it took were a few words spoken aloud for her to achieve her own freedom from Samuel, but Florence expresses her own sense of fearfulness about being able to speak out. When Florence states that Edgar has taken "the better part" of her life, Loureen replies, "Not yet, Florence."

Loureen calls the upstairs neighbor, Florence, to help her. (Shkurd / Shutterstock.com)

With this statement, the tone of the conversation shifts. Florence has been talking about escape, Loureen has done something more drastic, and now Loureen seems to be encouraging Florence to take a more aggressive approach in dealing with Edgar. Florence, for an instant, clutches at the straw of hope that Loureen seems to embody, hoping for an instant that by wishing something aloud, it might come true, and she asks Loureen to come with her, wait for Edgar, "and then you can spit out your words and . . . ." But Loureen interrupts and insists that it does not work like that.

The conversation shifts to the ways in which Loureen can protect herself from the police. Florence, offering her complicity in whatever Loureen has done, states, "I didn't see anything but a pile of ash." When Loureen still contemplates calling the police, Florence asks,

> Why? What are you gonna tell them? About all those times they refused to help, about all those nights you slept in my bed 'cause you were afraid to stay down here? About the time he

nearly took out your eye 'cause you flipped the television channel?

Florence's speech reveals her own suspicions about Loureen's possible fate if she makes that phone call. She does not believe that the police will accept Loureen's story but expects them to read into Loureen's history with Samuel a motive for murder rather than an act of self-defense.

Loureen's behavior, her confessions, her conversations with Florence about killing Samuel, and Florence's own clear doubts about Loureen's bizarre story of Samuel's combustion all contribute to the audience's sense of confusion about what really happened. Nottage seems to indicate that the truth about Samuel's death is irrelevant, because Loureen found her voice and realized the power of words; yet Nottage's play comes off as a dramatization of Loureen's wish fulfillment. Loureen does not have to do anything except verbally condemn her husband to escape a history of abuse.

In that the message of Nottage's play is an advocation to speak out, it is a good one, but the way in which events develop in the play provides an unclear message to readers and to domestic-abuse victims. Nottage does not portray Loureen speaking to authorities or to an organization such as a safe house, although she does suggest that in the past, the police have been unwilling to help Loureen. Nottage does not seem to be advocating murder, either. She claims that the power of words is the driving force of the play, but unless those words are spoken repeatedly and to people who can actually help rather than to the person who will continue to practice abuse, the magic that Nottage depicts in *Poof!* will not happen. Tragically, freedom from an abuser cannot be obtained through the victim's wishes alone, but it is this fantasy that Nottage portrays in her play.

Source: Catherine Dominic, Critical Essay on *Poof!*, in *Drama for Students*, Gale, Cengage Learning, 2012.

Randy Gener

In the following essay, Gener recalls discussions with Nottage in examining how her travel and worldview inform her dramatic endeavors.

Four years ago Lynn Nottage crossed the goat-filled countryside of Senegal and Gambia with her butt suspended in midair. It was her first journey to Africa; in the company of her husband, filmmaker Tony Gerber, she was crammed with other passengers inside a minibus rushing through the region's infernal traffic. "It was a hideous bus ride," she recalls, laughingly. "For 10 hours my ass did not touch the plastic-covered seat."

The secondhand Renault she was in, a staple of public transportation in Senegal, is popularly called a *car rapide*, which is dismaying and iron-ical since it is neither a car nor especially rapid; like the tap-taps of Haiti, these privately owned vans have been known to tip over, especially on the bush and savannah roads where they are typically piled high with luggage strapped to the roof. They might swerve madly to avoid a pothole in the road or stop unexpectedly to pick up another passenger. The *apprenti*, the guy hanging out the back of the vehicle, garbage-man style, keeps calling out: "Yes, come on. Get in."

"No matter how crowded the van got there was always room for one more person," Nottage says.

On the day she describes, however, her cul-turally constructed ideas of personal space weren't the only things that were challenged en route. "A woman was traveling with her five children," says Nottage, herself a mother of a seven-year-old. "I expected her children to be rowdy and noisy, like American kids, but they were very quiet and polite—stone silence." Then one of the kids in the tightly packed van began to throw up. Nottage was gripped by panic and disgust. "I have to get out of here, I told myself," she remembers. "The bus did not stop. Everyone in the bus cupped their hands and passed the vomit along toward a window."

Nottage thought she was going to become ill, but, strangely, what she took away from that

gruesome experience was a kind of revelation: "In that moment everyone in the bus became the parent," she explains. "It was grotesque and uncomfortable, but everyone was willing to help this sick boy. I found that phenomenal. I can't imagine that existing here in America." In that minibus, Nottage literally saw "the commu-nal spirit of Africans" at work, as opposed to the American individualism that decrees it's every man for himself. "There are real ideals to be taken from African culture," she posits. "You do discover in Africa that there is more Ameri-can in you than you thought existed."

Or, perhaps, more than you care to admit.

Going to Africa for three weeks was one of the seminal experiences in the 40-year-old play-wright's life. If you've never been, some of the crazy stories Nottage can tell you about that beautiful, complicated, turbulent, messy, ver-dant, tenacious continent will likely suffer in the telling. Her mother and grandmother, who made several trips to Kenya and other parts of Africa, had a powerful emotional and spiritual connection to the continent, and it lived in her imagination from the time she was two years old, although it took her until she was in her mid-thirties to get there. While her fascination for Africa remains undimmed ("It is home," she says. "You have this distant love for something. You meet it, and it exceeds your expectations"), her romantic notions of embracing the mother-land are nevertheless tinged with firsthand knowledge of the sheer brutal reality of its his-tory and politics, its civil wars and cycles of poverty, the powerful legacy of colonialism—as well as the aggressive human-rights abuses she studied while working for four years, straight out of Yale Drama School, as a press officer for Amnesty International.

"The issues that were prevalent when I left Amnesty International were the ethnic killings between Hutus and Tutsis in Rwanda," she says. "You couldn't get anyone to pay attention. Reporters were like, 'Where's Burundi?' Many people gave lip service. That's devastating when you're shouting and you're seeing these images from the field of bloated bodies floating down the rivers. I had a lot of anger and frustration—feelings of helplessness and hopelessness."

This past summer the Brooklyn-based play-wright traveled with her husband, her daughter, Ruby, and her father, Wallace, to Kenya and Uganda for a little over a month. She'd been there in the summer of 2004, with director Kate Whoriskey, in search of a play about the lives of refugee women and girls from Sudan and the Democratic Republic of the Congo, all victims of war, rape and torture at the hands of armed forces [see *American Theatre*, May/June '05]. Now, in 2005, she was planning to visit the all-female Kenyan village of Umoja. Founded 10 years ago by homeless women who had been abandoned by their husbands because they had been raped and thus shamed the community, Umoja (meaning "unity" in Swahili) has since prospered into a sanctuary for young women escaping violence, female genital mutilation and forced marriage.

"I'm trying to find a human way of dramatizing these women's experiences that will provoke thought," Nottage says. "The stories of these refugee women running away from rape and domestic abuse are so graphic, so heart-wrenching, that it will be difficult for people to spend two hours hearing them. It was emotionally difficult for me to hear when I interviewed over 15 women in Kampala." This work-in-progress, which she refers to as "my Africa play," is likely to be called *Ruined*. In it, she says, she will be careful to draw a line between reality and fiction: "Even though I am passionate about the subject, the play won't be testimonials from these women. They told me their stories—they didn't give me their stories—and they are sacred. I know the story I want to tell."

In her plays, as in her life, Lynn Nottage is an intrepid traveler. With a keenly perceptive eye and an unerring ear for dialogue, as well as a healthy appreciation for the unusual, the absurd and the hilariously ironic, she will go anywhere and try just about anything to make the theatrical experience full and rewarding. She is addicted to excursions and research, which she blames, in part, for her being so unprolific: The ground on which her numinous reputation stands consists of only six full-length creations and a memorable one-act, *Poof!* "I see writers who get produced constantly," she says. "They churn out plays year after year. I'm in awe of them. I'm the absolute opposite. I overindulge myself when it comes to research, because for me that's part of the joy of writing the play. Take the one I'm working on right now: This is my second trip to Africa, okay? Is that necessary? Would most playwrights go to this extreme to write a play?"

You never know exactly where the immersions will take Nottage's original mind next. One moment she's routing around in the Brooklyn of the Cold War 1950s (*Crumbs from the Table of Joy*), and in the next she's stuck in a hostage situation controlled by demobilized guerillas in a remote village in Mozambique (*Mud, River, Stone*). If she's not cavorting in hidden corners with court painters and ladies-in-waiting of the French court of Louis XIV (*Las Meninas*), she's locked herself inside an East New York apartment with a gang of terrorists who blow up an FBI building (*Por'knockers*). Often her plays pull a bait-and-switch. Possessed by a mischievous wit that she inherited from the maternal side of her family, Nottage lures you into settling in for a comic ride and then jars it with an unexpected shift in emotional tone or fantasy elements that seem to come out of left field. *Mud, River, Stone*, to pick one example, starts out as a fish-out-of-water satire about a middle-class African-American husband and wife who lose their way somewhere in Africa and land in a wilderness hotel—until harsh reality sets in and they are held at gunpoint, along with a United Nations representative, by a crazed ex-soldier bellhop. Says Seret Scott, a longtime friend who has directed most of Nottage's early plays: "It's almost like a sports event where you're having a great time and, all of a sudden, you hear a sickening, deafening sound, and you know somebody broke a leg. It stops you cold. You ask, 'But when did it stop being funny?' As a director I ask, 'Was it always serious all along?'" (And the wonder of it is that Nottage wrote *Mud, River, Stone* before she ever set foot in Africa.)

Even *Crumbs from the Table of Joy*, ostensibly a memory play about a teenage girl and her displaced southern family in post–World War II Brooklyn, disorients. Shot through with heavy political talk, including an allegorical disquisition on black separatism versus assimilation and sharp critiques of puritanical Christianity, this coming-of-age tale momentarily swerves when the father marries a German woman who may have survived the concentration camps. (When Daddy tells the outraged girls to calm down and take a seat, one of them retorts: "Why? She won't be white if we sit down?") Nottage's subversion tactics are not a deliberate strategy. "It's just the way my imagination works," she suggests. "It's like where you choose to sit when you get on the bus. Some like to sit safely next to the driver. Some like to sit far back. I don't always want to go into the familiar, easy place. I prefer to take the long, slow road, so I can do a lot of sightseeing. I enjoy that very difficult bus ride, with my ass suspended in the air, squeezed between lots of people. I'm going to learn more in a journey that's offering lots of surprises. That's how I approach my writing."

Though at heart a withering satirist, Nottage always goes beyond the external to get to the heart and soul of a place or an era, and she always shows a depth of understanding and respect for her characters—usually restless searchers, forgotten people and alienated folks who are trying to fit in or find a connection or are on a quest for identity.

A poetic purveyor of missed and made intimacies, Nottage also has a crush on strange romantic pairings as narrative devices; they're practically a sine qua non of her small but sturdily cantilevered body of work. Sometimes her infatuation for odd couples results in laughable hookups and ill-fated affairs, as when Undine, the high-powered flack of *Fabulation*, spirals from the ghetto arms of Mo' Dough, a gangsta rapper with gold teeth and progressively twisting baseball cap; to the errant affections of Herve, a swarthy Argentinean gigolo who eats crudites and knocks her up only to snatch all her money and abandon her; and finally to the sweet aspirations of Guy, the Brooklyn ex-addict she meets in drug therapy.

More frequently, as in *Crumbs from the Table of Joy* and *Las Meninas*, Nottage's unlikely lovers fly in the face of racial, social and sexual conventions after having been flung together by the caprices of history or politics: The God-fearing black father and his new German refugee bride in the former play, as well as Queen Marie-Thérèse of France (the wife of Louis XIV) and the African dwarf Nabo in the latter, are nothing if not mismatched souls who discover each other in moments of desperate need, estrangement and lonely vulnerability. (To put this point in extravagant relief, try casting *Las Meninas* with all black actors, mostly made up as white aristocrats in rococo masks, as in Jean Genet's *The Blacks*.) "These plays are making a statement about the nature of love, which is sometimes blind," Nottage muses. "We can't control or make decisions about how our hearts travel."

Few American dramatists aspire to such a panoramic view of the world or manage it so engagingly. Curious and imaginative, subtle and intricate, each Nottage play is richer and more incisive than the one before. Hers is not just a world of incident, intrigue and adventure but a cartography of complex human interactions that sardonically displays the outward sheen of life's absurdities but is capacious enough, in performance, to let its underlying dignity shine through.

"Lynn is pretty unpredictable," notes director Whoriskey, who shepherded Nottage's breakthrough play, *Intimate Apparel*, at South Coast Repertory in California and CENTER-STAGE in Baltimore, as well as its companion play, *Fabulation*, at Playwrights Horizons in New York City. "*Intimate Apparel*'s characters are so sensitively drawn that there's this evolution that happens for actors. *Fabulation*, on the other hand, is funny and very urban and fast. It's much more of a quick hit. Now she's coming up with another piece, *Ruined*—again it's going to be a different idea. More than any writer I know, Lynn is really able to transform. You're always curious to know where she's going to go next."

"I don't think there's necessarily a Lynn Nottage voice," muses director Daniel Sullivan, whose crowning Round-about Theatre Company production of *Intimate Apparel*, seen in New York City and Los Angeles, is responsible for solidifying Nottage's reputation as a dramatist of the first order. "She can go from the abstract world to the satirical, as she does in *Fabulation*. She can also create a thoroughly researched piece like *Intimate Apparel* that lives with great authority in the Victorian world. But it's not as though she will continue storytelling of any particular kind, because she will move on to new worlds."

To grasp Nottage's panoptic view of human affairs, you need only inspect the many private doors of class, race and gender that Esther Mills, the daughter of former slaves, is allowed to pass through at the turn of the past century in *Intimate Apparel*, the country's most produced play of the 2005–06 season. Then juxtapose the spectrum of social types (a Fifth Avenue bride, a tenderloin whore) in Esther's Gilded Age New York with the scenes of class struggle during Undine's rude fall from an upscale pedestal in *Fabulation*. Subtitled "The Re-Education of Undine," this latter play is a barbed satire about the perils of self-invention and social climbing, a picaresque fable about bourgeois comeuppance in black America, as flamboyant and full of tough-edged sarcasm as *Intimate Apparel* is elegant and full of delicacies. Steeped in Africanist elements, *Fabulation* tracks Undine's angry, panic-stricken descent from the snooty, self-righteous Manhattan "buppies" who boot her out of their club to her dreary working-class Brooklyn roots (Lotto-addicted security guards, welfare flunkies, a haughty crackhead granny), where she is known by her real name, Sharona Watkins. A surreal fusion of "Absolutely Fabulous" and a classic trickster fable, this very tall cautionary urban parable steals its title from a verse of an unfinished epic rap poem about Br'er Rabbit that Undine's maybe-crazy Desert Storm-vet brother, Flow, is composing, which goes:

> It 'bout who we be today
> And in our fabulating way.
> 'bout saying that we be
> Without a-pology.

The Yoruba have a saying: "One's destiny could not be magically averted, because it is a question of fate." Spiritually, *Fabulation* is an American descendant of the West African fable, whose animating verve lies in the psychic concept of *nyama* (energy of action), in which the erotics of laughter convey a moral theme: The past is never truly past.

The brooding, understated *Intimate Apparel* and the zany, over-the-top *Fabulation* represent the contradictory impulses and range of Nottage's big-hearted imagination. "The two plays are bookends: I wrote them at the exact same time," Nottage reveals. "For *Fabulation*, I tried to imagine Esther 100 years later, after she's enjoyed the benefits of the women's rights and civil rights movements and become a fully empowered African-American woman, like Condoleezza Rice—and that was Undine. Esther's journey is about becoming empowered, whereas Undine feels completely empowered, so I imagined the opposite journey for her. She falls on hard times, goes through this spiral downward, goes back to her roots. In the end, they both achieve the same thing, which is finding self."

Elaborately constructed out of a series of personal encounters, *Intimate Apparel* tells of the self-effacing Esther's proud pursuit of love in suggestive, novelistic strokes. The yearning to be touched and the tactile pleasures of fabric run woven as leitmotifs throughout. The reason audiences have been utterly captivated by the play, that critics have thrown a garland of major prizes at its feet, that theatre companies across the country have been powerfully drawn to it, has to do with its satisfying density: the rare skill by which it builds tension and pathos to a conclusion that is both quiet and emotionally shattering.

"People like plays about history, but people love doing *Intimate Apparel* because its characters are so pre-Freudian—they speak about their feelings through clothing and business relations," Whoriskey ventures. "Nobody actually talks about their emotional life. You're constantly guessing at how people are feeling as you witness their actions. Lynn has written specific stage directions, and it would be a good idea for them to be followed. The story is in the behavior."

Director Sullivan compares Nottage with David Mamet. "Certainly what is not spoken between Esther and the Jewish fabric-seller Mr. Marks is the heart of the play," he says. "The sadness of it is that theirs is the deepest relationship in the play. What Lynn understood, that Mamet did not understand when he attempted to put his rhythmic language within the Victorian framework of *Boston Marriage*, is what you don't say—the strictures of language that don't allow you to express yourself, and that can be dramatically viable."

Crafted with the lyricism, well-made structure and knowing touches of an extraordinarily fine work of period fiction, *Intimate Apparel* does more than thoroughly entertain—it informs and transports audiences in a way that would be second only to the experience itself. It deserves a place in the pantheon of American dramatic realism of Alice Childress, Lorraine Hansberry, Ntozake Shange and Pearl Cleage.

Written seven years after *Mud, River, Stone*, *Intimate Apparel* is an anomaly in Nottage's oeuvre. It is her most personal play to date, the by-product of a traumatic period that began in 1997 with the death of Nottage's mother, Ruby, of Lou Gehrig's disease followed two months later by the birth of her daughter Ruby.

"My mother taught me how to be an independent thinker, which I think impacts the way I approach my work," says Nottage, interviewed in the comfortably appointed living room of her

Brooklyn home in Boerum Hill. The walls are bedecked with artwork from her parents' friends, who include the painters Norman Lewis, Ernest Crichlow and Romare Bearden. "She encouraged me from the time I was very young to travel and explore the world. She was a passionate, beautiful woman, a humanist who lived by her convictions. She was politically active until the moment she literally couldn't expand her lungs full enough to exhale words."

In a way, Nottage's feelings of filial loss lend seriousness and urgency to *Intimate Apparel*, whose Esther is loosely based on her Barbadian great grandmother, Ethel Boyce, who arrived in New York alone in 1902 to work as a seamstress specializing in women's undergarments. Despite the family prediction that she would remain a spinster, Ethel began corresponding with a Barbadian laborer consigned to the Panama Canal, George Armstrong, who had seen a portrait of her hanging above her uncle's bunk. It was to be a short-lived marriage. In a perhaps apocryphal story, George died prematurely when a stone hit him on the head while he was proselytizing on a speaker's corner.

Not much else is known about Ethel and George. All that's left is a striking passport photograph of Ethel from the early 1920s. "For whatever reason—these are the idiosyncrasies of families—my grandmother became paranoid in her old age," Nottage says. "In addition to not wanting people to steal her precious things, she didn't want people to have these photographs. She began hiding them all over the house. You can find photographs in the weirdest places." After shaking out every polyester dress and tattered fur, Nottage found the sepia passport photo tucked carelessly into an old *Family Circle* magazine.

"It has taken me the act of writing a new play to rescue the members of my family from storage," Nottage wrote in an essay, "Lives Rescued from Silence," for the *Los Angeles Times*. "Sitting in the main hall of the New York Public Library, I had an epiphany: If my family hadn't preserved our stories, and history certainly had not, then who would?"

Since she lost her own mother and after she had become a parent herself, Nottage says, "I feel like a different writer. I can't tell you how I've changed, but motherhood has changed the way in which I view the world."

Her friend Seret Scott detects a new fluency—a blossoming—in Nottage's playwriting since she came out of her private shell in 2002 with *Intimate Apparel* and *Fabulation*. Scott says, "Lynn's writing was always elegant and humorous, but now I feel that she can put down the most ordinary person in the world—people who are otherwise considered uneducated or unintelligent—and invest them with nuance. In terms of character, those nuances are fluid. You don't feel any bumps. Her plays give working-class characters something that allows them to rise above the station our society generally boxes them in."

In her writing, as in her travels, Nottage has also been making bold political choices. Having embraced the role of theatrical preserver, Nottage is a modern-day por'knocker mining for gold among the buried stories, historical archives, faraway African villages and erased or discarded lives. But, she says, ultimately "I speak only for myself. When I look back at history, I'm very aware that I'm doing so through my own personal filter, which is that of an African-American woman living in the 21st century."

Source: Randy Gener, "Conjurer of Worlds: From Richly Imagined Epochs to Unsparing Satires, Lynn Nottage's Roving Imagination Channels History's Discards into Drama," in *American Theatre*, Vol. 22, No. 8, October 2005, pp. 22–26.

SOURCES

Ayres, Neil, "Magical Realism Defies Genres," in *The Man Booker Prizes*, http://www.themanbookerprize.com/perspective/articles/98 (accessed August 27, 2011).

Benford, M. Sue, "Implications of Plant Genome Research to Alternative Therapies: A Case for Radiogenic Metabolism in Humans," in *Journal of Theoretics*, Vols. 4–6, 2002, pp. 1–14, http://www.journaloftheoretics.com/Articles/4-6/MSB.pdf (accessed August 27, 2011).

"Bio," in *Lynn Nottage*, http://www.lynnnottage.net/about.html (accessed August 27, 2011).

"Does Spontaneous Human Combustion Exist?" in *BBC News*, November 21, 2005, http://news.bbc.co.uk/2/hi/uk_news/magazine/4456428.stm (accessed August 27, 2011).

Flavell, Judy, "*Poof!* From Drama to Discussion: A Tool for Talking about Domestic Violence," in *American Shorts*, Kentucky Educational Television, http://www.ket.org/americanshorts/poof/pdf/poof_discussion_guide.pdf (accessed August 27, 2011).

Gener, Randy, "Conjurer of Worlds: From Richly Imagined Epochs to Unsparing Satires, Lynn Nottage's Roving Imagination Channels History's Discards into

Drama," in *American Theatre*, Vol. 22, No. 8, October 2005, http://www.tcg.org/publications/at/oct05/nottage.cfm (accessed August 27, 2011).

"Herstory of Domestic Violence: A Timeline of the Battered Women's Movement," in *Minnesota Center against Violence and Abuse (MINCAVA) Electronic Clearinghouse*, 1999, http://www.mincava.umn.edu/documents/herstory/herstory.html (accessed August 27, 2011).

"History of VAWA," in *FaithTrust Institute*, http://www.ncdsv.org/images/HistoryofVAWA.pdf (accessed August 27, 2011).

"Intimate Partner Violence in the U.S.," in *Bureau of Justice Statistics*, http://bjs.ojp.usdoj.gov/content/intimate/victims.cfm (accessed August 27, 2011).

Isherwood, Charles, "August Wilson, Theater's Poet of Black America, Is Dead at 60," in *New York Times*, October 3, 2005, http://www.nytimes.com/2005/10/03/theater/newsandfeatures/03wilson.html (accessed August 27, 2011).

"Lynn Nottage," in *New York Times*, September 21, 2010, http://topics.nytimes.com/top/reference/timestopics/people/n/lynn_nottage/index.html (accessed August 27, 2011).

Nesmith, Eugene, "Four Bad Sisters," in *A Sourcebook of African American Performance: Plays, People, Movements*, edited by Annemarie Bean, Routledge, 1999, pp. 211–15.

Nottage, Lynn, *Poof!*, in *Crumbs from the Table of Joy, and Other Plays*, Theatre Communications Group, 2004, pp. 89–103.

Page, Yolanda W., "African American Drama," in *The Greenwood Encyclopedia of Multiethnic American Literature: A–C*, edited by Emmanuel Sampath Nelson, Greenwood Press, 2005, pp. 43–51.

Shannon, Sandra G., "An Intimate Look at the Plays of Lynn Nottage," in *Contemporary African American Women Playwrights: A Casebook*, Routledge, 2007, pp. 185–94.

Smalls, Shante T., "Nottage, Lynn (1965–)," in *The Columbia Encyclopedia of Modern Drama*, edited by Gabrielle H. Cody and Evert Sprinchorn, Vol. 2, Columbia University Press, 2007, pp. 978–79.

Snodgrass, Mary Ellen, "Domestic Abuse," in *Encyclopedia of Feminist Literature*, Facts on File, 2006, pp. 147–48.

FURTHER READING

Elam, Harry J., and David Krasner, eds., *African American Performance and Theater History: A Critical Reader*, Oxford University Press, 2001.
    Elam and Krasner gather critical essays about African American theater and the course of its

modern history. Discussions of individual plays, playwrights, and movements are included.

Kolin, Philip C., *Suzan-Lori Parks: Essays on the Plays and Other Works*, McFarland, 2010.
    Parks is one of Nottage's theatrical peers and a fellow winner of the Pulitzer Prize for Drama. Kolin's collection of critical essays on Parks's body of work examines her feminism, her voice as an African American playwright, individual plays and their themes, and her often-experimental style.

Miles, Al, *Ending Violence in Teen Dating Relationships*, Augsburg Books, 2005.
    Miles offers an overview of information about teen-dating violence. Using a variety of research methods, including interviews, Miles assesses the characteristics of violent teen relationships and explores ways in which harmful relationships can be recognized and teens can be guided toward healthier relationships.

Perkins, Kathy A., and Roberta Uno, eds., *Contemporary Plays by Women of Color*, Routledge, 1996.
    Published three years after Nottage's *Poof!* premiered, this collection features other dramas written in the 1990s by African American, Asian American, Latina, and Native American women playwrights.

Randles, Jenn, and Peter Hough, *Spontaneous Human Combustion*, Robert Hale, 2007.
    Paranormal researchers Randles and Hough examine evidence related to the phenomenon of spontaneous human combustion through interviews with fire officers, witnesses, and victims who have survived.

SUGGESTED SEARCH TERMS

Lynn Nottage AND Poof!

Lynn Nottage AND domestic violence

Lynn Nottage AND awards

Lynn Nottage AND African American drama

Lynn Nottage AND feminist drama

Lynn Nottage AND contemporary theater

Lynn Nottage AND one-act plays

Lynn Nottage AND Crumbs from the Table of Joy

Lynn Nottage AND experimental drama

Lynn Nottage AND spontaneous human combustion

A Raisin in the Sun

1961

When Lorraine Hansberry's play *A Raisin in the Sun* made the move from Broadway to film, the move preserved both the Broadway cast and author Hansberry as the screenwriter. Daniel Petrie, whose previous directing experience was largely on television, directed the film, which stars Sidney Poitier as Walter Lee, Ruby Dee as Walter Lee's wife Ruth, and Claudia McNeil as the family matriarch, Lena "Mama" Younger. David Susskind and Phillip Rose produced *A Raisin in the Sun* for Columbia Pictures, for release in 1961. Before filming began, Hansberry wrote several new scenes for inclusion in the film, including scenes to show Mama being exploited by a white grocer and being patronized by her white employer. Hansberry also included a scene where Walter Lee encounters similar patronizing treatment; but studio executives at Columbia Pictures vetoed any additions that they thought might alienate a white audience and make the story less sympathetic. As a result, the film version of *A Raisin in the Sun* is very little changed from the Broadway play.

A Raisin in the Sun was filmed in Chicago and also Los Angeles. Both the film and the play are set in 1950s Chicago and introduced white audiences to the plights of black Americans, whose efforts to improve their lives were severely limited by the society in which they lived. The film centers on the decision the Younger family must make about how to spend the insurance money left to Mama when her husband died.

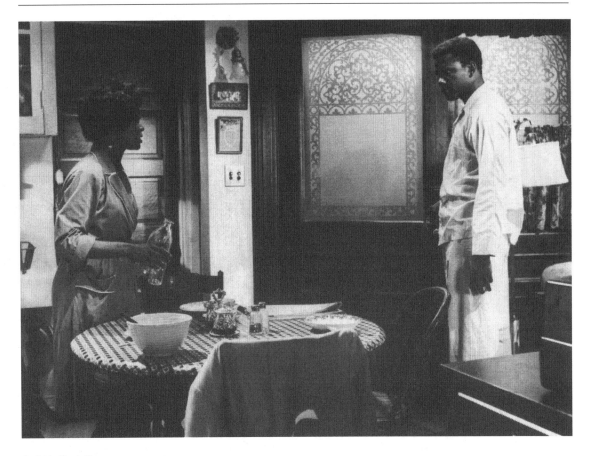

© *AF Archive | Alamy*

Important themes include the lack of opportunities for African Americans, segregation, and the importance of family and heritage. In 1962, the Hollywood Foreign Press nominated Poitier for a Golden Globe Award for Best Actor in a Motion Picture and McNeil for an award for Best Actress in a Motion Picture. *A Raisin in the Sun* was also awarded the Gary Cooper Award at the Cannes Film Festival. This award recognizes human valor in a film's content and treatment and has only been awarded twice since the festival began.

A Raisin in the Sun was first produced on Broadway in March 1959. Because the play has, with one exception, an all-black cast, *A Raisin in the Sun* was considered a risky investment when producer Philip Rose first sought to stage the play, and it took a year to raise enough money. Yet *A Raisin in the Sun* was well received and won the New York Drama Critics' Circle Award for Best Play. The drama was also nominated for four Tony Awards, including Best Play, Best

Actor in a Play for Poitier, Best Actress in a Play for McNeil, and Best Direction of a Play for Lloyd Richards. *A Raisin in the Sun* was the first play written by a black writer and directed by a black director to be staged on Broadway.

PLOT SUMMARY

A Raisin in the Sun is a black-and-white film, with exterior locations filmed in Chicago, Illinois, where the story is set, and also in Los Angeles, California. The initial setting is a small, crowded apartment. As the film opens, every member of the Younger family scrambles to use the communal bathroom outside the apartment, as they rush to get ready to leave for school and work. Walter Lee awakens and asks whether the $10,000 insurance check has arrived yet. Ruth, his wife, reminds him that the check is for his mother and not for him. A quarrel soon erupts between Walter Lee and Ruth. She is angry that he and his friends stayed up late

FILM TECHNIQUE

- Although by the 1960s color films had been popular for more than twenty years, Petrie chose to film *A Raisin in the Sun* in black and white. Black-and-white photography allows for greater emphasis on the use of light and darkness and shadows, which often cross characters' faces in times of stress. With black and white, the audience is not distracted by the use of color, which can dominate a film. Instead, the audience is forced to focus on the characters and what they are doing and saying. The setting of the apartment, for example, fades into the background. The apartment exists, but it does not demand the viewer's attention. In contrast, color photography makes everything on the screen important, and each item competes for the viewer's attention. Black-and-white photography means that the audience looks at each character's face and pays more attention to the dialogue. There is less distraction than when using color.

- In the play, the opening scene is of Travis sleeping on the sofa, which is a fold-down bed in the center of the room. In the film, the opening shot is a close-up of Sidney Poitier, as Walter Lee, sleeping. The camera is closely focused on his face, lingering on the sleeping star, when the jarring alarm clock causes his eyes to fly open. This shot of the relaxed and sleeping Walter Lee is one of the few times that his face is not filled with anger, frustration, or bitterness. Rather than beginning with the sleeping child, the film makes clear that it is Walter Lee who is the catalyst for the story. The camera also lingers on Ruth's face, showing her irritation at Walter Lee when he refuses to get out of bed. In the same shot, the camera also shows Ruth reflected in a mirror, further emphasizing her irritation and indicating her separation from her husband. Camera angles and close-up shots are useful for showing a character's emotional state, as in the case of Ruth, who is irritated with Walter Lee for spending the evening with his friends. Close-up shots allow the audience to share the characters' emotional turmoil, and they focus the audience's attention on whatever the director thinks is important. When Walter Lee picks up the insurance check for the first time, the camera focuses tightly on his face. Initially, his expression is one of wonderment, but then with a slight movement of his eyes and lips, the actor creates an impression of both cunning and happiness.

- The director also uses over-the-shoulder shots. For instance, when Mama and Asagai are talking, the camera is behind Beneatha and focuses the audience's attention on the interaction between Mama and Asagai. The over-the-shoulder shot is also used when Walter Lee rushes into the apartment to ask whether the check has arrived. This shot shifts the focus from him to Mama and Ruth and their dismay that Walter Lee is so singularly focused on the insurance check that he fails to greet his mother and his wife.

---

the night before, talking and drinking, which kept their son, Travis, who must sleep on the sofa in the living room, from sleeping. Walter Lee defends his friends, Willie and Bobo, who have a plan to help all of them become rich.

Walter Lee's sister Beneatha enters, angry that she cannot get into the bathroom. Walter Lee is angry that she is in school and not working to support the family. He accuses Beneatha of wanting the insurance money to pay for medical school, and a nasty fight breaks out between the two. Ruth intervenes and forces Walter Lee out the door and to work. The family matriarch, Mama, enters, and she and Ruth talk about the fact that Mama will be retiring and it is her last day of work.

In the next scene, Walter Lee is at work. He is a chauffeur, and he spends the day wiping down the boss's car to keep it clean and driving wherever he is told to drive. Walter Lee's resentment at being subject to his boss's needs is obvious in the angry expression on his face. This scene does not appear in the theatrical production, where all the action of the play occurs in the apartment. In the film version, the audience is able to leave the small apartment to see where Walter Lee works. This scene adds an important dimension to Walter Lee's personality, since the long days of wiping down the car and driving the boss reveal the mindless repetition of his job and help to account for both his anger and his frustration at the lifetime of drudgery stretching out before him.

The scene then shifts back to the apartment. Ruth is exhausted from ironing all day. She and Mama begin to talk about the insurance check that is expected to arrive the following day. Mama explains that it is her dream to live in a house with a yard and garden. She also talks about her deceased husband and how much he loved his children and how he felt that society holds back black men and keeps them from succeeding.

When Beneatha returns home, Mama and Ruth tell Beneatha that she should marry George, her rich boyfriend, but Beneatha says she has no plans to marry. She wants to be a doctor. Beneatha's many statements about God and how God has nothing to do with her success or her goal of being a doctor anger Mama, who claims that she did not bring up her children to speak about God in such a derogatory manner. She forces Beneatha to admit that there is still God in her mother's house, which finally ends the confrontation. Ruth then asks what Mama will do about Walter Lee's demand that the insurance money be used to buy a liquor store, and Mama replies that she will not use her husband's money for such a purpose.

The scene next shifts to Walter Lee, Willie, and Bobo, who sit in a bar drinking. They discuss their plan to invest in a liquor store. Willie tells Walter Lee that when a woman does not support a man it is time to break up. Walter Lee hesitates, and in his hesitation he seemingly agrees with his friend. This dialogue and this scene do not appear in the stage production, where the action never leaves the apartment. The scene's inclusion in the film further emphasizes the widening gulf between Walter Lee and Ruth and his dependence on his friends.

It is now Saturday, and Mama and Beneatha are busy cleaning. Joseph Asagai telephones, and Beneatha invites him to come to the apartment right away. Ruth arrives home and announces that she is pregnant. She has seen a female doctor, which concerns Mama. Ruth is upset, as is Beneatha, who worries about where another child will sleep in the crowded apartment. Ruth collapses in grief at this new burden and is led away by Mama, just as Beneatha's friend, Asagai, arrives.

Asagai brings Beneatha a dress from his native Nigeria. Asagai asks why Beneatha wears her hair mutilated in such an artificial style, when the women of Nigeria wear their hair in a more natural style. When Mama enters, Asagai easily wins her over, and in doing so he also wins Beneatha, who is suddenly interested in Asagai as a man and not just for what he can tell her about her African identity.

Soon Travis arrives home, and the check is delivered. Mama then asks Ruth why she did not go to the family doctor and instead went to a female doctor, one who is known in the neighborhood as being willing to end an unwanted pregnancy. The stage direction for this scene states that Ruth looks at Mama meaningfully and Mama opens her mouth to speak, but just then Travis comes in. (This implication that this woman doctor will perform an abortion is later made clearer when Mama tells Walter that she thinks that "Ruth is thinking 'bout getting rid of that child"; Ruth will then tell Walter that she gave the woman doctor a five-dollar down payment to end the pregnancy.) At the present moment, Walter Lee rushes in and grabs the check. When Mama refuses to give him the money for the liquor store, an angry confrontation erupts. Ruth tries to speak to Walter Lee, but he yells at her and tells his mother that marrying Ruth was a mistake. Walter Lee tries to rush out the door to go and drink, but Mama will not let him. She accuses him of drinking too much and of having another woman. Walter Lee tells his mother there is no other woman, but he is thirty-five years old and has nothing and will always be nothing. His job is nothing to him, just filled with days of waiting on another man. Walter Lee explains that money is life for him, and he must have the insurance money to survive. When Mama tells Walter Lee that Ruth is pregnant, he is stunned to learn that she is thinking of ending the pregnancy. Mama tells Walter Lee that it is time that he acts like a man; he should also tell his wife not to have an abortion. When Walter Lee walks out, Mama yells after him that he is a disgrace to his father's memory.

The next scene shifts to the bar, where Walter Lee sits drinking. Once again, this scene is a departure from the stage play, in which the audience may surmise that he has gone out drinking, but it is not shown. Back in the apartment, Beneatha models the Nigerian dress that Asagai has brought her; she puts on a record and dances to Nigerian music. As Beneatha dances, Walter Lee comes in and gets a beer from the refrigerator. He is drunk and begins to dance to the music, claiming he is a warrior. Beneatha encourages him. At that moment George arrives, and Walter Lee rushes out to throw up in the community toilet.

George and Beneatha begin to fight over her plan to go out with him in her Nigerian garb. Beneatha rushes out, and Walter Lee returns. Walter Lee makes fun of George's shoes, calling him a college boy, but when Ruth intervenes, Walter Lee calms down and tries to interest George in his plans for investing in a liquor store. When George rejects Walter Lee's plans, Walter Lee again insults George for going to college. George retaliates by telling Walter Lee he is bitter. The argument nearly escalates into a physical brawl before Beneatha returns, having changed from her Nigerian clothes into a dress that George finds acceptable. As Beneatha and George leave, George calls Walter Lee a Prometheus. In Greek mythology, Prometheus was a champion of humankind who stole fire from Zeus and gave it to humans. Prometheus was punished by Zeus by having to suffer a torturous punishment that was repeated every single day. In the film of *A Raisin in the Sun*, this is George's only appearance, but in the stage production, he appears in a later scene, where he tells Beneatha once again that he is not interested in African heritage. He wants a simple, attractive girl and not one who talks all the time about the past.

After Beneatha and George leave, Ruth tells Walter Lee that she will get rid of the baby. Before Walter Lee can respond, Mama arrives back at the apartment. She refuses Walter Lee's demands that she tell him what she did with the money. However, when Travis enters, Mama tells him that she used some of the money to buy a house. Walter Lee is not simply angry at Mama's use of the money to buy a house; he is

devastated. He is also shocked that the new house is in a white neighborhood. Ruth is simply happy to be leaving the small, miserable apartment, with its cockroaches. Mama tells Walter that the house is located at 4903 Clybourne Street in Clybourne Park. In the play, however, the address is 406 Clybourne Street. There is no explanation for why the address is changed in the screenplay.

After Ruth leaves the room, Mama pleads with Walter Lee to understand that she bought the house to try to mend the family. Walter Lee rejects her plea and tells her that she has rejected her children's dreams. Walter Lee tells his mother that he cannot be a man because she runs the house. Then he leaves.

In the next scene, Walter Lee's employer's wife calls and tells Ruth that they will replace Walter Lee if he does not come to work the next day. Mama goes to the bar to find her son, who is sitting in a back booth drinking by himself. Mama calls her son a bum who sits and drinks all day. Walter Lee asks why she left the South and why she is trying to stop him from leaving the prison in which he now lives. Mama is devastated by her son's questions and gives Walter Lee $6,500. He is told to put $3,000 in a saving account for Beneatha's medical school. The remaining $3,500 is to be put in a checking account that Walter Lee will control. He is to be the head of the family and needs to take over from his mama. This scene takes place in the apartment in the original stage production but is moved to a bar in the film, where its staging seems more realistic, given that Walter Lee has spent the past three days drinking at a bar.

The next scene is at the new house. The family excitedly enters and runs from room to room exploring the house. The change in Walter Lee's demeanor is striking. He is happy and confident as he presents his mother with a gift of gardening tools and Travis presents his grandmother with a gardening hat. This scene does not appear in the stage production, but its importance in the film is to visually present to the audience all that has been missing from the family's life in the apartment. The house is filled with sunlight. There is a yard and garden for Mama and a bedroom for Travis. The visit to the house makes real something that is only talked about in the stage production.

In the next scene, the family is packing their possessions and preparing to leave the apartment.

A knock at the door introduces Mr. Lindner, who tells the family that the neighborhood community organization has become aware of the Youngers' purchase of a house in their neighborhood. Lindner tries to explain that the neighborhood is filled with hardworking people who have a dream about what kind of neighborhood they want. They want everyone to share a common background. He tries to convince them that the neighborhood rejection of the Younger family is not about race, but that Negro families should live with other Negro families. The neighborhood is willing to buy the house from the Younger family and help them make a profit. Walter Lee throws Lindner out of the apartment. As he leaves, Lindner says that the Younger family is not wanted and that people will not change their hearts.

When Mama arrives back at the apartment, she learns about Lindner's visit. She is undeterred and begins to fix up her old plant to take it to the house. In spite of Lindner's visit, they are all happy to be leaving the apartment. They are singing and dancing, but the celebrating ends when Bobo arrives. He tells Walter Lee that Willie has run off with their money for the liquor store. Walter Lee is wild with anger. When Mama enters, Walter Lee confesses that he never went to the bank. He gave the entire $6,500 to Willie. Mama recalls all the sacrifices that her husband made, which ended his life prematurely. Her anger is out of control, and she nearly strikes Walter Lee before she collapses in his arms.

Later that afternoon, Asagai arrives to help with the packing for the move. Beneatha tells Asagai that her brother has lost the money, including her money for medical school. Asagai counters Beneatha's despair with a reminder that had her father not died, she would not have had the money. He offers her another option. She should come to Nigeria with him, where she can reclaim her African heritage as his wife. Initially, Beneatha tries to resist, but clearly she is happy about this proposal. Asagai offers to leave and allow her time to think.

Mama tells everyone to begin unpacking and cancel the move. Ruth protests, but Mama tells her they will all have to give up their dreams. Walter Lee enters and tells them he has called Lindner and asked him to come over. Walter Lee wants to sell the house back to the white neighbors. Walter Lee makes a speech about the importance of being a taker and not allowing

people to use them. He is willing to take the money from Lindner and not inflict black people on white people who do not want them. At the end of this speech, Walter Lee suddenly realizes what he has said: he seems to be accepting Lindner's bigoted view of the world and acting as if he and his family are not good enough to live in the white neighborhood.

Mama is devastated by Walter Lee's speech, but Beneatha simply rejects her brother as having no worth. Mama reminds her daughter that the time to love people is when they have made mistakes and when they are at their lowest point. Mr. Lindner arrives, and Mama tells Walter Lee, sarcastically, to go ahead and make his son, Travis, proud by assuming the role of the subservient black man who is not good enough to live in a white neighborhood. Walter Lee begins by telling Mr. Lindner that the Younger family is descended from proud people. Finally, Walter Lee tells Lindner that the family will move into the house and be good neighbors. His father sacrificed for that house and labored for every brick. Lindner tries to appeal to Mama, but she tells him that her son is the head of the family.

Lindner leaves, and the family finishes packing and getting ready to move into their new house. Beneatha tells them that Asagai has asked her to marry him, and Walter Lee says he is the head of the family and will decide whom she will marry. Mama is happy that Walter Lee has finally become a man. The film ends with Mama standing alone in the old apartment, physically and emotionally bidding it farewell.

CHARACTERS

Joseph Asagai

Joseph Asagai is played by Ivan Dixon, who would eventually earn considerable fame for the role he would play on the television series *Hogan's Heroes*. Asagai is a college student from Nigeria. He is very sociable and friendly, and he is infatuated with Beneatha, who initially resists his advances. Beneatha is more interested in Asagai as an African than as a man. He likes that Beneatha will change her appearance to more closely resemble Nigerian women. Asagai also gives Beneatha a dress worn by his sister. Asagai is always referred to by his last name and not by his first name; Lindner is the only other character in this film referred to by a last name.

Bobo

Joel Fluellen plays Walter Lee's friend Bobo. He appears twice in scenes at the bar, where he, Walter Lee, and Willie plan how they will get rich when they buy their liquor store. He also appears at Walter Lee's apartment to tell him that Willie has run off with their money. Bobo is as devastated as Walter Lee and has lost every bit of money he had, although he admits he did not invest as much money as Walter Lee. Rather than expressing anger at Willie, Bobo is filled with despair.

Willie Harris

Willie Harris is played by Roy Glenn. A friend of Walter Lee's, Willie steals the money that Walter Lee gives him to invest in a liquor store. In the theatrical production, he never appears onstage, and the audience learns about Willie's character based on what other characters say about him. In the film production, however, the audience is given the opportunity to meet Willie. He talks up the liquor store, but he also encourages Walter Lee to break with his wife and family, since the women in the Younger family are opposed to the liquor store. In the end, Willie is revealed as a swindler and con man.

Mrs. Johnson

Mrs. Johnson appears in a brief scene that is included in the stage play but eliminated from the film. In this scene, Mrs. Johnson describes the violence with which white neighbors greet black families who dare to move to a white neighborhood.

Mark Lindner

John Fiedler played the role of Mark Lindner in the 1959 Broadway theatrical production, and he was cast in the same role for both the 1961 film and a later 1989 television movie. Lindner is the spokesman for the white neighbors who oppose the Younger family's plan to move into a house in their white neighborhood. Lindner is the only white actor in the play and the film. His sole purpose is to report the view of the neighborhood association and to make clear that a black family is not wanted in the neighborhood. Initially, Lindner appears to be hesitant and uncomfortable as he delivers his message. He does not want to be seen as racist, even though that is certainly the reason for why the Younger family is not wanted in the neighborhood. He is also afraid that Walter Lee might attack him. On his second visit, he is more comfortable with the Younger family and more self-assured. In large part, his comfort stems from his misguided confidence that the Younger family will accept his offer to buy their new house.

Mama

See Lena Younger

George Murchison

George Murchison is played by Louis Gossett, Jr., in his first film role. Gossett also played the role of Murchison in the Broadway production of *A Raisin in the Sun*. George is another of Beneatha's friends. He is a college student from a wealthy family. George likes Beneatha but wants her to give up her interest in her African heritage. He is a snob about his wealth and thinks he is superior to Walter Lee, who has not gone to college and who works in a menial job. George is concerned about Beneatha's appearance, especially when he sees her in Nigerian dress. He is also worried about whether she will play the traditional role that he expects of a woman. George and Beneatha fight about her desire to discover and reclaim her heritage; George sees her desire as pointless compared with his own goals.

Beneatha Younger

Diana Sands plays Beneatha Younger, a role she originated in the Broadway production of the play and for which she received an Outer Critics Circle Award in 1959. Beneatha is Walter Lee's younger sister. She is about twenty years old and is a college student. She plans to attend medical school and become a doctor. Beneatha is the only Younger family member who has been able to attend college, which leads to some resentment on the part of Walter Lee, who thinks that his sister should have a job and help to support the family. In addition to her dream of attending medical school, Beneatha wants to learn about her African heritage, as a way to reclaim what was lost through the history of slavery and assimilation into American culture. She is first interested in Asagai because she wants to learn about her ethnic identity and her African origins. Beneatha is so focused on her African heritage that she is blind to the world in which she lives. For instance, when Walter Lee begins dancing with Ruth, Beneatha accuses them of dancing like old-time Negroes. For Beneatha, the correct way to dance is the way that Africans dance. She plays African music on her record player and practices dancing to it.

Lena Younger

Claudia McNeil, who also played this role in the 1959 Broadway production, plays Lena "Mama" Younger. She played the role of Mama again at the Candlelight Forum Theatre in Chicago, Illinois, in 1975. Mama is the matriarch of the Younger family. Her late husband's death and his insurance money enable her to retire after many years of hard work, but when Mama receives the check, she is upset, reminded that this money is all that remains of her husband's life. Mama is intent on using this insurance money to help both her children achieve greater success. She is also saddened that her children have not grown up to be what she had hoped they would be. Beneatha no longer believes in God, and all Walter Lee ever talks about is money.

Mama's dream is to move out of the crowded three-room apartment that the family shares and into a house, where there will be a yard in which her grandson, Travis, can play. Her dream of having a garden is represented by the single plant that she lovingly cares for each day. Mama and her husband struggled for years in menial jobs but were never able to save enough money to buy a house. His death makes it possible for her to make her dream of owning a house a reality, but she also buys the house because she thinks it will heal the rift that has developed in the family. Mama is so completely unselfish that it never occurs to her to use the $10,000 insurance money for herself. She will use it only to benefit her family.

Ruth Younger

Ruby Dee plays the role of Ruth Younger in the film; she had played this role in the Broadway theatrical production as well. Ruth, who is Walter Lee's wife, is a domestic worker; she labors in other women's homes. No matter how tired she is, she will not take a day off; she needs the job and feels a sense of responsibility to be a dependable worker. Ruth shares Mama's dream of owning a home with a yard. Ruth wants her family to be successful, strong, and happy. She wants her son, Travis, to have his own room and not have to sleep on the sofa in the living room. Ruth tries to negotiate peace between Beneatha and Walter Lee and helps to soothe tense situations. However, Ruth is also aware that she and Walter Lee are drifting apart. In one scene, she admits to Mama that she and Walter Lee seem to have lost the closeness they once shared. Ruth considers ending her pregnancy because she

thinks that Walter Lee will not want another child. Ruth is generally very quiet, but when she learns that Mama has bought a house, she is transformed into a different woman. She is excited and happy for the first time in the film.

Travis Younger

Travis Younger is played by Stephen Perry. Travis is the ten-year-old son of Walter Lee and Ruth. Because the apartment is so small, he must sleep on the sofa in the living room. He is a cheerful child, and he is excited to move to the family's new home. Travis is the catalyst for moving to the new house, since Mama wants him to be able to play outside and to have his own room in the house. Travis's role in the film is somewhat smaller than in the stage play; there, he appears in a scene that is missing from the movie, in which he is sent outside to play to escape the fumes from a spray being used to kill the cockroaches that infest the apartment.

Walter Lee Younger

Sidney Poitier's performance of Walter Lee Younger earned him both a Golden Globe nomination for Best Actor in a Motion Picture and a Best Actor nomination from the British Academy of Film and Television Arts. Poitier also played this role in the Broadway theatrical debut of *A Raisin in the Sun*. Walter Lee is a chauffeur. He sees the wealthy people he drives and wants the same wealth for his family. Walter Lee blames racism for his being stuck in a service job, but he also makes poor choices, such as investing $6,500 with a swindler. Walter Lee is not interested in either his sister's dream of medical school or his mother's and wife's dreams of living in a house instead of an apartment. He can only see his own dream of being rich. The insurance check is his sole focus, and he does not even notice that his wife is pregnant until his mother tells him. Walter Lee desperately wants the insurance check and impatiently asks for it a day before he knows it is due to arrive. He thinks that investing in the liquor store is his chance to "be someone" and to help his son reach the same position.

Walter Lee is brimming with anger and frustration throughout much of the film. Poitier's performance is one of barely controlled rage. The character's frustration and resentment boil over into his speech, with the use of tones that are alternately sarcastic and bitter. Walter Lee drinks to escape the hopelessness of his life but fails to understand that his drinking also limits him. When George calls Walter Lee a Prometheus, Walter Lee does not understand the insult, since he does not know that according to Greek mythology Prometheus was destined to spend his life being tortured every day. Had he understood the reference, it is likely that Walter Lee would have been even more depressed and frustrated than usual. It is only after Mama gives him the $6,500 that Walter Lee's anger evaporates and he finally reconciles with his wife, Ruth.

THEMES

Black Culture
In both the theatrical production of the play and the film, Hansberry probes difficult issues, such as black assimilation and identity. *Assimilation* refers to the absorption of a minority culture into that of the majority, replacing distinctive cultural traits with the dominant ones. Beneatha most clearly exhibits the tension created between the old ways and the struggle to forge a unique black identity that is not adopted from white culture. Her determination to go to medical school is one way in which she strives to create a unique identity for herself. Few women, and even fewer black women, attended medical school in the 1950s. In addition to her career plan, Beneatha actively seeks knowledge about her African heritage and uses what she learns about her African past to replace those parts of her life that she identifies as too white and too assimilated.

Asagai plays an important role in fulfilling Beneatha's quest to discover her identity. He provides her with a Nigerian dress and shows her how to wear it. He also gives her music records that contain African music. Later in the film, Beneatha plays the records and dances in an African style to the music. In addition to the robes and the records, in the play (but not the film version), Asagai gives her a Nigerian headdress. Asagai also teases Beneatha about her hair, which is chemically straightened. He asks her why she mutilates her hair, since wearing it natural is how her hair should be worn. The exclusion of the headdress from the film diminishes Beneatha's efforts to reclaim her African heritage and therefore makes her efforts to establish a new identity less of a focus in the

film. Later in the film, when Beneatha watches Ruth and Walter Lee dancing, she tells them that they dance like Negroes. The implication is that they should be dancing as Africans.

Family Relationships
In both the stage play and the film version of *A Raisin in the Sun*, several of the family relationships are defined by money. Mama became head of the family after her husband, Big Walter, died. Mama wants Walter Lee to be the head of the family but needs him to prove that he is capable of assuming that role. It never occurs to Mama that she is qualified to lead the family. In the 1950s, women did not head families if a man was available to do so. His mother's usurping of this traditional masculine role emasculates Walter Lee, causing him to question his ability to take care of his family. As a result, he thinks that opening his own liquor store and being his own boss will help to restore his sense of masculinity. One of the reasons that Mama gives Walter Lee the $6,500 is to restore him to his rightful position as head of the Younger family. Mama's display of trust in handing Walter Lee a roll of cash restores him to this traditional masculine role.

Another important Younger family relationship is the one portrayed by Walter Lee and Ruth. In the opening scene of the film, Ruth chastises Walter Lee for having his friends over and staying up late. Travis, who must sleep on the sofa, was unable to sleep on a school night. Ruth is angry, and Walter Lee's response is angry. Throughout much of the film, as well as in the play, Walter Lee and Ruth argue about money. When Ruth tells Travis that she cannot give him fifty cents for school, Walter steps up and gives his son a dollar. This is money that the family does not really have to spend, but Walter Lee wants his son to know that his father can provide for him.

The largest source of conflict between Walter Lee and Ruth centers on his plan to use the insurance money to invest in a liquor store. Ruth hates the idea of a liquor store. Too many men drink too much, and Walter Lee spends a great deal of time drinking in a bar. Because Ruth feels that Walter Lee no longer loves her, she visits a female doctor who is known to perform abortions. Walter Lee reconciles with Ruth only after Mama gives him a share of the insurance money and steps down from her role as head of the

READ, WATCH, WRITE

- Hansberry first wrote *A Raisin in the Sun* as a theatrical play. She then rewrote the play as a screenplay for the film production. Working in small groups with two or three classmates, create a glossary of film and camera terms. Some terms to consider are point of view; montage; dissolve; high angle; short, medium, and long shots; tracking shot; pan shot; and close-up shot. In your glossary, define each term and then provide an example of how it is used in the film. In addition to creating a written film glossary, work with a small group to prepare a video of examples to illustrate your glossary terms. If a film technique that you discuss in your glossary was not used in filming *A Raisin in the Sun*, provide an example from a different film with which you are familiar. Next, download the film clips that you have selected into a digital presentation to show to your classmates or post on your Web site.

- In one scene in the film, Beneatha plays African music and dances to the music that Asagai has given her. Research music from Nigeria, the country from which Asagai originated. Write a paper in which you discuss the various circumstances in which such music is performed and how it reflects the culture and values of Nigeria in the context of the movie.

- In *A Raisin in the Sun*, Beneatha values education, as does George. Both of these characters use language differently from Mama or Walter Lee or Ruth, who have less education. Lindner also has his own distinct speech patterns. Choose one speech by each of these characters. In an essay, compare the ways each character uses language and what these speech patterns reveal about each character's education, socioeconomic level, desires, dreams, and values.

- In this film, Mr. Lindner represents how white discrimination against blacks could be used to keep blacks out of the white world. As you watch this film, consider what you see and hear. How might the physical settings and the words spoken by these characters either reinforce or deny Lindner's fears? For example, is Lindner likely to be more impressed by the cleanliness of the apartment or the shabbiness of the Younger family belongings? Does Lindner respond more to what Beneatha says or to what Walter Lee says? Watch both of the scenes in which Lindner appears and carefully study both his speech and his mannerisms. Then prepare a presentation in which you use video clips of Lindner to thoroughly analyze his character and what he is revealing to the audience about racism and prejudice.

- After watching the film of *A Raisin in the Sun*, read the play. Much of the action of both play and film focuses on Walter Lee, who is alternately angry, frustrated, impatient, isolated, and explosive. Consider how the director chooses to reveal these moods to the audience. Watch Walter Lee's face as he speaks and when other characters speak to him. What do you learn from watching his face? How is it different from the experience of reading the play? Try watching the film with the sound muted. What do you learn about this character's moods from simply watching the camera shots? How is he dressed? What does his clothing say about the kind of person he is? Make a list of everything that you now know about Walter Lee and create a comprehensive character analysis chart, in which you explore this character's dreams and values in key scenes throughout the film.

The plot involves the use of restrictive covenants to prevent desegregation of neighborhoods in the south side of Chicago. (© *Visions of America, LLC | Alamy*)

family. The timing of this reconciliation suggests that Walter Lee needed money to give him stature. He also needed to be accepted as the head of the family before he could become the husband that Ruth thought him to be in the early years of their marriage.

Racism

Racism and the segregation and discrimination that often define racism are very evident in both the film and staged productions of *A Raisin in the Sun*. Mama works as a domestic servant. This is the only work she has ever performed. Ruth is also employed as a domestic, and Walter Lee is a chauffeur. No member of the family has been able to rise above the servant class. Walter's anguish at the lack of opportunities for black men is revealed in his desire to open his own liquor store, where his son Travis will see him achieve the same kind of success that white men achieve.

In addition to limiting employment opportunities, racism also limits where the Younger

family can live. Mama's choice to buy a home in a white neighborhood sets in motion the confrontation over segregation that dominates the last part of both the film and the play. Mama tells the family that she chose the house in Clybourne Park because it was the nicest house for the least amount of money. The homes being built for black families are farther from town and twice as expensive. The Lindner character represents white oppression of the black family. Lindner is played as unassuming and passive, but his role is to tell the Younger family that they are not the kind of people who will fit in with the neighborhood—in short, that they do not belong in a white neighborhood. He argues that black families are happier living with their own kind in their own communities, rather than living in a neighborhood where they are not wanted. Lindner represents an effort by a white neighborhood to clothe their racism in a quiet, passive voice, rather than making it overt, with threats.

Beneatha is the one member of the family to actively combat racism and discrimination. She attends college and has career plans that resist the employment pattern she sees at home. Rather than working as a domestic, Beneatha plans an education and a professional career in medicine. She is not satisfied with living as the kind of black woman she sees modeled by her mother and Ruth. Instead, Beneatha embraces her race as a unique gift and reaches back to her origins in pre-slavery Africa. She wants to learn about what it means to be an African woman because it affords an image not limited by racism and segregation.

STYLE

Music

The opening music is dramatic, with the opening filled with percussion instruments before the credits continue with the melodic sounds of strings. The music, by Lawrence Rosenthal, suggests the serious nature of the film. When Mama tells Ruth about her early years in the apartment with Big Walter, the music is sentimental and is so muted that it is easy to miss. When Asagai shows Beneatha how to wear traditional Nigerian dress, the music becomes more joyful, and the tempo picks up, with suggestions of African tribal sounds. The music disappears during serious conversations, such as when Walter Lee argues with Mama over giving him the money for the liquor store. Except for when Beneatha plays her record player, there is no direction for music noted in printed copies of the play.

Costuming

The actors' costumes are simple working clothes. Walter Lee wears a suit and a cap for his job as a chauffeur. Mama and Ruth are often shown wearing simple shirtwaist dresses, with aprons tied around their waists. Mama wears a hat with flowers when she comes in from shopping, but when at home, her hair is unadorned and neatly arranged in a bun at her neck. Beneatha's clothing is also simple, but it is obviously a bit neater, better kept, and seemingly of higher quality than that worn by the other women. She occasionally wears a shirtwaist dress without an apron, but much of the time, Beneatha wears dungarees and a button-down shirt, tied at the waist. The clothing worn by the Younger family suggests practicality, rather than an attempt to impress outsiders.

Setting

Although the film allows the drama to move off the stage and away from the Youngers' tiny apartment, much of the action still takes place in the apartment. The kitchen is small and crowded, with a table, four mismatched chairs, and a small refrigerator. A checkered cloth covers the table. A single plant sits on a windowsill, and a few kitchen tools hang on the wall. The ironing board is also visible in the kitchen. The other rooms are also simply decorated with well-worn furniture. What is especially noticeable is how clean and neat everything is. Nothing is out of place, and even though Travis sleeps on the sofa, the bedding is carefully put away every morning. The stage directions for the play describe the rooms as crowded but neat, with well-worn furniture that was undoubtedly nice many years ago when first purchased. The film adopts this stage direction and uses this setting to present the family as neat and orderly, clean and simple, which emphasizes their willingness to work hard, even though they have little to show for all their hard work.

CULTURAL CONTEXT

Segregated America

A Raisin in the Sun was one of the first Hollywood films to focus on the plights of black Americans. During the 1960s, the civil rights movement would gain momentum, and part of that effort centered on showing white audiences the inequalities that African Americans were enduring. This film shows the differences between the opportunities of blacks and whites for housing and employment in Chicago, and it helped awaken its audiences to injustice.

Although the U.S. Supreme Court had ruled that enforcement of racially restrictive neighborhood covenants was unconstitutional in 1948, Chicago in the 1950s was slow to accept these changes. The 1927 Chicago Municipal Code, which adopted racially restrictive housing covenants, was still being followed into the 1950s, in spite of several legal cases challenges these covenants. Many black residents of Chicago thus found it difficult to find housing and were forced to live in low-income housing projects that were often crime ridden. Efforts by Chicago's African American population to move out of the ghettos and into suburban neighborhoods were met with

Ruby Dee played Ruth Younger in the film.
(© AF Archive / Alamy)

resistance, much as Hansberry shows in *A Raisin in the Sun*. African American groups filed lawsuits against the Chicago Housing Authority in an attempt to integrate some Chicago neighborhoods, but these lawsuits failed to achieve their goals. Chicago was not the only city to have segregated housing, whether official or unofficial. When filming began in Los Angeles, Poitier attempted to rent a house but found that no one was willing to rent to a black man, not even one who was a movie star.

The small, crowded apartment that Hansberry depicts in both film and play was typical of the housing in which blacks lived in Chicago. Blacks paid the same amount in rent as whites for apartments that were less than one-fourth as large. It was not uncommon for black housing to lack electricity or hot water. The Younger apartment lacks a bathroom; instead, the family shares a community bathroom with the other inhabitants of their apartment building. Rats and cockroaches also inhabited these crowded apartments. In both the film and play, Beneatha sprays insecticide among the cracks in the apartment walls. In the play, there are two episodes

where Travis plays outside chasing rats. He also describes how the rats are killed. The references to rats and the scenes detailing the killing of rats, which are not included in the film version, are evidence of the family's poor living conditions and their deteriorating neighborhood. The film focuses on what happens inside the apartment and contrasts the crowded apartment with the spaciousness and cleanliness of the new house.

There were some efforts in the predominantly low-income black neighborhoods to increase police protection, eliminate overcrowding in schools, and prevent delinquency among black residents. There were also efforts to increase job opportunities through on-the-job training. However, during the 1950s and 1960s, segregation and discrimination toward blacks actually increased in Chicago. As a result, opportunities for black Chicagoans to have better access to education, employment, and housing decreased. Mama's description of how she and her husband had fled the violence of the South to create a better life for their children in Chicago reminds the audience of the danger of lynching that African Americans faced in the South. This film shows segregation being used to prevent blacks from achieving the kinds of success that they had dreamed of finding when they migrated to the North.

In *A Raisin in the Sun*, the audience sees the small apartment, the bathroom in the common hallway, and the need to spray for cockroaches. The audience also hears Walter Lee lament the lost opportunities for employment and voice his desire to run his own business. The film also shows the oppressors of black Chicagoans in the person of Lindner, the white chairman of the Clybourne Park Improvement Association, who tells audiences that "our Negro families are happier when they live in their own communities." This defense of neighborhood covenants, which had already been found unconstitutional by the Supreme Court, demonstrates how neighborhood associations were working to circumvent laws against discrimination. Lindner's angry departing words, "I hope you people know what you are getting into," expose the dangers that the Younger family will face in their new home. They are the same dangers that other black families faced when moving into white neighborhoods. In the original ending to the play, Hansberry wanted the family to be sitting in their new home in the dark, armed and waiting for a mob to come and attack them. She changed the ending before the play was ever produced, either on stage or film, at the producer's request. The happier ending keeps the audience from confronting the reality of what black families did face when hostile and angry mobs demanded that they move out of a neighborhood.

CRITICAL OVERVIEW

The film version of *A Raisin in the Sun* was eagerly awaited and released in 1961 to generally positive reviews. The play had been a hit on Broadway only two years earlier, winning the New York Drama Critics' Circle Award for Best Play in 1959. Two of the film's actors, Poitier and McNeil, had been nominees for Tony Awards in 1960, as was the play, which was nominated for best play of the year. In a 2004 revival of *A Raisin in the Sun*, both Audra McDonald and Phylicia Rashad received Tony Awards for their roles.

The success of the initial Broadway stage production set a high standard for the film to match; according to most film reviewers, it easily reached the same level. In Jesse H. Walker's review of *A Raisin in the Sun* for the *New York Amsterdam News*, the film is pronounced "even better than the award-winning play." In particular, Walker cites the film's ability to move outside the small Chicago apartment to show Walter Lee at work and drinking in a bar, as well as showing the audience the new home. Walker mentions that one of the strengths of the filmed version of *A Raisin in the Sun* is the cast retained from the Broadway play, led by Poitier, McNeil, Dee, and Sands, who create a "tender, loving portrayal of a family with a dream."

Other reviewers were similarly complimentary. In his review for the *Los Angeles Times*, John L. Scott states that *A Raisin in the Sun* was a "moving stage drama" that has now become "an equally affecting film melodrama." As did Walker, Scott notes the strengths of Poitier, McNeil, Dee, and Sands, whose performances Scott describes as "piercing" and "vivid." Bosley Crowther's review of the film for the *New York Times* is similarly complimentary of the cast, who he claims "can make Miss Hansberry's simple, telling words carry the heart-piercing eloquence of poetry or the bloodletting slash of knives." Crowther points out that the dialogue "has the

ring of authentic conversation and the authority of truth."

In a review of *A Raisin in the Sun* for the *Washington Post and Times-Herald*, a contributor echoes other reviewers who noted the strength and talent of the Broadway cast's appearance in the film production. In particular, this reviewer reassures audience members that they need not "fear a heavy-handed message from Miss Hansberry." Instead, the reviewer claims that Hansberry includes "rollicking humor" and a "family joke" in lieu of "sociological commentary." The inclusion of this humor, according to the reviewer, allows the audience to identify with the characters, who face a struggle familiar to all people who want to create better lives for their families.

CRITICISM

Sheri Metzger Karmiol
Karmiol is a university lecturer in interdisciplinary studies. In the following essay, she evaluates Sidney Poitier's performance in the film version of A Raisin in the Sun.

Lorraine Hansberry develops many important themes in *A Raisin in the Sun*. She focuses on the strength that women reveal as they struggle with poverty and negotiate the relationships that they have with their husbands and sons. There are scenes in the film that reveal Walter Lee's chauvinistic attitude toward the women in his family and scenes that highlight the generational conflict between mother and son. Hansberry also explores the importance of Africa as a source of racial pride and as a component of black heritage. However, the thwarted dreams of black Americans are what provide one of the most important themes in *A Raisin in the Sun*. Each adult member of the Younger family expresses a dream, but whether that dream can be fulfilled or whether it must die is the subject of the film. The title for *A Raisin in the Sun* is taken from a 1951 poem by Langston Hughes, "Harlem [2]." In this poem, Hughes asks whether a dream that is repeatedly put off dries up and withers like a raisin in the sun, whether it hurts and becomes infected like a wound, or whether it explodes. Hughes's poem proves to be an apt inspiration for Hansberry's film. In *A Raisin in the Sun*, Sidney Poitier's performance as Walter Lee Younger reveals a man teetering on a

WHAT DO I SEE NEXT?

- A made-for-television film of *A Raisin in the Sun* starring Sean (P. Diddy) Combs and Phylicia Rashad was released by Sony Pictures in 2008; it is available on DVD. It was directed by Kenny Leon and based on a script by Paris Qualles. This production earned good reviews and was watched by more than 12 million viewers on its ABC debut. This production was nominated for three Emmy Awards but failed to win.

- *To Be Young, Gifted, and Black* (1972) is a film based on the book of the same title, which is a compilation of Hansberry's short writings. The film includes scenes from *A Raisin in the Sun* as well as from several of Hansberry's short stories and essays. Blythe Danner, Ruby Dee, Claudia McNeil, and Roy Scheider star. This film was directed by Michael Schultz and was developed with input from Hansberry's husband, Robert Nemiroff. This film is available on VHS as part of PBS's "Great Performances" series.

- Sidney Poitier also starred in *To Sir with Love*, a 1967 British film that deals with racism and prejudice in inner-city schools. Poitier plays a new teacher who must confront racism in a school filled with students who do not expect to ever succeed in life. James Clavell wrote the screenplay and directed the film, which was based on a novel by E. R. Braithwaite. This film provides an interesting contrast to *A Raisin in the Sun* and illustrates that racism was an issue in Great Britain as well as the United States.

- *The Rosa Parks Story* is a 2002 television film starring Angela Bassett. The film dramatizes the life of Parks, who became a modern hero after she refused to give up her seat on a bus in Montgomery, Alabama, to a white man in 1955. Her refusal to obey this segregation law helped to fuel the civil rights movement. This film would pair nicely with *To Kill a Mockingbird*, a 1962 film starring Gregory Peck and appropriate for young-adult audiences, which also focuses on prejudice and racism in Alabama.

- *The Piano Lesson* is a 1995 film based on an August Wilson play of the same title. This film, which was a Hallmark Hall of Fame production, stars Charles S. Dutton and Alfre Woodard as a brother and sister who struggle to understand and retain their heritage. The piano in the title is a family heirloom, but the brother wants to sell it to buy farmland. There are clear parallels to the conflict in *A Raisin in the Sun*, in which Walter Lee wants his father's insurance money to buy a liquor store. *The Piano Lesson* was nominated for four Golden Globe Awards.

- *Nothing but a Man* (1963) was one of the earliest independent films with a mostly black cast created for an integrated audience. The film focuses on a black man who insists to his white bosses that he must be treated with dignity and respect. The film is not focused on civil rights for the African American community but rather is a plea for personal rights.

- *Martin Luther King, Jr.: "I Have a Dream"* (2005) includes King's memorable speech of August 28, 1968, as well as footage from his 1963 March on Washington for Jobs and Freedom. This DVD also includes news film from several early 1960s civil rights protests. News anchor Peter Jennings narrates much of the film. Although reading the speech is also important, the film allows viewers to hear King's stirring voice deliver his now-famous words.

---

precipice, nearly exploding into rage. Walter Lee is a man who sees his dream slipping away from him. Throughout the film, Poitier's performance illuminates Walter Lee's ever-present fear that his dream will be deferred until it withers and dies, just as Hughes describes in his poem.

The insurance check that motivates each character's action in *A Raisin in the Sun* seems to hold the power to make dreams become reality. Mama's plan will divide the money to make all their dreams come true: $3,500 buys the house in Clybourne Park, $3,000 will allow Beneatha to attend medical school, and $3,500 will give Walter Lee the opportunity to fulfill his dream of owning his own liquor store. Instead of setting aside money for Beneatha, however, Walter Lee proves greedy, discounting Beneatha's dream and investing her portion of the $6,500, which is subsequently lost to Willie. As a result, only Mama achieves her dream. In "'Measure Him Right': An Analysis of Lorraine Hansberry's *Raisin in the Sun*," Jeanne-Marie A. Miller suggests that the insurance check tests each member of the family. It is the catalyst that creates familial conflicts, but it also functions as a way to explore each family member's character. The need for money, which often seems to consume Walter Lee, illuminates the flaws in his character. Miller claims that when Mama uses some of the money to buy the house, she "destroys her son, and explodes his dream of a life of dignity as he defines it." Of course, had Mama not used some of the money to buy the house, Walter Lee would likely have given all $10,000 to Willie and thus lost it all. When Mama takes some of the money to buy a new home, she forces Walter Lee to acknowledge the validity of the dreams of others.

Although McNeil's Mama is a commanding presence in this film, it is Poitier's depiction of Walter Lee that forms the central focus for the actions of each of the other characters. As an example, several times in the opening scenes of *A Raisin in the Sun*, Ruth tells Walter Lee to "eat your eggs." The phrase "eat your eggs" is meant as a practical response to bring Walter Lee back into the present and to remind him that dreams

are just that—dreams. What the phrase actually does, however, is deny Walter's dream by substituting the practical necessity of eating breakfast. Ruth's repetition of this phrase is her effort to bring her husband back to earth, but for Walter Lee, Ruth's words are a reminder of the stifling atmosphere of their home. In the close confines of the apartment, there is no room for the man to dream. The liquor store is his dream: in owning his own business, he will be his own boss and achieve what many other black men at the time could not. In the early scenes of *A Raisin in the Sun*, Walter Lee characterizes the women in his life as not supportive of his dreams. At one point in the film, he exclaims,

> A man say to his woman: I got me a dream. She says: Eat your eggs, they getting cold. Man say to his woman: Help me now to take a hold of this here world and his woman say: eat your eggs and go to work.

Although the actual text of this scene makes clear Walter Lee's frustration, Poitier's command of the scene reveals to the audience the depth of Walter Lee's disappointment that his wife is too small-minded to appreciate and support his dreams. As the scene progresses, his anger builds. There is an intensity in Poitier's expressions, especially the way his eyes lock onto Ruth, as he tries to explain the importance of his dreams and why his father's insurance money is so important to him. When his anger shifts to Beneatha and threatens to explode as he berates her unwillingness to work to help the family, Ruth finally intervenes and pushes him toward the door and to work. At this point, Poitier's arms drop, and it is with mingled sadness and disappointment that he says, "Nobody in this house is ever going to understand me." Poitier's sagging posture and downcast expression make these words come to life.

What Walter Lee has failed to acknowledge is that every other member of his family also has a dream. Mama's dreams are different from his. At one time, her dream was to escape the South and live somewhere free of the risk of lynching. Now, her dream is to live in her own house, where she can walk on floors that she owns. She dreams of giving her grandson, Travis, his own room in which to sleep and a yard in which he can play safely, away from the risks of the inner city. Ruth's dream also centers on escaping the apartment and having a house. She also dreams of making her marriage whole again and recreating the closeness that she and Walter

Lee once shared. As a college student, Beneatha has already achieved more than any other member of the family, but she dreams of reaching higher still. She dreams of going to medical school but instead leans toward fulfilling another aspiration: finding her heritage in Africa. In time, only Walter Lee's dream will remain unfulfilled. His despair when he learns that Willie has stolen his dream is an important scene for Poitier, who must make the audience see that this man is more than just a lost cause. The audience has to feel his pain. Walter Lee's fear when he learns that the money has been stolen and he has been betrayed is revealed through Poitier's many nervous tics, his hyperactive movements, and his delivery of angst-ridden words: "Willie. Don't do it man. Not with that money. Not with that money. I trusted you. I put my whole life in your hands." His final scream, "Willie Willie," is two words filled with years of pain and disappointment. The sheer agony in Poitier's words, the anguish expressed on his face, his collapse to the ground—all of these combine to portray a man whose life has just collapsed around him. Walter Lee may have acted foolishly, but Poitier makes him more than a foolish man.

In reviews of the film version of *A Raisin in the Sun*, many of the actors are celebrated for their efforts to capture the essence of the characters they play, but it is Poitier's anguished portrayal of Walter Lee that demands the audience's attention. In his autobiography, *The Measure of a Man*, Poitier writes that he had a basic disagreement with Hansberry over his depiction of Walter Lee. Long before the play opened on Broadway and well before the decision was made to adapt it for film, Poitier resisted Hansberry's vision for the character. Poitier saw the son as "a man whose life is on the line," but Hansberry saw the story as centered on Mama, with the son as a "ne'er-do-well" whose mother ultimately makes him into a man. However, Poitier explains that he was not content to play the role that way. He wanted to bring a greater intensity to the role, to portray Walter Lee as a proud man who struggles with the limitations and role forced on him by an unjust world. Aram Goudsouzian discusses the intensity that Poitier brings to his role in this film in his book *Sidney Poitier: Man, Actor, Icon.* Goudsouzian claims that as Walter Lee, "Poitier is exquisitely expressive: pacing with anger, imitating an African warrior, shimmying to jazz, dropping to his

Sidney Poitier starred as Walter Lee Younger in the film. (© Moviestore collection Ltd / Alamy)

knees in torment, standing upright with reclaimed manhood." Poitier so "owns the film," according to Goudsouzian, that the other actors seem to fade into the background. Because much of the film takes place in the Younger family's tiny apartment, Poitier appears even larger and more forceful next to the smallness of the set.

By the end of the film, Mama, Ruth, and Beneatha all achieve some variation of their dreams, and it is only Walter Lee whose dreams have withered, like a raisin in the sun. Hughes's poem was a response to the racism that was so prevalent in American society prior to the civil rights movement that peaked in the 1960s. *A Raisin in the Sun* is also a response to racism, but it is through Poitier, whose tortured performance is designed to earn the audience's sympathy and concern, that the film becomes a statement about the injustice of racism. Poitier takes Hansberry's words and makes the effect of racism personal. The effect of the words as they are spoken in this film makes Poitier's character seem more tortured than they might when spoken by a lesser actor. Walter Lee is beaten down by his past and the emptiness of his future. He has been beaten down by the dreams that seem always just out of his grasp and by a world that appears intent on keeping black men from ever escaping the chains that hold their dreams just out of reach. Walter Lee's dream is to achieve dignity and a position in the world in which he can hold his head high, but he never achieves his dream. Nonetheless, Hansberry ends the film on a happy note, with the family moving out of their apartment and into their new home. There is no mention of the racism and perhaps even violence that will greet the family upon their arrival in this white neighborhood, nor are Walter Lee's future or his dream important any longer. His chauffeur's job awaits him, and he will not own his own business. But he has resisted the efforts of Mr. Lindner to buy out the family, and he must be satisfied that even though his dream has eluded him once again, he has achieved stature in his family's eyes.

Source: Sheri Metzger Karmiol, Critical Essay on *A Raisin in the Sun*, in *Drama for Students*, Gale, Cengage Learning, 2012.

Zachary Ingle

In the following excerpt, Ingle reviews elements of the play that were changed for the original screenplay and the effects of those on the final film.

. . . One should also note themes, characters, and scenes that Hansberry did not expand upon or include in her screenplay. Despite her Pan-Africanism and belief that changes for Blacks in Africa could also lead to changes for Blacks in America (Carter 47), she developed Asagai's character no further. She also omits the scenes included in the expanded text of the play, scenes written before the play was on Broadway but deleted for the sake of playing time (see Wilkerson). (Some of Asagai and Beneatha's expanded conversation in Act III did make the film.) Although these scenes were utilized in the play's twenty-fifth-anniversary revival and now serve as a curious novelty for fans and scholars of *A Raisin in the Sun*, they pale in comparison to what did make it into the play, and have subsequently fallen out of favor with audiences and critics.

Overall a marvel, Hansberry's screenplay ably bears comparison with the best screenplays adapted from previous material. Spike Lee was so impressed after reading the original screenplay that he now considers Hansberry an icon in African-American cinema as well, her name worthy of consideration along with Oscar Micheaux,

> THE UNIVERSAL THEMES IN *A RAISIN IN THE SUN* HELPED IT CROSS ALL RACIAL, CLASS, AGE, AND ETHNIC BOUNDARIES, WHILE STILL FITTING W. E. B. DUBOIS'S CRITERIA FOR NEGRO THEATRE AS BEING 'BY, FOR, ABOUT, AND NEAR [NEGROES].'"

Ossie Davis, Gordon Parks, and Melvin Van Peebles (Hansberry, *A Raisin* xlvi). However, the strength of her screenplay lies not in the new scenes (which offer little in the way of a "more radical critique of whiteness," contra Lipari), but rather in her direction. Hansberry's screenplay delights in its readability and flow; one can envision the film in the mind while reading it. I do not argue that Hansberry was an "establishment artist"; her other writings, not to mention the surveillance conducted by the FBI for her promotion of socialism, prove that she was anything but (Carter 39). Still, little evidence supports the notion that Hansberry's screenplay is any more sweeping in its condemnation of entrenched racism and capitalism than the play that first gave voice to these dissents. As Lipari herself admits, new dialogue about race is kept to a minimum, but the mise-en-scène and cinematography suggested in the script reflect Hansberry's scathing critique of racism and capitalism. Lipari forgets, however, that this is Hollywood—rarely will writers see their screenplays, as envisioned, on the screen. Rather than blame the studio executives, perhaps more criticism should be aimed at director Daniel Petrie.

With the screenplay complete, production for the film began 6 July 1960 and ended September 7. Most of the cast from the original stage production reprised their roles in the film, including Sidney Poitier as Walter, Claudia McNeil as Lena, Ruby Dee playing Ruth, Diana Sands as Beneatha, Ivan Dixon as Asagai, John Fiedler in the role of Lindner, and Louis Gossett, Jr., as George Murchison. Stage producer Phillip Rose served in the same capacity for the film, along with David Susskind. As mentioned above, Petrie was chosen as director. At that time, he had only done television work and one feature, *The Bramble Bush*, released in 1960.

Cuts to Hansberry's screenplay occurred in both pre-production (cut from the screenplay before filming) and post-production (filmed, but cut while editing). Regrettably, we do not know which category all the expunged scenes fall under, but the memoranda reveal a few answers. For example, the scene involving Lena at her employer's was cut in its entirety with suitable rationale from Sam Briskin, Columbia Pictures Vice President of Production: "It was agreed that [these pages] stopped the flow of the story, introduce a character—Mrs. Holiday—whom we never see again, and in general contain unnecessary exposition" (Lipari 92). Lena's shopping experience was also cut, but the film retained Hansberry's new lines for Lena pertaining to her distaste for supermarkets. Perhaps the filmmakers operated under this mindset: given the wealth of wonderful characters in Hansberry's play, if certain new scenes did not develop the characters further, or even amplify the tension, why include them?

Unfortunately, little is known about Hansberry's opinion about the cuts made. Even in her "informal autobiography," *To Be Young, Gifted and Black*, adapted by her husband and notable producer in African-American theatre, Robert Nemiroff, Hansberry fails to mention the film, favorably or otherwise. Nemiroff worked hard to also get Hansberry's original screenplay published. He died, however, months before its release. Needless to say, Nemiroff had unique insight into Hansberry's work:

> The Hansberry screenplay is [. . .] vastly different from the 1961 movie, which was essentially the stageplay with minor "openings out." At least forty percent of the text (not counting smaller variations within speeches—there are hundreds of these) is brand new, containing what all who've read it recently recognize as some of her finest [. . .] writing [. . .] While retaining the primary scenes, themes, and dialogue of the play, therefore, she sought to capture through the camera what the stageplay could only talk about: the full reality of the ghetto experience. (Hansberry, *A Raisin* xvii;)

So why were the cuts made? First of all, Nemiroff's estimate that forty percent of the text is new seems rather high; a close reading of both the screenplay and stageplay reveals that an estimate of twenty to thirty percent would be more accurate. Lipari places the blame on the Columbia studio executives who had most of the control over the film (90). Wilkerson maintains that Vice President Briskin's editorial notes,

speaking on behalf of "the movie studios who were incredibly cautious about offending the American (i.e., white) public," catalyzed the cuts (Hansberry, *A Raisin* xxxvi–xxxvii). Lipari makes much of the memoranda over *A Raisin in the Sun* that passed between studio executives. She particularly criticizes Columbia Pictures Corporation executive Arthur Kramer's memo to Susskind:

> In general, David, I am fearful of the written word, as opposed to a vis-à-vis conversation. I am fearful because notes expressed on paper seem so much colder and more remote than those expressed verbally. I should like you to remember while reading these notes the strong affirmative reaction we all had after reading the first draft screenplay. That reaction, as you recall, was that the author did a remarkable job of transferring a wonderful play to the screenplay medium. [. . .] this is particularly impressive when one considers the author has never before written a screenplay. (Lipari 90)

It is the phrase "fearful of the written word" that Lipari takes to task, finding that it "unintentionally evokes a long tradition of white fear of black writing" (82). Lipari argues that the studio missed an "opportunity to contest the Hollywood images of whiteness associated with goodness, universality, and innocence" (83) with the changes to the original screenplay.

The changes to Hansberry's screenplay resulted in a film closer to her original play. The film was received with somewhat mixed reviews, often divided over its "staginess." Arthur Knight of the *Saturday Review* said that the film transcends the "limitations of its single set and three-act construction" through the direction. Notable *New York Times* critic Bosley Crowther admitted that the film was "stagelike," but admired how Hansberry's play had been "turned into an equally fine screen drama." Phillip T. Hartung (*Commonweal*) declared the film "rather static [. . .] relying greatly on close-ups and dialogue." Anonymous reviewers in *Newsweek* and *Life* were much harsher, as they argued that the action is too confined to call it a "real movie" and is "too tightly limited to theater dimensions." In the end, however, *A Raisin in the Sun* was a success, garnering BAFTA Award and Golden Globe nominations for Poitier and McNeil, while Petrie acquired a Directors Guild of America nomination, and Dee won "Best Supporting Actress" by the National Board of Review. Hansberry also did not go overlooked, her screenplay nominated by the Writers Guild of America for "Best Written

American Drama." The film was also honored at Cannes, where it won the Gary Cooper Award for "human values" and Petrie was nominated for the coveted Palm d'Or.

A Raisin in the Sun was released when stage-to-screen adaptations may have been at their height, and a comparison to these other films should be made. Both *Inherit the Wind* (1960, based on a play by Jerome Lawrence and Robert E. Lee, film directed by Stanley Kramer) and *Long Day's Journey Into Night* (1962, a Eugene O'Neill play, directed by Sidney Lumet) pleased audiences and critics, as did *12 Angry Men* (1957, adapted from a teleplay, again by Sidney Lumet). Nor was *A Raisin in the Sun* the first major film based on a black play; United Artists released *Take a Giant Step* (Leacock, 1959) two years previous, and the film received two Golden Globe nominations, despite its failure at the box office.

Although *Inherit the Wind* contains some exterior scenes, *Long Day's Journey Into Night* is distinctively stage-bound. *12 Angry Men*, released four years prior, was a hit despite all of the film's action in the small jury room, save for a scant three minutes. One might reasonably conclude that the producers of *A Raisin in the Sun* saw little need to retain all of Hansberry's new exterior shots. A precedent had already been set for feature films that remained close to the plays from which they originated and were perhaps a bit stagy in the way they were filmed. Likewise, studio executives saw little need in tampering with Hansberry's play, a conventional, but unsurprising choice, given the notoriously conservative nature of studios of the era, who often operated with the principle "if it ain't broke, don't fix it." In remaining close to the play, they went so far as to keep the entire principal Broadway cast (save the role of Travis, whose age necessitated a new young actor).

Spike Lee, who contributed a commentary to the published screenplay, also believes that Hansberry's original screenplay was censored: "It seems to me all the cuts had to deal with softening a too defiant black voice" (Hansberry, *A Raisin* xlvi). Lee points out, "Of course, Columbia probably cited length as the reason for the deletions. But I feel Lorraine was right in her vision to 'open up' the play [. . .] She wanted to make it cinematic, to make it a film. In the final result, the film is very stagey" (Hansberry, *A Raisin* xlvi;). Despite Lee's opinion, *A*

Raisin in the Sun's length should be considered. The film runs 128 minutes, over thirty minutes longer than the average feature of that era. Indeed, Hansberry herself gave length as the reason for the cuts (Lipari 96). Hansberry's envisioned film may have been more potent and emotive in its depiction of racism in Chicago, but shorter films make safer investments: the shorter the film, the more showings in a day. It would not have been the first time that Hollywood favored profits over art; one recalls the decision to release a truncated (and disastrous) *Cleopatra* (Mankiewicz, 1963) rather than in two three-hour parts.

Lipari, Lee, and others criticize the film as if it were completely emasculated; a close viewing of the film reveals quite the opposite. Much race language from the play/screenplay made the transition to the film: Walter's statement about how "rich white people live"; Lena advising Ruth to call in sick with the flu, since it "sounds so respectable" to white people; Lena's statement about knowing she never was a "rich white woman"; all of Walter's talk about how black men and women are; both Lindner scenes preserved en toto; and Walter's plea to the "Great White Father [. . .] we's ain't gwine cum out deh and dirty up yo's white folks' neighborhood." In addition, the words "faggoty" and "crackers" are each used twice, fairly offensive vocabulary at that time. Although Lipari refers to the "studio's erasures of so-called 'race issues,'" (91) the film obviously preserves a significant black voice.

The notion of "white fear" (at least in this instance) is further invalidated when considering the abortion issue, a topic far more controversial at that time than any racial issues Hansberry brings up in her original screenplay. Columbia chose not to censor the scenes dealing with abortion, something they could have done easily. Why then would they consider a realistic portrayal of Chicago's black neighborhoods more controversial than abortion? This makes little sense, and those who have raised their ire over the changes to Hansberry's screenplay fail to notice this.

The Columbia executives receive little credit from those critical of their editing decisions. What about their decision to finance the picture? In a *New York Times* interview (17 July 1960) a Columbia spokesman stated, "Frankly, [*A Raisin in the Sun*] is a risky project for the studio.

Columbia decided to gamble on it because they felt it had a chance to be a great picture" (*Raisin DVD*). Thankfully, Columbia did finance *A Raisin in the Sun*, the first great black film of the 1960s and proof that black films could reach large audiences.

Unfortunately, we will never know what motivated Columbia's decision to edit *A Raisin in the Sun* to its final form, barely different from its stage form. Racism has become a simple scapegoat for the action the studio took. This author realizes the dangers in questioning the established opinion on the subject, but various factors must also be considered. To take the effortless course and assume "white fear" was the determining factor appears simplistic given the milieu in which the film *A Raisin in the Sun* was created. Critics of the film, ignoring 1961 post-McCarthyism Hollywood, impose the Hollywood of Stepin Fetchit, Mammy, and Prissy on this era.

Screenplays were often added or deleted to while filming, and Hansberry's screenplay (though brilliant) was no exception. No doubt length was a concern as it has always been, and scenes deemed unnecessary were deleted. Perhaps audiences would have responded favorably to a longer film; if so, this makes studio executives guilty of nothing more than ignorance. Although "white fear" (as articulated by Lipari) has existed in Hollywood, little suggests its involvement in the making of *A Raisin in the Sun*. Columbia executives admired Hansberry's play and attempted to remain true to her vision as much as possible. Also, critics who think Petrie and others dismissed Hansberry's screenplay entirely should watch the film again and take note of the new scenes and lines that were included (three scenes in the Kitty Kat Klub, including a new conversation among Walter, Willie, and Bobo, in addition to the aforementioned scenes). Lipari's view of *A Raisin in the Sun* as a production that "paradoxically contests, succumbs to, and perpetuates the demands of structural racism" (90–91) has here been refuted.

Finally then, *A Raisin in the Sun* stands as the greatest African-American play of the twentieth century, as well as one of the greatest American dramas, period. Black theatre historian James V. Hatch says, "*A Raisin in the Sun* confronted Whites for an acknowledgement that a black family could be fully human, 'just like us'"

(Hill and Hatch 370). The universal themes in *A Raisin in the Sun* helped it cross all racial, class, age, and ethnic boundaries, while still fitting W. E. B. DuBois's criteria for Negro theatre as being "by, for, about, and near [Negroes]." Furthermore, the film paved the way for future films, such as the films of 1963–1964 (*Nothing But a Man* [Roemer, 1964], *One Potato Two Potato* [Peerce, 1964], *The Cool World* [Clarke, 1964]) that took Blacks seriously (see Johnson). In *A Raisin in the Sun*, Blacks had a film truly their own, a film of which to be proud and that still holds up well 45 years later (quite unlike the black-cast musicals *The Green Pastures* [Connelly and Keighley, 1936], *Cabin in the Sky* [Minnelli, 1943], and *Carmen Jones* [Preminger, 1954] that perpetuated long-held African-American stereotypes). Those that have examined the controversy over Hansberry's original screenplay of *A Raisin in the Sun* have done us a great service; still, we must always separate the rational arguments from those influenced by imprudent blameworthiness on white racism and fear....

Source: Zachary Ingle, "'White Fear' and the Studio System: A Re-evaluation of Hansberry's Original Screenplay of *A Raisin in the Sun*," in *Literature Film Quarterly*, Vol. 37, No. 3, July 2009, pp. 184–93.

Lisbeth Lipari

In the following excerpt, Lipari examines the studio's suppression of the screenplay as an example of the maintenance, containment, and repair of the cultural production of whiteness.

THE FILM

. . . In the end, little of the screenplay's cinematic exposition was incorporated into the film, which is a nearly isomorphic visual and verbal replication of the play. Not only does the film rely exclusively on dialogue in ways that render the screenplay's critique of normative whiteness and white racism inaudible, but it also employs classical Hollywood conventions to the same effect. In contrast to the screenplay's opening montage of Southside ghetto scenes with the Langston Hughes poem superimposed on them, for example, the film opens with title and credits on a gray background reminiscent of early 1950s television graphics. The poem appears neither on the screen nor the sound track, and the music is a kind of Americana melody reminiscent of Aaron Copeland's *Appalachian Springs*. The opening strips the film of its Southside Chicago, African American context in

"

ALTHOUGH THE ACTIONS OF THE WHITE

CHARACTER LINDNER AND THE WHITE

NEIGHBORHOOD ASSOCIATION ARE CRITIQUED IN

THE FILM, THIS DEPICTION LIMITS THE

UNDERSTANDING OF RACISM TO THE OVERT ACTS OF

PREJUDICED INDIVIDUALS."

ways that make no connection between the title and the dramatic narrative. One fan letter that sings the film's praises ends with a query: "Please explain exactly the meaning of the title *A Raisin in the Sun*. I have a vague idea but am not sure!" This fan letter attests to the impact of Columbia Pictures' decision not to include Hughes's poem, which framed the play and the film in a way that emphasizes the impact of racism on the lives of black people.

Further, in contrast to the screenplay's introductory description, the film makes the Youngers' dark, cramped apartment look bright and comfortable. Although the grandson Travis sleeps on the couch as he did in the play, the furniture in the film appears nice and solid, the kitchen does not seem all that tiny, and light streams in from every window. Moreover, the film's opening action sequence follows Ruth as she moves from window to window opening the shades and bringing in radiant sunshine. The film also employs the saccharine conventions of classical Hollywood musical style in ways that transform the screenplay's intersectional critiques into nostalgia and romanticism. In scenes between Beneatha and her young African suitor Asagai, for example, who explicitly wrestle with normative gender and cultural politics throughout the drama, the strings swell in romantic, cresting waves in the classical Hollywood style of the 1950s. Similarly, Mama's two rhetorically masterful speeches are accompanied by flute and harp music that sentimentalizes and diminishes the power of her voice.

Thus, the film gives the lie to authorship, that in spite of Hansberry's screenplay credit and Petrie's role as director, the final authority was the studio. Yet in newspaper accounts and

the critical introduction to the 1992 publication of Hansberry's original screenplay, the received narrative about the making of the film version of *A Raisin* claims that the real authoring of the film occurred in the editing booth. In a 1961 newspaper article, for example, director Daniel Petrie expressed disappointment with *A Raisin's* receipt of a special Gary Cooper Award for human values at the Cannes Film Festival. Petrie described European complaints about the film's excessive dialogue, limited location, and inappropriate *mise-en-scène*, but he attributed these complaints to the final cutting of the film:

> There was so little visual emphasis on the poor living conditions of the Chicago Negro family that foreign audiences didn't see what they had to complain about... To shorten it, most of the visual description of the neighborhood was removed, while almost all of the play's dialogue remained. When I saw the foreign audience grow restless, I was convinced that the wrong things had been cut out.

Similarly, Hansberry was quoted in 1961 as saying that the screenplay was cut because it made the film too long, and this claim is repeated in the 1992 publication of the original screenplay. Although some exterior footage was shot and ultimately cut from the film, the studio memos indicate that most of the screenplay's editing was done in pre- not post-production; the Columbia Pictures executives ensured that no scenes of Southside Chicago or of new white characters would appear in the film long before the shooting even began. One wonders whether Petrie or Hansberry ever saw the production notes sent by Kramer to Susskind. According to Carter, Susskind shared Briskin's notes from the meeting with Hansberry, but Carter does not mention the Kramer memo. Yet examination of the two memos confirms what Spike Lee sensed when he read the original screenplay and then viewed the film. In his commentary on the published version of the original screenplay, Spike Lee writes: "It seems to me that all the cuts had to deal with softening a too defiant black voice."

The argument of this paper is not, however, that this rhetorical softening was an act of conscious old fashioned racism in the sense of the studio executives' conscious intention to deride or discriminate against African Americans. Rather, by eliminating the complex critique of race/class relations articulated in the screenplay, the executives participated in the ongoing enactment of modern racism, a symbolic process that conceals the conditions of production and the maintenance of white normativity and supremacy. Thus, the film participated in the cultural production of representations of whiteness that sustain the conditions by which racism remains unquestioned. Although the actions of the white character Lindner and the white neighborhood association are critiqued in the film, this depiction limits the understanding of racism to the overt acts of prejudiced individuals. The film thus perpetuates what Segrest refers to as the mythology that insists that racism only affects people of color: "Because racism normalizes whiteness and problematizes 'color,' we whites as 'generic humans' escape scrutiny for our accountability as a group for creating racism and as individuals for challenging it."

CONCLUSION

Without a doubt, both the play and film versions of *A Raisin in the Sun* were historically and culturally significant rhetorical productions. Given its historical context in the heart of the civil rights movement—the film production began the same year as the student sit-in movement, five years after the Montgomery bus boycott, and opened only months before the beginning of Freedom Summer—the film was being produced in an era when white racism and white innocence were being contested as never before. The fundamental structures of political, social, and economic oppression of African Americans were in the foreground of public life for white and black Americans alike. Further, Hollywood did not even produce films written by African American writers until the late 1950s, and *A Raisin* was only the second film in U.S. history (after the 1959 *Take a Giant Step*) to contest "blackface minstrel family films... which avoid dramatizing issues of race, gender, and class." Thus, given the political and cultural context of racist depictions of African Americans, such as the minstrel, *Amos n' Andy*, and what Marlon Riggs calls "ethnic notions," the wide-ranging success of the 1957 theater and 1961 film productions of *A Raisin* were significant achievements, and the studio executives are to be credited with producing the film at all. As Hansberry herself has noted, until *A Raisin*, never before had white people seen black characters talking together outside the presence of whites, nor had audiences, black or white, seen African Americans portrayed on the screen with dignity, humanity, and complexity.

At the same time, however, the suppression of the original screenplay supports Mark McPhail's supposition that "the failure of black Americans to rhetorically resolve this country's racial antagonisms lies less in the ability of African Americans to speak well than in the willingness of white Americans to listen." The Columbia Pictures executives' expurgation of Hansberry's screenplay illustrates a white unwillingness to listen that served the interests of white supremacy through two simultaneous and seemingly contradictory strategies. First, the erasures of the screenplay masked white privilege by rendering whiteness, which was confined only to one character and a pair of interactions, relatively invisible in the film. At the same time, the suppression of the screenplay normalized whiteness by presenting white cultural forms and values as universal norms; for example, by excising the screenplay's more Afrocentric rhetorical gestures and inserting white Hollywood conventions in their place. Importantly, both the masking and the normalizing ignored and marginalized the film's black audience, for whom whiteness is neither normal nor invisible but is the ubiquitous expression of social and political dominance. Thus, the studio deletions of the screenplay forestalled Hansberry's attempts to address two audiences simultaneously, to do what Henry Louis Gates, Jr., quoting Jean-Paul Sartre, refers to as "the double simultaneous postulation" of authors who write for a split public of black and white readers.

From the perspective of cultural politics, keeping whiteness *invisible to whites* has a variety of purposes, including the instrumental political purpose of perpetuating structures of domination, of maintaining the systematically asymmetrical allocation of material, cultural, and political resources to the benefits of whites, such as disparities in income and education. As Marilyn Frye remarks, white people's ignorance of white privilege is not a passive state; it is intentional and determined and "creates the conditions that ensure its continuance." Keeping whiteness invisible has another less overtly political and more inherently ethical purpose, however; it spares whites the pain of seeing ourselves as oppressors, as morally compromised and not innocent. Debian Marty has written that "white children born in the United States inherit the moral predicament of living in a white supremacist society." Frye has expressed this moral predicament in the question: "Does being white make it impossible for me to be a good person?" There is a wellspring of shame attached to the moral predicament of whiteness; maintaining what Du Bois dubbed the "veil" comes at a moral cost to blacks and whites. Thus, the studio's suppression of Hansberry's screenplay actively worked to maintain what McPhail calls the

> ideology of innocence....White Americans continue to dominate and define public discussions of race and their implications for social and political change, and that domination seems to reflect an attitude of indifference that cannot be adequately explained by the politics of complicity, but must be addressed in terms of an ideology of innocence.

Further, keeping whiteness *invisible to whites* involves the political, economic, and ideological imperatives of the conditions of representation. As Daniel Bernardi notes:

> U.S. cinema has consistently constructed whiteness, the representational and narrative form of Eurocentrism, as the norm by which all "Others" fail by comparison. People of color are generally represented as either deviant threats to white rule, thereby requiring civilizing or brutal punishment, or fetishized objects of exotic beauty, icons for a racist scopophilia.

That those who control the conditions of representation also control the conditions of production, both material and symbolic, has become a common presupposition of film, cultural, and media studies. In the case of *A Raisin*, keeping representations of whiteness as seen from a black perspective off the screen maintained the *white illusion* of *white invisibility* that derives from the white fear of being seen by people of color. David Roediger writes of the long history of white silencing of black views of white racism: "Discounting and suppressing the knowledge of whiteness held by people of color was not just a byproduct of white supremacy but an imperative of racial domination." To Hansberry, like Du Bois, racial transformation invites whites to own our complicity with racism and move from the stance of mythology and apology to the stance of recognition and accountability, our "guilty ears tingling with the truth." As bell hooks writes: "[M]any white people do not imagine the way whiteness makes its presence felt in black life, most often as a terrorizing imposition, a power that wounds, hurts, tortures." Although the original screenplay explored some of this terrorizing presence, the studio's suppression prevented audiences from seeing anything other than normative Hollywood constructions of whiteness. In the end, control of the cinematic depiction of

whiteness remained the exclusive prerogative of institutional Hollywood, which dictated who was to be subjected to whose gaze, and how.

Source: Lisbeth Lipari, "'Fearful of the Written Word': White Fear, Black Writing, and Lorraine Hansberry's *A Raisin in the Sun* Screenplay," in *Quarterly Journal of Speech*, Vol. 90, No. 1, February 2004, pp. 81–102.

SOURCES

Crowther, Bosley, "Poitier Heads Cast of Fine Adaptation," in *New York Times*, March 30, 1961, p. 24.

Goudsouzian, Aram, *Sidney Poitier: Man, Actor, Icon*, University of North Carolina Press, 2004, pp. 183–88.

Hansberry, Lorraine, *A Raisin in the Sun*, Random House, 1995.

Hughes, Langston, "Harlem [2]," in *Collected Poems of Langston Hughes*, Knopf, 2004, p. 426.

Marner, Bruce, *Film Production Technique: Creating the Accomplished Image*, Cengage, 2008, pp. 10–12, 28–31.

Miller, Jeanne-Marie A., "'Measure Him Right': An Analysis of Lorraine Hansberry's *Raisin in the Sun*," in *Teaching American Ethnic Literatures*, edited by John R. Maitino and David R. Peck, University of New Mexico Press, 1996, pp. 133–41.

Mitchell, Diana, "A Teacher's Guide to Lorraine Hansberry's *A Raisin in the Sun*," Penguin Group, http://us.penguingroup.com/static/pdf/teachersguides/raisinsun.pdf (accessed July 10, 2011).

Mjagkij, Nina, ed., *Organizing Black America: An Encyclopedia of African American Organizations*, Garland Press, 2001, pp. 122–23.

Moore, Natalie Y., and Lance Williams, *The Almighty Black P Stone Nation: The Rise, Fall, and Resurgence of an American Gang*, Lawrence Hill, 2011, pp. 11–12.

Norman, Brian, and Piper Kendrix Williams, eds., *Representing Segregation: Toward an Aesthetics of Living Jim Crow, and Other Forms of Racial Division*, State University of New York Press, 2010, pp. 119–25.

Poitier, Sidney, *The Measure of a Man*, HarperCollins, 2000, pp. 147–58.

A Raisin in the Sun, DVD, Sony Pictures Home Entertainment, 2000.

"*Raisin* Raised to New Heights," in *Washington Post and Times-Herald*, June 14, 1961, p. D10.

Santas, Constantine, *Responding to Film: A Text Guide for Students of Cinema Art*, Rowman & Littlefield, 2002, pp. 57–67.

Scott, John L., "*Raisin in the Sun* Stirring Film Play," in *Los Angeles Times*, April 21, 1961, p. 23.

Walker, Jesse H., "Hit Stage Play Now Hit Film," in *New York Amsterdam News*, March 11, 1961, p. 17.

FURTHER READING

Bolden, Tonya, *The Book of African American Women: 150 Crusaders, Creators, and Uplifters*, Adams Media, 2004.

This book is a collection of brief biographies, beginning with a 1619 biography of a slave brought to the Jamestown colony. Bolden includes biographies of famous women, but she also includes biographies of women, who made significant contributions to African American history and culture without ever becoming famous.

Effiong, Philip Uko, *In Search of a Model for African-American Drama*, University Press of America, 2000.

This book includes a very long critical chapter on Hansberry, with an emphasis on her use of African images in her works. In *A Raisin in the Sun*, Beneatha adopts a number of different African symbols, which are intended to forge a connection to Africa.

Hirsch, Arnold R., *Making the Second Ghetto: Race and Housing in Chicago: 1940–1960*, University of Chicago Press, 1998.

Hirsch relates the struggle for housing desegregation in Chicago following the end of World War II. He argues that Chicago established a model for other northern cities, as ethnic and racial minorities worked to create equal access to housing following the Great Migration of southern blacks to northern cities.

Leeson, Richard, *Lorraine Hansberry: A Research and Production Sourcebook*, Greenwood, 1997.

This book is a reference guide to Hansberry's life and career. There is an extensive chapter on *A Raisin in the Sun*, as well as a bibliography of source material to guide readers who wish to learn more about this playwright. The author has also included several interviews with Hansberry as well as reviews of her work.

Morrison, Toni, ed., *Race-ing Justice, En-gendering Power: Essays on Anita Hill, Clarence Thomas, and the Construction of Social Reality*, Pantheon, 1992.

Toni Morrison edited and wrote the introduction to this text, which is a collection of nineteen essays that deal with several aspects of African American identity, civil rights, equality, and the public perception of race and gender equality, centered on the Clarence Thomas controversy of the early 1990s. These essays explore important ideas about equality for African American women.

Sniderman, Paul M., and Thomas Piazza, *Black Pride and Black Prejudice*, Princeton University Press, 2004.

The authors of this text provide an often-provocative look at race relations in the United States. The focus is on how African Americans view themselves and how they perceive they are viewed by other groups. Among the topics covered are black pride, black intolerance and racism.

Wiese, Andrew, *Places of Their Own: African American Suburbanization in the Twentieth Century*, University of Chicago Press, 2005.

Wiese traces the movements of African Americans into the suburbs surrounding large cities. He points out that despite racism, poverty, and isolation, many blacks were determined to move into white communities to fulfill their dreams of better housing and schools.

Wilkerson, Isabel, *The Warmth of Other Suns: The Epic Story of America's Great Migration*, Random House, 2010.

Wilkerson describes what has come to be called the Great Migration, the mid-twentieth-century exodus from the South of some six million blacks who hoped to find a better life in the North. The journey was often undertaken as a way to escape Jim Crow laws; however, many of the people leaving the southern United States faced an uncertain future. This book contains many individual stories and is, in many ways, similar to the immigration stories of those who found haven in the United States during the nineteenth and twentieth centuries.

SUGGESTED SEARCH TERMS

Lorraine Hansberry AND Raisin in the Sun

Lorraine Hansberry

Hansberry AND Chicago housing

Hansberry AND dream

Langston Hughes AND Dream Deferred

Sidney Poitier AND Daniel Petrie

Sidney Poitier AND Raisin in the Sun

Claudia McNeil AND Raisin in the Sun

civil rights movement AND Lorraine Hansberry

Chicago AND segregated housing

Chicago AND black employment

South Side Chicago AND ghetto housing

African American dream AND segregation

The Stronger

AUGUST STRINDBERG

1889

August Strindberg's *The Stronger*, which premiered in 1889 at Strindberg's Scandinavian Experimental Theater in Copenhagen, Denmark, is one of the most commonly performed plays in the world, not only because of the importance of its author but also because of its brevity: it is intended to run for about fifteen minutes. It is highly unusual in that, while it has two characters, only one of them speaks, delivering what is effectively a monologue, while the other reacts only through gesture and expression.

Although the surface of the play gives every appearance of bourgeois gentility—its characters are two middle-class women meeting in a Victorian coffeehouse—it explores one of Strindberg's main themes, that interaction between human beings always was and still is a savage struggle for dominance and that the evolution of so-called polite society has merely replaced physical violence with psychological violence. In the brief action of the play, one of the characters is revealed as the "stronger," and the other is nearly destroyed by the psychological blows she delivers. The text is so subtle, however, that only the most determined untangling of the drama can reveal which is which.

August Strindberg (The Library of Congress)

AUTHOR BIOGRAPHY

Strindberg was born in Stockholm, Sweden, on January 22, 1849. His mother was a maid, and his father was a clerk in a shipping office. His relationship with his parents was deeply troubled. His mother resented his intellect, and his father resented his success. Throughout his life, Strindberg was indecisive and restless and marked by a strange combination of talent and failure. Supporting himself as a tutor, Strindberg switched back and forth between the liberal arts curriculum of the university in Uppsala and a premedical scientific education at the Institute of Technology in Stockholm, until his failure in chemistry exams settled the issue. However, he never completed a formal degree.

While still at school in the late 1860s, Strindberg began to publish articles in Swedish newspapers and magazines, and in 1870, his one-act play *In Rome* was performed at the Royal Theater in Stockholm. He continued to publish fiction, dramas, and essays, but in 1874, he became an

assistant librarian and soon considered himself a failed writer.

Strindberg married Siri von Essen in 1877, convincing her to leave her first husband, Baron Wrangel, for him. Her new marriage displaced her from the baron's aristocratic family circles and allowed her to work as an actress at the Royal Theater. By 1879, Strindberg had to declare bankruptcy, but two years later he published his novel *The Red Room*, which became a best-seller in Scandinavia and is today considered the beginning of modern Swedish literature. Strindberg was able to renew his career as a writer with considerably greater success, although he went through periods of wealth and poverty throughout his life. After living for many years in Switzerland and France, Strindberg and his wife moved to Copenhagen, Denmark, in 1889 and opened the Scandinavian Experimental Theater. The venture lasted for less than a year before collapsing, but *The Stronger* was one of the plays Strindberg wrote for it, with his wife playing the main character of Frau X.

Strindberg was a contradictory and unconventional man. Although at times in his life Strindberg said hateful things about women, at other points he advocated equal rights for women. His spiritual life moved from Lutheranism, to atheism, to mysticism (the belief that one can attain spiritual truth through direct communion with God or ultimate reality) and occultism (the belief in the influence of supernatural powers). Some of his work was shocking to Victorian audiences, and in 1884, he was tried for blasphemy for his writing and beliefs. He was acquitted, and following his trial, he intended to begin a new career as a scientist, but he suffered a mental collapse between 1892 and 1896. Then he published articles describing his alchemical experiments and his search for magical correspondences between heaven and earth.

Strindberg published over sixty plays throughout his life. His early work was more in the naturalist style, attempting to create onstage a perfect illusion of reality, but after his mental collapse he embraced a much less realistic style, producing plays, like *The Dream Play* (1901), that explore the unconscious mind and more abstract psychological concepts.

Strindberg divorced his first wife in 1890 and had two more short-lived marriages to actresses more than twenty-five years younger than himself. After he narrowly lost the Nobel Prize in

Literature for 1909, a charitable collection had to be taken up from his readers throughout Europe to avoid another bankruptcy; but he was soon able to sell the rights to reprint his life's work for the modern equivalent of several million dollars. However, even that could not save his Intimate Theater, founded in 1907, from financial collapse. Strindberg died in Stockholm on April 12, 1912, probably of cancer.

PLOT SUMMARY

The Stronger, though a complete play in itself, is no longer than a scene in an ordinary play. The play takes place in a coffeehouse where the two characters, both actresses, meet in a quiet corner. The two are identified in the dramatis personae (the list of characters that heads a play) as Frau (Mrs.) X. and Mlle. (Miss) Y. The first name of the younger woman is Amelia, as revealed in the play's dialogue, or rather monologue, because only Frau X. speaks. During the brief course of the play, Frau X. speaks to Mlle. Y. on the basis of their shared knowledge; therefore much of what the characters understand from the first only gradually becomes clear to the audience.

At the beginning of the play, Mlle. Y. is already reading in a quiet corner of a café, with a half-finished beer on her table. Frau X. comes in with a shopping basket and sits next to her. The two women are obviously well known to each other, and their acquaintance allows Mlle. Y. to greet Frau X. without speaking.

When Frau X. enters the café, she greets the other woman, calling her Amelia and noting that she is alone in a café on Christmas Eve, a seemingly offhand remark whose meaning will become clearer as the drama develops. Frau X. observes that the situation is sad and recalls another sad event, when she attended a wedding reception in Paris at which the bride sat alone reading a humor magazine while the groom played billiards: she could see the marriage was headed for disaster.

After a pause in the conversation while a waiter brings Frau X. her hot chocolate, she reveals (to the audience) that she was speaking of Mlle. Y.'s wedding. Mlle. Y. is now divorced, against the advice Frau X. gave her at the time. Frau X. seems almost to taunt the younger woman with the fact that she does not have a home and family of her own, the conventional aspirations of bourgeois women in the nineteenth

MEDIA ADAPTATIONS

- *The Stronger* was set as an opera in 1952 by Hugo Weisgall, with a libretto by Rochard Henry Hart. Weisgall's own recording of the opera with the Aeolian Chamber Players was re-released on CD by Composers Recording in 1997 and 2010.

- In 1971, a version of *The Stronger* directed by Patrick Garland and starring Britt Ekland and Marianne Faithful was aired by the British Broadcasting Corporation.

- In 1976, the American Film Institute commissioned a film version of *The Stronger* directed by Lee Grant.

- Minna Görandsdotter's version of *The Stronger* was produced by Aglepta and FAMU for European television in 1999.

- A 2004 production of *The Stronger*, adapted by Denniz Clontz and directed by Jan Marlyn Reesman, is available for viewing on the Internet Movie Database Web site.

- A performance of *The Stronger* by the Michigan Classical Repertory Company was recorded in 2007 and is available online on DVD (together with *Miss Julie*).

- A 2007 production of *The Stronger* directed by Steve Cleberg is available for viewing on the Internet Movie Database Web site.

century. It is reasonable to assume from the text that Mlle. Y. divorced because her husband committed adultery. Because it is now Christmas Eve and Mlle. Y. spent a Christmas with her then fiancée's parents, it would seem that the marriage must have been made and dissolved within the last year.

Frau X. shows Mlle. Y. the Christmas presents she is bringing her own children, perhaps a provocation after her mentioning the younger woman not understanding what it is to have children. One of them is a toy gun, which she fires unexpectedly at Mlle. Y., startling her.

This is a joke, but jokes often mask aggression that it would be impolite to reveal openly. Frau X. suggests that Mlle. Y. has more reason to want to shoot her. The reasons given are highly compressed and can be wholly understood only on the basis of later passages, but it seems that Mlle. Y. was romantically linked with Bob, Frau X.'s husband, at some time in the past, but he ended that relationship to marry his current wife. Further, Mlle. Y. must have been fired from a theater troupe she belonged to at that time (though she still seems to work as an actress elsewhere). Frau X. maintains that these things are coincidences but conceives that Mlle. Y. must nevertheless blame her for them.

Frau X. next takes out of her basket a pair of slippers that are her husband's Christmas present. She embroidered tulips on them because he wants tulips on everything, although she herself does not like them. She observes that Mlle. Y. will never have seen Bob wearing slippers, which causes the younger woman to laugh. Frau X. mocks her husband by imitating the way he walks with the slippers and then mimicking his cursing at the household servants. She tells Mlle. Y. that she ought to have a husband like Bob, and how Bob is undoubtedly faithful to her because he told her so himself. All of this makes Mlle. Y. laugh openly.

Frau X. thinks Mlle. Y. might be angry with her husband, believing that, in his role as a government minister, he might have been the one responsible for her losing her earlier job. To show there are no hard feelings, Frau X. invites her to come to dinner that evening (in Sweden, Christmas Eve is the main celebration of the holiday). Somehow she wants to make up for coming between Bob and Mlle. Y. Perhaps because they were professionally connected, however, the relationship with Mlle. Y. did not simply end when Bob's romantic attentions shifted. Frau X. tells Mlle. Y., "I was so afraid of you.... I couldn't risk being your enemy, so I became your friend." She thought her husband was upset to have Mlle. Y. in their social life, so she pushed Bob to make them remain friends, even made him kiss her at the christening of Bob and Frau X.'s son.

Frau X.'s demeanor suddenly changes as she follows a train of thought; she accuses Mlle. Y.: "Your eyes rolled out of me all these thoughts which lay like raw silk in their cocoon." She suddenly asks accusatory questions, about what really happened to Mlle. Y.'s engagement

to Bob, why she does not visit them any longer and will not visit tonight. Frau X. has just come to the conclusion that Bob and Mlle. Y. are having an affair, and that is why, as she thinks, Bob makes her do everything the way Mlle. Y. would want, from having tulips (Mlle. Y.'s favorite flower) everywhere on their home décor to naming their son Eskil (a very common name in Sweden) after Mlle. Y.'s father. Suddenly Frau X.'s life seems to her as if Mlle. Y.'s soul had entered into her own and eaten it from the inside like a parasitic worm. She describes the same feeling in a long string of other colorful metaphors.

Frau X. sees Mlle. Y. as incapable of finding a real marriage of her own but only able to lurk like a predatory stork outside a mouse hole waiting to gobble up the innocent men that come her way, or else lurking like a mousetrap waiting to destroy some innocent man. Just as suddenly, another change comes over Frau X., and now she pities Mlle. Y. as she would a wounded animal. She excuses her lashing out because of the pain of her wound. She dismisses the affair as a matter of no consequence because, after all, she is the one married to Bob. She now interprets all the ways she has been made to accept Mlle. Y.'s tastes as just something that makes her more attractive to her husband. She is, she believes, in the much stronger position because she can go home to her husband, while Mlle. Y. has no husband. She especially feels she is in a stronger place because she can go home to her children, which the younger woman is lacking.

CHARACTERS

The Waiter
The waiter brings Frau X. her chocolate shortly after the beginning of the play. He does not speak and in many productions is omitted, probably as an economy measure.

Bob X.
Bob is Frau X.'s husband. Presumably his name is Robert, but the English nickname Bob is used in the original Swedish text. This superficial linguistic borrowing speaks to the internationalist character of late nineteenth-century European culture. At some time before Bob and Frau X.'s marriage, Bob had been engaged to Mlle. Y. Given the nature of the play, the

audience can know very little of Bob's character beyond what his wife says, and the reliability of that is questionable.

Frau X. presents a curious dichotomy in her portrayal of her husband. On one hand, she thinks Bob is safe and domesticated; in fact, she believes he is hen-pecked ("He's a pretty good little husband" translates a Swedish idiom that is more explicitly to that effect). On the other hand, she believes that he has dictatorial control over her life and that he uses it to reshape her, forcing her to like tulips, and chocolate, and the mountains, for instance. This paradox represents how she views her husband even before realizing that Mlle. Y. is the model for this refashioning.

Perhaps more substantial is the characterization of Bob that comes about from the interaction between the two women. When Frau X. shows Mlle. Y. the slippers she is giving Bob as a Christmas present, she says, "You've never seen him in slippers." Mlle. Y. laughs, and at that point Frau X. must imagine it is funny because the idea of her husband being alone with another woman is ridiculous. Mlle. Y. may find it humorous for a different reason; perhaps when he is alone with her, he is not interested in doing anything as domestic as wearing slippers. This leads to the inference that Bob values his wife precisely for her domesticity and is happy to participate in it with her.

Perhaps Bob has depths of character that are quite different and that he never shows to his wife. Bob seems to be as happy to lie to Frau X. as she is to be lied to. She believes that he is faithful because he tells her about all the women who try to seduce him but whom he rebuffs on her behalf. If, in fact, he is lying, and he has slept with a number of these women, Bob must take an almost sadistic delight in deceiving his wife so shamelessly. Bob's possible dual nature is also constructed for the audience by Frau X. (Only by accepting what she says can one interpret Mlle. Y.'s reactions as supporting the wife's claims.) Her ultimate portrayal is a revision and an intensification of the split she already saw in Bob before she created or discovered her narrative of the affair.

Frau X.

Although she worked (and perhaps still works) as an actress, the main feature of Frau X. is her domesticity. She has completely internalized the values of her culture that tell her that her worth as a woman is to be found in home and family. She holds in pity (and perhaps contempt) any woman who does not attain the fulfillment of devoting herself to a husband and children. The delight that Frau X. takes in running her household is palpable in her description of her husband's complaints about the incompetence of the servants: she thinks it is precious to see Bob trying to interfere in her domain and floundering. She is just as enraptured with her children, her "little pigs" (in Sweden the pig is a symbol of good luck and fertility and so an apt nickname for children). While she is still being civil, she cannot help but talk about them and show off their Christmas presents.

However, the most salient characteristic Frau X. displays onstage is her hostility towards Mlle. Y. Bob had broken off his engagement to Mlle. Y. to marry his wife, so Frau X. naturally imagines that Mlle. Y. is filled with the same hostility she would feel in such a situation. Frau X. insists that she was blameless in the affair, which she must do to protect her own self-image. Her own hatred of Mlle. Y. she justifies by claiming it is defensive and more particularly by denying it. She tells Mlle. Y. what a good friend she has always been to her and how she looked out for her interests. Her denial of interfering with Mlle. Y.'s career makes more sense if it is something she has to say to keep an admission of her guilt form pouring out. She must be Mlle. Y.'s friend, she tells herself as well as Mlle. Y., because if she were not, then she would be her enemy, having succumbed to jealousy. Frau X. cannot admit, especially to herself, that she is indeed jealous and hostile, because that is outside the character she thinks she ought to have. Nevertheless, her passive-aggressive taunting of Mlle. Y. about her lack of children and her shooting her with the toy gun—a suspiciously hostile joke—reveal the depths of her hatred.

At the beginning of the play, Frau X.'s feelings for Mlle. Y. consist of a polite and highly forced friendship (as seen in how she made Bob kiss his former fiancée at a party), masking murderous intent. She hates the younger woman because she fears losing her husband to her but cannot bring herself to open hostility because it would mean facing that very fear. It is as though Frau X. is trapped in an emotional prison, unable to think and act freely. The underlying tension erupts like a riot in her accusation of the affair between Mlle. Y. and Bob. Frau X. must inevitably accuse Mlle. Y. of the thing she fears from her. It may even be true, but neither Frau X. nor the audience have any way of knowing.

Just as surely, after the release of aggression restores some inner calm, Frau X. must immediately retreat into a fantasy of domestic tranquility. The affair is real, she perhaps thinks or tells herself, but it makes no difference. Nothing can be allowed to compromise her image of herself as a perfect homemaker, so nothing will be allowed to do so. A moment before, she railed against Mlle. Y. for invading and destroying her home and her soul, but finally Frau X. simply dismisses the whole matter: Mlle. Y. remains powerless because she lacks a husband and children and so can pose no threat to Frau X.'s own home. Frau X. is confident that her world is going to go on just as it did before. This can only be described as a wish or a fantasy. She surely believes that the affair is real, the betrayal by her husband true, but she refuses to admit the terrible threat these things pose to her. She voluntarily returns to her prison, accepting that her husband's refashioning of her life on the model of his mistress's is somehow a guarantee that her marriage will be preserved.

Mlle. Amelia Y.

Mlle. Y. is the most enigmatic of the characters. Although she is present onstage throughout the whole play, she says nothing herself and is therefore almost completely defined by Frau X.'s monologue. The most dramatic thing that she does is to laugh at Frau X.'s remark about the slippers, and even this is very ambiguous. At the time, Frau X. believes, and the audience must also believe, that Mlle. Y. laughs at Frau X.'s joke, but by the end of the play this laughter is reinterpreted, so that she is laughing at Frau X. in contempt, because of her private knowledge that she has deceived the older woman.

Frau X. characterizes Mlle. Y. at first as a family friend whose situation, being without a husband or children, is to be pitied. Then, once Frau X. comes to believe in her husband's affair, Mlle. Y. blazes up in Frau X.'s mind as a ravening monster, "a giant crab ready to catch hold of me with your claws." After a moment's reflection, Frau X. again sees Mlle. Y. as pitiable, and for the same reasons as before, because nothing has changed in her essential circumstances.

The one true defining characteristic of Mlle. Y. is her silence. If Frau X. is correct in all of her reasoning and supposition—if the two women are locked in a battle of brains (and bodies) and Mlle. Y. is trying to destroy her through soul murder—then Mlle. Y. remains silent because her triumph is complete. She can tell from Frau X.'s desperation that she is completely destroyed, and to say anything in addition would spoil the completeness of her triumph. If, on the other hand, everything that Frau X. suspects is nothing more than her jumping to paranoid conclusions and there is no affair, then Mlle. Y. must simply be appalled beyond words by what she hears.

THEMES

Strength

The Stronger is like a duel in which the two characters struggle each to overcome the other, albeit through words and ideas rather than with swords or pistols. The strength of Frau X. consists of her social position. According to the conventions of her day, her home and children give her strong claims on her husband, a strength she can use once she recognizes Mlle. Y. as her rival. However, her strength is ultimately illusory. She believes that her position of strength makes it inevitable that she will win the struggle for her husband, but all she can do is to state this belief as if it were true.

It may well be, however, that there are parts of her husband that Frau X. knows nothing about, and it is precisely those parts on which Mlle. Y. has a claim. Her strength is demonstrated by the likelihood that Mlle. Y. is able to lure Bob away from the fortress of the home that Frau X. thinks is so strong and inviolable, that Bob has entered into a relationship with her against all the social pressure that stands in the way. Frau X. seems incapable of understanding or even imagining the true situation, and that, ultimately, is perhaps why Mlle. Y. does not speak: it would not do any good because her words would not even be understood.

Psychology

Thanks to the work being done by the psychologist Jean-Marie Charcot, the 1880s and 1890s saw a craze in European intellectual circles for hypnosis. The popular conception of hypnosis is

- Laura Wilson's *Daily Life in a Victorian House* (1998) is a lavishly illustrated young-adult guide to Victorian family life. Use this book as a guide, alongside traditional and online research, to construct a multimedia class presentation describing the daily life of Strindberg's Frau X.

- Craig Slaight and Jack Sharrar's *Short Plays for Young Actors* (1996) is an anthology of brief, one-scene plays drawn from cultures around the world. Select one of the plays and perform it for your class. After the presentation, lead a class discussion on how the play compares with *The Stronger*.

- Search the Internet for filmed performances of *The Stronger* (a very large number have been uploaded by both amateur and professional theater groups). Make a class presentation, if possible illustrated by clips, comparing several performances in terms of their historical authenticity (many are self-consciously updated and set in the contemporary world), their dramatic and editorial choices, and other points of contrast. Post your presentation on your online blog or Web page, and invite classmates to post their observations.

- Stage two class readings of *The Stronger*, one in which Frau X. is portrayed as being stronger and one in which Mlle. Y. is portrayed as being stronger. Write an essay detailing the theatrical techniques that were used to create each impression.

exemplified in George du Maurier's 1894 novel *Trilby* (then the best-selling novel in history), in which the evil gypsy mastermind Svengali (the origin of that term) is able to hypnotize the young girl Trilby. He first cures her headaches, then turns her into a great opera singer, and eventually takes over her mind and enslaves her.

In his 1887 essay "The Battle of the Brains," Strindberg takes from Charcot's work the idea that those with more sophisticated brains can dominate and control others with less sophisticated brains through their natural capacities, if not, strictly speaking, through hypnosis. Strindberg saw this mental domination playing out not only in the class divisions of society but also in the abilities of intellectuals, politicians, and orators to shape public opinion and sway crowds and of actors and magicians to control the responses of audiences.

Naturally, this put Strindberg the playwright firmly in the controlling part of mankind, as he imagined. He viewed social interactions as a struggle for power in which mental violence has replaced the physical violence of less advanced eras. Although he put no stock in the technique of hypnosis, Strindberg believed in many occult and supernatural agencies, such as spirit mediums and animal magnetism, and so conceived that such battles between minds were carried out not only through words and arguments but also by more direct mental contact, by which the unconscious energy of one mind could reach out directly to another and overcome it. Strindberg was quite ready to see events of this kind in his own life and certainly represented them in his dramas.

Strindberg's distinctive beliefs about psychology are reflected in *The Stronger* through Frau X.'s conscious attempts to dominate Mlle Y. but more especially in the charges that the older woman makes against the younger. Frau X. complains to Mlle Y., "Your soul crept into mine, like a worm into an apple, ate and ate, grubbed and grubbed, until nothing was left but the rind within." Although this image starts with the familiar idea of a worm in an apple, it grow beyond that and calls on Strindberg's specialized knowledge as a naturalist, suggesting an egg laid inside another organism that hatches into a parasitic grub that eats its host from the inside out, a common occurrence in the insect world. This horrible image stands nicely for Strindberg's ideas of psychological domination and control. Immediately after, he supplies a different image that suggests the occult tendencies of his psychological theories when Frau X. accuses, "You lay like a snake and enchanted me with your black eyes." This precisely suggests the domination of a person through animal magnetism with an image based on the folk belief that snakes entrance birds into standing still to await being eaten.

The entire play takes place in the café as the two women chat. (Konrad Bak | Shutterstock.com)

STYLE

Quart d'heure

Quart d'heure is French for "quarter of an hour" and is the name of a genre of very brief one-act plays. These plays became popular in France in the years after the Franco-Prussian War of 1870–1871. They frequently dealt with highly dramatic subject matter, often with rapid exchanges of dialogue and a twist ending. A typical example is Henry Lavedan's *Between Brothers*, which concerns a duel fought between two brothers.

The best known example of a *quart d'heure* in English is *The Hooligan*, by William S. Gilbert (famous for writing the libretti of the Savoy Operas composed by Arthur Sullivan). In *The Hooligan*, a young man is about to be executed for having murdered his fiancée, but because his humble background and disadvantaged life evoke pity, his sentence is commuted. He is in such a pitch of fear and excitement when he hears the good news that he dies of a heart attack on the spot.

This theatrical form interested Strindberg because of his interests in naturalism. It offers the possibility of preserving the dramatic unity of classical drama (i.e., telling a story that takes place in real time in a single location) while presenting a realistic conversation, producing a highly naturalistic effect, as if *The Stronger*, for instance, were a real conversation overheard in a coffeehouse. Strindberg heightened the novelty effect of the form by writing *The Stronger* as a monologue. Another consideration was that in 1888, Strindberg had founded the Scandinavian Experimental Theater as much as a business as an artistic venture, and such a simple play seemed to offer a greater potential for profit. Nevertheless, the theater failed. As a result, *The Stronger* was the only *quart d'heure* play he would write, and the last play of any kind he would write or stage for three years, until he had recovered from the personal disaster.

Monologue

The Stronger is a monologue, with all of the lines spoken by the single character of Frau X. It is an unusual technique, because the word *drama* itself at its root means "action" and usually implies interaction between characters. In the ancient theater of the Greeks and Romans, the only monologues came at the beginnings of plays, when a character (usually a god or a slave—both thought to be more observant of events around them than ordinary people) would explain to the audience the background information necessary to understanding the rest of the play. Much later, William Shakespeare began to use the soliloquy, in which a lone character on the stage speaks almost directly to the audience, revealing private, interior thoughts that in real life would remain hidden.

In *The Stronger*, Frau X.'s monologue makes up the whole action of the play itself. At length, it slowly reveals to the audience the past events that make the actions on stage meaningful; really, the main action that takes place is her own reinterpretation of past events. Frau X. never speaks aloud what she is actually thinking the way that, say, Hamlet does, but in a manner more in keeping with the psychological science of Strindberg's day, she seems to project her thoughts in statements that perhaps say the opposite of what she is thinking. Similarly, Mlle. Y.'s character is more built up by the thoughts and feelings attributed to her by Frau X. than by any pantomime the speechless actress on the stage can carry out.

COMPARE
&
CONTRAST

- **1880s:** Middle-class women who choose independent careers and lives, such as actresses, stand outside the traditional structures of family and society. Because they are not under the control of a man (a husband or father), they are typically stereotyped as transgressive of social norms and threatening in terms of breaking social mores, such as adultery.

  Today: Middle-class women are generally expected to pursue careers and integrate their independence into new family structures.

- **1880s:** Dramatic performances can only be experienced directly by audiences in live attendance.

  Today: Dramatic performances are typically viewed by mass audiences over television or recorded on film (or its digital equivalent).

For instance, more people saw Joseph Losey's film of *Don Giovanni* during its initial release in 1979 than had seen live performances of the opera during the preceding two centuries, and far more than that have since seen transfers of the film to VHS or DVD.

- **1880s:** Actors and actresses who do not fulfill traditionally productive roles in society are seen as socially transgressive and therefore suspected of being prone to immorality and vice.

  Today: Actors and actresses are still stereotyped as violating social norms, but because of the force of their celebrity created by the mass media, they are nevertheless widely seen as role models.

HISTORICAL CONTEXT

The Victorian Bourgeoisie

The bourgeoisie was a middle class that developed in Europe after the Renaissance. They were "middle" in being above (in the European understanding of class) farmers and laborers who lived from the work of their hands and below aristocrats whose wealth and power derived from owning land. In general, the bourgeoisie lived by trade or by controlling capital, that is, the means of production, such as factories. With the Industrial Revolution, industrial production radically increased the wealth of society and concentrated it in the hands of the bourgeoisie. They effectively assumed economic control over European culture and, in a series of revolutions between 1792 and 1870, also wrested political control from the landowners. The nineteenth century saw the cultural flowering of the bourgeoisie as well, with the creation of new art, new manners, and new mores all in line with bourgeois taste.

Strindberg began life at the very lowest rung of the bourgeois class but raised himself up through education, an acceptable means of bourgeois social advancement; this would have been particularly true if he had followed the career of a physician or scientist, but as a writer and a man of the theater, he could exist only on the fringe of the bourgeois world, in a profession that lacked respectability, regardless of his success, regardless even to what degree he acted to regulate and advance bourgeois taste through his novels and plays. Strindberg's audience, however, was entirely bourgeois.

The world portrayed in *The Stronger* expresses the very essence of bourgeoisie culture. Bourgeois society depended upon the amassing and control of wealth beyond what was necessary for daily needs, and this had to be signaled through the display of costly but useless objects and habits. These signs may, indeed, have been things that gave much pleasure but would not be necessary or useful in themselves. The quintessential bourgeoisie space was the sitting room

The slippers, a gift, are a major topic of conversation for Mlle. Y. and Frau X. *(robodread | Shutterstock.com)*

crammed with mass-produced, but nevertheless tasteful and expensive, items such as decorative porcelains and grandfather clocks.

The coffeehouse, where *The Stronger* takes place, is essentially a commercial sitting room where the same sorts of experiences and displays can be made. Part of the lure of coffee and chocolate comes from their being exotic, expensive, and foreign. Similarly, the "Japanese basket" Frau X. carries may have imitated the appearance of traditional Japanese handicrafts but was surely made in a factory workshop, whether in Europe or in rapidly industrializing Japan. The "illustrated newspaper" Mlle. Y. is reading functioned to regulate and propagate bourgeois taste. The very use of foreign appellations such as Frau and mademoiselle is a

marker of the international, sophisticated culture maintained by the bourgeoisie.

Christmas is the characteristic bourgeois holiday, because it celebrates the bourgeoisie nuclear family, involves the exchange of expensive but largely useless displays of wealth, and takes place, of course, in the sitting room. The ideals of possessing a home, children, and a husband, all of which Frau X. boasts of and teases Mlle. Y. for lacking, represent the aspirations of the bourgeois woman (as opposed to alternative ideals such as a career and autonomy, which Mlle. Y. possesses, in transgression of bourgeois norms).

The idea of the vacation, taken when it is convenient rather than as part of the cycle of work and rest of the agricultural year, is a supremely bourgeois invention; it was the bourgeoisie who first had to decide whether to visit the mountains or the shore merely for the sake of idle pleasure, using the new industrial product of the locomotive. At one of the deepest levels of meaning in the play, Frau X.'s realization that her life of bourgeois indulgence is based not on her own tastes but on Mlle. Y.'s is a general criticism of the bourgeois way of life, copied out of what one reads and sees in novels and magazines.

CRITICAL OVERVIEW

Almost every critical treatment of Strindberg's *The Stronger* follows the same pattern. Beginning with a derivation of the play's content from the playwright's essays "The Battle of the Brains" and "Soul Murder" and his keen interest in contemporary psychology, the analyses inevitably take as their main subject the discussion of which character is indeed the stronger, Frau X. or Mlle. Y. There is by no means a consensus of opinion, but rather each camp is well represented.

Frau X. is perhaps the more popular choice, as argued, for instance, by Walter Johnson in his biography *August Strindberg*. The answer, he thinks, comes in a letter from Strindberg to his first wife, Siri von Essen (on March 6, 1889, no. 232 in Michael Robinson's translation of Strindberg's letters). She was actualizing the role of Frau X. for the first time, and while he was out of town at the beginning of rehearsals, Strindberg advised her to "play it like this . . . [a]s the stronger." Moreover, in the text of the play, Frau X. explicitly claims to be the stronger. In Johnson's view, she goes on to prove that she is the stronger by deducing the affair between her husband and Mlle. Y.

Børge Gedsø Madsen, in *Strindberg's Naturalistic Theatre*, refines this perspective and posits that in the beginning of the play, Mlle. Y. has the upper hand and is able even to laugh at her rival's vulgarity and ignorance, because her knowledge of her affair with Bob gives a second, more significant meaning to much that Frau X. has to say. But by the end of the play, Frau X. has broken down her rival's position, gaining insight into the affair and not being destroyed by it.

This interpretation would seem certain, then, but in fact, it has been challenged increasingly by more recent critics, especially Egil Törnqvist, in

his *Strindbergian Drama*, who claims that Mlle. Y. begins and ends as the stronger. To begin, Törnqvist discusses some of the evidence adduced in favor of Frau X. While it is true that Strindberg wrote as quoted to his wife, at the same time he made a statement to the press that Mlle. Y., the non-speaking heroine, would be portrayed in his new drama as the stronger. Does he contradict that in his letter? Not at all. He instructs his wife to play Frau X. *as* the stronger, which means no more than that the character believes herself to be such, but people often believe false things about themselves.

Strindberg also instructed his wife to "give it 50% of the Charlatan . . . and suggest depths that don't exist!" This indicates more than a little that there is something false in Frau X.'s claims. Moreover, the fact that, in order to please her husband, Frau X. has had to do everything she can to imitate Mlle. Y., to become the other woman in her husband's eyes, hardly seems to leave her in a position of strength. Frau X.'s triumph over her rival is expressed in the words, "I believe you have lost him." People only believe what they cannot demonstrate to be true, so it seems that her triumph is little more than an aspiration or a hope. On these grounds Törnqvist builds his interpretation of Mlle. Y. as the stronger, but he concedes that it is no accident, but rather a testimony to Strindberg's dramatic skill, that the matter of which woman is the stronger is so balanced that each director can shape his production of the play according to either interpretation.

CRITICISM

Bradley A. Skeen

Skeen is a classicist. In the following essay, he examines The Stronger *in light of Strindberg's theory of soul murder.*

Strindberg stands among the greatest modern playwrights because he deals, like Franz Kafka or Philip K. Dick, with the great modern theme of paranoia, the individual's sense in the modern world that the very nature of reality is working against him, that everything around him is trying to destroy him. A few years after writing *The Stronger*, Strindberg suffered a temporary mental breakdown with clinical symptoms of paranoia, and his life and work was

WHAT DO I READ NEXT?

- Robert Louis Stevenson's *A Child's Garden of Verses* (1885) presents the ideal Victorian bourgeois culture in a didactic form intended for children.

- Buchi Emecheta's *The Bride Price* (2008) is a young-adult novel set in contemporary Nigeria, where traditional culture has been transformed by Western colonialism and where Western culture is taking on a new form by merging with tradition. The plot concerns a teenage girl who has to negotiate between the arranged marriage that her culture expects and Western ideas of romantic love. She uses deception and cunning to control her own destiny.

- *Inside the Victorian Home: A Portrait of Domestic Life in Victorian England* (2005), by Judith Flanders, gives a survey of daily life in Victorian bourgeois culture organized around the spaces of the house. The book gives a very quick introduction to the backgrounds of the characters in *The Stronger*.

- The twentieth-century Swedish filmmaker Ingmar Bergman was deeply influenced by

Strindberg. His 1982 film *Fanny and Alexander* is filled with homages to Strindberg's works, from *The Stronger* to *The Dream Play*. The main characters are a family of prominent actors in Stockholm theater around 1900. The film exists in a theatrical version (188 minutes) and a version originally shown on Swedish television (312 minutes). The published screenplay (1989) adds a nearly novelistic dimension to the story.

- Strindberg's *Inferno* and *From an Occult Diary*, translated by Mary Sandbach in 1979, give insight into Strindberg's paranoia, mental breakdown, and occultist beliefs. *Inferno*, in particular, is presented as a memoir of his life in Paris as part of a circle of famous intellectuals but is usually interpreted as a novel, all of whose characters happen to be real people—the book defies genre conventions.

- Per Hedström's *Strindberg: Painter and Photographer* (2001) is the catalog of an international 2001 exhibition of Strindberg's graphical works.

---

constantly animated by themes of paranoia. An example of this is the idea of soul murder, by which petty small people secretly attack great and important people (like himself) with the intent to damage them and if possible unhinge them to the point where they are ruined or even attempt to kill themselves. He outlines the idea in an essay in his collection *Vivisections* (1887) and made it an important theme in his plays, including *The Stronger*.

Strindberg's essay "Soul Murder (Apropos *Rosmersholm*)" was occasioned by his recognition that the main theme of Henrik Ibsen's play *Rosmersholm* was an idea that he calls soul murder, or psychic murder. The bulk of the essay is spent explaining the concept in general and exemplifying it with instances from his personal life; many

were things that truly happened to him, as his biographers have confirmed. Taking a familiar example from literature, he cites Iago's deception of Othello in Shakespeare's play. Iago fills Othello's minds with doubts and suspicions about his wife's fidelity until he is driven to kill her, resulting in his own execution. Strindberg lays out the pattern of Iago's killing Othello merely by the power of suggestion. Strindberg believed that the individual must make his way in society through a struggle for power, that each individual must either dominate or be dominated.

As open violence disappeared from modern European society (like most Europeans in the 1880s, Strindberg was convinced that there could never be another general European war), it was increasingly replaced by this kind of

> AN EXAMPLE OF THIS IS THE IDEA OF SOUL MURDER, BY WHICH PETTY SMALL PEOPLE SECRETLY ATTACK GREAT AND IMPORTANT PEOPLE (LIKE HIMSELF) WITH THE INTENT TO DAMAGE THEM AND IF POSSIBLE UNHINGE THEM TO THE POINT WHERE THEY ARE RUINED OR EVEN ATTEMPT TO KILL THEMSELVES."

psychic struggle. When one attacks a political rival, Strindberg states,

> Nowadays one ... 'prevails upon' him, exposes his intentions, ascribes to him intentions he does not have, deprives him of his livelihood, denies him social standing, makes him look ridiculous—in short, tortures him to death by lies or drives him insane instead of killing him.

Among attempts at psychic murder directed against himself, Strindberg mentions such things as manuscripts he had sent to publishers not being published or creditors that owed him money threatening to sue *him* if he did not stop asking for it. It was evidently impossible for Strindberg to conceive that these things might have happened randomly (e.g., a package being lost in the mail) or to view such situations from a perspective other than his own (a curious fault in a playwright). If any misfortune befell him, some human agency had to be the cause. When such beliefs advance beyond human causes, to lead one to think the universe itself is against one, that is a psychopathic condition, and Strindberg's paranoia makes his work an important precursor of postmodern literature, where this kind of paranoia will emerge as an important theme in the works of writers like Franz Kafka and Joseph Heller.

When Strindberg imagines his enemies making attacks of psychic murder against him, he sees himself as stronger than them, so they fail to destroy him. It is this paranoid conception of resistance to psychic murder that is at the heart of *The Stronger*. One of the characters, the weaker, is trying to commit psychic murder against the other, the stronger. Recalling what psychic murder entails for Strindberg, the audience

can see how one of the characters lies and confabulates, trying to convince the other that her position is really the weaker, that her life is meaningless and might as well be thrown away, trying to completely crush her and even drive her to commit suicide. It is clear, then, that the one trying to commit soul murder is Frau X. She is the weaker woman, trying, and failing, to attack Mlle. Y., whose silence is a symbol of her rising above and repelling the attack.

The text of *The Stronger* illustrates in dramatic form many of the points Strindberg makes in "Soul Murder." The victim of soul murder, he says,

> loses all ability to gauge a situation, all power to judge danger, all control over the passions, and the nerves of movement and feeling now react only to first impressions. False causal associations, erroneous ideas, conclusions without sufficient ground, hallucinations and finally a frenzy or constant state of defence that expresses itself in hostility, soon manifests itself.

This characterizes the whole shape of Frau X.'s discourse. Is she not the attacker? Certainly, but because soul murder is a struggle, a contest between two psyches, if the attack fails against the stronger, it must be the weaker who suffers. Accordingly, Frau X. turns a random encounter into a life-or-death struggle that she is hardly prepared for, as her emotions run away with her. One idea after another rapidly come into her mind, and she not only accepts them but blurts them out in a frenzy. In the space of a few minutes she goes from talking of her friendship with Mlle. Y. to feeling, and gratuitously showing, a vicious hatred. In short, it is the failed attempt at psychic murder that induces a sort of paranoid delusion in Frau X.'s mind.

Realizing that Strindberg conceived of her speech in this way complicates any understanding of the text. A simplistic interpretation might assume that the play is to be understood by taking whatever Frau X. says at face value, because she is, after all, the only voice creating the world for the viewer. In fact, her speech represents not the reality of the play, but at most her momentary and certainly distorted view of that reality. The viewer cannot know which of her accusations and assertions is true and is left struggling to understand the truth. It may well be that the affair between Bob and Mlle. Y. is entirely delusional. The point of the play is to communicate the character's fear and uncertainty, the feelings that so often overwhelm people in real life.

Frau X. tries to use the techniques of soul murder against Mlle. Y. In "Soul Murder," Strindberg asserts, "As is well known, there is nothing so destructive to the thinking process as shattered hopes, and a highly developed form of this torture can induce insanity." The main form of attack that Frau X. makes against Mlle. Y. consists of this dashing of hopes, although within the brief temporal unity of *The Stronger*, this kind of attack must be carried out retrospectively. Frau X. interprets Mlle. Y.'s life as filled with disappointment. She does not have any of the things that women traditionally want, and she is impeded even in pursuing her socially suspect (in Victorian eyes) career of an actress.

Mlle. Y. was engaged to be married twice, the first time to Bob, only to be tossed aside in favor of Frau X. The second time she succeeded in getting married but divorced over adultery. She should not have done that, Frau X. tells her, because it would have been better to put up with an adulterous husband than to have no home and no children. Although Mlle. Y. still works as an actress, it is, in Frau X.'s view, at a less prestigious theater than previously. Frau X. assures her that her husband's influence had nothing to do with that, which, by the logic of soul murder, is as good as telling Mlle. Y. that she worked behind the scenes to get her younger rival fired and succeeded, and there is nothing Mlle. Y. can do about it.

This kind of behind-the-scenes backstabbing is, in Strindberg's view, one of the key techniques of soul murder. Frau X. tells Mlle. Y. that she has even lost Bob as her lover (the most fanciful and least supported statement in the play, even if one assumes everything else is true), so she is without a home, without a husband, without children, even without a lover: "[E]verything in your hands [is] worthless and sterile." Everything the younger woman has failed to do, Frau X. has accomplished. Finally, Frau X. tells her, "You can't learn from another, you can't bend—and therefore you will be broken like a dry stalk—but I won't be!" Here, Frau X. wants to believe, the soul murder is complete, and the life that Mlle. Y. wanted for herself has been completely destroyed, whether or not she has a mental breakdown or kills herself. That is, if everything Frau X. has said is true, Mlle. Y. is destroyed. Frau X. says herself that the situation is conditional; one or the other of them will be broken. However, since Frau X. is suffering from the fevered symptoms of soul murder herself, it seems clear who is the stronger.

Source: Bradley A. Skeen, Critical Essay on *The Stronger*, in *Drama for Students*, Gale, Cengage Learning, 2012.

Harry G. Carlson

In the following excerpt, Carlson establishes that Strindberg experimented with occultism and the law of universal analogy in his writing.

> If we want a clear picture of how our... rational culture [today] has shrunk and constricted the definition of reality, at the same time that it banished whatever does not fit the definition to a shadow world of "psychic phenomena"—then we should turn to Strindberg, especially the painter and the poet Strindberg.
>
> —Ulf Linde, *Efter hand*

> What is religion?...I say religion is Anschlusz mit Jenseits, in our language: contact with the transcendental; contact with the source of power.
>
> —Strindberg, *Black Banners*

> The Eye altering alters all.
>
> —William Blake

MYSTICISM IN FIN DE SIÈCLE PARIS

The relationship between Strindberg's interests in occult ideas and phenomena and his later plays and novels has been debated by scholars for more than half a century. On the one hand, Martin Lamm and Göran Stockenström argued that major concepts in Strindberg's post-Inferno art were patterned on occult principles that were widely accepted by artists at the turn of the century. On the other, Gunnar Brandell, taking an autobiographical and psychoanalytical view, was skeptical. He concluded that in Strindberg's case such exotic interests were motivated primarily by personal, deep-seated psychological problems. "Perhaps one should not take such fantasies as seriously as Lamm seems to do," says Brandell, "when he surmises that the 'gods' and the 'powers'" that Strindberg wrote about were derived from occult images. "The God and demons [he]...struggled against sprang...from his own inner conflicts." But Brandell's evaluation of the "powers" does not preclude the possibility that Strindberg's demons were both personal and in accord with occult models. To understand the appeal and importance of the occult, not only to Strindberg, but to a whole artistic generation, it is necessary to understand the heightened spiritual/religious atmosphere that pervaded Paris when he

"BUT AN ARTIST DID NOT HAVE TO BE EITHER A DEDICATED AESTHETE OR A DEVOUT MYSTIC TO FIND ASPECTS OF THE OCCULT USEFUL, AS BOTH STRINDBERG AND YEATS DISCOVERED."

arrived for an extended stay in 1894. In this context his interests were not at all eccentric. For more than a decade the French capital had been a world center of revived interest in the occult. Many of the artists and intellectuals who migrated there to be exposed to the ancient, esoteric "secret wisdom" shared with Strindberg an enormous hunger for more evocative sources of inspiration than the positivist materialism of the day. In fact, by 1894, some in the occult movement were worried that it had become too fashionable—the esoteric was becoming exoteric. Papus, one of the leaders and editor of the most important of the occult journals, *L'Initiation* (to which Strindberg later contributed), decided that it was time for initiates "to leave the society folk to amuse one another and to retreat more than ever into the closed groups from which we were obliged to emerge in 1882 only to stop the propagation of doctrines that were leading the nation's intellectual life to destruction." There were others, however, especially in the arts, who felt that the esoteric should become exoteric and that occult teachings should be broadcast to all. This would inaugurate the new age that Kandinsky described in 1911 as "the Era of the Great Spiritual in Art."

In Strindberg's 1904 novel *The Gothic Rooms* is a glowing description of the inspirational mood he says he found in 1890s Paris.

> It was then that people discovered they were on the wrong path; at the next crossroads they veered in a new direction. They had collected facts and phenomena but could explain nothing. Explaining meant finding out what lay behind the phenomenon, and when people noticed that what lay behind it was on the "other side," they logically sought *Jenseits* [the Beyond]. This was called mysticism. And it was then that Swedenborg arose after a sleep of a hundred years in the grave.

> (*SS* [*Samlade skrifter*] 40:112)

Not everyone was impressed by the quality and character of the mystical climate. French literary critic Camille Mauclair reported that

> the Salons bulged with Holy Women at the Sepulchre, Seas of Galilee, crucifixions, roads to Emmaus, pardons, and benedictions, all executed in the same leached-out tones and with the same magic lantern lighting effects.... An appalling and unending plethora of missals, chasubles, monstrances, and lilies.... All the external signs of faith were dragged in, and only faith itself was left out.... The theaters put on Passions in verse, or as tableaux vivants. Poems sagged beneath the weight of knights errant, palfreys, crenelations, and troubadours. The same label was used to cover Liberty fabrics, anemia, the Virgin Mary, stained glass, Edgar Poe, the Primitives, Sarah Bernhardt (in any role), braided hair,...slender waists, M. Péladan, waistless dresses, and M. Huysman's latest books. Such was the arsenal of mysticism: a jumble sale stall.

Strindberg, however, participated very selectively in the mystical revival so exploited by Decadentism. He admired Poe, Péladan, and Huysmans but had no taste for the affected aestheticism that "dethroned life and put art in its place," as Jean Pierrot has described the phenomenon. But an artist did not have to be either a dedicated aesthete or a devout mystic to find aspects of the occult useful, as both Strindberg and Yeats discovered....

RENDERING VISIBLE THE INVISIBLE WORLD: THE "MAGIC WAND OF ANALOGY"

The primary artistic boon that many writers and painters derived from Theosophy and other aspects of the occult was an ancient cosmology that had striking implications for the way they thought about their art. For dramatists like Strindberg it meant new choices in the handling of character and the conventions of time and space that challenged the dominant realism of the contemporary theatre and anticipated the development of Surrealism and Expressionism. For painters like Kandinsky and Mondrian it meant new freedom in the handling of subject matter that challenged the dominant figurative tradition in the visual arts and initiated an interest in abstractionism.

Three basic premises of occult cosmology must have seemed especially appealing and useful to Strindberg, premises shared by both occult camps, Western and Eastern. The first was that the universe was divided into two worlds, one visible and terrestrial, the other invisible and spiritual, and that it was up to the artist to reveal the relationships between them. The second premise identified potential tools of expression for the artist: the correspondences or analogies that existed and created bonds both within and between the worlds, such as the analogy that views a human being as a microcosm, or diminutive mirror image of "the greater being," the universe as macrocosm. The third premise posited the existence of an intermediate state of being or world between matter and spirit, termed the "astral light" by Papus's group and the "astral plane" by the Theosophists.

The idea of an invisible world beyond the one we see was a Platonic concept (some critics, in fact, rename the occult tradition the Platonic tradition) that had also been vital to the earlier Romantics. Carlyle cited German idealistic philosopher Johann Fichte's allusion to "the divine idea of the world" that lies "at the bottom of appearance" and asserted that "all appearance, from the starry sky to the grass of the field, but especially the appearance of man and his work, is but the *vesture*, the embodiment that renders it visible."

The second premise entailed preparing to see in a new way, becoming an "initiate" uniquely equipped to detect the correspondences between appearance and what was "at the bottom of appearance." Once again, the Romantics had led the way. Novalis, in a passage underlined and accentuated in the margin of Strindberg's copy of his works, stressed the necessity of learning "to use the Magic Wand of Analogy." Affirming analogies or correspondences—through axioms like "as above, so below" and "as within, so without"—created bonds between all elements and phenomena in the universe, making the artist's mission, as William Blake described it,

> To see a World in a Grain of Sand
> And a Heaven in a Wild Flower
> Hold Infinity in the palm of your hand
> And Eternity in an hour

Strindberg's Occultist mentors and colleagues worked diligently to revalidate the traditional "law of universal analogy." Papus wrote in his *L'Occultisme* that "analogy permits, given one sole phenomenon, to deduce with certainty one general law applicable to all phenomena, even those of a totally different order." And Guaita asserted that it was by virtue of analogies

"that the mollusk secretes the mother-of-pearl and the human heart love"; "the same law rules the communion of the sexes and gravitation of the suns." The analogies drawn were not simply curiosities: they were evidence of humanity's intimate relationship with every part of the natural order. For Strindberg they became, as they had been for the Romantics, a means of making the universe organic again. Just as the Romantics reacted against eighteenth-century mechanistic rationalism, Strindberg and other fin de siècle Occultist enthusiasts reacted against positivist materialism.

Neither Papus nor Guaita, however, received primary credit from Strindberg for demonstrating to him the spiritual and poetic power of analogy—that he gave to eighteenth-century mystics Emanuel Swedenborg and Louis-Claude de Saint-Martin (*Brev* 12:315), also popular with the Theosophists. Swedenborg, the first to apply the terminology of correspondences to the older theory of universal analogy, was the model and inspiration for generations of Romantic artists from Blake through Balzac, Baudelaire, and Yeats. And Saint-Martin, a philosopher and friend of Rousseau, was much admired by both the German and French Romantics. Like Swedenborg, he too emphasized an analogical view of the universe that moved toward a restoration of material and spiritual harmony. Both Saint-Martin (called the "Luther of Occultism") and Swedenborg probably offered Strindberg what he felt was lacking in other occult theorists: a way of appreciating the ancient wisdom within an orthodox religious tradition, untainted by high-powered aestheticism, magic, or satanism. While Saint-Martin criticized the superstitious practices of the mystical Illuminist tradition, Swedenborg stressed a Christian interpretation of Occultist principles. More importantly, they provided Strindberg, as they had provided the Romantics before him, with a new rationale for the artist as a poet-seer who possesses, as Sainte-Beuve put it, "the key to the symbols and the knowledge of the figures, for whom what to others seems incoherent and contradictory is only a harmonic contrast, a chord on the universal lyre."

In 1896 Strindberg experimented with the poetic potential in the law of universal analogy in essays for *L'Initiation*, experiments that would later be put to good use in his post-Inferno drama. In one of these essays, the author reveals his Neoplatonic purpose in using correspondences with an epigraph credited to the Talmud: "If you want to know the invisible, look carefully at the visible" (*SS* 27:357). Another essay, "A Look into Space," relates the results of a test the author said he conducted on himself to investigate the mysteries of "primordial light" ("*urlijuset*"). In it we find the same perceptive, self-proclaimed Naturalist who had written so eloquently about Swedish nature a decade earlier. But now, his visual acuity sharpened by his painting and his imagination reawakened, he is no longer concerned about the dangers of "hallucinations." Without hesitation, he pursues his objective observations beyond the natural, using analogy and correspondence to create bonds between the images flashing on his own retina and the spectacular energies of outer space. The imaginative "woodnymphistic" improvisations he practiced as a painter had become scientific and occult:

> When I press against my eyeballs in the dark, I see first a chaos of light, stars, and sparks, which gradually condense and collect into a shining, rotating disk. This disk then begins to throw out sheaves of red light, imitating the sun's faculae, but also resembling the vortex of a sunspot or the spiral nebulae in the constellation Virgo or Orion.... When the pain provoked by the pressure is at its maximum, the sun disappears, and a single, dazzling star remains. As the pressure diminishes, the light phenomenon ceases, and a play of colors begins. In the center a *Scabiosa* purple depression appears, surrounded by soft sulfur yellow, and resembling a sunspot in design. Is this, then, what the astronomer renders in words and pictures—the interior of the eye...? Where does the self begin, and where does it end? Did the eye conform to the sun? Or is the eye the creative phenomenon we call the sun?

(*SS* 27:354)

The implications of the questions raised were discussed approvingly in an "amendment" to the article signed by "Buddhist Guymiot," who mingles images from East and West: "The eye is a reduction of Brahma's egg.... Everything that takes place in our solar system is analogous with what takes place it one of our eyes.... In the play of light in our eyes we can study the play of light in the cosmos.... One must take seriously the expression macrocosm and microcosm in order to arrive at a knowledge of nature. There is nothing outside man which is not also inside man and in other forms of existence" (*SS* 27:355–57).

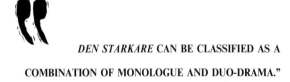

DEN STARKARE CAN BE CLASSIFIED AS A COMBINATION OF MONOLOGUE AND DUO-DRAMA."

Strindberg had at last found a way to regain a center of meaning in his life. He was beginning to discover, in his own words, "the infinite coherence" in "the great chaos" (*Brev* 11:153) of existence, echoing probably unknowingly similar feelings expressed by French Romantic Gérard Nerval forty years earlier in his novel *Aurélia*:

> How can I have existed so long, I said to myself, outside Nature without identifying myself with her? Everything lives, everything acts, everything corresponds; the magnetic rays emanating from myself or others traverse unimpeded the infinite chain of created things; it is a transparent network which covers the world, and its fine threads communicate from one to another to the planets and the stars. I am now a captive on the earth, but I converse with choiring stars, who share my joys and sorrows! . . .

Source: Harry G. Carlson, "The Romance of the Occult," in *Out of Inferno: Strindberg's Reawakening as an Artist*, University of Washington Press, 1996, pp. 187–222.

Egil Törnqvist

In the following excerpt, Törnqvist discusses the importance of Den starkare *(The Stronger) in Strindberg's oeuvre of one-act plays.*

Strindberg's international reputation as a dramatist is usually connected with two enterprises. Before the so-called Inferno Crisis in the mid-1890s, he was an eminent representative of naturalist drama. His famous preface to *Fröken Julie* [*Miss Julie*] is generally recognized along with Zola's *Le Naturalisme au théâtre* as its most important manifesto. After the Inferno Crisis, he penned his preexpressionist plays, in which the protagonists are more in conflict with themselves and with the Powers, as Strindberg termed them, than with each other. Both enterprises have been rather extensively researched.

Strindberg's two other notable contributions to modern drama have received considerably less attention and recognition. I refer to his cycle of plays about the Swedish royals—we would have to go to Shakespeare to find a counterpart—and to his commitment to the one-act play as a serious and independent form of drama, our concern at the moment.

One of the relatively few scholarly works devoted to the one-act play as a genre unequivocally states that "seit Strindbergs theoretischem Debüt von 1889 muss der Einakter als eigenständige Gattung gelten" (Schnetz, 24) [since Strindberg's theoretical debut in 1889, the one-act play must count as an independent genre]. Such a statement certainly invites more attention to Strindberg's one-act plays than has hitherto been bestowed on them.

Schnetz speaks of the one-act play (*der Einakter*), not of the short play (*das Kurzdrama*). The distinction, although important, is rarely made. To qualify as a one-act play, I would suggest, a play must not contain any intermission, curtain, or black-out indicating a change of time and/or place. The "short play" or *Kurzdrama* is of another order. It is of course true that most one-act plays are fairly short, but their length, which is usually considered of great importance, is in fact irrelevant to the question of whether they are one-act plays. Thus Strindberg's *Fröken Julie* and *Fordringsägare* [*Creditors*], both plays that fill a whole evening, formally qualify as one-act plays, although *Fröken Julie,* with its intermediate "Ballet," is arguably a disguised two-act play. Strindberg's Chamber Plays, on the other hand, whose performance time is about the same, do not qualify as one-act plays; lacking a unity of time and to some extent of place, they are divided into different parts separated by, one must assume, a curtain or a black-out.

According to this single, intersubjective criterion, Strindberg penned fourteen one-act plays. Of these, two—the verse drama *I Rom* [*In Rome*] and the historical play *Den fredlöse* [*The Outlaw*]—belong to Strindberg's earliest period, while the puppet play *Kaspers fettisdag* [*Casper's Shrove Tuesday*] is relatively late. The remaining eleven were all written between 1888 and 1892 during the playwright's so-called naturalist period. In the following, I shall limit myself to these eleven one-act plays of the middle period and focus on two of them: *Den starkare* and *Inför döden* [*In the Face of Death*].

When Schnetz speaks of Strindberg's debut as a theoretician in 1889, she refers to the article "Om modernt drama och modern teater" ["On Modern Drama and Modern Theater"] published in the Danish journal *Ny jord*. But Strindberg had, in fact, commented on the one-act form the year before. In his preface to *Fröken Julie*, he says:

> As for the technical aspects of composition, I have experimented with eliminating act divisions. The reason is that I believe our dwindling capacity for accepting illusion is possibly further disturbed by intermissions, during which the spectator has time to reflect and thereby escape the suggestive influence of the author-hypnotist.... My hope for the future is to so educate audiences that they can sit through a one-act play that lasts an entire evening. But this will require experimentation.

(*Five Plays*, 72–3)

The quotation suggests that Strindberg's interest in the one-act play is directly related to his ambition, as a naturalist playwright, to create maximal illusion.

In "Om modernt drama och modern teater," he notes that the "new"—i.e. naturalist—drama pays more attention to character description than to plot, that the unities of time and place are observed, and that in "det betydelsefulla motivets uppsökande," ["searching for the significant motif"], the playwrights focus on,

> life's two poles, life and death...the fight for the spouse, for the means of subsistence, for honor, all these struggles—with their battlefield cries of woe, wounded and dead during which one heard a new philosophy of life conceived as a struggle, blow its fertile winds from the south.

> These were tragedies such as had not been seen before. The young authors...seemed reluctant to impose their suffering on others more than was absolutely necessary. Therefore, they made the suffering as brief as possible, let the pain pour forth in one act, sometimes in a single scene.

(Cole, 18–9)

Strindberg then sketches the history of the short one-act play, the *quart d'heure*, which he sees as the paradigmatic form for the presentation of modern man. At the same time, he regards "den utforda enaktaren" ["the fully executed one-act play"] as "det kommande dramats formule" ["the formula of the drama to come"]. Using Musset's proverbs as a model, one might, he declares, "[m]ed hjälp av ett bord och två stolar...få framställda de starkaste konflikter livet bjuder" ["by means of a table and two chairs...present the most powerful conflicts of life"], and this by resorting to "den moderna psykologiens upptäcter" (*Samlade skrifter*, 17: 301) ["the discoveries of modern psychology"] (Cole, 20–1).

At the time, Strindberg was strongly influenced by the so-called psychology of suggestion and was extremely anxious to be staged in Paris, where Zolaesque naturalism was *en vogue*. At the same time, he was trying to establish his Scandinavian Experimental Theater. These three facts explain why Strindberg precisely at this moment was so concerned with psychological, naturalistic one-act drama. As always, he desired to be abreast of the most recent developments, especially when they related to scientific achievements.

The demand of naturalism that staged events should mirror real ones is eminently fulfilled in the one-act play in the sense that unity of time and place are usually observed—so much so that the playing time (Germ. *Spielzeit*) often precisely corresponds with the scenic time (Germ. *gespielte Zeit*, the time assumed to pass between the raising and lowering of the curtain), a circumstance that does not occur in plays of more than one act.

Although Strindberg never became an out-and-out naturalist and definitely rejects what he calls petty naturalism, the eleven one-act plays he wrote between 1888 and 1892 may for want of a better label be considered naturalistic dramas. A congruence of playing time and scenic time characterizes *Den starkare*, *Paria*, and *Första varningen*: in all three the unity of place is also strictly observed. In *Första varningen*, Strindberg even alludes to this synchronism when, in the beginning, he has the Gentleman state that he is to leave in half an hour. The reason for observing these unities may well be a naturalist endeavor on Strindberg's part to heighten the slice-of-life character of these plays. Contrary to what is often assumed, *Fröken Julie* is in this respect less faithful to the requirements of naturalist verisimilitude. The drama is marked by a certain discrepancy between the playing time (around an hour and a half) and the scenic time (around twelve hours). But significantly the playwright disguises this discrepancy by having dancing peasants invade the kitchen midway through the play. The time seems extended, and there is no need for a curtain which means that the illusion of the spectator is never broken.

Given its brevity, the one-act play offers little possibility for varied description of characters and environment. The naturalistic emphasis on inherited traits and environment as determining factors is in many respects better suited to the narrative, as for example novel cycles like Zola's

Les Rougon-Macquart, than to the concise and stylized form that the one-act play exemplifies. Here even the main characters tend to be types rather than individuals, and the limited scenic time prevents or at least obstructs the depiction of decisive mental changes. On the other hand, the fact that drama-in-performance by definition is a sensuous form presenting not by way of narration but in flesh and blood means that the drama in this sense concords better with the demands of naturalism than the epic. Yet this is more true of the play in several acts than of the one-act play. And in principle even more true of the modern equivalent of the nineteenth-century serial, the television soap opera. The one-act play, by contrast, lends itself to depicting parabolic situations. Here we deal not so much with people in conflict with each other as with man in conflict with an outward or inward fate. Existential and universal problems reign supreme.

It is hardly surprising, therefore, that in the studies devoted to the one-act play as genre, the naturalist one-act play has received only modest attention. While Schnetz focuses on the absurdist one-act play, Rudolf Halbritter discusses what he sees as the three main categories of the (Anglo-American) short play—the symbolist (Yeats), the epic-didactic (Wilder), and the grotesque (Pinter), and there are "vergleichweise wenige naturalistische und impressionistische Kurzdramen" (Halbritter, 28) [relatively few naturalistic and impressionistic short plays].

The question arises whether naturalism is inimical to the one-act form. If so, are Strindberg's "naturalist" one-act plays less faithful to naturalism than one generally assumes? Or, if we maintain that Strindberg's one-act plays are indeed naturalistic, do they represent a blind alley avoided by later playwrights? I believe there is something to be said for both. On one hand, Strindberg's one-act plays are more stylized and less naturalistic than usually thought. On the other, since the general trend in modern drama has been away from naturalism, we cannot expect any flourishing of this type of drama in plays intended for the stage, but rather in other media—radio, television....

[I]n the lists of *dramatis personae*, Strindberg sometimes designates his characters by name, sometimes only by blood or other relationship (father, daughter, son-in-law), sometimes by profession, and sometimes by abstraction (Mr. X, Miss Y). The unavoidable conclusion is that the naturalistic Strindbergian one-act play is a protean phenomenon. Its homogeneity depends not so much on formal characteristics, as on thematic coherence—not surprisingly considering the author's own situation at the time, matrimonial relations stand central—coupled with an exceedingly dense dialogue, rich in subtext, and an almost cynical tone associated with the *comédie rosse.*

Strindberg's pioneering contribution is perhaps most noticeable in the shortest of his one-act plays, the monodrama *Den starkare* [*The Stronger*], where the author dramatizes the coincidental meeting between two actresses in a cafe on Christmas Eve. At the end of Mrs. X's long monologue—Miss Y does not say a word—it is clear that Miss Y has been, and perhaps still is, the mistress of Mrs. X's husband.

Den starkare can be classified as a combination of monologue and duo-drama. Miss Y's reactions are extremely important, since they both motivate and qualify Mrs. X's statements. But the monodrama form is not unproblematic. While the exposition in a normal play usually is handled by secondary characters, whose "objective" information often ironically contrasts with the versions of the main characters, in *Den starkare* the protagonist, Mrs. X, must provide the exposition herself. As a result she presents both factual information and subjective interpretation of this information. Indeed part of the play's suggestive power lies in the fact that it is so hard to separate the one from the other.

Impressed by the French *quart d'heure* plays, Strindberg wrote *Den starkare* for the Scandinavian Experimental Theater he had founded in November 1888. It is likely that he wrote both parts in the play for his wife Siri von Essen; in performances in Sweden Siri, who was a Swedish-speaking Finn, could do the speaking part; in performances in Denmark she could do the silent one. The fact that the little theater group consisted of both Swedish- and Danish-speaking actors may, in fact, have contributed to Strindberg's choice of the monodrama form. According to another hypothesis, Strindberg wrote *Den starkare* to demonstrate that the monologue need not be banished from naturalist drama (*Strindbergs dramer*, 4:7). In the preface to *Fröken Julie* he notes: "Monologen är nu av våra realister bannlyst såsom osannolik, men om jag motiverar den, får jag den sannolik, och kan således begagna den med fördel" (*Samlade Verk*, 27:110) ["Our realists

today condemn the monologue as implausible, but if I motivate it, I can make it plausible and use it to advantage"] (*Five Plays*, 72). By including Miss Y in the play, Strindberg could motivate Mrs. X's long monologue from a naturalist *tranche-de-vie* point of view, despite the fact that Mrs. X at times seems to be thinking aloud rather than addressing Miss Y. Far from a shortcoming, these fluctuations between soliloquy and monologue add to the suggestiveness and psychological depth of the playlet.

What is the relationship between Strindberg's one-act play and those in more than one act? In his influential *Theorie des modernen Dramas*, Peter Szondi devotes a short chapter to the one-act play under the telling title "Rettungsversuche" ["Rescue Attempts"]. When a number of leading playwrights began to write one-act plays in the 1880s, it was, according to Szondi, a symptom that the traditional form of drama had by that time become so undramatic that it had become problematic. The one-act play is an attempt to replace the tension based on diluted interhuman conflicts with a tension outside human relations. Instead of a conflict between the characters, the one-act play offers an existential or metaphysical conflict between man and some force outside him which he cannot master, fate, providence, or, to use Strindberg's expression, the Powers. . . .

Source: Egil Törnqvist, "The Strindbergian One-Act Play," in *Scandinavian Studies,* Vol. 68, No. 3, Summer 1996, pp. 356–69.

August Strindberg
In the following excerpt, Strindberg explains his character creation process with regard to his play Fröken Julie.

. . . Thus I have neither been one-sidedly physiological nor one-sidedly psychological in my procedure. Nor have I merely delivered a moral preachment. This multiplicity of motives I regard as praiseworthy because it is in keeping with the views of our own time. And if others have done the same thing before me, I may boast of not being the sole inventor of my paradoxes—as all discoveries are named.

In regard to the character-drawing I may say that I have tried to make my figures rather "characterless," and I have done so for reasons I shall now state.

In the course of the ages the word character has assumed many meanings. Originally it signified probably the dominant groundnote in the

> OF COURSE, I HAVE NO ILLUSIONS ABOUT GETTING THE ACTORS TO PLAY *FOR* THE PUBLIC AND NOT *AT* IT, ALTHOUGH SUCH A CHANGE WOULD BE HIGHLY DESIRABLE."

complex mass of the self, and as such it was confused with temperament. Afterward it became the middle-class term for an automaton, so that an individual whose nature had come to a stand-still, or who had adapted himself to a certain part in life—who had ceased to grow, in a word—was named a character; while one remaining in a state of development—a skilful navigator on life's river, who did not sail with closetied sheets, but knew when to fall off before the wind and when to luff again—was called lacking in character. And he was called so in a depreciatory sense, of course, because he was so hard to catch, to classify, and to keep track of. This middle-class notion about the immobility of the soul was transplanted to the stage, where the middle-class element has always held sway. There a character became synonymous with a gentleman fixed and finished once for all—one who invariably appeared drunk, jolly, sad. And for the purpose of characterisation nothing more was needed than some physical deformity like a clubfoot, a wooden leg, a red nose; or the person concerned was made to repeat some phrase like "That's capital!" or "Barkis is willin'," or something of that kind. This manner of regarding human beings as homogeneous is preserved even by the great Molière. . . . I do not believe . . . in simple characters on the stage. And the summary judgments of the author upon men—this one stupid, and that one brutal, this one jealous, and that one stingy—should be challenged by the naturalists, who know the fertility of the soul-complex, and who realise that "vice" has a reverse very much resembling virtue.

Because they are modern characters, living in a period of transition more hysterically hurried than its immediate predecessor at least, I have made my figures vacillating, out of joint, torn between the old and the new. And I do not think it unlikely that, through newspaper reading and overheard conversations, modern ideas may have leaked down to the strata where domestic servants belong.

My souls (or characters) are conglomerates, made up of past and present stages of civilisation, scraps of humanity, torn-off pieces of Sunday clothing turned into rags—all patched together as is the human soul itself. And I have furthermore offered a touch of evolutionary history by letting the weaker repeat words stolen from the stronger, and by letting different souls accept "ideas"—or suggestions, as they are called—from each other.

In regard to the dialogue, I want to point out that I have departed somewhat from prevailing traditions by not turning my figures into catechists who make stupid questions in order to call forth witty answers. I have avoided the symmetrical and mathematical construction of the French dialogue, and have instead permitted the minds to work irregularly as they do in reality, where, during conversation, the cogs of one mind seem more or less haphazardly to engage those of another one, and where no topic is fully exhausted. Naturally enough, therefore, the dialogue strays a good deal as, in the opening scenes, it acquires a material that later on is worked over, picked up again, repeated, expounded, and built up like the theme in a musical composition.

The plot is pregnant enough, and as, at bottom, it is concerned only with two persons, I have concentrated my attention on these, introducing only one subordinate figure, the cook, and keeping the unfortunate spirit of the father hovering above and beyond the action. I have done this because I believe I have noticed that the psychological processes are what interest the people of our own day more than anything else. Our souls, so eager for knowledge, cannot rest satisfied with seeing what happens, but must also learn how it comes to happen! What we want to see are just the wires, the machinery. We want to investigate the box with the false bottom, touch the magic ring in order to find the suture, and look into the cards to discover how they are marked.

In this I have taken for models the monographic novels of the brothers de Goncourt, which have appealed more to me than any other modern literature.

Turning to the technical side of the composition, I have tried to abolish the division into acts. And I have done so because I have come to fear that our decreasing capacity for illusion might be unfavourably affected by intermissions during which the spectator would have time to reflect and to get away from the suggestive influence of the author-hypnotist. My play will probably last an hour and a half, and as it is possible to listen that length of time, or longer, to a lecture, a sermon, or a debate, I have imagined that a theatrical performance could not become fatiguing in the same time. As early as 1872, in one of my first dramatic experiments, *The Outlaw*, I tried the same concentrated form, but with scant success. The play was written in five acts and wholly completed when I became aware of the restless, scattered effect it produced. Then I burned it, and out of the ashes rose a single, well-built act, covering fifty printed pages, and taking an hour for its performance. Thus the form of the present play is not new, but it seems to be my own, and changing aesthetical conventions may possibly make it timely.

My hope is still for a public educated to the point where it can sit through a whole-evening performance in a single act. But that point cannot be reached without a great deal of experimentation. In the meantime I have resorted to three art forms that are to provide resting-places for the public and the actors, without letting the public escape from the illusion induced. All these forms are subsidiary to the drama. They are the monologue, the pantomime, and the dance, all of them belonging originally to the tragedy of classical antiquity. For the monologue has sprung from the monody, and the chorus has developed into the ballet.

Our realists have excommunicated the monologue as improbable, but if I can lay a proper basis for it, I can also make it seem probable, and then I can use it to good advantage. It is probable, for instance, that a speaker may walk back and forth in his room practising his speech aloud; it is probable that an actor may read through his part aloud, that a servant-girl may talk to her cat, that a mother may prattle to her child, that an old spinster may chatter to her parrot, that a person may talk in his sleep. And in order that the actor for once may have a chance to work independently, and to be free for a moment from the author's pointer, it is better that the monologues be not written out, but just indicated. As it matters comparatively little what is said to the parrot or the cat, or in one's sleep—because it cannot influence the

action—it is possible that a gifted actor, carried away by the situation and the mood of the occasion, may improvise such matters better than they could be written by the author, who cannot figure out in advance how much may be said, and how long the talk may last, without waking the public out of their illusions.

It is well known that, on certain stages, the Italian theatre has returned to improvisation and thereby produced creative actors—who, however, must follow the author's suggestions—and this may be counted a step forward, or even the beginning of a new art form that might well be called *productive*.

Where, on the other hand, the monologue would seem unreal, I have used the pantomime, and there I have left still greater scope for the actor's imagination—and for his desire to gain independent honours. But in order that the public may not be tried beyond endurance, I have permitted the music—which is amply warranted by the Midsummer Eve's dance—to exercise its illusory power while the dumb show lasts. And I ask the musical director to make careful selection of the music used for this purpose, so that incompatible moods are not induced by reminiscences from the last musical comedy or topical song, or by folk-tunes of too markedly ethnographical distinction.

The mere introduction of a scene with a lot of "people" could not have taken the place of the dance, for such scenes are poorly acted and tempt a number of grinning idiots into displaying their own smartness, whereby the illusion is disturbed. As the common people do not improvise their gibes, but use ready-made phrases in which stick some double meaning, I have not composed their lampooning song, but have appropriated a little known folk-dance which I personally noted down in a district near Stockholm. The words don't quite hit the point, but hint vaguely at it, and this is intentional, for the cunning (*i.e.*, weakness) of the slave keeps him from any direct attack. There must, then, be no chattering clowns in a serious action, and no coarse flouting at a situation that puts the lid on the coffin of a whole family.

As far as the scenery is concerned, I have borrowed from impressionistic painting its asymmetry, its quality of abruptness, and have thereby in my opinion strengthened the illusion. Because the whole room and all its contents are not shown, there is a chance to guess at things—

that is, our imagination is stirred into complementing our vision. I have made a further gain in getting rid of those tiresome exits by means of doors, especially as stage doors are made of canvas and swing back and forth at the lightest touch. They are not even capable of expressing the anger of an irate *pater familias* who, on leaving his home after a poor dinner, slams the door behind him "so that it shakes the whole house." (On the stage the house sways.) I have also contented myself with a single setting, and for the double purpose of making the figures become parts of their surroundings, and of breaking with the tendency toward luxurious scenery. But having only a single setting, one may demand to have it real. Yet nothing is more difficult than to get a room that looks something like a room, although the painter can easily enough produce waterfalls and flaming volcanoes. Let it go at canvas for the walls, but we might be done with the painting of shelves and kitchen utensils on the canvas. We have so much else on the stage that is conventional, and in which we are asked to believe, that we might at least be spared the too great effort of believing in painted pans and kettles.

I have placed the rear wall and the table diagonally across the stage in order to make the actors show full face and half profile to the audience when they sit opposite each other at the table.

Another novelty well needed would be the abolition of the footlights. The light from below is said to have for its purpose to make the faces of the actors look fatter. But I cannot help asking: why must all actors be fat in the face? Does not this light from below tend to wipe out the subtler lineaments in the lower part of the face, and especially around the jaws? Does it not give a false appearance to the nose and cast shadows upward over the eyes? If this be not so, another thing is certain: namely, that the eyes of the actors suffer from the light, so that the effective play of their glances is precluded. Coming from below, the light strikes the retina in places generally protected (except in sailors, who have to see the sun reflected in the water), and for this reason one observes hardly anything but a vulgar rolling of the eyes, either sideways or upwards, toward the galleries, so that nothing but the white of the eye shows. Perhaps the same cause may account for the tedious blinking of which especially the actresses are guilty. And

when anybody on the stage wants to use his eyes to speak with, no other way is left him but the poor one of staring straight at the public, with whom he or she then gets into direct communication outside of the frame provided by the setting. . . . Would it not be possible by means of strong side-lights (obtained by the employment of reflectors, for instance) to add to the resources already possessed by the actor? Could not his mimicry be still further strengthened by use of the greatest asset possessed by the face: the play of the eyes?

Of course, I have no illusions about getting the actors to play *for* the public and not *at* it, although such a change would be highly desirable. I dare not even dream of beholding the actor's back throughout an important scene, but I wish with all my heart that crucial scenes might not be played in the centre of the proscenium, like duets meant to bring forth applause. Instead, I should like to have them laid in the place indicated by the situation. Thus I ask for no revolutions, but only for a few minor modifications. To make a real room of the stage, with the fourth wall missing, and a part of the furniture placed back toward the audience, would probably produce a disturbing effect at present.

In wishing to speak of the facial make-up, I have no hope that the ladies will listen to me, as they would rather look beautiful than lifelike. But the actor might consider whether it be to his advantage to paint his face so that it shows some abstract type which covers it like a mask.

In modern psychological dramas, where the subtlest movements of the soul are to be reflected on the face rather than by gestures and noise, it would probably be well to experiment with strong side-light on a small stage, and with unpainted faces, or at least with a minimum of make-up.

If, in addition, we might escape the visible orchestra, with its disturbing lamps and its faces turned toward the public; if we could have the seats on the main floor (the orchestra or the pit) raised so that the eyes of the spectators would be above the knees of the actors; if we could get rid of the boxes with their tittering parties of diners; if we could also have the auditorium completely darkened during the performance; and if, first and last, we could have a small stage and a small house: then a new dramatic art might rise, and the theatre might at least become an institution for the entertainment of people with culture.

While waiting for this kind of theatre, I suppose we shall have to write for the "ice-box," and thus prepare the repertory that is to come.

I have made an attempt. If it prove a failure, there is plenty of time to try over again.

Source: August Strindberg, Preface to *Fröken Julie*, in *Plays, Second Series*, Charles Scribner's Sons, 1913, pp. 96–112.

SOURCES

du Maurier, George, *Trilby*, 2 vols., Berhnhard Tauchnitz, 1894, pp. 92–104.

Gay, Peter, *Pleasure Wars: The Bourgeois Experience, Victoria to Freud*, Vol. 5, W. W. Norton, 1999, pp. 46–164.

Johnson, Walter, *August Strindberg*, Twayne, 1978, pp. 148–49.

Lagercrantz, Olof, *August Strindberg*, translated by Anselm Hollo, Farrar, Straus, Giroux, 1984.

Madsen, Børge Gedsø, *Strindberg's Naturalistic Theatre: Its Relation to French Naturalism*, University of Washington Press, 1962, pp. 120–22.

Strindberg, August, "The Battle of the Brains," in *Selected Essays*, selected, edited, and translated by Michael Robinson, Cambridge University Press, 1996, pp. 25–46.

———, *Strindberg's Letters*, Vol. 1, selected, edited, and translated by Michael Robinson, University of Chicago Press, 1992, pp. 307–309.

———, "Soul Murder (Apropos *Rosmersholm*)," in *Selected Essays*, selected, edited, and translated by Michael Robinson, Cambridge University Press, 1996, pp. 64–72.

———, *The Stronger: A Play in One Act*, translated by F. I. Ziegler, in *Poet Lore: A Quarterly Magazine of Letters*, Spring 1906, pp. 47–50.

Törnqvist, Egil, *Strindbergian Drama: Themes and Structure*, Alqvist & Wiskell, 1982, pp. 64–70.

FURTHER READING

Meyer, Michael Leverson, *Strindberg*, Random House, 1985.
> This is one of the two standard biographies of Strindberg.

Robinson, Michael, ed., *The Cambridge Companion to August Strindberg*, Cambridge University Press, 2009.
> This collection of essays contains a variety of topics related to Strindberg's life and art written by leading Strindberg specialists.

Strindberg, August, *Plays*, 4 vols., translated by Edwin Björkman, Charles Scribner's Sons, 1912–1916.
> Although no complete translation of Strindberg's plays has ever been published in English, this is the most extensive collection in translation.

———, *Strindberg on Drama and Theater: A Sourcebook*, selected, translated, and edited by Egil Törnqvist and Brigitta Steene, Amsterdam University Press, 2007.
> Drawn from Strindberg's essays and letters, this is a narrowly focused anthology of passages bearing directly on theatrical theory and production.

SUGGESTED SEARCH TERMS

August Strindberg

The Stronger AND August Strindberg

realism

hypnosis

bourgeoisie

Émile François Zola

Jean-Martin Charcot

monodrama

Fanny and Alexander AND August Strindberg

Soul Murder AND August Strindberg

naturalism AND August Strindberg

They Knew What They Wanted

SIDNEY HOWARD

1924

They Knew What They Wanted is a play by the American dramatist Sidney Howard. It was first produced in New York in 1924 and won the Pulitzer Prize for Drama the following year. It was Howard's first truly successful play, and throughout the 1920s and 1930s he would be regarded as one of the most accomplished dramatists of the period. Even thirty or forty years later, some critics still regarded *They Knew What They Wanted* as one of the finest plays in the American theater.

The play is marked by the social realism that was popular in American drama in the first decades of the twentieth century. Issues such as Prohibition and labor relations form a significant background for the plot, which is about an aging Italian immigrant named Tony, a California winegrower, who is about to marry a young woman named Amy whom he saw working in a restaurant in San Francisco but has not yet met. Too shy to approach her in person, he courted her by mail, getting his handsome young foreman, Joe, whose English is much better than his, to write the letters. Unbeknownst to Joe, he also sent a photograph of Joe to Amy, allowing her to assume that the picture was of him. When Amy arrives at Tony's farmhouse for the wedding, she at first mistakes Joe for Tony, a situation that leads to further complications as the play develops.

Although it is seldom performed today, *They Knew What They Wanted* remains of interest as a

Sidney Howard (© *Corbis*)

well-constructed comedy with realistic characters. Howard's compassionate attitude toward those characters as they get caught up in a potentially explosive situation, and his emphasis on forgiveness rather than revenge, make the play as relevant and enjoyable for twenty-first-century readers as it was for playgoers in the 1920s. Although currently out of print, the play can be found in *Famous American Plays of the 1920s*, selected and introduced by Kenneth Macgowan, published in 1988.

AUTHOR BIOGRAPHY

Howard was born on June 26, 1891, in Oakland, California, the son of John Lawrence and Helen Louise Howard. His father was a steamship executive, and his mother was a musician. Howard began to write seriously when he was nineteen years old and recovering from tuberculosis in a

Swiss sanatorium. Later he attended the University of California at Berkeley, where he edited a literary periodical. He received a bachelor of arts degree in 1915 and a master of arts degree from Harvard University in 1916. It was while he was at Harvard that he decided he wanted to be a dramatist. In World War I, he served in the American Ambulance Corps, the U.S. Army, and the U.S. Air Service, in which he became a captain. After the war, in 1919, he began working as a journalist for *Life* magazine, becoming literary editor in 1922.

Howard published *Three Flights Up*, a collection of short stories, in 1924, but after that it was as a dramatist that he made his mark. He had three plays produced from 1921 to 1924 before writing *They Knew What They Wanted*, the play for which he is best known. The play was turned down sixteen times by producers but was finally produced in New York by the Theater Guild in November 1924 and published the following year. It ran for 414 performances and was awarded the Pulitzer Prize in 1925.

Howard continued to work as a journalist throughout the 1920s and also as a translator of European plays for the American stage. He was fluent in French and Spanish. In 1921, Howard married Clare Eames, an actress. They were divorced in 1930, and Howard married Leopoldine Blaine Damrosch in 1931. He had one child by his first wife and two by his second.

During his career as a dramatist, Howard wrote more than twenty-five plays, including *Lucky Sam McCarver* (produced 1925), *The Silver Cord* (1926), *Half Gods* (1929), *Yellow Jack* (1934), *Dodsworth* (1934), *The Ghost of Yankee Doodle* (1937), and *Madame, Will You Walk?* (produced posthumously in 1953). Howard also wrote many screenplays, the most famous of which was his adaptation of Margaret Mitchell's novel *Gone with the Wind* (1939), for which he won a posthumous Academy Award in 1940. Howard died in a farming accident on August 23, 1939, in Tyringham, Massachusetts, at the age of forty-eight.

PLOT SUMMARY

Act 1

The play is set in Tony's farmhouse in Napa Valley, California, in the 1920s. Tony's foreman, Joe, tells Father McKee that he is about to leave

MEDIA ADAPTATIONS

- *They Knew What They Wanted* was adapted as the 1930 film *A Lady to Love*, which was released by MGM and featured Edward G. Robinson as Tony.

- In 1940, a second film version, titled *They Knew What They Wanted*, was released by RKO Radio Pictures. It starred Carole Lombard, Charles Laughton as Tony, and William Gargan.

- Frank Loesser wrote the book, music, and lyrics for the musical production *The Most Happy Fella*, with a libretto based on Howard's play. It opened on Broadway in 1956 and ran for 676 performances.

Tony's employment but does not want to go until he has seen Tony get married that same day. Tony enters, dressed to the nines, ready to drive to the railroad station to pick up the bride he has seen but never actually met. Father McKee says he disapproves of the marriage because the woman is not a Catholic and also because she is a young woman and Tony is sixty years old. When the priest asks him why he never got married before, Tony says he was always poor, but during Prohibition he has become rich, for, as a result of bootlegging, the price of wine has gone up, so now he wants a wife. He also wants to have children.

Tony leaves so he can drive to collect Amy. Joe tells the priest that he has advised Tony against the marriage also. He has not met Amy but personally wrote all Tony's letters to her for him, since his English is better than Tony's. It transpires that Tony saw Amy working as a waitress in a cheap spaghetti joint in San Francisco and decided on the spot that he wanted to marry her, although he was too scared to speak to her. He found out her name and wrote to her, sending a picture, and asked her to marry him.

The R.F.D. (Rural Free Delivery) man arrives with Amy. It turns out that Tony was

not at the station in time to meet her, and the R.F.D. gave her a ride to the farmhouse. Joe and the R.F.D. assume Tony was just late, and the R.F.D. says he will look for him. Amy is put out at first about not being met but then she settles down and forgets about it. She likes the wedding decorations they have put up.

Father McKee and the R.F.D. exit, leaving Joe alone with Amy. Amy says that she likes the place and the view. She tells Joe she used to live on a farm in Santa Clara; her father took to drink, and they lost the farm after her mother died. Joe says he used to be an organizer for the Wobblies, a labor group, and Amy says she is glad he is no longer. She likes Italians, she says, but adds that she never thought she would marry one. She decided to take a chance and now she is happy that she did. She touches Joe's sleeve and says she feels very comfortable about the arrangement. She thinks they will get along and everything will turn out fine. She calls him Tony. Joe is dismayed and starts to protest, but he is interrupted by the sound of a car arriving.

Tony has been in a car accident and has broken both his legs. He is carried inside. Amy has no idea who he is until Joe tells her. Stunned, she accuses them of tricking her. She pulls from her trunk a photograph of Joe, which had been sent to her in the letter from Tony. Joe realizes that Tony sent the photo because he feared rejection if he sent one of himself. Joe says he knew nothing about the deception. Amy is angry and says she quit her job to come to marry Tony, thinking he looked like Joe. Joe says Tony meant no harm. Amy says she is leaving and talks about finding a lawyer. Joe goes into another room to see how Tony is doing, and when he returns, he finds that Amy has changed her mind. She still likes the place and will go through with the marriage.

Act 2

It is evening on the same day. The wedding celebration outside the house is winding down. Tony talks with the Doctor, and then Joe comes in with Ah Gee, and they go to the cellar for more wine. The Doctor tells Tony that it will take six months for him to recover, but Tony does not want Amy to have to look after him. He says he will hire a nurse instead. The Doctor leaves, and Tony and Joe talk. Tony is worried about whether Amy is still angry, but Joe reassures him that everything will be all right as long as he is good to her. All she needs is a good home, and Tony is lucky that he picked a girl as good as Amy. But Tony is convinced that God will punish him for playing a trick on Amy. He shows Joe some expensive diamond earrings he has bought for her.

Joe calls Amy in. She is still wearing her wedding dress. Tony gives her the diamonds, and she begins to cry. Then she puts them on and declares them to be beautiful. Joe makes a remark, and Amy gets angry with him for interrupting. She gives the photograph back to Joe and indicates that she has no hard feelings about it. On Tony's instructions, Joe tears the photo up.

Tony mentions that Joe is about the leave the farm and tries to persuade him to stay. Joe says he must leave, and Amy expresses her dislike of Wobblies and their migratory lifestyles.

The Doctor and Father McKee enter, arguing about Prohibition. Some guests come in from outside, including a small boy and girl and their mothers. The Doctor and Joe shoo them out. The Doctor gives Tony some medicine to help him sleep, and Amy says there is no need for a nurse. She will be glad to look after Tony herself. Joe and the Doctor carry Tony out on a stretcher, leaving Amy alone with Father McKee. The priest indicates that he approves of her. The Doctor returns, and Amy again insists that she can look after Tony without the help of a nurse. The Doctor and the priest exit, leaving Amy alone with Joe. Joe says he is definitely leaving next morning. He is fond of Tony and he wants to make sure that Amy likes him. He does not want Tony to have his feelings hurt. Amy is indignant that he should question her about it. She says she knows what is expected of her and tells him to mind his own business. Joe apologizes, but they both become angry before calming down and shaking hands. Amy starts to cry and Joe comforts her, putting his hands on her shoulders. Amy remains upset and says she thinks everyone must be laughing at her, adding that she wishes she were dead. Joe kisses her. She breaks loose when she hears Tony calling for her from the bedroom. She turns toward the bedroom door, but Joe prevents her from going in. She breaks free of him and runs out of the house. Joe runs after her.

Act 3

Three months have passed. Father McKee, Joe, and Tony are talking about current affairs and

exchanging views on society and government. Joe, as a Wobbly, supports progressive change through the labor movement, but Father McKee says that nothing much ever changes as far as government is concerned. Political activism accomplishes nothing, and he thinks that the radical pamphlets Joe reads are stupid. He thinks Joe should be more concerned about his duties than his rights. Tony does not want things to change either, since he is making a lot of money as a bootlegger. He is not interested in politics, although he does his duty by voting. Joe says he is about to leave for San Francisco and wants to participate in the struggle of labor against the capitalists. Tony warns him he may end up in jail, but Joe replies that there are worse places to be.

Amy enters and says she has no interest in reforming the world. She is too busy running the house. She gives Tony an affectionate hug and sits next to him as she peels some apples that will be made into apple pie for dinner. The Doctor arrives and congratulates Tony on his recovery. He can now walk with the aid of crutches. Tony praises the work Amy has done as his nurse. Everyone exits to sit outside, except for the Doctor and Joe. The Doctor tells Joe that Amy went to see him last week because she was sick. The Doctor knows she is pregnant, but he has not told her. The Doctor knows that the injured Tony cannot be the father. Joe is dismayed and admits that he and Amy made love just once, on the night of the wedding. The Doctor and Joe have to decide who is to tell Tony. Joe decides to do it immediately and tells Amy he must see her alone. He informs her about the pregnancy. She is horrified. She refuses to consider an abortion, and they decide they must go away together, as the Doctor suggested. Amy is reluctant but sees no other option. She feels sorry for Tony, who has been so good to her. She goes to pack a few things, and they plan to leave immediately. When she returns, she tells Tony that Joe is leaving, and then confesses the whole story to Tony. She says it is better that he know everything straightaway. She insists that she does not want to go, and that she loves him, but she must leave. Tony is furious when he hears what has happened. He grabs a shotgun and says he will kill Joe. Amy tries to persuade him not to. Joe enters and wrenches the gun from Tony. Tony falls and is then helped into a chair. He is still trying to fight Joe.

Tony asks where she is going, and she says San Francisco. She denies that she will be living with Joe. Tony wants to know how she will support herself and a baby. He is concerned about her. He tries to talk her into staying, knowing that she loves him and does not love Joe. Tony says he will accept the baby and they will raise it as if it were his own. Amy says it would not work, but Tony insists that he can forgive her for her mistake. Amy relents and agrees to stay. Joe is relieved and leaves for good. Tony embraces Amy.

CHARACTERS

Amy

Amy is an attractive woman in her early twenties who has agreed to leave her job as a waitress at a cheap Italian restaurant in San Francisco to marry Tony. She has never met him in person but has been corresponding with him after he asked her by letter to marry him. Even when she finds out that she was deceived into thinking that Tony was a young man (because she was sent a picture of Joe rather than Tony) she agrees to go through with the marriage. She likes the farmhouse and thinks she can make a life for herself there. She is fed up with living in the city and wants to create a home for herself. Since her general philosophy of life is to forgive and forget, she is willing to drop the issue of the fake photograph. Even when Tony breaks both his legs, she says she will devote herself to nursing him back to health.

All the men in the play approve of Amy, since she impresses them as being of good character, with much common sense, and likely to make an ideal wife. She is the kind of person who makes the best of things in whatever situation she happens to find herself. She has no regrets about the past and makes a point of not keeping mementos or souvenirs. Ever since she was a child she has thrown away all such reminders— actions that suggest a painful past. Indeed, it transpires that Amy has had a difficult life. She is of Swiss descent and grew up on a farm in Santa Clara, California. Her quarreling parents used to take out their anger on her; then her father took to drink, and her mother died, and she had to move to Mountain View.

Amy keeps her promise to Tony, and for three months she flourishes, looking after him and running the household. A genuine affection

develops between them. They are happily married. Then comes the devastating revelation that she is pregnant. She is in anguish because she knows the baby is Joe's, the result of one indiscretion on the wedding night. She does not love Joe, however; she loves her husband, and she is relieved when Tony, to her great surprise, agrees to raise the child as if it were his own.

Angelo

Angelo is one of the two Italian farmhands who report to Tony. When Amy first arrives, he greets her effusively in Italian.

The Doctor

The Doctor is a young man recently out of medical school, and he has a practice in this rural area that keeps him busy. He takes care of Tony immediately after the car accident. The Doctor does not drink alcohol and strongly supports Prohibition, calling it the best reform since the ending of slavery, which brings him into disagreement with Father McKee, who has no objection to alcohol in moderation.

First Italian Mother

The First Italian Mother enters briefly in act 2, while the wedding celebrations are still going on. She speaks only in Italian and is upset when the Second Italian Mother says that her daughter Maria is not as beautiful as the other woman's son. A brief quarrel ensues.

First Italian Mother's Daughter

The First Italian Mother's Daughter rushes in soon after her mother and embraces Tony and kisses him. Her name is Maria.

Ah Gee

Ah Gee is the Chinese cook. He is a silent man of uncertain age.

Georgio

Georgio is one of the two Italian farmhands who report to Tony. He is seen when Amy first arrives, and he talks excitedly in Italian.

Joe

Joe is the foreman in Tony's vineyard. Italian by descent, he was born in San Francisco. He is a migrant worker who has been at Tony's for five months when the play begins, which is a long time for him to stay in one place. He is always thinking of moving on, and when the play begins, he is set on leaving as soon as Tony is married. He is fond of Tony, who has treated him well. He does not think the marriage to Amy is a good idea but does not try to dissuade Tony from it. Indeed, it is Joe who writes letters to Amy on Tony's behalf, since his English is so much better than Tony's.

Joe is a member and former organizer of the Wobblies, and he supports the labor movement. He thinks he may move to San Francisco and get involved in some of the bitter labor disputes there. He has read a lot of socialist literature and opposes the capitalist system. He likes to talk about standing up for workers' rights and claims to be ready to go to jail for them if necessary. When Tony refers to the United States as a free country, Joe replies that "the only freedom we got left is the freedom to choose which one of our rights we'll go to jail for."

Joe has something of a reputation as a womanizer, but he wants to behave decently toward Amy and promises Father McKee that he will not chase after her. He thinks he knows a lot about women, but he has a rather patronizing attitude toward them. He is not opposed to women's rights, which he knows about through his work with the labor movement, but he thinks that women are far more interested in acquiring a nice home than in pursuing any rights they might have. Despite Joe's best efforts to behave well, however, there is at first an attraction between him and Amy, which, for just one night, neither is able to resist.

Father McKee

Father McKee is a Catholic priest. He is rather severe in his judgments and prefers to denounce rather than praise, although he has a basically kind nature. He does not approve of Tony's marriage because Amy is not a Catholic and Tony does not know her well, but he agrees to marry them, and when he meets Amy he has to admit that she appears to be an outstanding young woman. Father McKee does not approve of Joe's activities in the labor movement because he believes that nothing much ever changes, at least as far as government is concerned. As a religious man, he thinks that people should be more concerned about their duties to one another than with their political rights.

The R.F.D. Man

The R.F.D. (Rural Free Delivery) man gives Amy a ride from the railroad station to Tony's farmhouse, since there is no one else there to help her. After dropping her off, he goes to look for Tony. He is an old man who chews tobacco.

Second Italian Mother

The Second Italian Mother appears briefly in act 2. She is the mother of Giovannino, and she upsets the First Italian Mother when she says in Italian that Giovannino is more beautiful than Maria, the other woman's daughter.

Second Italian Mother's Son

The Second Italian Mother's Son is named Giovannino, and he is nine years old.

Tony

Tony is a sixty-year-old winegrower. He is stout but energetic and outgoing, and at the beginning of the play he is very excited about his forthcoming wedding. Tony is originally from Italy, but he has been in the United States for twenty years and is an American citizen. He is proud of his Italian heritage and keeps a portrait of the Italian patriot Giuseppe Garibaldi hanging on the wall, but he is also proud to be an American, as can be seen from the portrait of George Washington that also hangs on the wall. However, unlike Joe, Tony has no interest in politics.

Formerly poor, Tony has flourished since Prohibition began, because that has forced the price of wine up, and he has become rich. He is now able to fulfill his ambition to marry, because now any woman he marries will not have to work, and he also wants to have children. He could find no suitable woman locally, but when he first saw Amy waiting on tables in San Francisco, he decided he wanted to marry her but was too shy to approach her in person. Instead, he proposed by letter, getting Joe to write for him because Joe's English is much better than his own. Fearing rejection from Amy, Tony sent along a photograph of Joe with the letter, allowing Amy to think the photo was of him. Knowing he has deceived her, he is worried that God will punish him for it and that things will not work out with Amy.

On his way to collect Amy, Tony crashes his car and breaks both legs. It takes him months to recover, but Amy sticks by him. He is kind to her and generous as well, buying her four-hundred-dollar earrings, the equivalent of many thousands of dollars in today's money.

TOPICS FOR FURTHER STUDY

- Organize a class debate on the parallels between the Prohibition era and the modern era's war on drugs. One side should argue that the war on drugs is similar to Prohibition in that it brings about negative consequences for society as a whole, and that some currently illegal drugs should be legalized. The other side should argue that the two situations are very different and certain types of drugs should remain illegal. Conduct online and traditional research to find statistics and facts to back up your side of the argument.

- In an essay, analyze the different positions taken by Father McKee and Joe at the beginning of act 3 of *They Knew What They Wanted* regarding political action. Joe wants to create necessary change through political action, but the priest believes that political change cannot alter the way people are. Who do you think gets the better of the argument?

- How are romantic relationships and dating different now from what they were in the 1920s? Write a humorous short story in which you imagine you are going back in time and end up visiting Tony and also meeting with Amy and Joe. You observe them for a while, and after you have overcome your surprise at the way they talk and act, what would you say to Amy in particular about how women's roles and attitudes have changed since the 1920s? Consider also the possibility that the way Tony and Amy initially develop their relationship has something in common with the way young people today meet through online dating sites.

- Consult *Teen Love: On Relationships; A Book for Teenagers*, by Kimberley Kirberger, which is based on letters sent by teenagers and answers provided by the author. Create a blog and write fictional letters from Joe and Amy of the play to Kirberger, expressing their feelings about the situation they are in and seeking advice. Specify at what stage of the plot the letters are written. Then write a one-paragraph reply to each fictional letter. Share your blog with classmates who are doing the same project and see who comes up with the best letters and answers.

When Tony discovers that Amy is pregnant by Joe, he is furious and loses control of himself. He threatens to kill Joe, but then he calms down and shows some concern for Amy's future. He decides to forgive her one mistake and accept the baby and raise it as his own.

THEMES

Forgiveness

Forgiveness is the main theme of the play, emerging right at the end. As the drama develops, it is not obvious that there will be a happy ending. There is some dramatic tension as Amy and Joe contemplate the fact that she is to bear his child, and the play could as easily have finished as a tragedy rather than a comedy. The fact that it does not is a tribute to the characters of Amy and Tony. Regretting the mistake she made on the wedding night, Amy is determined that Tony must be told the truth, even though that will be painful for both of them. She is not expecting him to forgive her; she does not ask him to. In fact, it seems like forgiveness is the furthest thing from her mind. She knows Tony will feel angry and betrayed, and she has decided that she will leave the home immediately; she believes she has no other option. Naturally enough, when Tony hears her confession, he is angry. He loses self-control, and when he

Tony, an aging vintner, falls in love with a San Francisco waitress. *(StockLite / Shutterstock.com)*

threatens to shoot Joe, the play appears as if it might be heading for a tragic denouement. However, when Tony's initial rush of anger subsides, his basically good, kind nature resurfaces. This is in keeping with how he has been presented throughout the play. He is a man with a good heart, and in this testing moment he is given a chance to show it. Reason triumphs over passion, and forgiveness triumphs over revenge. When he is back in his right mind after his explosion of temper, Tony quickly realizes that forgiveness on his part is in everyone's best interest. After all, he has always wanted a child, and soon there will be one that he can call his own, if he can bring himself to do so. Amy has no desire to leave because she loves her husband, so forgiveness on Tony's part will allow her to stay. Finally, Tony's forgiveness will allow Joe to leave without being racked by remorse and guilt. This is appropriate because in the five months that Joe has been living in Tony's house, the two men have developed an affection and respect for each other. Forgiveness of Joe's one selfish act will allow them to part on good terms. Forgiveness, then, allows life to flow on

smoothly, in contrast to revenge, which would have destroyed the lives of all three major characters.

The theme of forgiveness is well expressed by Amy as the guiding philosophy of her life. This comes early in the play, before she realizes how relevant her words will later become, when she forgives Tony for not coming to meet her at the railroad station: "All right, then, I'll forgive you. That's the way I am. Forgive and forget! I always believe in letting bygones be bygones."

Deception

Audience sympathy may well be with Tony in the last act of the play, because in this highly unusual situation, he is the wronged husband. However, there is a kind of rough poetic justice in what happens. When Tony wooed Amy by letter, he sent her a picture of the handsome Joe, leading her to believe that the picture was of him, Tony. It is then not surprising that Amy should feel an attraction toward Joe when she arrives at the house, since she has no doubt been looking often at that photograph of the man she assumes is her husband-to-be. At that point her sense of duty—she has made a commitment to marry—seems in concert with her natural desire, which is for Joe.

When the deception is uncovered, Amy forgives Tony for it (another example of forgiveness in this play). But in act 3, another, far more serious deception is uncovered. Tony, the initial deceiver, is now the deceived. Had he been more honest in the first place, he might not have found himself in the position he is in. But his act of forgiveness presents a neat reversal of roles and a pleasing symmetry: in act 1, Amy forgives Tony his deception; in act 3, Tony forgives Amy her deception, which followed quite logically from his.

STYLE

Comedy

Comedy refers to a light form of drama that has a happy ending. According to M. H. Abrams in *A Glossary of Literary Terms*, the purpose of a comedy is "to interest and amuse us: the characters and their discomfitures engage our delighted attention rather than our profound concern; we feel confident that no great disaster will occur." Comedy is contrasted with tragedy, which has an unhappy ending, often one in which the protagonist dies. Traditional romantic comedies, such as those written by Shakespeare, often end with weddings. Obstacles to love are overcome, harmony is restored, and there is the promise of new life.

Because *They Knew What They Wanted* ends happily, it may be thought of as a comedy. Although it begins rather than ends with a wedding, the resolution, in which Tony accepts Amy's pregnancy, is filled with the promise of harmony and new life. The play also exploits the frequent comic device of mistaken identity (the photograph in act 1) and achieves resolution through an act of forgiveness, another common plot device used in comedy to facilitate the inevitable happy ending.

Social Realism

Realism was a literary movement that began in the nineteenth century. Social realism was a characteristic of American drama in the first two decades of the twentieth century. Realism means greater naturalness in dialogue, with characters talking the way people talk in real life rather than in the more literary language that had been fashionable in earlier periods of American drama. This can be seen in Tony's ungrammatical English, still flecked with Italian speech patterns, and Joe's ungrammatical, down-to-earth, working-class way of speaking, including his habit of dropping the final *g* in present participles (*goin*) and the final *d* in words such as *and*.

Social drama also shows awareness of social, cultural, moral, economic, and political issues and problems of the day. In this play, that element of social realism can be seen in the discussions between the characters on politics and labor relations and in the fact that Prohibition is the reality of the day and has relevance for Tony's situation.

Foreshadowing

In order to make the last moments of act 2, when Amy and Joe unite for their one-time-only tryst, convincing and not arbitrary, the dramatist must subtly prepare the audience for it. He accomplishes this through careful foreshadowing. For example, in act 1 Joe is presented as having had a lot of girlfriends. Tony tells the priest that there are no local women left for him to choose because Joe has been with them all. He also admits to Father McKee that he does "go chasin' women plenty." Tony is anxious that Joe leave immediately (although it soon turns out that this is because he does not want Amy to see that the photograph he sent was of Joe, not because he does not trust Joe).

The sudden coming together of Joe and Amy is also prepared for psychologically, because several times Amy is irritable with Joe for no good reason, which suggests that her discomfort with him may be an attraction in disguise. There is also the moment at the end of act 1 when Amy almost decides to place the photograph of Joe in the bosom of her dress but thinks better of it and pushes the photo away.

At the same time, the dramatist provides a counterbalance to these hints and foreshadowing. There is Joe's obvious sincerity and affection for Tony, his promise to Father McKee not to chase after Amy, and the absolutely correct way in which he deals with Amy when she first arrives. The counterbalance is necessary because the dramatist does not want the audience simply to assume that Joe will misbehave. When he does, it is a genuine surprise (as it must be for the moment to work as drama), but on reflection the audience will realize that it is in fact not all that surprising and has been well prepared for.

HISTORICAL CONTEXT

The Wobblies

The Industrial Workers of the World, known as the Wobblies, was a labor union founded in Chicago in 1905. This is the organization that Joe is a member of in *They Knew What They Wanted*. The Wobblies were a radical organization. Unlike other labor unions of the period, who worked to improve pay and working conditions within their industries, the Wobblies wanted to create an international workers' movement that would overthrow the capitalist system. They regarded the interests of labor as irrevocably opposed to those of the owners of capital, and they advocated a class war aimed at creating a completely new economic system.

The aims of the IWW and its radical but idealistic vision are described in the article "The IWW," on the Lucy Parsons Project Web site:

> The IWW aimed to unite workers around the world, lock arms, and walk off their jobs in a mass general strike, rendering factory owners powerless, effectively overthrowing capitalism. In its place would be the new society based on industrial unionism, in which workers controlled their own destinies and the fruits of labor could be enjoyed by all.

The Wobblies were known for their stirring songs, like "Remember," which Joe is singing as *They Knew What They Wanted* opens. The lyrics tell of two hundred union men who are in jail because they protested laws favoring employers that turned them into virtual slaves. The song was written by Harrison George, a Wobbly member, from his jail cell in Cook County, Illinois (Chicago area), in 1917. Wobblies sang their songs in picket lines and at mass meetings.

During the peak of their activities from their founding into the 1910s and 1920s, the Wobblies were known for their ability to bring out workers on strikes. According to Wobbly historian Joyce L. Kornbluh, the Wobblies led 150 strikes in a number of different industries in the period leading up to World War I. Textile workers, lumber workers, silk workers, miners, and ironworkers were all involved, in disputes that took place

across many different states, including Nevada, Massachusetts, Louisiana, Arkansas, New Jersey, and Minnesota. There was also a 1912 Wobbly-inspired dockworkers' strike in San Pedro, California, which Joe mentions in the play when he says he wishes he had been involved in it.

The Wobblies opposed U.S. participation in World War I and continued to lead strikes during the war, unlike other unions. This meant that Wobblies were regarded by the authorities as subversives and were subject to arrest. In 1917, 165 Wobblies were arrested across the nation, and in the following year over eighty men received prison sentences of between five and twenty years for espionage. (In the play, Joe tells Tony and Father McKee that a man in California was arrested and imprisoned simply because he carried a Wobbly membership card.) Kornbluh comments on the extent of attacks on the Wobblies during this period:

> Little judicial effort went into protecting IWW members from community hysteria. Employer-funded vigilante groups and patriotic leagues were as likely as police units to raid IWW halls, homes, gatherings, and meetings with impunity. The persecution was soon intensified by criminal syndicalism laws passed in many states with the specific objective of destroying the IWW. Every form of intimidation was employed.

Prohibition

Prohibition began in January 1920, as required by the Eighteenth Amendment to the Constitution, which was ratified in 1919, and the Volstead Act of the same year. Under these provisions, the manufacture, distribution, and sale of alcohol in the United States were banned.

Prohibition was the culmination of many years of campaigning by temperance groups such as the Anti-Saloon League, formed in 1893. The league worked to enact local laws banning alcohol, and this was followed by a concerted effort to extend the ban nationally.

There were many factors that contributed to Prohibition. The banning of alcohol was supported by many religious groups, especially Protestant denominations such as Baptists and Methodists, who thought drinking alcohol was a sin and lauded the virtues of hard work and sobriety. Another factor was prejudice against the large number of recent immigrants clustered in the cities, who were thought to indulge in excessive drinking and possess low morals.

COMPARE
&
CONTRAST

- **1920s:** The Industrial Workers of the World (also known as the IWW, or the Wobblies) declines in membership as some members switch their allegiance to the Communist Party, and many employers try to suppress the organization. However, the Wobblies remain a significant force in the labor movement and lead a strike in Colorado coal mines in 1928.

  Today: Membership of the IWW is believed to be less than a thousand, but the organization continues to support and promote the interests of workers. The Wobblies remain headquartered in Chicago and publish a monthly newspaper, the *Industrial Worker,* described as the "Voice of Revolutionary Industrial Unionism."

- **1920s:** The manufacture and sale of alcohol in the United States, known as Prohibition, is illegal throughout the decade by ratification of the Eighteenth Amendment, passed in 1919.

Today: The Twenty-first Amendment repealed Prohibition in 1933. Today alcohol is legally manufactured and sold in the United States, but many regard the so-called war on drugs, in which drugs such as marijuana are illegal, to be a parallel to Prohibition. Illegal drugs are not difficult to obtain, and drug gangs and drug smuggling operations flourish. Criminal convictions of people who sell or use illegal drugs swell prison populations.

- **1920s:** Women's rights is an issue throughout the decade. In 1920, the Nineteenth Amendment is passed, granting women the right to vote. In 1923, the equal rights amendment is introduced in the U.S. Congress, but during the 1920s it is never brought to a vote.

  Today: Many laws exist to safeguard women's rights. In 2009, the Lilly Ledbetter Fair Pay Act makes it easier for women to sue their employer for pay discrimination based on gender.

High crime rates in the cities were blamed by temperance groups on high alcohol consumption. Many employers believed that alcohol had a negative effect on worker productivity. Supporters of Prohibition also thought it would improve people's health.

Prohibition did not work quite as its supporters envisioned, however. Although in the early years consumption of alcohol did go down, Prohibition also brought about or exacerbated several social problems. It created a large black market for alcohol, which led to the rise of organized crime syndicates that were able to supply the need. There was money to be made from bootlegging, as Tony in *They Knew What They Wanted* has found out; he has become rich from it. Along with organized crime came corruption, in which public officials either looked the other way or actively collaborated in the illegal trade.

During the later years of Prohibition, alcohol consumption was on the rise. More people were willing to flout the law, and illegal liquor was more easily available. Prohibition was repealed in 1933 with the ratification of the Twenty-first Amendment, the only amendment that repeals another amendment. Most historians today consider Prohibition a disaster, since it did not accomplish its goals and led to serious and unanticipated social problems. According to the economist Mark Thornton, in his essay, "Alcohol Prohibition Was a Failure," the effects of Prohibition were entirely negative:

> Alcohol became more dangerous to consume; crime increased and became "organized"; the court and prison systems were stretched to the breaking point; and corruption of public officials was rampant. No measurable gains were made in productivity or reduced absenteeism. Prohibition removed a significant source of tax revenue and greatly increased government

Tony proposes marriage in a letter to Amy. *(Dewayne Flowers | Shutterstock.com)*

spending. It led many drinkers to switch to opium, marijuana, patent medicines, cocaine, and other dangerous substances that they would have been unlikely to encounter in the absence of Prohibition.

CRITICAL OVERVIEW

When first produced in 1924, *They Knew What They wanted* was favorably received by critics. Alexander Woolcott, in the New York *Evening Sun*, describes it as "a true, living, salty comedy . . . a colorful piece cut from the genuine fabric of American life. It is one of those comedies which move uneasy on the edge of tragedy." In the *New Republic*, Stark Young comments approvingly on the play's "kindly glowing atmosphere and the sense of the children, of songs and the vine and the sun that Mr. Howard achieves in the characters." The play was an equal success when it was produced in London in 1926.

Despite its success, some controversy became attached to the play when Howard was accused of plagiarism. The three authors of a play titled *The Full of the Moon* sued him, claiming he had stolen the plot from their play. Their suit was dismissed in court in 1927, however, when it was shown that Howard's play was in fact derived from sources such as the Tristan and Iseult legend rather than from any contemporary play.

Since the 1920s, the play has been revived several times. In 1949, twenty-five years after its first production, a revival was mounted in Philadelphia. The production met with approval from Maurie Orodenker in *Billboard*, who deemed the play "a drama rich in warmth and vitality and understanding." The part of "the grizzled but golden-hearted Tony" was played by Paul Muni, and Orodenker praises his performance, noting that "he endows his character with a warmth and depth to make it a major theatrical experience."

The play was revived again in 1994 at the Rainbow Theater in Stamford, Connecticut, but for Alvin Klein in the *New York Times*, the production was not a success. Klein describes the play as a "curio" that after winning the Pulitzer Prize has "fad[ed] into oblivion." In his opinion, the evening would have been livened up by some of the songs from *The Most Happy Fella*, the successful 1956 Broadway musical by Frank Loesser that was based on the play.

CRITICISM

Bryan Aubrey

Aubrey holds a PhD in English. In the following essay, he examines the similarities between They Knew What They Wanted *and the legend of Tristan and Iseult.*

Broadway fans may know something of Sidney Howard's play *They Knew What They Wanted*, since there are still plenty of recordings available of the 1956 musical *A Most Happy Fella*, which is based on the play. The Pulitzer Prize–winning play was also popular enough in its own day to spawn two movie versions, but since then revivals have been few and far between, and twenty-first-century playgoers who wish to familiarize themselves with the work of this dramatist must head for the library rather than the theater.

Any reader of the play will quickly notice that some of the language belongs very much to another era. This is particularly noticeable in the ethnic stereotyping. Amy and Tony both refer to Ah Gee, the Chinese cook, as a "chink," and Ah Gee says very little, in keeping with the stereotype of the inscrutable Chinaman. Italians are presented not only as excitable and emotional but are repeatedly referred to as "wops." Today, the term "wop" is considered an ethnic slur, but in the play no one objects to it. "A regular wop wedding!" says Amy when she see the way the house has been decorated for the occasion. She immediately apologizes to Joe for using the term, but he does not mind. Indeed, when he talks to Father McKee, he uses the term himself to refer to Tony. Modern readers might be particularly startled when the Doctor says to Tony, "Half of what you have been through to-day would have killed a white man! You wops are crazy." This remark opens a window on how Italian immigrants to the United States were regarded at the

> HOWARD ALSO PRESERVES THE ELEMENT OF FORGIVENESS IN THE TRISTAN MYTH. JUST AS KING MARKE FORGIVES THE TWO LOVERS THEIR TRANSGRESSIONS, SO TONY IN THE PLAY IS WILLING TO FORGIVE AMY HER ONE MISTAKE."

time. There was large-scale immigration to the United States from Italy during the late nineteenth and early twentieth centuries, and Italians and other immigrants from southern Europe were not considered "white" and had to face a lot of prejudice on that account.

However, the play also shows the process of cultural assimilation. Tony, a twenty-year resident of the United States, still speaks ungrammatical, accented English and identifies strongly with his home country as well as his adopted one, but Joe, on the other hand, who was born in San Francisco of Italian descent, shows little trace of his ancestry. "You don't talk one bit like an Italian," Amy observes. The play thus shows how the "melting pot" of America works: second- and third-generation immigrants like Joe become part of the American mainstream.

Interesting though it may be for the reader to note prevailing attitudes in the 1920s toward ethnicity, they are not really part of the dramatist's concern. Tony, after all, is doing pretty well as a bootlegger, and his ethnicity is not an issue for any of the characters. Of course, Howard was concerned with contemporary social issues such as Prohibition and labor relations, but for the engine of the plot and the play's major themes he was interested primarily in love and passion and the curious triangle created by his three characters Tony, Joe, and Amy. In that, he acknowledged that he had a mythological parallel in mind, the medieval legend of Tristan and Iseult. This is a story that has proved endlessly fascinating to the Western mind for centuries. Richard Wagner's nineteenth-century opera *Tristan und Isolde* (1865) is probably the most well-known modern version of the story.

In the Tristan legend, as in Howard's play, there are three main characters. These are King

WHAT DO I READ NEXT?

- Howard's play *The Silver Cord* was first produced in 1926, two years after *They Knew What They Wanted*, and is considered one of his best plays. It is a drama about family relationships, particularly the bond between mother and son. The mother concerned is Mrs. Phelps, who wants to control her two adult sons, David and Robert, and does not react well when she thinks she is going to lose David to his new wife, Christine, and Robert to his fiancée, Hester.

- *Porgy*, a play by DuBose and Dorothy Heyward, was first produced in New York City in 1927. It was adapted from a novel of the same title published by DuBose Heyward in 1925. Like *They Knew What They Wanted*, *Porgy* was one of the outstanding plays of the 1920s and was the basis for a musical adaptation, George Gershwin's famous opera *Porgy and Bess* (1935). The story tells of Porgy, a crippled African American man who lives in the tenements of Charleston, South Carolina, in the 1920s.

- *The Romance of Tristan and Iseult*, as retold by Joseph Bédier from a translation by Hilaire Belloc in a 2005 edition, is a rendering of one of the most enduring stories of the Western world. Often retold in various versions in medieval times, the legend of Tristan and Iseult has had an enormous influence on literature, art, and music. This tale of love, passion, and tragedy is compellingly told in this modern version.

- *The Face of America: Plays for Young People* (2011), edited by Peter Brosius and Elissa Adams, contains four plays written for the Children's Theatre Company of Minneapolis. Each play is set in the United States and deals with issues of cultural and ethnic diversity. In one play, a young African American and a Somali-born immigrant overcome their initial difficulties in understanding each other; another play shows the daughter of a Russian immigrant learning how to connect with neighbors from Puerto Rico and the West Indies. A third play deals with Mexican immigrant farmworkers, both legal and illegal, and the last play shows interactions between Native American and white culture.

- Part of the "Perspectives on History" series, *The Roaring Twenties* (1997), by David King, is a collection of primary documents from the 1920s, including letters, diaries, interviews, and poetry. There are many illustrations, and the book as a whole gives a fascinating picture of all aspects of life in the 1920s, from Prohibition and gangsters to jazz, movies, and sports.

- *A Streetcar Named Desire* is a play by an even greater name than Sidney Howard in American theater: Tennessee Williams. Many of Williams's plays are still performed today, and this one, first produced in 1947, is one of his most famous. Like *They Knew What They Wanted*, it is a drama about love and passion that involves three principal characters, although unlike in Howard's play, there are no acts of forgiveness to resolve the intense drama that unfolds.

Marke of Cornwall; his trusted knight, Tristan; and the Irish princess, Iseult (Isolde in Wagner's opera). Tristan goes on an expedition to Ireland, where he kills in combat a troublesome Irish warlord. During the battle, Tristan sustains a wound, and the only one who can heal it is Iseult, the niece of the conquered warlord. After being healed by Iseult, who does not know who he is, Tristan returns to the Cornish court. King Marke does not have a wife or heir, so some time later Tristan resolves, with Marke's permission, to return to Ireland and persuade Iseult to

Embarrassed by his age, Tony encloses a picture of his young farm hand, Joe, in the letter. (tandem / Shutterstock.com)

become Marke's wife. Iseult consents, and they set sail back to Cornwall. Before they leave, Iseult's mother gives a love potion to Iseult's maid, Brangien. Whenever a man and woman drink the potion together, they will fall in love. Brangien is told to give the potion to Marke and Iseult on their wedding night. Unfortunately, Tristan and Iseult, feeling thirsty on the voyage, drink the love potion, and before the voyage is over, they have become lovers.

The story continues with many complications in various different versions, but the essence is that King Marke is for a while deceived about the relationship between Tristan and Iseult. Then, in Wagner's version of the story, Tristan is betrayed by his friend Melot and wounded. King Marke reproaches Tristan for his lack of loyalty. Tristan makes his way to Brittany and again sends for Iseult to heal him. Iseult arrives too late, and Tristan dies. Then

Marke arrives. He has forgiven the lovers, but he arrives too late to avert the tragedy. Iseult dies of grief.

In his modern-day version of the Tristan myth, Howard retained some central elements while discarding anything that did not suit his purpose. The trick with the photograph, in which Tony sends a photograph of Joe rather than of himself to Amy, is an ingenious twist on the central incident in which Tristan woos Iseult on behalf of Marke. Because of the misidentified photograph, Amy is predisposed to fall in love with Joe rather than Tony, and this is the equivalent of the love potion drunk unawares, since neither Joe nor Amy knows of the deception involving the photo, and they get something that neither had bargained for. The central idea in the Tristan myth, of duty at war with passion or desire, is thus replicated in the play at least for a short while: like Iseult, Amy makes a journey to marry a man she has not seen, and she feels it her duty to stick to an agreement she has made. Nevertheless, she is unable to deny, at least on the first night that she stays at Tony's house, the attraction she feels toward Joe.

Howard also preserves the element of forgiveness in the Tristan myth. Just as King Marke forgives the two lovers their transgressions, so Tony in the play is willing to forgive Amy her one mistake. However, there is a big difference between the two works in this respect. The legend of Tristan and Iseult is a tragedy, since the lovers die. Marke's forgiveness comes too late, and all he can do is lament the situation. But in *They Knew What They Wanted*, Tony overcomes his anger and dismay at what has happened and is able to make the best of the situation. Tragedy, the dramatization of the pain of the human condition, is thus turned into comedy, the celebration of life. The difference between the legend and the play is also the difference between romance and realism. In the Tristan legend, the two lovers are laid side by side in the grave. From Tristan's grave grows a vine, and from Iseult's grave grows a rose, and the two become entwined forever, a timeless symbol of passionate, doomed love that still somehow cannot be defeated. Howard's play ends not with death but with real life continuing as best it can: husband and wife, at home, a child to come, and the prospect of some measure of happiness.

When Howard opted for this dramatic turnaround right at the last, he transcended a moralistic stance that would have punished adultery in favor of showing the way that people are able to adapt positively to the realities of the situation they find themselves in, even when that situation is fraught with the dangerous emotions of jealousy and betrayal. This life-affirming quality is part of what makes the play moving, and it is not difficult to see why it was awarded the Pulitzer Prize and was so popular with audiences in the 1920s and in two film versions. Readers who have some skill in staging a play in their minds as they read will also note how well the play is constructed, with each act, rather like each act in Wagner's *Tristan und Isolde*, coming to a splendidly dramatic climax: the discovery of Tony's deception, alongside the veiled attraction between Joe and Amy (act 1); Joe and Amy's sudden embrace (act 2); and the disclosure of Amy's pregnancy and Tony's subsequent anger and forgiveness (act 3).

Bearing all this in mind, it is to be hoped that some enterprising theater company will decide that *They Knew What They Wanted* is worth a twenty-first-century airing. Talk of "wops" and "chinks" may be excised or left to mark it as a period piece, but the central elements of love, passion, duty, and desire form as potent a mix as ever they did, and Howard's skillful treatment of them is still worth the price of admission.

Source: Bryan Aubrey, Critical Essay on *They Knew What They Wanted*, in *Drama for Students*, Gale, Cengage Learning, 2012.

Sidney Howard White

In the following excerpt, White provides a plot overview of They Knew What They Wanted *and speculates on the play's possible sources and its role in the social realism of 1920s drama.*

The title of Howard's most famous play, *They Knew What They Wanted*, tells nearly as much about the author as it does about the play. Ever forthright and well known for his dynamic, positive manner, Howard succeeded admirably in fashioning a play which champions the same virtues. A matter-of-fact certainty and blunt pragmatism rule the lives of his three principals. What finally resolves the issues at the end of the play is simply the agreement *not* to resolve them at all, that is, not to resolve them in the usual searing probes into human nature. Resolution here is simply a comic standstill, an acceptance of things as they seem to be for better or for

> WE MUST BE CONVINCED IN SO MANY LINES, MOVEMENTS, AND STAGE BUSINESS THAT THEIR COMING TOGETHER IS COMPLETELY INEVITABLE."

worse. This, in effect, is what differentiates the play from that other success of 1924, O'Neill's *Desire Under the Elms*, with which it is often compared. Amazingly similar in plot, they do, nevertheless, derive from two distinctly different concepts. O'Neill writes a modern tragedy; Howard writes a modern comedy.

The play is set in the Napa Valley in California, an area which the young Howard knew very well. The grape growing communities fill the low hills and wide valleys north of San Francisco Bay, providing an excellent choice for a story about essentially simple, warm-hearted people. At first Howard had the thought of writing a short story about an Italian who wanted to establish a dynasty like the Goulds or Astors. Experiments in trying to approximate the rich Italian dialect in words convinced him that it would be better as a spoken piece for the theater. And, of course, the conception of Tony as the prosperous, middle-aged owner of the vineyard, never developed into a story of economic power; Tony remains a modestly content rancher. He does, however, have a great style. Howard describes his first entrance: "Magnificently Tony enters from the bedroom. He is stout, floridly bronzed, sixty years old, vigorous, jovial, simple, and excitable. His great gift is for gesture. Today we meet him in his Sunday best, a very brilliant, purple suit with a more than oriental waistcoat which serves to display a stupendous gold watch chain. He wears a boiled shirt, an emerald-green tie, and a derby hat. He carries his new patent-leather shoes in his hand. He seems to be perspiring rather freely." The "Sunday best" is to meet his mail-order bride, Amy, who is arriving today from San Francisco. We learn that Joe, his young and handsome assistant, has actually written the letters for him and that it is his picture, not Tony's, that has won the older man a bride.

These complexities are enough to provide the basis for the comedy of confusion and discovery which fills Act One. The initial characterizations of Tony and his partner in duplicity, the carefree Joe, are exceptionally well done. The introductory scenes are cleverly arranged, with Father McKee, the local Catholic priest, serving as a catalyst to bring out the situation. He is there to question the propriety of such a wedding under such unusual circumstances; primarily, he's concerned about the age difference. Interesting ambiguities instantly set in: Tony is anxious to have Joe leave after the wedding because of the deception; Father McKee, not knowing the entire story, believes the departure is simply a practical precaution since Joe is widely known as a lusty romancer. To Father McKee's opinion that Tony should have found someone in his own parish, Tony has a ready reply: "Joe is sleepin' with evra one." To the basic question of Father McKee: "There ain't no good in no old man marryin' with no young woman," Tony has the best answer: "You think anybody marry with old woman?"

Tony's deepest feelings are honestly expressed in a winning simplicity: "She [Amy] is like a rose, all wilt. You puttin' water on her an' she come out most beautiful. I'm goin' marry with my Amy, Padre, an' I don' marry with nobody else." Tony had seen her once in San Francisco as a waitress, never talked to her but simply got her address. Somehow, as we know Tony better, the utter foolishness of his courtship seems almost an irrelevant issue. The character is so well drawn that we never ask the wrong (or right) questions. He never married earlier, he tells Father McKee, because he was too poor, he didn't want a wife "for mak' her work all da time." That would be no good, "Da's mak' her no more young no more prett.'" But now that Prohibition has come, which is "dam' fool law," since "God mak' dees country for growin' da grape," Tony has become prosperous and can now afford a wife. It is hard to refute his logic. His plans are, he concludes, "fine for God an' evrabody! I tell you, Padre, Tony knows w'at he want!"

Tony leaves for the station to meet Amy, but somehow they miss each other and Amy arrives at the ranch on her own. Immediately we sense the presence of another person who seems to know what she wants. At first angry at not being met, she quickly alters her mood before Father McKee and Joe: "All right, then, I'll forgive you. That's the way I am. Forgive and forget! I always believe in letting bygones be bygones." In her own way she astounds them; she is all that Tony had said of her, very pretty, small, with golden hair and a "face like morning sunshine." Howard describes her as shining "with an inner, constitutional energy. Her look is, to be sure, just a little tired. She probably is not more than twenty-two or -three, but she seems older. Her great quality is definiteness. It lends pathos to her whole personality." She also talks along at a rather brisk pace, perhaps to keep up her courage. Alone now with Joe when the others have to leave, she sets off an excellent comic scene by assuming that Joe is Tony. In Joe's rather natural reluctance to explain we have the sufficient delays for many double meanings and comic lines.

An uproar quickly ensues with the excited arrival of Tony who has been in a serious auto accident. They bring him in on a bench, both legs in compound fractures; otherwise, he's as talkative as ever and full of apologies for Amy. At first horrified when she finally learns who Tony really is, she quickly calms down and tries to take the situation in hand. Here, of course, we meet the typical Howard heroine again. Somewhat like the pathetic Mrs. Vietch (in the short story of the same year) she pulls herself up out of seeming adversity and confusion and takes a stand. While the others stare in admiration, she firmly announces her decision as the first act curtain falls. "No. I ain't going. Why should I go? I like the country. This place suits me all right. It's just what I was looking for. I'm here and I might as well stick. I guess he ain't so bad, at that. I guess I could have done a lot worse. If he wants to marry me, I'm game. I'm game to see it through. It's nice up here."

The wedding takes place; the festivities go on long into the night despite the seriousness of Tony's condition and the doctor's protestations. He will, however, be laid up at least six months. Joe consoles Tony with his "philosophy of women," emphasizing that they need caring for—"knockin' around just raises hell with a girl"—since they can't stand the rough times a man can take. To Tony Joe seems very smart about women. Amy, however, is obviously bothered by Joe's presence, and it quickly becomes apparent that she is trying to deny the effect he has on her. The scene develops well between the three of them: Tony is pressing an expensive set of earrings on his Amy; Joe is trying somehow to back off, reduce his presence; Amy, tearful, still snaps at Joe—perhaps again to keep up her courage. Tony is determined now that Joe stay on even though he would rather leave. Amy attempts to feign indifference. They continue to spar with each other when alone, which increases the audience's anticipation of things to come. This scene, the seduction scene, which closes the second act, is obviously not an easy scene to write. We must be convinced in so many lines, movements, and stage business that their coming together is completely inevitable. It is made to work by the clever running out of nearly all of Amy's desperate thoughts—why she left San Francisco, what she is determined to do here for Tony, even without love. "I got all I bargained for," she tells Joe, "and then some. I'm fixed. I'm satisfied. I didn't come up here . . . like I did . . . looking for love . . . or . . . or . . . anything like that." She finally softens toward Joe when he admits he never knew of the photo deception. And in her contriteness (or weariness) she stumbles into his aims—and rather believably, passion quickly takes hold. The act ends, as he determinedly runs after her out of the house.

Three months later, as Act Three opens, we find the house markedly changed by the presence of a woman. Curtains, lamp shades, some embroidered works—all indicate a kind of domestic tranquility. While the others talk politics, Amy seems privately content: "Well, the world may need reforming but I got no kick." Quickly we learn in the doctor's accusation of Joe, that Amy is pregnant; and perhaps the best thing to do is for the two to leave. Amy takes the news as a kind of moral judgment: "If you go wrong, you're sure to get it sooner or later, I got it sooner." The attitude is completely characteristic of Amy in her rather pitiless view of life and things. Take everything as it comes seems to be her philosophy of life. Apparently, there is no other course but to leave together, which they agree reluctantly to do. The traumatic effect on Tony is well prepared for with the following dialogue:

> Amy: Joe's going away.
> Tony: He's no' goin' without sayin' goo'-by?
> Amy: I dunno. . . . Maybe he is. . . .
> Tony: That boy mak' me verra unhappy. I been lovin' Joe like he was my own son an' he's goin' away like dat. He's no good.
> Amy: People who ain't no good ain't worth worrying about. The thing to do is let 'em go and forget 'em.
> Tony: Da's no' so easy like you think, Amy. I been lovin' Joe like my own son.

> Amy: Joe ain't no worse than other people I could mention.
> Tony: I love Joe but he don' love me.
> Amy: I love you, Tony! I love you!
> Tony: I know, Amy, I know.
> Amy: And you ain't never going to believe that I do again.

This scene, of course, becomes the most challenging for Howard. When Tony finally learns the truth he goes completely berserk, even accusing her of being a whore. In another sense, the excitement of the scene adds up to good sentiment and melodrama as Amy pleads in her defense and gradually wears Tony down. Tony and Joe first scuffle over the gun on the wall and finally Tony is quieted. He now sees what must be done: he begs Amy to stay with him and have her baby. After all, it "ees good sense! Eees w'at is evrabody wantin' here! You an' Joe an' me!" His conviction mounts as his anger subsides; there's no denying the eminent practicality of his suggestion, which of course holds the entire meaning of the play. Moral judgments aside, Tony has his own reassurance in answer to Amy's confession of guilt: "What you done was mistake in da head, not in da heart. . . . Mistake in da head is no matter." And so—with Joe's departure—the comedy comes to a happy ending. . . .

There were many speculations about the source of the plot. Although Howard denied "hotly" its relationship to the legend of Paola and Francesca, there are still the obvious parallels. In Dante's *Divine Comedy* the story is related of the deformed Giancotto who has Paola woo Francesca for him by proxy. Following the marriage, the husband discovers their attachment and kills them both. In the Preface to the published edition, Howard admitted his reliance on Wagner's great romantic opera, *Tristan und Isolde*, and particularly the earlier medieval tale: "It [the play] is shamelessly, consciously, and even proudly derived from the legend of Tristran and Yseult, and the difference between the legend of Tristran and Yseult and that of Paola and Francesca is simply that the Italian wronged husband killed everybody in sight while his northern counterpart forgave everybody—which amounts to the monumental difference between a bad temper and tolerance." A marvelous explanation; and obviously written in Howard's characteristic high, buoyant style—the style, incidentally, of many of his personal letters.

The difference, then, between the two legends is that all important one to Howard, the tolerance of the wronged husband. Even though in bare outline the Paola story is actually closer to the facts of Howard's play, it is the Tristran story ending that concerns Howard. According to the original medieval romance Tristran has the charge to woo Yseult (Isolde) for his lord. By accident they drink a love potion and become lovers. Exiled to another land, he lies dying and asks for Yseult to heal him. She arrives with her husband, who miraculously had come to unite the unhappy lovers, but they find Tristran dead. Forgiveness, understanding—not a mistake of "da heart"—underlie both stories. It is as if Howard is saying in his modern morality tale that we all make mistakes, that circumstances often mislead us, but that we must not be judged too harshly.

There is a touch of the naturalistic philosophy in the plight of Amy and Joe, somewhat reminiscent of Dreiser's trapped people—caught not so much by their own internal weaknesses but by the inexorable forces of the world they live in. Much of the play is given to the 1920 context, Prohibition, the IWW (International Workers of the World) issues in particular with the attendant hates and violence. Joe sings at the beginning of the play, "Remember," an IWW song.

> We speak to you from jail to-day,
> Two hundred union men,
> We're here because the bosses' laws
> Bring slavery again.

The opening, lengthy scene of Act Three is a full scale discussion among Father McKee, Joe, and Tony on government today and the threat from radicals such as Joe. With Father McKee on one side and Joe on the other and Tony somewhat in the middle ("I don' want changin' nothing.") we get a rather accurate picture of the turbulent times. The young man of little means is restless with the capitalistic structure, the man of the church wants stability, and the happy winegrower makes money by the bushel.

> Father McKee: You radicals, Joe, you're always an' forever hollerin' an' carryin' on 'bout your rights. How about your duties? There ain't no one to prevent your doin' your duties but you ain't never done 'em in your life.
> Joe: I'm savin' my duties for the brotherhood of man.
> Tony: Dio mio!

> Father McKee: You're talkin' a lot of balderdash. Mind your own business an' leave the brotherhood of man to me. Brothers is *my* job.
> Tony: You think evrabody's goin' be brother like dat an' don' scrap no more? Eees crazy idea! You ain't got no good sense, Joe, you an' dos goddam Wobblies.

Essentially, however, Joe *is* the radical of the 1920's. "Maybe I don't mean nothin' at all. Maybe I'm just restless an' rarin' to go." There are scraps, like the dock strike at San Pedro, that he should get into. "The only freedom we got left" Joe tells the others, "is the freedom to choose which one of our rights we'll go to jail for." This, then, is the kind of anti-hero of the times so popular in contemporary literature. Match Joe up with the hapless Amy and we have a worthy pair for sympathy—not censure.

We stress "pathetic" with Amy only in the sense that she can really do so very little to order her life. Within a rather narrow box she struts her independence but it is always, no matter what, still a box. Her great strength is her pragmatism, the undeniable power to make the best of things. "Well, the world may need reforming," she bravely tells the philosophers as she joins them, "but I got no kick. The grapes is near ripe and ready for picking. The nights is getting longer, the mornings is getting colder, and Tony's getting better. Down town they're putting up the posters for the circus and I hear the show's going into winter quarters just the other side of Napa. I guess that's all the remarks I got to make now." Howard admitted to Barrett Clark that this opening scene of Act Three was what he liked best in the play—the chance for Amy in her simple way to put down the others (Clark, p. 202)....

Source: Sidney Howard White, "*They Knew What They Wanted* (1924)," in *Sidney Howard*, Twayne, 1977, pp. 49–59.

Walter J. Meserve

In the following excerpt, Meserve maintains that American social drama of the 1920s combined comedy, realism, and melodrama and finds that Howard's plays, though not intellectually weighty, were well served by this genre.

Underlying a great portion of the American plays written after the turn of the twentieth century there is a social consciousness and a concern for realism that distinguishes a trend in American drama. At its beginning it was a dual and almost parallel movement, the most significant in late 19th century American drama: the development of a social comedy, and the Rise of Realism in the drama. Numerous plays began to caricature aspects of society and also to reflect the literary interest in realism. Later, after the shock resulting from the American production of Ibsen's *Ghosts* in 1889, Ibsenism lent a certain unifying force to these trends. But it was not until the 1920's that social drama became a serious and dominant trend, part of a national growth in American drama which was reflected in the plays of Maxwell Anderson, Philip Barry, Paul Green, Rachael Crothers, Eugene O'Neill, S. N. Behrman, Elmer Rice, and Sidney Howard. Of these dramatists, only Sidney Howard produced his most significant plays during the twenties. During this decade which is now remembered mainly for the work of the Provincetown Players and the plays of Eugene O'Neill, Sidney Howard emerged as the first major writer of social drama in a long line of development that leads from James A. Herne to Tennessee Williams.

Writing a preface to *Lucky Sam McCarver*, Howard admitted that as a thinker he was neither profound nor original. In an age which makes every man his own "puffer" such modesty and honesty is refreshing in any writer, and one is perhaps tempted to be overly charitable in the face of such self-depreciation.

But after some thought one must conclude that Sidney Howard was right. This does not mean, of course, that he was superficial or that he was a poor dramatist, but rather that his plays do not lend themselves to searching literary criticism. Generally, his plays do not emphasize intellectual depth or imaginative development, but they do suggest a potent new force for a movement in American drama. To this trend he added an artistic mastery which deserves a certain critical acclaim.

The social drama of the twenties seems to have developed from several existing categories of early twentieth century drama, fused by the term *social* but vaguely distinguished as social comedy, social realism, and social melodrama—all of which showed the influence of Ibsenism. In 1890 Alfred Hennequin in "Characteristics of American Drama" (*Arena*, I [May, 1890], 700–709) maintained that French melodrama and English melodrama had combined to produce a new type of American play—the social melodrama. That such a social drama was not

MAINLY HOWARD'S CHARACTERS KNOW WHAT THEY WANT, BUT HOWARD INVARIABLY CONTROLLED THEIR DESTINIES."

popular at this time, however, is made clear by the frightened and frigid reception given James A. Herne's *Margaret Fleming* and by declarations like Daniel Frohman's in "The Tendencies of the American Stage" (*Cosmopolitan*, XXXVIII [November, 1904], 15–22) that American audiences looked for "vivacity and rapid sequence" in plays rather than the "food for thought" which the French and Germans preferred. Seven years after this comment, Clayton Hamilton, writing on "Melodrama, Old and New" (*Bookman*, XXXIII [May, 1911], 309–14), re-emphasized the same idea as he moaned the changes in modern melodrama. In the past he had enjoyed the melodrama of Augustin Daly, David Belasco, and Owen Davis—all vivid and violent, sweet and sentimental. Now Hamilton found "a new species of melodrama that is ashamed of itself" as it takes the form of "a serious study of contemporary social problems."

With this fusion of comedy, realism, and melodrama, touched lightly by Ibsenism, social drama was being born in America. It was a slow process, but by the first decade of the twentieth century, attitudes and issues had become accepted materials for plays—social, political, economic, religious, or moral. Among the numerous writers of what must be called realistic social melodrama before World War I, one of the most successful was Eugene Walter whose drama, *The Easiest Way*, 1908, was a striking portrayal of a woman who was unable to overcome her own basic weakness and the temptations of society. *Fine Feathers*, 1913, another Walter play, dramatized with some effect the evils of greed and temptation in the modern world. The only playwrights of this period, in fact, whose names are likely to be recalled, wrote seriously of social problems: William Vaughn Moody, *The Great Divide*, 1909; Edward Sheldon, *The Boss*, 1916; Charles Rann Kennedy, and Rachael Crothers. Kennedy's *The Servant in the House*, 1908, might be called a social gospel play, a denunciation of weak and ineffective Christianity; while *The Idol Breakers*, 1914, a much underrated play, quite profoundly dramatized in symbolic fantasy the struggle of the idealist to obtain that freedom which is both truth and beauty. Starting with *He and She* in 1911 and continuing for the next twenty odd years, Miss Crothers concerned herself with the social problems of her day and almost every year contributed a play of some pleasure and value to American theater. In a theater where profundity was not a common ingredient of drama, Eugene Walter, Charles Rann Kennedy, Jessie Lynch Williams, Owen Davis, and Rachael Crothers infused into their plays both serious thought and some skill in handling the problems of dramaturgy.

Into this stream of American drama, Sidney Howard launched his plays and by so doing, added an imagination and talent, which, guided by a new sense of realism, gave social drama a new dignity and position in the eyes of the audiences and critics, both in America and abroad. The 1920's were his years of major achievement, and his most worthy plays of the decade were *They Knew What They Wanted*, *Lucky Sam McCarver*, *Ned McCobb's Daughter*, and *The Silver Cord*. Later plays of the 1930's *The Late Christopher Bean*, *Alien Corn*, and *The Ghost of Yankee Doodle*, showed his continued interest in his main theme but also suggested a decline in dramatic power. Yet Charles Whitman in his 1936 edition of *Representative Modern Dramas* could call Sidney Howard "one of the most accomplished of living American playwrights." And Joseph Wood Krutch in *American Drama Since 1918* could write that "Mr. Howard's plays are among the best ever written in America."

Although one finds Sidney Howard's plays of major significance in the development of modern social drama in America and his themes still vital and meaningful, candor forces one to agree with Mr. Krutch on only two Howard plays. In spite of obvious defects, *They Knew What They Wanted* is an epoch-marking play for its sense of humanity and its insights into social morality. Statements by Howard and current critics notwithstanding, however, it is a modern version of the Paola-Francesca love story or Wagner's *Tristam and Isolde* only in a very vague fashion. No characters in the ancient or modern stories bear close comparison, and the plots have only a vague resemblance at one or two points. The conflict in Howard's play, in fact, is completely different from that of the tragic lovers whom Dante celebrates. One might more advantageously compare the play with James A. Herne's *Margaret Fleming*. Margaret and Phillip Fleming no less than Tony and Amy, know what they want, and have either the strength to arrange it (as Tony and Margaret do) or the weakness to accept it (as Amy and Philip). Although parts of *They Knew What They Wanted* are talky and even irrelevant to the main action of the play, in Tony, Howard created his most successful character. Most appealing, most real, most expedient among Howard's people, Tony is also the one most able to deal with the exigencies of the world. After struggling with his pride, Tony makes a discovery, acts upon it in both a socially expedient and Christian manner, and becomes not the most miserable of men but a "most happy fella."

. . . During the twenties Howard adapted seven plays and wrote seven more of which only four seem worth analysis. Next in significance to *They Knew What They Wanted* and *The Silver Cord* are *Lucky Sam McCarver* and *Ned McCobb's Daughter*—one a theater failure and the other a success but both examples of the social drama in which Howard excelled. Each is concerned with a strong character in a series of situations contrived to dramatize those personal qualities which react powerfully to social conditions and frustrations. *Lucky Sam McCarver* starts out as an analysis of Sam McCarver but is more effective as the story of a woman who desperately wants love from a man who has only money to give. Unlike *Ned McCobb's Daughter*, it is an unhappy social drama of irresponsible people: a frustrated woman and a materialistic man who will always be, as one person tells him, "disappointed in the universe." Social conditions provide the background for Ned McCobb's daughter, Carrie, to show the superiority of her character and her Yankee determination to get what she wants. Mainly Howard's characters know what they want, but Howard invariably controlled their destinies. Although he frequently tempered his moral judgments with real mercy, within his definitions of right and wrong he was completely conventional in meting out rewards and punishments.

It was perhaps inevitable that Sidney Howard should write social drama. Man's social problems interested him before he became a playwright, although his services in World War I, first as an ambulance driver and then as an aviator concerned with destroying life perhaps reflect some confusion as to how he would satisfy his idealism. After the war he became a radical reporter for the *New Republic* before joining the editorial staff of the old *Life* and later working as a feature writer for Hearst's *International Magazine*. His personal idealism as a crusader, therefore, may explain Joe's polemic on individual rights in *They Knew What They Wanted*, the Keystone Cops Federal men in *Ned McCobb's Daughter*, and the bitter attitudes toward war in *The Ghost of Yankee Doodle*. Certainly his independence of spirit may be traced in the theme of individual freedom which permeates his plays.

This independence of spirit, however, did not extend to the form in which he wrote his plays. He was not an experimenter at a time when many were experimenting. It is commonplace, of course, to call him a traditionalist, but his attitude toward the dignity of the dramatist seems to carry him beyond this position. For him the dramatist was only a "vicarious actor" who depended upon the actor to make his work meaningful. "The best that any dramatist can hope," he stated, "is that his play may prove to be a worthy vehicle." With this attitude he followed the theories of Augustin Daly and Daniel Frohman, and the "Laws of Dramatic Construction" put forth in 1886 by Bronson Howard who disregarded literary value and thought of a play only as stage production. As a result both Howards emphasized, among other things, the "satisfactory" ending of a play—that which would satisfy the audience whether or not it revealed true character. Sidney Howard, however, was never able to leave his play completely in the hands of the actors. His technique suggests, perhaps unconsciously, the inadequacy of some of his lines as well as his distrust of actors or readers to interpret his ideas correctly. One immediately recalls his innumerable and sometimes insufferably clever stage directions. When reprimanding Tony in *They Knew What They Wanted*, Father McKee becomes a "very severe shepherd." Mrs. Phelps' "wee mousie" activities indicate the part that stage directions play in *The Silver Cord*. Clearly some of his stage directions were a vain attempt to be witty and/or "literary" in the most common sense of the term. Too often, however, stage directions in his plays,

rather than simply describing movements, indicate a definite interpretation which perhaps only reinforces Howard's position as a "vicarious actor."

Generally Howard followed the realistic patterns established by his American predecessors, but he cannot be denied the courage—and the success—with which he brought new points of view to the theater and strengthened some of the old. With the strong realistic social morality of *They Knew What They Wanted* he followed the trend of the past but revolted from it in the same way that Sinclair Lewis made use of the realism of William Dean Howells and yet rebelled from its narrowness. In *The Silver Cord* he insinuated a Freudian interpretation with such success that the illustration, at least, remains enduring in the history of American drama. Carrie McCobb is, of course, not an innovation but another realistic Yankee character, who ranks above James A. Herne's Uncle Nat Berry, memorable Downeaster in *Shore Acres* and Owen Davis' forceful Yankee girl, Jane, in his Pulitzer Prize winner, *Icebound*.

As a craftsman of the theater Howard found his greatest success in creating social drama from a mixture of realism, melodrama, and comedy. His major interest in his plays, however, was the people, as the titles of his plays indicate. Psychological interpretation of character becomes a part of his two best plays. More exuberant than thoughtful, however, he was frequently satisfied to have his characters simply react emotionally to strong stimuli. In *They Knew What They Wanted*, for example, Tony controls his passion, rises above his pride, and in strength rather than in weakness rationalizes the situation which confronts him: "What you have done is mistake in da head, not in da heart"; he says, "Mistake in head is no matter." Howard himself showed in his characters that he agreed with this idea: emotion is more important than intellect—and certainly easier to dramatize. A biologist with a Ph.D., Christina in *The Silver Cord* at first tries to resolve her difficulties with Mrs. Phelps through reason, but her attempts fail; intellect is not enough. Even after she tries to combine intellect and emotion, she does not become a completely satisfying heroine because her argument is cooled by the force of intelligence rather than heated by emotional conviction. Howard forgot one of his basic rules in this play. Consequently, the audience cannot accept without question the positive victory of "life" which Howard obviously indicates in his conclusion.

. . . A dominant idea in Howard's plays is presented in the title of his first popular success: *They Knew What They Wanted.* With this idea he reflects the distinctive and positive individualism of the social drama of the 1920's and also distinguishes this social drama from what came before and what eventually followed. Social drama and melodrama before and during World War I generally emphasized the force of social conventions. Before *Nice People* in 1920 and *Expressing Willie* in 1924 Rachael Crothers did not allow her characters to assert themselves beyond social acceptability. Nor did Jessie Lynch William's *Why Marry?* suggest anything more than the acceptance of social custom. With very few exceptions playwrights dramatized the subjection of the individual to the conventions of society. During the 1930's the tone of American social drama again changed, although the individualism of the twenties did not completely die out. A strong trend in the thirties, however, dramatized man as representative of a social class and frequently victimized by the social structures.

Although characters in American social drama of the 1920's generally knew what they wanted, not all were successful in achieving their desire. For example, S. N. Behrman's hero, Clark Storey, in *The Second Man,* 1927, knew what he wanted and kept it. So did Mary and Jim Hutton in Philip Barry's *Paris Bound,* 1927, as well as Lissa in his earlier play *In a Garden,* 1924. Maxwell Anderson's *Saturday's Children,* 1927, discover what they want and try, although in a very romantic fashion, to get it. Earlier, 1923, Jane in Davis's *Icebound* was successful in getting what she wanted. On the other hand, Paul Green's Abraham McCrannie from *In Abraham's Bosom,* 1926, knew exactly what he wanted but couldn't gain it. Even the characters in Elmer Rice's *The Adding Machine,* 1923, and Sophie Treadwell's *Machinal* fit into this thesis. Exceptions can be found, of course, but Howard should be credited with putting his finger upon an idea which helps define the social drama of the 1920's.

During a decade in which the achievement of one dramatist overshadowed the work of all others, Sidney Howard escapes notice as the first major writer of social drama in modern American drama. Although he generally followed an established trend in American drama, Howard, in his best plays, brought an artistic mastery to the creation of his characters, a social perspective which made his plays transcend the limitations of a contemporary social drama, and an attitude toward life which helped characterize the social drama of the twenties.

Source: Walter J. Meserve, "Sidney Howard and the Social Drama of the Twenties," in *Modern Drama,* Vol. 6, No. 3, December 1963, pp. 256–66.

Barrett H. Clark

In the following excerpt, Clark reminisces through quotes from letters to Howard about They Knew What They Wanted *and the controversy that surrounded it.*

. . . But the later missives are more revealing, and most of them need little explanation. The next one I am printing has to do with my short review of *They Knew What They Wanted,* and was written in the spring of 1924.

No description of Sid Howard would do him justice that left out his comments on the books and persons he disliked, or that failed to show him in moments of disgust or anger. I have of course no right to leave in these letters some of the unflattering strictures he passed on plays and writers, and I am sorry I cannot print them. However, I am at liberty to recall how (in 1922 or 1923) he and I, having taken St. John Ervine and his wife to lunch at the Algonquin, were engaged in a terribly earnest conversation over our coffee. Two strange figures came over to a table next to ours—one short and stout, the other tall and not so stout as he became later on. Without introducing themselves they spoke over Sidney's head and mine to our guests, and one of them (I think it was the taller) solemnly announced, "You'd better come over to our table when you're bored." It was perfectly clear to me that Messrs. Woollcott and Heywood Broun were in a facetious mood, but Sidney was mad through and through. The Ervines and I laughed, but Sidney was ready to fight.

Another time he had asked me to introduce him to ———, a fairly well-known playwright whose work he liked. The luncheon at the Harvard Club was a failure. I can't explain it, but every topic of conversation ended up some blind alley, and after a short time Sid just sat back in his chair, bit his lip and fidgeted with his moustache. Maybe it was because our guest hadn't wanted a cocktail. He got up and left early, and

"THE SUCCESS OF THAT PLAY AND OF SO MANY OTHERS THAT FOLLOWED IT BROUGHT THE INEVITABLE LAWSUIT FOR ALLEGED PLAGIARISM AND THE THREAT OF ANOTHER FROM PERSONS WHO BELIEVED SIDNEY CAPABLE OF STEALING THEIR IDEAS."

Sidney and I laughed. "There's a dumb cluck! Let's get our drinks now! I wonder who wrote his play for him?"

This last is characteristic, not of his occasional lack of sympathy with a man he didn't like, but of his quick reaction to a given situation. Another man we had both known did something that in my own way I resented and described to Sid as "not very decent." "Not very decent?" he snapped. "Barrett, our friend——— is just a plain son of a bitch." This expression, you will understand, was not so widely used in the 20's as it is today.

And now for the next letter:

> Thanks for your note and the grand notice you gave the play. As to cutting Joe, there you raise the most interesting point that has been raised yet. I did cut him a good deal because he tended to overbalance the others . . . which was not good because the play is really about Tony and Amy. I daresay you agree to that, and I don't think that I cut anything of any value. I am inclined to think that the trouble may be in his being *too* actual. I knew the man and reported him overfaithfully and there were moments when I stuck so close to him that, odd as it may seem, he ceased to be theatric and became improbable. After all, the play is a little (and unimportant) treatise on the obsessions which make the world go round. The woman's obsession for security—the man's, for a dynasty—on the one hand (Tony) and for rebellion on the other (Joe's). It is always dangerous to stick too closely to an original and I may have got Joe into the trouble you find by just that process. Another thing is that Anders, admirable as his performance is, does not quite understand the inarticulate quality of his part—the groping . . . ideas. He often makes a transition in Joe's mind sound like a cut. For myself, I like best in the play my medieval morality at the opening of the 3rd act, where capital, rebellion & the facts of the case—pragmatic church—are all worsted by the woman's knowledge of the day of the week. I'm boring you with all this because your review is the very best thing the play has had, the most searching and the most understanding. When Bob Benchley covered both *Desire Under the Elms* & *They Knew What They Wanted* as French triangles I was outraged for both O'Neill and myself. I'm delighted, too, at your review of *Desire*. There's a fine play! There's rather a showing, these days, for American plays, isn't there? There may not be any *great* ones—though Stallings & Anderson are pretty near—but there are four of them—doing big business and earning at least serious respect—and that's *not* bad. Isn't Pauline Lord a great actress? *Really* a great actress? She's had an awful effect on me. Every word I write seems absolutely flat. I hear her say 'let go of my skirt,' and I'm gone, absolutely gone for the day. I can't get her out of my mind. Love to Cecile from both of us. When do we eat again? . . . Wednesday (which is chicken and waffles day at the Coffee House) I do recommend. Affection.

These words about Pauline Lord came back to me (I hadn't thought of them for years) when I saw Miss Lord at Sidney's funeral; she stood motionless in the cemetery, with the air of having just arrived from nowhere at all, precisely as she did in the first act of *They Knew What They Wanted*. I realized then what Sidney meant.

The success of that play and of so many others that followed it brought the inevitable lawsuit for alleged plagiarism and the threat of another from persons who believed Sidney capable of stealing their ideas. I think that in both cases the plaintiffs were not the ordinary kind of snipers who file claim and hope for a settlement from an author who may be willing to pay a few hundred dollars to avoid the greater expense and worry of maintaining his innocence in court. I testified in the one case that came to trial and prepared testimony and reports for the other case, which was dropped when Sidney categorically assured the author he had never seen, read, or even heard of her play. I can't imagine how anyone, looking into his blue-gray eyes, could possibly imagine him capable of plagiarizing anything. On the title page of the MS of *The Rivet* he wrote my name boldly above his own, and if I had not insisted that that of the man who had done four-fifths of the work should stand first, it would so have remained; *Dodsworth*, to judge from the title page, would seem to be a hack job that Sidney did a little work on; and *Yellow Jack*, as "original" as any play I know, was announced as written "in collaboration with Paul de Kruif."

The next letter came from Wiscasset, Maine, I think in the summer of 1930:

> Specifically, I need in my plagiarism suit a play in which the wife takes a lover because her husband is an invalid. Anything in that direction will do. I have just read the ridiculous affair which I was accused of robbing and I can destroy it finally and forever—though it bears no resemblance to *They Knew What They Wanted*—if I can show that their story is not original. Their story—I retail it, because I am asking you for help—is briefly this. A Swiss guide and his bride come home from their wedding and find there a Chasseur Alpin vagabond who makes an immediate set for the lady. The husband is called out to rescue some mountain climbers who have fallen into a crevasse and himself falls and is brought home paralyzed. The Chasseur stays in the house to help while the bride nurses her husband for seven months and falls in love with the Chasseur (bad sentence, very). The upshot is sex and the paralytic miraculously cured so that he can murder the lover and violate his wife, much against her will. That is the play which I want to prove is not at all original in plot, basic plot of course. Aside from the story, it is a pathetic effort which would play only about forty five minutes with all its big scenes. It has no characterization, reality or merit of any kind. But there is the accident motive. The differences are obvious between that play and mine. The wife in mine does not love her husband, has never seen him. Does not love her seducer. Has the mistaken identity theme. I have the baby motive. The plays have no real similarity of any kind. Even the accident, in their play, occurs *after* the marriage. But I want to make assurance doubly sure by discrediting the originality of their play. Or, for that matter, of my own. But theirs, I think, is the easier to discredit. I have, already, an Edith Wharton story. I want a French play in which a wife, married to an invalid, turns to a lover for consolation. Just that much is enough. Can you provide, Lord?

A few days later these two notes arrived:

> The complaint says: '. . . the unique portion of the triangle being that the husband of the woman is incapacitated from marital duties on his wedding night, thus giving the other man a chance of pleading love for the woman while the husband is helpless . . .' All of your examples, including *Le Chemineau*, are valuable and germane as destroying the uniqueness, still, if you think of one in which anything happens on the wedding night, I shall then be perfectly happy. I can't believe that the smutty minded Frogs and the old Italian comedy passed up anything as rich as that.

> I feel sure now that the brief reference to so many plays will clear all my difficulties away. I can say, granting the accidental slight similarity which *They Knew What They Wanted* bears to *The Full of the Moon*, allow me to show that *The Full of the Moon* is not exactly an original composition. Bless you for all your help. Now, one other thing. There was an old play made from Mark Twain's famous character, Colonel Mulberry Sellers. I believe it was called *The Mighty Dollar*. One John C. Raymond, a great comedian of the seventies, played it. . . . I'm thinking there might be something in it. The Colonel was a great old boy.

The trial, ably handled by Sidney's old friend and attorney Ernest Angell, was rather exciting. Until I was called to the witness stand I sat with Clare Eames in the "audience," doing my best to keep her from interrupting the proceedings. Sidney, when on the stand or sitting at the table with Angell, cast anxious glances in our direction, while Clare muttered audible stage whispers. At one point in the argument of the opposition she almost shouted, "What damn nonsense!", and the Judge thumped his gavel, though he didn't seem to be much in earnest; he too was enjoying the show. I had prepared what we all thought was pretty good defense testimony in the shape of several plots from 15th and 16th century French farces. When I went on the stand Angell, looking very business-like and sharp, asked me to give the Judge, in brief form, a few examples of Gallic plots which would show that *They Knew What They Wanted*, if it was "stolen," was based on common literary property in existence centuries before the plaintiffs play was even thought of. Reduced to brief synopses, most of these sounded like short tales from *The Decameron*, and at one point I hesitated. Sidney smiled, and from the far end of the courtroom I could see Clare, her elbows on the bench in front of her, encouraging me to go ahead. She was grinning. After I had offered three or four examples the Judge told me that that was enough, and hinted jokingly that he might have to clear the court if I went on. The case was dismissed. . . .

Source: Barrett H. Clark, "Sidney Howard," in *Intimate Portraits, Being Recollections of Maxim Gorky, John Galsworthy, Edward Sheldon, George Moore, Sidney Howard & Others*, Dramatists Play Service, 1951, pp. 181–226.

SOURCES

Abrams, M. H., *A Glossary of Terms*, 4th ed., Holt, Rinehart and Winston, 1981, p. 25.

Coffey, Thomas M., *The Long Thirst: Prohibition in America, 1920–1933*, W. W. Norton, 1975, pp. ix–x.

Eisner, Sigmund, *The Tristan Legend: A Study in Sources*, Northwestern University Press, 1969, pp. 23–29.

Howard, Sidney, *They Knew What They Wanted*, in *Famous American Plays of the 1920s*, selected and introduced by Kenneth Macgowan, Dell Publishing, 1988, pp. 133–206.

"The IWW," in *The Lucy Parsons Project*, http://www.lucyparsonsproject.org/iww.html (accessed June 1, 2011).

"IWW Chronology (1916–1920)," in *Industrial Workers of the World*, May 1, 2005, http://www.iww.org/en/culture/chronology/chronology3.shtml (accessed June 2, 2011).

"The IWW Songbook," http://www.sacredchao.net/iww/ (accessed June 6, 2011).

Klein, Alvin, "A Pulitzer Winner in Revival," in *New York Times*, May 22, 1994, http://theater.nytimes.com/mem/theater/treview.html?res=9D01E4DF1238F931A15756C0A962958260 (accessed June 2, 2011).

Kornbluh, Joyce L., "Industrial Workers of the World," in *The Lucy Parsons Project*, http://www.lucyparsonsproject.org/iww/kornbluh_iww.html (accessed June 1, 2011).

Orodenker, Maurie, Review of *They Knew What They Wanted*, in *Billboard*, January 29, 1949, p. 47.

SoRelle, Cynthia M., "Sidney Howard," in *Dictionary of Literary Biography*, Vol. 7, *Twentieth-Century American Dramatists*, edited by John MacNicholas, Gale Research, 1981, pp. 308–14.

Thornton, Mark, "Alcohol Prohibition Was a Failure," in *Cato Institute*, July 17, 1991, http://www.cato.org/pub_display.php?pub_id=1017 (accessed June 30, 2011).

"Why Prohibition?" in *Temperance and Prohibition*, Ohio State University College of Arts and Sciences Web site, http://prohibition.osu.edu/content/why_prohibition.cfm (accessed June 30, 2011).

Woolcott, Alexander, Review of *They Knew What They Wanted*, in *Sidney Howard*, by Sidney Howard White, Twayne Publishers, 1977, p. 56; originally published in *Evening Sun* (New York, NY), November 25, 1924, p. 24.

"Women's Rights Timeline," in *Leonore Annenberg Institute for Civics*, http://www.annenbergclassroom.org/Files/Documents/Timelines/WomensRightstimeline.pdf (accessed June 30, 2011).

Young, Stark, Review of *They Knew What They Wanted*, in *Sidney Howard and Clare Eames: American Theater's Perfect Couple of the 1920s*, McFarland, 2004, p. 61; originally published in *New Republic*, January 25, 1924.

FURTHER READING

Behr, Edward, *Prohibition: Thirteen Years That Changed America*, Arcade, 2011.

> This is a history of Prohibition. Behr tells a lively story of the corruption and violence that characterized the era, emphasizing how it led to the rise of organized crime.

Carnevale, Nancy C., *A New Language, a New World: Italian Immigrants in the United States, 1890–1945*, University of Illinois Press, 2009.

> Zeroing in on a time period that encompasses the milieu of Howard's play, Carnevale's book focuses on Italian Americans' experiences in adapting to the language of their new home nation.

O'Rear, Charles, Janice Fuhrman, and Robert Mondavi, *Napa Valley: The Land, the Wine, the People*, Ten Speed Press, 2001.

> In this volume, *National Geographic* photographer O'Rear, who lived in the Napa Valley for over twenty years, presents images that bring the luscious valley to life for readers everywhere.

Schwartz, Michael, "No Kick Coming: The Staging and Taming of the I.W.W. in Sidney Howard's *They Knew What They Wanted*," in *Text and Presentation, 2010*, edited by Kiki Gounaridou, McFarland, 2010, pp. 69–76.

> Schwartz discusses Howard's treatment of the Wobblies in *They Knew What They Wanted*.

SUGGESTED SEARCH TERMS

Sidney Howard

They Knew What They Wanted AND Sidney Howard

They Knew What They Wanted AND drama

Prohibition

Wobblies

social realism

Tristan and Iseult

Tristan and Isolde

Industrial Workers of the World

Roaring Twenties

Italian immigration AND United States

Time Flies

DAVID IVES

1997

Time Flies is a one-act play written by David Ives. It was first performed in 1997 at Primary Stages, an off-Broadway theater in New York City. ("Off-Broadway" is a term used to refer to New York City theatrical productions that are not staged in the major theaters in the district surrounding Broadway; usually the term describes avant-garde, experimental plays or productions, often written by new or unknown authors, performed before smaller audiences.) The production was part of an evening of six one-acts by Ives titled *Mere Mortals and Others*. Although Ives has written a number of full-length plays, he is best known for his one-act sketches, including those in *Mere Mortals and Others* and an earlier collection, *All in the Timing*, consisting of plays he wrote between 1987 and 1993.

In discussing Ives's work, critics often use such words as witty, madcap, snappy, and dizzying, as well as intelligent, to refer to the author's comic sensibility. Indeed, most, but not all, of his plays are comedic, usually capturing brief moments in time and examining them from quirky and unusual perspectives. *Time Flies* is no exception. The play features two lonely young mayflies, Horace and May, who meet and are immediately attracted to each other. Sadly, though, as the two try to live out a courtship ritual at May's pond, they turn on a television to watch a broadcast of "Swamp Life," a nature documentary narrated by real-life environmentalist and television host Sir David Attenborough. Quickly they discover that

David Ives (Getty Images)

the subject of the show is May's pond—and themselves. As the two watch themselves on television, they discover that, as with all mayflies, they have only one day to live.

Times Flies contains some adult language and themes, particularly in the presentation of a kind of sexual encounter between the two major characters, the mayflies. The context of both the language and the themes, however, is lighthearted and comic rather than gritty and realistic, making the play suitable for older high-school and college students. *Time Flies* can be found in an anthology of Ives's one-act plays, *Time Flies and Other Short Plays*, published in 2001.

AUTHOR BIOGRAPHY

Ives was born on January 1, 1950, in Chicago, Illinois. After attending a seminary, he enrolled at Northwestern University. Later, he was an

editor for the journal *Foreign Affairs* before enrolling at the Yale School of Drama in 1981, where he received a master of fine arts degree in playwriting. His earliest play, *Canvas*, was first produced in 1972. He also wrote humor pieces for such publications as *Spy*, the *New York Times Magazine*, and the *New Yorker*. By the late 1980s, he was regularly writing one-act plays, including *Sure Thing*, *Variations on the Death of Trotsky*, *Philip Glass Buys a Loaf of Bread*, *The Universal Language*, and *Words, Words, Words*.

Among his most popular works have been the one-act plays included in *All in the Timing*, first produced onstage in 1993. *Mere Mortals*, which includes *Time Flies*, is similarly a collection of one-acts, first performed in 1997. In addition to one-acts, Ives has written full-length plays, including *Polish Joke*, *Is He Dead?* (an adaptation of a work by Mark Twain) and *New Jerusalem: The Interrogation of Baruch de Spinoza*, a play that chronicles the 1656 punishment of Spinoza, a philosopher expelled from his Jewish community for his radical ideas.

In the 1990s, Ives branched out into musical theater. He is an artistic associate at Encores! a forum in New York City for American musicals. There, he has adapted more than a dozen shows for musical theater, including David Copperfield's magic show *Dreams and Nightmares* for Broadway. He wrote the script for the Broadway musical *Dance of the Vampires* and cowrote the script for *Irving Berlin's White Christmas*. Other musical-theater credits include Frances Hodgson Burnett's *A Secret Garden*, Cole Porter's *Jubilee*, and an adaptation of Rogers and Hammerstein's *South Pacific* (starring famed singer Reba McEntire). Ives's play *Venus in Fur* debuted in 2010.

Additionally, Ives has turned his hand to classic drama, including translations of Georges Feydeau's farce *A Flea in Her Ear* and Pierre Corneille's *The Liar*. Ives has also written three young-adult novels: *Monsieur Eek* (2001), *Scrib: Some Characters, Adventures, Letters, and Conversations from the Year 1863, Including a Deadly Chase in the Wilderness of the Fearsome Canyon, as Told by Billy Christmas, Who Was There* (2005), and *Voss: How I Come to America and Am Hero, Mostly* (2008).

Ives has been the recipient of numerous awards. His play *Don Juan in Chicago* received the Outer Critics Circle's John Gassner Playwriting

Award and a Drama Desk nomination for outstanding play. He won the 1994 George and Elizabeth Martin Playwriting Award. *New York* magazine named him one of the "100 Smartest New Yorkers," but in characteristically comic fashion, Ives responded by dismissing the compliment in the magazine itself: "Lists are anti-democratic, discriminatory, elitist, and sometimes the print is too small." He has been an adjunct professor at Columbia University in New York City, where he conducted a "lab" for playwrights.

PLOT SUMMARY

Time Flies opens with Horace and May, two mayflies, arriving at May's pond, which is actually little more than a puddle. There is a full moon, and cuckooing, such as that of a cuckoo clock, can be heard. Horace and May have met at a party, and May thanks Horace for flying her home. The two engage in awkward conversation as they get to know one another. They discover that both their parents had died at around dawn that morning. Horace indicates that he wants to leave, but May offers him a drink. For light, May turns on fireflies by tickling their undersides. As the conversation continues, they talk about having both been born at about seven-thirty that morning and having molted earlier in the day. May offers to turn on some music, and the two observe the full moon.

The sound of a frog can be heard coming from offstage, and Horace and May become fearful, knowing that frogs prey on mayflies. To settle Horace's nerves, May offers him a cocktail, but Horace says that he would be happy with just some stagnant water. Ironically, Horace toasts May by saying "Long life."

May asks Horace whether he would like to watch television. Among the choices is "Swamp Life," an episode of *Life on Earth* hosted and narrated by naturalist Sir David Attenborough. As they watch the program, they discover that the episode's subject is their puddle and themselves. Attenborough's narration emphasizes that the mayfly, along with other species of insects, engages in a desperate struggle for survival and that its biological imperative is to mate and reproduce. Horace and May are offended because Attenborough keeps referring to the mayfly as "lowly." As the show continues, May offers Horace something to eat, including

plankton and gnats. Horace and May learn from the television program that mayflies are a major food source for trout, salmon, and frogs. Once again the sound of a frog is heard from offstage.

The television program turns to mating behaviors. Attenborough describes how mayflies palpate their proboscises, which leads to a kind of sexual encounter between Horace and May. Attenborough then notes that the life span of a mayfly is just a single day, long enough to mate, produce offspring, and then die. Horace and May are disturbed by what they have just learned. In his distress, Horace seems to be having an asthma attack and asks for a paper bag in which to breathe. Meanwhile, the "cuckoo" sound reminds them of the passage of time. Their tension causes them to have something of an argument about the brevity of their sex lives and attitude of males to females. Yet again, a frog is heard, along with the "cuckoo" sound. Horace and May both apologize for their testiness to each other.

May then says that she had plans—plans that will never come to fruition because she is going to die. She says that she wanted to see Paris, even though she has no idea what Paris is. When May says that she is scared, Horace gives voice to the theme of the play:

> You know, May, we don't have much time, and really, we hardly know each other—but I'm going to say it. I think you're swell. I think you're divine.... And I say who cares if life is a swamp and we're just a couple of small bugs in a very small pond. I say live, May! I say... darn it... live!

When May asks how, Attenborough appears onstage and addresses them, suggesting that they fly to Paris. May says "Carpe diem," and when Horace asks the meaning of the phrase, Attenborough replies that it means "bon voyage." As the stage darkens, Horace and May fly off to Paris.

CHARACTERS

Sir David Attenborough

Sir David Attenborough (1926–) is a real-life figure. He began his career working for the BBC (British Broadcasting Corporation), and in time he produced and narrated a large number of television series about the natural world.

The major joke of the play is that when Horace and May turn on the television, they watch a program hosted by Attenborough and discover that the subject of the program is their pond—and themselves. Through Attenborough, Horace and May learn that they have only one day to live and that their biological imperative is to mate to carry on the species. At the end of the play, Attenborough appears onstage and addresses the characters, suggesting to them that they fly off to Paris. After May exclaims "Carpe diem!" and Horace asks what that means, Attenborough replies that it means "bon voyage," a French phrase commonly used to wish people well when they are embarking on a journey.

Horace

Horace is the lead male character in *Time Flies*. Like May, he is a mayfly, so any stage presentation of the play will feature him in a costume with antennae and a long nose. He has met May at a party (a "swarm") and has offered to "fly" May to her home in a pond, which is actually just a puddle. Horace is depicted as slightly awkward. Like any young man who has gone to an apartment with a young woman for the first time, he is uncertain how to behave. He apologizes to May for bumping into her, and he worries that his wing is in May's way when the two sit on a lily pad. When the two are threatened by a frog, he appears initially to be more frightened than May is, but when the frog later reappears, he seems more courageous and willing to confront the frog. Horace expresses the major theme of the play when he says, "And I say who cares if life is a swamp and we're just a couple of small bugs in a very small pond. I say live, May! I say . . . darn it . . . live!"

May

May, also a mayfly, is the lead female character in *Time Flies*. She has met Horace at a party (a "swarm") and has apparently asked him to "fly" her home to her pond, where she has a lily pad that functions as a couch. She becomes frightened after she and Horace learn that they have only a day to live, and her fear grows when the sun begins to come up, signaling the end of their day. May, though, is the source of some hope at the play's end, for she has a desire to fly to Paris. She reiterates the play's theme, "Carpe diem," and at the end of the play she and Horace in fact fly off to Paris.

THEMES

Life

The premise of *Time Flies* is that the two major characters, Horace and May, are mayflies and hence have only a single day to be born, mature, mate, and then die. Throughout the play, the phrase "carpe diem" is used. *Carpe diem* is a Latin phrase usually translated as "seize the day" but sometimes translated as "pluck," "enjoy," or "grasp the day." The phrase originated with the classical Roman poet Horace, who wrote an ode that contains the line "Carpe diem, quam minimum credula postero," or "Enjoy today, putting as little trust as possible in tomorrow." The phrase "carpe diem" caught on and continues to be used, even today, to refer to a philosophy of life that urges people to immerse themselves in today rather than worrying about the future. Sometimes, the phrase is used to suggest leading a life of pure pleasure based on the notion that death could lie just around the corner. This is a misinterpretation of Horace, who was calling not for a life of dissipation but for one filled with energy, drive, purpose, and enthusiasm.

The applicability of the theme of carpe diem is clear in *Time Flies*. Horace and May learn that they have just a single day to life. They are attracted to one another, but they learn that their mating has just one purpose: to produce more mayflies. In the meantime, they face threats from predators such as frogs. They are dismayed to learn that they have no real future, although at the end of the play a more fulfilling future is hinted at as the two fly off to Paris.

Love

Time Flies is at bottom a love story, although one with an unusual twist. Horace and May, although nominally mayflies, are depicted as similar to any two humans who meet and are attracted to each other. They have met at a party ("quite a swarm"), and Horace has flown May back to her home, a pond, just as a young man might go back to a woman's apartment with her. As a play, *Time Flies* relies on the skill of the actors as they buzz, bump into each other, and otherwise express their awkwardness as they have a sexual encounter. Their story, though, is bittersweet. Although they have found each other, they learn from watching a television program that they have only a single day to live. This knowledge drives their determination to make their

TOPICS FOR FURTHER STUDY

- The ode featured in *Horace Odes I: Carpe Diem*, translated by David West (1995), is a highly readable modern English translation of the ode by classical Roman poet Horace, who gave the phrase *carpe diem* ("seize the day") to the West. Read the ode, then write a brief essay comparing it to *Time Flies*.

- The heavy metal band Metallica recorded the song "Carpe Diem Baby," available on the Internet as a free MP3 download. The song's lyrics, also widely available on the Internet, express a theme of living life to the fullest. Imagine that you are directing a production of *Time Flies*. Prepare "production notes" in which you incorporate Metallica's "Carpe Diem Baby" into the production at various points. Alternatively, locate the song "Seize the Day," by heavy-metal band Avenged Sevenfold, available as a free MP3 download. Prepare an oral presentation in which you explain how "Seize the Day" expresses themes similar to those found in *Time Flies*.

- Numerous poets have taken up the theme of "seize the day." Among them are British poets Andrew Marvell, author of "To His Coy Mistress"; Robert Herrick, author of "To the Virgins, to Make Much of Time"; and Sir John Suckling (incidentally, the inventor of cribbage), author of "Song," also known by its first line "Why So Pale and Wan, Fond Lover?" Locate one or more of these widely available poems. Perform the poem for your classmates on your social networking site or Web page and invite them to comment on the poem's thematic similarities to *Time Flies*.

- In numerous countries, a medieval Latin song variously titled "Gaudeamus Igitur" ("Let Us Rejoice") or "De Brevitate Vitae" ("On the Shortness of Life") continues to be frequently performed as a school song, often at graduations. Various versions of the song and its lyrics, which embody the seize-the-day theme of *Time Flies*, are widely available on the Internet. Locate a performance of the song and play it for your classmates, providing them with an English translation. Write a letter to the editor of your school newspaper urging that the song be performed by your school's choir at graduation.

- *Dead Poets Society* is the title of a 1989 film starring Robin Williams as a literature teacher at a boys' boarding school. The teacher delivers a memorable line when, reflecting on former students at the school, he tells his current students: "But if you listen real close, you can hear them whisper their legacy to you. Go on, lean in. Listen, you hear it?—Carpe—hear it?—Carpe, carpe diem, seize the day boys, make your lives extraordinary." Using this movie as your inspiration, prepare a multimedia presentation or one-act play in which you urge your classmates to "seize the day."

relationship more intense. The audience knows that, on a literal level, their love affair will last only for a few hours. On a figurative level, though, the audience is invited to think about the shortness of life and the need for people to avoid putting aside their emotions out of caution, reticence, or fear. Life is filled with dangers, such as ravenous frogs and salmon. The only thing that makes life worth living is love, which has to be seized and held fast.

Irony

Time Flies is simultaneously humorous and highly ironic. The irony, of course, stems from the dramatic situation: the two characters have found love, only to learn that their love and their lives are destined to last for only a day. This understanding is a source of considerable humor. Both characters learn that their parents died just that morning. Both went through the process of molting and growing wings that

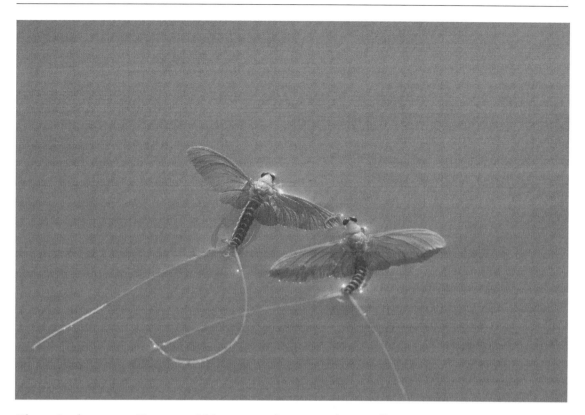

The main characters, Horace and May, are anthropomorphic mayflies. *(Laky_981 / Shutterstock.com)*

afternoon. Neither has any experience beyond the day in which they have been alive; neither knows what "Tuesday" is because neither has lived through a Tuesday. However, at the same time both characters have been recipients of a cultural inheritance. They know about frogs. May has a television. Horace knows about sex therapist Dr. Ruth Westheimer. Like humans, the two characters are sentient and can draw on previous experience, even if it is not their own. The span of the characters' lives is very limited, so they are not going to experience the joys and sorrows of a long life. Thus, while the audience members will laugh at the absurdity of the drama's premise, they will also recognize the ironic sadness of life's limitations.

STYLE

Anthropomorphism

The term *anthropomorphism*, derived from the Greek word for "human form," refers to a literary technique by which animals (or objects) are given human shape or human characteristics. The fables of Aesop and many Walt Disney animated films feature anthropomorphic characters, but perhaps the most famous such work is George Orwell's *Animal Farm*. Clearly, *Time Flies* draws on the tradition of anthropomorphism in literature by featuring two mayflies as the central characters. The selection of mayflies was likely no accident. Mayflies belong to the order Ephemeroptera, which comes from the Greek *ephemeros*, meaning "short lived," and *pteron*, meaning "wing." By selecting a creature with a short life span, Ives is able to put into play his ironic and humorous take on the theme of "seize the day."

Puns

Time Flies relies heavily on puns and other forms of language play. This language play starts with the names of the characters. May would seem to be a suitable name for a female mayfly, and Ives makes a comic play on the name when Horace mistakenly calls her "April." The name Horace is a direct allusion to the first-century BCE Roman author Horace (or, more fully, Quintus Horatius

Flaccus), but again Ives plays with the name by having May call him Vergil (often spelled Virgil), the name of another classical Roman author.

This type of wordplay, much of it having to do with insects, continues throughout the play. Horace and May meet at a party that was "quite a swarm." The two turn on fireflies for light. For music, the choices are the Beatles, the Byrds, and the Crickets. When May offers Horace something to drink, the choices are a grasshopper or a stinger (the names of two alcoholic cocktails). One of the choices on television is *The Fly*, a 1958 science-fiction/horror movie remade in 1986 starring actor Jeff Goldblum; the movie is about a scientist who accidentally merges himself with a housefly during a teleportation experiment. Food choices include various forms of gnats, including "Gnat King Cole," a play on the name Nat King Cole, a famous singer, and when Horace says that he could not finish a whole one, May replies "'Gnat' to worry."

The use of a lily pad as May's home recalls the word *pad*, slang for an apartment with connotations of the resident being hip and cool. When the television does not seem to work right, May adjusts the antennae—on her head. When Horace indicates that he is attracted to May, she replies with an outrageous pun, "I think it was larva at first sight." As Horace and May rub their antennae together, Horace quotes Shakespeare's *Hamlet* by saying "There's the rub. There's the rub." This type of verbal play adds to the humor of the piece, using laughter to draw the audience into the play's more serious theme.

Allegory

Allegory is a literary technique in which characters, settings, and situations represent things or abstract ideas and are used to convey a message or teach a lesson. Allegory is typically used to teach moral, ethical, or religious lessons—as it does in what is perhaps the most famous of allegories, John Bunyan's *Pilgrim's Progress*—but is sometimes used for satiric or political purposes. At bottom, *Time Flies* is an allegorical play. Despite all the humor, puns, and comic stage business, the play teaches a serious lesson about the power of love and the need to take full advantage of the time one has on earth. While Horace and May do not, strictly speaking, stand for abstractions, they are representative of the human condition.

HISTORICAL CONTEXT

Although *Time Flies* does not explicitly advance an environmental theme, the presence of Sir David Attenborough as a character suggests that the play was written in an era of heightened environmental consciousness and awareness of the natural world, both in the United States and in many countries throughout the world. Attenborough is a British naturalist who rose through the ranks at the BBC (British Broadcasting Corporation) to produce and host a number of series about wildlife and the natural world. Among these series were *Life on Earth*, *The Living Planet*, *The Life of Birds*, *The Life of Mammals*, *The First Eden*, *Wildlife on One* ("One" referring to the BBC channel), *The World About Us*, *The Blue Planet*, and *Saving Planet Earth*. Virtually all of these shows attracted huge audiences in Great Britain, and many of them were successfully broadcast in the United States, making Attenborough almost a household name.

This heightened awareness of the natural world, depicted comically in *Time Flies*, was reflected by a number of events that took place during the 1990s. In 1992, for example, the first Earth Summit was held in Rio de Janiero, Brazil, to focus on a number of worldwide environmental concerns. The following year, the National Biological Service was established at the U.S. Department of the Interior, and President Bill Clinton signed a bill limiting logging in old growth forests. A major event was the release of the initial report of the United Nations Intergovernmental Panel on Climate Change, which predicted severe long-term impacts from the buildup of greenhouse gases in the atmosphere. In 1995, wolves were reintroduced into Yellowstone National Park, and during the mid-1990s, various organizations were calling for a worldwide phase-out of lead in gasoline to reduce air pollution.

In 1997, the world mourned the death of Jacques Cousteau, a leading oceanographer and environmental activist, and that year 122 nations adopted the Kyoto Protocol, a major worldwide environmental initiative. That same year, scientists announced that they had cloned an adult sheep, Dolly. In 1999, the Worldwatch Institute reported that 70 percent of scientists believed that the world is experiencing the largest mass extinction of species in history. This is just a sampling of some of the environmental

COMPARE
&
CONTRAST

- **1997:** Many of the world's nations sign the Kyoto Protocol, a major environmental initiative. The U.S. Congress, however, does not ratify the treaty.

  Today: Many environmentalists adhere to the conclusions about greenhouse gases and global warming reached by the United Nations Intergovernmental Panel on Climate Change.

- **1997:** Scientists announce that an adult sheep named Dolly has been successfully cloned, bringing issues involving biology and the natural world to worldwide attention.

Today: Cloning of molecular fragments and single-celled organisms is commonplace, usually for the purpose of medical and biological research, but the cloning of higher forms of life is still rare.

- **1997:** The Toyota Prius is the first hybrid gas-electric vehicle, designed to use less fuel and therefore produce less pollution, to go into full production.

Today: In 2010, about 28,500 hybrid vehicles are sold in the United States.

and natural events and developments that would likely have been of importance to Ives's initial New York audiences as they watched a play about insects shedding light on the human condition.

By the 1990s, few people would have regarded the sexual innuendo of *Time Flies* as at all shocking. Many prominent Americans made it into the news because of extramarital relationships and other kinds of behavior that in former generations might have been considered scandalous. By 1997, President Bill Clinton was widely regarded as a "womanizer" because of his relationships with Gennifer Flowers, Paula Jones, and Monica Lewinsky. Speaker of the U.S. House of Representatives Newt Gingrich attracted attention because of his relationship with a much younger staffer (whom he later married). Also in the mid-1990s, "America's mayor," Rudy Giuliani, was found to have possibly been involved in extramarital affairs.

Additionally, few Americans would have failed to recognize Horace's reference to "Dr. Ruth," that is, Dr. Ruth Westheimer, a diminutive (about four feet, seven inches tall), funny, enthusiastic sex therapist who often appeared on radio and television. Dr. Ruth was widely parodied because of her German-Jewish accent, but she fostered an atmosphere of frank, lighthearted

discussion of sexual matters. Although events and personalities such as these had no direct impact on Ives or on *Time Flies*, they were indicative of an ongoing loosening of standards of personal behavior, a theme that was increasingly finding its way into the popular culture. In this way, the sexual content of *Time Flies* became accepted and hardly worthy of note—despite May's comment about "the filth on television these days."

CRITICAL OVERVIEW

Ives's plays have been popular with both actors and audiences. Actors and acting students enjoy the plays because they are compact and enable actors to exhibit a wide range of skills, particularly comic skills. Audiences enjoy them for the simple reason that they tend to be simultaneously funny, thought provoking, and touching.

It is difficult to separate reactions to *Time Flies* as a text from reactions to performances of the plays. Reviewers see the play in production; they do not read it in the same way that a critic would read and review a novel. Thus, for example, Elyse Sommer, writing for *CurtainUp*, saw a performance that failed to excite her, saying that the plays of *Mere Mortals* "zoom away full of vinegar and sass, but they tend to stagger as

The mayflies live on a pond and are getting ready for an evening out. (Anton Petrus | Shutterstock.com)

often as they soar." Nevertheless, she says, "the plays are as quick as ever" in their examination of an "idiosyncratic landscape." In a similar vein, G. L. Horton, in a review of a Boston production for *Aisle Say*, declares that the plays of *Mere Mortals* are "the amusing products of a distinctive voice and an acute ear," but Norton also says that "the Ives quirks become predictable" and that "the quality of Ives' word play . . . isn't quite up to supplying the surprises the plotting lacks."

Generally, though, reactions to productions of *Time Flies* have been very positive. Jason Zinoman, writing for the *New York Times*, calls the play a "sweet romance" and says that it balances Ives's "gentle absurdist tone with its Borsht Belt sensibility." (*Borscht Belt* is a colloquial term referring to summer resorts in the Catskill Mountains popular with Jewish vacationers in earlier generations; performances by comedians were common at these resorts.) Commenting on a production in San Diego,

Bill Eadie, writing for *SanDiego.com*, says that "none of these plays ever attains the comic philosophical level of, say, Chekhov. Rather, several of them play like sketches on *Saturday Night Live* or Second City improv bits." Nevertheless, Eadie concludes that Ives "plays with human understanding of social conventions and probes how those conventions might be different if we were born, matured, mated, and died in a single day."

Commenting on the same production, a reviewer for the San Diego *North County Times* refers to Ives's "word-drunk playlets" and calls the author "one-of-a-kind, the creator of playful, compact comedies." The reviewer says that "the distinctive Ives tone is lightly absurdist" and calls the plays "brisk, often brilliant." *Time Flies*, according to the reviewer, is "one of Ives' most popular pieces." In response to a later production in San Diego, Charlene Baldridge, in the online journal *Turbula*, calls *Time Flies* the "best of the lot" and sees the play as "hilarious and touching." Back in the East, Peter Marks reviewed a production of *Mere Mortals* for the *New York Times*. He writes that the plays are "fast and ferociously funny" and refers to Ives's "gratifying ability to unharness the intoxicating power of language."

CRITICISM

Michael J. O'Neal

O'Neal holds a PhD in English. In the following essay, he examines references to time as the motif that holds Time Flies *together.*

Sometimes it can be difficult to say what a work of literature is "about." One answer to the question of what *Time Flies* is about might be that it is about two mayflies who meet, fall in love, and then discover that they have only a day to live, but that would be a restatement of the obvious. More fundamentally, *Time Flies*, as its title suggests, is a play about time and its passage. Ives uses a number of references to time as the glue that holds the play together.

The first, obviously, is the title. What is less obvious, though, is that "time flies"—which is a form of wordplay given that the play is about two mayflies—is the English translation of *tempus fugit*. This was a phrase given to Western literature in a poem titled *Georgics* by the classical Roman poet Virgil (the same Virgil, or Vergil,

WHAT DO I READ NEXT?

- Ives's young-adult novel *Voss: How I Come to America and Am Hero, Mostly* (2008) uses letters to tell the story of the comic misadventures of Vospop ("Voss") Vsklzwczdztwczky, a fifteen-year-old who smuggles himself into the United States hidden in a crate of black-market cheese puffs.

- Ives is the author of numerous one-act plays. One that is popular with directors and actors is *Words, Words, Words*, included in his collection *All in the Timing* (available in *All in the Timing: Fourteen Plays*, 1994). The play features three intelligent chimpanzees who are locked in a cage with the task of hitting typewriter keys at random and in doing so, eventually reproducing Shakespeare's play *Hamlet*.

- Autumn Cornwall's young-adult novel *Carpe Diem* (2009) is a fictional take on the theme of Ives's *Time Flies*. The novel tells the story of a sixteen-year-old girl whose bohemian grandmother persuades the girl's parents to allow her to accompany her grand-

mother on a trip through southwest Asia that turns the heroine's world upside down.

- *Seize the Day*, a phrase that captures the central theme of *Time Flies*, is the title of a novella by Saul Bellow (1956). The novella tells the story of a day in the life of a man who has fallen on hard times and is forced to examine his life.

- Famed comedian Bill Cosby is the author of a book also called *Time Flies* (1988). The book is a warm, humorous romp through the tribulations of aging.

- *Life in the Undergrowth* (2006) is Sir David Attenborough's book written for the layperson about the insect world.

- Gary Soto's *Accidental Love* (2006) is a young-adult novel that tells the story of Marissa Rodriguez, a fourteen-year-old Hispanic girl who accidentally meets and falls in love with a nerdy boy from another school. Under the power of love and in the face of surrounding dangers that would thwart that love, Marissa transforms her life.

---

whose name May mistakenly assigns to Horace, whose name is that of another classical Roman poet). The line in Virgil's poem is "Sed fugit interea fugit irreparabile tempus, singula dum capti circumvectamur amore," which can be translated as: "But time meanwhile is flying, flying irreparably, while entranced by love we linger around each detail." The phrase can frequently be found on clocks, and it has entered the popular culture: Eulalie Mackecknie Shinn, the mayor's wife in the play *The Music Man*, frequently utters it, and "Tempus Fugit" is the title of an episode of *The X-Files*. As such, "time flies" neatly parallels the use of *carpe diem*, or "seize the day," a phrase popularized by Horace (the Roman poet) and used by both of the characters in *Time Flies*.

Another important marker of the passage of time is the "cuckoo" sound that comes from

offstage. The cuckoo, of course, is a species of bird, but the cuckoo has been used in clocks since at least the mid-nineteenth century. With the passing of each hour, the cuckoo emerges from the clock to give its distinctive call. The cuckoo clock has become a cultural icon used to mark the passage of time in poetry, fiction, movies, cartoons, music, paintings, and television shows. Many who have taken piano lessons have probably played "The Cuckoo Clock," as in John Thompson's *The First Grade Book*. In *Time Flies*, the appearance and reappearance of the cuckoo serve to remind the characters of the passage of time and that their time is limited.

The play makes numerous other references to time. Horace and May discover that they were both born at seven thirty that morning—and in

The mayflies fear the frogs, who symbolize death. *(Wolfgang Eichentopf / Shutterstock.com)*

fact, Horace notes more precisely that he was born at seven thirty-three. May's name calls attention to the month, and Ives underlines the time connotation of her name by having Horace mistakenly call her April. After May provides Horace with a drink, he toasts her by clinking glasses with her and saying, "Long life, May." David Attenborough notes in his television program that the mayfly first appeared some three hundred fifty million years ago, and he points out that the mayfly belongs to the "order Ephemeroptera, meaning 'living for a single day.'"

At one point, Horace asks May what time it is, but May responds that she does not have a watch. Later Horace says, "Time is moving so fast now" as the cuckoo continues to sound. He then says, "This explains everything. We were born this morning, we hit puberty in midafternoon, our biological clocks went BONG, and here we are." Later still he says, "Wait a minute, wait a minute," and he and May talk about the brevity of their sexual encounter. As the play draws to a climax, Horace says, "I was just hoping to live till Tuesday." Throughout the play, the moon hangs over the characters, but at

the end, the sun is coming up, marking the end of Horace's and May's one day of life.

Ives makes a subtle reference to the passage of time when Horace and May are rubbing their antennae together. In response, an excited Horace says, "There's the rub. There's the rub." Theatergoers are likely to recognize this as a phrase in "To be or not to be," the title character's famous soliloquy in Shakespeare's *Hamlet*. In this soliloquy, Hamlet debates within himself the question of whether or not it would be better for him to die rather than live. The full quotation reads as follows: "To die, to sleep; / To sleep, perchance to dream. Ay, there's the rub, / For in that sleep of death what dreams may come, / When we have shuffled off this mortal coil, / Must give us pause." The "rub" is that Hamlet does not know what comes after death, just as the audience may speculate that Horace and May have no idea of the "fate" to which they refer.

Through it all, though, is the phrase *carpe diem*, or "seize the day." Horace and May have only a single day to live—and as a play with allegorical elements, *Time Flies* suggests to audience members that in the span of time and history, they too have only a limited time to live and take advantage of the benefits, like Paris, that life has to offer. All of the human markers of time are included in the play: minutes, hours, mornings, afternoons, days (like Tuesday), and the millennia in which the mayfly has carried out its biological destiny. The moon and the sun, along with the cuckoo, mark the passage of time in the absence of a wristwatch.

Within this immense span of time, Horace and May have their moment, the moment in which they can make a connection and, as Horace puts it, "live." The dictates of biology conspire against them, just as against all living creatures, who are born, mature, mate (perhaps), and die. The reader imagines that the next night, another pair of mayflies will inhabit May's puddle and carry on with life, in much the same way higher species, including humans, do. They, too, will face the inevitability of the passage of time and death, and there's the rub. But the play's ending suggests a source of hope: It is to be hoped that all will seize the opportunity to fly to Paris, the city of light and love, and wrest something meaningful out of life.

Source: Michael J. O'Neal, Critical Essay on *Time Flies*, in *Drama for Students*, Gale, Cengage Learning, 2012.

David Ives

In the following interview, Ives discusses a new play and some of the writing secrets that keep his dramas fresh.

New York playwright David Ives continues his long association with director Walter Bobbie as *Venus in Fur*, presented at Classic Stage Company last season, goes to Broadway in early 2011. Bobbie will also helm Ives's *The School for Lies*, a new adaptation of Moliere's *The Misanthrope*, at CSC in April. Plus, Ives is working on his 29th and 30th concert-musical adaptations, *Bells Are Ringing* and *Lost in the Stars*, for the Encores! series at City Center.

Were there any scenes in Venus in Fur *where Walter Bobbie surprised you with his choices?*

There was a moment I thought epitomized his brilliance, when the woman in the play says to the man, "Bring me my other shoes." I wrote the stage direction "He changes her shoes for her." Walter turned it into this extraordinary five-minute silent scene of the man putting an incredible pair of fetish boots on her. One night an audience member walked down the aisle and

leaned over the stage to get a better view. The costume designer [Anita Yavich] had found those boots in a catalogue—but because of a fetish convention going on in Germany, they were out of stock. Some secret supplier of fetish boots managed to find her a pair.

Do you and Walter have running jokes?

We call each other "Buddy" ever since we collaborated on an Encores! script by Buddy DaSilva, We sign everything "Buddy"; we never use our names. When you mentioned him, actually, I was surprised to hear his name is still Walter.

When you were casting Venus, *was it confusing to have a play within an audition within an audition?*

No—it was highly suspenseful, because we couldn't find anybody to play these parts. After six months, we had a general call. In walked this young woman from NYU, Nina Arianda. She threw down her stuff, opened her mouth and five seconds later we knew we had found her. It was uncanny, because she was auditioning to play an actress in a play for which the playwright can't find an actress. I seem to be specializing these days in erasing the line between reality and illusion.

Do you remember the first musical you ever saw?

Until I started adapting musicals for Encores!, I'd only seen six musicals in my entire life, and two of them were *Sweeney Todd*. The first one I saw was probably *Candide*, the Hal Prince environmental production, back in the 1970s.

Does humor from past eras usually need updating?

Certain jokes are immortal. Like in Aristophanes where somebody has to go on a trip to Hell, and he stops a corpse being carried by in a funeral procession to ask the way—and then the corpse asks for money to carry the bags. That will never be stale—I think the Three Stooges used it. But, yes, a standard job in adapting comedy is you have to take out the wife-beating jokes. Our tastes in these things have changed.

The thing about adapting, for me—maybe because I'm egotistical, or greedy—is that I always have to make it my own. It's my job to bring to an adaptation the energy of a playwright working on a new play. I've done the work on *The Misanthrope* that Moliere himself might have done had he lived another 350 years. I'm looking forward to working on it with Walter Bobbie and [designer] John Lee Beatty and getting back to couplets.

Do you have a rhyming dictionary?

I was just thinking I'm tired of marking up my rhyming dictionary. It doesn't have all the rhymes in it, so I end up writing in the margins, and doing that breaks its spine and then I have to buy a new one and re-edit the rhyming dictionary.

You should sell the old one—I bet you'd pull in some cash on eBay for The David Ives Hand-Annotated Rhyming Dictionary. Speaking of books, you've written some for kids. What did you read growing up?

I didn't read children's books; I read Mickey Spillane and Agatha Christie. I didn't know *The Wind in the Willows* till I was in my twenties, and a girlfriend read it out loud to me. Which was certainly the end of *The Wind in the Willows*, for me.

What's the secret to keeping a kid's attention?

The secret for keeping anyone's attention is me keeping my attention. If I'm not amused or moved, I know nobody else is going to be. I don't try to write for kids, I try to write about kids—but I've stopped writing children's books, because the world of children's publishing is a jungle that makes the theatre look like Utopia.

Who makes you laugh now?

I can tell you nothing depresses me like comedians.

What artist do you wish could paint your portrait?

David Hockney. There's an extraordinary exhilaration that comes off his paintings.

What's your ideal dinner party?

It's big. You'd have to have the Great Hall of the Metropolitan Museum for it. Corneille would be there. The essayist Charles Lamb. Henry Fielding. Horace. And Shakespeare, of course—though he'd only talk about box-office receipts.

Source: David Ives, "20 Questions: David Ives," in *American Theatre*, Vol. 27, No. 8, October 2010, p. 152.

Joel Hirschhorn

In the following excerpted review, Hirschhorn examines a San Diego production of a sextet of the Time Flies *plays, including* Time Flies.

...It's said time flies when you're having fun, and the fun quotient is sky-high in David Ives' sextet of comic plays at the Old Globe. Moving from anthropomorphic mayflies to British detectives and inept biblical construction workers, the author maintains a warped, witty tone; he even manages to humanize some of his screwball protagonists. Not all six plays within *Time Flies* work perfectly, but director Matt August and a peerless cast capture the distinctive notes in Ives' literary voice.

Easily the evening's highlight is *The Mystery of Twicknam Vicarage*, a sendup of stiff-upper-lip British drawing-room mysteries. Channeling suave Ray Milland and bumbling Peter Sellers, David Adkins is a rector who's among the suspects in the murder of ladies' man Jeremy (Jeffrey Brick). Other suspects include contemptuous wife Sarah (Nancy Bell) and the corpse's widow, Mona (Mia Barron), who cries in wonderfully cliched fashion, "He was so alive!" A marvelous bit of direction has the actors walking rapidly in reverse-rewind fashion to represent a flashback.

In the opener, which takes place on David Ledsinger's ingenious marsh-and-lilypad set, mayflies Horace (Mark Setlock) and May (Barron) adopt inspired buzzing sounds that signal imminent mating. This love affair is interrupted when David Attenborough (Adkins) drops down to the stage via rope and informs them they have one day to live. "I can rule out multiple orgasms," Barron comments, as the brokenhearted bugs try to find a solution and decide they should use their final hours flying to Paris. Their costumes by Holly Poe Durbin—silver wings; big, round black glasses; antennae; iridescent vests—are as clever as the dialogue.

Show's second episode takes place in the desert circa 1000 B.C., as Gorph (Setlock) and Cannaphilt (Adkins) lug a heavy stone and begin building the Tower of Babel. Along comes a tyrannical business-woman (Bell) who demands the overworked duo complete the tower quickly "or else you die," prompting them to reflect, "Why should we get sucked into some pyramid scheme?" The sequence has an outlandish Monty Python flavor, with shades of comic strip "The Wizard of Id," and there are enjoyably campy turns by Bell and by Brick as a lanky eunuch. Pacing here isn't as snappy as in Part One, but the sequence delivers plentiful laughs.

The Green Hill embraces Somerset Maugham *Razor's Edge* territory, as Jake (Adkins) visualizes a green hill where he can find peace and dashes all over the world trying to locate it. His girlfriend, Sandy (Bell), is understandably dismayed, but it doesn't stop Jake from searching for his lost horizon, encountering 16,973 hills in the process. A sensational visual has Jake standing on a green parachute that spreads on every side, and Ives pulls off a major feat—he emotionally involves us in Jake's Spiritual odyssey.

Bolero is about a woman (Bell) panicking over noises she hears. Her bedmate (Setlock), who shrugs them off, builds mild suspense but falls short on humor and peters out with a weak punch-line.

Final one-act, set in a church basement, *Lives of the Saints* is a well-acted character study of two women, Flo (Barron) and Edna (Bell), preparing for a funeral. But it is too low-key a climax after its high-powered predecessors. Fortunately, the lesser entries don't dim our awareness of Ives as a major satirist and playwright.

Source: Joel Hirschhorn, Review of *Time Flies*, in *Variety*, Vol. 392, No. 1, August 18, 2003, p. 28.

Celia Wren

In the following review, Wren critiques the short one-act collected as Lives of the Saints.

Don't count on entropy in David Ives territory. The laws of thermodynamics—physical and cultural—operate differently there. A writerly monkey can crank out the script of *Hamlet*. Marie Antoinette and the Lindbergh baby may share lunch on a construction girder, 50 stories above the ground. And Leon Trotsky has been sighted pondering politics as he sits with an axe sticking out of his skull. Ives's brief, frequently hilarious, sometimes brilliant plays are excursions into a unique landscape, where multiple universes propagate wildly, and language bottoms out into dizzying crevasses.

In January, the Philadelphia Theatre Company introduced the newest installment in the writer's loopy oeuvre: five short one-acts collected under the title *Lives of the Saints*. As with previous Ives assemblages, including the national hit *All in the Timing*, the new show juggles existential abstractions as dexterously as easygoing snippets of Americana and bad puns—as if a group of Harvard philosophy

professors had staged a coup at *Saturday Night Live*. The pieces vary in quality—the goofiness of the Old Testament sendup *Babel's in Arms*, for example, seems arbitrary and somewhat juvenile next to *The School of Natural Philosophy*, a metaphysical spy caper packed with high-voltage paradoxes. But the Philadelphia cast, well-stocked with Ives veterans like actress Nancy Opel, polishes off even the slighter pieces with zest. As directed by John Rando, who staged *Mere Mortals* in New York in 1997, the production vaults smoothly from philosophical conceits to deadpan takes, with Russell Metheny's streamlined sets (a few modern chairs and a wall for a doctor's office, for example) giving the ideas lots of room to breathe.

Ives at his best leaves you with a sense that you've been stunned by a heavy object. That's the impact of the strongest playlet in the new collection: *Enigma Variations*. The work's premise sets banality hurtling against mystical speculations: a series of patients visit their respective doctors to complain of rarefied malaise, like déjà vu or the elusive presence of a doppelganger. Heady speculations fly thick and fast. Time may not be linear; reality may be illusory; and, to make matters worse, the doctor's truculent bisexual assistant (Danton Stone) may be Aphrodite, goddess of love. But the real genius of the piece lies in high-concept physical humor. Two identically dressed doctors and two identically dressed patients (Arnie Burton, Bradford Cover, Anne O'Sullivan and Opel) act out each medical consultation, executing small movements—crossed arms, the insertion of a pen into a pocket—in tandem, with startling coordination. This twinning effect allows the skit to reflect visually the kind of havoc Ives wreaks with words and ideas.

A more clownish version of this mayhem is at work in *The School of Natural Philosophy*, which parodies espionage movies while gnawing away at the nature of truth. Who are the cartoonish spies who have broken into the eponymous school's blandly modern office? What is their mission, and who are they working for? Well, the so-called Mr. Smith, Ms. Jones and Mr. Brrrowwwn (Cover, Opel and Burton, respectively) would probably like answers to those questions, too. Trench-coated symbols for the riddle of existence, these spies wield ludicrously camouflaged weapons—a bouquet of flowers may be a Kalashnikov; coffee may be truth serum; a gummy bear may be a knockout drop. Words are booby-trapped as well: "It's deep!" Ms. Jones says, plunging a hand into a book with a false bottom. "It's Dostoyevsky," replies the loud, disembodied voice that has been giving the spies instructions.

If this kind of cerebral high-wire act is what you might expect from Ives, the show's title sketch is more inscrutable. The rambling, plotless *Lives of the Saints* sets two pious elderly women tottering around a church basement as they prepare a funeral breakfast. Edna and Flo (Opel and Sullivan) mime the sifting of sugar, the decanting of potato chips, and so on, but their actions sound hyperrealistic. As the scene straggles on, a retracting panel explains why: Other cast members, concealed above the stage, are supplying the noises, crinkling bags of chips, drizzling a pitcher of water into a basin, and so on.

With its shaggy-dog-story rhythm, its reliance on the hackneyed life-is-theatre trope, and its lack of verbal and intellectual pyrotechnics, *Lives of the Saints* feels downright un-Ivesian. One is tempted to fish for significance: Perhaps the point is to deconstruct spirituality, the way *The School of Natural Philosophy* deconstructs language and the search for truth. Perhaps the marionette doves that finally hover over Flo's and Edna's heads condemn religion as a hoax. Perhaps the skit is debunking reverent attitudes that turn theatre into worship.

Then again, perhaps the point is simply wackiness, as it is in *Soap Opera*, about a man's star-crossed romance with a washing machine. The collection *Lives of the Saints* proves once again that Ives can be preposterous in many sundry veins. Those who find his work too clever by half should give the new show a wide berth. But his fans will find another reason to say, in the words of an ancient theologian, "It is to be believed because it is absurd."

Source: Celia Wren, "Irrational Exuberance," in *American Theatre*, Vol. 16, No. 4, April 1999, pp. 37–38.

SOURCES

Baldridge, Charlene, "Smart Skits Make Their Point," Review of *Time Flies*, in *Turbula*, Summer 2003, http://turbula.net/2003-summer/theater-globe-timeflies.php (accessed September 6, 2011).

"David Ives," in *American Theatre Wing*, May 2010, http://americantheatrewing.org/biography/detail/david_ives (accessed September 2, 2011).

"David Ives," in HarperCollins Children's Web site, http://www.harpercollinschildrens.com/Kids/AuthorsAndIllustrators/ContributorDetail.aspx?CId=20275 (accessed September 2, 2011).

"David Ives," in *Saipan.com*, http://www.saipan.com/edu/mhs/S.&%20D.%20Web%20Page/PERFORMANCE-NMC-David%20Ives.htm (accessed September 2, 2011).

"David Ives Offers 'Lab' for Playwrights, Just Off Broadway," in *Columbia University Record*, February 10, 1995, http://www.columbia.edu/cu/record/archives/vol20/vol20_iss16/record2016.16.html (accessed September 2, 2011).

"December 2010 Dashboard: Year End Tally," in *Hybrid-Cars*, January 7, 2011, http://www.hybridcars.com/hybrid-clean-diesel-sales-dashboard/december-2010.html (accessed September 4, 2011).

Eadie, Bill, "Time Flies at New Village Arts," in *SanDiego.com*, August 2, 2009, http://local.sandiego.com/arts/time-flies-at-new-village-arts (accessed September 6, 2011).

Horton, G. L., Review of *Mere Mortals*, in *Aisle Say Boston*, http://www.stagepage.info/reviews/MereM.html (accessed September 2, 2011).

Ives, David, *Time Flies*, in *Time Flies and Other Short Plays*, Grove Press, 2001, pp. 3–18.

Kaminer, Ariel, Larissa MacFarquhar, and Liesl Schillinger, "The 100 Smartest New Yorkers," in *New York*, January 30, 1995, p. 43.

"Laughs Fly in New Village Arts' Treatment of David Ives' Words," Review of *Time Flies*, in *North County Times* (San Diego, CA), August 6, 2009.

Marks, Peter, Review of *Mere Mortals and Others*, in *New York Times Theater Reviews, 1997–1998*, Psychology Press, 2001, p. 79; originally published in *New York Times*, May 13, 1997.

"Mayflies (Ephemeroptera)," in State Hygienic Laboratory at the University of Iowa Web site, http://www.shl.uiowa.edu/services/limnology/macroinvertebrates/ephemeroptera.xml (accessed on September 6, 2011).

"Memorable Quotes for *Dead Poets Society*," in *Internet Movie Database*, http://www.imdb.com/title/tt0097165/quotes (accessed September 7, 2011).

"The Nineties," in *Environmental History Timeline*, Radford University Web site, http://www.radford.edu/~wkovarik/envhist/11nineties.html (accessed September 5, 2011).

Robinson, Simon, "The Dozen Most Important Cars of All Time," in *Time*, January 10, 2008, http://www.time.com/time/specials/2007/article/0,28804,1701729_1701728_1701722,00.html (accessed September 5, 2011).

Shakespeare, William, *Hamlet: The Prince of Denmark*, in *The Complete Works of William Shakespeare*, Vol. 3, edited by David Bevington, Bantam, 1980, act 3, scene 1, lines 65–69.

Sommer, Elyse, Review of *Mere Mortals*, in *CurtainUp*, 1996, http://www.curtainup.com/mortals.html (accessed September 2, 2011).

Verrall, Arthur Woollgar, *Studies Literary and Historical in the Odes of Horace*, Macmillan, 1884, p. 188.

Wilkinson, L. P., *The Georgics of Virgil: A Critical Survey*, Cambridge University Press Archive, 1978, p. 49.

Zinoman, Jason, "Warning: Don't Swat That Fly, She May Be One of the Stars," in *New York Times*, June 7, 2007, http://ilikecollin.com/wp-content/uploads/2011/05/Time-Flies-Others-by-Ives-Theater-Review-New-York-Times-print.pdf (accessed September 6, 2011).

FURTHER READING

Bottoms, Stephen J., *Playing Underground: A Critical History of the 1960s Off-Off-Broadway Movement*, University of Michigan Press, 2006.

> This volume explores the genesis of the off-off-Broadway theater movement in the 1960s, referring to very small-scale experimental productions. Readers interested in the intersection between theater and the free-speech movement of the 1960s—the era when Ives was coming of age—will find here a compendium of information about this theatrical movement.

Fisher, James, *Historical Dictionary of Contemporary American Theater: 1930–2010*, Scarecrow Press, 2011.

> Readers interested more generally in contemporary theater will find in this volume discussion of the plays, people, movements, and institutions that have shaped the American stage. The book includes a chronology, an introductory essay, an extensive bibliography, and more than fifteen hundred cross-referenced dictionary entries.

Hischak, Thomas S., *Off-Broadway Musicals since 1919: From "Greenwich Village Follies" to "The Toxic Avenger,"* Scarecrow Press, 2011.

> Readers interested in off-Broadway musical theater will find in this volume examinations of hundreds of musicals. Among them are such influential words as *The Fantasticks* and *Little Shop of Horrors*, along with many other important but perhaps forgotten musicals.

Polsky, Milton E., *You Can Write a Play*, Applause Books, 2002.

> Polsky, like Ives, is a teacher of the art of playwriting. This highly respected book offers insights into ways to shape a dramatic vision into a play with exercises, suggestions, and examples from established playwrights. The book has often served as a textbook or classroom supplement.

SUGGESTED SEARCH TERMS

David Ives

David Ives AND Mere Mortals

David Ives AND Time Flies

carpe diem

carpe diem AND David Ives

Horace ode AND carpe diem

de brevitate vitae

gaudeamus igitur

John Gassner Playwriting Award

musical theater

Broadway theater

off-Broadway theater

Outer Critics Circle

seize the day

mayflies

Trying to Find Chinatown

DAVID HENRY HWANG

1996

David Henry Hwang's *Trying to Find Chinatown* was first produced in 1996 for the Humana Festival, which is held at the Actors Theatre in Louisville, Kentucky. It was published along with another one of the author's short plays, *Bondage*, that same year. The volume *Trying to Find Chinatown: The Selected Plays* was released in 1999. It is a collection of eight short plays by the playwright.

Like many of Hwang's plays, *Trying to Find Chinatown* focuses on the concepts of ethnicity and identity in the United States. It is a brief one-act play that only casts two actors. An encounter between two strangers on the streets of New York leads to important questions about what defines an individual's culture and ethnicity, as the two characters share their conflicting points of view about what it means to be Asian American. Within this single act, Hwang skillfully explores the concepts of ethnicity, assimilation, and self-identity.

AUTHOR BIOGRAPHY

Hwang was born in Los Angeles, California, in 1957. His parents, Henry and Dorothy Hwang, were first-generation Chinese immigrants. Henry was a banker, and Dorothy was a music teacher. Hwang studied the violin as a child and developed an interest in music and performing arts. Hwang

David Henry Hwang *(© Everett Collection Inc | Alamy)*

Along with his theatrical dramas, Hwang has worked on the books for Broadway musicals, including *Flower Drum Song* and *Aida*. He has also collaborated with different composers to create opera librettos, including *The Voyage*, *Alice in Wonderland*, and *The Fly*. In 1993, the movie version of *M. Butterfly* was released. Hwang wrote the screenplay adaptation for his drama and soon penned other screenplays, including *Possession* and the television miniseries *The Lost Empire*.

Over the course of his career, Hwang has earned numerous honors and grants, including a Guggenheim Fellowship, a National Endowment for the Arts award, and a Rockefeller Foundation Fellowship. He was appointed to the President's Committee on the Arts and the Humanities in 1994 and held the position until 2001. In 1998, the David Henry Hwang Theater in Los Angeles, dedicated to the influential playwright, became the new main stage for the East West Players, the oldest Asian American theater company in the United States. As of 2011, Hwang lived in Brooklyn, New York, with his wife and children.

earned a bachelor of arts degree from Stanford University in 1979. He then attended the Yale University School of Drama from 1980 to 1981.

Hwang's successful career as a playwright began in the 1980s. He staged his first play, *F.O.B.*, at Stanford and showcased it at other venues, including in New York. The play won an Obie Award in 1981; the Obie Awards are presented by the *Village Voice* to new and creative productions performed off-Broadway. This success was quickly followed by *The Dance & the Railroad*, which was nominated for a Drama Desk Award in 1982. Hwang, however, is best known for his groundbreaking play *M. Butterfly*. *M. Butterfly* won an Antoinette Perry Award in 1988, making Hwang the first Asian American playwright to win a Tony Award. He was also a finalist for the 2008 Pulitzer Prize for *Yellow Face*. Hwang's plays are known for their themes of personal, sexual, and ethnic identity as well as their ability to effectively encompass both Asian and American culture.

PLOT SUMMARY

Trying to Find Chinatown tells the story of a chance encounter between two men who have very different ideas about what it means to be Chinese American. Their debate occurs in a single act, which is separated into two different locations or scenes. Two male actors play the characters Ronnie and Benjamin. Ronnie is a Chinese American street musician, and Benjamin is a blond-haired, blue-eyed tourist. Both are in their twenties, but Benjamin is a little younger than Ronnie. Ronnie is dressed in 1960s-style clothing with 1990s piercings, which emphasize his artistic personality and rebellion against societal norms.

The play takes place on a street corner in the Lower East Side of New York City. Ronnie is playing the violin as the play begins. His musical style is influenced by jazz and classic rock 'n' roll. This first song is specifically compared to the style of Jimi Hendrix. Both Ronnie and Benjamin make assumptions about each other based on appearance, and the play explores the complexities associated with personal and public identity.

MEDIA ADAPTATIONS

- A trailer for *Trying to Find Chinatown* was posted on YouTube (http://www.youtube.com/watch?v = ifV4HjUEsdo) on June 27, 2007.

- A portion of Hwang's interview with *Asia Pacific Arts*, where he describes his views of ethnic identity, was posted on YouTube (http://video.search.yahoo.com/search/video;_ylt = A0oG7iW421JOADoA.nJXNyoA?p = David + Henry + Hwang&fr2 = piv-web) on November 15, 2010.

Benjamin, a tourist from the Midwest, encounters Ronnie playing on the street corner as he holds a paper, obviously looking for an address. He stops to listen to Ronnie play his violin and applauds when the musician is done. Benjamin compliments Ronnie for how well he plays his "fiddle" and begins to walk away when Ronnie clears his throat. He rejects the coins that Benjamin first pulls out but is willing to accept a dollar bill. The first words Ronnie says to Benjamin are, "And don't call it a 'fiddle,' OK?" He then goes on to insult Benjamin's intelligence by conjuring up Midwest stereotypes.

Benjamin points out that he has never given anyone on the street a dollar before and asks for Ronnie's help finding an address. Ronnie agrees, but he becomes outraged when he sees that the address is in Chinatown. He accuses Benjamin of racial profiling because he is asking an Asian American the way to Chinatown. Benjamin is confused by Ronnie's anger, at first, but he slowly understands the thought process behind it.

Benjamin responds to the angry rant by saying, "Brother, I can absolutely relate to your anger." He then goes on to describe the history of Asian oppression and stereotypes in the United States in an attempt to promote solidarity. Ronnie interrupts Benjamin as he attempts to explain that he was not "motivated by the

sorts of racist assumptions." Ronnie cannot understand how or why Benjamin would know about Asian American history because he is not of Asian descent.

Benjamin tells Ronnie that he took Asian American studies in college, and Ronnie is surprised to find out that the University of Wisconsin even has Asian American studies. Benjamin explains that the program was created after the Third World Unity Hunger Strike. Ronnie confronts his own stereotypes about people from the Midwest when he says, "It just never occurred to me, the idea of Asian students in the Midwest going on a hunger strike." He still does not, however, understand why Benjamin would be interested in Asian American studies.

Benjamin explains, "Just like everyone else. I wanted to explore my roots." He tells Ronnie how proud he is of his Asian heritage but is interrupted. Ronnie sarcastically asks, "Did they bother to teach you that in order to find your Asian 'roots,' it's a good idea to first be Asian?" Benjamin is confused by Ronnie's insistence that he is not Asian but white. Benjamin finally recognizes why Ronnie makes such assumptions and explains that his name is Benjamin Wong. Ronnie calls himself the "Bow Man." Here, each character defines who he believes he is: Benjamin is convinced that he is a Chinese American, and Ronnie sees himself as a musician.

Benjamin was adopted by Chinese American parents and considers himself Asian American. Ronnie questions if Benjamin can be Asian because he has blond hair and blue eyes. Benjamin, who has fully embraced the culture of his parents, tells Ronnie that no one can "judge my race by my genetic heritage alone." Ronnie questions what determines race if not genetics. Benjamin, however, counters that it would be a charade for him to believe that he is white when the culture that he understands is Asian American. He says that he wants what Ronnie already has, "A home. With your people." Benjamin is looking for a sense of camaraderie, but he will not find it with Ronnie.

When referring to Chinatown, Ronnie says, "Those places don't tell you a thing about who *I* am." Benjamin accuses Ronnie of being assimilated and hating himself. He offers to help Ronnie discover who he is by recommending Asian identity books. Benjamin, who refuses to let his genetics define his culture, is insisting that Ronnie embrace the culture of his ancestors.

Ronnie rejects Benjamin's help and calls him an "ethnic fundamentalist." He insists that ethnicity does not equal identity, but Benjamin believes that rejecting ethnic identity is "like saying you *have* no identity." Ronnie launches into a monologue, giving a brief history of music, specifically jazz and blues in relation to the violin. "Now tell me, could any legacy be more rich[?]" he asks. Again, Ronnie identifies himself by his profession. He begins playing his own composition, and Benjamin drops the dollar in the violin case before leaving.

Ronnie's music provides the background to Benjamin's monologue, which will end the play. In the stage directions, Hwang questions whether Ronnie's music begins to show a Chinese influence. A director who chooses to play music with Chinese influence would indicate that Ronnie's heritage is still part of his identity. Although Ronnie and Benjamin continue to share the stage, they are no longer aware of each other.

Benjamin finds the address in Chinatown without Ronnie's help. It is the tenement house where his father was born. Here, he connects with his family's history and feels his father's ghost as he eats a *hua moi* or sugared plum. Benjamin has taken this pilgrimage to his father's home six months after his death. He considers this location the home of his father's ghost and also the home of "the dutiful hearts of all his descendants," making it his home as well. Benjamin ends his monologue by reinforcing the theme of the play. As he considers the ghosts of the tenement, Benjamin is saddened to think of those who were not given the chance "to know who they truly are."

CHARACTERS

Ronnie Chang

Ronnie is a Chinese American in his mid twenties. He is also a New York street musician who plays the violin. He is described in the scene directions as someone who wears "retro-'60s clothing and has a few requisite '90s body mutilations." Ronnie has an artistic personality, and he is an excellent musician whose musical ability impresses Benjamin. The musical style of Jimi Hendrix influences his opening song, and the audience later learns that jazz and rock artists inspire him and heavily influence his own musical compositions.

He meets Benjamin as the young tourist stops to hear Ronnie play. Ronnie makes assumptions about Benjamin because he is a Caucasian tourist from the Midwest who calls a violin a "fiddle." Ronnie agrees to help Benjamin find an address, but he becomes furious when Benjamin asks him the way to a building in Chinatown. Ronnie accuses Benjamin of employing racial stereotypes and refuses to help him. He is surprised when Benjamin identifies himself as an Asian American. Ronnie insists that Benjamin cannot be an Asian American because he is white. He and Benjamin argue about what it means to be Asian and what defines a person's ethnic identity. When Ronnie does not show the same sense of pride in his family's heritage that Benjamin feels, Benjamin accuses him of assimilation and self-hatred. Ronnie, however, identifies himself as a musician, believing that his ethnicity alone cannot define who he is. He draws his identity from the musical subculture. The stage directions do hint, however, that Ronnie's heritage still influences his music and, therefore, his identity.

Benjamin Wong

Benjamin is described as "blond, blue-eyed, a Midwestern tourist in the big city." He runs across Ronnie as he is looking for an address. He is impressed by Ronnie's musical skill, and he stops to applaud and compliment Ronnie. Benjamin makes the mistake of calling Ronnie's violin a "fiddle" and listens to the musician insult him with hick stereotypes. Benjamin agrees to pay Ronnie a dollar for the song, but he also asks the native New Yorker for directions to an address in Chinatown. He is confused by Ronnie's angry reply and accusations of racism. Benjamin attempts to apologize, and he identifies himself as Chinese American because Chinese Americans adopted him. The audience learns that Benjamin is originally from Tribune, Kansas, and that he took Asian American studies at the University of Wisconsin. Benjamin refuses to be defined by his genes and argues with Ronnie that he is not white but a Chinese American.

Benjamin is horrified to discover that Ronnie does not completely identify himself as Asian American. He offers to help Ronnie find himself in his Chinese roots, but Ronnie rejects his concept of ethnic identity. Benjamin gives Ronnie a dollar and leaves. On his own, he finds his father's birthplace and childhood home in Chinatown. There, he feels a connection with his family and chosen culture. He feels at home. Ronnie explains that his father has been dead for six months and that going on this pilgrimage helps him sense his father's spirit.

THEMES

Cultural Identity

Trying to Find Chinatown explores the concept of cultural identity in light of racial constructs. The *Merriam-Webster Dictionary* defines culture as "the customary beliefs, social forms, and material traits of a racial, religious, or social group." Hwang shows his audience that one does not need to share a gene pool to identify with a particular social group or culture. Although Benjamin is genetically Caucasian, he identifies with the adopted culture of his parents. He defines himself as Chinese American, arguing, "you can't judge my race by my genetic heritage alone." Benjamin may look "white" to Ronnie, but he refuses to be defined by the genetic heritage of his birth parents.

Similarly, Ronnie does not believe that his family's ethnicity can define him. While Ronnie is Asian American, his chosen identity is that of a musician. An artistic social group forms his cultural identity. Ronnie considers his forebears to be musical icons such as Son Sims and Louis Armstrong. Both characters choose to align their identities with the cultures that they feel best define them and enable them to be themselves.

Self-Identity

Hwang explores the concept of self-identity in *Trying to Find Chinatown*. Both Ronnie and Benjamin attempt to retain a sense of self beyond their genetic features. Benjamin explains, "a society wedded to racial constructs constantly forces me to explain my very existence." Benjamin calls himself "Chinese-American." His self-identity, however, goes beyond culture; Benjamin sees himself as his father's son. He is fiercely proud of everything that his father overcame. His pilgrimage to Chinatown is not

simply an attempt to connect with his cultural heritage; it is how he connects to his family's history. He takes a deeply personal journey to his father's birthplace. In finding the tenement his father came from, Benjamin feels a connection to his spirit, which cements his identity as a dutiful son.

Ronnie's personal identity stems from what he does rather than who his parents are. His given name is Ronnie Chang, but he calls himself "The Bow Man," which shows how he chooses to view himself as a musician. Hwang explained in an interview for *US Asians* that Ronnie "finds his identity in an activity not related to his ethnic background." His ethnic background, however, does remain part of him. The character chooses to play jazz or rock music, but the stage instructions indicate that Chinese music could influence Ronnie's final song, which is his own creation. This indicates that Ronnie accepts his heritage, but he does not allow his ethnicity alone to define him.

Stereotypes

Ronnie and Benjamin are each guilty of stereotyping in *Trying to Find Chinatown*. Ironically, both characters battle against stereotypes as they place them on each other. Ronnie makes assumptions about Benjamin based on his accent and physical appearance. He first presumes that Benjamin is uneducated and backwards because he is from the Midwest rather than New York. Ronnie is insulting about Benjamin's home and family. In reality, Benjamin is well educated. Additionally, Ronnie's belief that people from the Midwest do not care about the Asian American experience is challenged when he learns that the University of Wisconsin teaches Asian American studies.

Ronnie also assumes that Benjamin is a racist because he is a Caucasian who asks an Asian American for directions to Chinatown. Benjamin, however, has no racist feelings toward Ronnie. As the adopted son of Chinese Americans, Benjamin considers himself Asian American. He calls Ronnie "Brother" twice as he explains who he is. In fact, Benjamin embraces his parents' culture in a way Ronnie does not.

Benjamin assumes that Ronnie passionately embraces his Chinese heritage and culture simply because he is biologically a Chinese American. He tells Ronnie, "I'm just trying to find what you've already got." Ronnie,

TOPICS FOR FURTHER STUDY

- Read *The Red Umbrella*, Christina Gonzalez's young-adult story about a Cuban teenager, Lucia Alvarez, who is sent to America with her brother during Operation Pedro Pan. Create social network pages (Twitter, Facebook, Myspace, Google+) for Lucia, Ronnie, and Benjamin, and with two friends respond as the characters. What advice would Ronnie and Benjamin give to Lucia about living in America? What would she say to them about the importance of family and culture?

- Research American society and culture in the 1990s using online and traditional resources. What societal changes occurred during this decade, and how did they affect Asian Americans? Create a video or multimedia presentation of the time that focuses on these sociological changes. Include a history of Hwang's plays and their reception within the presentation. Explain why you think some of his plays were poorly reviewed in light of the sociology of the times.

- Research the history of Asian Americans in the theater and other performing arts.

Examine the development of Asian American stereotypes. Create a Web site that provides a time line of Asian American theater. Provide links to important events and individuals within your timeline.

- Read Frank Chin's *The Chickencoop Chinaman*, the first Asian American play produced off Broadway. Write a one-act play in which one of Chin's characters and one of Hwang's characters meet each other. How would the characters relate to each other? Ask a classmate to perform the play with you. Record the performance, and post it on a Web site, YouTube, or online blog. Invite classmates to review the performance.

- Read through *Zoot Suit, and Other Plays*, by Luis Valdez. Choose one of the plays, possibly *Los Vendidos*, to compare with *Trying to Find Chinatown*. Write a paper that focuses the on similarities and differences between the characters, style, or themes. Explain what you think accounts for the differences and similarities between the two plays.

---

however, does not identify with his ethnicity in a way that satisfies Benjamin. Benjamin cannot understand anyone walking away from the community that he has worked so hard to be a part of. He goes on to accuse Ronnie of hating himself because he does not identify with his race and cultural heritage. In this way, Benjamin places his own stereotype on Ronnie and any other Asian American who does not share his feelings and point of view.

Assimilation

Benjamin accuses Ronnie of being assimilated because he does not identify with his Chinese heritage the same way that Benjamin does.

Assimilation is a common theme in Asian American and other ethnic literature. The *Merriam-Webster Dictionary* definition of assimilation is "the process of receiving new facts or of responding to new situations in conformity with what is already available to consciousness."

Immigrants to new countries often try to fit in with the dominant culture. There is some fear that people assimilate at the expense of ignoring their cultural heritage and family traditions. Benjamin considers Ronnie's attitude to be a sign of assimilation. In his opinion, Ronnie is rejecting his ethnicity and part of his heritage to fit into mainstream American culture.

Two men argue over which can claim Chinatown as home. (sepavo | Shutterstock.com)

STYLE

One-Act Play

Trying to Find Chinatown is a brief one-act play. According to an entry in the ninth edition of *A Handbook to Literature*, one-act plays became prominent in the 1890s as part of the little theater movement. Before this time they were relegated to vaudeville theater and opening acts. A one-act play only contains a single act, but the act may be broken into more than one scene. The dialogue between Benjamin and Ronnie takes place in a single scene on a New York street corner. Benjamin exits this scene to finds his father's birthplace, where he delivers the final monologue.

Irony

Irony is a device that has been used by writers for centuries. In drama, irony occurs when characters behave in a way that the audience considers unsuitable in the circumstances.

Benjamin embodies irony. He is a Caucasian American who was adopted by Chinese Americans, which is a twist on the increasing numbers of Caucasian Americans adopting children from Asia in the 1990s. According to research published by the Evan B. Donaldson Adoption Institute, the majority of international adoptions between 1971 and 2001 involved children from Asian countries. The irony continues as Benjamin discusses white oppression and accuses a Chinese American of ignoring his ethnicity and assimilating into mainstream culture.

Drama

Any acted story or play is an example of drama in its simplest definition. Over the centuries, however, plays have evolved into different categories such as comedy and tragedy. Plays that do not deal with tragic or comical themes and still focus on serious issues are considered dramas. *Trying to Find Chinatown* fits this definition of a drama. The play addresses social issues such as racial stereotypes without relying on comical or tragic plot devices. It also causes the audience to consider how a person can define his or her ethnic and personal identity.

Two-Person Play

A two-person play is the term used to describe plays, movies, or other performances that rely on two main characters. The British vernacular refers to it as a two-hander play. The conflict is explored through the dialogue of the actors. As with many other two-person plays, the main characters in *Trying to Find Chinatown* have different perspectives. The play relies on the debate between Ronnie and Benjamin to drive the plot forward.

HISTORICAL CONTEXT

1990s

The 1990s were a time of social change throughout the world. The Berlin Wall fell in 1989, effectively beginning the end of the decades-old cold war between America and the Soviet Union. After the Soviet Union fell in 1992, capitalism spread throughout the world. Even China made allowances for private markets. Many international markets flourished, and technology advanced. This is the decade when the Internet became accessible to the public.

COMPARE
&
CONTRAST

- **1990s:** The Asian American population in the United States doubles between 1980 and 1990. Asian Americans make up a small but quickly growing minority. There is racial tension, and many Asian Americans and other minorities are targeted in the Los Angeles race riots in 1992.

  Today: The Asian American Alliance reports that 40 percent of immigrants to the United States are Asian. There is controversy around the issue of immigration, and the Asian American Justice Center works with the U.S. government to solve the problems associated with illegal immigration.

- **1990s:** The Asian American presence in mainstream theater grows as more Asian American writers and actors are recognized for their talent. Criticism occurs over how Asian Americans are portrayed, and Caucasian actors are

still given Asian roles, such as in the 1991 Broadway production of *Miss Saigon*.

  Today: More opportunities are available for Asian American artists, but there is still debate over how Asian Americans are portrayed. Debate over assigning Asian roles to Caucasian actors, such as in the movie *The Last Airbender*, is still relevant.

- **1990s:** The cold war with the Soviet Union ends, but the United States becomes involved in the Gulf War in Iraq and other international conflicts. The World Trade Center is bombed in 1993 and severely damaged by Middle Eastern terrorists.

  Today: The terrorist attacks on September 11, 2001, lead to the war on terror. This is the first large-scale attack on American soil in decades. A military presence remains in Afghanistan, Iraq, and other countries as of late 2011.

Despite the end of the cold war, there were still international conflicts. Iraq invaded Kuwait in 1990, leading to the Gulf War, which ended in 1991. The United States was also involved in the Kosovo War from 1998 to 1999.

America, however, also saw its share of internal conflicts. People grew increasingly aware of social problems, such as gang violence and the AIDS epidemic. There were race riots in Los Angeles in 1992 after Los Angeles police officers were acquitted for beating Rodney King, an African American, during an arrest. In 1993, there was a violent conflict between the Bureau of Alcohol, Tobacco and Firearms and David Koresh's Branch Davidians in Waco, Texas, leading to an FBI raid and the deaths of most of the Branch Davidians. In 1995, Timothy McVeigh and Terry Nichols carried out the bombing of a federal building in Oklahoma City, Oklahoma, in response to the Waco incident. The United States hosted the Olympics in Atlanta in 1996, and a bomb went off in a

parking lot near the Olympic venues. The latter part of the decade saw a rise in school violence, and school shootings such as the 1999 Columbine massacre changed security on campuses.

Many of the teenagers and young adults of the decade (labeled Generation X) lived through the recession of the early 1980s and did not share the ideals of their parents. Relaxed clothing, body piercings, and tattoos became fashionable with young people, according to Peggy Whitely and others in *American Cultural History*. During this turbulent time, music evolved into different genres that reflected the attitudes of young listeners. In the 1990s, rock music branched out into different styles such as grunge, goth, punk, and indie. Rap, hip-hop, and dance music also gained popularity. More female musicians entered the music industry, having come out of the feminist movement. Ronnie's character, dress, and musical style reflect the attitude of rebellion and individuality seen in the rock artists of the decade.

Benjamin is a Caucasian Asian American. (3355m | Shutterstock.com)

Asian American Theater

Asian Americans have a long, complex history with theater and the performing arts. Although Asian Americans have been in the country for generations, they were not often represented in the arts. There were different reasons for this. As Misha Berson explains in *Between Worlds: Contemporary Asian-American Plays*, "Many immigrant parents (Asian and non-Asian) actively discouraged their first-generation children from having anything to do with 'show business.'" American theater was also different from the Asian art forms of epic and dance. Additionally, there were not many opportunities for Asian American actors and writers.

Before the 1950s, Asian Americans were relegated to Chinese opera, vaudeville acts called "chop suey," and B-movie stereotypes like Charlie Chan. Caucasian actors in makeup often played Asian American roles. The first mainstream play to depict Asian Americans was the 1958 Rodgers and Hammerstein musical *Flower*

Drum Song. The Chinese characters were bland stereotypes. A Caucasian actor played the main character, and all of the other actors cast were Japanese.

The civil rights movement of the 1960s led to the creation of the first Asian American theater, the East West Players, in 1965. Frank Chin and other writers formed the Asian American Theater Workshop in 1973. Chin wrote the first play by an Asian American to appear in New York, *The Year of the Dragon*, which debuted in 1977. Asian American theaters and workshops have provided opportunities for playwrights and actors, but Asian Americans have become more accepted in other venues. Hwang's first play, for example, was produced at Stanford.

Third World Liberation Front

Benjamin mentions the Third World Hunger Strike when he explains how the University of Wisconsin began its Asian American studies program. He is referring to the influence of the Third World Liberation Front, a multicultural group of students who demanded that the University of California at Berkeley teach the history and culture of different ethnic groups. The group was born out of the African American civil rights movement, as Diane C. Fujino points out in an article for *Social Justice*. The front was particularly active at Berkeley between 1967 and 1969 and organized sit-ins, hunger strikes, and other forms of social protests. Benjamin explains that students in the Midwest worked to add ethnic studies, particularly Asian studies, to curricula as well. The activities at Berkeley prompted students at other colleges to take similar actions; political activism was not limited to Berkeley.

The Third World Liberation Front at Berkeley originally demanded that a Third World College be created. The Third World College was not possible, according to the Web site for Berkeley's ethnic studies department, but other concessions were made to include the histories of marginalized groups. Initially, four programs were created, and a comparative ethnic studies program was added later. Similar actions were taken at colleges and universities across the country.

CRITICAL OVERVIEW

In 1988, William A. Henry III wrote in *Time* that Hwang "has the potential to become the first important dramatist of American public life since Arthur Miller, and maybe the best of them all." Hwang has been praised and criticized for his portrayals of Asian and Asian American characters. Amy Ling notes in *MELUS* that his first play, *F.O.B.*, effectively blends Chinese and American culture "to create a mixed genre, a kaleidoscopic, exciting, beautiful production." His Tony Award–winning play *M. Butterfly* earned high praise on Broadway. In his *New York Times* review, Frank Rich calls it a "visionary work that bridges the history and culture of two worlds."

Some critics, however, have argued that Hwang's plays help reinforce Asian stereotypes by exploring them. In *Theatre Journal*, Karen Shimakawa, for example, argues that *M. Butterfly* "contradicts the Orientalist stereotypes at the same time it reinscribes them." C. W. E. Bigsby

points out in *Modern American Drama, 1945–2000* that Hwang had a series of "poorly received" plays.

Trying to Find Chinatown and other plays written for the Humana Festival at the Actors Theatre of Louisville, however, had predominantly positive feedback. *Trying to Find Chinatown* is popular in class settings because it is short and contains themes that students from different cultures can easily understand.

Critical reviews of Hwang's recent works have been largely positive. Ben Brantley of the *New York Times* calls Hwang's 2007 production *Yellow Face* a "lively, messy and provocative cultural self-portrait of a play." *Chicago Tribune* reviewer Chris Jones writes that the 2011 release of Hwang's comedy *Chinglish* is "Hwang's best work since *M. Butterfly*." Regardless of how critics view Hwang, there is no denying his influence on American theater.

CRITICISM

April Paris

Paris is a freelance writer who has an extensive background working with literature and educational materials. In the following essay, she argues that in Trying to Find Chinatown, *both Ronnie and Benjamin claim the right to choose their own identities.*

David Henry Hwang's *Trying to Find Chinatown* addresses important social questions regarding ethnicity and personal identity. The play shows how easily people judge each other based solely on appearance. Although each character argues against racism and stereotyping, each one is guilty of making assumptions about the other based on his ethnicity. Ronnie and Benjamin argue about the significance of their ethnicity, but in reality, they both want the same thing: neither one wants to be defined by his physical appearance. They are incapable, however, of giving the acceptance that they desire. As each character attempts to free himself from the other's racial constraints, he is unwilling to release the other from his own. Benjamin expects Ronnie to live up to his Asian heritage, and Ronnie is reluctant to accept the Caucasian Benjamin as a Chinese American. By observing the intolerance of the characters, the audience can hopefully learn to give other people the

WHAT DO I READ NEXT?

- Oscar G. Brockett and Franklin J. Hildy's tenth edition of *History of the Theatre*, published in 2007, provides an overview of theater history across the globe. This is a useful reference book for anyone interested in learning about theatrical styles from different cultures.

- Sucheng Chan's *Asian Americans: An Interpretive History* ("Immigrant Heritage of America" series) examines the history of Asian Americans in the United States up through its publication in 1991. The volume does explore racial discrimination, but it also shows how individuals have been able to overcome their circumstances.

- Khaled Hosseini's 2003 novel *The Kite Runner* examines the relationship between family and culture in the modern immigration experience. Amir, who is a successful writer in California, tells the story of his childhood in Afghanistan and his immigration to the United States.

- *F.O.B. and Other Plays*, is a collection of Hwang's early works. Compiled by Hwang and Maxine Hong Kingston in 1990, these early plays show his evolution as a playwright over the years.

- Published in 2004, *Kira Kira* is Cynthia Kadohata's Newbery Award–winning young-adult novel that tells the story of Katie and her family as they move from a large Japanese community to a small town in Georgia where there are few Japanese

Americans. The book explores the themes of culture and stereotypes.

- George Ochoa's *America in the 1990s* ("Decades of American History" series) is a nonfiction book published in 2005 that explains events of the 1990s and their impact on society. It helps explain the setting and culture of *Trying to Find Chinatown*.

- *The Columbia Guide to Asian American History*, by Gary Y. Okihiro, was published in 2001. This nonfiction volume examines the history of Asian Americans over the past two hundred years and provides a valuable list of other helpful resources.

- Matt de la Peña's *Mexican WhiteBoy* was published in 2008. This young-adult novel explores the concept of ethnic identity and self-identity as Danny Lopez, a teenager who is both Mexican and Caucasian, learns how to find himself in both cultures.

- *Asian American Studies: A Reader*, edited by Min Song and Jean Yu-wen Shen Wu in 2000, is an anthology that explores the history, literature, and culture of Asian Americans from different countries. Students will find it a useful introduction to Asian American studies.

- *Version 3.0: Contemporary Asian American Plays*, edited by Chay Yew in 2011, is a collection of modern plays by different Asian American authors. The diverse subject matter of these plays shows the versatility of the Asian American experience.

---

freedom to be themselves and stop making quick judgments based on ethnicity or appearance.

In an interview for *US Asians*, Hwang admitted to personally identifying with the character Ronnie because Ronnie identifies himself by his profession as a musician; his actions define who he is more than his culture does. Ronnie is insulted by the idea that he should

know about everything about Chinese culture simply because he is Chinese American. His anger at Benjamin's request to give him directions to a Chinatown address reflects how sensitive Ronnie is on the subject. His reply to Benjamin indicates that other tourists have probably made the same assumptions that he accuses Benjamin of making: "What are you

RONNIE AND BENJAMIN ARGUE ABOUT THE SIGNIFICANCE OF THEIR ETHNICITY, BUT IN REALITY, THEY BOTH WANT THE SAME THING: NEITHER ONE WANTS TO BE DEFINED BY HIS PHYSICAL APPEARANCE."

gonna ask me next? Where you can find the best dim sum in the city?"

Ronnie's defensive attitude stems from his own conjectures concerning Benjamin. The fact that Benjamin is genetically Caucasian and from the Midwest leads Ronnie to automatically believe that the young tourist is judging him based on his race, but Ronnie is only partially correct in this assessment. Benjamin considers himself a Chinese American because he is the adopted son of Chinese Americans. He does not consider Ronnie foreign or racially different from himself. Benjamin does, however, assume that he shares a cultural connection with Ronnie because of his Chinese ancestry. He goes so far as to call Ronnie "Brother."

After trying to persuade Ronnie to accept him as a Chinese American, Benjamin becomes critical of Ronnie's self-identity. He simply assumes that Ronnie, and indeed all Asian Americans, would want to identify with their cultural heritage and be involved in the Asian American community. Benjamin places expectations on Ronnie because of his race despite his complaint that "a society wedded to racial constructs constantly forces me to explain my very existence." Benjamin demands that Ronnie conform to his definition of who and what a Chinese American should be.

Ronnie, however, tells Benjamin that Chinatown and its culture do not define him. Ronnie shatters Benjamin's expectations of him, and they argue about the importance of ethnicity in general. The argument between Ronnie and Benjamin echoes some of the criticism that Hwang has experienced from different Asian American critics. William A. Henry III points out common Asian American criticisms of

Hwang in his article for *Time*: "Those on the left see him as having sold out to white ways. Those on the right criticize him for airing the dirty linen of the Asian subculture." Benjamin calls Ronnie "one of those self-hating *assimilated* Chinese-Americans." In a moment of pure irony, a genetically Caucasian man accuses a genetically Asian man of being too white.

Ronnie has obviously heard criticism similar to Benjamin's before and responds in a way that mirrors the playwright's own feelings. He does not deny his ancestry, but he believes that identity is much more complex than his ethnicity. "Sure I'm Chinese. But folks like you act like that means something. Like, all of a sudden, you know who I am." He goes on to argue that identity is not "skin-deep." To Ronnie, his personal identity is much more complex than his ethnicity. Hwang's *American Theatre* interview with Misha Berson, quoted in C. W. E. Bigsby's *Modern American Drama, 1945–2000*, confirms the author's concept of identity: "The romanticization, the glorification of the root culture just seems very simplistic to me now.... Real life is far more complicated than that." Ronnie wants to be judged for what he does rather than what he looks like, but he simultaneously makes assumptions about people based solely on their appearance.

He accuses Benjamin of being an "ethnic fundamentalist," but a similar argument could be made about Ronnie. Earlier in the play, when Benjamin explains that he is Chinese American and that genes cannot limit his race, Ronnie is incredulous. Although Ronnie does not fully embrace ethnicity as his own identity, he has a problem with Benjamin going beyond his genetics in defining himself as Asian. He asks, "If genes don't determine race, what does?" The question indicates that Ronnie has issues with accepting Benjamin outside of his predetermined racial construct. Benjamin chooses to identify with the culture of his adopted parents rather than the culture of his birth parents. Still, Ronnie argues that genes do play a factor in your identity: "You can't just wake up and say 'Gee, I *feel* black today.'" Interestingly, Hwang does not share Ronnie's hesitation in accepting someone's self-determined ethnicity. When asked about *Trying to Find Chinatown* by *US Asians*, Hwang said if an "individual identified himself as an APA (Asian Pacific American), I would accept his self-categorization."

Ronnie finally seems to accept Benjamin's identity, but he does so in a sarcastic and dismissive way: "OK, knock yourself out, learn to use chopsticks, big deal." He appears to reverse his views on genetics when Benjamin questions Ronnie's identity in light of his Chinese heritage. He feels that Benjamin is limiting his identity to ethnicity and argues, "You go skin-deep, and call it a day." He calls Benjamin "folks like you" after Benjamin tries to help him find his Asian identity, referring to Chinese Americans who believe in the extreme importance of one's heritage. This indicates that Ronnie now recognizes Benjamin as a Chinese American, specifically one who disapproves of his personal choices.

The play ends with monologues from both characters. The monologues explain how each one views his personal identity. Ronnie's identity comes from his music. His alternative name is "The Bow Man," which refers to his skill playing the violin. Ronnie identifies with the musical subculture and tells Benjamin that he needs to "hear with [his] ears." As Ronnie holds his violin, he describes the history of the violin, jazz, and rock music. This history comprises his heroes and his personal mythology. As he plays his own composition, Ronnie asks, "Does it have to sound like Chinese opera before people like you decide I know who I am?" Again, he refers to the way that people attempt to categorize him based on his ethnicity.

Although jazz and rock musicians have contributed to Ronnie's style, Hwang's open-ended scene directions imply that his heritage may have, in part, shaped him: "As the music continues, does it slowly begin to reflect the influence of Chinese music?" While Ronnie's ethnicity does not define him, it remains part of him, and the music that he composes reflects that influence. Music with a Chinese influence would also provide the appropriate background for Benjamin's monologue.

Benjamin's monologue begins after he finds the tenement where his father was born. It is here where Benjamin reaffirms his identity as a Chinese American. He feels a sense of belonging in New York's Chinatown as he listens to different dialogues and smells the spices and food: "I felt immediately that I had entered a world where all things were finally familiar." As he sucks on a *hua-moi*, or sugared plum, Benjamin further establishes his identity by connecting with his father's spirit. He ends his monologue by

considering the "lost souls, denied this most important of revelations: to know who they truly are." This is the last line of the play and reinforces the central theme of self-identity. The characters ignore each other at the end as they engage in the activities that define them as individuals. Ronnie plays his violin while Benjamin sucks on a sugared plum and considers his father's family history.

Hwang wrote in "The Myth of Immutable Cultural Identity" that "we may be victims of racism but we may also be its perpetrators." Ronnie and Benjamin effectively illustrate this point as they present both the positive and negative views of ethnic identity. While each character fights against racial stereotypes, he enforces them on the other. Benjamin refuses to identify himself as white and immerses himself in his parents' culture. He is unwilling, however, to see beyond Ronnie's ethnicity. He practically demands that Ronnie have the same level of commitment to Chinese American culture that he has. Any deviation from these expectations automatically equals a sense of shame or self-loathing in Benjamin's mind. Ironically, Benjamin serves as the voice of other Asian Americans who disapprove of Ronnie's behavior.

Ronnie, who finds the idea of being defined by his ethnic appearance insulting, argues that genes define race and ethnic identity. He is, initially, unwilling to accept Benjamin as Chinese American because of his appearance. As each character searches for a personal identity within and beyond ethnicity, he misses the opportunity to accept others for who they are. The audience, however, can learn from the mistakes of Ronnie and Benjamin and discover how to give each other the same freedom that we seek. As Hwang explained to Howard Ho in an interview for *Asia Pacific Arts*, "I feel that ultimately we should be going for a society where people can be part of cultures that they're attracted to."

Source: April Paris, Critical Essay on *Trying to Find Chinatown*, in *Drama for Students*, Gale, Cengage Learning, 2012.

Bonnie Lyons

In the following excerpted interview, Lyons and Hwang examine the cultural forces that influence his playwriting.

IN A LOT OF MY PLAYS, INCLUDING *F.O.B.*,

A DESIRE TO BE UPWARDLY MOBILE DOVETAILS

WITH ABANDONMENT OF CULTURAL ROOTS, AND

SO DESIRE FOR STATUS TURNS OUT TO BE A

SIGNPOST OF GENERAL ABANDONMENT OF

PRINCIPLES."

Raised in a wealthy Los Angeles suburb by a first generation, Chinese American fundamentalist Christian family, David Henry Hwang wrote and directed his first play, *F.O.B.* (slang for "fresh off the boat"), which explores the tensions within and between recent and assimilated Chinese immigrants. *F.O.B.* won an Obie when it moved to New York in 1980 and since then many of Hwang's plays, including *The Dance of the Railroad* (1981), *Family Devotions* (1981), *The Sound of a Voice* (1983), *The House of Sleeping Beauties* (1983), *Rich Relations* (1986), *M. Butterfly* (1988), and *Bondage* (1992), have addressed issues of individual identity, group identity, and as he explains in this interview, fluidity of identity. Hwang's most famous play, his Tony Award–winning *M. Butterfly*, exposes Western attitudes toward Asia by deconstructing one of the most powerful and seductive images of the Orient, Puccini's opera *Madame Butterfly*. Far more than contributions to ethnic theater, Hwang's plays provide brilliant and complex analyses of the politics of race, gender, class, and sexuality.

The following interview took place on September 7, 1996, a few months before his most recent play, *Golden Child*, opened in New York.

BL: You've written in many styles and many kinds of plays. Do you see anything linking all your work? What about the issue of identity? Autonomy and community?

DHH: It's probably true that all my work in some sense confronts the issue of fluidity of identity and explores the idea that who we are is the result of circumstance, the result of things that are not necessarily inherent but instead come out of our interaction with our contacts. Many of the plays suggest that if the contact

changes, the individual becomes a different person, so to speak. Much of my work is about Asian-Americans, but even in the plays that aren't, you can trace that theme of fluidity of identity. The notion of community vs. the individual is interesting; it's not an idea I've really thought of before in relation to my work. As an Asian-American whose parents are immigrants, one of the dilemmas I feel most strongly in my own life is trying to figure out that issue. I was raised with a mentality that was concerned with group identity and about doing things for the group. But I was also raised as an American, which is essentially about individual identity. So I know that personally the issue of the individual vs. community has been a struggle for me, so it would not be surprising if that came through one way or another in my plays. But it's not actually a theme I've ever set down and traced through.

Do you tend to look back at your body of work and see aspects that you didn't see earlier?

If I compare writing plays to raising children (perhaps I'm inclined to that analogy since my wife and I have an infant!), I'd say that while you're in the process, there's not a lot of time or inclination to reflect on how your parenting style has changed while raising different children. Rather than look back, I'm more interested in focusing on what's next.

How does your interest in fluidity of identity relate to the current notion of the self as theater or self as performer?

In many of my plays there is at least one character playing some role, whether it's a predetermined role that exists in literature like Gallimard playing Pinkerton in *M. Butterfly* or Steve in *F.O.B.* playing Gwan Gung. The characters take on various mythologies and try to find themselves in relation to those mythologies, almost as if the search for identity is so difficult and complex that it is easier to hang your hat on a preestablished identity and try to have that become you or you become that thing.

Some critics have said that many of your plays can be seen as confrontations between two opposing forces or two opposing characters in which the seemingly weaker one triumphs. Do you agree?

Most of my plays do have an ideological duality to them; *M. Butterfly* has a series of them. *Golden Child*, my most recent play, is a real change—it's my first real ensemble play. But

I don't think it is always the case that my plays follow the pattern of the weaker one triumphing over the stronger like Pinter's servant becoming the master. In *The Dance and the Railroad*, for instance, it's more an issue of the two characters trading positions. But the two positions are not defined relative to one another in terms of power in the same way Pinkerton and Butterfly are defined. Switching places is a very common aspect of my work, and I've been conscious of that when I set out to write them. *Golden Child* develops the Chinese vs. Christian theme that was in *Family Devotions* and *Rich Relations*. I'm not entirely satisfied with those plays; this is my attempt to trace back the roots of the Chinese/Christian conflict. It's about my great-grandfather who converted to Christianity in China in the 20s and the effects of his conversion on his three wives. The conversion obviously created a conflict, so in a sense *Golden Child* ends up being an ensemble piece about the opposition between Christianity and ancestor worship in terms of dualities.

So the big change with the new play is that it's an ensemble piece?

I think there are four good female roles and one strong male role and that the characters are more developed than in my earlier plays. About four or five years ago I decided that I had developed my ability to write plays with interesting structures and interesting ideas but that I hadn't paid enough attention to the detail that gives characters full human richness. So with this play I consciously set out to be more Chekhovian.

Years ago you said, "I'm not interested in subtext or subtleties. I'm more interested in creating layers of a structure that have reverberations, one upon the other." Is your new play a kind of repudiation of that earlier position?

Yes, I'm trying to make up for what I now perceive as a certain deficiency in my work. I want to continue to grow as a writer, and character complexity is the area I have consciously been focusing on.

Elsewhere you've said that "except for a little more equal opportunities in theater" you were "loath to set out an aesthetic or political agenda" for other people. Do you have an aesthetic or political agenda for yourself?

Because I work with Asian themes and material I've become involved in various cultural

debates like the *Miss Saigon* controversy that you can call a debate over multiculturalism or political correctness, depending on how you look at it. I think I've probably become an old-fashioned 60s integrationist. I've become rather antinationalistic and antiseparatist in my middle age. I'm in a mixed marriage and I have a biracial child. In my earlier years I agreed with the nationalistic argument that one shouldn't be assimilated, that it is pathetic to try to mimic the white man. At this point in my life I would say that the argument against assimilation wrongly assumes that culture is static. It doesn't make any sense to me; culture is what people create at any given time, culture lives and changes. So I think it's accurate to say that while society is going to change me, I am also going to change society. In a model of dynamic assimilation we're constantly moving to create culture, and this I think essentially has been the history of America with the exception of certain groups that have not been included. To expand on the model of dynamic assimilation and to include all the excluded groups is perhaps my personal political agenda these days.

Your own political thinking has gone through three stages: an early, unquestioning assimilationist position, then a stage of isolationism and nationalism, and now your current thinking about dynamic assimilation. Do you think young writers have to repeat the same three stages?

People are always going to have to work through issues, the question is what they have to work through. And that has a lot to do with the particular context of your time. When I was in college it was the birth of the isolationist/nationalist period, and that was the car I got into to begin this journey. Nowadays it seems to me college-age people recognize the importance of race but also see that it is not the whole picture. That seems to me to be a different place from which to start than it was in the 70s.

A critic has said that you have "the potential to become the first important dramatist of American public life since Arthur Miller." Do you see yourself as a dramatist of American public life?

I don't see my work as consciously pursuing public themes like Tony Kushner's. I'm more caught up in my own perhaps self-indulgent personal journey. My own journey happens to have a public dimension to it in that it deals with some of the issues that the country is involved in right now. But I don't approach it from that direction; my personal concerns happen to spill over into the public arena.

The characters in your first play F.O.B. *were in their twenties, that is, around your own age. Has it gotten easier to write about older characters as you've gotten older yourself?*

Because my work is personal, the plays tend to focus on characters that are about the same age I am. Even the great-grandfather who is the center of *Golden Child* is about the age I am now. The real problem is different. For example at this point in my life, if someone asked me to work on something that involved high school kids I'd have a problem. I don't know what it is to be a high school kid in the 1990s.

Your plays have been quite sympathetic to women characters and aware of sexism and gender issues. Any idea why?

I grew up with a lot of strong women. One of the funny things about being Chinese-American is that everyone else believes that Asian women are submissive and defer to men. My mom and aunt were both exceptions to that, and if everybody is an exception, then clearly something is wrong with the general rule. Traditional Chinese culture is really oppressive towards women; at the same time, growing up in a Chinese family, experientially you feel you are part of a matriarchy. I don't think Chinese women are victimized by their oppressive circumstances; I think they figure out a way to survive powerfully within those conditions. I grew up in a fundamentalist background; it was something I had to rebel against and get out of. Because of that I have been really sensitive to any kind of fundamentalism and have a kind of instinctive recoil. It seemed to me that if I was going to write about Asian characters and try to affirm their value vis-à-vis white culture, I would have to look at the entire picture, which involved me as a man trying to regard women with the same respect I would like white culture to regard me. It has never made sense to me to separate racism and sexism. Maybe that's the explanation for what you flatteringly call my sensitivity to women and gender issues.

In The Dance and the Railroad *Lone says about the workers, "They are dead. Their muscles work only because the white man forces them. I live because I can still force my muscles to work for me." I thought that was a very powerful*

statement about the desire for autonomy and metaphorically spoke about many of your characters' desire to have their minds working for themselves rather than being controlled by cultural forces or other people's ideas.

The characters are often clinging for security to a certain identity based on a stereotype or literary archetype and simultaneously trying to go past them to something that is more personal and individual. In act 3, scene 2 of *M. Butterfly* when Song disrobes, Song is really trying to say, "Look at me, get past the make-up, get past the archetype. You were in love with me." Now Song is doing that for somewhat egotistical reasons, but he is trying to get to something personal.

Some of your plays such as Family Devotions *and* Rich Relations *seem concerned with American materialism and class. Do you consider class and materialism central concerns in your work?*

I think I've chickened out a bit on the issue of class and race. The English are obsessed with class; we Americans are obsessed with race. Race and racism have allowed white society to perceive itself as classless, because it is classless in relation to the black underclass.

As an Asian I've had to deal with racism, but it's qualitatively different from what African-Americans face; it's more like anti-Semitism. That puts me in a strange position in dealing with class, because as an Asian American I can't transcend my race but I can transcend my class. I am upwardly mobile in a way that is difficult for African-Americans. In *Rich Relations* and *Family Devotions* obsession with class status seems to be part of Christianity; the characters who are interested in Christianity are also very interested in material status. I think that functions to some extent as a critique of the religion and exposes some of the hypocrisy. In a lot of my plays, including *F.O.B.*, a desire to be upwardly mobile dovetails with abandonment of cultural roots, and so desire for status turns out to be a signpost of general abandonment of principles.

In one of your introductions you talk about F.O.B., The Dance and the Railroad, *and* Family Devotions *as your trilogy on Chinese-America. Do they represent three stages—*F.O.B. *as a repudiation of self-hatred;* The Dance and the Railroad *as a positive embrace of ignored aspects of a* *culture's history and cultural forms; and* Family Devotions *as a complicated grappling with the issues of the past, tradition, and remembering?*

I agree with your characterization of *F.O.B.* and *The Dance and the Railroad.* I'm not entirely happy with *Family Devotions.* It sets out some questions, but I don't know that it's really able to answer those questions, so I can't talk about it with the same assurance.

. . . Do the three generations of Family Devotions *represent your reading of the typical Chinese-American immigrant pattern—the first generation is tied to the past whether a false sense of the past or not, the second generation repudiates the past and accepts American values, and the third generation tries to come to some accommodation with the past and with America?*

I think that's a pretty general sociological pattern for most American immigrant groups, but my own personal pattern is more complicated because I am not actually third generation. Even though my parents were immigrants, they chose to assimilate to a large extent—so they were like the first two generations in a way. My whole personal political development is largely a reaction to the fact that my parents did assimilate. If they had been more traditional and tied to the root culture, I would probably be a completely different person.

In recent years you've written screen plays as well as plays. Can you talk a bit about your career as a screen writer?

Since *M. Butterfly* my play output has been quite slim. I think that's because I was living in L.A. and writing screen plays. Now that I'm living back in New York I feel like I have a better balance between my playwriting life and my screenwriting life.

. . . At one time you said that you felt pressure from both sides of the Asian-American community. From the right for airing dirty laundry in public, and from the left for being too "whited out." Has that changed over the years?

Pressure from the right has eased off because of the success of *M. Butterfly*—it's something like "If the whites like you, we have to like you too." Some leftist people have accused *M. Butterfly* of perpetuating negative notions about Asians, male emasculation for instance. Some people are unhappy that I have this Asian guy on stage in a dress for two acts. And

certainly I've been criticized for inappropriate use of Chinese mythology. Nobody likes to be criticized, but the debate over my plays seems to be useful for the Asian-American community. It allows Asian-American audiences to define themselves in relation to a particular artist by either rejecting or accepting that person's vision. They can say, "I like *The Joy Luck Club* but I don't like David's work" or vice versa. My work like Amy Tan's or Maxine's can be used as a way of thinking about Asian-American culture. And those kinds of comparisons are useful to undermine the notion of the Official Asian-American voice. . . .

Source: Bonnie Lyons, "Making His Muscles Work for Himself: An Interview with David Henry Hwang," in *Literary Review: An International Journal of Contemporary Writing*, Vol. 42, No. 2, 1999, pp. 230–44.

David Henry Hwang

In the following foreword, Hwang articulates his view of Asian Americans as evidenced in the content of his play Face Value.

> Glenn (a white supremacist): I'm not going to shoot anyone who's not Chinese! Now—
> Pastor (Glenn's follower): But maybe . . . I am?
> Glenn: No . . . race is—based on color—OK, well, maybe that can change, but—genetics! It's firmly rooted in genetics!
> Linda (an Asian American woman): Scientifically, that's not true either.
> Glenn: Then it's faith! As long as you believe you're white, you'll never turn Chinese!!

With my 1993 play *Face Value*, I sought to question the mythology of race. The plot hinges on two Asian Americans who go in white face to disrupt the opening night of a Broadway musical in which an Anglo actor has been cast as a Chinese. Obviously, this premise recalls the *Miss Saigon* casting controversy of 1990, when the British actor Jonathan Pryce was cast as a "Eurasian." In *Face Value*, matters are further complicated with the arrival of two white supremacists, who believe the lead actor actually *is* Asian, and kidnap him for stealing jobs from white people. The result is a farce of mistaken identity, suggesting that race is a construct that has no inherent meaning other than that which we choose to assign it.

Face Value was thoroughly panned in its Boston tryout, and closed on Broadway in previews. Though I concede the play had artistic flaws (I'm currently rewriting it for a future production), I also felt the material struck a chord

> AS WE MOVE TOWARD EMPOWERMENT,
HOWEVER, WE FIND OURSELVES FACING AN
ENTIRELY NEW SET OF REALITIES AND
RESPONSIBILITIES."

that made white Boston critics nervous and defensive.

The struggle to balance art, commerce, and political activism has preoccupied me throughout my career as a playwright and screenwriter. Some Asian Americans find my work progressive and ground-breaking, others accuse me of perpetuating stereotypes and selling out to the white establishment. My intention is to hold my art up as a mirror to my own evolution as an Asian American. "Evolution" is the operative word here. I do not believe that I will ever become a "fully actualized" Asian American, indeed such a state would be death, creatively and politically. The only constant in our lives is change, and as we approach the new challenges of the 1990s, we must reevaluate and question old assumptions to progressively harness such change.

As I consider the state of Asian America in the 1990s, many of the assumptions that had once seemed inviolate to me are open to reconsideration. Primary among these, in my view, is the desirability of nationalism and isolationism. At one point in my life, I wanted only to write about Asian Americans, work only with Asian American artists, and aim exclusively toward Asian American audiences. I don't mean in any way to disparage that period, for it helped to heal many of the wounds Euro-American racism had inflicted on me. Having passed through that period, however, it now seems to me imperative to engage society at large, to grapple with it, challenge it, bully and cajole it toward change.

As a native of Los Angeles, I felt the profound limitations of the isolationist/nationalist model during the 1992 uprising that followed the first Rodney King verdict. In the wake of simmering tensions between African American and Korean American communities in New York as well as Los Angeles, repressed

hostilities exploded into outright violence. One cannot help but feel that "multiculturalism," as defined during the late 1970s and 1980s, had not been sufficiently inclusive; it operated under the assumption of a Euro-majority nation. Under such circumstances, to "explain ourselves" seemed a pathetic attempt to win favor from whites, the very people who had taught us self-loathing.

In the 1990s, however, we see the rise of a new demographic reality: a nation with no majority race. Certainly whites continue to control a wildly disproportionate amount of power in the United States; that injustice has not changed. But the fact that people of color will soon numerically dominate this nation means that in "explaining ourselves," we are now building bridges to Latino, African, and Native Americans as well as those of European origin. The need to forge such bonds speaks to the explosion of another belief from an earlier decade: the myth of "Third World" solidarity. White America has traditionally set minorities to war against each other over scraps from its pie. As Anglos react to their shrinking powerbase, such battles will become fiercer and more commonplace. Thus, "multiculturalism," it seems to me, must evolve into a sort of "interculturalism" which attempts to outline commonalities as well as differences. For example, the question, "What do Asian American and African American cultures have in common?" has not yet been properly posed. In the past we may have replied, "We're all non-white." Such a reactionary response is of limited value as we approach the new millennium.

In fact, the 1990s seem to me to question the very definition of Asian America itself. With increasing bi- and multiracialism among our children, with the expanding diversity of Asian Americans among us, the boundaries of our community have become blurred. When a Caucasian woman who was adopted and raised by working-class *nisei* parents argues with a college student whose parents are wealthy Japanese diplomats, who is the "real" Asian American? Does it matter? Addressing such questions forces us to confront an issue many of us have sidestepped: class. To say that an upper-class Chinese-American corporate lawyer has more in common with a newly arrived Laotian cabdriver than, say, a wealthy African American Ivy Leaguer is a necessary lie. It is necessary because

Asians are perceived monolithically in America and must therefore band together. It is a lie, however, because it ignores the line that class cuts through our community and that many Asian Americans, myself included, have often swept under the carpet.

In *Face Value*, I attempted to deal with some of these ambiguities, the fact that definitions of race are meaningless, except as a reaction to the meaningless racism of society as a whole. I believe this message was particularly uncomfortable for whites. Some of my Anglo friends told me the first act of my play made them feel "guilty." One Caucasian woman leaving a performance was overheard saying, "How could they do a play about race in the 1990s and make it about Asians? Asians don't have any problems!" The notion that racial distinctions may be absurd can be disturbing even to Asian Americans. But, in my experience with *Face Value*, it is far more disturbing to whites. Unsurprising, since power in America has historically been distributed along racial lines, and Anglos now feel their influence diminishing before new demographic and cultural realities.

In fact, what most irks white America in the 1990s is that it is increasingly losing control of the political agenda. In the sixties and seventies, white liberalism could be dispensed from above, the majority magnanimously handing over a larger piece of the pie to powerless minorities. In the nineties, people of color are making our own rules, re-defining a national identity that certainly includes European Americans, but as only one element in a diverse picture. As we move toward empowerment, however, we find ourselves facing an entirely new set of realities and responsibilities. It is this evolution that makes the following essays so vital and necessary. In the 1990s, Asian American activism and resistance looks into the mirror, and discovers something frightening and wonderful: Our faces are changing.

Source: David Henry Hwang, Foreword to *The State of Asian America: Activism and Resistance in the 1990s*, edited by Karin Aguilar-San Juan, South End Press, 1994, pp. ix–xii.

SOURCES

"About the OBIES," in *Village Voice*, http://www.villagevoice.com/obies/about/ (accessed August 6, 2011).

"Asian Americans Taking a Stand on the Illegal Immigration Battle," in *Asian American Alliance*, http://www. asianamericanalliance.com/Immigration.html (accessed August 5, 2011).

"Assimilation," in *Merriam-Webster Dictionary*, http://www.merriam-webster.com/dictionary/assimilation (accessed August 3, 2011).

Berson, Misha, ed., *Between Worlds: Contemporary Asian-American Plays*, Theatre Communications Group, 1990, pp. ix–xiv.

——, "The Demon in David Hwang," in *Modern American Drama, 1945–2000*, by C. W. E. Bigsby, Cambridge University Press, 2000, p. 353; originally published in *American Theatre*, April 1998.

Bigsby, C. W. E., *Modern American Drama: 1945–2000*, Cambridge University Press, 2000, pp. 348–53.

Brantley, Ben, "A Satirical Spin on Stereotypes, at Home, Abroad and on Broadway," in *New York Times*, http://theater2.nytimes.com/2007/12/11/theater/reviews/11yellow.html?ref=davidhenryhwang (accessed August 2, 2011).

"Culture," in *Merriam-Webster Dictionary*, http://www.merriam-webster.com/dictionary/culture (accessed August 3, 2011).

"David Henry Hwang," in Steven Barclay Agency Web site, http://www.barclayagency.com/hwang.html (accessed August 2, 2011).

"David Henry Hwang Biography," in *Film Reference*, http://www.filmreference.com/film/89/David-Henry-Hwang.html (accessed August 3, 2011).

Fujino, Diane C., "Race, Place, Space, and Political Development: Japanese-American Radicalism in the 'Pre-Movement' 1960s," in *Social Justice*, Vol. 35, No. 2, 2008, pp. 57–79.

Henry, William A., III, "David Henry Hwang: When East and West Collide," in *Time*, August 14, 1989, http://www.time.com/time/magazine/article/0,9171,958369-1,00.html (accessed August 1, 2011).

"History," in *Department of Ethnic Studies*, College of Letters & Sciences, University of California, Berkeley Web site, http://ethnicstudies.berkeley.edu/history.php (accessed August 5, 2011).

Ho, Howard, "Multicultural Absurdities: An Interview with David Henry Hwang," in *Asia Pacific Arts*, http://asiapacificarts.usc.edu/w_apa/showarticle.aspx?articleID=16302&AspxAutoDetectCookieSupport=1 (accessed August 2, 2011).

Hwang, David Henry, "The Myth of Immutable Cultural Identity," in *Asian American Drama: 9 Plays from the Multiethnic Landscape*, edited by Brian Nelson, Applause Theatre, 1997, pp. vii–viii.

——, *Trying to Find Chinatown*, in *Trying to Find Chinatown: The Selected Plays*, Theatre Communications Group, 1999, pp. 281–94.

"International Adoption Facts," in Evan B. Donaldson Adoption Institute Web site, http://www.adoptioninstitute.org/FactOverview/international.html (accessed August 3, 2011).

"Irony," in *A Glossary of Literary Terms*, 7th ed., edited by M. H. Abrams, Harcourt Brace College Publishers, 1999, p. 137.

"It's OK to Be Wrong and/or It's OK to Be Hwang," in *US Asians*, http://usasians-articles.tripod.com/davidhenryhwang-theater.html (accessed August 1, 2011).

Jones, Chris, "Theatre Review: 'Chinglish,'" in *Chicago Tribune*, June 2011, http://leisureblogs.chicagotribune.com/the_theater_loop/2011/06/theater-review-chinglishthrough-july-24-at-the-goodman-theatre-170-n-dearborn-st-2-hours-25-minutes-25-.html (accessed August 2, 2011).

Ling, Amy, "A Perspective on Chinamerican Literature," in *MELUS*, Vol. 8, No. 2, Summer 1981, pp. 76–81.

"One-Act Play," in *A Handbook to Literature*, 9th ed., edited by William Harmon and Hugh Holman, Prentice Hall, 2003, p. 352.

Rich, Frank, "*M. Butterfly*: A Story of a Strange Love, Conflict and Betrayal," in *New York Times*, March 21, 1998, http://www.nytimes.com/1988/03/21/theater/review-theater-m-butterfly-a-story-of-a-strange-love-conflict-and-betrayal.html?src=pm (accessed August 1, 2011).

Shimakawa, Karen, "'Who's to Say?' or, Making Space for Gender and Ethnicity in *M. Butterfly*," in *Theatre Journal*, Vol. 45, No. 3, October 1993, pp. 349–62.

Whitley, Peggy, Becky Bradley, Bettye Sutton, and Sue Goodwin, "1990–1999," in *American Cultural History*, http://wwwappskc.lonestar.edu/popculture/decade90.html (accessed August 2, 2011).

FURTHER READING

Aguilar-San Juan, Karin, ed., *The State of Asian America: Activism and Resistance in the 1990s*, South End Press, 1994.
This book is a collection of essays written by activists and academics who explore political activism in the Asian American community from the 1960s through the 1990s. David Henry Hwang is the author of the foreword of this volume.

Han, Ara, and John Tsu, eds., *Asian American X: An Intersection of Twenty-first Century Asian American Voices*, University of Michigan Press, 2004.
This diverse collection of essays gives different perspectives about self-identity within the Asian American community, as well as the conflict between Asian and American cultures.

Huping, Ling, and Allan Austin, eds., *Asian American History and Culture: An Encyclopedia*, M. E. Sharpe, 2009.
This reference book explores different Asian cultures and their histories within the United States. The encyclopedia is a useful source for students interested in the events and people responsible for shaping Asian American history.

Hwang, David Henry, *Yellow Face*, Theatre Communications Group, 2009.
Hwang's comical play is an autobiographical mock documentary that examines American culture. The play takes up the issues of racism, ethnic identity, and self-identity that *Trying to Find Chinatown* addresses.

Kim Lee, Esther, *A History of Asian American Theatre*, Cambridge University Press, 2006.
This nonfiction text compiles source documents and interviews to provide an overview of Asian American theater from 1965 to 2005. Students will find the history of the evolution of Asian American theater insightful.

Na, An, *A Step from Heaven*, Front Street Imprint of Boyds Mills Press, 2001.
Na's young-adult fiction work won the Michael L. Printz award in 2002. It tells the story of a young girl, Ju, who emigrates with her family from Korea and faces the difficulties of living in a new country and between two different cultures.

Nguyen, Mimi Thi, and Thuy Linh Nguyen Tu, eds., *Alien Encounters: Popular Culture in Asian America*, Duke University Press, 2007.
The nonfiction essays in this volume examine the roles of Asian Americans in popular culture. This is one of the few books to provide in-depth analysis of pop culture in the United States and how Asian Americans have influenced it as both creators and consumers.

Wei, William, *The Asian American Movement*, Temple University Press, 1993.
Wei describes the events of the 1960s and 1970s and how they affected the Asian American movement in his nonfiction book. As the first book to explore the Asian American movement, it is a useful resource for anyone interested in this period of American history.

SUGGESTED SEARCH TERMS

David Henry Hwang

Trying to Find Chinatown

David Henry Hwang AND Trying to Find Chinatown

David Henry Hwang AND criticism

Trying to Find Chinatown AND criticism

Asian American theater

Asian American theater AND history

Asian American AND history

one-act play

America AND 1990s

David Henry Hwang AND Asian American theater

Workout

WENDY WASSERSTEIN

1995

Wendy Wasserstein's *Workout* (1995) is a one-act play, composed entirely of a monologue by a zealous workout instructor who jumps, thrusts, and twists her way through the script. The character is an exaggerated version of the modern "superwoman," the woman who has it all—career, husband, kids—and handles it all perfectly. Through the main character's mini-meltdown ("my moment"), Wasserstein illustrates the toll that maintaining such a persona exacts on a woman, even one as "super" as this one. Through this very brief play (the script is just a page and a half long), Wasserstein uses her trademark wit to satirize the unrealistic standards set for women in American society and illustrate the resentment these standards kindle in "ordinary" women who struggle to reach them. The play was published in Wasserstein's *Seven One-Act Plays* in 2000.

AUTHOR BIOGRAPHY

Wasserstein was born on October 18, 1950, in Brooklyn, New York, the youngest child of Morris and Lola Wasserstein. She grew up in Manhattan, where she attended private school. Her mother, a dancer, enrolled her in dance classes at the June Taylor School of Dance and after classes took her to the theater. Wasserstein's father was a successful manufacturer

Wendy Wasserstein *(AP Images)*

of textiles who invented the fabric known as velveteen.

Wasserstein enjoyed the theater but did not consider a career in writing until college. While attending Mount Holyoke College in Massachusetts, a girlfriend talked her into taking a class in playwriting. As Wasserstein described in an interview with Jackson Bryer in *Theatre History Studies*, "My friend Ruth said to me, 'Why don't we take playwriting at Smith and then we can go shopping?' I answered, 'I don't know much about fashion, but I'm sort of interested in shopping. This is a good idea.'" In the end, the class with Len Berkman resulted in a lot more than a fun shopping trip; it was the beginning of Wasserstein's career as a playwright.

Although Wasserstein proceeded to write, she did not immediately decide to become a playwright. She briefly enrolled in a dance program at California State University, Long Beach, but then returned to New York, where she attended City College and earned a master's degree in creative writing. A play she wrote during this time, *Any Woman Can't*, became Wasserstein's first produced play. The thrill of seeing her work performed on stage prompted Wasserstein to

apply to Yale Drama School. She was accepted and received her master of fine arts degree from Yale in 1976.

While at Yale, Wasserstein wrote the play *Uncommon Women and Others*, a one-act play she later expanded. The play was produced off-Broadway, receiving several awards. It was later produced as a telecast on PBS. The characters are all graduates of Mount Holyoke College who meet six years later for a reunion. Wasserstein's next play, *Isn't It Romantic* (1983), features similar characters but is set later in life.

Wasserstein received a grant from the British American Arts Association and moved to London, where she wrote her most acclaimed and well-known play, *The Heidi Chronicles*. *The Heidi Chronicles* spans over two decades in the life of its protagonist Heidi Holland. Heidi, committed to feminist ideals of independence and equality, watches with dismay as her friends, once also committed to such principles, gradually compromise to attract husbands and begin families. *The Heidi Chronicles* was a hit with both critics and audiences and won the Pulitzer Prize for Drama in 1989.

In 1992, Wasserstein's next play, *The Sisters Rosensweig*, was first performed at New York's Lincoln Center. In this play, Wasserstein tells of three sisters and the differing relationships they have with their Jewish faith. Favorably received, the play was nominated for a 1993 Tony Award. After *The Sisters Rosensweig*, Wasserstein wrote the children's book *Pamela's First Musical*, the story of a girl whose aunt takes her to see her first Broadway production.

In April 1997, Wasserstein's play *An American Daughter* was performed at the Lincoln Center. The play chronicles the difficulties of a female nominee for the office of surgeon general and the struggles of her friend, an African American Jewish oncologist. The nomination is sabotaged by a comment from the main character's own husband, who reveals that she ignored a summons for jury duty. The situation is similar to the real-life travails of attorney general nominee Zoe Baird. *An American Daughter*, a darker and more serious play for Wasserstein, met with mixed reviews and had a relatively short run. Later that same year, Wasserstein was dealt a personal blow when her older sister Sandra, a successful business executive, died of breast cancer.

Wasserstein wrote the screenplay to the movie *The Object of My Affection*, adapted from the novel by Stephen McCauley and released in 1998, after it took several years to find a studio interested in the quirky story of a pregnant woman in love with a gay man. The movie starred Jennifer Aniston and Paul Rudd but received mixed reviews.

Wasserstein dealt with a much more significant production in 1999: the birth of her daughter Lucy Jane. Wasserstein had been trying for eight years to have a child through fertility treatments. As she wrote in the *New Yorker*, "When I had first contemplated becoming a mother, I was involved with a man who I hoped would be the father. But when we stopped seeing each other I felt there was no reason to abandon the project." Unfortunately, Lucy Jane was three months premature and had a shaky beginning. However, ten weeks after her birth, she came home.

Motherhood did little to slow Wasserstein down. Her next play, *Old Money*, premiered in December 2000, and in 2001, a collection of her essays, *Shiksa Goddess; or, How I Spent My Forties*, was published. She wrote the play *Psyche in Love* for the 2003 Tribeca Theater Festival and another play, *Third*, in 2005.

In December 2005, Wasserstein was hospitalized. She had been suffering from lymphoma for some time, though few people outside a close circle of family and friends knew of her illness. She died on January 29, 2006. Her six-year-old daughter Lucy Jane went to live with her brother Bruce, a wealthy investment banker, and his wife. On January 30, 2006, the lights on Broadway were dimmed in Wasserstein's honor.

PLOT SUMMARY

As *Workout* opens, a woman in leotards enters a room, switches on music with a driving disco beat, and begins working out. As she exercises, she talks, alternating between stories of her own life and exhortations to her unseen class of fellow exercisers to "feel the burn" and "push it."

As the main character talks, it becomes clear that she is a rabid overachiever. She tells the audience that in the day to come, she will work on a novel, open a chain of appliance stores, begin learning ancient Egyptian, announce the publication of her new workout book, attend her

daughter's dance recital, support her husband in announcing his candidacy for governor, visit some friends, and feed her children an assortment of health foods ("I like to think about the brewer's yeast I gave my children for breakfast"). The character offers signs that, perhaps, her life is not as exemplary as it sounds. Her favorite time of day, she says, is when she takes a moment to sit down with her favorite quilt, take a deep breath, and cry.

The hostility that many women feel toward such unrealistic "superwomen" models is illustrated through the unseen character Denise. Throughout her monologue, the main character makes comments such as "Really squeeze it, Denise," and "Just keep bouncing, Denise." The audience learns how Denise really feels about her workout leader when the main character says, "Denise, put the gun down. Your life isn't my fault!"

After the character's brief moment of vulnerability, admitting to crying with her quilt, she composes herself and begins doing jumping jacks, encouraging Denise to jump along.

CHARACTERS

Children
The workout woman mentions her children, although they do not appear in the play. She does not speak about them affectionately. Instead, the brief references to them only reveal more of her efforts to be a superwoman. She attempts to be an ideal mother by feeding them health foods and allowing them to play only "nonviolent" games.

Denise
Denise is one of the unseen exercisers in the workout woman's class. Although Denise never actually appears onstage or speaks any lines in the play, the workout woman repeatedly addresses her, encouraging her to push harder and feel the burn. When the frenzied main character tells Denise to "put the gun down," the audience recognizes Denise as a normal, "non-superwoman" who resents the unrealistic standards set by the overachieving workout leader.

Husband

The workout woman's husband (who does not appear onstage) is also an overachiever who is planning to announce his candidacy for governor that evening and also helps prepare dinner while simultaneously "debating with Connie Chung and the six o'clock news team by satellite."

Woman

The main character, whose name is never mentioned, is the workout leader who takes the stage at the opening of Wasserstein's one-act play. She is an overachieving superwoman, the epitome of the woman who "has it all"—vibrant career, happy family, creative pursuits, enriching relationships. Her frenetic pace (both during the workout and in her life) and near-pathological need to achieve more and more exemplify the insecurities felt by women of the era. The heirs to the rights and privileges secured by the feminist movement, women of the 1980s and 1990s felt the obligation to have it all, even if it meant sacrificing the time and leisure to enjoy it. The sad revelation that her "very favorite part of the day" is curling up in a quilt and weeping "just a little" demonstrates that her superwoman persona is just a facade and that she is prey to the same human foibles as any normal woman.

THEMES

Overachievement

The main character in *Workout* is an exaggerated portrayal of the classic overachiever. Many women in the 1980s and 1990s, aware of the sacrifices and struggles made by women in previous generations to open new avenues of career opportunity for women, felt the obligation to take advantage of every such opportunity. At the same time, by the 1990s women had begun to question the viability of "having it all": many working women were stressed, overscheduled, and exhausted and came to resent the unrealistic "superwoman" standard. The language used by the workout woman—"Don't give in. Push it. Push it"—illustrates the relentless pressure these women put on themselves.

The main character of *Workout* is a cartoon of the superwoman, a woman who does it all, has it all, and juggles it all with aplomb. However, Wasserstein shows the audience that the workout woman's outer image does not match her internal emotions. Once her children are outside playing and her husband is occupied making dinner and debating by satellite, she finally has time for "my moment," when she wraps herself in a favorite quilt and cries.

Repression and Control

The repression of emotion is a necessary component of the overachieving superwoman lifestyle. Fully experiencing emotions requires time for reflection, something not in the overachiever's schedule (except during her "moment"). The relentlessly cheery facade presented by the play's main character must give way at some point; as she gets closer to her "favorite time of the day," her exercise instructions reflect her anticipation: "Feel it all over," she says, "get ready to release."

The "release" is necessary because all genuine feeling has been repressed the rest of the day. She is allowed just this one moment to "feel it all over" and release the white-knuckled grip she has over her emotions. Then she picks herself up and begins again: "Now we're ready for fifty more jumping jacks." Even sex with her husband, normally an experience of emotional release, is something to be controlled: "It's better now than when we first got married because we're organized," she says. This statement expresses the ludicrous nature of the superwoman's quest for control, as it presents what should be an entirely sensual and emotional experience as something that can be "organized."

The workout woman's need for control extends beyond her own emotions, however. She is opening a chain of appliance stores because "it's so important that we take charge of our own appliances." She even controls regional infrastructure: "Last week I restored the electricity for the city of Fresno." It is not enough for her to star in the story of Nefertiti, she is "also producing, directing, writing, editing, and distributing."

Even the workout woman's children are spoken of in terms of her control over them, not in terms of affection. She speaks of the foods they are not allowed ("the words 'french toast' are never used in our house") and the restricted activities they are allowed ("nonviolent baseball with radishes and zucchinis"). The daughter's dance recital is not experienced as a moment of pride in her accomplishment but is usurped as an opportunity for the father to announce his candidacy for governor.

TOPICS FOR FURTHER STUDY

- Write a version of *Workout* that includes other characters onstage (Denise, for instance, or the main character's husband). With your classmates, perform this play, or have someone film it. Does the addition of other characters improve the play? Change the meaning? Post your film to YouTube or your Web page and invite classmates to discuss the previous questions.

- Research the feminist movement in the United States and create a PowerPoint presentation on its history. Include an interactive time line of important events and people with links to major event Web sites, brief descriptions of the major figures involved (Betty Friedan and Gloria Steinem, for instance), and why they are significant to the movement.

- Watch the DVD of the 1978 television production of *Uncommon Women and Others*, one of Wasserstein's early plays, starring Meryl Streep, Jill Eikenberry, and Swoosie Kurtz. What similar themes do you see in both this play and *Workout*? What major differences? Write an essay comparing the two plays.

- Read the young-adult novel *Good Enough* (2008), by Paula Yoo. Can you relate to the main character's situation? Why do you think her parents put so much pressure on her to succeed? Are there any positive results to this pressure? Stage a debate in your classroom. Have half the class argue in favor of such high expectations and standards and the other half argue against. Research, using online and print sources, the effects of parental pressure on teens for information to use in your debate.

- Wasserstein's Tony Award for best play in 1989 was notable because few women playwrights have won this award. Go to the Web site for the Tony Awards, and determine the number of women playwrights and directors who have been nominated for this award in the past ten years. Make a bar graph showing the number of women nominated in each year, versus the number of men. Then create a second graph showing the number of female winners versus female nominees.

- *Workout* is a short one-act play, consisting of a spoken monologue by one character. How would you turn it into a musical? Team up with some of your classmates to write a song the main character would sing about her busy day. Perform your song for your class, or record it and put it on a CD.

Resentment

For the majority of this brief play, the workout woman comes across not as a real woman but as an unattainable ideal. This superwoman ideal presented to women by the media, and sometimes by other women, stirred resentment in those women who struggled and failed to achieve it. For instance, one perfume commercial from the 1980s featured a model-perfect woman singing, "I can bring home the bacon, fry it up in a pan, and never let you forget you're a man."

The resentment felt toward those who espoused this ideal is personified in the play by Denise. About halfway through the workout, shortly after the main character announces her intention to learn ancient Egyptian so she can star in, write, direct, produce, and distribute the movie about Nefertiti, she pauses in her directions to say, "Denise, put the gun down. Your life isn't my fault!" Some might argue that in perpetuating the ideal of the flawless overachieving woman, Denise's struggles may very well be her fault, at least in part.

The main character in Workout *performs amazing feats while working out.* (*Benis Arapovic /*
Shutterstock.com)

STYLE

Hyperbole
Much of the humor of *Workout* is achieved through hyperbole (exaggeration used for effect). Obviously no woman (no human being at all, for that matter) could fit all the activities the main character describes into a single day. Likewise, the breadth of the main character's pursuits would stagger even Leonardo da Vinci: novel writing, screenwriting, acting, producing, directing, business management, and electrical engineering.

Just as the main character's overachievement is exaggerated, Denise's reaction—actually threatening her with a gun—is also extreme. The main character handles Denise's threat casually, telling her, "Be angry with your buttocks."

Metaphor
The main character's intense workout is a metaphor for the way she lives her life: pushing,

squeezing, and punishing herself ("I felt the burn that time"). She sublimates any feelings of anger or frustration into her exercise. She says at the opening of the play that "buttock tucks" are her favorite exercise, and many of the times she refers to the exercises she is doing, they are buttocks-related: she goes from buttock tucks to fire hydrant lifts, another buttocks-related exercise, and tells Denise, "Be angry with your buttocks." This parallels the character's anal-retentive nature (an obsessive need for order and control).

Monologue
A monologue is defined as a long speech by one actor in a play, as opposed to dialogue, which refers to a conversation between two or more characters. *Workout* is a very brief one-act play that is entirely a monologue by the main character. Although she refers to other characters throughout her speech—her husband, her children, Denise—she is the only character seen or heard throughout. This technique fits in well with the main character's need for control; if other characters were permitted to speak, this would require relinquishing control of the topic, if only for a moment.

HISTORICAL CONTEXT

Women's Issues
The early 1990s were an eventful time for women's issues. In 1991, the subject of sexual harassment in the workplace took center stage when Clarence Thomas, a nominee for Supreme Court associate justice, was accused of sexually harassing Anita Hill, a lawyer who had worked for him in the 1980s. Over three days of televised hearings, Hill described various inappropriate comments made to her by Thomas, including descriptions of scenes from pornographic films. Thomas flatly denied all accusations. Despite Hill's testimony, Thomas was confirmed as an associate justice of the Supreme Court. The case, however, was instrumental in raising awareness of sexual harassment, and afterward, more women were willing to come forward and speak out against such behavior by employers or co-workers.

Also in 1991, Susan Faludi's controversial book *Backlash: The Undeclared War against American Women* asserted that opponents of feminism were exploiting reports of career women's alleged

COMPARE
&
CONTRAST

- **1990s:** The deadline for ratification of the equal rights amendment, to grant women equality of rights under the law, was in 1982. The amendment was still three states short when the deadline passed. The amendment continues to be introduced in every session of Congress. The ratification of the Twenty-seventh Amendment (an amendment concerning changes in Congressional pay) in 1992, after 203 years (it was first approved by Congress in 1789), gives women new hope and a precedent for extending the ratification period.

  Today: In March 2011, Representative Tammy Baldwin of Wisconsin introduces a resolution that would remove the ratification deadline and make the equal rights amendment part of the Constitution as soon as three more states ratify.

- **1990s:** The main character in *Workout* leads a group workout class, popularized in the 1980s (the Jane Fonda workout video of 1982 being the first huge exercise video hit). In the 1990s, home-exercise equipment such as treadmills and rowing machines increase in popularity, while step aerobics adds a new twist to group exercise classes.

  Today: Yoga has reached new heights of popularity, as has Zumba, a dance-exercise class featuring Latin dance music. Boot-camp-style exercise classes are also popular.

- **1990s:** In 1989, Wendy Wasserstein is the first solo woman to win the Tony Award for Best Play with *The Heidi Chronicles*. In the entire decade of the 1990s, just one woman wins this award: Yasmina Reza, for her play *Art*.

  Today: Through 2011, only one more woman wins a Tony Award for Best Play, and it is once again Yasmina Reza, for her play *God of Carnage* (2009).

---

difficulties—burnout, loneliness, infertility—as evidence that feminism was a failed experiment that should be shelved. Faludi argued that it was the lack of equality that persisted, not the achievement of equality, that was responsible for more of these problems. (For instance, she says that women "still shoulder 70 percent of the household duties," despite men's claims that they were pitching in.)

In 1992, Vice President Dan Quayle attacked TV sitcom character Murphy Brown for becoming a single mother, claiming that she was "mocking the importance of fathers." Feminists protested the characterization, and future first lady Hillary Clinton asserted that the statement was proof the Bush administration was out of touch with America. The incident had special relevance for Wasserstein, who had already begun the first in a long series of fertility treatments that would result in her becoming a single mother in 1999.

In 1993, the Clinton administration began lifting restrictions on abortion counseling and funding and also established the Family Leave Act, which allows workers to take up to twelve weeks of unpaid leave after the birth of a child or to care for an ill family member. In 1994, Clinton signed the Violence against Women Act, providing increased resources for the prosecution of violent crimes against women, harsher penalties for these crimes, and increased funding for battered women's shelters.

The Workout Craze
Although Wasserstein's play was first performed in the 1990s, the workout craze was born in the 1980s, beginning with Jane Fonda's book titled simply *Workout* in 1981. At about the same time, *The Richard Simmons Show* offered support and diet tips for overweight viewers. Phrases such as "feel the burn" (coined by Fonda) became part of everyday conversation. Workout wear such

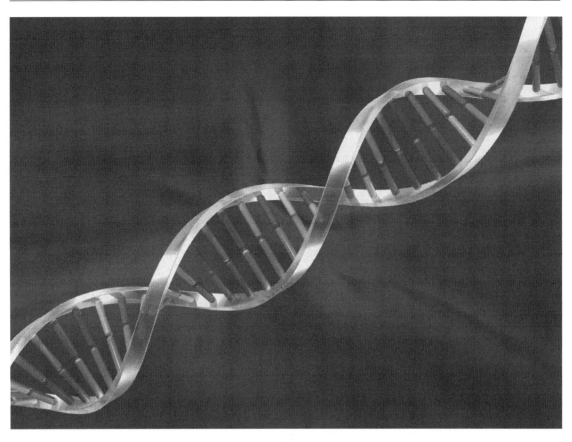

The woman unravels the secret of DNA while working out. (*Paul Fleet | Shutterstock.com*)

as leg warmers, cropped sweatshirts, and leotards became fashion trends for everyone, not just exercisers. Olivia Newton-John jumped on the workout bandwagon with her hit "Let's Get Physical"; the video for the song featured Newton-John in a headband and leotard at a health club.

The craze was not as intense during the 1990s, but new workouts kept Americans interested. Step aerobics, Tae-Bo, and strength-training workouts with free weights all became popular in the 1990s. Nike's "Just Do It" ads, which began in the late 1980s, became an iconic campaign for the company during the 1990s, selling millions of dollars' worth of exercise apparel.

CRITICAL OVERVIEW

Most of Wasserstein's plays were popular successes, although not all were received as well critically as commercially. Audiences loved the humor and warmth of her plays, and in her

lifetime Wasserstein became one of those rare playwrights that the American public actually knows by name. In fact, the commercial success of her plays became a sticking point with some critics, who complained that Wasserstein's plays were lacking in substance, like sitcoms for the stage, and did little to challenge the audience intellectually. In a particularly harsh review of *The Heidi Chronicles* in the *Nation*, Moira Hodgson states, "It's a harmless play, perfect for Broadway since there is nothing in it to offend deeply or shake up the house, but just enough to make the audience feel knowing." She asserts that Wasserstein's Pulitzer Prize for the play is evidence of "the sorry state of Broadway this year."

Wasserstein's breakthrough play was 1977's *Uncommon Women and Others*. Depicting frustration among women who feel that the promises of feminism have not been fulfilled, the play deals with subjects rarely seen on the stage at that time and featured an almost entirely female cast. The play attracted a lot of attention and many favorable reviews, including one from John Simon of *New York* magazine, a critic with a reputation for harsh reviews. 1983's *Isn't It Romantic* received some favorable notice, although it suffered, some critics felt, from a lack of substance. In a later favorable review of *The Heidi Chronicles* in the *New Republic*, Robert Brustein remarks, "*The Heidi Chronicles* is not yet the work of a mature playwright, but it is a giant step beyond the cute dating games and Jewish mother jokes of *Isn't It Romantic*."

The Heidi Chronicles, of course, was an enormous hit, winning both the Pulitzer Prize and the Tony Award for Best Play in 1989. Reviews were largely positive. Many critics felt Wasserstein matured even further with her 1991 play *The Sisters Rosensweig*, the story of three sisters coping with their Jewish heritage. David Sheward, in *Back Stage*, calls it "the perfect example of a production which is both popular and intelligent." The play was nominated for the Tony Award for Best Play. *Workout* was written between *The Sisters Rosensweig* and *An American Daughter* and features the familiar Wasserstein theme of the pressures placed on women by unrealistic standards.

Reviews of Wasserstein's plays *An American Daughter* (1997) and *Old Money* (2000) were mixed because neither had lengthy runs. Her last play, *Third*, was reviewed positively by many critics. David Rooney, in *Daily Variety*, calls the play "her best in years," and Ben Brantley of the *New York Times*, while describing the play as "imbalanced," also notes, "Yet *Third* exhales a gentle breath of autumn, a rueful awareness of death and of seasons past, that makes it impossible to dismiss as a quick-sketch comedy of political manners."

Overall, though some critics felt that Wasserstein sometimes sacrificed substance for laughs and entertainment, most believed that her work continued to mature throughout her career. Her ability to bring women's issues to the stage with both respect and humor made her a pioneer in American theater.

CRITICISM

Laura Beth Pryor

Pryor is a professional writer with more than twenty-five years of experience and a special interest in literature. In the following essay, she examines how the main character's exercise regimen in Wasserstein's play Workout *parallels her daily life in its movements and pace and how she represents an impossible ideal that women strive for, to their own detriment.*

The one-act play *Workout*, by Wendy Wasserstein, deals with some of the same themes featured in her longer plays: the new opportunities available to women as a result of feminism, the restrictions still placed upon them, and the difficulties of establishing one's identity within these shifting paradigms. The main character, with her ridiculous daily schedule, seems to feel that because these new avenues are open to her, she must take advantage of all of them; the buffet of choices is not all you *want* to eat, but all you *can* eat.

Such is the dilemma of Wasserstein's "new woman." If a woman chooses to stay home with her children, is she showing disrespect for the struggles of feminists before her? If she decides to forgo a family and concentrate on career, is she perpetuating the stereotype of the mannish, driven, hard-edged feminist? If she does both, can she do both as well as she would like? The superwoman can.

Although women of the twenty-first century are finding more realistic ways to navigate these challenges (telecommuting is on the rise, flex-time is offered at more and more companies, and day-care options have improved since the writing of Wasserstein's play), the image of the superwoman still persists. The term is very appropriate for Wasserstein's protagonist here, because she spends the entire play flexing her muscles and building her strength. She rattles off items on her to-do list alternately with exercises in the workout. Her life *is* a workout, and what she does to her body throughout the play parallels the way she lives her life.

She begins by taking a deep breath. As she allows herself this moment to breathe, she says, "Mmmmmm," as though a deep breath is a treat on par with a bar of chocolate or a massage. This moment of relaxation is short-lived, however, because she then launches into buttock tucks. Most of the workout is devoted to buttocks exercises; she directs her followers to "squeeze" five times in the next two short paragraphs. She is holding in, contracting, controlling. The words "tuck" and "tuck in" are used several times throughout the play.

WHAT DO I READ NEXT?

- Julie Salamon's 2011 biography *Wendy and the Lost Boys: The Uncommon Life of Wendy Wasserstein* illuminates Wasserstein's personal life: her eccentric family, her large circle of friends, her difficulties in romance, and her decision to become a single mother. The biography includes much new information, including Wasserstein's 1999 discovery of an institutionalized older brother, Abner, who she never knew existed.

- The book *The Heidi Chronicles, and Other Plays* (1990) includes not only the Pulitzer Prize–winning work but also her earlier plays *Uncommon Women and Others* and *Isn't It Romantic*. The plays are introduced by André Bishop, Wasserstein's close friend and the former artistic director of Playwrights Horizons, which produced many of Wasserstein's plays, including her first, *Any Woman Can't*.

- *Jar the Floor*, a 1999 play by Cheryl West, is a comedy/drama that profiles four generations of women in an African American family. The character Maydee is intent on academic achievement, while her mother is bent on finding a man (or several). The play demonstrates how views of race and gender have evolved over time and shows the difficulties some women have in coping with these changes.

- Wasserstein cites Anton Chekhov as her favorite playwright. She wrote a stage adaptation of one of his short stories, "The Man in a Case." *The Complete Plays: Anton Chekhov*, translated by Laurence Senelick, was published in 2005 and provides many annotations to enhance readers' understanding of the plays.

- Playwright Suzan Lori-Parks, like Wasserstein, graduated from Mount Holyoke College, and she cites Wasserstein as an inspiration. She won the Pulitzer Prize in 2002 for her play *Topdog/Underdog*. The script of this play was published that year.

- Wasserstein's only novel, *Elements of Style*, was published posthumously in 2006. A satirical look at New York society after the terrorist attacks of September 11, 2001, it tells the story of pediatrician Frankie Weissman and her shallow, self-obsessed acquaintances. Although reviews of the novel were lukewarm, Wasserstein's trademark wit makes it an entertaining read.

- Wasserstein had a long-standing relationship with Playwrights Horizons theater in New York. They produced many of her plays, including *The Heidi Chronicles*. A more recent collection of the theater's plays is available in the book *Plays from Playwrights Horizons*, Vol. 2 (2010). The volume contains six plays, including *The Moment When*, a play by Wasserstein's friend James Lapine.

- Kit Reed's satirical novel *Thinner Than Thou* (2005) tells of a future society so obsessed with perfecting one's physical appearance that it has become a religion, presided over by Reverend Earl, who advocates dietary supplements, punishing exercise regimens, and cosmetic surgery. Underweight or overweight individuals are sent to "convents" for intervention, which are more like concentration camps. When their anorexic sister Annie is sent to one, teen twin brothers Betz and Danny set out on a rescue mission. The novel won a 2005 Alex Award.

- The 2001 young-adult novel *Homeless Bird*, by Gloria Whelan, tells the story of Koly, an Indian girl whose parents arrange a marriage for her at thirteen and send her to live with her husband and in-laws in a faraway village. Her husband dies shortly after, and Koly is abandoned by her in-laws and left to fend for herself in the city of Vrindavan. Her struggle and eventual triumph in a male-dominated society underscore the novel's feminist theme.

The woman opens a chain of department stores while working out. *(Felix Mizioznikov / Shutterstock.com)*

It is interesting to note that these terms can have homey, positive connotations: we can tuck in to a good meal or get tucked into bed. However, the character uses them only to indicate physical contraction. At no point does the character describe any warmth or genuine emotion within her family unit. The activities the whole family does together—the dance recital and a visit to a friend's house—sound more like a political agenda than fun outings (the dance recital is used to announce the main character's latest book and her husband's candidacy for governor). If her workout is literally anal, the rest of her life is figuratively so.

The workout is also highly masochistic. She tells her unseen fellow exercisers, "make the muscles burn," "don't give in," and "push it." When Denise threatens her with a gun, she instructs her to turn her anger on herself: "Be angry with your buttocks. Let them know your feelings." In other words, squeeze the emotion back in and repress it.

Her admonition to Denise to "put the gun down" is one of the punch lines of the

play. The humor stems not just from the hyperbole represented by Denise's extreme reaction but also from the recognition and empathy the women in the audience will inevitably feel toward Denise. Women everywhere have met at least one alleged superwoman, Wasserstein knew, and perhaps even wanted to threaten her. In contrast to all the tucking, squeezing, and contracting, Denise posits the explosion and catharsis of a gunshot, a release in the imagination, though tragic for everyone if realized.

The self-abuse perpetuated by the main character (and recommended to Denise) throughout the workout persists in the rest of her day. She runs five miles at four-thirty in the morning. After her children have been fed brewer's yeast, she does the workout, after which she will work on a novel for two hours, open a chain of appliance stores, and then learn ancient Egyptian. One can almost imagine that she cheers herself on throughout the day the same way she does during the workout, telling herself to push it and not give in.

She began the workout by taking a deep breath; the next time she mentions breathing again is when she allows herself "my moment," around six o'clock in the evening. She sits down with her favorite quilt, "And I take a deep breath, and I cry . . . But just a little." At first, it appears the character has finally cracked and shown us some humanity. However, note how closely the "moment" resembles one more exercise: she takes a deep breath (just as she did before the buttock tucks), performs the exercise (crying), takes one more breath, and launches into fifty jumping jacks. Even her meltdown is carefully programmed; to quote the overachieving coed in Rob Reiner's 1985 film *The Sure Thing*, "Spontaneity has its time and place."

The *Workout* character's lack of warmth and emotion when speaking about her family, her nonstop movement, and her precise programming of her day make her seem more like a robot than a superwoman, and that is the point: this is not a real woman. This is the ideal held up for women by a conflict of generations. For Wasserstein's generation, this conflict was a defining one. Their mothers encouraged marriage and children; their feminist peers pushed for equality and high-powered careers. The effort to "have it all" pushed women to take on a load that was often, ironically, far heavier than men's, not equal to it. Like her carefully programmed life, the main character's husband, who makes half the dinner and shares half the spotlight, was (and, some would argue, still is) an elusive ideal. For millions of American women, the attempt to become the superwoman ideal is simply not working out.

Source: Laura Beth Pryor, Critical Essay on *Workout*, in *Drama for Students*, Gale, Cengage Learning, 2012.

Stephen J. Whitfield

In the following excerpt, Whitfield investigates the thematic significance of Jewish identity in Wasserstein's major plays, comparing the verisimilitude of their autobiographical dimensions with the collective experience of Jewish Americans.

Born in Brooklyn on 18 October 1950, Wendy Wasserstein has drawn on features of her family life to inspire all four of her major plays. She was the youngest of four children, including two other daughters—one of whom became a high executive at Citicorp, while another married a doctor and raised three children. "She did the best," the "bachelor girl" playwright once sardonically announced,

> THE PLAYS OF WENDY WASSERSTEIN ARE POPULATED WITH JEWS BUT ARE EVEN MORE FREQUENTLY FILLED WITH WOMEN."

in comparing the siblings whose lives would be transmuted into *The Sisters Rosensweig* (1992). The Wassersteins themselves were very solidly and successfully middle class—"a sort of traditional family, eccentric but traditional," the playwright later recalled. Morris was a successful textile manufacturer; and among the fabrics that he patented was velveteen, which Holly Kaplan's father has invented, according to *Uncommon Women and Others* (177). In *Isn't It Romantic* (1983), Janie Blumberg's father manufactures stationery. Wendy Wasserstein's bohemian and liberated mother, Lola, was a devotee of theater and of dance classes, which Tasha Blumberg, the aerobically inclined mother in *Isn't It Romantic*, continues to take.

When Wendy was twelve, the family moved to the Upper East Side of Manhattan, reinforcing the expectations of high academic and professional achievement with the presumptions of a future combining maternity and domesticity. Beginning at the Yeshivah of Flatbush, she hit the ground running, and already by the second grade, she realized that she was funny: "I was good company . . . an elementary school Falstaff." She graduated from the Calhoun School and went on to major in history, class of 1971, at Mount Holyoke College. (The eponymous protagonist of *The Heidi Chronicles* [1988] becomes an art historian.) Wasserstein got a master's degree in creative writing at City University of New York in 1973 (studying with playwright Israel Horovitz and novelist Joseph Heller) and then studied at the Yale School of Drama, from which she received a Master of Fine Arts in 1976. Drawing on her undergraduate experience, she had submitted a thesis play at Yale, a one-act acorn that would grow into the Obie-winning oak entitled *Uncommon Women and Others*. Moving back to New York City, which is where the two young women in *Isn't It Romantic* inaugurate a similar stage in their lives, Wasserstein was soon recognized as among the most sparkling playwrights of her generation.

Luck did not hurt: when *Uncommon Women* was elevated to the Public Broadcasting System's Great Performances series a year after opening at the Marymount Manhattan Theatre, her Yale classmate Meryl Streep played Leilah, replacing another soon-to-be legendary actress, Glenn Close. Talent mattered too: Wasserstein's first play won the *Village Voice* Off-Broadway Award; her third to be staged won the Pulitzer Prize for drama and the Antoinette Perry (or Tony) Award, plus honors from the New York Drama Critics' Circle, the Outer Critics Circle and the Drama Desk—just about everything but the Heisman Trophy. *The Heidi Chronicles* was also her first to prove Broadway-bound. And when *The Sisters Rosensweig* opened there, the character of Sara Goode was played by Jane Alexander, whom President Clinton soon appointed to head the National Endowment for the Arts. Though Wasserstein's total output has not been huge (and has inspired little extensive scholarly criticism), she merits attention for another reason besides the recognition and acclaim that her gifts have elicited. Perhaps more than in the work of any major American dramatist of this century (even including Clifford Odets, for example), the vicissitudes of Jewish identity should be included among the primary themes of Wendy Wasserstein's work.

Its ethnicity is not emphatic. The author herself has not advanced a communal agenda, nor does she insist that her dramaturgy be used for Jewish purposes. She has not assigned herself the responsibility of speaking for the Jewish people—or even necessarily *to* it. The first noteworthy Jewish American leader, Mordecai Manuel Noah, also happened to be a playwright, yet his melodramas were not overtly placed in the service of Jewish interests and were even barren of Jewish characters. Although Wasserstein may not have Jewish audiences (or critics) primarily in mind and does not wish to be judged primarily as a Jewish playwright, neither is she Lillian Hellman, whose plays betray no obvious signs of Jewish origins, idiom, or purposes. Wasserstein is also a product of the *Zeitgeist*. Born five years after Bess Myerson of the Sholom Aleichem Cooperatives Houses of the Bronx had become Miss America, Wasserstein is heir to the legitimation

of ethnicity—including Jewish ethnicity. Born five years before Will Herbert's *Protestant Catholic Jew* (1955) inflated his own Judaism to tripartite status as one of the nation's three presumptive if unofficial faiths, she grew up in an era of frictionless integration into American society, in which its Jews did not feel in *galut*.

Unlike the bleak desperation that animates the Berger family during the Great Depression in Odets' *Awake and Sing!* (1935), unlike the rapacity that motivates the Hubbards in the ruined, post-Reconstruction South of Hellman's *The Little Foxes* (1939), Wasserstein's Jews need not worry where the next meal is coming from or how best to stay ahead in an ambience haunted by the experience and the fear of poverty. In the Group Theatre of the 1930s, the edgy characters played by Jules Garfinkle (a.k.a. John Garfield) faced the problem of how to make money. For Larry "the Liquidator" Garfinkle (called Larry Garfield in the movie version of Jerry Sterner's 1989 play, *Other People's Money*), the problem was how to make his money make money. The trajectory is thus sharply upward, from the working-class Bergers to the lower-middle-class Lomans in *Death of a Salesman* (1949) to the sisters Rosensweig, whose roles in life range from an international banker based in London to an international travel writer living in exotic Asia to a leader of the Temple Beth El women's auxiliary. Its Sisterhood may not be powerful, but at least it is based in posh Newton, Massachusetts. Theatrical history thus reflects the gravity-defying upward mobility of American Jewry. It is almost too good to be true that the only brother to the sisters Wasserstein became a Master of the Universe, using other people's money to specialize in leveraged buyouts. In 1988 Bruce Wasserstein was an architect of the $25 billion RJR-Nabisco merger that capped the buccaneering, let's-make-a-deal capitalism of the Reagan era. No wonder his sister's characters, who have attended the best schools and have inherited the comforts of young urban professionals, come out ahead of the progeny of the Bergers and the Lomans.

The accident of birth also made Wasserstein the beneficiary of enhanced sensitivity to the female condition and to the injustices of gender. "I can't understand not being a feminist," she admits, having turned thirteen when Betty Friedan's *The Feminine Mystique* was published and "the problem with no name" specified. If the perplexities of peoplehood do not spring to mind when considering the thrust of Wasserstein's work, that is because, though multifarious identities need not be incompatible, she writes far more directly as a woman than as a Jew. The perspective that her plays offer is feminist (and not Judaic); and in them feminist speeches are given even to men like the faux furrier Mervyn Kant, who punctures the cliché that Jews Do Not Drink: "I think it's a myth made up by our mothers to persuade innocent women that Jewish men make superior husbands. In other words, it's worth it to put up with my crankiness, my hypochondria, my opinions on world problems, because I don't drink." Some evidence suggests that Heidi Holland herself is not Jewish, and the contemporary challenge that she faces would be familiar to virtually any young professional American woman thrown off balance when the rules of engagement keep shifting.

Though the social problem that *Isn't It Romantic* addresses is defined with a New York Jewish accent, Janie is not exactly looking (in theater critic Carolyn Clay's pun) for Mr. Good Bar Mitzvah. The protagonist is deft at playing back the mixed messages that Tasha Blumberg, who has already inhaled the air of emancipation even as she was raising Janie, has communicated to her daughter. "Mother, think about it," Janie announces. "Did you teach me to marry a nice Jewish doctor and make chicken for him? You order up breakfast from a Greek coffee shop every morning. Did you teach me to go to law school and wear gray suits at a job that I sort of like every day from nine to eight? You run out of here in leg warmers and tank tops to dancing school. Did you teach me to compromise and lie to the man I live with and say I love you when I wasn't sure? You live with your partner; you walk Dad to work every morning." It is hard not to detect here a note of envy for an earlier generation that at its luckiest managed to combine intimacy with security and to reconcile expanded vocational and avocational possibilities with conventional middle-class comforts.

The plays of Wendy Wasserstein are populated with Jews but are even more frequently filled with women. Her oeuvre has constituted, according to one critic, "comedies of feminine survival that explore the ambiguous effectiveness of the women's movement during the past quarter of a century. Using the pattern of her own life as a paradigm, she has dramatized with a sharply satiric wit the problematic intersection of the individual experience and the collective feminist ideology that would explain and transform it." Though the special burden of expectation for women to marry is a recurrent theme in Wasserstein's work, an even more special burden that is placed upon Jewish women privileges marriage within the faith. World Jewry is not even a blip on the demographic screen, no bigger than the margin of statistical error in the Chinese census; and continuity requires philoprogenitiveness and endogamy, values that are not quintessential either to the ideology of feminism or to the pleasures of romantic love. The pressure comes from parents who do not want their own child to be *aharon ha-aharonim* (the last of the last), a terminal Jew; and that anxiety is erratically conveyed, with mixed and uncertain results.

Thus Holly Kaplan phones (or pretends to phone) a young Jewish physician in Minneapolis, but fears to establish such a connection even as she seeks it. Thus Janie Blumberg is comically fixed up with a Russian cab driver. And isn't it romantic that Heidi Holland, though probably not Jewish (but not specified as a gentile either), cannot escape from the clutches of Scoop Rosenbaum, even at the raucous Jewish wedding that ratifies his compromising decision to marry someone else. In the controversial climax to the play, Heidi has adopted a daughter and become a single mother. Thus Gorgeous Teitelbaum wishes that her sister's loneliness might be cured, and tells Tess Goode, her niece: "I always said to mother, if only Sara would meet a furrier or a dentist." The fifty-four-year-old Sara is permitted to wonder whether her one-night-stand gentleman caller merits a longer commitment. "You're just like all the other men I went to high school with," she tells Merv Kant. "You're smart, you're a good provider, you read *The Times* every day, you started running at fifty to recapture your youth, you worry a little too much about your health, you thought about having affairs, but you never actually did it, and now that she's departed, your late wife, Roslyn, is a saint." Men like him and Scoop Rosenbaum and perhaps even the unseen and unheard Doctor Mark Silverstein have the right business and professional credentials to embody success and security. But they also threaten the autonomy and egalitarianism that a feminist vision encourages and an expanding economy sanctions.

The ideology of the women's movement can collide with the dictates of patriarchal Judaism. Though Wasserstein's writing betrays no awareness of such tension, not even her most militant sisters would confuse a conclave of the Union for Traditional Conservative Judaism with the boys-will-be-boys raunchiness of a Tailhook convention. Religious faith and ritual have nevertheless become diminished in the observably Jewish but unobservant families that are dissected in Wasserstein's satire. Few can be classified among the "good ga davened," whom Holly Kaplan, the lone Jew among the *femmes savantes* at Mount Holyoke, defines as "those who davened or prayed right. Girls who good ga davened did well. They marry doctors and go to Bermuda for Memorial Day weekends. These girls are also doctors but they only work part-time because of their three musically inclined children, and weekly brownstone restorations." It is akin to "a 'did well' list published annually, in New York, Winnetka, and Beverly Hills, and distributed on High Holy Days...." Upward mobility and a securely middle-class status have become so central to the ethos of American Jewry that even a far less savvy undergraduate than Holly cannot fail to notice.

Of course anti-Semitism has not entirely evaporated; when the uncommon women play conjugal games with one another, Samantha Stewart realizes that she cannot "marry" Holly because back home "there would be a problem at the club." But secularism has narrowed the gap between Jew and gentile. Holly would never concur with an earlier Jew, a Venetian who declines an invitation to dine with Bassanio: "I will buy with you, sell with you, talk with you, walk with you... but I will not eat with you, drink with you, nor pray with you" (*The Merchant of Venice* 1.3). Secularism is also powered by the sexual revolution. Filling a diaphragm with Orthocreme, Holly announces: "Now...whenever I see a boy with a yarmulke, I think he has a diaphragm on his head. I shouldn't have said that. I'll be struck down by a burning bush."

Wanting to connect (by telephone) with Dr. Mark Silverstein, whom she had met at the Fogg Museum the previous summer, Holly reveals through her monologue her insecurity, her smarts, her uncertainties, her taste in culture,

and her yearning for both interdependence and intimacy, as well as her need to forge her own future. In 1978, six years after graduating, Holly is unmarried, her life in limbo. "I haven't made any specific choices," she tells her college friends. "My parents used to call me three times a week at seven A.M. to ask me, 'Are you thin, are you married to a root-canal man, are *you* a root-canal man?' And I'd hang up and wonder how much longer I was going to be in 'transition.'" She may still be unattached because of the historical factors beyond her control. To find the right (Jewish) man has become dicey. Jet planes had already made Miami no harder to visit than the Catskills, narrowing the distinctive sites for dating and mating, as Kutsher's came to be considered a last resort. Reluctant to compromise, Holly may have to remain single. Refusing to compromise, her creator forfeited a chance to bring *Uncommon Women and Others* to Broadway. One producer considered the play "too wistful" and proposed a revised ending: "When everyone asks Holly, 'What's new with you?' she should pull out a diamond ring and say, 'Guess what? I'm going to marry Dr. Mark Silverstein.'" The playwright herself thought: "Well, she'd have to have a lobotomy, and I'd have to have a lobotomy too."...

Source: Stephen J. Whitfield, "Wendy Wasserstein and the Crisis of (Jewish) Identity," in *Daughters of Valor: Contemporary Jewish American Women Writers*, edited by Jay L. Halio and Ben Siegel, University of Delaware Press, 1997, pp. 226–46.

SOURCES

Bigsby, Christopher, "Wendy Wasserstein," in *Contemporary American Playwrights*, Cambridge University Press, 1999, pp. 330–68.

Brantley, Ben, "As Feminism Ages, Uncertainty Still Wins," Review of *Third*, in *New York Times*, October 25, 2005.

Brustein, Robert, Review of *The Heidi Chronicles*, in *New Republic*, April 17, 1989, p. 32.

Bryer, Jackson, "An Uncommon Woman: An Interview with Wendy Wasserstein," in *Theatre History Studies*, Vol. 29, 2009, p. 1.

"The Clinton Presidency: Timeline of Major Actions," in *Welcome to the White House*, http://clinton5.nara.gov/WH/Accomplishments/eightyears-02.html (accessed August 25, 2011).

"Dan Quayle vs. Murphy Brown," in *Time*, June 1, 1992, http://www.time.com/time/magazine/article/0,9171, 975627,00.html (accessed August 25, 2011).

"The Equal Rights Amendment," in *Equal Rights Amendment Home Page*, http://www.equalrightsamendment .org (accessed August 25, 2011).

Faludi, Susan, *Backlash: The Undeclared War against American Women*, Anchor Books, 1991, pp. ix–xxiii.

Foley, Michele, "Fitness Trends for 2011," in *FitSugar*, American College of Sports Medicine, November 2, 2010, http://www.fitsugar.com/2011-Fitness-Trends-From-American-College-Sports-Medicine-11764553 (accessed August 25, 2011).

Hodgson, Moira, Review of *The Heidi Chronicles*, in *Nation*, May 1, 1989, p. 605.

Isherwood, Charles, "Wendy Wasserstein Dies at 55; Her Plays Spoke to a Generation," in *New York Times*, January 31, 2006, http://www.nytimes.com/2006/01/ 31/theater/31wasserstein.html?ref = wendywasserstein (accessed August 25, 2011).

"Memorable Quotes for *The Sure Thing*," in *Internet Movie Database*, http://www.imdb.com/title/tt0090103/ quotes (accessed September 1, 2011).

"Mini-Case Study: Nike's 'Just Do It' Campaign," in *Center for Applied Research*, www.cfar.com/Documents/ nikecmp.pdf (accessed August 25, 2011).

"9 Trends of the 1990s," in *CBS Money Library*, http:// findarticles.com/p/articles/mi_m0675/is_2_18/ai_60589328/ (accessed August 25, 2011).

"1990s: The Fighting Back Decade," in *Elizabeth A. Sackler Center for Feminist Art: Feminist Timeline*, http://www.brooklynmuseum.org/eascfa/feminist_timeline/ 1990.php (accessed August 25, 2011).

"Retro Enjoli Commercial," in *YouTube*, http://www. youtube.com/watch?v = 4X4MwbVf5OA (accessed September 1, 2011).

Rooney, David, Review of *Third*, in *Daily Variety*, October 25, 2005, p. 4.

Salamon, Julie, *Wendy and the Lost Boys: The Uncommon Life of Wendy Wasserstein*, Penguin, 2011, pp. 167–85, 413–27.

Sheward, David, Review of *The Sisters Rosensweig*, in *Back Stage*, April 16, 1993, p. 21.

Simon, John, Review of *Uncommon Women and Others*, in *New York*, Vol. 27, No. 44, November 7, 1994, p. 102.

Smolowe, Jill, "Sex, Lies and Politics: He Said, She Said," in *Time*, October 21, 1991, http://www.time.com/ time/magazine/article/0,9171,974096-1,00.html (accessed August 25, 2011).

"Tony Awards," in *Internet Broadway Database*, http:// www.ibdb.com/advSearchAwards.php (accessed August 25, 2011).

Wasserstein, Wendy, "Complications," in *New Yorker*, February 21, 2000, http://www.newyorker.com/archive/ 2000/02/21/2000_02_21_087_TNY_LIBRY_000020250? printable = true&currentPage = 1 (accessed August 25, 2011).

———, *Workout*, in *Seven One-Act Plays*, Dramatists Play Service, 2000, pp. 43–44.

FURTHER READING

Balakian, Jan, *Reading the Plays of Wendy Wasserstein*, Applause Theater and Cinema Books, 2010.

> Balakian takes a historical approach to analyzing Wasserstein's plays, viewing them as cultural artifacts shaped by the times in which they were written. Using this frame of reference, she analyzes how feminism, politics, and Wasserstein's Jewish heritage informed the plots and characterization of her major plays.

Ciociola, Gail, *Wendy Wasserstein: Dramatizing Women, Their Choices and Their Boundaries*, McFarland, 1998.

> Ciociola looks at five of Wasserstein's plays from a feminist perspective, showing how feminist political views shaped and changed her characters, even though Wasserstein herself declined to define herself as a feminist.

Durang, Christopher, *27 Short Plays*, Smith and Kraus, 1995.

> Durang was a close friend of Wasserstein's. She met him at Yale Drama School and later based a character in *The Heidi Chronicles* on him. Durang is known for his absurd comedies, such as *Sister Mary Ignatius Explains It All for You* (included in this collection). The volume also contains the one-act play *Medea*, a collaboration between Wasserstein and Durang.

Hellman, Lillian, *An Unfinished Woman: A Memoir*, Back Bay Books, 1999.

> Wasserstein was an admirer of Hellman and her work, and she wrote the foreword to this edition of Hellman's 1969 autobiography, for which Hellman won the National Book Award (though some critics claim she invented many of the supposedly autobiographical tales). Hellman, who wrote the plays *The Children's Hour* and *The Little Foxes* (among many others), was also the longtime lover of author Dashiell Hammett.

Murphy, Brenda, ed., *The Cambridge Companion to American Women Playwrights*, Cambridge University Press, 1999.

> This volume of scholarly essays covers a wide range of playwrights, beginning with a section on "pioneers" such as Mercy Otis Warren and Susannah Haswell Rowson, both born in the eighteenth century; progressing through

early-twentieth-century playwrights such as Frances Hodgson Burnett, Rachel Crothers, and Lillian Hellman; and finally featuring Wendy Wasserstein, among others, in the section titled "New Feminists."

Wasserstein, Wendy, *Shiksa Goddess; or, How I Spent My Forties*, Knopf, 2001.

This collection of essays, many of which first appeared in magazines such as the *New Yorker* and *Harper's Bazaar*, covers a wide range of topics, from an interview with Bette Midler to the death of Wasserstein's older sister Sandra. It also includes a piece that chronicles the difficult conception and premature birth of her daughter Lucy Jane.

SUGGESTED SEARCH TERMS

Wendy Wasserstein

Wendy Wasserstein AND Workout

Wendy Wasserstein AND feminism

Wendy Wasserstein AND Playwrights Horizons

Wendy Wasserstein AND Broadway

Wendy Wasserstein AND Yale Drama

Wendy Wasserstein AND Christopher Durang

Wendy Wasserstein AND Pulitzer Prize

Wendy Wasserstein AND Lucy Jane

Wendy Wasserstein AND drama

Glossary of Literary Terms

A

Abstract: Used as a noun, the term refers to a short summary or outline of a longer work. As an adjective applied to writing or literary works, abstract refers to words or phrases that name things not knowable through the five senses. Examples of abstracts include the *Cliffs Notes* summaries of major literary works. Examples of abstract terms or concepts include "idea," "guilt" "honesty," and "loyalty."

Absurd, Theater of the: See *Theater of the Absurd*

Absurdism: See *Theater of the Absurd*

Act: A major section of a play. Acts are divided into varying numbers of shorter scenes. From ancient times to the nineteenth century plays were generally constructed of five acts, but modern works typically consist of one, two, or three acts. Examples of five-act plays include the works of Sophocles and Shakespeare, while the plays of Arthur Miller commonly have a three-act structure.

Acto: A one-act Chicano theater piece developed out of collective improvisation. *Actos* were performed by members of Luis Valdez's Teatro Campesino in California during the mid-1960s.

Aestheticism: A literary and artistic movement of the nineteenth century. Followers of the movement believed that art should not be mixed with social, political, or moral teaching.

The statement "art for art's sake" is a good summary of aestheticism. The movement had its roots in France, but it gained widespread importance in England in the last half of the nineteenth century, where it helped change the Victorian practice of including moral lessons in literature. Oscar Wilde is one of the best-known "aesthetes" of the late nineteenth century.

Age of Johnson: The period in English literature between 1750 and 1798, named after the most prominent literary figure of the age, Samuel Johnson. Works written during this time are noted for their emphasis on "sensibility," or emotional quality. These works formed a transition between the rational works of the Age of Reason, or Neoclassical period, and the emphasis on individual feelings and responses of the Romantic period. Significant writers during the Age of Johnson included the novelists Ann Radcliffe and Henry Mackenzie, dramatists Richard Sheridan and Oliver Goldsmith, and poets William Collins and Thomas Gray. Also known as Age of Sensibility

Age of Reason: See *Neoclassicism*

Age of Sensibility: See *Age of Johnson*

Alexandrine Meter: See *Meter*

Allegory: A narrative technique in which characters representing things or abstract ideas are used to convey a message or teach a lesson.

Allegory is typically used to teach moral, ethical, or religious lessons but is sometimes used for satiric or political purposes. Examples of allegorical works include Edmund Spenser's *The Faerie Queene* and John Bunyan's *The Pilgrim's Progress.*

Allusion: A reference to a familiar literary or historical person or event, used to make an idea more easily understood. For example, describing someone as a "Romeo" makes an allusion to William Shakespeare's famous young lover in *Romeo and Juliet.*

Amerind Literature: The writing and oral traditions of Native Americans. Native American literature was originally passed on by word of mouth, so it consisted largely of stories and events that were easily memorized. Amerind prose is often rhythmic like poetry because it was recited to the beat of a ceremonial drum. Examples of Amerind literature include the autobiographical *Black Elk Speaks,* the works of N. Scott Momaday, James Welch, and Craig Lee Strete, and the poetry of Luci Tapahonso.

Analogy: A comparison of two things made to explain something unfamiliar through its similarities to something familiar, or to prove one point based on the acceptedness of another. Similes and metaphors are types of analogies. Analogies often take the form of an extended simile, as in William Blake's aphorism: "As the caterpillar chooses the fairest leaves to lay her eggs on, so the priest lays his curse on the fairest joys."

Angry Young Men: A group of British writers of the 1950s whose work expressed bitterness and disillusionment with society. Common to their work is an anti-hero who rebels against a corrupt social order and strives for personal integrity. The term has been used to describe Kingsley Amis, John Osborne, Colin Wilson, John Wain, and others.

Antagonist: The major character in a narrative or drama who works against the hero or protagonist. An example of an evil antagonist is Richard Lovelace in Samuel Richardson's *Clarissa,* while a virtuous antagonist is Macduff in William Shakespeare's *Macbeth.*

Anthropomorphism: The presentation of animals or objects in human shape or with human characteristics. The term is derived from the Greek word for "human form." The fables of Aesop, the animated films of Walt Disney, and Richard Adams's *Watership Down* feature anthropomorphic characters.

Anti-hero: A central character in a work of literature who lacks traditional heroic qualities such as courage, physical prowess, and fortitude. Anti-heros typically distrust conventional values and are unable to commit themselves to any ideals. They generally feel helpless in a world over which they have no control. Anti-heroes usually accept, and often celebrate, their positions as social outcasts. A well-known anti-hero is Yossarian in Joseph Heller's novel *Catch-22.*

Antimasque: See *Masque*

Antithesis: The antithesis of something is its direct opposite. In literature, the use of antithesis as a figure of speech results in two statements that show a contrast through the balancing of two opposite ideas. Technically, it is the second portion of the statement that is defined as the "antithesis"; the first portion is the "thesis." An example of antithesis is found in the following portion of Abraham Lincoln's "Gettysburg Address"; notice the opposition between the verbs "remember" and "forget" and the phrases "what we say" and "what they did": "The world will little note nor long remember what we say here, but it can never forget what they did here."

Apocrypha: Writings tentatively attributed to an author but not proven or universally accepted to be their works. The term was originally applied to certain books of the Bible that were not considered inspired and so were not included in the "sacred canon." Geoffrey Chaucer, William Shakespeare, Thomas Kyd, Thomas Middleton, and John Marston all have apocrypha. Apocryphal books of the Bible include the Old Testament's Book of Enoch and New Testament's Gospel of Peter.

Apollonian and Dionysian: The two impulses believed to guide authors of dramatic tragedy. The Apollonian impulse is named after Apollo, the Greek god of light and beauty and the symbol of intellectual order. The Dionysian impulse is named after Dionysus, the Greek god of wine and the symbol of the unrestrained forces of nature. The Apollonian impulse is to create a rational, harmonious world, while the Dionysian is to express the irrational forces of personality. Friedrich Nietzche uses these terms in *The Birth of Tragedy* to designate contrasting elements in Greek tragedy.

Apostrophe: A statement, question, or request addressed to an inanimate object or concept or to a nonexistent or absent person. Requests for inspiration from the muses in poetry are examples of apostrophe, as is Marc Antony's address to Caesar's corpse in William Shakespeare's *Julius Caesar*: "O, pardon me, thou bleeding piece of earth, That I am meek and gentle with these butchers!... Woe to the hand that shed this costly blood!..."

Archetype: The word archetype is commonly used to describe an original pattern or model from which all other things of the same kind are made. This term was introduced to literary criticism from the psychology of Carl Jung. It expresses Jung's theory that behind every person's "unconscious," or repressed memories of the past, lies the "collective unconscious" of the human race: memories of the countless typical experiences of our ancestors. These memories are said to prompt illogical associations that trigger powerful emotions in the reader. Often, the emotional process is primitive, even primordial. Archetypes are the literary images that grow out of the "collective unconscious." They appear in literature as incidents and plots that repeat basic patterns of life. They may also appear as stereotyped characters. Examples of literary archetypes include themes such as birth and death and characters such as the Earth Mother.

Argument: The argument of a work is the author's subject matter or principal idea. Examples of defined "argument" portions of works include John Milton's *Arguments* to each of the books of *Paradise Lost* and the "Argument" to Robert Herrick's *Hesperides*.

Aristotelian Criticism: Specifically, the method of evaluating and analyzing tragedy formulated by the Greek philosopher Aristotle in his *Poetics*. More generally, the term indicates any form of criticism that follows Aristotle's views. Aristotelian criticism focuses on the form and logical structure of a work, apart from its historical or social context, in contrast to "Platonic Criticism," which stresses the usefulness of art. Adherents of New

Criticism including John Crowe Ransom and Cleanth Brooks utilize and value the basic ideas of Aristotelian criticism for textual analysis.

Art for Art's Sake: See *Aestheticism*

Aside: A comment made by a stage performer that is intended to be heard by the audience but supposedly not by other characters. Eugene O'Neill's *Strange Interlude* is an extended use of the aside in modern theater.

Audience: The people for whom a piece of literature is written. Authors usually write with a certain audience in mind, for example, children, members of a religious or ethnic group, or colleagues in a professional field. The term "audience" also applies to the people who gather to see or hear any performance, including plays, poetry readings, speeches, and concerts. Jane Austen's parody of the gothic novel, *Northanger Abbey*, was originally intended for (and also pokes fun at) an audience of young and avid female gothic novel readers.

Avant-garde: A French term meaning "vanguard." It is used in literary criticism to describe new writing that rejects traditional approaches to literature in favor of innovations in style or content. Twentieth-century examples of the literary *avant-garde* include the Black Mountain School of poets, the Bloomsbury Group, and the Beat Movement.

B

Ballad: A short poem that tells a simple story and has a repeated refrain. Ballads were originally intended to be sung. Early ballads, known as folk ballads, were passed down through generations, so their authors are often unknown. Later ballads composed by known authors are called literary ballads. An example of an anonymous folk ballad is "Edward," which dates from the Middle Ages. Samuel Taylor Coleridge's "The Rime of the Ancient Mariner" and John Keats's "La Belle Dame sans Merci" are examples of literary ballads.

Baroque: A term used in literary criticism to describe literature that is complex or ornate in style or diction. Baroque works typically express tension, anxiety, and violent emotion. The term "Baroque Age" designates a period in Western European literature beginning in the late sixteenth century and ending about one hundred years later. Works of this period often mirror the qualities of works more generally associated with the label "baroque" and sometimes feature elaborate conceits. Examples of Baroque works include John Lyly's *Euphues: The Anatomy of Wit,* Luis de Gongora's *Soledads,* and William Shakespeare's *As You Like It.*

Baroque Age: See *Baroque*

Baroque Period: See *Baroque*

Beat Generation: See *Beat Movement*

Beat Movement: A period featuring a group of American poets and novelists of the 1950s and 1960s—including Jack Kerouac, Allen Ginsberg, Gregory Corso, William S. Burroughs, and Lawrence Ferlinghetti—who rejected established social and literary values. Using such techniques as stream of consciousness writing and jazz-influenced free verse and focusing on unusual or abnormal states of mind—generated by religious ecstasy or the use of drugs—the Beat writers aimed to create works that were unconventional in both form and subject matter. Kerouac's *On the Road* is perhaps the best-known example of a Beat Generation novel, and Ginsberg's *Howl* is a famous collection of Beat poetry.

Black Aesthetic Movement: A period of artistic and literary development among African Americans in the 1960s and early 1970s. This was the first major African-American artistic movement since the Harlem Renaissance and was closely paralleled by the civil rights and black power movements. The black aesthetic writers attempted to produce works of art that would be meaningful to the black masses. Key figures in black aesthetics included one of its founders, poet and playwright Amiri Baraka, formerly known as LeRoi Jones; poet and essayist Haki R. Madhubuti, formerly Don L. Lee; poet and playwright Sonia Sanchez; and dramatist Ed Bullins. Works representative of the Black Aesthetic Movement include Amiri Baraka's play *Dutchman,* a 1964 Obie award-winner; *Black Fire: An Anthology of Afro-American Writing,* edited by Baraka and playwright Larry Neal and published in 1968; and Sonia Sanchez's poetry collection *We a BaddDDD People,* published in 1970. Also known as Black Arts Movement.

Black Arts Movement: See *Black Aesthetic Movement*

Black Comedy: See *Black Humor*

Black Humor: Writing that places grotesque elements side by side with humorous ones in an attempt to shock the reader, forcing him or her to laugh at the horrifying reality of a disordered world. Joseph Heller's novel *Catch-22* is considered a superb example of the use of black humor. Other well-known authors who use black humor include Kurt Vonnegut, Edward Albee, Eugene Ionesco, and Harold Pinter. Also known as Black Comedy.

Blank Verse: Loosely, any unrhymed poetry, but more generally, unrhymed iambic pentameter verse (composed of lines of five two-syllable feet with the first syllable accented, the second unaccented). Blank verse has been used by poets since the Renaissance for its flexibility and its graceful, dignified tone. John Milton's *Paradise Lost* is in blank verse, as are most of William Shakespeare's plays.

Bloomsbury Group: A group of English writers, artists, and intellectuals who held informal artistic and philosophical discussions in Bloomsbury, a district of London, from around 1907 to the early 1930s. The Bloomsbury Group held no uniform philosophical beliefs but did commonly express an aversion to moral prudery and a desire for greater social tolerance. At various times the circle included Virginia Woolf, E. M. Forster, Clive Bell, Lytton Strachey, and John Maynard Keynes.

Bon Mot: A French term meaning "good word." A *bon mot* is a witty remark or clever observation. Charles Lamb and Oscar Wilde are celebrated for their witty *bon mots.* Two examples by Oscar Wilde stand out: (1) "All women become their mothers. That is their tragedy. No man does. That's his." (2) "A man cannot be too careful in the choice of his enemies."

Breath Verse: See *Projective Verse*

Burlesque: Any literary work that uses exaggeration to make its subject appear ridiculous, either by treating a trivial subject with profound seriousness or by treating a dignified subject frivolously. The word "burlesque" may also be used as an adjective, as in "burlesque show," to mean "striptease act."

Examples of literary burlesque include the comedies of Aristophanes, Miguel de Cervantes's *Don Quixote*, Samuel Butler's poem "Hudibras," and John Gay's play *The Beggar's Opera*.

C

Cadence: The natural rhythm of language caused by the alternation of accented and unaccented syllables. Much modern poetry—notably free verse—deliberately manipulates cadence to create complex rhythmic effects. James Macpherson's "Ossian poems" are richly cadenced, as is the poetry of the Symbolists, Walt Whitman, and Amy Lowell.

Caesura: A pause in a line of poetry, usually occurring near the middle. It typically corresponds to a break in the natural rhythm or sense of the line but is sometimes shifted to create special meanings or rhythmic effects. The opening line of Edgar Allan Poe's "The Raven" contains a caesura following "dreary": "Once upon a midnight dreary, while I pondered weak and weary...."

Canzone: A short Italian or Provencal lyric poem, commonly about love and often set to music. The *canzone* has no set form but typically contains five or six stanzas made up of seven to twenty lines of eleven syllables each. A shorter, five- to ten-line "envoy," or concluding stanza, completes the poem. Masters of the *canzone* form include Petrarch, Dante Alighieri, Torquato Tasso, and Guido Cavalcanti.

Carpe Diem: A Latin term meaning "seize the day." This is a traditional theme of poetry, especially lyrics. A *carpe diem* poem advises the reader or the person it addresses to live for today and enjoy the pleasures of the moment. Two celebrated *carpe diem* poems are Andrew Marvell's "To His Coy Mistress" and Robert Herrick's poem beginning "Gather ye rosebuds while ye may...."

Catharsis: The release or purging of unwanted emotions—specifically fear and pity—brought about by exposure to art. The term was first used by the Greek philosopher Aristotle in his *Poetics* to refer to the desired effect of tragedy on spectators. A famous example of catharsis is realized in Sophocles's *Oedipus Rex,* when Oedipus discovers that his wife, Jacosta, is his own mother and that

the stranger he killed on the road was his own father.

Celtic Renaissance: A period of Irish literary and cultural history at the end of the nineteenth century. Followers of the movement aimed to create a romantic vision of Celtic myth and legend. The most significant works of the Celtic Renaissance typically present a dreamy, unreal world, usually in reaction against the reality of contemporary problems. William Butler Yeats's *The Wanderings of Oisin* is among the most significant works of the Celtic Renaissance. Also known as Celtic Twilight.

Celtic Twilight: See *Celtic Renaissance*

Character: Broadly speaking, a person in a literary work. The actions of characters are what constitute the plot of a story, novel, or poem. There are numerous types of characters, ranging from simple, stereotypical figures to intricate, multifaceted ones. In the techniques of anthropomorphism and personification, animals—and even places or things—can assume aspects of character. "Characterization" is the process by which an author creates vivid, believable characters in a work of art. This may be done in a variety of ways, including (1) direct description of the character by the narrator; (2) the direct presentation of the speech, thoughts, or actions of the character; and (3) the responses of other characters to the character. The term "character" also refers to a form originated by the ancient Greek writer Theophrastus that later became popular in the seventeenth and eighteenth centuries. It is a short essay or sketch of a person who prominently displays a specific attribute or quality, such as miserliness or ambition. Notable characters in literature include Oedipus Rex, Don Quixote de la Mancha, Macbeth, Candide, Hester Prynne, Ebenezer Scrooge, Huckleberry Finn, Jay Gatsby, Scarlett O'Hara, James Bond, and Kunta Kinte.

Characterization: See *Character*

Chorus: In ancient Greek drama, a group of actors who commented on and interpreted the unfolding action on the stage. Initially the chorus was a major component of the presentation, but over time it became less significant, with its numbers reduced and its role eventually limited to commentary between acts. By the sixteenth century the chorus—if employed at all—was typically a single person who provided a prologue and an epilogue and occasionally appeared between acts to introduce or underscore an important event. The chorus in William Shakespeare's *Henry V* functions in this way. Modern dramas rarely feature a chorus, but T. S. Eliot's *Murder in the Cathedral* and Arthur Miller's *A View from the Bridge* are notable exceptions. The Stage Manager in Thornton Wilder's *Our Town* performs a role similar to that of the chorus.

Chronicle: A record of events presented in chronological order. Although the scope and level of detail provided varies greatly among the chronicles surviving from ancient times, some, such as the *Anglo-Saxon Chronicle,* feature vivid descriptions and a lively recounting of events. During the Elizabethan Age, many dramas—appropriately called "chronicle plays"—were based on material from chronicles. Many of William Shakespeare's dramas of English history as well as Christopher Marlowe's *Edward II* are based in part on Raphael Holinshead's *Chronicles of England, Scotland, and Ireland.*

Classical: In its strictest definition in literary criticism, classicism refers to works of ancient Greek or Roman literature. The term may also be used to describe a literary work of recognized importance (a "classic") from any time period or literature that exhibits the traits of classicism. Classical authors from ancient Greek and Roman times include Juvenal and Homer. Examples of later works and authors now described as classical include French literature of the seventeenth century, Western novels of the nineteenth century, and American fiction of the mid-nineteenth century such as that written by James Fenimore Cooper and Mark Twain.

Classicism: A term used in literary criticism to describe critical doctrines that have their roots in ancient Greek and Roman literature, philosophy, and art. Works associated with classicism typically exhibit restraint on the part of the author, unity of design and purpose, clarity, simplicity, logical organization, and respect for tradition. Examples of literary classicism include Cicero's prose,

the dramas of Pierre Corneille and Jean Racine, the poetry of John Dryden and Alexander Pope, and the writings of J. W. von Goethe, G. E. Lessing, and T. S. Eliot.

Climax: The turning point in a narrative, the moment when the conflict is at its most intense. Typically, the structure of stories, novels, and plays is one of rising action, in which tension builds to the climax, followed by falling action, in which tension lessens as the story moves to its conclusion. The climax in James Fenimore Cooper's *The Last of the Mohicans* occurs when Magua and his captive Cora are pursued to the edge of a cliff by Uncas. Magua kills Uncas but is subsequently killed by Hawkeye.

Colloquialism: A word, phrase, or form of pronunciation that is acceptable in casual conversation but not in formal, written communication. It is considered more acceptable than slang. An example of colloquialism can be found in Rudyard Kipling's *Barrack-room Ballads:* When 'Omer smote 'is bloomin' lyre He'd 'eard men sing by land and sea; An' what he thought 'e might require 'E went an' took—the same as me!

Comedy: One of two major types of drama, the other being tragedy. Its aim is to amuse, and it typically ends happily. Comedy assumes many forms, such as farce and burlesque, and uses a variety of techniques, from parody to satire. In a restricted sense the term comedy refers only to dramatic presentations, but in general usage it is commonly applied to nondramatic works as well. Examples of comedies range from the plays of Aristophanes, Terrence, and Plautus, Dante Alighieri's *The Divine Comedy,* Francois Rabelais's *Pantagruel* and *Gargantua,* and some of Geoffrey Chaucer's tales and William Shakespeare's plays to Noel Coward's play *Private Lives* and James Thurber's short story "The Secret Life of Walter Mitty."

Comedy of Manners: A play about the manners and conventions of an aristocratic, highly sophisticated society. The characters are usually types rather than individualized personalities, and plot is less important than atmosphere. Such plays were an important aspect of late seventeenth-century English comedy. The comedy of manners was revived in the eighteenth century by Oliver

Goldsmith and Richard Brinsley Sheridan, enjoyed a second revival in the late nineteenth century, and has endured into the twentieth century. Examples of comedies of manners include William Congreve's *The Way of the World* in the late seventeenth century, Oliver Goldsmith's *She Stoops to Conquer* and Richard Brinsley Sheridan's *The School for Scandal* in the eighteenth century, Oscar Wilde's *The Importance of Being Earnest* in the nineteenth century, and W. Somerset Maugham's *The Circle* in the twentieth century.

Comic Relief: The use of humor to lighten the mood of a serious or tragic story, especially in plays. The technique is very common in Elizabethan works, and can be an integral part of the plot or simply a brief event designed to break the tension of the scene. The Gravediggers' scene in William Shakespeare's *Hamlet* is a frequently cited example of comic relief.

Commedia dell'arte: An Italian term meaning "the comedy of guilds" or "the comedy of professional actors." This form of dramatic comedy was popular in Italy during the sixteenth century. Actors were assigned stock roles (such as Pulcinella, the stupid servant, or Pantalone, the old merchant) and given a basic plot to follow, but all dialogue was improvised. The roles were rigidly typed and the plots were formulaic, usually revolving around young lovers who thwarted their elders and attained wealth and happiness. A rigid convention of the *commedia dell'arte* is the periodic intrusion of Harlequin, who interrupts the play with low buffoonery. Peppino de Filippo's *Metamorphoses of a Wandering Minstrel* gave modern audiences an idea of what *commedia dell'arte* may have been like. Various scenarios for *commedia dell'arte* were compiled in Petraccone's *La commedia dell'arte, storia, technica, scenari*, published in 1927.

Complaint: A lyric poem, popular in the Renaissance, in which the speaker expresses sorrow about his or her condition. Typically, the speaker's sadness is caused by an unresponsive lover, but some complaints cite other sources of unhappiness, such as poverty or fate. A commonly cited example is "A Complaint by Night of the Lover Not Beloved" by Henry Howard, Earl of Surrey.

Thomas Sackville's "Complaint of Henry, Duke of Buckingham" traces the duke's unhappiness to his ruthless ambition.

Conceit: A clever and fanciful metaphor, usually expressed through elaborate and extended comparison, that presents a striking parallel between two seemingly dissimilar things— for example, elaborately comparing a beautiful woman to an object like a garden or the sun. The conceit was a popular device throughout the Elizabethan Age and Baroque Age and was the principal technique of the seventeenth-century English metaphysical poets. This usage of the word conceit is unrelated to the best-known definition of conceit as an arrogant attitude or behavior. The conceit figures prominently in the works of John Donne, Emily Dickinson, and T. S. Eliot.

Concrete: Concrete is the opposite of abstract, and refers to a thing that actually exists or a description that allows the reader to experience an object or concept with the senses. Henry David Thoreau's *Walden* contains much concrete description of nature and wildlife.

Concrete Poetry: Poetry in which visual elements play a large part in the poetic effect. Punctuation marks, letters, or words are arranged on a page to form a visual design: a cross, for example, or a bumblebee. Max Bill and Eugene Gomringer were among the early practitioners of concrete poetry; Haroldo de Campos and Augusto de Campos are among contemporary authors of concrete poetry.

Confessional Poetry: A form of poetry in which the poet reveals very personal, intimate, sometimes shocking information about himself or herself. Anne Sexton, Sylvia Plath, Robert Lowell, and John Berryman wrote poetry in the confessional vein.

Conflict: The conflict in a work of fiction is the issue to be resolved in the story. It usually occurs between two characters, the protagonist and the antagonist, or between the protagonist and society or the protagonist and himself or herself. Conflict in Theodore Dreiser's novel *Sister Carrie* comes as a result of urban society, while Jack London's short story "To Build a Fire" concerns the protagonist's battle against the cold and himself.

Connotation: The impression that a word gives beyond its defined meaning. Connotations may be universally understood or may be significant only to a certain group. Both "horse" and "steed" denote the same animal, but "steed" has a different connotation, deriving from the chivalrous or romantic narratives in which the word was once often used.

Consonance: Consonance occurs in poetry when words appearing at the ends of two or more verses have similar final consonant sounds but have final vowel sounds that differ, as with "stuff" and "off." Consonance is found in "The curfew tolls the knells of parting day" from Thomas Grey's "An Elegy Written in a Country Church Yard." Also known as Half Rhyme or Slant Rhyme.

Convention: Any widely accepted literary device, style, or form. A soliloquy, in which a character reveals to the audience his or her private thoughts, is an example of a dramatic convention.

Corrido: A Mexican ballad. Examples of *corridos* include "Muerte del afamado Bilito," "La voz de mi conciencia," "Lucio Perez," "La juida," and "Los presos."

Couplet: Two lines of poetry with the same rhyme and meter, often expressing a complete and self-contained thought. The following couplet is from Alexander Pope's "Elegy to the Memory of an Unfortunate Lady": 'Tis Use alone that sanctifies Expense, And Splendour borrows all her rays from Sense.

Criticism: The systematic study and evaluation of literary works, usually based on a specific method or set of principles. An important part of literary studies since ancient times, the practice of criticism has given rise to numerous theories, methods, and "schools," sometimes producing conflicting, even contradictory, interpretations of literature in general as well as of individual works. Even such basic issues as what constitutes a poem or a novel have been the subject of much criticism over the centuries. Seminal texts of literary criticism include Plato's *Republic,* Aristotle's *Poetics,* Sir Philip Sidney's *The Defence of Poesie,* John Dryden's *Of Dramatic Poesie,* and William Wordsworth's "Preface" to the second edition of his *Lyrical Ballads.* Contemporary schools of criticism include deconstruction, feminist, psychoanalytic, poststructuralist, new historicist, postcolonialist, and reader-response.

D

Dactyl: See *Foot*

Dadaism: A protest movement in art and literature founded by Tristan Tzara in 1916. Followers of the movement expressed their outrage at the destruction brought about by World War I by revolting against numerous forms of social convention. The Dadaists presented works marked by calculated madness and flamboyant nonsense. They stressed total freedom of expression, commonly through primitive displays of emotion and illogical, often senseless, poetry. The movement ended shortly after the war, when it was replaced by surrealism. Proponents of Dadaism include Andre Breton, Louis Aragon, Philippe Soupault, and Paul Eluard.

Decadent: See *Decadents*

Decadents: The followers of a nineteenth-century literary movement that had its beginnings in French aestheticism. Decadent literature displays a fascination with perverse and morbid states; a search for novelty and sensation—the "new thrill"; a preoccupation with mysticism; and a belief in the senselessness of human existence. The movement is closely associated with the doctrine Art for Art's Sake. The term "decadence" is sometimes used to denote a decline in the quality of art or literature following a period of greatness. Major French decadents are Charles Baudelaire and Arthur Rimbaud. English decadents include Oscar Wilde, Ernest Dowson, and Frank Harris.

Deconstruction: A method of literary criticism developed by Jacques Derrida and characterized by multiple conflicting interpretations of a given work. Deconstructionists consider the impact of the language of a work and suggest that the true meaning of the work is not necessarily the meaning that the author intended. Jacques Derrida's *De la grammatologie* is the seminal text on deconstructive strategies; among American practitioners of this method of criticism are Paul de Man and J. Hillis Miller.

Deduction: The process of reaching a conclusion through reasoning from general premises to a specific premise. An example of deduction is present in the following syllogism: Premise: All mammals are animals. Premise: All whales are mammals. Conclusion: Therefore, all whales are animals.

Denotation: The definition of a word, apart from the impressions or feelings it creates in the reader. The word "apartheid" denotes a political and economic policy of segregation by race, but its connotations—oppression, slavery, inequality—are numerous.

Denouement: A French word meaning "the unknotting." In literary criticism, it denotes the resolution of conflict in fiction or drama. The *denouement* follows the climax and provides an outcome to the primary plot situation as well as an explanation of secondary plot complications. The *denouement* often involves a character's recognition of his or her state of mind or moral condition. A well-known example of *denouement* is the last scene of the play *As You Like It* by William Shakespeare, in which couples are married, an evildoer repents, the identities of two disguised characters are revealed, and a ruler is restored to power. Also known as Falling Action.

Description: Descriptive writing is intended to allow a reader to picture the scene or setting in which the action of a story takes place. The form this description takes often evokes an intended emotional response—a dark, spooky graveyard will evoke fear, and a peaceful, sunny meadow will evoke calmness. An example of a descriptive story is Edgar Allan Poe's *Landor's Cottage,* which offers a detailed depiction of a New York country estate.

Detective Story: A narrative about the solution of a mystery or the identification of a criminal. The conventions of the detective story include the detective's scrupulous use of logic in solving the mystery; incompetent or ineffectual police; a suspect who appears guilty at first but is later proved innocent; and the detective's friend or confidant—often the narrator—whose slowness in interpreting clues emphasizes by contrast the detective's brilliance. Edgar Allan Poe's "Murders in the Rue Morgue" is commonly regarded as the earliest example of this type

of story. With this work, Poe established many of the conventions of the detective story genre, which are still in practice. Other practitioners of this vast and extremely popular genre include Arthur Conan Doyle, Dashiell Hammett, and Agatha Christie.

Deus ex machina: A Latin term meaning "god out of a machine." In Greek drama, a god was often lowered onto the stage by a mechanism of some kind to rescue the hero or untangle the plot. By extension, the term refers to any artificial device or coincidence used to bring about a convenient and simple solution to a plot. This is a common device in melodramas and includes such fortunate circumstances as the sudden receipt of a legacy to save the family farm or a last-minute stay of execution. The *deus ex machina* invariably rewards the virtuous and punishes evildoers. Examples of *deus ex machina* include King Louis XIV in Jean-Baptiste Moliere's *Tartuffe* and Queen Victoria in *The Pirates of Penzance* by William Gilbert and Arthur Sullivan. Bertolt Brecht parodies the abuse of such devices in the conclusion of his *Threepenny Opera.*

Dialogue: In its widest sense, dialogue is simply conversation between people in a literary work; in its most restricted sense, it refers specifically to the speech of characters in a drama. As a specific literary genre, a "dialogue" is a composition in which characters debate an issue or idea. The Greek philosopher Plato frequently expounded his theories in the form of dialogues.

Diction: The selection and arrangement of words in a literary work. Either or both may vary depending on the desired effect. There are four general types of diction: "formal," used in scholarly or lofty writing; "informal," used in relaxed but educated conversation; "colloquial," used in everyday speech; and "slang," containing newly coined words and other terms not accepted in formal usage.

Didactic: A term used to describe works of literature that aim to teach some moral, religious, political, or practical lesson. Although didactic elements are often found in artistically pleasing works, the term "didactic" usually refers to literature in which the message is more important than the form.

The term may also be used to criticize a work that the critic finds "overly didactic," that is, heavy-handed in its delivery of a lesson. Examples of didactic literature include John Bunyan's *Pilgrim's Progress,* Alexander Pope's *Essay on Criticism,* Jean-Jacques Rousseau's *Emile,* and Elizabeth Inchbald's *Simple Story.*

Dimeter: See *Meter*

Dionysian: See *Apollonian and Dionysian*

Discordia concours: A Latin phrase meaning "discord in harmony." The term was coined by the eighteenth-century English writer Samuel Johnson to describe "a combination of dissimilar images or discovery of occult resemblances in things apparently unlike." Johnson created the expression by reversing a phrase by the Latin poet Horace. The metaphysical poetry of John Donne, Richard Crashaw, Abraham Cowley, George Herbert, and Edward Taylor among others, contains many examples of *discordia concours.* In Donne's "A Valediction: Forbidding Mourning," the poet compares the union of himself with his lover to a draftsman's compass: If they be two, they are two so, As stiff twin compasses are two: Thy soul, the fixed foot, makes no show To move, but doth, if the other do; And though it in the center sit, Yet when the other far doth roam, It leans, and hearkens after it, And grows erect, as that comes home.

Dissonance: A combination of harsh or jarring sounds, especially in poetry. Although such combinations may be accidental, poets sometimes intentionally make them to achieve particular effects. Dissonance is also sometimes used to refer to close but not identical rhymes. When this is the case, the word functions as a synonym for consonance. Robert Browning, Gerard Manley Hopkins, and many other poets have made deliberate use of dissonance.

Doppelganger: A literary technique by which a character is duplicated (usually in the form of an alter ego, though sometimes as a ghostly counterpart) or divided into two distinct, usually opposite personalities. The use of this character device is widespread in nineteenth- and twentieth- century literature, and indicates a growing awareness among authors that the "self" is really a composite of many "selves." A well-known story containing a *doppelganger* character is Robert Louis Stevenson's *Dr. Jekyll and Mr. Hyde,* which dramatizes an internal struggle between good and evil. Also known as The Double.

Double Entendre: A corruption of a French phrase meaning "double meaning." The term is used to indicate a word or phrase that is deliberately ambiguous, especially when one of the meanings is risque or improper. An example of a *double entendre* is the Elizabethan usage of the verb "die," which refers both to death and to orgasm.

Double, The: See *Doppelganger*

Draft: Any preliminary version of a written work. An author may write dozens of drafts which are revised to form the final work, or he or she may write only one, with few or no revisions. Dorothy Parker's observation that "I can't write five words but that I change seven" humorously indicates the purpose of the draft.

Drama: In its widest sense, a drama is any work designed to be presented by actors on a stage. Similarly, "drama" denotes a broad literary genre that includes a variety of forms, from pageant and spectacle to tragedy and comedy, as well as countless types and subtypes. More commonly in modern usage, however, a drama is a work that treats serious subjects and themes but does not aim at the grandeur of tragedy. This use of the term originated with the eighteenth-century French writer Denis Diderot, who used the word *drame* to designate his plays about middle- class life; thus "drama" typically features characters of a less exalted stature than those of tragedy. Examples of classical dramas include Menander's comedy *Dyscolus* and Sophocles' tragedy *Oedipus Rex.* Contemporary dramas include Eugene O'Neill's *The Iceman Cometh,* Lillian Hellman's *Little Foxes,* and August Wilson's *Ma Rainey's Black Bottom.*

Dramatic Irony: Occurs when the audience of a play or the reader of a work of literature knows something that a character in the work itself does not know. The irony is in the contrast between the intended meaning of the statements or actions of a character and the additional information understood by the audience. A celebrated example of dramatic irony is in Act V of William Shakespeare's *Romeo and Juliet,* where two young lovers meet their end as a result of a tragic misunderstanding. Here, the audience has full knowledge that Juliet's apparent "death" is merely temporary; she will regain her senses when the mysterious "sleeping potion" she has taken wears off. But Romeo, mistaking Juliet's drug-induced trance for true death, kills himself in grief. Upon awakening, Juliet discovers Romeo's corpse and, in despair, slays herself.

Dramatic Monologue: See *Monologue*

Dramatic Poetry: Any lyric work that employs elements of drama such as dialogue, conflict, or characterization, but excluding works that are intended for stage presentation. A monologue is a form of dramatic poetry.

Dramatis Personae: The characters in a work of literature, particularly a drama. The list of characters printed before the main text of a play or in the program is the *dramatis personae.*

Dream Allegory: See *Dream Vision*

Dream Vision: A literary convention, chiefly of the Middle Ages. In a dream vision a story is presented as a literal dream of the narrator. This device was commonly used to teach moral and religious lessons. Important works of this type are *The Divine Comedy* by Dante Alighieri, *Piers Plowman* by William Langland, and *The Pilgrim's Progress* by John Bunyan. Also known as Dream Allegory.

Dystopia: An imaginary place in a work of fiction where the characters lead dehumanized, fearful lives. Jack London's *The Iron Heel,* Yevgeny Zamyatin's *My,* Aldous Huxley's *Brave New World,* George Orwell's *Nineteen Eighty-four,* and Margaret Atwood's *Handmaid's Tale* portray versions of dystopia.

E

Eclogue: In classical literature, a poem featuring rural themes and structured as a dialogue among shepherds. Eclogues often took specific poetic forms, such as elegies or love poems. Some were written as the soliloquy of a shepherd. In later centuries, "eclogue" came to refer to any poem that was in the pastoral tradition or that had a dialogue or monologue structure. A classical example of an eclogue is Virgil's *Eclogues,* also known as *Bucolics.* Giovanni Boccaccio, Edmund Spenser, Andrew Marvell, Jonathan Swift, and Louis MacNeice also wrote eclogues.

Edwardian: Describes cultural conventions identified with the period of the reign of Edward VII of England (1901-1910). Writers of the Edwardian Age typically displayed a strong reaction against the propriety and conservatism of the Victorian Age. Their work often exhibits distrust of authority in religion, politics, and art and expresses strong doubts about the soundness of conventional values. Writers of this era include George Bernard Shaw, H. G. Wells, and Joseph Conrad.

Edwardian Age: See *Edwardian*

Electra Complex: A daughter's amorous obsession with her father. The term Electra complex comes from the plays of Euripides and Sophocles entitled *Electra,* in which the character Electra drives her brother Orestes to kill their mother and her lover in revenge for the murder of their father.

Elegy: A lyric poem that laments the death of a person or the eventual death of all people. In a conventional elegy, set in a classical world, the poet and subject are spoken of as shepherds. In modern criticism, the word elegy is often used to refer to a poem that is melancholy or mournfully contemplative. John Milton's "Lycidas" and Percy Bysshe Shelley's "Adonais" are two examples of this form.

Elizabethan Age: A period of great economic growth, religious controversy, and nationalism closely associated with the reign of Elizabeth I of England (1558-1603). The Elizabethan Age is considered a part of the general renaissance—that is, the flowering of arts and literature—that took place in Europe during the fourteenth through sixteenth centuries. The era is considered the golden age of English literature. The most important dramas in English and a great deal of lyric poetry were produced during this period, and modern English criticism began around this time. The notable authors of the period—Philip Sidney, Edmund Spenser, Christopher Marlowe, William Shakespeare, Ben Jonson, Francis Bacon, and John Donne—are among the best in all of English literature.

Elizabethan Drama: English comic and tragic plays produced during the Renaissance, or more narrowly, those plays written during the last years of and few years after Queen Elizabeth's reign. William Shakespeare is considered an Elizabethan dramatist in the broader sense, although most of his work was produced during the reign of James I. Examples of Elizabethan comedies include John Lyly's *The Woman in the Moone,* Thomas Dekker's *The Roaring Girl, or, Moll Cut Purse,* and William Shakespeare's *Twelfth Night.* Examples of Elizabethan tragedies include William Shakespeare's *Antony and Cleopatra,* Thomas Kyd's *The Spanish Tragedy,* and John Webster's *The Tragedy of the Duchess of Malfi.*

Empathy: A sense of shared experience, including emotional and physical feelings, with someone or something other than oneself. Empathy is often used to describe the response of a reader to a literary character. An example of an empathic passage is William Shakespeare's description in his narrative poem *Venus and Adonis* of: the snail, whose tender horns being hit, Shrinks backward in his shelly cave with pain. Readers of Gerard Manley Hopkins's *The Windhover* may experience some of the physical sensations evoked in the description of the movement of the falcon.

English Sonnet: See *Sonnet*

Enjambment: The running over of the sense and structure of a line of verse or a couplet into the following verse or couplet. Andrew Marvell's "To His Coy Mistress" is structured as a series of enjambments, as in lines 11-12: "My vegetable love should grow/ Vaster than empires and more slow."

Enlightenment, The: An eighteenth-century philosophical movement. It began in France but had a wide impact throughout Europe and America. Thinkers of the Enlightenment valued reason and believed that both the individual and society could achieve a state of perfection. Corresponding to this essentially humanist vision was a resistance to religious authority. Important figures of the Enlightenment were Denis Diderot and Voltaire in France, Edward Gibbon and David Hume in England, and Thomas Paine and Thomas Jefferson in the United States.

Epic: A long narrative poem about the adventures of a hero of great historic or legendary importance. The setting is vast and the action is often given cosmic significance through the intervention of supernatural forces such as gods, angels, or demons. Epics are typically written in a classical style of grand simplicity with elaborate metaphors and allusions that enhance the symbolic importance of a hero's adventures. Some well-known epics are Homer's *Iliad* and *Odyssey,* Virgil's *Aeneid,* and John Milton's *Paradise Lost.*

Epic Simile: See *Homeric Simile*

Epic Theater: A theory of theatrical presentation developed by twentieth-century German playwright Bertolt Brecht. Brecht created a type of drama that the audience could view with complete detachment. He used what he termed "alienation effects" to create an emotional distance between the audience and the action on stage. Among these effects are: short, self-contained scenes that keep the play from building to a cathartic climax; songs that comment on the action; and techniques of acting that prevent the actor from developing an emotional identity with his role. Besides the plays of Bertolt Brecht, other plays that utilize epic theater conventions include those of Georg Buchner, Frank Wedekind, Erwin Piscator, and Leopold Jessner.

Epigram: A saying that makes the speaker's point quickly and concisely. Samuel Taylor Coleridge wrote an epigram that neatly sums up the form: What is an Epigram? A Dwarfish whole, Its body brevity, and wit its soul.

Epilogue: A concluding statement or section of a literary work. In dramas, particularly those of the seventeenth and eighteenth centuries, the epilogue is a closing speech, often in verse, delivered by an actor at the end of a play and spoken directly to the audience. A famous epilogue is Puck's speech at the end of William Shakespeare's *A Midsummer Night's Dream.*

Epiphany: A sudden revelation of truth inspired by a seemingly trivial incident. The term was widely used by James Joyce in his critical writings, and the stories in Joyce's *Dubliners* are commonly called "epiphanies."

Episode: An incident that forms part of a story and is significantly related to it. Episodes may be either self-contained narratives or events that depend on a larger context for their sense and importance. Examples of episodes include the founding of Wilmington, Delaware in Charles Reade's *The Disinherited Heir* and the individual events comprising the picaresque novels and medieval romances.

Episodic Plot: See *Plot*

Epitaph: An inscription on a tomb or tombstone, or a verse written on the occasion of a person's death. Epitaphs may be serious or humorous. Dorothy Parker's epitaph reads, "I told you I was sick."

Epithalamion: A song or poem written to honor and commemorate a marriage ceremony. Famous examples include Edmund Spenser's "Epithalamion" and e. e. cummings's "Epithalamion." Also spelled Epithalamium.

Epithalamium: See *Epithalamion*

Epithet: A word or phrase, often disparaging or abusive, that expresses a character trait of someone or something. "The Napoleon of crime" is an epithet applied to Professor Moriarty, arch-rival of Sherlock Holmes in Arthur Conan Doyle's series of detective stories.

Exempla: See *Exemplum*

Exemplum: A tale with a moral message. This form of literary sermonizing flourished during the Middle Ages, when *exempla* appeared in collections known as "example-books." The works of Geoffrey Chaucer are full of *exempla*.

Existentialism: A predominantly twentieth-century philosophy concerned with the nature and perception of human existence. There are two major strains of existentialist thought: atheistic and Christian. Followers of atheistic existentialism believe that the individual is alone in a godless universe and that the basic human condition is one of suffering and loneliness. Nevertheless, because there are no fixed values, individuals can create their own characters—indeed, they can shape themselves—through the exercise of free will. The atheistic strain culminates in and is popularly associated with the works of Jean-Paul Sartre. The Christian existentialists, on the other hand,

believe that only in God may people find freedom from life's anguish. The two strains hold certain beliefs in common: that existence cannot be fully understood or described through empirical effort; that anguish is a universal element of life; that individuals must bear responsibility for their actions; and that there is no common standard of behavior or perception for religious and ethical matters. Existentialist thought figures prominently in the works of such authors as Eugene Ionesco, Franz Kafka, Fyodor Dostoyevsky, Simone de Beauvoir, Samuel Beckett, and Albert Camus.

Expatriates: See *Expatriatism*

Expatriatism: The practice of leaving one's country to live for an extended period in another country. Literary expatriates include English poets Percy Bysshe Shelley and John Keats in Italy, Polish novelist Joseph Conrad in England, American writers Richard Wright, James Baldwin, Gertrude Stein, and Ernest Hemingway in France, and Trinidadian author Neil Bissondath in Canada.

Exposition: Writing intended to explain the nature of an idea, thing, or theme. Expository writing is often combined with description, narration, or argument. In dramatic writing, the exposition is the introductory material which presents the characters, setting, and tone of the play. An example of dramatic exposition occurs in many nineteenth-century drawing-room comedies in which the butler and the maid open the play with relevant talk about their master and mistress; in composition, exposition relays factual information, as in encyclopedia entries.

Expressionism: An indistinct literary term, originally used to describe an early twentieth-century school of German painting. The term applies to almost any mode of unconventional, highly subjective writing that distorts reality in some way. Advocates of Expressionism include dramatists George Kaiser, Ernst Toller, Luigi Pirandello, Federico Garcia Lorca, Eugene O'Neill, and Elmer Rice; poets George Heym, Ernst Stadler, August Stramm, Gottfried Benn, and Georg Trakl; and novelists Franz Kafka and James Joyce.

Extended Monologue: See *Monologue*

F

Fable: A prose or verse narrative intended to convey a moral. Animals or inanimate objects with human characteristics often serve as characters in fables. A famous fable is Aesop's "The Tortoise and the Hare."

Fairy Tales: Short narratives featuring mythical beings such as fairies, elves, and sprites. These tales originally belonged to the folklore of a particular nation or region, such as those collected in Germany by Jacob and Wilhelm Grimm. Two other celebrated writers of fairy tales are Hans Christian Andersen and Rudyard Kipling.

Falling Action: See *Denouement*

Fantasy: A literary form related to mythology and folklore. Fantasy literature is typically set in non-existent realms and features supernatural beings. Notable examples of fantasy literature are *The Lord of the Rings* by J. R. R. Tolkien and the Gormenghast trilogy by Mervyn Peake.

Farce: A type of comedy characterized by broad humor, outlandish incidents, and often vulgar subject matter. Much of the "comedy" in film and television could more accurately be described as farce.

Feet: See *Foot*

Feminine Rhyme: See *Rhyme*

Femme fatale: A French phrase with the literal translation "fatal woman." A *femme fatale* is a sensuous, alluring woman who often leads men into danger or trouble. A classic example of the *femme fatale* is the nameless character in Billy Wilder's *The Seven Year Itch,* portrayed by Marilyn Monroe in the film adaptation.

Fiction: Any story that is the product of imagination rather than a documentation of fact. characters and events in such narratives may be based in real life but their ultimate form and configuration is a creation of the author. Geoffrey Chaucer's *The Canterbury Tales,* Laurence Sterne's *Tristram Shandy,* and Margaret Mitchell's *Gone with the Wind* are examples of fiction.

Figurative Language: A technique in writing in which the author temporarily interrupts the order, construction, or meaning of the writing for a particular effect. This interruption takes the form of one or more figures of speech such as hyperbole, irony, or simile.

Figurative language is the opposite of literal language, in which every word is truthful, accurate, and free of exaggeration or embellishment. Examples of figurative language are tropes such as metaphor and rhetorical figures such as apostrophe.

Figures of Speech: Writing that differs from customary conventions for construction, meaning, order, or significance for the purpose of a special meaning or effect. There are two major types of figures of speech: rhetorical figures, which do not make changes in the meaning of the words, and tropes, which do. Types of figures of speech include simile, hyperbole, alliteration, and pun, among many others.

Fin de siecle: A French term meaning "end of the century." The term is used to denote the last decade of the nineteenth century, a transition period when writers and other artists abandoned old conventions and looked for new techniques and objectives. Two writers commonly associated with the *fin de siecle* mindset are Oscar Wilde and George Bernard Shaw.

First Person: See *Point of View*

Flashback: A device used in literature to present action that occurred before the beginning of the story. Flashbacks are often introduced as the dreams or recollections of one or more characters. Flashback techniques are often used in films, where they are typically set off by a gradual changing of one picture to another.

Foil: A character in a work of literature whose physical or psychological qualities contrast strongly with, and therefore highlight, the corresponding qualities of another character. In his Sherlock Holmes stories, Arthur Conan Doyle portrayed Dr. Watson as a man of normal habits and intelligence, making him a foil for the eccentric and wonderfully perceptive Sherlock Holmes.

Folk Ballad: See *Ballad*

Folklore: Traditions and myths preserved in a culture or group of people. Typically, these are passed on by word of mouth in various forms—such as legends, songs, and proverbs—or preserved in customs and ceremonies. This term was first used by W. J. Thoms in 1846. Sir James Frazer's *The Golden Bough* is the record of English folklore; myths about the frontier and the Old South exemplify American folklore.

Folktale: A story originating in oral tradition. Folktales fall into a variety of categories, including legends, ghost stories, fairy tales, fables, and anecdotes based on historical figures and events. Examples of folktales include Giambattista Basile's *The Pentamerone,* which contains the tales of Puss in Boots, Rapunzel, Cinderella, and Beauty and the Beast, and Joel Chandler Harris's Uncle Remus stories, which represent transplanted African folktales and American tales about the characters Mike Fink, Johnny Appleseed, Paul Bunyan, and Pecos Bill.

Foot: The smallest unit of rhythm in a line of poetry. In English-language poetry, a foot is typically one accented syllable combined with one or two unaccented syllables. There are many different types of feet. When the accent is on the second syllable of a two syllable word (con-*tort*), the foot is an "iamb"; the reverse accentual pattern (*tor*-ture) is a "trochee." Other feet that commonly occur in poetry in English are "anapest," two unaccented syllables followed by an accented syllable as in in-ter-*cept,* and "dactyl," an accented syllable followed by two unaccented syllables as in *su*-i-cide.

Foreshadowing: A device used in literature to create expectation or to set up an explanation of later developments. In Charles Dickens's *Great Expectations,* the graveyard encounter at the beginning of the novel between Pip and the escaped convict Magwitch foreshadows the baleful atmosphere and events that comprise much of the narrative.

Form: The pattern or construction of a work which identifies its genre and distinguishes it from other genres. Examples of forms include the different genres, such as the lyric form or the short story form, and various patterns for poetry, such as the verse form or the stanza form.

Formalism: In literary criticism, the belief that literature should follow prescribed rules of construction, such as those that govern the sonnet form. Examples of formalism are found in the work of the New Critics and structuralists.

Fourteener Meter: See *Meter*

Free Verse: Poetry that lacks regular metrical and rhyme patterns but that tries to capture the cadences of everyday speech. The form allows a poet to exploit a variety of rhythmical effects within a single poem. Free-verse techniques have been widely used in the twentieth century by such writers as Ezra Pound, T. S. Eliot, Carl Sandburg, and William Carlos Williams. Also known as *Vers libre.*

Futurism: A flamboyant literary and artistic movement that developed in France, Italy, and Russia from 1908 through the 1920s. Futurist theater and poetry abandoned traditional literary forms. In their place, followers of the movement attempted to achieve total freedom of expression through bizarre imagery and deformed or newly invented words. The Futurists were self-consciously modern artists who attempted to incorporate the appearances and sounds of modern life into their work. Futurist writers include Filippo Tommaso Marinetti, Wyndham Lewis, Guillaume Apollinaire, Velimir Khlebnikov, and Vladimir Mayakovsky.

G

Genre: A category of literary work. In critical theory, genre may refer to both the content of a given work—tragedy, comedy, pastoral—and to its form, such as poetry, novel, or drama. This term also refers to types of popular literature, as in the genres of science fiction or the detective story.

Genteel Tradition: A term coined by critic George Santayana to describe the literary practice of certain late nineteenth-century American writers, especially New Englanders. Followers of the Genteel Tradition emphasized conventionality in social, religious, moral, and literary standards. Some of the best-known writers of the Genteel Tradition are R. H. Stoddard and Bayard Taylor.

Gilded Age: A period in American history during the 1870s characterized by political corruption and materialism. A number of important novels of social and political criticism were written during this time. Examples of Gilded Age literature include Henry Adams's *Democracy* and F. Marion Crawford's *An American Politician.*

Gothic: See *Gothicism*

Gothicism: In literary criticism, works characterized by a taste for the medieval or morbidly attractive. A gothic novel prominently features elements of horror, the supernatural, gloom, and violence: clanking chains, terror, charnel houses, ghosts, medieval castles, and mysteriously slamming doors. The term "gothic novel" is also applied to novels that lack elements of the traditional Gothic setting but that create a similar atmosphere of terror or dread. Mary Shelley's *Frankenstein* is perhaps the best-known English work of this kind.

Gothic Novel: See *Gothicism*

Great Chain of Being: The belief that all things and creatures in nature are organized in a hierarchy from inanimate objects at the bottom to God at the top. This system of belief was popular in the seventeenth and eighteenth centuries. A summary of the concept of the great chain of being can be found in the first epistle of Alexander Pope's *An Essay on Man,* and more recently in Arthur O. Lovejoy's *The Great Chain of Being: A Study of the History of an Idea.*

Grotesque: In literary criticism, the subject matter of a work or a style of expression characterized by exaggeration, deformity, freakishness, and disorder. The grotesque often includes an element of comic absurdity. Early examples of literary grotesque include Francois Rabelais's *Pantagruel* and *Gargantua* and Thomas Nashe's *The Unfortunate Traveller,* while more recent examples can be found in the works of Edgar Allan Poe, Evelyn Waugh, Eudora Welty, Flannery O'Connor, Eugene Ionesco, Gunter Grass, Thomas Mann, Mervyn Peake, and Joseph Heller, among many others.

H

Haiku: The shortest form of Japanese poetry, constructed in three lines of five, seven, and five syllables respectively. The message of a *haiku* poem usually centers on some aspect of spirituality and provokes an emotional response in the reader. Early masters of *haiku* include Basho, Buson, Kobayashi Issa, and Masaoka Shiki. English writers of *haiku* include the Imagists, notably Ezra Pound, H. D., Amy Lowell, Carl Sandburg, and William Carlos Williams. Also known as *Hokku.*

Half Rhyme: See *Consonance*

Hamartia: In tragedy, the event or act that leads to the hero's or heroine's downfall. This term is often incorrectly used as a synonym for tragic flaw. In Richard Wright's *Native Son,* the act that seals Bigger Thomas's fate is his first impulsive murder.

Harlem Renaissance: The Harlem Renaissance of the 1920s is generally considered the first significant movement of black writers and artists in the United States. During this period, new and established black writers published more fiction and poetry than ever before, the first influential black literary journals were established, and black authors and artists received their first widespread recognition and serious critical appraisal. Among the major writers associated with this period are Claude McKay, Jean Toomer, Countee Cullen, Langston Hughes, Arna Bontemps, Nella Larsen, and Zora Neale Hurston. Works representative of the Harlem Renaissance include Arna Bontemps's poems "The Return" and "Golgotha Is a Mountain," Claude McKay's novel *Home to Harlem,* Nella Larsen's novel *Passing,* Langston Hughes's poem "The Negro Speaks of Rivers," and the journals *Crisis* and *Opportunity,* both founded during this period. Also known as Negro Renaissance and New Negro Movement.

Harlequin: A stock character of the *commedia dell'arte* who occasionally interrupted the action with silly antics. Harlequin first appeared on the English stage in John Day's *The Travailes of the Three English Brothers.* The San Francisco Mime Troupe is one of the few modern groups to adapt Harlequin to the needs of contemporary satire.

Hellenism: Imitation of ancient Greek thought or styles. Also, an approach to life that focuses on the growth and development of the intellect. "Hellenism" is sometimes used to refer to the belief that reason can be applied to examine all human experience. A cogent discussion of Hellenism can be found in Matthew Arnold's *Culture and Anarchy.*

Heptameter: See *Meter*

Hero/Heroine: The principal sympathetic character (male or female) in a literary work. Heroes and heroines typically exhibit admirable traits: idealism, courage, and integrity, for example. Famous heroes and heroines include Pip in Charles Dickens's *Great Expectations,* the anonymous narrator in Ralph Ellison's *Invisible Man,* and Sethe in Toni Morrison's *Beloved.*

Heroic Couplet: A rhyming couplet written in iambic pentameter (a verse with five iambic feet). The following lines by Alexander Pope are an example: "Truth guards the Poet, sanctifies the line,/ And makes Immortal, Verse as mean as mine."

Heroic Line: The meter and length of a line of verse in epic or heroic poetry. This varies by language and time period. For example, in English poetry, the heroic line is iambic pentameter (a verse with five iambic feet); in French, the alexandrine (a verse with six iambic feet); in classical literature, dactylic hexameter (a verse with six dactylic feet).

Heroine: See *Hero/Heroine*

Hexameter: See *Meter*

Historical Criticism: The study of a work based on its impact on the world of the time period in which it was written. Examples of postmodern historical criticism can be found in the work of Michel Foucault, Hayden White, Stephen Greenblatt, and Jonathan Goldberg.

Hokku: See *Haiku*

Holocaust: See *Holocaust Literature*

Holocaust Literature: Literature influenced by or written about the Holocaust of World War II. Such literature includes true stories of survival in concentration camps, escape, and life after the war, as well as fictional works and poetry. Representative works of Holocaust literature include Saul Bellow's *Mr. Sammler's Planet,* Anne Frank's *The Diary of a Young Girl,* Jerzy Kosinski's *The Painted Bird,* Arthur Miller's *Incident at Vichy,* Czeslaw Milosz's *Collected Poems,* William Styron's *Sophie's Choice,* and Art Spiegelman's *Maus.*

Homeric Simile: An elaborate, detailed comparison written as a simile many lines in length. An example of an epic simile from John Milton's *Paradise Lost* follows: Angel Forms, who lay entranced Thick as autumnal leaves that strow the brooks In Vallombrosa, where the Etrurian shades High over-arched embower; or scattered sedge Afloat, when with fierce winds Orion armed Hath vexed the Red-Sea coast, whose waves o'erthrew Busiris and his Memphian chivalry, While with perfidious hatred they pursued The sojourners of Goshen, who beheld From the safe shore their floating carcasses And broken chariot-wheels. Also known as Epic Simile.

Horatian Satire: See *Satire*

Humanism: A philosophy that places faith in the dignity of humankind and rejects the medieval perception of the individual as a weak, fallen creature. "Humanists" typically believe in the perfectibility of human nature and view reason and education as the means to that end. Humanist thought is represented in the works of Marsilio Ficino, Ludovico Castelvetro, Edmund Spenser, John Milton, Dean John Colet, Desiderius Erasmus, John Dryden, Alexander Pope, Matthew Arnold, and Irving Babbitt.

Humors: Mentions of the humors refer to the ancient Greek theory that a person's health and personality were determined by the balance of four basic fluids in the body: blood, phlegm, yellow bile, and black bile. A dominance of any fluid would cause extremes in behavior. An excess of blood created a sanguine person who was joyful, aggressive, and passionate; a phlegmatic person was shy, fearful, and sluggish; too much yellow bile led to a choleric temperament characterized by impatience, anger, bitterness, and stubbornness; and excessive black bile created melancholy, a state of laziness, gluttony, and lack of motivation. Literary treatment of the humors is exemplified by several characters in Ben Jonson's plays *Every Man in His Humour* and *Every Man out of His Humour.* Also spelled Humours.

Humours: See *Humors*

Hyperbole: In literary criticism, deliberate exaggeration used to achieve an effect. In William Shakespeare's *Macbeth,* Lady Macbeth hyperbolizes when she says, "All the perfumes of Arabia could not sweeten this little hand."

I

Iamb: See *Foot*

Idiom: A word construction or verbal expression closely associated with a given language. For example, in colloquial English the construction "how come" can be used instead of "why" to introduce a question. Similarly, "a piece of cake" is sometimes used to describe a task that is easily done.

Image: A concrete representation of an object or sensory experience. Typically, such a representation helps evoke the feelings associated with the object or experience itself. Images are either "literal" or "figurative." Literal images are especially concrete and involve little or no extension of the obvious meaning of the words used to express them. Figurative images do not follow the literal meaning of the words exactly. Images in literature are usually visual, but the term "image" can also refer to the representation of any sensory experience. In his poem "The Shepherd's Hour," Paul Verlaine presents the following image: "The Moon is red through horizon's fog;/ In a dancing mist the hazy meadow sleeps." The first line is broadly literal, while the second line involves turns of meaning associated with dancing and sleeping.

Imagery: The array of images in a literary work. Also, figurative language. William Butler Yeats's "The Second Coming" offers a powerful image of encroaching anarchy:
Turning and turning in the widening gyre
The falcon cannot hear the falconer;
Things fall apart....

Imagism: An English and American poetry movement that flourished between 1908 and 1917. The Imagists used precise, clearly presented images in their works. They also used common, everyday speech and aimed for conciseness, concrete imagery, and the creation of new rhythms. Participants in the Imagist movement included Ezra Pound, H. D. (Hilda Doolittle), and Amy Lowell, among others.

In medias res: A Latin term meaning "in the middle of things." It refers to the technique of beginning a story at its midpoint and then using various flashback devices to reveal previous action. This technique originated in such epics as Virgil's *Aeneid.*

Induction: The process of reaching a conclusion by reasoning from specific premises to form a general premise. Also, an introductory portion of a work of literature, especially a play. Geoffrey Chaucer's "Prologue" to the *Canterbury Tales,* Thomas Sackville's "Induction" to *The Mirror of Magistrates,* and the opening scene in William Shakespeare's *The Taming of the Shrew* are examples of inductions to literary works.

Intentional Fallacy: The belief that judgments of a literary work based solely on an author's stated or implied intentions are false and misleading. Critics who believe in the concept of the intentional fallacy typically argue that the work itself is sufficient matter for interpretation, even though they may concede that an author's statement of purpose can be useful. Analysis of William Wordsworth's *Lyrical Ballads* based on the observations about poetry he makes in his "Preface" to the second edition of that work is an example of the intentional fallacy.

Interior Monologue: A narrative technique in which characters' thoughts are revealed in a way that appears to be uncontrolled by the author. The interior monologue typically aims to reveal the inner self of a character. It portrays emotional experiences as they occur at both a conscious and unconscious level. images are often used to represent sensations or emotions. One of the best-known interior monologues in English is the Molly Bloom section at the close of James Joyce's *Ulysses.* The interior monologue is also common in the works of Virginia Woolf.

Internal Rhyme: Rhyme that occurs within a single line of verse. An example is in the opening line of Edgar Allan Poe's "The Raven": "Once upon a midnight dreary, while I pondered weak and weary." Here, "dreary" and "weary" make an internal rhyme.

Irish Literary Renaissance: A late nineteenth- and early twentieth-century movement in Irish literature. Members of the movement aimed to reduce the influence of British culture in Ireland and create an Irish national literature. William Butler Yeats, George Moore, and Sean O'Casey are three of the best-known figures of the movement.

Irony: In literary criticism, the effect of language in which the intended meaning is the opposite of what is stated. The title of Jonathan Swift's "A Modest Proposal" is ironic because what Swift proposes in this essay is cannibalism—hardly "modest."

Italian Sonnet: See *Sonnet*

J

Jacobean Age: The period of the reign of James I of England (1603-1625). The early literature of this period reflected the worldview of the Elizabethan Age, but a darker, more cynical attitude steadily grew in the art and literature of the Jacobean Age. This was an important time for English drama and poetry. Milestones include William Shakespeare's tragedies, tragi-comedies, and sonnets; Ben Jonson's various dramas; and John Donne's metaphysical poetry.

Jargon: Language that is used or understood only by a select group of people. Jargon may refer to terminology used in a certain profession, such as computer jargon, or it may refer to any nonsensical language that is not understood by most people. Literary examples of jargon are Francois Villon's *Ballades en jargon,* which is composed in the secret language of the *coquillards,* and Anthony Burgess's *A Clockwork Orange,* narrated in the fictional characters' language of "Nadsat."

Juvenalian Satire: See *Satire*

K

Knickerbocker Group: A somewhat indistinct group of New York writers of the first half of the nineteenth century. Members of the group were linked only by location and a common theme: New York life. Two famous members of the Knickerbocker Group were Washington Irving and William Cullen Bryant. The group's name derives from Irving's *Knickerbocker's History of New York.*

L

Lais: See *Lay*

Lay: A song or simple narrative poem. The form originated in medieval France. Early French *lais* were often based on the Celtic legends and other tales sung by Breton minstrels—thus the name of the "Breton lay." In

fourteenth-century England, the term "lay" was used to describe short narratives written in imitation of the Breton lays. The most notable of these is Geoffrey Chaucer's "The Minstrel's Tale."

Leitmotiv: See *Motif*

Literal Language: An author uses literal language when he or she writes without exaggerating or embellishing the subject matter and without any tools of figurative language. To say "He ran very quickly down the street" is to use literal language, whereas to say "He ran like a hare down the street" would be using figurative language.

Literary Ballad: See *Ballad*

Literature: Literature is broadly defined as any written or spoken material, but the term most often refers to creative works. Literature includes poetry, drama, fiction, and many kinds of nonfiction writing, as well as oral, dramatic, and broadcast compositions not necessarily preserved in a written format, such as films and television programs.

Lost Generation: A term first used by Gertrude Stein to describe the post-World War I generation of American writers: men and women haunted by a sense of betrayal and emptiness brought about by the destructiveness of the war. The term is commonly applied to Hart Crane, Ernest Hemingway, F. Scott Fitzgerald, and others.

Lyric Poetry: A poem expressing the subjective feelings and personal emotions of the poet. Such poetry is melodic, since it was originally accompanied by a lyre in recitals. Most Western poetry in the twentieth century may be classified as lyrical. Examples of lyric poetry include A. E. Housman's elegy "To an Athlete Dying Young," the odes of Pindar and Horace, Thomas Gray and William Collins, the sonnets of Sir Thomas Wyatt and Sir Philip Sidney, Elizabeth Barrett Browning and Rainer Maria Rilke, and a host of other forms in the poetry of William Blake and Christina Rossetti, among many others.

M

Mannerism: Exaggerated, artificial adherence to a literary manner or style. Also, a popular style of the visual arts of late sixteenth-century Europe that was marked by elongation of the human form and by intentional spatial distortion. Literary works that are self-consciously high-toned and artistic are often said to be "mannered." Authors of such works include Henry James and Gertrude Stein.

Masculine Rhyme: See *Rhyme*

Masque: A lavish and elaborate form of entertainment, often performed in royal courts, that emphasizes song, dance, and costumery. The Renaissance form of the masque grew out of the spectacles of masked figures common in medieval England and Europe. The masque reached its peak of popularity and development in seventeenth-century England, during the reigns of James I and, especially, of Charles I. Ben Jonson, the most significant masque writer, also created the "antimasque," which incorporates elements of humor and the grotesque into the traditional masque and achieved greater dramatic quality. Masque-like interludes appear in Edmund Spenser's *The Faerie Queene* and in William Shakespeare's *The Tempest.* One of the best-known English masques is John Milton's *Comus.*

Measure: The foot, verse, or time sequence used in a literary work, especially a poem. Measure is often used somewhat incorrectly as a synonym for meter.

Melodrama: A play in which the typical plot is a conflict between characters who personify extreme good and evil. Melodramas usually end happily and emphasize sensationalism. Other literary forms that use the same techniques are often labeled "melodramatic." The term was formerly used to describe a combination of drama and music; as such, it was synonymous with "opera." Augustin Daly's *Under the Gaslight* and Dion Boucicault's *The Octoroon, The Colleen Bawn,* and *The Poor of New York* are examples of melodramas. The most popular media for twentieth-century melodramas are motion pictures and television.

Metaphor: A figure of speech that expresses an idea through the image of another object. Metaphors suggest the essence of the first object by identifying it with certain qualities of the second object. An example is "But soft, what light through yonder window breaks?/ It is the east, and Juliet is the sun" in William Shakespeare's *Romeo and Juliet.* Here, Juliet, the first object, is identified with qualities of the second object, the sun.

Metaphysical Conceit: See *Conceit*

Metaphysical Poetry: The body of poetry produced by a group of seventeenth-century English writers called the "Metaphysical Poets." The group includes John Donne and Andrew Marvell. The Metaphysical Poets made use of everyday speech, intellectual analysis, and unique imagery. They aimed to portray the ordinary conflicts and contradictions of life. Their poems often took the form of an argument, and many of them emphasize physical and religious love as well as the fleeting nature of life. Elaborate conceits are typical in metaphysical poetry. Marvell's "To His Coy Mistress" is a well-known example of a metaphysical poem.

Metaphysical Poets: See *Metaphysical Poetry*

Meter: In literary criticism, the repetition of sound patterns that creates a rhythm in poetry. The patterns are based on the number of syllables and the presence and absence of accents. The unit of rhythm in a line is called a foot. Types of meter are classified according to the number of feet in a line. These are the standard English lines: Monometer, one foot; Dimeter, two feet; Trimeter, three feet; Tetrameter, four feet; Pentameter, five feet; Hexameter, six feet (also called the Alexandrine); Heptameter, seven feet (also called the "Fourteener" when the feet are iambic). The most common English meter is the iambic pentameter, in which each line contains ten syllables, or five iambic feet, which individually are composed of an unstressed syllable followed by an accented syllable. Both of the following lines from Alfred, Lord Tennyson's "Ulysses" are written in iambic pentameter: Made weak by time and fate, but strong in will To strive, to seek, to find, and not to yield.

Mise en scene: The costumes, scenery, and other properties of a drama. Herbert Beerbohm Tree was renowned for the elaborate *mises en scene* of his lavish Shakespearean productions at His Majesty's Theatre between 1897 and 1915.

Modernism: Modern literary practices. Also, the principles of a literary school that lasted from roughly the beginning of the twentieth century until the end of World War II. Modernism is defined by its rejection of the literary conventions of the nineteenth century and by its opposition to conventional morality, taste, traditions, and economic values. Many writers are associated with the concepts of Modernism, including Albert Camus, Marcel Proust, D. H. Lawrence, W. H. Auden, Ernest Hemingway, William Faulkner, William Butler Yeats, Thomas Mann, Tennessee Williams, Eugene O'Neill, and James Joyce.

Monologue: A composition, written or oral, by a single individual. More specifically, a speech given by a single individual in a drama or other public entertainment. It has no set length, although it is usually several or more lines long. An example of an "extended monologue"—that is, a monologue of great length and seriousness—occurs in the one-act, one-character play *The Stronger* by August Strindberg.

Monometer: See *Meter*

Mood: The prevailing emotions of a work or of the author in his or her creation of the work. The mood of a work is not always what might be expected based on its subject matter. The poem "Dover Beach" by Matthew Arnold offers examples of two different moods originating from the same experience: watching the ocean at night. The mood of the first three lines—The sea is calm tonight The tide is full, the moon lies fair Upon the straights.... is in sharp contrast to the mood of the last three lines—And we are here as on a darkling plain Swept with confused alarms of struggle and flight, Where ignorant armies clash by night.

Motif: A theme, character type, image, metaphor, or other verbal element that recurs throughout a single work of literature or occurs in a number of different works over a period of time. For example, the various manifestations of the color white in Herman Melville's *Moby Dick* is a "specific" *motif*, while the trials of star-crossed lovers is a "conventional" *motif* from the literature of all periods. Also known as *Motiv* or *Leitmotiv*.

Motiv: See *Motif*

Muckrakers: An early twentieth-century group of American writers. Typically, their works exposed the wrongdoings of big business and government in the United States. Upton Sinclair's *The Jungle* exemplifies the muckraking novel.

Muses: Nine Greek mythological goddesses, the daughters of Zeus and Mnemosyne (Memory). Each muse patronized a specific area of the liberal arts and sciences. Calliope presided over epic poetry, Clio over history, Erato over love poetry, Euterpe over music or lyric poetry, Melpomene over tragedy, Polyhymnia over hymns to the gods, Terpsichore over dance, Thalia over comedy, and Urania over astronomy. Poets and writers traditionally made appeals to the Muses for inspiration in their work. John Milton invokes the aid of a muse at the beginning of the first book of his *Paradise Lost:* Of Man's First disobedience, and the Fruit of the Forbidden Tree, whose mortal taste Brought Death into the World, and all our woe, With loss of Eden, till one greater Man Restore us, and regain the blissful Seat, Sing Heav'nly Muse, that on the secret top of Oreb, or of Sinai, didst inspire That Shepherd, who first taught the chosen Seed, In the Beginning how the Heav'ns and Earth Rose out of Chaos....

Mystery: See *Suspense*

Myth: An anonymous tale emerging from the traditional beliefs of a culture or social unit. Myths use supernatural explanations for natural phenomena. They may also explain cosmic issues like creation and death. Collections of myths, known as mythologies, are common to all cultures and nations, but the best-known myths belong to the Norse, Roman, and Greek mythologies. A famous myth is the story of Arachne, an arrogant young girl who challenged a goddess, Athena, to a weaving contest; when the girl won, Athena was enraged and turned Arachne into a spider, thus explaining the existence of spiders.

N

Narration: The telling of a series of events, real or invented. A narration may be either a simple narrative, in which the events are recounted chronologically, or a narrative with a plot, in which the account is given in a style reflecting the author's artistic concept of the story. Narration is sometimes used as a synonym for "storyline." The recounting of scary stories around a campfire is a form of narration.

Narrative: A verse or prose accounting of an event or sequence of events, real or invented. The term is also used as an adjective in the sense "method of narration." For example, in literary criticism, the expression "narrative technique" usually refers to the way the author structures and presents his or her story. Narratives range from the shortest accounts of events, as in Julius Caesar's remark, "I came, I saw, I conquered," to the longest historical or biographical works, as in Edward Gibbon's *The Decline and Fall of the Roman Empire,* as well as diaries, travelogues, novels, ballads, epics, short stories, and other fictional forms.

Narrative Poetry: A nondramatic poem in which the author tells a story. Such poems may be of any length or level of complexity. Epics such as *Beowulf* and ballads are forms of narrative poetry.

Narrator: The teller of a story. The narrator may be the author or a character in the story through whom the author speaks. Huckleberry Finn is the narrator of Mark Twain's *The Adventures of Huckleberry Finn.*

Naturalism: A literary movement of the late nineteenth and early twentieth centuries. The movement's major theorist, French novelist Emile Zola, envisioned a type of fiction that would examine human life with the objectivity of scientific inquiry. The Naturalists typically viewed human beings as either the products of "biological determinism," ruled by hereditary instincts and engaged in an endless struggle for survival, or as the products of "socioeconomic determinism," ruled by social and economic forces beyond their control. In their works, the Naturalists generally ignored the highest levels of society and focused on degradation: poverty, alcoholism, prostitution, insanity, and disease. Naturalism influenced authors throughout the world, including Henrik Ibsen and Thomas Hardy. In the United States, in particular, Naturalism had a profound impact. Among the authors who embraced its principles are Theodore Dreiser, Eugene O'Neill, Stephen Crane, Jack London, and Frank Norris.

Negritude: A literary movement based on the concept of a shared cultural bond on the part of black Africans, wherever they may be in the world. It traces its origins to the former French colonies of Africa and the Caribbean. Negritude poets, novelists, and essayists generally stress four points in their writings: One, black alienation from traditional African culture can lead to feelings of inferiority. Two, European colonialism and Western education should be resisted. Three, black Africans should seek to affirm and define their own identity. Four, African culture can and should be reclaimed. Many Negritude writers also claim that blacks can make unique contributions to the world, based on a heightened appreciation of nature, rhythm, and human emotions—aspects of life they say are not so highly valued in the materialistic and rationalistic West. Examples of Negritude literature include the poetry of both Senegalese Leopold Senghor in *Hosties noires* and Martiniquais Aime-Fernand Cesaire in *Return to My Native Land.*

Negro Renaissance: See *Harlem Renaissance*

Neoclassical Period: See *Neoclassicism*

Neoclassicism: In literary criticism, this term refers to the revival of the attitudes and styles of expression of classical literature. It is generally used to describe a period in European history beginning in the late seventeenth century and lasting until about 1800. In its purest form, Neoclassicism marked a return to order, proportion, restraint, logic, accuracy, and decorum. In England, where Neoclassicism perhaps was most popular, it reflected the influence of seventeenth- century French writers, especially dramatists. Neoclassical writers typically reacted against the intensity and enthusiasm of the Renaissance period. They wrote works that appealed to the intellect, using elevated language and classical literary forms such as satire and the ode. Neoclassical works were often governed by the classical goal of instruction. English neoclassicists included Alexander Pope, Jonathan Swift, Joseph Addison, Sir Richard Steele, John Gay, and Matthew Prior; French neoclassicists included Pierre Corneille and Jean-Baptiste Moliere. Also known as Age of Reason.

Neoclassicists: See *Neoclassicism*

New Criticism: A movement in literary criticism, dating from the late 1920s, that stressed close textual analysis in the interpretation of works of literature. The New Critics saw little merit in historical and biographical analysis. Rather, they aimed to examine the text alone, free from the question of how external events—biographical or otherwise—may have helped shape it. This predominantly American school was named "New Criticism" by one of its practitioners, John Crowe Ransom. Other important New Critics included Allen Tate, R. P. Blackmur, Robert Penn Warren, and Cleanth Brooks.

New Negro Movement: See *Harlem Renaissance*

Noble Savage: The idea that primitive man is noble and good but becomes evil and corrupted as he becomes civilized. The concept of the noble savage originated in the Renaissance period but is more closely identified with such later writers as Jean-Jacques Rousseau and Aphra Behn. First described in John Dryden's play *The Conquest of Granada,* the noble savage is portrayed by the various Native Americans in James Fenimore Cooper's "Leatherstocking Tales," by Queequeg, Daggoo, and Tashtego in Herman Melville's *Moby Dick,* and by John the Savage in Aldous Huxley's *Brave New World.*

O

Objective Correlative: An outward set of objects, a situation, or a chain of events corresponding to an inward experience and evoking this experience in the reader. The term frequently appears in modern criticism in discussions of authors' intended effects on the emotional responses of readers. This term was originally used by T. S. Eliot in his 1919 essay "Hamlet."

Objectivity: A quality in writing characterized by the absence of the author's opinion or feeling about the subject matter. Objectivity is an important factor in criticism. The novels of Henry James and, to a certain extent, the poems of John Larkin demonstrate objectivity, and it is central to John Keats's concept of "negative capability." Critical and journalistic writing usually are or attempt to be objective.

Occasional Verse: poetry written on the occasion of a significant historical or personal event. *Vers de societe* is sometimes called occasional verse although it is of a less serious nature. Famous examples of occasional verse include Andrew Marvell's "Horatian Ode upon Cromwell's Return from England," Walt Whitman's "When Lilacs Last in the Dooryard Bloom'd"—written upon the death of Abraham Lincoln—and Edmund Spenser's commemoration of his wedding, "Epithalamion."

Octave: A poem or stanza composed of eight lines. The term octave most often represents the first eight lines of a Petrarchan sonnet. An example of an octave is taken from a translation of a Petrarchan sonnet by Sir Thomas Wyatt: The pillar perisht is whereto I leant, The strongest stay of mine unquiet mind; The like of it no man again can find, From East to West Still seeking though he went. To mind unhap! for hap away hath rent Of all my joy the very bark and rind; And I, alas, by chance am thus assigned Daily to mourn till death do it relent.

Ode: Name given to an extended lyric poem characterized by exalted emotion and dignified style. An ode usually concerns a single, serious theme. Most odes, but not all, are addressed to an object or individual. Odes are distinguished from other lyric poetic forms by their complex rhythmic and stanzaic patterns. An example of this form is John Keats's "Ode to a Nightingale."

Oedipus Complex: A son's amorous obsession with his mother. The phrase is derived from the story of the ancient Theban hero Oedipus, who unknowingly killed his father and married his mother. Literary occurrences of the Oedipus complex include Andre Gide's *Oedipe* and Jean Cocteau's *La Machine infernale,* as well as the most famous, Sophocles' *Oedipus Rex.*

Omniscience: See *Point of View*

Onomatopoeia: The use of words whose sounds express or suggest their meaning. In its simplest sense, onomatopoeia may be represented by words that mimic the sounds they denote such as "hiss" or "meow." At a more subtle level, the pattern and rhythm of sounds and rhymes of a line or poem may be onomatopoeic. A celebrated example of onomatopoeia is the repetition of the word "bells" in Edgar Allan Poe's poem "The Bells."

Opera: A type of stage performance, usually a drama, in which the dialogue is sung. Classic examples of opera include Giuseppi Verdi's *La traviata*, Giacomo Puccini's *La Boheme*, and Richard Wagner's *Tristan und Isolde*. Major twentieth-century contributors to the form include Richard Strauss and Alban Berg.

Operetta: A usually romantic comic opera. John Gay's *The Beggar's Opera*, Richard Sheridan's *The Duenna*, and numerous works by William Gilbert and Arthur Sullivan are examples of operettas.

Oral Tradition: See *Oral Transmission*

Oral Transmission: A process by which songs, ballads, folklore, and other material are transmitted by word of mouth. The tradition of oral transmission predates the written record systems of literate society. Oral transmission preserves material sometimes over generations, although often with variations. Memory plays a large part in the recitation and preservation of orally transmitted material. Breton lays, French *fabliaux*, national epics (including the Anglo-Saxon *Beowulf*, the Spanish *El Cid*, and the Finnish *Kalevala*), Native American myths and legends, and African folktales told by plantation slaves are examples of orally transmitted literature.

Oration: Formal speaking intended to motivate the listeners to some action or feeling. Such public speaking was much more common before the development of timely printed communication such as newspapers. Famous examples of oration include Abraham Lincoln's "Gettysburg Address" and Dr. Martin Luther King Jr.'s "I Have a Dream" speech.

Ottava Rima: An eight-line stanza of poetry composed in iambic pentameter (a five-foot line in which each foot consists of an unaccented syllable followed by an accented syllable), following the abababcc rhyme scheme. This form has been prominently used by such important English writers as Lord Byron, Henry Wadsworth Longfellow, and W. B. Yeats.

Oxymoron: A phrase combining two contradictory terms. Oxymorons may be intentional or unintentional. The following speech from William Shakespeare's *Romeo and Juliet* uses several oxymorons: Why, then, O brawling love! O loving hate! O anything, of nothing first create! O heavy lightness! serious vanity! Mis-shapen chaos of well-seeming forms! Feather of lead, bright smoke, cold fire, sick health! This love feel I, that feel no love in this.

P

Pantheism: The idea that all things are both a manifestation or revelation of God and a part of God at the same time. Pantheism was a common attitude in the early societies of Egypt, India, and Greece—the term derives from the Greek *pan* meaning "all" and *theos* meaning "deity." It later became a significant part of the Christian faith. William Wordsworth and Ralph Waldo Emerson are among the many writers who have expressed the pantheistic attitude in their works.

Parable: A story intended to teach a moral lesson or answer an ethical question. In the West, the best examples of parables are those of Jesus Christ in the New Testament, notably "The Prodigal Son," but parables also are used in Sufism, rabbinic literature, Hasidism, and Zen Buddhism.

Paradox: A statement that appears illogical or contradictory at first, but may actually point to an underlying truth. "Less is more" is an example of a paradox. Literary examples include Francis Bacon's statement, "The most corrected copies are commonly the least correct," and "All animals are equal, but some animals are more equal than others" from George Orwell's *Animal Farm*.

Parallelism: A method of comparison of two ideas in which each is developed in the same grammatical structure. Ralph Waldo Emerson's "Civilization" contains this example of parallelism: Raphael paints wisdom; Handel sings it, Phidias carves it, Shakespeare writes it, Wren builds it, Columbus sails it, Luther preaches it, Washington arms it, Watt mechanizes it.

Parnassianism: A mid nineteenth-century movement in French literature. Followers of the movement stressed adherence to well-defined artistic forms as a reaction against the often chaotic expression of the artist's ego that dominated the work of the Romantics. The Parnassians also rejected the moral, ethical, and social themes exhibited in the works of French Romantics such as Victor Hugo. The aesthetic doctrines of the Parnassians strongly influenced the later symbolist and decadent movements. Members of the Parnassian school include Leconte de Lisle, Sully Prudhomme, Albert Glatigny, Francois Coppee, and Theodore de Banville.

Parody: In literary criticism, this term refers to an imitation of a serious literary work or the signature style of a particular author in a ridiculous manner. A typical parody adopts the style of the original and applies it to an inappropriate subject for humorous effect. Parody is a form of satire and could be considered the literary equivalent of a caricature or cartoon. Henry Fielding's *Shamela* is a parody of Samuel Richardson's *Pamela*.

Pastoral: A term derived from the Latin word "pastor," meaning shepherd. A pastoral is a literary composition on a rural theme. The conventions of the pastoral were originated by the third-century Greek poet Theocritus, who wrote about the experiences, love affairs, and pastimes of Sicilian shepherds. In a pastoral, characters and language of a courtly nature are often placed in a simple setting. The term pastoral is also used to classify dramas, elegies, and lyrics that exhibit the use of country settings and shepherd characters. Percy Bysshe Shelley's "Adonais" and John Milton's "Lycidas" are two famous examples of pastorals.

Pastorela: The Spanish name for the shepherds play, a folk drama reenacted during the Christmas season. Examples of *pastorelas* include Gomez Manrique's *Representacion del nacimiento* and the dramas of Lucas Fernandez and Juan del Encina.

Pathetic Fallacy: A term coined by English critic John Ruskin to identify writing that falsely endows nonhuman things with human intentions and feelings, such as "angry clouds" and "sad trees." The pathetic fallacy is a required convention in the classical poetic form of the pastoral elegy, and it is used in the modern poetry of T. S. Eliot, Ezra Pound, and the Imagists. Also known as Poetic Fallacy.

Pelado: Literally the "skinned one" or shirtless one, he was the stock underdog, sharp-witted picaresque character of Mexican vaudeville and tent shows. The *pelado* is found in such works as Don Catarino's *Los effectos de la crisis* and *Regreso a mi tierra*.

Pen Name: See *Pseudonym*

Pentameter: See *Meter*

Persona: A Latin term meaning "mask." *Personae* are the characters in a fictional work of literature. The *persona* generally functions as a mask through which the author tells a story in a voice other than his or her own. A *persona* is usually either a character in a story who acts as a narrator or an "implied author," a voice created by the author to act as the narrator for himself or herself. *Personae* include the narrator of Geoffrey Chaucer's *Canterbury Tales* and Marlow in Joseph Conrad's *Heart of Darkness*.

Personae: See *Persona*

Personal Point of View: See *Point of View*

Personification: A figure of speech that gives human qualities to abstract ideas, animals, and inanimate objects. William Shakespeare used personification in *Romeo and Juliet* in the lines "Arise, fair sun, and kill the envious moon,/ Who is already sick and pale with grief." Here, the moon is portrayed as being envious, sick, and pale with grief—all markedly human qualities. Also known as *Prosopopoeia*.

Petrarchan Sonnet: See *Sonnet*

Phenomenology: A method of literary criticism based on the belief that things have no existence outside of human consciousness or awareness. Proponents of this theory believe that art is a process that takes place in the mind of the observer as he or she contemplates an object rather than a quality of the object itself. Among phenomenological critics are Edmund Husserl, George Poulet, Marcel Raymond, and Roman Ingarden.

Picaresque Novel: Episodic fiction depicting the adventures of a roguish central character ("picaro" is Spanish for "rogue"). The picaresque hero is commonly a low-born but clever individual who wanders into and out of various affairs of love, danger, and farcical intrigue. These involvements may take place at all social levels and typically present a humorous and wide-ranging satire of a given society. Prominent examples of the picaresque novel are *Don Quixote* by Miguel de Cervantes, *Tom Jones* by Henry Fielding, and *Moll Flanders* by Daniel Defoe.

Plagiarism: Claiming another person's written material as one's own. Plagiarism can take the form of direct, word-for-word copying or the theft of the substance or idea of the work. A student who copies an encyclopedia entry and turns it in as a report for school is guilty of plagiarism.

Platonic Criticism: A form of criticism that stresses an artistic work's usefulness as an agent of social engineering rather than any quality or value of the work itself. Platonic criticism takes as its starting point the ancient Greek philosopher Plato's comments on art in his *Republic*.

Platonism: The embracing of the doctrines of the philosopher Plato, popular among the poets of the Renaissance and the Romantic period. Platonism is more flexible than Aristotelian Criticism and places more emphasis on the supernatural and unknown aspects of life. Platonism is expressed in the love poetry of the Renaissance, the fourth book of Baldassare Castiglione's *The Book of the Courtier,* and the poetry of William Blake, William Wordsworth, Percy Bysshe Shelley, Friedrich Holderlin, William Butler Yeats, and Wallace Stevens.

Play: See *Drama*

Plot: In literary criticism, this term refers to the pattern of events in a narrative or drama. In its simplest sense, the plot guides the author in composing the work and helps the reader follow the work. Typically, plots exhibit causality and unity and have a beginning, a middle, and an end. Sometimes, however, a plot may consist of a series of disconnected events, in which case it is known as an "episodic plot." In his *Aspects of the Novel,* E. M. Forster distinguishes between a story, defined as a "narrative of events arranged in their time- sequence," and plot, which organizes the events to a "sense of causality." This definition closely mirrors Aristotle's discussion of plot in his *Poetics.*

Poem: In its broadest sense, a composition utilizing rhyme, meter, concrete detail, and expressive language to create a literary experience with emotional and aesthetic appeal. Typical poems include sonnets, odes, elegies, *haiku,* ballads, and free verse.

Poet: An author who writes poetry or verse. The term is also used to refer to an artist or writer who has an exceptional gift for expression, imagination, and energy in the making of art in any form. Well-known poets include Horace, Basho, Sir Philip Sidney, Sir Edmund Spenser, John Donne, Andrew Marvell, Alexander Pope, Jonathan Swift, George Gordon, Lord Byron, John Keats, Christina Rossetti, W. H. Auden, Stevie Smith, and Sylvia Plath.

Poetic Fallacy: See *Pathetic Fallacy*

Poetic Justice: An outcome in a literary work, not necessarily a poem, in which the good are rewarded and the evil are punished, especially in ways that particularly fit their virtues or crimes. For example, a murderer may himself be murdered, or a thief will find himself penniless.

Poetic License: Distortions of fact and literary convention made by a writer—not always a poet—for the sake of the effect gained. Poetic license is closely related to the concept of "artistic freedom." An author exercises poetic license by saying that a pile of money "reaches as high as a mountain" when the pile is actually only a foot or two high.

Poetics: This term has two closely related meanings. It denotes (1) an aesthetic theory in literary criticism about the essence of poetry or (2) rules prescribing the proper methods, content, style, or diction of poetry. The term poetics may also refer to theories about literature in general, not just poetry.

Poetry: In its broadest sense, writing that aims to present ideas and evoke an emotional experience in the reader through the use of meter, imagery, connotative and concrete words, and a carefully constructed structure based on rhythmic patterns. Poetry typically relies on words and expressions that have several layers of meaning. It also makes use of the effects of regular rhythm on the ear and may make a strong appeal to the senses through the use of imagery. Edgar Allan Poe's "Annabel Lee" and Walt Whitman's *Leaves of Grass* are famous examples of poetry.

Point of View: The narrative perspective from which a literary work is presented to the reader. There are four traditional points of view. The "third person omniscient" gives the reader a "godlike" perspective, unrestricted by time or place, from which to see actions and look into the minds of characters. This allows the author to comment openly on characters and events in the work. The "third person" point of view presents the events of the story from outside of any single character's perception, much like the omniscient point of view, but the reader must understand the action as it takes place and without any special insight into characters' minds or motivations. The "first person" or "personal" point of view relates events as they are perceived by a single character. The main character "tells" the story and may offer opinions about the action and characters which differ from those of the author. Much less common than omniscient, third person, and first person is the "second person" point of view, wherein the author tells the story as if it is happening to the reader. James Thurber employs the omniscient point of view in his short story "The Secret Life of Walter Mitty." Ernest Hemingway's "A Clean, Well-Lighted Place" is a short story told from the third person point of view. Mark Twain's novel *Huck Finn* is presented from the first person viewpoint. Jay McInerney's *Bright Lights, Big City* is an example of a novel which uses the second person point of view.

Polemic: A work in which the author takes a stand on a controversial subject, such as abortion or religion. Such works are often extremely argumentative or provocative. Classic examples of polemics include John Milton's *Aeropagitica* and Thomas Paine's *The American Crisis*.

Pornography: Writing intended to provoke feelings of lust in the reader. Such works are often condemned by critics and teachers, but those which can be shown to have literary value are viewed less harshly. Literary works that have been described as pornographic include Ovid's *The Art of Love*, Margaret of Angouleme's *Heptameron*, John Cleland's *Memoirs of a Woman of Pleasure; or, the Life of Fanny Hill*, the anonymous *My Secret Life*, D. H. Lawrence's *Lady Chatterley's Lover*, and Vladimir Nabokov's *Lolita*.

Post-Aesthetic Movement: An artistic response made by African Americans to the black aesthetic movement of the 1960s and early '70s. Writers since that time have adopted a somewhat different tone in their work, with less emphasis placed on the disparity between black and white in the United States. In the words of post-aesthetic authors such as Toni Morrison, John Edgar Wideman, and Kristin Hunter, African Americans are portrayed as looking inward for answers to their own questions, rather than always looking to the outside world. Two well-known examples of works produced as part of the post-aesthetic movement are the Pulitzer Prize-winning novels *The Color Purple* by Alice Walker and *Beloved* by Toni Morrison.

Postmodernism: Writing from the 1960s forward characterized by experimentation and continuing to apply some of the fundamentals of modernism, which included existentialism and alienation. Postmodernists have gone a step further in the rejection of tradition begun with the modernists by also rejecting traditional forms, preferring the anti-novel over the novel and the anti-hero over the hero. Postmodern writers include Alain Robbe-Grillet, Thomas Pynchon, Margaret Drabble, John Fowles, Adolfo Bioy-Casares, and Gabriel Garcia Marquez.

Pre-Raphaelites: A circle of writers and artists in mid nineteenth-century England. Valuing the pre-Renaissance artistic qualities of religious symbolism, lavish pictorialism, and natural sensuousness, the Pre-Raphaelites cultivated a sense of mystery and melancholy that influenced later writers associated with the Symbolist and Decadent movements. The major members of the group include Dante Gabriel Rossetti, Christina Rossetti, Algernon Swinburne, and Walter Pater.

Primitivism: The belief that primitive peoples were nobler and less flawed than civilized peoples because they had not been subjected to the tainting influence of society. Examples of literature espousing primitivism include Aphra Behn's *Oroonoko: Or, The History of the Royal Slave*, Jean-Jacques Rousseau's *Julie ou la Nouvelle Heloise*,

Oliver Goldsmith's *The Deserted Village,* the poems of Robert Burns, Herman Melville's stories *Typee, Omoo,* and *Mardi,* many poems of William Butler Yeats and Robert Frost, and William Golding's novel *Lord of the Flies.*

Projective Verse: A form of free verse in which the poet's breathing pattern determines the lines of the poem. Poets who advocate projective verse are against all formal structures in writing, including meter and form. Besides its creators, Robert Creeley, Robert Duncan, and Charles Olson, two other well-known projective verse poets are Denise Levertov and LeRoi Jones (Amiri Baraka). Also known as Breath Verse.

Prologue: An introductory section of a literary work. It often contains information establishing the situation of the characters or presents information about the setting, time period, or action. In drama, the prologue is spoken by a chorus or by one of the principal characters. In the "General Prologue" of *The Canterbury Tales,* Geoffrey Chaucer describes the main characters and establishes the setting and purpose of the work.

Prose: A literary medium that attempts to mirror the language of everyday speech. It is distinguished from poetry by its use of unmetered, unrhymed language consisting of logically related sentences. Prose is usually grouped into paragraphs that form a cohesive whole such as an essay or a novel. Recognized masters of English prose writing include Sir Thomas Malory, William Caxton, Raphael Holinshed, Joseph Addison, Mark Twain, and Ernest Hemingway.

Prosopopoeia: See *Personification*

Protagonist: The central character of a story who serves as a focus for its themes and incidents and as the principal rationale for its development. The protagonist is sometimes referred to in discussions of modern literature as the hero or anti-hero. Well-known protagonists are Hamlet in William Shakespeare's *Hamlet* and Jay Gatsby in F. Scott Fitzgerald's *The Great Gatsby.*

Protest Fiction: Protest fiction has as its primary purpose the protesting of some social injustice, such as racism or discrimination. One example of protest fiction is a series of five novels by Chester Himes, beginning in 1945 with *If He Hollers Let Him Go* and ending in 1955 with *The Primitive.* These works depict the destructive effects of race and gender stereotyping in the context of interracial relationships. Another African American author whose works often revolve around themes of social protest is John Oliver Killens. James Baldwin's essay "Everybody's Protest Novel" generated controversy by attacking the authors of protest fiction.

Proverb: A brief, sage saying that expresses a truth about life in a striking manner. "They are not all cooks who carry long knives" is an example of a proverb.

Pseudonym: A name assumed by a writer, most often intended to prevent his or her identification as the author of a work. Two or more authors may work together under one pseudonym, or an author may use a different name for each genre he or she publishes in. Some publishing companies maintain "house pseudonyms," under which any number of authors may write installations in a series. Some authors also choose a pseudonym over their real names the way an actor may use a stage name. Examples of pseudonyms (with the author's real name in parentheses) include Voltaire (Francois-Marie Arouet), Novalis (Friedrich von Hardenberg), Currer Bell (Charlotte Bronte), Ellis Bell (Emily Bronte), George Eliot (Maryann Evans), Honorio Bustos Donmecq (Adolfo Bioy-Casares and Jorge Luis Borges), and Richard Bachman (Stephen King).

Pun: A play on words that have similar sounds but different meanings. A serious example of the pun is from John Donne's "A Hymne to God the Father": Sweare by thyself, that at my death thy sonne Shall shine as he shines now, and hereto fore; And, having done that, Thou haste done; I fear no more.

Pure Poetry: poetry written without instructional intent or moral purpose that aims only to please a reader by its imagery or musical flow. The term pure poetry is used as the antonym of the term "didacticism." The poetry of Edgar Allan Poe, Stephane Mallarme, Paul Verlaine, Paul Valery, Juan Ramoz Jimenez, and Jorge Guillen offer examples of pure poetry.

Q

Quatrain: A four-line stanza of a poem or an entire poem consisting of four lines. The following quatrain is from Robert Herrick's "To Live Merrily, and to Trust to Good Verses": Round, round, the root do's run; And being ravisht thus, Come, I will drink a Tun To my *Propertius.*

R

Raisonneur: A character in a drama who functions as a spokesperson for the dramatist's views. The *raisonneur* typically observes the play without becoming central to its action. *Raisonneurs* were very common in plays of the nineteenth century.

Realism: A nineteenth-century European literary movement that sought to portray familiar characters, situations, and settings in a realistic manner. This was done primarily by using an objective narrative point of view and through the buildup of accurate detail. The standard for success of any realistic work depends on how faithfully it transfers common experience into fictional forms. The realistic method may be altered or extended, as in stream of consciousness writing, to record highly subjective experience. Seminal authors in the tradition of Realism include Honore de Balzac, Gustave Flaubert, and Henry James.

Refrain: A phrase repeated at intervals throughout a poem. A refrain may appear at the end of each stanza or at less regular intervals. It may be altered slightly at each appearance. Some refrains are nonsense expressions—as with "Nevermore" in Edgar Allan Poe's "The Raven"—that seem to take on a different significance with each use.

Renaissance: The period in European history that marked the end of the Middle Ages. It began in Italy in the late fourteenth century. In broad terms, it is usually seen as spanning the fourteenth, fifteenth, and sixteenth centuries, although it did not reach Great Britain, for example, until the 1480s or so. The Renaissance saw an awakening in almost every sphere of human activity, especially science, philosophy, and the arts. The period is best defined by the emergence of a general philosophy that emphasized the importance of the intellect, the individual, and world affairs. It contrasts strongly with the medieval worldview, characterized by the dominant concerns of faith, the social collective, and spiritual salvation. Prominent writers during the Renaissance include Niccolo Machiavelli and Baldassare Castiglione in Italy, Miguel de Cervantes and Lope de Vega in Spain, Jean Froissart and Francois Rabelais in France, Sir Thomas More and Sir Philip Sidney in England, and Desiderius Erasmus in Holland.

Repartee: Conversation featuring snappy retorts and witticisms. Masters of *repartee* include Sydney Smith, Charles Lamb, and Oscar Wilde. An example is recorded in the meeting of "Beau" Nash and John Wesley: Nash said, "I never make way for a fool," to which Wesley responded, "Don't you? I always do," and stepped aside.

Resolution: The portion of a story following the climax, in which the conflict is resolved. The resolution of Jane Austen's *Northanger Abbey* is neatly summed up in the following sentence: "Henry and Catherine were married, the bells rang and every body smiled."

Restoration: See *Restoration Age*

Restoration Age: A period in English literature beginning with the crowning of Charles II in 1660 and running to about 1700. The era, which was characterized by a reaction against Puritanism, was the first great age of the comedy of manners. The finest literature of the era is typically witty and urbane, and often lewd. Prominent Restoration Age writers include William Congreve, Samuel Pepys, John Dryden, and John Milton.

Revenge Tragedy: A dramatic form popular during the Elizabethan Age, in which the protagonist, directed by the ghost of his murdered father or son, inflicts retaliation upon a powerful villain. Notable features of the revenge tragedy include violence, bizarre criminal acts, intrigue, insanity, a hesitant protagonist, and the use of soliloquy. Thomas Kyd's *Spanish Tragedy* is the first example of revenge tragedy in English, and William Shakespeare's *Hamlet* is perhaps the best. Extreme examples of revenge tragedy, such as John Webster's *The Duchess of Malfi,* are labeled "tragedies of blood." Also known as Tragedy of Blood.

Revista: The Spanish term for a vaudeville musical revue. Examples of *revistas* include Antonio Guzman Aguilera's *Mexico para* *los mexicanos,* Daniel Vanegas's *Maldito jazz,* and Don Catarino's *Whiskey, morfina y marihuana* and *El desterrado.*

Rhetoric: In literary criticism, this term denotes the art of ethical persuasion. In its strictest sense, rhetoric adheres to various principles developed since classical times for arranging facts and ideas in a clear, persuasive, appealing manner. The term is also used to refer to effective prose in general and theories of or methods for composing effective prose. Classical examples of rhetorics include *The Rhetoric of Aristotle,* Quintillian's *Institutio Oratoria,* and Cicero's *Ad Herennium.*

Rhetorical Question: A question intended to provoke thought, but not an expressed answer, in the reader. It is most commonly used in oratory and other persuasive genres. The following lines from Thomas Gray's "Elegy Written in a Country Churchyard" ask rhetorical questions: Can storied urn or animated bust Back to its mansion call the fleeting breath? Can Honour's voice provoke the silent dust, Or Flattery soothe the dull cold ear of Death?

Rhyme: When used as a noun in literary criticism, this term generally refers to a poem in which words sound identical or very similar and appear in parallel positions in two or more lines. Rhymes are classified into different types according to where they fall in a line or stanza or according to the degree of similarity they exhibit in their spellings and sounds. Some major types of rhyme are "masculine" rhyme, "feminine" rhyme, and "triple" rhyme. In a masculine rhyme, the rhyming sound falls in a single accented syllable, as with "heat" and "eat." Feminine rhyme is a rhyme of two syllables, one stressed and one unstressed, as with "merry" and "tarry." Triple rhyme matches the sound of the accented syllable and the two unaccented syllables that follow: "narrative" and "declarative." Robert Browning alternates feminine and masculine rhymes in his "Soliloquy of the Spanish Cloister": Gr-r-r—there go, my heart's abhorrence! Water your damned flower-pots, do! If hate killed men, Brother Lawrence, God's blood, would not mine kill you! What? Your myrtle-bush wants trimming? Oh, that rose has prior claims— Needs its leaden vase filled brimming? Hell dry you up with flames!

Triple rhymes can be found in Thomas Hood's "Bridge of Sighs," George Gordon Byron's satirical verse, and Ogden Nash's comic poems.

Rhyme Royal: A stanza of seven lines composed in iambic pentameter and rhymed *ababbcc.* The name is said to be a tribute to King James I of Scotland, who made much use of the form in his poetry. Examples of rhyme royal include Geoffrey Chaucer's *The Parlement of Foules,* William Shakespeare's *The Rape of Lucrece,* William Morris's *The Early Paradise,* and John Masefield's *The Widow in the Bye Street.*

Rhyme Scheme: See *Rhyme*

Rhythm: A regular pattern of sound, time intervals, or events occurring in writing, most often and most discernably in poetry. Regular, reliable rhythm is known to be soothing to humans, while interrupted, unpredictable, or rapidly changing rhythm is disturbing. These effects are known to authors, who use them to produce a desired reaction in the reader. An example of a form of irregular rhythm is sprung rhythm poetry; quantitative verse, on the other hand, is very regular in its rhythm.

Rising Action: The part of a drama where the plot becomes increasingly complicated. Rising action leads up to the climax, or turning point, of a drama. The final "chase scene" of an action film is generally the rising action which culminates in the film's climax.

Rococo: A style of European architecture that flourished in the eighteenth century, especially in France. The most notable features of *rococo* are its extensive use of ornamentation and its themes of lightness, gaiety, and intimacy. In literary criticism, the term is often used disparagingly to refer to a decadent or over-ornamental style. Alexander Pope's "The Rape of the Lock" is an example of literary *rococo.*

Roman à clef: A French phrase meaning "novel with a key." It refers to a narrative in which real persons are portrayed under fictitious names. Jack Kerouac, for example, portrayed various real-life beat generation figures under fictitious names in his *On the Road.*

Romance: A broad term, usually denoting a narrative with exotic, exaggerated, often idealized characters, scenes, and themes. Nathaniel Hawthorne called his *The House of the Seven Gables* and *The Marble Faun* romances in order to distinguish them from clearly realistic works.

Romantic Age: See *Romanticism*

Romanticism: This term has two widely accepted meanings. In historical criticism, it refers to a European intellectual and artistic movement of the late eighteenth and early nineteenth centuries that sought greater freedom of personal expression than that allowed by the strict rules of literary form and logic of the eighteenth-century neoclassicists. The Romantics preferred emotional and imaginative expression to rational analysis. They considered the individual to be at the center of all experience and so placed him or her at the center of their art. The Romantics believed that the creative imagination reveals nobler truths—unique feelings and attitudes—than those that could be discovered by logic or by scientific examination. Both the natural world and the state of childhood were important sources for revelations of "eternal truths." "Romanticism" is also used as a general term to refer to a type of sensibility found in all periods of literary history and usually considered to be in opposition to the principles of classicism. In this sense, Romanticism signifies any work or philosophy in which the exotic or dreamlike figure strongly, or that is devoted to individualistic expression, self-analysis, or a pursuit of a higher realm of knowledge than can be discovered by human reason. Prominent Romantics include Jean-Jacques Rousseau, William Wordsworth, John Keats, Lord Byron, and Johann Wolfgang von Goethe.

Romantics: See *Romanticism*

Russian Symbolism: A Russian poetic movement, derived from French symbolism, that flourished between 1894 and 1910. While some Russian Symbolists continued in the French tradition, stressing aestheticism and the importance of suggestion above didactic intent, others saw their craft as a form of mystical worship, and themselves as mediators between the supernatural and the mundane. Russian symbolists include Aleksandr Blok, Vyacheslav Ivanovich Ivanov, Fyodor Sologub, Andrey Bely, Nikolay Gumilyov, and Vladimir Sergeyevich Solovyov.

S

Satire: A work that uses ridicule, humor, and wit to criticize and provoke change in human nature and institutions. There are two major types of satire: "formal" or "direct" satire speaks directly to the reader or to a character in the work; "indirect" satire relies upon the ridiculous behavior of its characters to make its point. Formal satire is further divided into two manners: the "Horatian," which ridicules gently, and the "Juvenalian," which derides its subjects harshly and bitterly. Voltaire's novella *Candide* is an indirect satire. Jonathan Swift's essay "A Modest Proposal" is a Juvenalian satire.

Scansion: The analysis or "scanning" of a poem to determine its meter and often its rhyme scheme. The most common system of scansion uses accents (slanted lines drawn above syllables) to show stressed syllables, breves (curved lines drawn above syllables) to show unstressed syllables, and vertical lines to separate each foot. In the first line of John Keats's *Endymion,* "A thing of beauty is a joy forever:" the word "thing," the first syllable of "beauty," the word "joy," and the second syllable of "forever" are stressed, while the words "A" and "of," the second syllable of "beauty," the word "a," and the first and third syllables of "forever" are unstressed. In the second line: "Its loveliness increases; it will never" a pair of vertical lines separate the foot ending with "increases" and the one beginning with "it."

Scene: A subdivision of an act of a drama, consisting of continuous action taking place at a single time and in a single location. The beginnings and endings of scenes may be indicated by clearing the stage of actors and props or by the entrances and exits of important characters. The first act of William Shakespeare's *Winter's Tale* is comprised of two scenes.

Science Fiction: A type of narrative about or based upon real or imagined scientific theories and technology. Science fiction is often peopled with alien creatures and set on other planets or in different dimensions. Karel Capek's *R.U.R.* is a major work of science fiction.

Second Person: See *Point of View*

Semiotics: The study of how literary forms and conventions affect the meaning of language. Semioticians include Ferdinand de Saussure, Charles Sanders Pierce, Claude Levi-Strauss, Jacques Lacan, Michel Foucault, Jacques Derrida, Roland Barthes, and Julia Kristeva.

Sestet: Any six-line poem or stanza. Examples of the sestet include the last six lines of the Petrarchan sonnet form, the stanza form of Robert Burns's "A Poet's Welcome to his love-begotten Daughter," and the sestina form in W. H. Auden's "Paysage Moralise."

Setting: The time, place, and culture in which the action of a narrative takes place. The elements of setting may include geographic location, characters' physical and mental environments, prevailing cultural attitudes, or the historical time in which the action takes place. Examples of settings include the romanticized Scotland in Sir Walter Scott's "Waverley" novels, the French provincial setting in Gustave Flaubert's *Madame Bovary,* the fictional Wessex country of Thomas Hardy's novels, and the small towns of southern Ontario in Alice Munro's short stories.

Shakespearean Sonnet: See *Sonnet*

Signifying Monkey: A popular trickster figure in black folklore, with hundreds of tales about this character documented since the 19th century. Henry Louis Gates Jr. examines the history of the signifying monkey in *The Signifying Monkey: Towards a Theory of Afro-American Literary Criticism,* published in 1988.

Simile: A comparison, usually using "like" or "as," of two essentially dissimilar things, as in "coffee as cold as ice" or "He sounded like a broken record." The title of Ernest Hemingway's "Hills Like White Elephants" contains a simile.

Slang: A type of informal verbal communication that is generally unacceptable for formal writing. Slang words and phrases are often colorful exaggerations used to emphasize the speaker's point; they may also be shortened versions of an often-used word or phrase. Examples of American slang from the 1990s include "yuppie" (an acronym for Young Urban Professional), "awesome" (for "excellent"), wired (for "nervous" or "excited"), and "chill out" (for relax).

Slant Rhyme: See *Consonance*

Slave Narrative: Autobiographical accounts of American slave life as told by escaped slaves. These works first appeared during the abolition movement of the 1830s through the 1850s. Olaudah Equiano's *The Interesting Narrative of Olaudah Equiano, or Gustavus Vassa, The African* and Harriet Ann Jacobs's *Incidents in the Life of a Slave Girl* are examples of the slave narrative.

Social Realism: See *Socialist Realism*

Socialist Realism: The Socialist Realism school of literary theory was proposed by Maxim Gorky and established as a dogma by the first Soviet Congress of Writers. It demanded adherence to a communist worldview in works of literature. Its doctrines required an objective viewpoint comprehensible to the working classes and themes of social struggle featuring strong proletarian heroes. A successful work of socialist realism is Nikolay Ostrovsky's *Kak zakalyalas stal* (*How the Steel Was Tempered*). Also known as Social Realism.

Soliloquy: A monologue in a drama used to give the audience information and to develop the speaker's character. It is typically a projection of the speaker's innermost thoughts. Usually delivered while the speaker is alone on stage, a soliloquy is intended to present an illusion of unspoken reflection. A celebrated soliloquy is Hamlet's "To be or not to be" speech in William Shakespeare's *Hamlet.*

Sonnet: A fourteen-line poem, usually composed in iambic pentameter, employing one of several rhyme schemes. There are three major types of sonnets, upon which all other variations of the form are based: the "Petrarchan" or "Italian" sonnet, the "Shakespearean" or "English" sonnet, and the "Spenserian" sonnet. A Petrarchan sonnet consists of an octave rhymed *abbaabba* and a "sestet" rhymed either *cdecde, cdccdc,* or *cdedce.* The octave poses a question or problem, relates a narrative, or puts forth a proposition; the sestet presents a solution to the problem, comments upon the narrative, or applies the proposition put forth in the octave. The Shakespearean sonnet is divided into three quatrains and a couplet rhymed *abab cdcd efef gg.* The couplet provides an epigrammatic comment on the narrative or problem put forth in the quatrains. The Spenserian sonnet uses three quatrains and a couplet like the Shakespearean, but links their three rhyme schemes in this way: *abab bcbc cdcd ee*. The Spenserian sonnet develops its theme in two parts like the Petrarchan, its final six lines resolving a problem, analyzing a narrative, or applying a proposition put forth in its first eight lines. Examples of sonnets can be found in Petrarch's *Canzoniere,* Edmund Spenser's *Amoretti,* Elizabeth Barrett Browning's *Sonnets from the Portuguese,* Rainer Maria Rilke's *Sonnets to Orpheus,* and Adrienne Rich's poem "The Insusceptibles."

Spenserian Sonnet: See *Sonnet*

Spenserian Stanza: A nine-line stanza having eight verses in iambic pentameter, its ninth verse in iambic hexameter, and the rhyme scheme ababbcbcc. This stanza form was first used by Edmund Spenser in his allegorical poem *The Faerie Queene.*

Spondee: In poetry meter, a foot consisting of two long or stressed syllables occurring together. This form is quite rare in English verse, and is usually composed of two monosyllabic words. The first foot in the following line from Robert Burns's "Green Grow the Rashes" is an example of a spondee: Green grow the rashes, O.

Sprung Rhythm: Versification using a specific number of accented syllables per line but disregarding the number of unaccented syllables that fall in each line, producing an irregular rhythm in the poem. Gerard Manley Hopkins, who coined the term "sprung rhythm," is the most notable practitioner of this technique.

Stanza: A subdivision of a poem consisting of lines grouped together, often in recurring patterns of rhyme, line length, and meter. Stanzas may also serve as units of thought in a poem much like paragraphs in prose. Examples of stanza forms include the quatrain, *terza rima, ottava rima,* Spenserian, and the so-called *In Memoriam* stanza from Alfred, Lord Tennyson's poem by that title. The following is an example of the latter form: Love is and was my lord and king, And in his presence I attend To hear the tidings of my friend, Which every hour his couriers bring.

Stereotype: A stereotype was originally the name for a duplication made during the printing process; this led to its modern definition as a person or thing that is (or is assumed to be) the same as all others of its type. Common stereotypical characters include the absent-minded professor, the nagging wife, the troublemaking teenager, and the kind-hearted grandmother.

Stream of Consciousness: A narrative technique for rendering the inward experience of a character. This technique is designed to give the impression of an ever-changing series of thoughts, emotions, images, and memories in the spontaneous and seemingly illogical order that they occur in life. The textbook example of stream of consciousness is the last section of James Joyce's *Ulysses.*

Structuralism: A twentieth-century movement in literary criticism that examines how literary texts arrive at their meanings, rather than the meanings themselves. There are two major types of structuralist analysis: one examines the way patterns of linguistic structures unify a specific text and emphasize certain elements of that text, and the other interprets the way literary forms and conventions affect the meaning of language itself. Prominent structuralists include Michel Foucault, Roman Jakobson, and Roland Barthes.

Structure: The form taken by a piece of literature. The structure may be made obvious for ease of understanding, as in nonfiction works, or may obscured for artistic purposes, as in some poetry or seemingly "unstructured" prose. Examples of common literary structures include the plot of a narrative, the acts and scenes of a drama, and such poetic forms as the Shakespearean sonnet and the Pindaric ode.

Sturm und Drang: A German term meaning "storm and stress." It refers to a German literary movement of the 1770s and 1780s that reacted against the order and rationalism of the enlightenment, focusing instead on the intense experience of extraordinary individuals. Highly romantic, works of this movement, such as Johann Wolfgang von Goethe's *Gotz von Berlichingen,* are typified by realism, rebelliousness, and intense emotionalism.

Style: A writer's distinctive manner of arranging words to suit his or her ideas and purpose in writing. The unique imprint of the author's personality upon his or her writing, style is the product of an author's way of arranging ideas and his or her use of diction, different sentence structures, rhythm, figures of speech, rhetorical principles, and other elements of composition. Styles may be classified according to period (Metaphysical, Augustan, Georgian), individual authors (Chaucerian, Miltonic, Jamesian), level (grand, middle, low, plain), or language (scientific, expository, poetic, journalistic).

Subject: The person, event, or theme at the center of a work of literature. A work may have one or more subjects of each type, with shorter works tending to have fewer and longer works tending to have more. The subjects of James Baldwin's novel *Go Tell It on the Mountain* include the themes of father-son relationships, religious conversion, black life, and sexuality. The subjects of Anne Frank's *Diary of a Young Girl* include Anne and her family members as well as World War II, the Holocaust, and the themes of war, isolation, injustice, and racism.

Subjectivity: Writing that expresses the author's personal feelings about his subject, and which may or may not include factual information about the subject. Subjectivity is demonstrated in James Joyce's *Portrait of the Artist as a Young Man,* Samuel Butler's *The Way of All Flesh,* and Thomas Wolfe's *Look Homeward, Angel.*

Subplot: A secondary story in a narrative. A subplot may serve as a motivating or complicating force for the main plot of the work, or it may provide emphasis for, or relief from, the main plot. The conflict between the Capulets and the Montagues in William Shakespeare's *Romeo and Juliet* is an example of a subplot.

Surrealism: A term introduced to criticism by Guillaume Apollinaire and later adopted by Andre Breton. It refers to a French literary and artistic movement founded in the 1920s. The Surrealists sought to express unconscious thoughts and feelings in their works. The best-known technique used for achieving this aim was automatic writing—transcriptions of spontaneous outpourings from the unconscious. The Surrealists proposed to unify the contrary levels of conscious and unconscious, dream and reality, objectivity and subjectivity into a new level of "super-realism." Surrealism can be found in the poetry of Paul Eluard, Pierre Reverdy, and Louis Aragon, among others.

Suspense: A literary device in which the author maintains the audience's attention through the buildup of events, the outcome of which will soon be revealed. Suspense in William Shakespeare's *Hamlet* is sustained throughout by the question of whether or not the Prince will achieve what he has been instructed to do and of what he intends to do.

Syllogism: A method of presenting a logical argument. In its most basic form, the syllogism consists of a major premise, a minor premise, and a conclusion. An example of a syllogism is: Major premise: When it snows, the streets get wet. Minor premise: It is snowing. Conclusion: The streets are wet.

Symbol: Something that suggests or stands for something else without losing its original identity. In literature, symbols combine their literal meaning with the suggestion of an abstract concept. Literary symbols are of two types: those that carry complex associations of meaning no matter what their contexts, and those that derive their suggestive meaning from their functions in specific literary works. Examples of symbols are sunshine suggesting happiness, rain suggesting sorrow, and storm clouds suggesting despair.

Symbolism: This term has two widely accepted meanings. In historical criticism, it denotes an early modernist literary movement initiated in France during the nineteenth century that reacted against the prevailing standards of realism. Writers in this movement aimed to evoke, indirectly and symbolically, an order of being beyond the material world of the five senses. Poetic expression of personal emotion figured strongly in the movement, typically by means of a private set of symbols uniquely identifiable with the individual poet. The principal aim of the Symbolists was to express in words the highly complex feelings that grew out of everyday contact with the world. In a broader sense, the term "symbolism" refers to the use of one object to represent another. Early members of the

Symbolist movement included the French authors Charles Baudelaire and Arthur Rimbaud; William Butler Yeats, James Joyce, and T. S. Eliot were influenced as the movement moved to Ireland, England, and the United States. Examples of the concept of symbolism include a flag that stands for a nation or movement, or an empty cupboard used to suggest hopelessness, poverty, and despair.

Symbolist: See *Symbolism*

Symbolist Movement: See *Symbolism*

Sympathetic Fallacy: See *Affective Fallacy*

T

Tale: A story told by a narrator with a simple plot and little character development. Tales are usually relatively short and often carry a simple message. Examples of tales can be found in the work of Rudyard Kipling, Somerset Maugham, Saki, Anton Chekhov, Guy de Maupassant, and Armistead Maupin.

Tall Tale: A humorous tale told in a straightforward, credible tone but relating absolutely impossible events or feats of the characters. Such tales were commonly told of frontier adventures during the settlement of the west in the United States. Tall tales have been spun around such legendary heroes as Mike Fink, Paul Bunyan, Davy Crockett, Johnny Appleseed, and Captain Stormalong as well as the real-life William F. Cody and Annie Oakley. Literary use of tall tales can be found in Washington Irving's *History of New York,* Mark Twain's *Life on the Mississippi,* and in the German R. F. Raspe's *Baron Munchausen's Narratives of His Marvellous Travels and Campaigns in Russia.*

Tanka: A form of Japanese poetry similar to *haiku.* A *tanka* is five lines long, with the lines containing five, seven, five, seven, and seven syllables respectively. Skilled *tanka* authors include Ishikawa Takuboku, Masaoka Shiki, Amy Lowell, and Adelaide Crapsey.

Teatro Grottesco: See *Theater of the Grotesque*

Terza Rima: A three-line stanza form in poetry in which the rhymes are made on the last word of each line in the following manner: the first and third lines of the first stanza, then the second line of the first stanza and the first and third lines of the second stanza, and so on with the middle line of any stanza rhyming with the first and third lines of the following stanza. An example of *terza rima* is Percy Bysshe Shelley's "The Triumph of Love": As in that trance of wondrous thought I lay This was the tenour of my waking dream. Methought I sate beside a public way Thick strewn with summer dust, and a great stream Of people there was hurrying to and fro Numerous as gnats upon the evening gleam,...

Tetrameter: See *Meter*

Textual Criticism: A branch of literary criticism that seeks to establish the authoritative text of a literary work. Textual critics typically compare all known manuscripts or printings of a single work in order to assess the meanings of differences and revisions. This procedure allows them to arrive at a definitive version that (supposedly) corresponds to the author's original intention. Textual criticism was applied during the Renaissance to salvage the classical texts of Greece and Rome, and modern works have been studied, for instance, to undo deliberate correction or censorship, as in the case of novels by Stephen Crane and Theodore Dreiser.

Theater of Cruelty: Term used to denote a group of theatrical techniques designed to eliminate the psychological and emotional distance between actors and audience. This concept, introduced in the 1930s in France, was intended to inspire a more intense theatrical experience than conventional theater allowed. The "cruelty" of this dramatic theory signified not sadism but heightened actor/audience involvement in the dramatic event. The theater of cruelty was theorized by Antonin Artaud in his *Le Theatre et son double* (*The Theatre and Its Double*), and also appears in the work of Jerzy Grotowski, Jean Genet, Jean Vilar, and Arthur Adamov, among others.

Theater of the Absurd: A post-World War II dramatic trend characterized by radical theatrical innovations. In works influenced by the Theater of the Absurd, nontraditional, sometimes grotesque characterizations, plots, and stage sets reveal a meaningless universe in which human values are irrelevant. Existentialist themes of estrangement, absurdity, and futility link many of the works of this movement. The principal writers of the Theater of the Absurd are Samuel Beckett, Eugene Ionesco, Jean Genet, and Harold Pinter.

Theater of the Grotesque: An Italian theatrical movement characterized by plays written around the ironic and macabre aspects of daily life in the World War I era. Theater of the Grotesque was named after the play *The Mask and the Face* by Luigi Chiarelli, which was described as "a grotesque in three acts." The movement influenced the work of Italian dramatist Luigi Pirandello, author of *Right You Are, If You Think You Are.* Also known as *Teatro Grottesco.*

Theme: The main point of a work of literature. The term is used interchangeably with thesis. The theme of William Shakespeare's *Othello*—jealousy—is a common one.

Thesis: A thesis is both an essay and the point argued in the essay. Thesis novels and thesis plays share the quality of containing a thesis which is supported through the action of the story. A master's thesis and a doctoral dissertation are two theses required of graduate students.

Thesis Play: See *Thesis*

Three Unities: See *Unities*

Tone: The author's attitude toward his or her audience may be deduced from the tone of the work. A formal tone may create distance or convey politeness, while an informal tone may encourage a friendly, intimate, or intrusive feeling in the reader. The author's attitude toward his or her subject matter may also be deduced from the tone of the words he or she uses in discussing it. The tone of John F. Kennedy's speech which included the appeal to "ask not what your country can do for you" was intended to instill feelings of camaraderie and national pride in listeners.

Tragedy: A drama in prose or poetry about a noble, courageous hero of excellent character who, because of some tragic character flaw or *hamartia*, brings ruin upon him- or herself. Tragedy treats its subjects in a dignified and serious manner, using poetic language to help evoke pity and fear and bring about catharsis, a purging of these emotions. The tragic form was practiced extensively by the ancient Greeks. In the Middle Ages, when classical works were virtually unknown, tragedy came to denote any works about the fall of persons from exalted to low conditions due to any reason: fate, vice, weakness, etc. According to the classical definition of tragedy, such works present the "pathetic"—that which evokes pity—rather than the tragic. The classical form of tragedy was revived in the sixteenth century; it flourished especially on the Elizabethan stage. In modern times, dramatists have attempted to adapt the form to the needs of modern society by drawing their heroes from the ranks of ordinary men and women and defining the nobility of these heroes in terms of spirit rather than exalted social standing. The greatest classical example of tragedy is Sophocles' *Oedipus Rex.* The "pathetic" derivation is exemplified in "The Monk's Tale" in Geoffrey Chaucer's *Canterbury Tales.* Notable works produced during the sixteenth century revival include William Shakespeare's *Hamlet, Othello,* and *King Lear.* Modern dramatists working in the tragic tradition include Henrik Ibsen, Arthur Miller, and Eugene O'Neill.

Tragedy of Blood: See *Revenge Tragedy*

Tragic Flaw: In a tragedy, the quality within the hero or heroine which leads to his or her downfall. Examples of the tragic flaw include Othello's jealousy and Hamlet's indecisiveness, although most great tragedies defy such simple interpretation.

Transcendentalism: An American philosophical and religious movement, based in New England from around 1835 until the Civil War. Transcendentalism was a form of American romanticism that had its roots abroad in the works of Thomas Carlyle, Samuel Coleridge, and Johann Wolfgang von Goethe. The Transcendentalists stressed the importance of intuition and subjective experience in communication with God. They rejected religious dogma and texts in favor of mysticism and scientific naturalism. They pursued truths that lie beyond the "colorless" realms perceived by reason and the senses and were active social reformers in public education, women's rights, and the abolition of slavery. Prominent members of the group include Ralph Waldo Emerson and Henry David Thoreau.

Trickster: A character or figure common in Native American and African literature who uses his ingenuity to defeat enemies and escape difficult situations. Tricksters are most often animals, such as the spider, hare, or coyote, although they may take the form of humans as well. Examples of trickster tales include Thomas King's *A Coyote Columbus Story,* Ashley F. Bryan's *The Dancing Granny* and Ishmael Reed's *The Last Days of Louisiana Red.*

Trimeter: See *Meter*

Triple Rhyme: See *Rhyme*

Trochee: See *Foot*

U

Understatement: See *Irony*

Unities: Strict rules of dramatic structure, formulated by Italian and French critics of the Renaissance and based loosely on the principles of drama discussed by Aristotle in his *Poetics.* Foremost among these rules were the three unities of action, time, and place that compelled a dramatist to: (1) construct a single plot with a beginning, middle, and end that details the causal relationships of action and character; (2) restrict the action to the events of a single day; and (3) limit the scene to a single place or city. The unities were observed faithfully by continental European writers until the Romantic Age, but they were never regularly observed in English drama. Modern dramatists are typically more concerned with a unity of impression or emotional effect than with any of the classical unities. The unities are observed in Pierre Corneille's tragedy *Polyeucte* and Jean-Baptiste Racine's *Phedre.* Also known as Three Unities.

Urban Realism: A branch of realist writing that attempts to accurately reflect the often harsh facts of modern urban existence. Some works by Stephen Crane, Theodore Dreiser, Charles Dickens, Fyodor Dostoyevsky, Emile Zola, Abraham Cahan, and Henry Fuller feature urban realism. Modern examples include Claude Brown's *Manchild in the Promised Land* and Ron Milner's *What the Wine Sellers Buy.*

Utopia: A fictional perfect place, such as "paradise" or "heaven." Early literary utopias were included in Plato's *Republic* and Sir Thomas More's *Utopia,* while more modern utopias can be found in Samuel Butler's *Erewhon,* Theodor Herzka's *A Visit to Freeland,* and H. G. Wells' *A Modern Utopia.*

Utopian: See *Utopia*

Utopianism: See *Utopia*

V

Verisimilitude: Literally, the appearance of truth. In literary criticism, the term refers to aspects of a work of literature that seem true to the reader. Verisimilitude is achieved in the work of Honore de Balzac, Gustave Flaubert, and Henry James, among other late nineteenth-century realist writers.

Vers de societe: See *Occasional Verse*

Vers libre: See *Free Verse*

Verse: A line of metered language, a line of a poem, or any work written in verse. The following line of verse is from the epic poem *Don Juan* by Lord Byron: "My way is to begin with the beginning."

Versification: The writing of verse. Versification may also refer to the meter, rhyme, and other mechanical components of a poem. Composition of a "Roses are red, violets are blue" poem to suit an occasion is a common form of versification practiced by students.

Victorian: Refers broadly to the reign of Queen Victoria of England (1837-1901) and to anything with qualities typical of that era. For example, the qualities of smug narrowmindedness, bourgeois materialism, faith in social progress, and priggish morality are often considered Victorian. This stereotype is contradicted by such dramatic intellectual developments as the theories of Charles Darwin, Karl Marx, and Sigmund Freud (which stirred strong debates in England) and the critical attitudes of serious Victorian writers like Charles Dickens and George Eliot. In literature, the Victorian Period was the great age of the English novel, and the latter part of the era saw the rise of movements such as decadence and symbolism. Works of Victorian literature include the poetry of Robert Browning and Alfred, Lord Tennyson, the criticism of Matthew Arnold and John Ruskin, and the novels of Emily Bronte, William Makepeace Thackeray, and Thomas Hardy. Also known as Victorian Age and Victorian Period.

Victorian Age: See *Victorian*

Victorian Period: See *Victorian*

W

Weltanschauung: A German term referring to a person's worldview or philosophy. Examples of *weltanschauung* include Thomas Hardy's view of the human being as the victim of fate, destiny, or impersonal forces and circumstances, and the disillusioned and laconic cynicism expressed by such poets of the 1930s as W. H. Auden, Sir Stephen Spender, and Sir William Empson.

Weltschmerz: A German term meaning "world pain." It describes a sense of anguish about the nature of existence, usually associated with a melancholy, pessimistic attitude. *Weltschmerz* was expressed in England by George Gordon, Lord Byron in his *Manfred* and *Childe Harold's Pilgrimage,* in France by Viscount de Chateaubriand, Alfred de Vigny, and Alfred de Musset, in Russia by Aleksandr Pushkin and Mikhail Lermontov, in Poland by Juliusz Slowacki, and in America by Nathaniel Hawthorne.

Z

Zarzuela: A type of Spanish operetta. Writers of *zarzuelas* include Lope de Vega and Pedro Calderon.

Zeitgeist: A German term meaning "spirit of the time." It refers to the moral and intellectual trends of a given era. Examples of *zeitgeist* include the preoccupation with the more morbid aspects of dying and death in some Jacobean literature, especially in the works of dramatists Cyril Tourneur and John Webster, and the decadence of the French Symbolists.

Cumulative Author/Title Index

Cumulative Nationality/Ethnicity Index

Cumulative Nationality/Ethnicity Index

Cumulative Nationality/Ethnicity Index

Wilson, Lanford
Angels Fall: V20
Burn This: V4
Hot L Baltimore: V9
The Mound Builders: V16
Talley's Folly: V12
Wright, Doug
I Am My Own Wife: V23
Zindel, Paul
The Effect of Gamma Rays on Man-in-the-Moon Marigolds: V12

Argentinian
Dorfman, Ariel
Death and the Maiden: V4

Asian American
Hwang, David Henry
M. Butterfly: V11
The Sound of a Voice: V18
Trying to Find Chinatown: V29

Austrian
von Hofmannsthal, Hugo
Electra: V17
The Tower: V12

Bohemian (Czechoslovakian)
Capek, Karel
The Insect Play: V11

Canadian
Highway, Tomson
The Rez Sisters: V2
MacDonald, Ann-Marie
Goodnight Desdemona (Good Morning Juliet): V23
Pollock, Sharon
Blood Relations: V3
Thompson, Judith
Habitat: V22

Chilean
Dorfman, Ariel
Death and the Maiden: V4

Chinese
Xingjian, Gao
The Other Shore: V21

Cuban
Cruz, Nilo
Anna in the Tropics: V21
Fornes, Maria Irene
Fefu and Her Friends: V25
Prida, Dolores
Beautiful Señoritas: V23

Cuban American
Cruz, Nilo
Anna in the Tropics: V21

Czechoslovakian
Capek, Joseph
The Insect Play: V11
Capek, Karel
The Insect Play: V11
R.U.R.: V7
Havel, Vaclav
The Memorandum: V10
Stoppard, Tom
Arcadia: V5
Dogg's Hamlet, Cahoot's Macbeth: V16
Indian Ink: V11
The Real Thing: V8
Rosencrantz and Guildenstern Are Dead: V2
Travesties: V13

Dutch
de Hartog, Jan
The Fourposter: V12

English
Anonymous
Arden of Faversham: V24
The Second Shepherds' Play: V25
Arden, John
Serjeant Musgrave's Dance: V9
Ayckbourn, Alan
A Chorus of Disapproval: V7
Barnes, Peter
The Ruling Class: V6
Behn, Aphra
The Forc'd Marriage: V24
The Rover: V16
Bolt, Robert
A Man for All Seasons: V2
Bond, Edward
Lear: V3
Saved: V8
Christie, Agatha
The Mousetrap: V2
Churchill, Caryl
Cloud Nine: V16
Light Shining on Buckinghamshire: V27
Serious Money: V25
Top Girls: V12
Collins, Wilkie
The Frozen Deep: V28
Congreve, William
Love for Love: V14
The Way of the World: V15
Coward, Noel
Hay Fever: V6
Private Lives: V3

Cowley, Hannah
The Belle's Stratagem: V22
Delaney, Shelagh
A Taste of Honey: V7
Duffy, Maureen
Rites: V15
Edgar, David
The Life and Adventures of Nicholas Nickleby: V15
Fielding, Henry
Tom Thumb: V28
Ford, John
'Tis Pity She's a Whore: V7
Frayn, Michael
Copenhagen: V22
Noises Off: V28
Gems, Pam
Stanley: V25
Goldsmith, Oliver
She Stoops to Conquer: V1
Hare, David
Blue Room: V7
Plenty: V4
The Secret Rapture: V16
Holmes, Rupert
The Mystery of Edwin Drood: V28
Jonson, Ben(jamin)
The Alchemist: V4
Volpone: V10
Kyd, Thomas
The Spanish Tragedy: V21
Lavery, Bryony
Frozen: V25
Lessing, Doris
Play with a Tiger: V20
Marlowe, Christopher
Doctor Faustus: V1
Edward II: The Troublesome Reign and Lamentable Death of Edward the Second, King of England, with the Tragical Fall of Proud Mortimer: V5
The Jew of Malta: V13
Tamburlaine the Great: V21
Maugham, Somerset
For Services Rendered: V22
Middleton, Thomas
The Changeling: V22
A Chaste Maid in Cheapside: V18
Nicholson, William
Shadowlands: V11
Orton, Joe
Entertaining Mr. Sloane: V3
What the Butler Saw: V6
Osborne, John
Inadmissible Evidence: V24
Look Back in Anger: V4
Luther: V19
Pinter, Harold
The Birthday Party: V5
The Caretaker: V7
The Dumb Waiter: V25

308

Drama for Students, Volume 29

Subject/Theme Index

H

Happiness
  They Knew What They Wanted: 194
Hatred
  The Stronger: 160, 168
Hell
  Look Homeward Angel: 79
Helplessness
  The Cuban Swimmer: 38
Heritage
  The Cuban Swimmer: 27, 32, 36, 37, 40
  Los Vendidos: 85
  A Raisin in the Sun: 132, 135–137, 144, 147
  Trying to Find Chinatown: 225–227, 233–234
Hispanic American culture
  The Cuban Swimmer: 25, 27, 31, 34, 37
  Los Vendidos: 101–105
Hispanic American literature
  Los Vendidos: 101–105
Honesty
  Los Vendidos: 100
  Poof!: 117
Honor
  The Cuban Swimmer: 39
Hope
  The Cuban Swimmer: 39
Hopelessness
  Poof!: 114
  A Raisin in the Sun: 138
Humor
  Los Vendidos: 85, 92, 97, 100
  Poof!: 111, 118
  Time Flies: 210
  Workout: 249, 252
Husband-wife relationships
  Look Homeward Angel: 79
Hyperbole
  Workout: 247, 252

I

Identity
  12 Angry Men: 9–10
  The Cuban Swimmer: 22, 23, 27, 28–30, 36–37
  Look Homeward Angel: 71
  Los Vendidos: 93–94, 98–99
  Trying to Find Chinatown: 223
Ideology
  Workout: 255–256
Illusion (Philosophy)
  12 Angry Men: 18
Imagery (Literature)
  The Cuban Swimmer: 38, 40
Immigrant life
  The Cuban Swimmer: 22, 23, 27, 37, 39
  Los Vendidos: 85, 90

  They Knew What They Wanted: 192
  Trying to Find Chinatown: 227, 235, 238
Imprisonment
  The Stronger: 160–161
Insecurity
  Workout: 245
Insight
  12 Angry Men: 19
Intelligence
  12 Angry Men: 7
  They Knew What They Wanted: 201
Intimidation
  Poof!: 14, 115
Irony
  Look Homeward Angel: 83
  Time Flies: 210–211
  Trying to Find Chinatown: 228
Isolation
  The Cuban Swimmer: 35

J

Jealousy
  The Stronger: 160
  They Knew What They Wanted: 195
Justice
  12 Angry Men: 1, 8, 9, 13–14, 19, 20
  Los Vendidos: 106

K

Kindness
  They Knew What They Wanted: 185

L

Language and languages
  The Cuban Swimmer: 32, 35
  They Knew What They Wanted: 192
  Time Flies: 211–212, 214
Liberalism
  12 Angry Men: 19, 20
Life (Philosophy)
  Time Flies: 209
Loneliness
  The Cuban Swimmer: 38
Longing
  The Cuban Swimmer: 38
Love
  Guys and Dolls: 51–52, 59
  Look Homeward Angel: 69
  A Raisin in the Sun: 136
  They Knew What They Wanted: 184, 194, 197, 204
  Time Flies: 209–210, 214, 218

M

Magic
  Poof!: 121, 122

Magical realism
  The Cuban Swimmer: 22, 31–32, 34–37
  Poof!: 118
Marriage
  Guys and Dolls: 49, 50, 54
  Look Homeward Angel: 79
  The Stronger: 160–161
  They Knew What They Wanted: 182, 184, 185, 196
Masculinity
  A Raisin in the Sun: 139
Masochism
  Workout: 252
Memory
  12 Angry Men: 5
Metaphors
  The Cuban Swimmer: 30, 39
  Los Vendidos: 92–94
  The Stronger: 159
  Workout: 247
Metaphysics
  The Stronger: 175
Mexican American culture
  Los Vendidos: 85–86, 90, 93–95, 97–105
Middle class
  The Stronger: 164–166
Midwestern United States
  Trying to Find Chinatown: 224
Mistakes
  They Knew What They Wanted: 201
Morality
  Guys and Dolls: 59
  Los Vendidos: 93
  A Raisin in the Sun: 153–154
  They Knew What They Wanted: 201
Mother-child relationships
  Look Homeward Angel: 70, 77–81
Motivation
  They Knew What They Wanted: 204
Multiculturalism
  Trying to Find Chinatown: 231
Music
  A Raisin in the Sun: 142
Mysticism
  The Cuban Swimmer: 22, 26, 30–32, 36–37, 40

N

Narcissism
  Look Homeward Angel: 66
Naturalism (Literature)
  The Stronger: 174
Nostalgia
  Guys and Dolls: 63

O

Occult. *See* Supernatural
Oppression
   Los Vendidos: 89, 90, 92
   Trying to Find Chinatown: 224, 228
Outsiders
   Look Homeward Angel: 83
Overachievement
   Workout: 245

P

Paradoxes
   The Stronger: 160
Paranoia
   The Stronger: 166–168
Passion
   They Knew What They Wanted: 201
Point of view (Literature)
   12 Angry Men: 14–16
Politics
   Los Vendidos: 85, 92, 100, 101,
     105–109
   A Raisin in the Sun: 153
   They Knew What They Wanted:
     183, 185
Popular culture
   The Cuban Swimmer: 28
   Guys and Dolls: 63
Postmodernism
   The Cuban Swimmer: 34–35
Postwar society
   Guys and Dolls: 57
Poverty
   12 Angry Men: 7
   A Raisin in the Sun: 144
Power (Philosophy)
   The Cuban Swimmer: 34, 39
   Look Homeward Angel: 82
   Poof!: 114
   The Stronger: 156, 167
Pragmatism
   They Knew What They Wanted: 198
Prejudice
   12 Angry Men: 8, 9, 18–19
   The Cuban Swimmer: 26
   Los Vendidos: 89, 94, 97
Pride
   The Cuban Swimmer: 26, 37, 39
   A Raisin in the Sun: 144, 147
   They Knew What They Wanted: 201
   Trying to Find Chinatown: 225
Psychoanalysis
   Look Homeward Angel: 77–81
Psychology
   Look Homeward Angel: 77–81
   The Stronger: 161–162

Q

Questing
   The Cuban Swimmer: 36–40

R

Race relations
   A Raisin in the Sun: 151–154
Racism
   A Raisin in the Sun: 132, 136, 138,
     141–144, 147, 148, 150–154
   Trying to Find Chinatown: 225,
     237, 240
Rationality
   12 Angry Men: 20
   They Knew What They Wanted: 201
Reality
   The Cuban Swimmer: 38
   The Stronger: 168
Reason
   12 Angry Men: 19, 20
   They Knew What They Wanted:
     187, 201
Rebellion
   They Knew What They Wanted: 203
Reform
   They Knew What They Wanted: 184
Religion
   The Cuban Swimmer: 22, 25–26,
     30–31
   Look Homeward Angel: 73
Remorse
   Look Homeward Angel: 80–81
Representation
   A Raisin in the Sun: 154
Repression
   Look Homeward Angel: 71, 72
   Workout: 245, 252
Rescue
   Look Homeward Angel: 83
Resentment
   A Raisin in the Sun: 134
   Workout: 242, 246
Resistance
   Poof!: 121
Respect
   They Knew What They Wanted: 187
Responsibility
   12 Angry Men: 10–11
   The Cuban Swimmer: 39, 40
Resurrection
   The Cuban Swimmer: 39–40
Retribution. *See* Revenge
Revenge
   Poof!: 111
Right and wrong
   They Knew What They Wanted:
     200
Romantic love
   Guys and Dolls: 44, 46, 48–52, 54

S

Sadness
   Time Flies: 211
Salvation
   The Cuban Swimmer: 38

Sarcasm
   Trying to Find Chinatown: 234
Satire
   Los Vendidos: 90–92, 97
   Workout: 242
Security
   They Knew What They Wanted: 203
Self identity
   Trying to Find Chinatown: 222,
     226, 231, 233
Self image
   The Stronger: 161, 166
Self worth
   Look Homeward Angel: 82
Setting (Literature)
   12 Angry Men: 14–17
   Los Vendidos: 93
   A Raisin in the Sun: 142
Sex roles
   The Cuban Swimmer: 26–28, 32,
     34, 38
   Guys and Dolls: 57
   A Raisin in the Sun: 139, 141
   The Stronger: 160
Sexual behavior
   Time Flies: 206–208
Shame
   Poof!: 114
   A Raisin in the Sun: 154
Silence
   The Stronger: 161
Sin
   Guys and Dolls: 48
Skepticism
   Guys and Dolls: 56
   Poof!: 115
Social change
   Los Vendidos: 90, 92, 97–101
Social criticism
   The Stronger: 166
Social realism
   They Knew What They Wanted:
     180, 188, 198–202
Sorrow
   Look Homeward Angel: 83
Spirituality
   The Cuban Swimmer: 38
Stereotypes (Psychology)
   Los Vendidos: 85, 86, 89, 90, 94, 97
   They Knew What They Wanted:
     192
   Trying to Find Chinatown:
     224–227, 234, 237
Strength
   The Cuban Swimmer: 26, 27, 38
   A Raisin in the Sun: 144
   The Stronger: 161, 166
   They Knew What They Wanted: 201
Struggle
   The Cuban Swimmer: 35, 39
   A Raisin in the Sun: 144–145
   The Stronger: 168

Submission
   The Cuban Swimmer: 26, 27
Success
   The Cuban Swimmer: 35, 38, 40
   Look Homeward Angel: 72
   A Raisin in the Sun: 138
Suffering
   Look Homeward Angel: 82
   A Raisin in the Sun: 147
   They Knew What They Wanted:
      184
Supernatural
   The Stronger: 170–172
Suspicion
   Poof!: 123, 124
Symbolism
   The Cuban Swimmer: 26, 32, 35, 38
   Look Homeward Angel: 74, 79, 80,
      82, 83

T

Tension
   12 Angry Men: 17
   Los Vendidos: 90, 92, 100
   A Raisin in the Sun: 139
   The Stronger: 161, 175
   Time Flies: 208

Time
   Time Flies: 208, 214, 215–217
Tradition
   The Cuban Swimmer: 25, 27–28,
      30–32, 34, 36, 37, 39, 40
   Trying to Find Chinatown: 227
Transformation
   Guys and Dolls: 53, 61
Triumph
   The Cuban Swimmer: 27
   The Stronger: 161, 166
Truth
   The Stronger: 168
   They Knew What They Wanted:
      186, 197

U

Uncertainty
   12 Angry Men: 17
   The Stronger: 168
Universality
   The Stronger: 174

V

Victimization
   Poof!: 114

Violence
   12 Angry Men: 4
   The Stronger: 156

W

Wealth
   Look Homeward Angel: 79
   A Raisin in the Sun: 138
   The Stronger: 164
   They Knew What They Wanted:
      185
Wishes
   Poof!: 122
Work
   Look Homeward Angel: 71–72
Workers
   Los Vendidos: 85, 88, 95–96,
      105–106
   They Knew What They Wanted:
      183, 185, 189
Working class
   12 Angry Men: 16

Y

Youth
   12 Angry Men: 13–14

LONGWOOD PUBLIC LIBRARY
800 Middle Country Road
Middle Island, NY 11953
(631) 924-6400
mylpl.net

LIBRARY HOURS

Monday-Friday	9:30 a.m. - 9:00 p.m.
Saturday	9:30 a.m. - 5:00 p.m.
Sunday (Sept-June)	1:00 p.m. - 5:00 p.m.